The Digital Video Tape Recorder

D0920327

For Chrissie

The Digital Video Tape Recorder

John Watkinson

Focal Press
An imprint of Butterworth-Heinemann Ltd
Linacre House, Jordan Hill, Oxford OX2 8DP

 A member of the Reed Elsevier plc group

OXFORD   LONDON   BOSTON
MUNICH   NEW DELHI   SINGAPORE   SYDNEY
TOKYO   TORONTO   WELLINGTON

First published 1994

British Library Cataloguing in Publication Data
Watkinson, John
  The Digital Video Tape Recorder
  I. Title
  621.38833

ISBN 0 240 51373 8

Library of Congress Cataloging in Publication Data
Watkinson, John.
  The digital video tape recorder/John Watkinson.
  p.   cm.
  Includes bibliographical references and index.
  ISBN 0 240 51373 8
  1. Digital video tape recorders. I. Title.
  TK6655.V5W54   94–15099
  621.388'33–dc20   CIP

Composition by Genesis Typesetting, Laser Quay, Rochester, Kent
Printed and bound in Great Britain by Clays, St Ives plc

Contents

Chapter 3 Video signals and conversion   **88**

Preface

The adoption of digital techniques in broadcast and facility equipment has been extremely swift. Only a few years ago, the digital video recorder was regarded as unusual and special, and the equipment was expensive in comparison to analog equipment. But in a fast-moving technology like this, a few years makes a lot of difference. In that time, recording densities have risen, VLSI chips have become cheaper, mechanical design has been refined, mistakes have been made and learned from, and today's digital VTR is the better for it.

The promise of better picture and sound quality was the original spur to the development of the digital recorder, but in the early formats this quality came with a price tag to match. Now it is economy which is the strength of digital VTRs. The quality is taken for granted; the low capital and running costs are the consideration in a world where accountability seems to be the watchword.

In the same way that the Compact Disc eliminated the vinyl disk, from now on, the digital VTR will take over and become the norm. It will no longer be a specialist device, but it will enter the mainstream of everyday use. Whilst the job of a VTR is unchanged, the technology inside a digital machine is almost unrecognizable to those familiar with analog machines, and years of experience are suddenly of little assistance.

The purpose of this book is to explain all of the technology of the DVTR, so that newcomers to the subject can find here everything they need to know in one volume.

One of the things I find rewarding about the DVTR is the range of technologies it embraces. Precision engineering, sophisticated servos, aerodynamics, magnetics, channel coding, high frequencies, error correction, transform coding, converters, microprocessor control are just some of the ingredients which go into a modern machine.

None of these fields is new, and the information in each is plentiful. The problem is that each field adopts its own specialist terms and resorts to mathematics with unfailing regularity. In this book I have taken each subject and explained it in plain English, defining the specialist terms as they are met. I have drawn heavily on explanations developed and tested in the many training courses I have given on the subject.

The essential theory of the DVTR is interspersed with practical examples drawn from specific formats and tips on operational practice, maintenance and troubleshooting.

As the DVTR is going to become a commonplace item, this book has to be accessible to a wide range of readers with a variety of backgrounds. With that in mind, chapter 1 is a tutorial introduction to the subject which assumes very little prerequisite knowledge. It helps to build a framework on which to put the remaining chapters.

Acknowledgements

Many people from all of the major manufacturers and elsewhere have gone out of their way to help provide material for this book and to answer my endless questions. My thanks go to all of them. I must mention in particular the following: Fraser Morrison and John Watney of Ampex, Takeo Eguchi, Jim Wilkinson, Dave Huckfield and Jeff Davis of Sony, Steve Owen of Panasonic, Yoshinobu Oba of NHK and Tom Cavanagh of CBC.

John Watkinson
Burghfield Common

Chapter 1

Introduction to the DVTR

Many of the chapters in this book explain specific aspects of the DVTR in detail. In contrast, this chapter considers the entire machine as a concept and excess detail is neither necessary nor desirable here.

1.1 What is a DVTR?

One of the vital concepts to grasp is that a digital recorder is simply an alternative means of recording a conventional video waveform. An ideal DVTR has the same characteristics as an ideal analog machine: both of them are totally transparent and reproduce the original applied waveform without error. One need only compare high-quality analog and digital equipment side by side with the same signals to realize how transparent modern equipment can be. Needless to say, in the real world ideal conditions seldom prevail, so analog and digital equipment both fall short of the ideal. Digital recording simply falls short of the ideal by a smaller distance and at lower cost, or, if the designer chooses, can have the same performance as analog at much lower cost.

Although there are a number of ways in which video waveforms can be represented digitally, there is one system, known as pulse code modulation (PCM), which is in virtually universal use[1]. Figure 1.1 shows how PCM works. Instead of being continuous, the time axis is represented in a discrete, or stepwise, manner. The waveform is not carried by continuous representation, but by measurement at regular intervals. This process is called sampling and the frequency with which samples are taken is called the sampling rate or sampling frequency F_s. It should be stressed that sampling is an analog process. Each sample still varies infinitely as the original waveform did. Sampled analog devices are well known in video; the charge-coupled sensor in a television camera is one example. To complete the conversion to PCM, each sample is then represented to finite accuracy by a discrete number in a process known as quantizing.

In television systems the input image which falls on the camera sensor will be continuous in time, and continous in two spatial dimensions corresponding to the height and width of the sensor. In analog video systems, the time axis is sampled into frames, and the vertical axis is sampled into lines. Digital video simply adds a third sampling process which takes place along the lines.

There is a direct connection between the concept of temporal sampling, where the input changes with respect to time at some frequency and is sampled at some

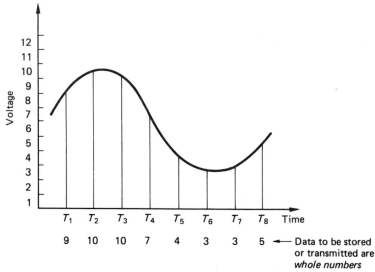

Figure 1.1 In pulse code modulation (PCM) the analog waveform is measured periodically at the sampling rate. The voltage (represented here by the height) of each sample is then described by a whole number. The whole numbers are stored or transmitted rather than the waveform itself.

other frequency, and spatial sampling, where an image changes a given number of times per unit distance and is sampled at some other number of times per unit distance. The connection between the two is the process of scanning. Temporal frequency can be obtained by multiplying spatial frequency by the speed of the scan. Figure 1.2 shows a hypothetical image sensor which has 1000 discrete sensors across a width of 1 centimetre. The spatial sampling rate of this sensor is thus 1000 per centimetre. If the sensors are measured sequentially during a scan which takes 1 millisecond to go across the 1 centimetre width, the result will be a temporal sampling rate of 1 MHz. In the spatial domain we refer to resolution, whereas in the time domain we refer to frequency response. The two are linked by the scanning speed.

Whilst any sampling rate which is high enough could be used for video, it is common to make the sampling rate a whole multiple of the line rate. Samples are then taken in the same place on every line. If this is done, a monochrome digital image is a rectangular array of points at which the brightness is stored as a

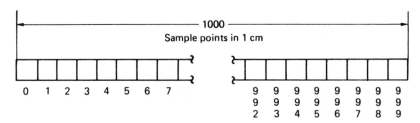

Figure 1.2 If the above spatial sampling arrangement of 1000 points per centimetre is scanned in 1 millisecond, the sampling rate will become 1 megahertz.

number. The points are known as picture cells, generally abbreviated to pixels, although sometimes the abbreviation is more savage and they are known as pels. As shown in Figure 1.3(a), the array will generally be arranged with an even spacing between pixels, which are in rows and columns. By placing the pixels close together, it is hoped that the observer will perceive a continuous image. Obviously the finer the pixel spacing, the greater the resolution of the picture will be, but the amount of data needed to record one picture will increase as the square of the resolution, and with it the costs.

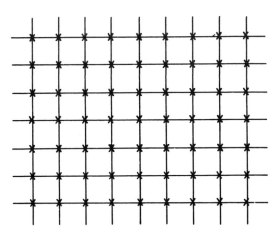

Figure 1.3(a) A picture can be stored digitally by representing the brightness at each of the above points by a binary number. For a colour picture each point becomes a vector and has to describe the brightness, hue and saturation of that part of the picture. Samples are usually but not always formed into regular arrays of rows and columns, and it is most efficient if the horizontal and vertical spacing are the same.

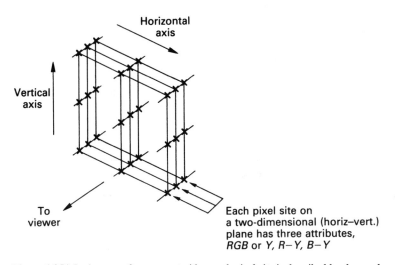

Figure 1.3(b) In the case of component video, each pixel site is described by three values and so the pixel becomes a vector quantity.

If it is desired to convey a coloured image, then it will be seen from Figure 1.3(b) that each image consists of three superimposed layers of samples, one for each component. The pixel is no longer a single number representing a scalar brightness value, but a vector which describes in some way the brightness, hue and saturation of that point in the picture. In *RGB*, the pixels contain three unipolar numbers representing the proportion of each of the three primary colours at that point in the picture. In colour difference working, each pixel again contains three numbers, but one of these is a unipolar number representing the luminance and the other two are bipolar numbers representing the colour difference values.

In order to produce moving pictures, the value of every pixel must be updated periodically. This effectively results in a three-dimensional array, where two of the axes are spatial and the third is temporal.

Since it is possible to represent any analog waveform digitally, composite video can also be digitized. Owing to the critical nature of chroma phase, the sampling rate will generally be locked to subcarrier so that it can be readily created from burst. It should be stressed that digital composite is simply another way of conveying composite video, and all of the attributes of composite, such as colour framing sequences, are still present in the resulting data.

At the ADC (Analog-to-Digital Converter), every effort is made to rid the sampling clock of jitter, or time instability, so every sample is taken at an exactly even time step. Clearly if there is any subsequent timebase error, the instants at which samples arrive will be changed and the effect can be detected. If samples arrive at some destination with an irregular timebase, the effect can be eliminated by storing the samples temporarily in a memory and reading them out using a stable, locally generated clock. This process is called timebase correction and all properly engineered DVTRs must use it. Analog VTRs employed timebase correctors, but the accuracy of these units was restricted by the fact that they could only use sync or burst timing references once per line. Disturbances within the line could not be detected. In a digital machine, every sample can be individually reclocked, so timebase error is not reduced; it is totally eliminated. As a result there is little point measuring the timebase stability of a digital recorder. This advantage of digital recording is particularly evident in composite digital formats, where precise chroma phase stability is obtained with ease.

Those who are not familiar with digital principles often worry that sampling takes away something from a signal because it is not taking notice of what happened between the samples. This would be true in a system having infinite bandwidth, but no analog signal can have infinite bandwidth. All analog signal sources from cameras, VTRs and so on have a resolution or frequency response limit, as indeed do devices such as CRTs and human vision. When a signal has finite bandwidth, the rate at which it can change is limited, and the way in which it changes becomes predictable. When a waveform can only change between samples in one way, it is then only necessary to convey the samples and the original waveform can be reconstructed from them. A more detailed treatment of the principle will be given in Chapter 3.

As stated, each sample is also discrete, or represented in a stepwise manner. The length of the sample, which will be proportional to the voltage of the video signal, is represented by a whole number. This process is known as quantizing and results in an approximation, but the size of the error can be controlled until it is negligible. If, for example, we were to measure the height of humans to the nearest metre, virtually all adults would register 2 metres high and obvious difficulties would result. These are generally overcome by measuring height to the nearest centimetre. Clearly there is no advantage in going further and expressing our height in a whole number of millimeters or even micrometres. The point is that an appropriate resolution can also be found for video signals, and a higher figure is not beneficial. The link between video quality and sample resolution is explored in Chapter 3.

The advantage of using whole numbers is that they are not prone to drift. If a whole number can be recorded and reproduced without numerical error, it has not changed at all. By recording video waveforms numerically, the original information has been expressed in a way which is better able to resist unwanted changes.

Essentially, a DVTR carries the original waveform numerically. The number of the sample is an analog of time, which itself is an analog of position across the screen, and the magnitude of the sample is (in the case of luminance) an analog of the brightness at the appropriate point in the image. In fact the succession of samples in a DVTR is actually *an analog* of the original waveform. This sounds like a contradiction and as a result some authorities prefer the term 'numerical video' to 'digital video' and in fact the French for DVTR is *magnetoscope numérique*. The term 'digital' is so well established in English that it is unlikely to change.

As both axes of the digitally represented waveform are discrete, the waveform can be accurately restored from numbers as if it were being drawn on graph paper. If we require greater accuracy, we simply choose paper with smaller squares. Clearly more numbers are then required and each one could change over a larger range.

In simple terms, the video waveform is conveyed in a digital recorder as if the voltage had been measured at regular intervals with a digital meter and the readings had been written down on a roll of paper. The rate at which the measurements were taken and the accuracy of the meter are the only factors which determine the quality, because once a parameter is expressed as a discrete number, a series of such numbers can be conveyed unchanged. Clearly in this example the handwriting used and the grade of paper have no effect on the information. The quality is determined only by the accuracy of conversion and is independent of the quality of the signal path.

1.2 Why binary?

Humans insist on using numbers expressed to the base of ten, having evolved with that number of digits. Other number bases exist; most people are familiar with the duodecimal system which uses the dozen and the gross. The most minimal system is binary, which has only two digits, 0 and 1. BInary digiTS are universally contracted to bits. These are readily conveyed in switching circuits by an 'on' state and an 'off' state, and relate readily to the two directions of magnetization for recording. With only two states, there is little chance of error.

In decimal systems, the digits in a number (counting from the right, or least significant end) represent ones, tens, hundreds, thousands, etc. Figure 1.4 shows that in binary, the bits represent one, two, four, eight, sixteen, etc. A multidigit binary number is commonly called a word, and the number of bits in the word is called the wordlength. The right-hand bit is called the least significant bit (LSB) whereas the bit on the left-hand end of the word is called the most significant bit (MSB). Clearly more digits are required in binary than in decimal, but they are more easily handled. A word of 8 bits is called a byte, which is a contraction of 'by eight'. The capacity of memories and storage media is measured in bytes, but to avoid large numbers, kilobytes, megabytes and gigabytes are often used. As memory addresses are themselves binary numbers, the wordlength limits the address range. The range is found by raising two to the power of the wordlength. Thus a 4 bit word has 16 combinations, and could address a memory having 16 locations. A 10 bit word has 1 024 combinations, which is close to 1000. In digital terminology, 1K = 1 024, so a kilobyte of memory contains 1 024 bytes. A megabyte (1MB) contains 1 024 kilobytes and a gigabyte contains 1 024 megabytes.

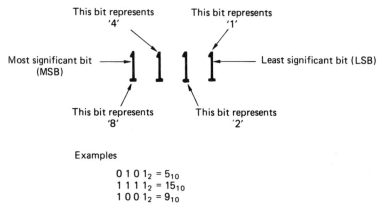

Examples

$$0\ 1\ 0\ 1_2 = 5_{10}$$
$$1\ 1\ 1\ 1_2 = 15_{10}$$
$$1\ 0\ 0\ 1_2 = 9_{10}$$

Figure 1.4 In a binary number, the digits represent increasing powers of 2 from the LSB. Also defined here are MSB and wordlength. When the wordlength is 8 bits, the word is a byte. Binary numbers are used as memory addresses, and the range is defined by the address wordlength. Some examples are shown here.

In the circuitry of a DVTR, the whole number representing the length of the sample is expressed in binary. The signals sent have two states, and change at predetermined times according to some stable clock. Figure 1.5 shows the consequences of this form of transmission. If the binary signal is degraded by noise, this will be rejected by the receiver, which judges the signal solely by whether it is above or below the half-way threshold, a process known as slicing. The signal will be carried in a channel with finite bandwidth, and this limits the slew rate of the signal; an ideally upright edge is made to slope. Noise added to a sloping signal can change the time at which the slicer judges that the level passed through the threshold. This effect is also eliminated when the output of the slicer is reclocked. However many stages the binary signal passes through, it still comes out the same, only later.

There is only one way in which data can practically be recorded at high density and that is where successive digits from each sample are laid down serially. This is the definition of pulse code modulation. Clearly the bit rate must now be considerably higher than the sampling rate. Whilst the recording of video in this

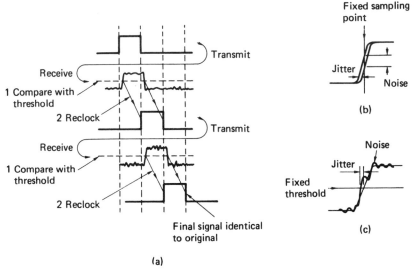

Figure 1.5 (a) A binary signal is compared with a threshold and relocked on receipt; thus the meaning will be unchanged. (b) Jitter on a signal can appear as noise with respect to fixed timing. (c) Noise on a signal can appear as jitter when compared with a fixed threshold.

way is advantageous, there is a penalty that a high-quality colour difference signal requires around 200 million bits per second. Clearly the DVTR could only become commonplace when such a data rate could be handled economically. Further applications become possible when means to reduce the data rate become economic.

1.3 Why digital?

There are two main answers to this question, and it is not possible to say which is the most important, as it will depend on one's standpoint.

(1) The quality of audio and video reproduction of a well-engineered DVTR is independent of the medium and depends only on the quality of the conversion processes.

(2) The conversion of audio and video to the digital domain allows tremendous opportunities which were denied to analog signals.

Someone who is only interested in sound and picture quality will judge the former the most relevant. If good-quality converters can be obtained, all of the shortcomings of analog recording can be eliminated to great advantage. One's greatest effort is expended in the design of converters, whereas those parts of the system which handle data need only be workmanlike. Timebase error, tape noise, print-through, dropouts, moiré and wow and flutter are all history. When a digital recording is copied, the same numbers appear on the copy: it is not a dub, it is a clone. If the copy is indistinguishable from the original, there has been no generation loss. Digital recordings can be copied indefinitely without loss of quality.

In the real world everything has a cost, and one of the greatest strengths of digital technology is low cost. If copying causes no quality loss, recorders do not need to be far better than necessary in order to withstand generation loss. They need only be adequate on the first generation whose quality is then maintained. There is no need for the great size and extravagant tape consumption of professional analog recorders. When the information to be recorded is discrete numbers, they can be packed densely on the medium without quality loss. Should some bits be in error because of noise or dropout, error correction can restore the original value. Digital recordings take up less space than analog recordings for the same or better quality. Tape costs are far less and storage costs are reduced.

Digital circuitry costs less to manufacture. Switching circuitry which handles binary can be integrated more densely than analog circuitry. More functionality can be put in the same chip. Analog circuits are built from a host of different component types which have a variety of shapes and sizes and are costly to assemble and adjust. Digital circuitry uses standardized component outlines and is easier to assemble on automated equipment. Little if any adjustment is needed.

Once video is in the digital domain, it becomes data, and as such is indistinguishable from any other type of data. Systems and techniques developed in other industries for other purposes can be used for video. Many of the techniques used in a DVTR, such as error correction, were originally developed for other purposes, but can be readily adapted.

Digital equipment can have self-diagnosis programs built-in. The machine points out its own failures. The days of chasing a signal with an oscilloscope are over. Even if a faulty component in a digital circuit could be located with such a primitive tool, it is well nigh impossible to replace a chip having 60 pins soldered through a six-layer circuit board. The cost of finding the fault may be more than the board is worth. Routine, mind-numbing adjustment of analog circuits to counteract drift is no longer needed. The cost of maintenance falls. It should be borne in mind, however, that the DVTR still uses tape which is in contact with moving heads and periodic cleaning is still a necessity.

As a result of the above, the cost of ownership of a modern DVTR is less than that of its analog predecessors. Debates about quality are academic; analog equipment can no longer compete economically, and it will dwindle away.

1.4 History of DVTRs

Whilst numerous experimental machines were built previously, the first production DVTR, launched in 1987, used the D-1 format which recorded colour difference data according to CCIR-601 on $\frac{3}{4}$ inch tape. Whilst it represented a tremendous achievement, the D-1 format was too early to take advantage of high-coercivity tapes and its recording density was quite low, leading to large cassettes and high running costs. The majority of broadcasters then used composite signals, and a component recorder could not easily be used in such an environment. Where component applications existed, the D-1 format could not compete economically with Betacam SP and M-II analog formats. As a result D-1 found application only in high-end post production suites.

The D-2 format came next, but this was a composite digital format, handling conventional PAL and NTSC signals in digital form, and derived from a format developed by Ampex for an automated cart. machine. The choice of composite recording was intended to allow broadcasters directly to replace analog recorders with a digital machine. D-2 retained the cassette shell of D-1 but employed higher-coercivity tape and azimuth recording (see Chapter 4) to improve recording density and playing time. Early D-2 machines had no flying erase heads, and difficulties arose with audio edits. D-2 was also hampered by the imminent arrival of the D-3 format.

D-3 was designed by NHK, and put into production by Panasonic. This had twice the recording density of D-2 and three times that of D-1. This permitted the use of $\frac{1}{2}$ inch tape, making a digital camcorder a possibility. D-3 used the same sampling structure as D-2 for its composite recordings. Coming later, D-3 had learned from earlier formats and had a more powerful error-correction strategy than earlier formats, particularly in the audio recording.

By this time the economics of VLSI chips had made made data reduction in VTRs viable, and the first application was the Ampex DCT format which used approximately 2:1 data reduction so that component video could be recorded on an updated version of the $\frac{3}{4}$ inch cassettes and transports designed for D-2.

When Sony were developing the Digital Betacam format, compatibility with the existing analog Betacam format was a priority. Digital Betacam uses the same cassette shells as the analog format, and certain models of the digital recorder can play existing analog tapes. Sony also adopted data reduction, but this was in order to allow the construction of a digital component VTR which offered sufficient playing time within the existing cassette dimensions.

The D-5 component format is backward compatible with D-3. The same cassettes are used and D-5 machines can play D-3 tapes. However, data reduction is not used; the tape speed is doubled in the component format in order to increase the bit rate.

In the future recording technology will continue to advance and further formats are inevitable as manufacturers perceive an advantage over their competitors. This does not mean that the user need slavishly change to every new format, as the cost of format change is high. The astute user retains his or her current format for long enough to allow a number of new formats to be introduced. The user will then make a quantum leap to a format which is much better than the present one, missing out those between and minimizing the changeover costs.

1.5 Some digital video processes outlined

Whilst the DVTR is a complex device, it is not necessarily difficult to understand. The machine can be broken down into major areas and then the processes performed there can be further broken down into smaller steps, each of which is relatively easy to follow. The main difficulty with study is to appreciate where the small steps fit in the overall picture. Subsequent chapters of this book will describe the key processes found in DVTRs in some detail, whereas this chapter illustrates why these processes are necessary and shows how they are combined in various ways in real equipment. Once the general structure of the DVTR is appreciated, the following chapters can be put in perspective.

Figure 1.6(a) shows a minimal digital video system. This is no more than a point-to-point link which conveys analog video from one place to another. It consists of a pair of converters and hardware to serialize and deserialize the

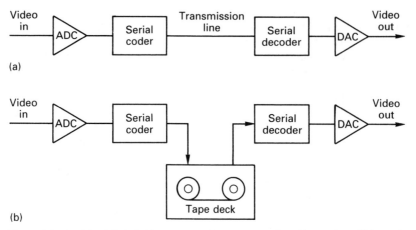

(a)

(b)

Figure 1.6. A minimal digital video system at (a) converts analog video to data which are then serialized for cable transmission. A recorder might in principle be one shown at (b) which simply records the serial waveform of (a). A practical recorder will be much more complex.

samples. There is a need for standardization in serial transmission so that various devices can be connected together. These standards for digital interfaces are described in chapter 3.

Figure 1.6(b) shows that in theory a DVTR could be made by recording the serial waveforms on tape and reproducing them later. In practice such a simple arrangement is doomed to failure because it takes no account of shortcomings in the recording process. Practical machines will be much more complex in order to deal with each of the problems.

1.6 Timebase correction

One of the characteristics of tape recording is that the time axis is not particularly stable owing to the flexibility of the tape. A solution is to extend the system of Figure 1.6 by the addition of some random access memory (RAM) as shown in Figure 1.7. The operation of RAM is described in Chapter 2. The relationship

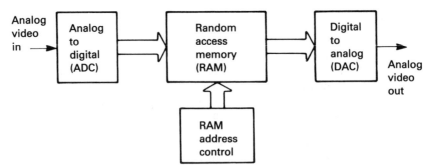

Figure 1.7 In the frame store, the recording medium is a random access memory (RAM). Recording time available is short compared with other media, but access to the recording is immediate and flexible as it is controlled by addressing the RAM.

between the read and write addresses makes the RAM into a variable delay. The addresses are generated by counters which overflow to zero after they have reached a maximum count. As a result the memory space appears to be circular as shown in Figure 1.8. The read and write addresses chase one another around the circle. If the read address follows close behind the write address, the delay is short. If it just stays ahead of the write address, the maximum delay is reached. If the input and output have an identical data rate, the address relationship will be constant. When a DVTR is playing back there will be variations in the

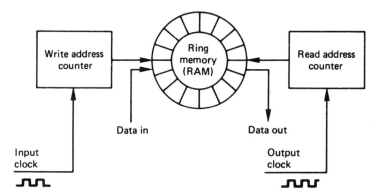

Figure 1.8 If the memory address is arranged to come from a counter which overflows, the memory can be made to appear circular. The write address then rotates endlessly, overwriting previous data once per revolution. The read address can follow the write address by a variable distance (not exceeding one revolution) and so a variable delay takes place between reading and writing.

instantaneous data rate from the tape. The timebase corrector absorbs these variations by varying its delay in the opposite sense. The write address changes at the varying rate from the tape, but the read address changes at a stable rate.

1.7 Time compression

When video signals are converted, the ADC must run at a constant clock rate and it outputs an unbroken stream of samples during the active line. Following a break during blanking, the sample stream resumes. In digital audio, the sample stream has no breaks at all. Time compression allows such sample streams to be broken into blocks for convenient handling.

Figure 1.9 shows an ADC feeding a pair of RAMs. When one is being written by the ADC, the other can be read, and vice versa. As soon as the first RAM is full, the ADC output switches to the input of the other RAM so that there is no loss of samples. The first RAM can then be read at a higher clock rate than the sampling rate. As a result the RAM is read in less time than it took to write it, and the output from the system then pauses until the second RAM is full. The samples are now time compressed. Instead of being an unbroken stream which is difficult to handle, the samples are now arranged in blocks with convenient pauses in between them. In these pauses numerous processes can take place. A rotary-head recorder can switch from one track to another in order to spread the

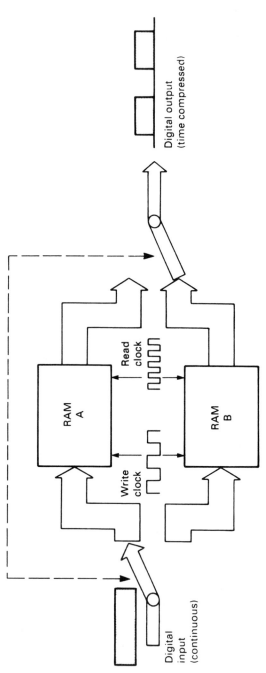

Figure 1.9 In time compression, the unbroken real-time stream of samples from an ADC is broken up into discrete blocks. This is accomplished by the configuration shown here. Samples are written into one RAM at the sampling rate by the write clock. When the first RAM is full, the switches change over, and writing continues into the second RAM whilst the first is read using a higher-frequency clock. The RAM is read faster than it was written and so all of the data will be output before the other RAM is full. This opens spaces in the data flow which are used as described in the text.

data from a field over several tape tracks. The time compression of the samples also makes space for synchronizing patterns, subcode and error-correction words to be recorded.

In DVTRs, the video data are time compressed so that part of the track is left for audio data. Figure 1.10 shows that heavy time compression of the audio data raises the instantaneous audio data rate up to that of the video data so that the same tracks, heads and much common circuitry can be used to record both.

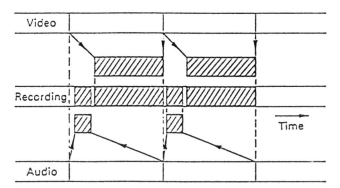

Figure 1.10 Time compression is used to shorten the length of track needed by the video. Heavily time-compressed audio samples can then be recorded on the same track using common circuitry.

Subsequently, any time compression can be reversed by time expansion. Samples are written into a RAM at the incoming clock rate, but read out at the standard sampling rate. Unless there is a design fault, time compression is totally indetectable. In a practical DVTR, the time expansion stage can be combined with the timebase-correction stage so that speed variations in the medium can be eliminated at the same time. The use of time compression is universal in digital recording. In general the *instantaneous* data rate at the medium is not the same as the rate at the converters, although clearly the *average* rate must be the same.

Another application of time compression is to allow several channels of audio to be carried along with video on a single cable. This technique is used in the serial digital interface (SDI) which is explained in Chapter 3.

1.8 Error correction and concealment

As anyone familiar with analog recording will know, magnetic tape is an imperfect medium. It suffers from noise and dropouts, which in analog recording are visible. Upon reproduction of binary data, a bit is either correct or wrong, with no intermediate stage. Small amounts of noise are rejected, but, inevitably, infrequent noise impulses cause some individual bits to be in error. Dropouts cause a larger number of bits in one place to be in error. An error of this kind is called a burst error. Whatever the medium and whatever the nature of the mechanism responsible, data either are recovered correctly, or suffer some combination of bit errors and burst errors.

The visibility of a bit error depends upon which bit of the sample is involved. If the LSB of one sample was in error in a detailed, contrasty picture, the effect would be totally masked and no-one could detect it. Conversely, if the MSB of one sample was in error in a flat field, no-one could fail to notice the resulting spot. Clearly a means is needed to render errors from the medium inaudible. This is the purpose of error correction.

In binary, a bit has only two states. If it is wrong, it is only necessary to reverse the state and it must be right. Thus the correction process is trivial and perfect. The main difficulty is in identifying the bits which are in error. This is done by coding the data by adding redundant bits. Adding redundancy is not confined to digital technology: airliners have several engines and cars have twin braking systems. Clearly the more failures which have to be handled, the more redundancy is needed. If a four-engined airliner is designed to fly normally with one engine failed, three of the engines have enough power to reach cruise speed, and the fourth one is redundant. The amount of redundancy is equal to the amount of failure which can be handled. In the case of the failure of two engines, the airliner can still fly, but it must slow down; this is graceful degradation. Clearly the chances of a two-engine failure on the same flight are remote.

In digital recording, the amount of error which can be corrected is proportional to the amount of redundancy, and it will be shown in Chapter 5 that within this limit, the samples are returned to exactly their original value. Consequently *corrected* samples are indetectable. If the amount of error exceeds the amount of redundancy, correction is not possible, and, in order to allow graceful degradation, concealment will be used. Concealment is a process where the value of a missing sample is estimated from those nearby. The estimated sample value

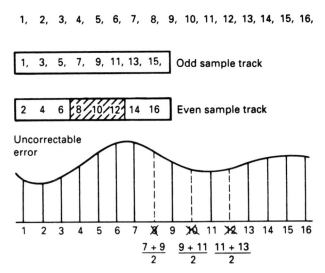

Figure 1.11 In cases where the error correction is inadequate, concealment can be used provided that the samples have been ordered appropriately in the recording. Odd and even samples are recorded in different places as shown here. As a result an uncorrectable error causes incorrect samples to occur singly, between correct samples. In the example shown, sample 8 is incorrect, but samples 7 and 9 are unaffected and an approximation to the value of sample 8 can be had by taking the average value of the two. This interpolated value is substituted for the incorrect value.

is not necessarily exactly the same as the original, and so under some circumstances concealment can be audible, especially if it is frequent. However, in a well-designed system, concealments occur with negligible frequency unless there is an actual fault or problem.

Concealment is made possible by rearranging the sample sequence prior to recording. This is shown in Figure 1.11 where odd-numbered samples are separated from even-numbered samples prior to recording. The odd and even sets of samples may be distributed over two tape tracks, so that an uncorrectable burst error only affects one set. On replay, the samples are recombined into their natural sequence, and the error is now split up so that it results in every other sample being lost in a two-dimensional structure. The picture is now described half as often, but can still be reproduced with some loss of accuracy. This is better than not being reproduced at all even if it is not perfect. Almost all digital recorders use such an odd/even distribution for concealment. Clearly if errors are fully correctable, the distribution pattern is of no consequence; it is only needed if correction is not possible.

The presence of an error-correction system means that the video (and audio) quality is independent of the tape/head quality within limits. There is no point in trying to assess the health of a machine by watching a monitor or listening to the audio, as this will not reveal whether the error rate is normal or within a whisker of failure. The only useful procedure is to monitor the frequency with which errors are being corrected, and to compare it with normal figures. Professional DVTRs have an error rate display for this purpose and in addition most allow the error-correction system to be disabled for testing.

1.9 Product codes

The higher the recording density, the more data are lost in a given sized dropout. Adding redundancy equal to the size of a dropout to every code is inefficient. Figure 1.12(a) shows that the efficiency of the system can be raised using interleaving. Following distribution, sequential samples from the ADC are assembled into codes, but these are not recorded in their natural sequence. A number of sequential codes are assembled along rows in a memory. When the memory is full, it is copied to the medium by reading down columns. On replay, the samples need to be de-interleaved to return them to their natural sequence. This is done by writing samples from tape into a memory in columns, and when it is full, the memory is read in rows. Samples read from the memory are now in their original sequence so there is no effect on the recording. However, if a burst error occurs on the medium as is shown shaded on the diagram, it will damage sequential samples in a vertical direction in the de-interleave memory. When the memory is read, a single large error is broken down into a number of small errors whose size is exactly equal to the correcting power of the codes and the correction is performed with maximum efficiency.

An extension of the process of interleave is where the memory array has not only rows made into codewords, but also columns made into codewords by the addition of vertical redundancy. This is known as a product code. Figure 1.12(b) shows that in a product code the redundancy calculated first and checked last is called the outer code, and the redundancy calculated second and checked first is called the inner code. The inner code is formed along tracks on the medium. Random errors due to noise are corrected by the inner code and do not impair the

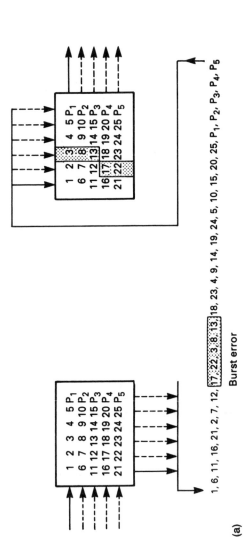

1, 6, 11, 16, 21, 2, 7, 12, 17, 22, 3, 8, 13, 18, 23, 4, 9, 14, 19, 24, 5, 10, 15, 20, 25, P_1, P_2, P_3, P_4, P_5

Burst error

(a)

Figure 1.12(a) Interleaving is essential to make error correction schemes more efficient. Samples written sequentially in rows into a memory have redundancy P added to each row. The memory is then read in columns and the data sent to the recording medium. On replay the non-sequential samples from the medium are de-interleaved to return them to their normal sequence. This breaks up the burst error (shaded) into one error symbol per row in the memory, which can be corrected by the redundancy P.

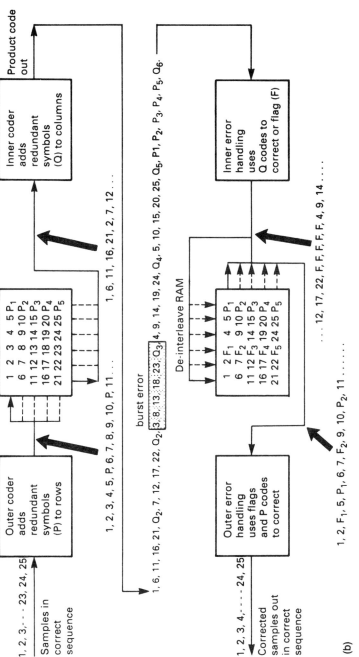

Figure 1.12(b) In addition to the redundancy P on rows, inner redundancy Q is also generated on columns. On replay, the Q code checker will pass on flags F if it finds an error too large to handle itself. The flags pass through the de-interleave process and are used by the outer error correction to identify which symbol in the row needs correcting with P redundancy. The concept of crossing two codes in this way is called a product code.

(b)

burst-correcting power of the outer code. Burst errors are declared uncorrectable by the inner code which flags the bad samples on the way into the de-interleave memory. The outer code reads the error flags in order to locate the erroneous data. As it does not have to compute the error locations, the outer code can correct more errors.

The interleave, de-interleave, time compression and timebase-correction processes cause delay and this is evident in the timing of the confidence replay output of DVTRs.

1.10 Shuffling

When a product-code-based recording suffers an uncorrectable error the result is a rectangular block of failed sample values which require concealment. Such a regular structure would be visible even after concealment, and an additional process is necessary to reduce the visibility. Figure 1.13 shows that a shuffle

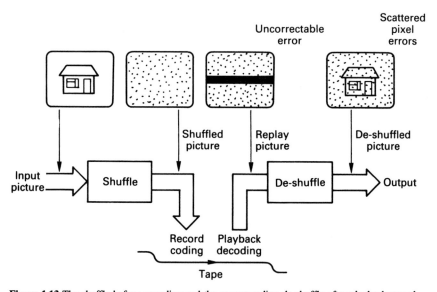

Figure 1.13 The shuffle before recording and the corresponding de-shuffle after playback cancel out as far as the picture is concerned. However, a block of errors due to dropout only experiences the de-shuffle, which spreads the error randomly over the screen. The pixel errors are then easier to conceal.

process is performed prior to product coding in which the pixels are moved around the picture in a pseudo-random fashion. The reverse process is used on replay, and the overall effect is nullified. However, if an uncorrectable error occurs, this will only pass through the de-shuffle and so the regular structure of the failed data blocks will be randomized. The errors are spread across the picture as individual failed pixels in an irregular structure. Chapter 7 treats shuffling techniques in more detail.

1.11 Channel coding

In most recorders used for storing digital information, the medium carries a track which reproduces a single waveform. Clearly data words representing audio samples contain many bits and so they have to be recorded serially, a bit at a time. DVTRs usually have two or four tracks which are read or written simultaneously. At high recording densities, physical tolerances cause phase shifts, or timing errors, between tracks and so it is not possible to read them in parallel. Each track must still be self-contained until the replayed signal has been timebase corrected.

Recording data serially is not as simple as connecting the serial output of a shift register to the head. In typical data, samples may contain strings of identical bits. If a shift register is loaded with such a sample and shifted out serially, the output stays at a constant level for the period of the identical bits, and no event is recorded on the track. On replay there is nothing to indicate how many bits were present, or even how fast to move the medium. Clearly serialized raw data cannot be recorded directly; it has to be modulated into a waveform which contains an embedded clock irrespective of the values of the bits in the samples. On replay a circuit called a data separator can lock to the embedded clock and use it to separate strings of identical bits.

The process of modulating serial data to make it self-clocking is called channel coding. Channel coding also shapes the spectrum of the serialized waveform to make it more efficient. With a good channel code, more data can be stored on a given medium. Spectrum shaping is used in certain DVTRs to allow re-recording without erase heads.

All of the techniques of channel coding are covered in detail in Chapter 4.

1.12 Video data reduction

Digital video operates with an extremely high data rate, particularly in high definition, and one approach to the problem is to reduce that rate without affecting the subjective quality of the picture. The human eye is not equally sensitive to all spatial frequencies, so some coding gain can be obtained by quantizing more coarsely the frequencies which are less visible. Video images typically contain a great deal of redundancy where flat areas contain similar pixel values repeated many times. Furthermore, in many cases there is little difference between one field and the next, and inter field data reduction can be achieved by sending only the differences. Whilst this may achieve considerable reduction, the result is difficult to edit because individual fields can no longer be identified in the data stream. Thus for production purposes, data reduction is restricted to exploiting the redundancy within each field individually. Production DVTRs such as Sony's Digital Betacam and the Ampex DCT use only very mild compression of about 2:1. This allows simple algorithms to be used and also permits multiple generations without artifacts being visible. Data reduction is discussed in Chapter 2.

Clearly a consumer DVTR needs only single-generation operation and has simple editing requirements. A much greater degree of compression can then be used, which might also take advantage of redundancy between fields.

Data reduction requires an encoder prior to the recording medium and a decoder after it. Unless the matching decoder is available, the recording cannot be played. Data reduction and the corresponding decoding are complex processes and take time, adding to existing delays in signal paths. Concealment of uncorrectable errors is also more difficult on reduced data.

1.13 The rotary-head tape transport

The high bit rate of digital video could be accommodated by a conventional tape deck having many parallel tracks, but each would need its own read/write electronics and the cost would be high. However, the main problem with such an approach is that the data rate is proportional to the tape speed. The provision of stunt modes such as still frame or picture-in-shuttle are difficult or impossible. The rotary head recorder has the advantage that the spinning heads create a high head-to-tape speed offering a high-bit-rate recording with a small number of heads and without high tape speed. The head-to-tape speed is dominated by the rotational speed, and the linear tape speed can vary enormously without changing the frequencies produced by the head by very much. Whilst mechanically complex, the rotary-head transport has been raised to a high degree of refinement and offers the highest recording density and thus lowest cost per bit of all digital recorders. Rotary-head transports are considered in detail in Chapter 6. Figure 1.14 shows that the tape is led around a rotating drum in a helix such that the

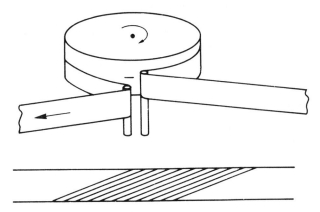

Figure 1.14 The tape is led in a helix around the revolving head drum. This results in long diagonal tracks across the tape.

entrance and exit heights are different. As a result the rotating heads cross the tape at an angle and record a series of slanting tracks. The rotating heads turn at a speed which is locked to the video field rate so that a whole number of tracks results in each input field. Time compression can be used so that the switch from one track to the next falls within a gap between data blocks. Clearly the slant tracks can only be played back properly if linear tape motion is controlled in some way. This is the job of the linear control track which carries a pulse corresponding to every slant track. The control track is played back in order to control the capstan. The breaking up of fields into several tracks is called segmentation and it is used to keep the tracks reasonably short. The segments are invisibly reassembled in memory on replay to restore the original fields.

1.14 DVTR block diagram

Figure 1.15(a) shows a representative block diagram of a full bit-rate DVTR. Following the converters will be the distribution of odd and even samples and a shuffle process for concealment purposes. An interleaved product code will be formed prior to the channel coding stage which produces the recorded waveform. On replay the data separator decodes the channel code and the inner and outer codes perform correction as in Section 1.11. Following the de-shuffle the data channels are recombined and any necessary concealment will take place. Figure 1.15(b) shows the block diagram of a DVTR using data reduction. Data from the converters are rearranged from the normal raster scan to sets of pixel blocks upon which the data reduction unit works. A common size is eight pixels horizontally by four vertically. The blocks are then shuffled for concealment purposes. The shuffled blocks are passed through the data reduction unit. The output of this is distributed and then assembled into product codes and channel coded as for a conventional recorder. On replay data separation and error correction takes place as before, but there is now a matching data expansion unit which outputs pixel blocks. These are then de-shuffled prior to the error concealment stage. As concealment is more difficult with pixel blocks, data from another field may be employed for concealment as well as data within the field.

Chapter 7 treats the signal systems of DVTRs in some detail.

1.15 Operating modes of a DVTR

A simple recorder needs to do little more than record and play back, but the sophistication of modern production processes requires a great deal more flexibility. A production DVTR will need to support most if not all of the following:

- Offtape confidence replay must be available during recording.
- Timecode must be recorded and this must be playable at all tape speeds. Full remote control is required so that edit controllers can synchronize several machines via timecode.
- A high-quality video signal is required over a speed range of $-1 \times$ to $+3 \times$ normal speed. Audio recovery is required in order to locate edit points from dialogue.
- A picture of some kind is required over the whole shuttle speed range (typically $\pm 50 \times$ normal speed).
- Assembly and insert editing must be supported, and it must be possible to edit the audio and video channels independently.
- It must be possible slightly to change the replay speed in order to shorten or lengthen programs. Full audio and video quality must be available in this mode, known as tape speed override (TSO).
- For editing purposes, there is a requirement for the DVTR to be able to play back the tape with heads fitted in advance of the record head. The playback signal can be processed in some way and re-recorded in a single pass. This is known as pre-read, or read–modify–write operation.

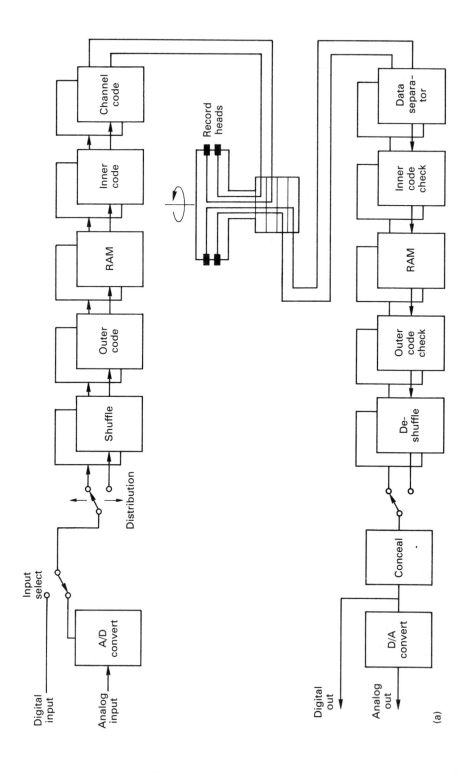

(a)

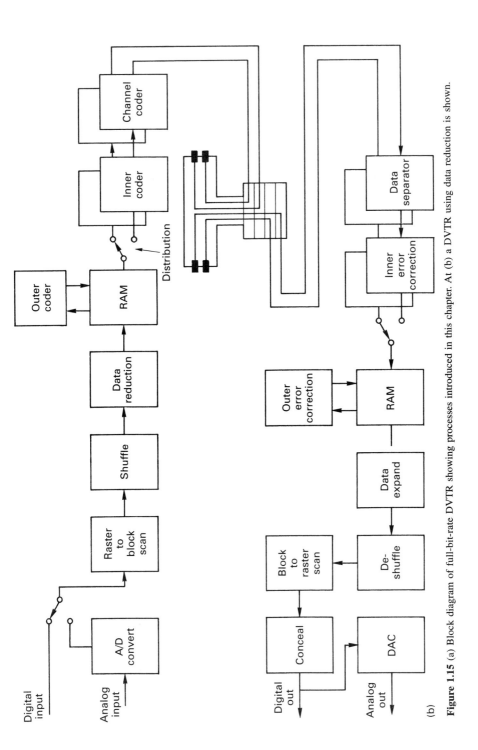

Figure 1.15 (a) Block diagram of full-bit-rate DVTR showing processes introduced in this chapter. At (b) a DVTR using data reduction is shown.

1.16 Confidence replay

It is important to be quite certain that a recording is being made, and the only way of guaranteeing that this is so is actually to play the tape as it is being recorded. Extra heads are fitted to the revolving drum in such a way that they pass along the slant tracks directly behind the record heads. The drum must carry additional rotary transformers so that signals can simultaneously enter and leave the rotating head assembly. As can be seen in Figure 1.16 the input signal will be made

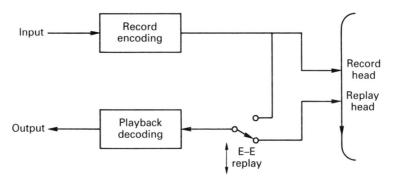

Figure 1.16 A professional DVTR uses confidence replay, where the signal recorded is immediately played back. If the tape is not running, the heads are bypassed in E-E mode so that all of the circuitry can be checked.

available at the machine output if all is well. In analog machines it was traditional to assess the quality of the recording by watching a picture monitor connected to the confidence replay output during recording. With a digital machine this is not necessary, and instead the rate at which the replay channel performs error corrections should be monitored. In some machines the error rate is made available at an output socket so that remote or centralized data reliability logging can be used. It will be seen from Figure 1.16 that when the machine is not running, a connection is made which bypasses the record and playback heads. The output signal in this mode has passed through every process in the machine except the actual tape/head system. This is known as E–E (Electronics to Electronics) mode, and is a good indication that the circuitry is functioning.

1.17 Colour framing

As will be seen in Chapter 3, composite video has a subcarrier added to the luminance in order to carry the colour difference signals. The frequency of this subcarrier is critical if it is to be invisible on monochrome TV sets, and as a result it does not have a whole number of cycles within a frame, but only returns to its starting phase once every two frames in NTSC and every four frames in PAL. These are known as colour framing sequences. When playing back a composite recording, the offtape colour frame sequence must be synchronized with the reference colour frame sequence, otherwise composite replay signals cannot be mixed with signals from elsewhere in the facility. When editing composite recordings, the subcarrier phase must not be disturbed at the edit point and this puts constraints on the edit control process. In both cases the solution is to record the start of a colour frame sequence in the control track of the tape. There is also a standardized algorithm linking the timecode with the colour framing sequences. Colour framing will be detailed in Chapter 7.

1.18 Timecode

Timecode is simply a label attached to each frame on the tape which contains the time at which it was recorded measured in hours, minutes, seconds and frames. There are two ways in which timecode data can be recorded. The first is to use a dedicated linear track, usually alongside the control track, in which there is one timecode entry for every tape frame. Such a linear track can easily be played back over a wide speed range by a stationary head. Timecode of this kind is known as linear timecode (LTC).

LTC clearly cannot be replayed when the tape is stopped or moving very slowly. In DVTRs with track-following heads, particularly those which support pre-read, head deflection may result in a frame being played which is not the one corresponding to the timecode from the stationary head. The player software needs to modify the LTC value as a function of the head deflection.

An alternative timecode is where the information is recorded in the video field itself, so that the above mismatch cannot occur. This is known as vertical interval timecode (VITC) because it is recorded in a line which is in the vertical blanking period. VITC has the advantage that it can be recovered with the tape stopped, but it cannot be recovered in shuttle because the rotary heads do not play entire tracks in this mode. DVTRs do not record the whole of the vertical blanking period, and if VITC is to be used, it must be inserted in a line which is within the recorded data area of the format concerned.

1.19 Picture-in-shuttle

A rotary-head recorder cannot follow the tape tracks properly when the tape is shuttled. Instead the heads cross the tracks at an angle and intermittently pick up short data blocks. Each of these blocks is an inner error-correcting codeword and this can be checked to see if the block was properly recovered. If this is the case, the data can be used to update a frame store which displays the shuttle picture. Clearly the shuttle picture is a mosaic of parts of many fields. In addition to helping the concealment of errors, the shuffle process is beneficial to obtaining picture-in-shuttle. Owing to shuffle, a block recovered from the tape contains data from many places in the picture, and this gives a better result than if many pixels were available from one place in the picture. The twinkling effect seen in shuttle is due to the updating of individual pixels following de-shuffle.

When data reduction is used, the picture is processed in blocks, and these will be visible as mosaicing in the shuttle picture as the frame store is updated by the blocks.

In composite recorders, the subcarrier sequence is only preserved when playing at normal speed. In all other cases, extra *colour processing* is required to convert the disjointed replay signal into a continuous subcarrier once more.

1.20 Digital audio in DVTRs

Audio was traditionally the poor relation in television, and the situation was not helped by the characteristics of rotary-head video recorders which had low linear tape speed by audio standards and high flutter. Most of the advantages attributed to digital video also apply to audio, and have recently helped to transform TV sound. Digital audio eliminates wow, flutter and phase errors between channels, and the use of error correction eliminates dropouts. Any signal-to-noise ratio required can be had by choice of a suitable sample wordlength. In fact most DVTRs can record 20 bit audio and thus outperform many audio-only formats. The Compact Disc served to raise the consumer's expectations in audio and this was shortly followed by the NICAM 728 digital transmission system. In view of the importance of audio in today's television productions, the entire contents of Chapter 8 are devoted to it.

Reference

1. BETTS, J.A., *Signal Processing Modulation and Noise*, Ch. 6. Sevenoaks: Hodder and Stoughton (1970)

Chapter 2

Essential principles

The conversion process expresses the analog input as a numerical code, but the choice of code for video will be shown to be governed by the processing requirements. Within the circuitry of a DVTR, all signal processing must be performed by arithmetic manipulation of the code values in suitable logic circuits. All of the necessary principles of such processing are shown here, beginning with basic logic and progressing to data reduction.

2.1 Pure binary code

For digital video use, the prime purpose of binary numbers is to express the values of the samples which represent the original analog video waveform. Figure 2.1 shows some binary numbers and their equivalent in decimal. The radix point has the same significance in binary: symbols to the right of it represent one-half, one-quarter and so on. Binary is convenient for electronic circuits, which do not get tired, but numbers expressed in binary become very long, and writing them is tedious and error prone. The octal and hexadecimal notations are both used for writing binary since conversion is so simple. Figure 2.1 also shows that a binary number is split into groups of three or four digits starting at the least significant end, and the groups are individually converted to octal or hexadecimal digits. Since 16 different symbols are required in hex. the letters A–F are used for the numbers above nine.

There will be a fixed number of bits in a PCM video sample, and this number determines the size of the quantizing range. In the 8 bit samples used in much digital video equipment, there are 256 different numbers. Each number represents a different analog signal voltage, and care must be taken during conversion to ensure that the signal does not go outside the converter range, or it will be clipped. In Figure 2.2(a) it will be seen that in an 8 bit pure binary system, the number range goes from 00 hex, which represents the smallest voltage, through to FF hex, which represents the largest positive voltage. The video waveform must be accommodated within this voltage range, and Figure 2.2(b) shows how this can be done for a PAL composite signal. A luminance signal is shown in Figure 2.2(c). As component digital systems only handle the active line, the quantizing range is optimized to suit the gamut of the unblanked luminance. There is a small offset in order to handle slightly misadjusted inputs.

Colour difference signals are bipolar and so blanking is in the centre of the signal range. In order to accommodate colour difference signals in the quantizing

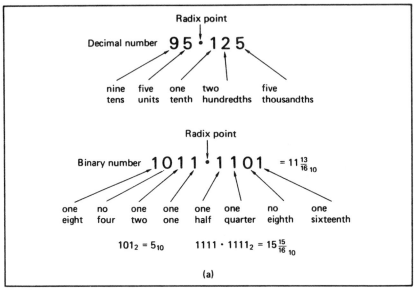

Binary   Octal
000000   00
000001   01
000010   02
000011   03
000100   04
000101   05
000110   06
000111   07 ◄──Overflow
001000   10
001001   11
etc.   etc.

10101   011 · 011   Binary
 2 5   3 · 3   Octal
× ×   ×   ×
64 8   1 $\frac{1}{8}$

= 171$\frac{3}{8}$ $_{10}$

There is no 8 or 9 in Octal

(b)

Binary	Hex	Decimal
0000	0	0
0001	1	1
0010	2	2
0011	3	3
0100	4	4
0101	5	5
0110	6	6
0111	7	7
1000	8	8
1001	9	9
1010	A	10
1011	B	11
1100	C	12
1101	D	13
1110	E	14
1111	F	15

1100 0000 1111 1111 1110 1110   Binary
 C   0   F   F   E   E   Hex

       0   15   15   14   14
       ×   ×   ×   ×
    65 536 4096 256   16

12
×
1048576   = 12 648 430$_{10}$

(c)

Figure 2.1 (a) Binary and decimal. (b) In octal, groups of 3 bits make one symbol 0–7. (c) In hex, groups of 4 bits make one symbol 0–F. Note how much shorter the number is in hex.

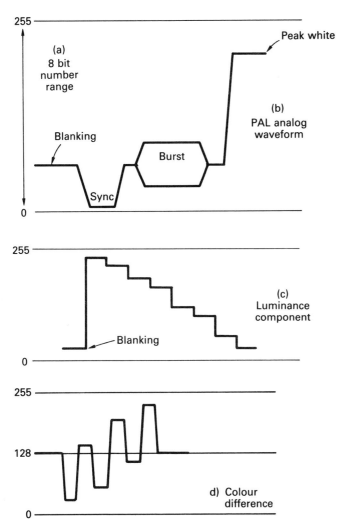

Figure 2.2 The unipolar quantizing range of an 8 bit pure binary system is shown at (a). The analog input must be shifted to fit into the quantizing range, as shown for PAL at (b). In component, sync pulses are not digitized, so the quantizing intervals can be smaller as at (c). An offset of half scale is used for colour difference signals (d).

range, the blanking voltage level of the analog waveform has been shifted as in Figure 2.2(d) so that the positive and negative voltages in a real audio signal can be expressed by binary numbers which are only positive. This approach is called offset binary. Strictly speaking both the composite and luminance signals are also offset binary because the blanking level is part way up the quantizing scale.

Offset binary is perfectly acceptable where the signal has been digitized only for recording or transmission from one place to another, after which it will be converted directly back to analog. Under these conditions it is not necessary for the quantizing steps to be uniform, provided both the ADC and DAC are

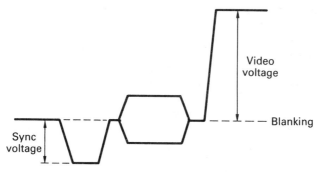

Figure 2.3 All video signal voltages are referred to blanking and must be added with respect to that level.

constructed to the same standard. In practice, it is the requirements of signal processing in the digital domain which make both non-uniform quantizing and offset binary unsuitable.

Figure 2.3 shows that analog video signal voltages are referred to blanking. The level of the signal is measured by how far the waveform deviates from blanking, and attenuation, gain and mixing all take place around blanking level. Digital vision mixing is achieved by adding sample values from two or more different sources, but unless all of the quantizing intervals are of the same size and there is no offset, the sum of two sample values will not represent the sum of the two original analog voltages. Thus sample values which have been obtained by non-uniform or offset quantizing cannot readily be processed because the binary numbers are not proportional to the signal voltage.

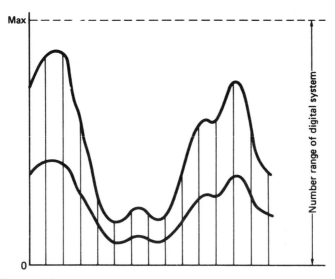

Figure 2.4 The result of an attempted attenuation in pure binary code is an offset. Pure binary cannot be used for digital video processing.

If two offset binary sample streams are added together in an attempt to perform digital mixing, the result will be that the offsets are also added and this may lead to an overflow. Similarly, if an attempt is made to attenuate by, say, 6.02 dB by dividing all of the sample values by two, Figure 2.4 shows that the offset is also divided and the waveform suffers a shifted baseline. This problem can be overcome with digital luminance signals simply by subtracting the offset from each sample before processing as this results in numbers truly proportional to the luminance voltage. This approach is not suitable for colour difference or composite signals because negative numbers would result when the analog voltage goes below blanking and pure binary coding cannot handle them. The problem with offset binary is that it works with reference to one end of the range. What is needed is a numbering system which operates symmetrically with reference to the centre of the range.

2.2 Two's complement

In the two's complement system, the upper half of the pure binary number range has been redefined to represent negative quantities. If a pure binary counter is

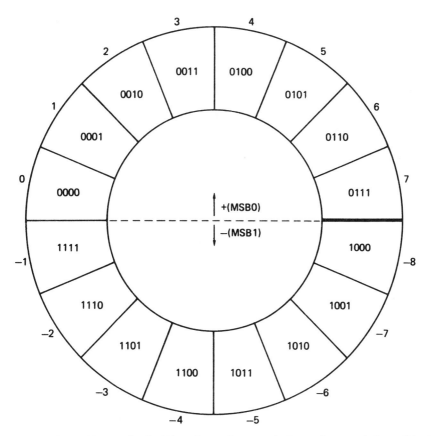

Figure 2.5 In this example of a 4 bit two's complement code, the number range is from −8 to +7. Note that the MSB determines polarity.

constantly incremented and allowed to overflow, it will produce all the numbers in the range permitted by the number of available bits, and these are shown for a 4 bit example drawn around the circle in Figure 2.5. As a circle has no real beginning, it is possible to consider it to start wherever it is convenient. In two's complement, the quantizing range represented by the circle of numbers does not start at zero, but starts on the diametrically opposite side of the circle. Zero is midrange, and all numbers with the MSB (Most Significant Bit) set are considered negative. The MSB is thus the equivalent of a sign bit where 1 = minus. Two's complement notation differs from pure binary in that the MSB is inverted in order to achieve the half circle rotation.

Figure 2.6 shows how a real ADC is configured to produce two's complement output. At (a) an analog offset voltage equal to one-half the quantizing range is added to the bipolar analog signal in order to make it unipolar as at (b). The ADC produces positive-only numbers at (c) which are proportional to the input voltage. The MSB is then inverted at (d) so that the all-zeros code moves to the centre of the quantizing range. The analog offset is often incorporated in the ADC as is the MSB inversion. Some converters are designed to be used in either pure binary or two's complement mode. In this case the designer must arrange the appropriate DC conditions at the input. The MSB inversion may be selectable by an external logic level. In the digital video interface standards the colour difference signals use offset binary because the codes of all zeros and all ones are at the end of the range and can be reserved for synchronizing. A digital vision mixer simply inverts the MSB of each colour difference sample to convert it to two's complement.

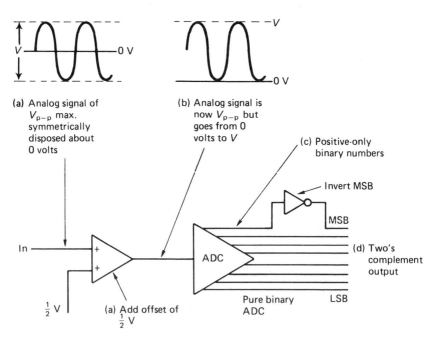

Figure 2.6 A two's complement ADC. At (a) an analog offset voltage equal to one-half the quantizing range is added to the bipolar analog signal in order to make it unipolar as at (b). The ADC produces positive only numbers at (c), but the MSB is then inverted at (d) to give a two's complement output.

The two's complement system allows two sample values to be added, or mixed in video parlance, and the result will be referred to the system midrange; this is analogous to adding analog signals in an operational amplifier.

Figure 2.7 illustrates how adding two's complement samples simulates a bipolar mixing process. The waveform of input A is depicted by solid black samples, and that of B by samples with a solid outline. The result of mixing is the linear sum of the two waveforms obtained by adding pairs of sample values. The dashed lines depict the output values. Beneath each set of samples is the calculation which will be seen to give the correct result. Note that the calculations are pure binary. No special arithmetic is needed to handle two's complement numbers.

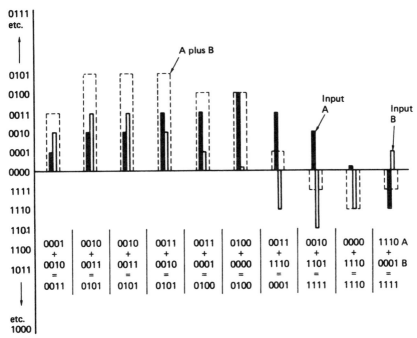

Figure 2.7 Using two's complement arithmetic, single values from two waveforms are added together with respect to midrange to give a correct mixing function.

It is sometimes necessary to phase-reverse or invert a digital signal. The process of inversion in two's complement is simple. All bits of the sample value are inverted to form the one's complement, and one is added. This can be checked by mentally inverting some of the values in Figure 2.5. The inversion is transparent and performing a second inversion gives the original sample values.

Using inversion, signal subtraction can be performed using only adding logic. The inverted input is added to perform a subtraction, just as in the analog domain. This permits a significant saving in hardware complexity, since only carry logic is necessary and no borrow mechanism need be supported.

In summary, two's complement notation is the most appropriate scheme for bipolar signals, and allows simple mixing in conventional binary adders. It is in virtually universal use in digital video and audio processing.

Two's complement numbers can have a radix point and bits below it just as pure binary numbers can. It should, however, be noted that in two's complement, if a radix point exists, numbers to the right of it are added. For example 1100.1 is not −4.5, it is −4 + 0.5 = −3.5.

2.3 Introduction to digital processes

However complex a digital process, it can be broken down into smaller stages until finally one finds that there are really only two basic types of element in use, and these can be combined in some way and supplied with a clock to implement virtually any process. Figure 2.8 shows that the first type is a *logical* element. This produces an output which is a logical function of the input with minimal delay. The second type is a *storage* element which samples the state of the input(s) when clocked and holds or delays that state. The strength of binary logic

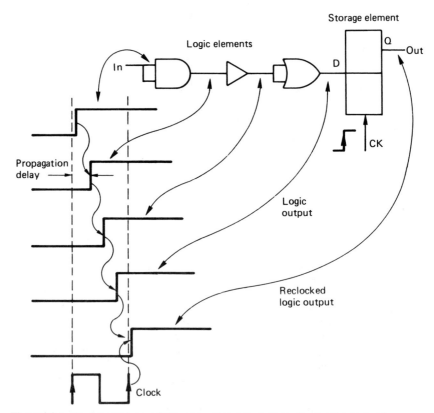

Figure 2.8 Logic elements have a finite propagation delay between input and output and cascading them delays the signal an arbitrary amount. Storage elements sample the input on a clock edge and can return a signal to near coincidence with the system clock. This is known as reclocking. Reclocking eliminates variations in propagation delay in logic elements.

is that the signal has only two states, and considerable noise and distortion of the binary waveform can be tolerated before the state becomes uncertain. At every logical element, the signal is compared with a threshold, and thus can pass through any number of stages without being degraded. In addition, the use of a storage element at regular locations throughout logic circuits eliminates time variations or jitter. Figure 2.8 shows that if the inputs to a logic element change, the output will not change until the *propagation delay* of the element has elapsed. However, if the output of the logic element forms the input to a storage element, the output of that element will not change until the input is sampled *at the next clock edge*. In this way the signal edge is aligned to the system clock and the propagation delay of the logic becomes irrelevant. The process is known as reclocking.

2.4 Logic elements

The two states of the signal when measured with an oscilloscope are simply two voltages, usually referred to as high and low. The actual voltage levels will depend on the type of logic family in use, and on the supply voltage used. Within logic, these levels are not of much consequence, and it is only necessary to know them when interfacing between different logic families or when driving external devices. The pure logic designer is not interested at all in these voltages, only in their meaning. Just as the electrical waveform from a microphone represents sound velocity, so the waveform in a logic circuit represents the truth of some statement. As there are only two states, there can only be *true* or *false* meanings. The true state of the signal can be assigned by the designer to either voltage state. When a high voltage represents a true logic condition and a low voltage represents a false condition, the system is known as *positive logic*, or *high true* logic. This is the usual system, but sometimes the low voltage represents the true condition and the high voltage represents the false condition. This is known as *negative logic* or *low true* logic. Provided that everyone is aware of the logic convention in use, both work equally well.

Negative logic is often found in the TTL (Transistor Transistor-Logic) family, because in this technology it is easier to sink current to ground than to source it from the power supply. Figure 2.9 shows that if it is necessary to connect several logic elements to a common bus so that any one can communicate with any other, an open-collector system is used, where high levels are provided by pull-up resistors and the logic elements only pull the common line down. If positive logic were used, when no device was operating the pull-up resistors would cause the common line to take on an absurd true state; whereas if negative logic were used, the common line would pull up to a sensible false condition when there is no device using the bus. Whilst the open collector is a simple way of obtaining a shared bus system, it is limited in frequency of operation due to the time constant of the pull-up resistors charging the bus capacitance. In the so called tri-state bus systems, there are both active pull-up and pull-down devices connected in the so-called totem-pole output configuration. Both devices can be disabled to a third state, where the output assumes a high impedance, allowing some other driver to determine the bus state.

In logic systems, all logical functions, however complex, can be configured from combinations of a few fundamental logic elements or *gates*. It is not profitable to spend too much time debating which are the truly fundamental ones,

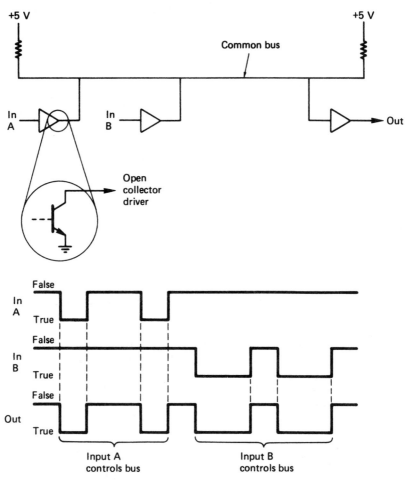

Figure 2.9 Using open-collector drive, several signal sources can share one common bus. If negative logic is used, the bus drivers turn off their output transistors with a false input, allowing another driver to control the bus. This will not happen with positive logic.

since most can be made from combinations of others. Figure 2.10 shows the important simple gates and their derivatives, and introduces the logical expressions to describe them, which can be compared with the truth-table notation. The figure also shows the important fact that when negative logic is used, the OR gate function interchanges with that of the AND gate. Sometimes schematics are drawn to reflect which voltage state represents the true condition. In the so-called intentional logic scheme, a negative logic signal always starts and ends at an inverting 'bubble'. If an AND function is required between two negative logic signals, it will be drawn as an AND symbol with bubbles on all the terminals, even though the component used will be a positive logic OR gate. Opinions vary on the merits of intentional logic.

If numerical quantities need to be conveyed down the two-state signal paths described here, then the only appropriate numbering system is binary, which has

Positive logic name	Boolean expression	Positive logic symbol	Positive logic truth table	Plain English
Inverter or NOT gate	$Q = \overline{A}$	A ──▷○── Q	$\begin{array}{c\|c} A & Q \\ \hline 0 & 1 \\ 1 & 0 \end{array}$	Output is opposite of input
AND gate	$Q = A \cdot B$	A, B ──⟩── Q	$\begin{array}{cc\|c} A & B & Q \\ \hline 0 & 0 & 0 \\ 0 & 1 & 0 \\ 1 & 0 & 0 \\ 1 & 1 & 1 \end{array}$	Output true when both inputs are true only
NAND (Not AND) gate	$Q = \overline{A \cdot B}$ $= \overline{A} + \overline{B}$	A, B ──⟩○── Q	$\begin{array}{cc\|c} A & B & Q \\ \hline 0 & 0 & 1 \\ 0 & 1 & 1 \\ 1 & 0 & 1 \\ 1 & 1 & 0 \end{array}$	Output false when both inputs are true only
OR gate	$Q = A + B$	A, B ──⟩── Q	$\begin{array}{cc\|c} A & B & Q \\ \hline 0 & 0 & 0 \\ 0 & 1 & 1 \\ 1 & 0 & 1 \\ 1 & 1 & 1 \end{array}$	Output true if either or both inputs true
NOR (Not OR) gate	$Q = \overline{A + B}$ $= \overline{A} \cdot \overline{B}$	A, B ──⟩○── Q	$\begin{array}{cc\|c} A & B & Q \\ \hline 0 & 0 & 1 \\ 0 & 1 & 0 \\ 1 & 0 & 0 \\ 1 & 1 & 0 \end{array}$	Output false if either or both inputs true
Exclusive OR (XOR) gate	$Q = A \oplus B$	A, B ──⟩⟩── Q	$\begin{array}{cc\|c} A & B & Q \\ \hline 0 & 0 & 0 \\ 0 & 1 & 1 \\ 1 & 0 & 1 \\ 1 & 1 & 0 \end{array}$	Output true if inputs are different

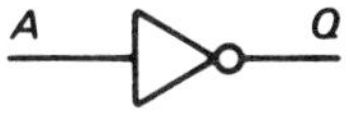

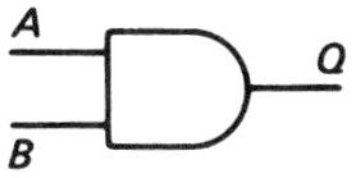

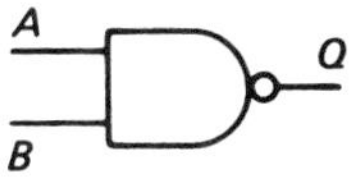

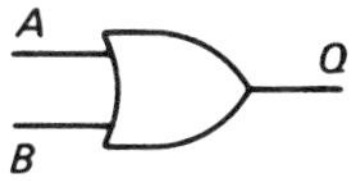

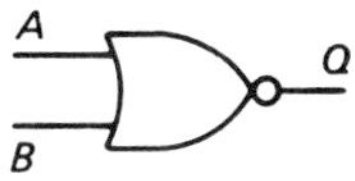

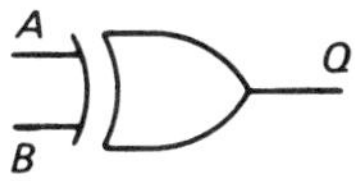

Figure 2.10 The basic logic gates compared.

only two symbols, 0 and 1. Just as positive or negative logic could be used for the truth of a logical binary signal, it can also be used for a numerical binary signal. Normally, a high voltage level will represent a binary 1 and a low voltage will represent a binary 0, described as a 'high for a one' system. Clearly a 'low for a one' system is just as feasible. Decimal numbers have several columns, each of which represents a different power of ten; in binary the column position specifies the power of two.

Several binary digits or bits are needed to express the value of a binary video sample. These bits can be conveyed at the same time by several signals to form a parallel system, which is most convenient inside equipment or for short distances because it is inexpensive, or one at a time down a single signal path, which is more complex, but convenient for cables between pieces of equipment because the connectors require fewer pins. When a binary system is used to convey numbers in this way, it can be called a digital system.

2.5 Storage elements

The basic memory element in logic circuits is the latch, which is constructed from two gates as shown in Figure 2.11(a), and which can be set or reset. A more useful variant is the D-type latch shown at (b) which remembers the state of the input at the time a separate clock either changes state for an edge-triggered device, or after it goes false for a level-triggered device. D-type latches are commonly available with four or eight latches to the chip. A shift register can be made from a series of latches by connecting the Q output of one latch to the D input of the next and connecting all of the clock inputs in parallel. Data are delayed by the number of stages in the register. Shift registers are also useful for converting between serial and parallel data transmissions.

Where large numbers of bits are to be stored, cross-coupled latches are less suitable because they are more complicated to fabricate inside integrated circuits than dynamic memory, and consume more current.

In large random access memories (RAMs), the data bits are stored as the presence or absence of charge in a tiny capacitor as shown in Figure 2.11(c). The capacitor is formed by a metal electrode, insulated by a layer of silicon dioxide from a semiconductor substrate; hence the term MOS (Metal Oxide Semiconductor). The charge will suffer leakage, and the value would become indeterminate after a few milliseconds. Where the delay needed is less than this, decay is of no consequence, as data will be read out before they have had a chance to decay. Where longer delays are necessary, such memories must be refreshed periodically by reading the bit value and writing it back to the same place. Most modern MOS RAM chips have suitable circuitry built in. Large RAMs store thousands of bits, and it is clearly impractical to have a connection to each one. Instead, the desired bit has to be addressed before it can be read or written. The size of the chip package restricts the number of pins available, so that large memories use the same address pins more than once. The bits are arranged internally as rows and columns, and the row address and the column address are specified sequentially on the same pins.

2.6 The phase-locked loop

All digital video systems need to be clocked at the appropriate rate in order to function properly. Whilst a clock may be obtained from a fixed-frequency oscillator such as a crystal, many operations in video require *genlocking* or synchronizing the clock to an external source. The phase-locked loop excels at this job, and many others, particularly in connection with recording and transmission.

In phase-locked loops, the oscillator can run at a range of frequencies according to the voltage applied to a control terminal. This is called a voltage-controlled oscillator or VCO. Figure 2.12 shows that the VCO is driven by a phase error measured between the output and some reference. The error changes the control voltage in such a way that the error is reduced, such that the output eventually has the same frequency as the reference. A low-pass filter is fitted in

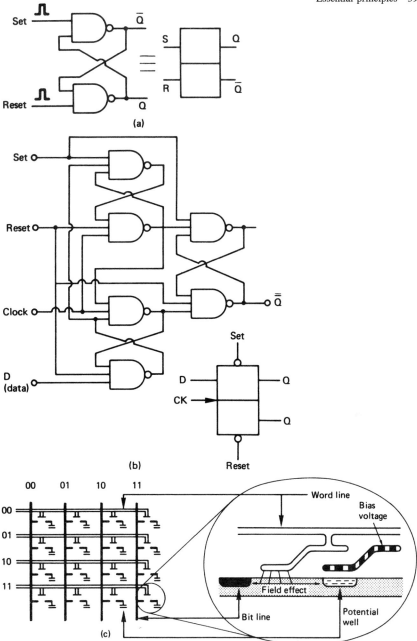

Figure 2.11 Digital semiconductor memory types. In (a), one data bit can be stored in a simple set–reset latch, which has little application because the D-type latch in (b) can store the state of the single data input when the clock occurs. These devices can be implemented with bipolar transistors of FETs, and are called static memories because they can store indefinitely. They consume a lot of power.

In (c), a bit is stored as the charge in a potential well in the substrate of a chip. It is accessed by connecting the bit line with the field effect from the word line. The single well where the two lines cross can then be written or read. These devices are called dynamic RAMs because the charge decays, and they must be read and rewritten (refreshed) periodically

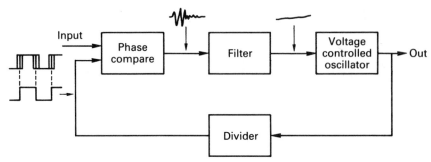

Figure 2.12 A phase-locked loop requires these components as a minimum. The filter in the control voltage serves to reduce clock jitter.

the control voltage path to prevent the loop becoming unstable. If a divider is placed between the VCO and the phase comparator, as in the figure, the VCO frequency can be made to be a multiple of the reference. This also has the effect of making the loop more heavily damped, so that it is less likely to change frequency if the input is irregular.

In digital video, the frequency multiplication of a phase-locked loop is extremely useful. Figure 2.13 shows how the 13.5 MHz clock of component

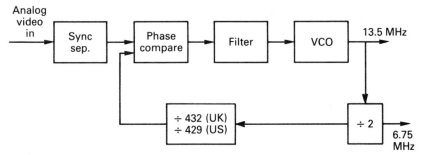

Figure 2.13 In order to obtain 13.5 MHz from input syncs, a PLL with an appropriate division ratio is required.

digital video is obtained from the sync pulses of an analog reference by such a multiplication process. In composite systems, a phase locked loop may lock to subcarrier instead.

2.7 Binary adding

The circuitry necessary for adding pure binary or two's complement numbers is shown in Figure 2.14. Addition in binary requires 2 bits to be taken at a time from the same position in each word, starting at the least significant bit. Should both be ones, the output is zero, and there is a *carry-out* generated. Such a circuit is called a half adder, shown in Figure 2.14(a), and is suitable for the least significant bit of the calculation. All higher stages will require a circuit which can

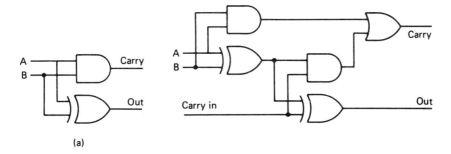

(a)

Data A	Bits B	Carry in	Out	Carry out
0	0	0	0	0
0	0	1	1	0
0	1	0	1	0
0	1	1	0	1
1	0	0	1	0
1	0	1	0	1
1	1	0	0	1
1	1	1	1	1

(b)

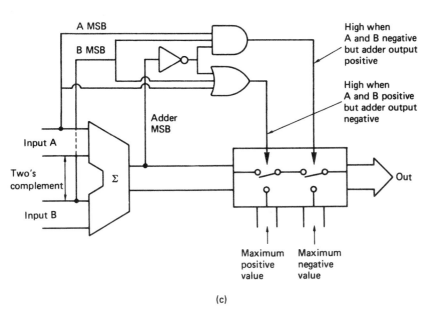

(c)

Figure 2.14 (a) Half adder; (b) full-adder circuit and truth table; (c) comparison of sign bits prevents wraparound on adder overflow by substituting clipping level.

accept a carry input as well as two data inputs. This is known as a full adder (Figure 2.14(b)). Multibit full adders are available in chip form, and have carry-in and carry-out terminals to allow them to be cascaded to operate on long wordlengths. Such a device is also convenient for inverting a two's complement number, in conjunction with a set of inverters. The adder chip has one set of inputs grounded, and the carry-in permanently held true, such that it adds one to the one's complement number from the inverter.

When mixing by adding sample values, care has to be taken to ensure that if the sum of the two sample values exceeds the number range the result will be clipping rather than wraparound. In two's complement, the action necessary depends on the polarities of the two signals. Clearly if one positive and one negative number are added, the result cannot exceed the number range. If two positive numbers are added, the symptom of positive overflow is that the most significant bit sets, causing an erroneous negative result, whereas a negative overflow results in the most significant bit clearing. The overflow control circuit will be designed to detect these two conditions, and override the adder output. If the MSB of both inputs is zero, the numbers are both positive; thus if the sum has the MSB set, the output is replaced with the maximum positive code (0111 . . .). If the MSB of both inputs is set, the numbers are both negative, and if the sum has no MSB set, the output is replaced with the maximum negative code (1000 . . .). These conditions can also be connected to warning indicators. Figure 2.14(c) shows this system in hardware. The resultant clipping on overload is sudden, and sometimes a PROM is included which translates values around and beyond maximum to soft-clipped values below or equal to maximum.

A storage element can be combined with an adder to obtain a number of useful functional blocks which will crop up frequently in video equipment. Figure 2.15(a) shows that a latch is connected in a feedback loop around an adder. The latch contents are added to the input each time it is clocked. The configuration is known as an accumulator in computation because it adds up or accumulates values fed into it. In filtering, it is known as a discrete-time integrator. If the input is held at some constant value, the output increases by that amount on each clock. The output is thus a sampled ramp.

Figure 2.15(b) shows that the addition of an inverter allows the difference between successive inputs to be obtained. This is digital differentiation. The output is proportional to the slope of the input.

2.8 Gain control by multiplication

When making a digital recording, the gain of the analog input will usually be adjusted so that the quantizing range is fully exercised in order to make a recording of maximum signal-to-noise ratio. During post production, the recording may be played back and mixed with other signals, and the desired effect can only be achieved if the level of each can be controlled independently. Gain is controlled in the digital domain by multiplying each sample value by a coefficient. If that coefficient is less than one, attenuation will result; if it is greater than one, amplification can be obtained.

Multiplication in binary circuits is difficult. It can be performed by repeated adding, but this is too slow to be of any use. In fast multiplication, one of the inputs will be simultaneously multiplied by one, two, four, etc., by hard-wired bit shifting. Figure 2.16 shows that the other input bits will determine which of these

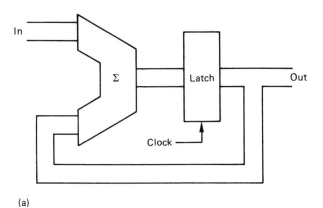

(a)

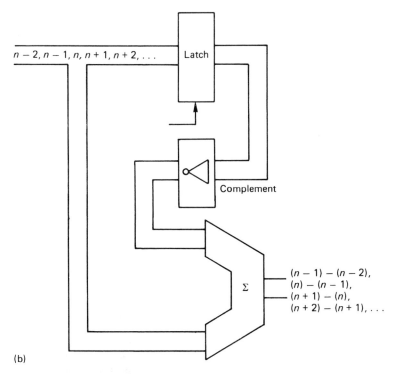

(b)

Figure 2.15 Two configurations which are common in processing. In (a) the feedback around the adder adds the previous sum to each input to perform accumulation or digital integration. In (b) an inverter allows the difference between successive inputs to be computed. This is differentiation.

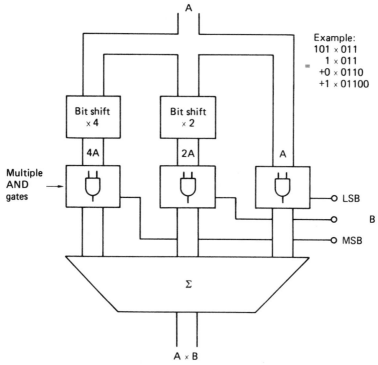

Figure 2.16 Structure of fast multiplier: the input A is multiplied by 1, 2, 4, 8, etc., by bit shifting. The digits of the B input then determine which multiples of A should be added together by enabling AND gates between the shifters and the adder. For long wordlengths, the number of gates required becomes enormous, and the device is best implemented in a chip.

powers will be added to produce the final sum, and which will be neglected. If multiplying by five, the process is the same as multiplying by four, multiplying by one, and adding the two products. This is achieved by adding the input to itself shifted two places. As the wordlength of such a device increases, the complexity increases exponentially, so this is a natural application for an integrated circuit. It is probably true that digital video would not have been viable without such chips.

2.9 Digital level controls

In an analog machine, level controls were invariably implemented as a variable resistance at some point in the circuitry. In a DVTR all operational signal level adjustments are performed by changing the gain coefficients supplied to a multiplier. In the case of preset controls, the operator will select the preset using the control system menu. The motion of a hand control of some kind will then be digitized to change the coefficient. The position of other controls, such as jog wheels on VTRs or editors, will also need to be digitized. In many cases the jog wheel is a multifunction device which is assigned like a soft key to control a number of parameters, depending on the selected menu. Controls can be linear or rotary, and absolute or relative. In an absolute control, the position of the knob determines the output directly. In a relative control, the knob can be moved to increase or decrease the output, but its absolute position is meaningless. Most DVTR jog wheels use the relative mode of operation.

Figure 2.17 shows a rotary incremental encoder. This produces a sequence of pulses whose number is proportional to the angle through which it has been

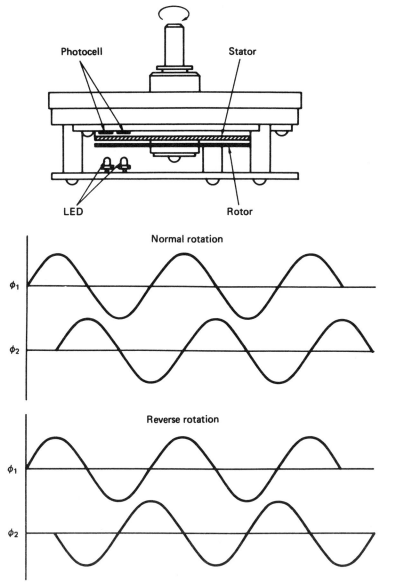

Figure 2.17 The fixed and rotating gratings produce moiré fringes which are detected by two light paths as quadrature sinusoids. The relative phase determines the direction, and the frequency is proportional to speed of rotation.

turned. The rotor carries a radial grating over its entire perimeter. This turns over a second, fixed, radial grating whose bars are not parallel to those of the first grating. The resultant moiré fringes travel inwards or outwards depending on the direction of rotation. Two suitably positioned light beams falling on photocells will produce outputs in quadrature. The relative phase determines the direction and the frequency is proportional to speed. The encoder outputs can be connected to a counter whose contents will increase or decrease according to the direction the rotor is turned. The counter provides the coefficient output.

The wordlength of the gain coefficients requires some thought as this determines the number of discrete gains available. If the coefficient wordlength is inadequate, the gain control becomes 'steppy' particularly towards the end of a fadeout. A compromise between performance and the expense of high-resolution faders is to insert a digital interpolator having a low-pass characteristic between the fader and the gain control stage. This will compute intermediate gains to higher resolution than the coarse fader scale so that the steps cannot be discerned.

Some thought must also be given to the wordlength of the system. If a sample is attenuated, it will develop bits which are below the radix point. For example, if an 8 bit sample is attenuated by 24 dB, the sample value will be shifted four places down. Extra bits must be available within the system to accommodate this shift. Digital video processors may have an internal wordlength of 16 bits or more. As the output will generally need to be of the same format as the input, the wordlength must be shortened. Shortening the wordlength of samples effectively makes the quantizing intervals larger and can thus be called requantizing. This must be done very carefully to avoid artifacts and the necessary processes will be treated in Section 2.11.

2.10 Blanking

It is often necessary to blank the ends of active line smoothly to prevent out-of-band signals being generated. Blanking consists of sloping off the active line by

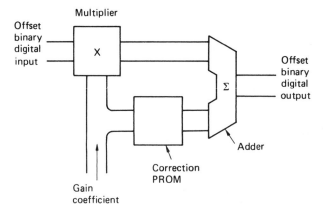

Figure 2.18 In order to fade an offset binary signal, a correction term from a PROM can be added to remove the level shift caused by fading.

multiplying the sample values by successively smaller coefficients until blanking is reached. This is easy where the sample values have been normalized so that zero represents black, but where the usual offset of 16_{10} is present, multiplication by descending coefficients will cause a black-level shift. The solution is to use a correction PROM which can be seen in Figure 2.18. This is addressed by the multiplier coefficient and adds a suitable constant to the multiplier output. If the multiplier were to have a gain of one-half, this would shift the black level by eight quantizing intervals, and so the correction PROM would add eight to the output. Where the multiplier has fully blanked, the output will be zero, and the correction PROM has to add 16_{10} to the output.

2.11 Requantizing and digital dither

Recent ADC technology allows the resolution of video samples to be raised from 8 bits to 10 or even 12 bits. The situation then arises that an existing 8 bit device such as a digital VTR needs to be connected to the output of an ADC with greater wordlength. The words need to be shortened in some way.

When a sample value is attenuated, the extra low-order bits which come into existence below the radix point preserve the resolution of the signal and the dither in the least significant bit(s) which linearizes the system. The same word extension will occur in any process involving multiplication, such as digital filtering. It will subsequently be necessary to shorten the wordlength. Low-order bits must be removed in order to reduce the resolution whilst keeping the signal magnitude the same. Even if the original conversion was correctly dithered, the random element in the low-order bits will now be some way below the end of the intended word. If the word is simply truncated by discarding the unwanted low-order bits or rounded to the nearest integer, the linearizing effect of the original dither will be lost.

Shortening the wordlength of a sample reduces the number of quantizing intervals available without changing the signal amplitude. As Figure 2.19 shows, the quantizing intervals become larger and the original signal is *requantized* with the new interval structure. This will introduce requantizing distortion having the same characteristics as quantizing distortion in an ADC. It then is obvious that when shortening the wordlength of a 10 bit converter to 8 bits, the two low-order bits must be removed in a way that displays the same overall quantizing structure as if the original converter had been only of 8 bit wordlength. It will be seen from Figure 2.19 that truncation cannot be used because it does not meet the above requirement but results in signal-dependent offsets because it always rounds in the same direction. Proper numerical rounding is essential in video applications because it accurately simulates analog quantizing to the new interval size. Unfortunately the 10 bit converter will have a dither amplitude appropriate to quantizing intervals one-quarter the size of an 8 bit unit and the result will be highly non-linear.

In practice, the wordlength of samples must be shortened in such a way that the requantizing error is converted to noise rather than distortion. One technique which meets this requirement is to use digital dithering[1] prior to rounding. This is directly equivalent to the analog dithering described in Chapter 3 in connection with ADCs.

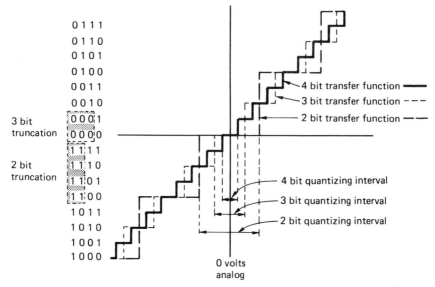

Figure 2.19 Shortening the wordlength of a sample reduces the number of codes which can describe the voltage of the waveform. This makes the quantizing steps bigger; hence the term requantizing. It can be seen that simple truncation or omission of the bits does not give analogous behaviour. Rounding is necessary to give the same result as if the larger steps had been used in the original conversion.

Digital dither is a pseudo-random sequence of numbers. If it is required accurately to simulate analog dither, then the digital dither must be bipolar so that it can have an average voltage of zero. Two's complement coding must be used for the dither values.

Figure 2.20 shows a simple digital dithering system for shortening sample wordlength. The output of a two's complement pseudo-random sequence generator (see Section 2.14) of appropriate wordlength is added to input samples prior to rounding. The most significant of the bits to be discarded is examined in order to determine whether the bits to be removed sum to more or less than half a quantizing interval. The dithered sample is either rounded down, i.e. the unwanted bits are simply discarded, or rounded up, i.e. the unwanted bits are discarded but one is added to the value of the new short word. The rounding process is no longer deterministic because of the added dither which provides a linearizing random component.

If this process is compared with that of Figure 3.31 it will be seen that the principles of analog and digital dither are identical; the processes simply take place in different domains using numbers which are rounded or voltages which are quantized as appropriate. In fact quantization of an analog dithered waveform is identical to the hypothetical case of rounding after bipolar digital dither where the number of bits to be removed is infinite, and remains identical for practical purposes when as few as 8 bits are to be removed. Analog dither may actually be generated from bipolar digital dither (which is no more than random numbers with certain properties) using a DAC.

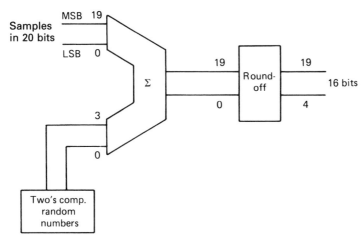

Figure 2.20 In a simple digital dithering system, two's complement values from a random number generator are added to low-order bits of the input. The dithered values are then rounded up or down according to the value of the bits to be removed. The dither linearizes the requantizing.

2.12 Timebase correction

A strength of digital technology is the ease with which delay can be provided. Accurate control of delay is the essence of timebase correction, necessary whenever the instantaneous time of arrival or rate from a data source does not match the destination. In digital video, the destination will almost always have perfectly regular timing, namely the sampling-rate clock of the final DAC. Timebase correction consists of aligning jittery signals from the tape or interface cable with that stable reference.

A further function of timebase correction is to reverse the time compression applied prior to recording or transmission. As was shown in Section 1.7, digital recorders compress data into blocks to facilitate editing and error correction as well as to permit head switching between blocks in rotary-head machines. Owing to the spaces between blocks, data arrive in bursts on replay, but must be fed to the output converters in an unbroken stream at the sampling rate. The time expansion used in the D-1 recorder to reduce the frequency at the heads is a further example of the use of the principle (see Chapter 6).

Although delay is easily implemented, it is not possible to advance a data stream. Most real machines cause instabilities balanced about the correct timing: the output jitters between too early and too late. Since the information cannot be advanced in the corrector, only delayed, the solution is to run the machine in advance of real time. In this case, correctly timed output signals will need a nominal delay to align them with reference timing. Early output signals will receive more delay, and late output signals will receive less delay.

Section 2.5 showed the principles of digital storage elements which can be used for delay purposes. The shift-register approach and the RAM approach to delay are very similar, as a shift register can be thought of as a memory whose address increases automatically when clocked. The data rate and the maximum delay determine the capacity of the RAM required. Figure 2.21 shows that the addressing of the RAM is by a counter that overflows endlessly from the end of the memory back to the beginning, giving the memory a ring-like structure. The write address is determined by the incoming data, and the read address is determined by the outgoing data. This means that the RAM has to be able to read and write at the same time. The switching between read and write involves not only a data multiplexer but also an address multiplexer. In general the arbitration between read and write will be done by signals from the stable side of the TBC

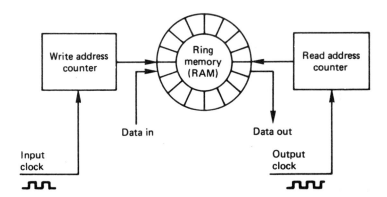

Figure 2.21 If the memory address is arranged to come from a counter which overflows, the memory can be made to appear circular. The write address then rotates endlessly, overwriting previous data once per revolution. The read address can follow the write address by a variable distance (not exceeding one revolution) and so a variable delay takes place between reading and writing.

as Figure 2.22 shows. In the replay case the stable clock will be on the read side. The stable side of the RAM will read a sample when it demands, and the writing will be locked out for that period. The input data cannot be interrupted in many applications, however, so a small buffer silo is installed before the memory, which fills up as the writing is locked out, and empties again as writing is permitted. Alternatively, the memory will be split into blocks, as was shown in Chapter 1, such that when one block is reading a different block will be writing and the problem does not arise.

In most digital video applications, the sampling rate exceeds the rate at which economically available RAM chips can operate. The solution is to arrange several video samples into one longer word, known as a superword, and to construct the memory so that it stores superwords in parallel.

2.13 Modulo-n arithmetic

Conventional arithmetic which is in everyday use relates to the real world of counting actual objects, and to obtain correct answers the concepts of borrow and carry are necessary in the calculations.

There is an alternative type of arithmetic which has no borrow or carry and which is known as modulo arithmetic. In modulo-n no number can exceed n. If it does, n or whole multiples of n are subtracted until it does not. Thus 25

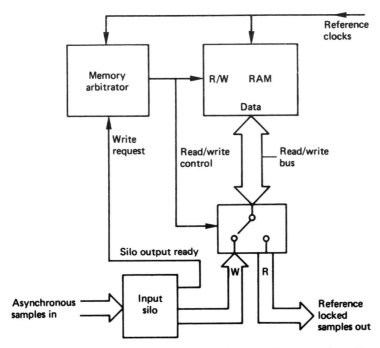

Figure 2.22 In a RAM-based TBC, the RAM is reference synchronous, and an arbitrator decides when it will read and when it will write. During reading, asynchronous input data back up in the input silo, asserting a write request to the arbitrator. Arbitrator will then cause a write cycle between read cycles.

modulo-16 is 9 and 12 modulo-5 is 2. The count shown in Figure 2.5 is from a 4 bit device which overflows when it reaches 1111 because the carry-out is ignored. If a number of clock pulses m are applied from the zero state, the state of the counter will be given by m mod.16. Thus modulo arithmetic is appropriate to systems in which there is a fixed wordlength, and this means that the range of values the system can have is restricted by that wordlength. A number range which is restricted in this way is called a finite field.

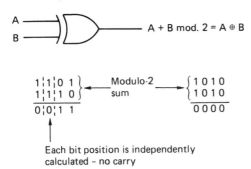

Each bit position is independently calculated - no carry

Figure 2.23 In modulo-2 calculations, there can be no carry or borrow operations and conventional addition and subtraction become identical. The XOR gate is a modulo-2 adder.

Modulo-2 is a numbering scheme which is used frequently in digital processes. Figure 2.23 shows that in modulo-2 the conventional addition and subtraction are replaced by the XOR function such that: A + B mod.2 = A XOR B. When multibit values are added mod.2, each column is computed quite independently of any other. This makes mod.2 circuitry very fast in operation as it is not necessary to wait for the carries from lower-order bits to ripple up to the high-order bits.

Modulo-2 arithmetic is not the same as conventional arithmetic and takes some getting used to. For example, adding something to itself in mod.2 always gives the answer zero.

2.14 The Galois field

Figure 2.24 shows a simple circuit consisting of three D-type latches which are clocked simultaneously. They are connected in series to form a shift register. At (a) a feedback connection has been taken from the output to the input and the result is a ring counter where the bits contained will recirculate endlessly. At (b) one XOR gate is added so that the output is fed back to more than one stage. The result is known as a twisted-ring counter and it has some interesting properties. Whenever the circuit is clocked, the left-hand bit moves to the right-hand latch, the centre bit moves to the left-hand latch and the centre latch becomes the XOR of the two outer latches. The figure shows that whatever the starting condition of the 3 bits in the latches, the same state will always be reached again after seven clocks, except if zero is used. The states of the latches form an endless ring of non-sequential numbers called a Galois field after the French mathematical prodigy Evariste Galois who discovered them. The states of the circuit form a maximum length

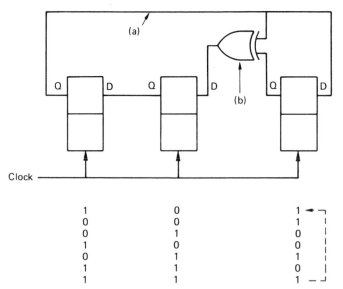

Figure 2.24 The circuit shown is a twisted-ring counter which has an unusual feedback arrangement. Clocking the counter causes it to pass through a series of non-sequential values. See text for details.

sequence because there are as many states as are permitted by the wordlength. As the states of the sequence have many of the characteristics of random numbers, yet are repeatable, the result can also be called a pseudo-random sequence (p.r.s). As the all-zeros case is disallowed, the length of a maximum length sequence generated by a register of m bits cannot exceed (2^m-1) states. The Galois field, however, includes the zero term. It is useful to explore the bizarre mathematics of Galois fields which use modulo-2 arithmetic. Familiarity with such manipulations is helpful when studying the error correction, particularly the Reed–Solomon codes used in recorders and treated in Chapter 6. They will also be found in processes which require pseudo-random numbers such as digital dither, and randomized channel codes used in many DVTR formats.

The circuit of Figure 2.24 can be considered as a counter and the four points shown will then be representing different powers of 2 from the MSB on the left to the LSB on the right. The feedback connection from the MSB to the other stages means that whenever the MSB becomes 1, two other powers are also forced to 1 so that the code of 1011 is generated.

Each state of the circuit can be described by combinations of powers of x, such as:

$$x^2 = 100$$
$$x = 010$$
$$x^2 + x = 110, \text{ etc.}$$

The fact that three bits have the same state because they are connected together is represented by the Mod.2 equation:

$$x^3 + x + 1 = 0$$

Let $x = a$, which is a primitive element. Now:

$$a^3 + a + 1 = 0$$

In modulo-2:

$$a + a = a^2 + a^2 = 0$$
$$a = x = 010$$
$$a^2 = x^2 = 100$$
$$a^3 = a + 1 = 011 \text{ from (2.11)}$$
$$a^4 = a^3 \times a = a(a + 1) = a^2 + a = 110$$
$$a^5 = a^2 + a + 1 = 111$$
$$a^6 = a^5 \times a = a(a^2 + a + 1)$$
$$= a^3 + a^2 + a = a + 1 + a^2 + a$$
$$= a^2 + 1 = 101$$
$$a^7 = a(a^2 + 1) = a^3 + a$$
$$= a + 1 + a = 1 = 001$$

In this way it can be seen that the complete set of elements of the Galois field can be expressed by successive powers of the primitive element. Note that the twisted-ring circuit of Figure 2.24 simply raises a to higher and higher powers as it is clocked; thus the seemingly complex multibit changes caused by a single clock of the register become simple to calculate using the correct primitive and the appropriate power.

The numbers produced by the twisted-ring counter are not random; they are completely predictable if the equation is known. However, the sequences produced are sufficiently similar to random numbers that in many cases they will be useful. They are thus referred to as pseudo-random sequences. The feedback connection is chosen such that the expression it implements will not factorize. Otherwise a maximum length sequence could not be generated because the circuit might sequence around one or other of the factors depending on the initial condition. A useful analogy is to compare the operation of a pair of meshed gears. If the gears have a number of teeth which is relatively prime, many revolutions are necessary to make the same pair of teeth touch again. If the number of teeth have a common multiple, far fewer turns are needed.

2.15 Noise and probability

Probability is a useful concept when dealing with processes which are not completely predictable. Thermal noise in electronic components is random, and although under given conditions the noise power in a system may be constant, this value only determines the heat that would be developed in a resistive load. In digital systems, it is the instantaneous voltage of noise which is of interest, since it is a form of interference which could alter the state of a binary signal if it were large enough. Unfortunately the instantaneous voltage cannot be predicted; indeed if it could the interference could not be called noise. Noise can only be quantified statistically, by measuring or predicting the likelihood of a given noise amplitude.

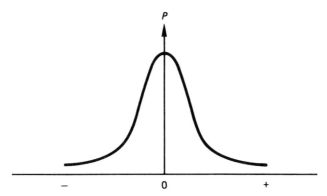

Figure 2.25 White noise in analog circuits generally has the Gaussian amplitude distribution shown.

Figure 2.25 shows a graph relating the probability of occurrence to the amplitude of noise. The noise amplitude increases away from the origin along the horizontal axis, and for any amplitude of interest, the probability of that noise amplitude occurring can be read from the curve. The shape of the curve is known as a Gaussian distribution, which crops up whenever the overall effect of a large number of independent phenomena is considered. Thermal noise is due to the contributions from countless molecules in the component concerned. Magnetic recording depends on superimposing some average magnetism on vast numbers of magnetic particles.

If it were possible to isolate an individual noise-generating microcosm of a tape or a head on the molecular scale, the noise it could generate would have physical limits because of the finite energy present. The noise distribution might then be rectangular as shown in Figure 2.26(a), where all amplitudes below the physical limit are equally likely. The output of a twisted-ring counter such as that in Figure 2.24 can have a uniform probability. Each value occurs once per sequence. The outputs are positive only but do not include zero, but every value from 1 up to $2^n - 1$ is then equally likely.

The output of a prs generator can be made into the two's complement form by inverting the MSB. This has the effect of exchanging the missing all-zeros value for a missing fully negative value as can be seen by considering the number ring in Figure 2.5. In this example, inverting the MSB causes the code of 1000 representing -8 to become 0000. The result is a 4 bit prs generating uniform probability from -7 to $+7$ as shown in Figure 2.26(a).

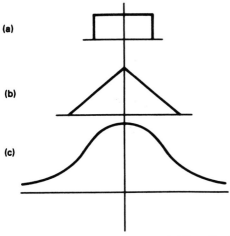

(a)

(b)

(c)

Figure 2.26 At (a) is a rectangular probability; all values are equally likely but between physical limits. At (b) is the sum of two rectangular probabilities, which is triangular, and at (c) is the Gaussian curve which is the sum of an infinite number of rectangular probabilities.

If the combined effect of two of these uniform probability processes is considered, clearly the maximum amplitude is now doubled, because the two effects can add, but provided the two effects are uncorrelated, they can also subtract, so the probability is no longer rectangular, but becomes triangular as in Figure 2.26(b). The probability falls to zero at peak amplitude because the chances of two independent mechanisms reaching their peak value with the same polarity at the same time are understandably small.

If the number of mechanisms summed together is now allowed to increase without limit, the result is the Gaussian curve shown in Figure 2.26(c), where it will be seen that the curve has no amplitude limit, because it is just possible that all mechanisms will simultaneously reach their peak value together, although the chances of this happening are incredibly remote. Thus the Gaussian curve is the overall probability of a large number of uncorrelated uniform processes.

2.16 Digital filtering

Earlier sections of this chapter have described how delay and gain control are achieved in the digital domain. These are the vital components required for digital filtering. One of the strengths of digital filtering is that it can be performed with stable binary logic instead of the inductors and capacitors needed for analog filters. In analog filtering, the frequency response is usually the most quoted parameter, followed by the phase response and the impulse response. These last two are the most difficult to get right in an analog filter.

Figure 2.27 shows that impulse response testing tells a great deal about a filter. In a perfect filter, all frequencies should experience the same time delay; this is the group delay. If not, there is a group-delay error. As an impulse contains an infinite spectrum, a filter fed with an impulse will separate the different frequencies in time if it suffers from group-delay error. Group-delay error is particularly unacceptable in video, because it causes the different frequencies in a sharp edge to appear at different places across the screen.

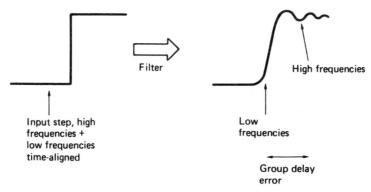

Figure 2.27 Group delay time-displaces signals as a function of frequency.

A pure delay will cause a phase shift proportional to frequency, and a filter with this characteristic is said to be phase-linear. The impulse response of a phase-linear filter is symmetrical. If a filter suffers from group delay error it cannot be phase-linear. It is almost impossible to make a phase linear analog filter, and many filters have a group-delay equalization stage following them which is often as complex as the filter itself. In the digital domain it is reasonably straightforward to make a phase linear filter, and phase equalization becomes unnecessary. Because of the sampled nature of the signal, whatever the response at low frequencies may be, all digital channels act as low-pass filters cutting off at the Nyquist limit, or half the sampling frequency.

2.17 FIR and IIR filters compared

Filters can be described in two main classes, as shown in Figure 2.28, according to the nature of the impulse response. Finite-impulse response (FIR) filters are always stable and, as their name suggests, respond to an impulse once, as they have only a forward path. In the temporal domain, the time for which the filter

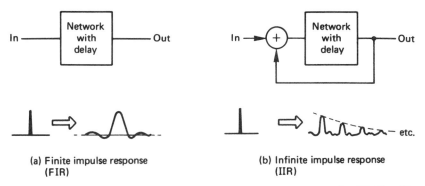

(a) Finite impulse response
(FIR)

(b) Infinite impulse response
(IIR)

Figure 2.28 An FIR filter (a) responds only to an input, whereas the output of an IIR filter (b) continues indefinitely rather like a decaying echo.

responds to an input is finite, fixed and readily established. The same is therefore true about the distance over which an FIR filter responds in the spatial domain.

Most filters intended for video use fall into this category. Infinite-impulse response (IIR) filters respond to an impulse indefinitely and are not necessarily stable, as they have a return path from the output to the input. For this reason they are also called recursive filters. Digital noise reducers and effects units which generate trails employ recursive filters, but since these processes are not necessary in recorders, the subject of IIR filters will not be explored here.

2.18 FIR filters

An FIR filter works by graphically constructing the impulse response for every input sample. It is first necessary to establish the correct impulse response. Figure 2.29(a) shows an example of a low-pass filter which cuts off at one-quarter of the sampling rate. The impulse response of a perfect low-pass filter is a $\sin x/x$ curve, where the time between the two central zero crossings is the reciprocal of the cut-off frequency. According to the mathematics, the waveform has always existed, and carries on for ever. The peak value of the output coincides with the input impulse. This means that the filter is not causal, because the output has changed before the input is known. Thus in all practical applications it is necessary to truncate the extreme ends of the impulse response, which causes an aperture effect, and to introduce a time delay in the filter equal to half the duration of the truncated impulse in order to make the filter causal. As an input impulse is shifted through the series of registers in Figure 2.29(b), the impulse response is created, because at each point it is multiplied by a coefficient as in Figure 2.29(c). These coefficients are simply the result of sampling and quantizing the desired impulse response. Clearly the sampling rate used to sample the impulse must be the same as the sampling rate for which the filter is being designed. In practice the coefficients are calculated, rather than attempting to sample an actual impulse response. The coefficient wordlength will be a compromise between cost and performance. Because the input sample shifts across the system to create the shape of the impulse response, the configuration is also known as a transversal filter. In operation with real sample streams, there will be several consecutive

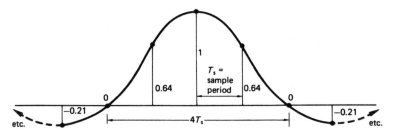

Figure 2.29(a) The impulse response of an LPF is a sin x/x curve which stretches from −∞ to +∞in time. The ends of the response must be neglected, and a delay introduced to make the filter causal.

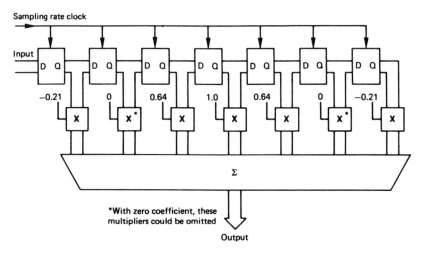

*With zero coefficient, these multipliers could be omitted

Figure 2.29(b) The structure of an FIR LPF. Input samples shift across the register and at each point are multiplied by different coefficients.

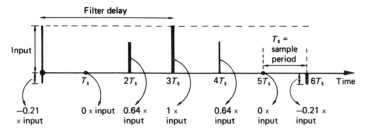

Figure 2.29(c) When a single unit sample shifts across the circuit of Figure 2.36(b), the impulse response is created at the output as the impulse is multiplied by each cofficient in turn.

sample values in the filter registers at any time in order to convolve the input with the impulse response.

Simply truncating the impulse response causes an abrupt transition from input samples which matter and those which do not. This aperture effect results in a tendency for the response to peak just before the cut-off frequency. This peak is known as Gibb's phenomenon; it causes ripples in both passband and stopband.[2,3] As a result, the length of the impulse which must be considered will depend not only on the frequency response, but also on the amount of ripple which can be tolerated. If the relevant period of the impulse is measured in sample periods, the result will be the number of points or multiplications needed in the filter.

Figure 2.30 compares the performance of filters with different numbers of points. A typical digital video FIR filter may need eight points.

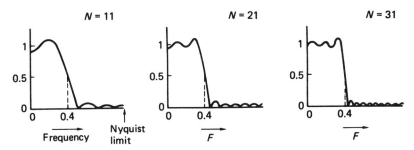

Figure 2.30 The truncation of the impulse in an FIR filter caused by the use of a finite number of points (N) results in ripple in the response. Shown here are three different numbers of points for the same impulse response. The filter is an LPF which rolls off at 0.4 of the fundamental interval. (Courtesy *Philips Technical Review*).

Rather than simply truncate the impulse response in time, it is better to make a smooth transition from samples which do not count to those that do. This can be done by multiplying the coefficients in the filter by a window function which peaks in the centre of the impulse. Figure 2.31 shows some different window functions and their responses. Clearly the rectangular window is the same as truncation, and the response is shown at I. A linear reduction in weight from the centre of the window to the edges characterizes the Bartlett window II, which trades ripple for an increase in transition-region width. At III is shown the Hanning window, which is essentially a raised cosine shape. Not shown is the similar Hamming window, which offers a slightly different trade-off between ripple and the width of the main lobe. The Blackman window introduces an extra cosine term into the Hamming window at half the period of the main cosine period, reducing Gibb's phenomenon and ripple level, but increasing the width of the transition region. The Kaiser window is a family of windows based on the Bessel function, allowing various trade-offs between ripple ratio and main lobe width. Two of these are shown in IV and V. The drawback of the Kaiser windows is that they are complex to implement.

Filter coefficients can be optimized by computer simulation. One of the best-known techniques used is the Remez exchange algorithm, which converges on the optimum coefficients after a number of iterations.

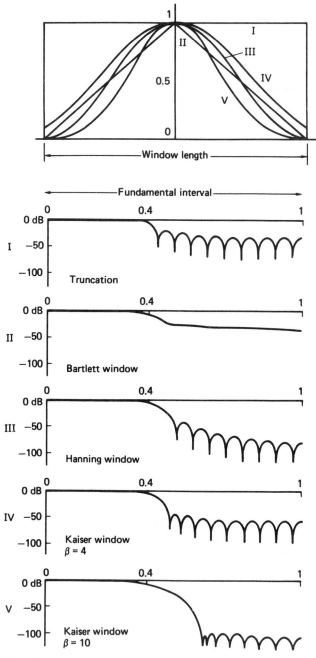

Figure 2.31 The effect of window functions. At top, various window functions are shown in continuous form. Once the number of samples in the window is established, the continuous functions shown here are sampled at the appropriate spacing to obtain window coefficients. These are multiplied by the truncated impulse response coefficients to obtain the actual coefficients used by the filter. The amplitude responses I–V correspond to the window functions illustrated. (Responses courtesy *Philips Technical Review*).

In the example of Figure 2.32, the low-pass filter of Figure 2.29 is shown with a Bartlett window. Acceptable ripple determines the number of significant sample periods embraced by the impulse. This determines in turn both the number of points in the filter, and the filter delay. As the impulse is symmetrical, the delay will be half the impulse period. The impulse response is a sin x/x function, and this has been calculated in the figure. The sin x/x response is next multiplied by the window function to give the windowed impulse response. If the coefficients

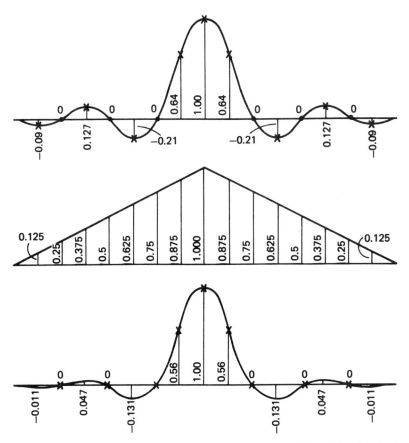

Figure 2.32 A truncated sin x/x impulse (top) is multiplied by a Bartlett window function (centre) to produce the actual coefficients used (bottom).

are not quantized finely enough, it will be as if they had been calculated inaccurately, and the performance of the filter will be less than expected. Figure 2.33 shows an example of quantizing coefficients. Conversely, raising the wordlength of the coefficients increases cost.

The FIR structure is inherently phase linear because there is rigid time control due to the way samples are shifted through the filter. The individual samples in a digital system do not know in isolation what frequency they represent, and they can only pass through the filter at a rate determined by the clock. Because of this inherent phase linearity, an FIR filter can be designed for a specific impulse response, and the frequency response will follow.

The frequency response of the filter can be changed at will by changing the coefficients. A programmable filter only requires a series of PROMs to supply the coefficients; the address supplied to the PROMs will select the response. The frequency response of a digital filter will also change if the clock rate is changed, so it is often less ambiguous to specify a frequency of interest in a digital filter in terms of a fraction of the fundamental interval rather than in absolute terms. This approach also helps in spatial filters where the fundamental interval is a spatial frequency of one-half the number of pixels per unit distance. The configuration shown in Figure 2.29 serves to illustrate the principle. The units used on the diagrams are sample periods, but these could be replaced by pixel spacings for a spatial filter. The response is proportional to these periods or spacings, and so it is not necessary to use actual figures.

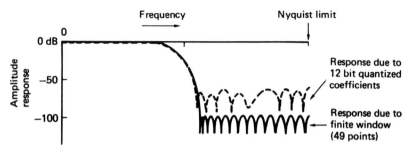

Figure 2.33 Frequency response of a 49 point transversal filter with infinite precision (solid line) shows ripple due to finite window size. Quantizing coefficients to 12 bits reduces attenuation in the stopband. (Responses courtesy *Philips Technical Review*).

Where the impulse response is symmetrical, it is often possible to reduce the number of multiplications, because the same product can be used twice, at equal distances before and after the centre of the window. This is known as folding the filter. A folded filter is shown in Figure 2.34.

2.19 Applications of digital filters in DVTRs

Digital filters are found in numerous places in the signal system of a DVTR. In order to take advantage of oversampling converters, an increase in sampling rate is necessary for DACs and a reduction in sampling rate is necessary for ADCs. In oversampling the factors by which the rates are changed are simple: either two or four. The timing of the system is thus simplified because all samples (input and output) are present on edges of the higher-rate sampling clock.

When a composite VTR plays at other than normal speed, the subcarrier sequence will be broken by the omitting or repeating of fields, and it will be necessary to filter chroma from luminance so that the chroma phase can be corrected. Additionally, the VTR may play an odd field when an even field is required, and a digital interpolator working in the vertical dimension is required to produce the required lines from those which are available.

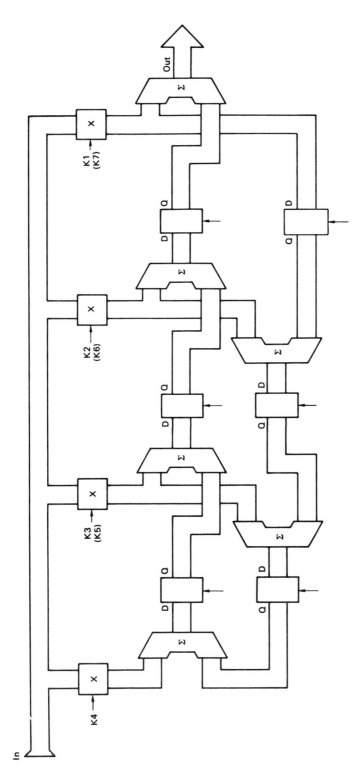

Figure 2.34 A seven-point folded filter for a symmetrical impulse response. In this case K1 and K7 will be identical, and so the input sample can be multiplied once, and the product fed into the output shift system in two different places. The centre coefficient K4 appears once. In an even-numbered filter the centre coefficient would also be used twice.

When an uncorrectable error occurs, it will be necessary to use the values of adjacent pixels to estimate a value for the missing pixel in order to conceal the error. A digital filter will be used for this purpose, and it may work in up to three dimensions in the case where data from adjacent fields are employed.

2.20 Oversampling filters

As will be seen, oversampling allows the use of simpler and less critical analog anti-aliasing and reconstruction filters, but requires a digital sampling-rate conversion stage at each converter. The rate conversion is simplified if an integer ratio is used, as this means that certain input samples are simply passed to the output unchanged.

Sampling-rate reduction by an integer factor following an oversampling ADC is dealt with first. Figure 2.35(a) shows the spectrum of a typical sampled system where the sampling rate is a little more than twice the analog bandwidth. Attempts to reduce the sampling rate by simply omitting samples, a process known as decimation, will result in aliasing, as shown in Figure 2.35(b). Intuitively it is obvious that omitting samples is the same as if the original sampling rate was

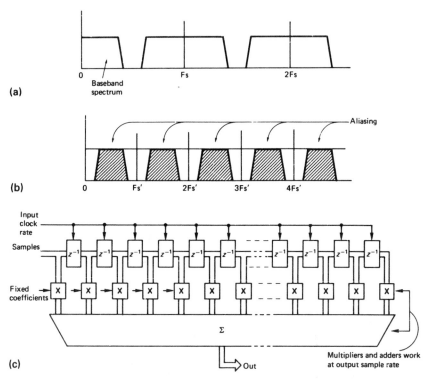

Figure 2.35 The spectrum of a typical digital sample stream at (a) will be subject to aliasing as in (b) if the baseband width is not reduced by an LPF. At (c) an FIR low-pass filter prevents aliasing. Samples are clocked transversely across the filter at the input rate, but the filter only computes at the output sample rate. Clearly this will only work if the two are related by an integer factor.

lower. In order to prevent aliasing, it is necessary to incorporate low-pass filtering into the system where the cut-off frequency reflects the new, lower, sampling rate. An FIR-type low-pass filter could be installed, as described earlier in this chapter, immediately prior to the stage where samples are omitted, but this would be wasteful, because for much of its time the FIR filter would be calculating sample values which are to be discarded. The more effective method is to combine the low-pass filter with the decimator so that the filter only calculates values to be retained in the output sample stream. Figure 2.35(c) shows how this is done. The filter makes one accumulation for every output sample, but that accumulation is the result of multiplying all relevant input samples in the filter window by an appropriate coefficient. The number of points in the filter is determined by the number of *input* samples in the period of the filter window, but the number of multiplications per second is obtained by multiplying that figure by the *output* rate. If the filter is not integrated with the decimator, the number of points has to be multiplied by the input rate. The larger the rate-reduction factor the more advantageous the decimating filter ought to be, but this is not quite the case, as the greater the reduction in rate, the longer the filter window will need to be to accommodate the broader impulse response.

When the sampling rate is to be increased by an integer factor, additional samples must be created at even spacing between the existing ones. There is no need for the bandwidth of the input samples to be reduced since, if the original sampling rate was adequate, a higher one must also be adequate.

Figure 2.36 shows that the process of sampling-rate increase can be thought of in two stages. First the correct rate is achieved by inserting samples of zero value

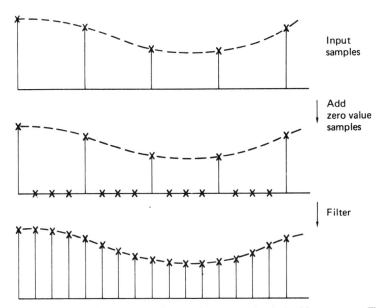

Figure 2.36 In integer-ratio sampling, rate increase can be obtained in two stages. First zero-value samples are inserted to increase the rate, and then filtering is used to give the extra samples real values. The filter necessary will be an LPF with a response which cuts off at the Nyquist frequency of the input samples.

at the correct instant, and then the additional samples are given meaningful values by passing the sample stream through a low-pass filter which cuts off at the Nyquist frequency of the original sampling rate. This filter is known as an interpolator, and one of its tasks is to prevent images of the lower input-sampling spectrum from appearing in the extended baseband of the higher-rate output spectrum.

How do interpolators work? Remember that, according to sampling theory, all sampled systems have finite bandwidth. An individual digital sample value is obtained by sampling the instantaneous voltage of the original analog waveform, and because it has zero duration, it must contain an infinite spectrum. However, such a sample can never be heard in that form because of the reconstruction process, which limits the spectrum of the impulse to the Nyquist limit. After reconstruction, one infinitely short digital sample ideally represents a sin x/x pulse whose central peak width is determined by the response of the reconstruction filter, and whose amplitude is proportional to the sample value. This implies that, in reality, one sample value has meaning over a considerable timespan, rather than just at the sample instant. If this were not true, it would be impossible to build an interpolator.

As in rate reduction, performing the steps separately is inefficient. The bandwidth of the information is unchanged when the sampling rate is increased; therefore the original input samples will pass through the filter unchanged, and it is superfluous to compute them. The combination of the two processes into an interpolating filter minimizes the amount of computation.

As the purpose of the system is purely to increase the sampling rate, the filter must be as transparent as possible, and this implies that a linear-phase configuration is mandatory, suggesting the use of an FIR structure. Figure 2.37

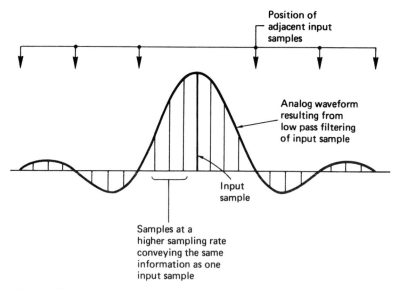

Figure 2.37 A single sample results in a sin x/x waveform after filtering in the analog domain. At a new, higher, sampling rate, the same waveform after filtering will be obtained if the numerous samples of differing size shown here are used. It follows that the values of these new samples can be calculated from the input samples in the digital domain in an FIR filter.

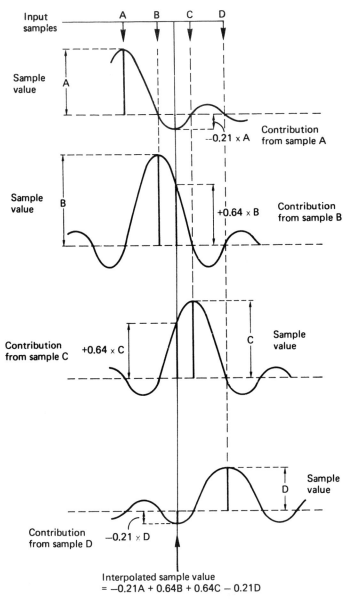

Input samples: A B C D

Sample value A

Contribution from sample A
−0.21 × A

Sample value B

+0.64 × B Contribution from sample B

Contribution from sample C +0.64 × C

Sample value C

Sample value D

Contribution from sample D −0.21 × D

Interpolated sample value
= −0.21A + 0.64B + 0.64C − 0.21D

Figure 2.38 A two times oversampling interpolator. To compute an intermediate sample, the input samples are imagined to be sin x/x impulses, and the contributions from each at the point of interest can be calculated. In practice, rather more samples on either side need to be taken into account.

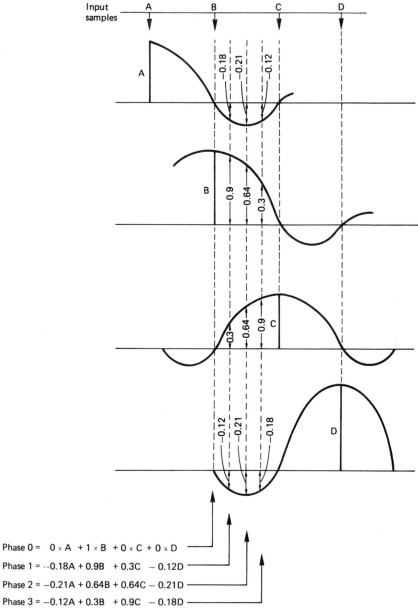

Figure 2.39 In 4× oversampling, for each set of input samples, four phases of coefficients are necessary, each of which produces one of the oversampled values.

shows that the theoretical impulse response of such a filter is a sin x/x curve which has zero value at the position of adjacent input samples. In practice this impulse cannot be implemented because it is infinite. The impulse response used will be truncated and windowed as described earlier. To simplify this discussion, assume that a sin x/x impulse is to be used. There is a strong parallel with the operation of a DAC where the analog voltage is returned to the time-continuous state by summing the analog impulses due to each sample. In a digital interpolating filter, this process is duplicated.[4]

If the sampling rate is to be doubled, new samples must be interpolated exactly half-way between existing samples. The necessary impulse response is shown in Figure 2.38; it can be sampled at the *output* sample period and quantized to form coefficients. If a single input sample is multiplied by each of these coefficients in turn, the impulse response of that sample at the new sampling rate will be obtained. Note that every other coefficient is zero, which confirms that no computation is necessary on the existing samples; they are just transferred to the output. The intermediate sample is computed by adding together the impulse responses of every input sample in the window. The figure shows how this mechanism operates. If the sampling rate is to be increased by a factor of four, three sample values must be interpolated between existing input samples. Figure 2.39 shows that it is only necessary to sample the impulse response at one-quarter the period of input samples to obtain three sets of coefficients which will be used in turn. In hardware-implemented filters, the input sample which is passed straight to the output is transferred by using a fourth filter phase where all coefficients are zero except the central one which is unity.

2.21 The Fourier transform

The Fourier transform is a processing technique which analyses signals changing with respect to time or distance and expresses them in the form of a temporal or spatial spectrum. Any waveform can be broken down into frequency components. Figure 2.40 shows that if the amplitude and phase of each frequency component is known, linearly adding the resultant components in an inverse transform results in the original waveform.

The Fourier transform may be performed on a continuous analog waveform, in which case a continuous spectrum results. However, in digital systems the waveform is expressed as a number of discrete samples. As a result the Fourier transform analyses the signal into an equal number of discrete frequencies. This is known as a discrete Fourier transform or DFT. The fast Fourier transform is no more than an efficient way of computing the DFT[5].

It will be evident from Figure 2.40 that knowledge of the phase of the frequency component is vital, as changing the phase of any component will seriously alter the reconstructed waveform. Thus the DFT must accurately analyse the phase of the signal components.

There are a number of ways of expressing phase. Figure 2.41 shows a point which is rotating about a fixed axis at constant speed. Looked at from the side, the point oscillates up and down at constant frequency. The waveform of that motion is a sine wave, and that is what we would see if the rotating point were to translate along its axis whilst we continued to look from the side.

One way of defining the phase of a waveform is to specify the angle through which the point has rotated at time zero (T = 0). If a second point is made to

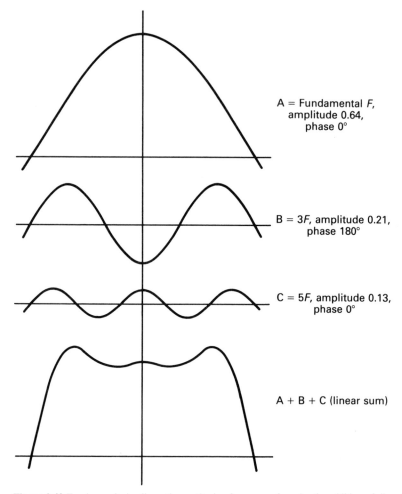

A = Fundamental F,
amplitude 0.64,
phase 0°

B = 3F, amplitude 0.21,
phase 180°

C = 5F, amplitude 0.13,
phase 0°

A + B + C (linear sum)

Figure 2.40 Fourier analysis allows the synthesis of any waveform by the addition of discrete frequencies of appropriate amplitude and phase.

revolve at 90° to the first, it would produce a cosine wave when translated. It is possible to produce a waveform having arbitrary phase by adding together the sine and cosine waves in various proportions and polarities. For example, adding the sine and cosine waves in equal proportion results in a waveform lagging the sine wave by 45°.

Figure 2.41 shows that the proportions necessary are respectively the sine and the cosine of the phase angle. Thus the two methods of describing phase can be readily interchanged.

The discrete Fourier transform spectrum-analyses a block of samples by searching separately for each discrete target frequency. It does this by multiplying the input waveform by a sine wave having the target frequency and adding up or integrating the products. Figure 2.42(a) shows that multiplying by

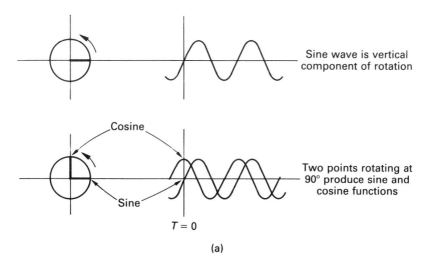

Sine wave is vertical
component of rotation

Cosine

Two points rotating at
90° produce sine and
cosine functions

Sine

$T = 0$

(a)

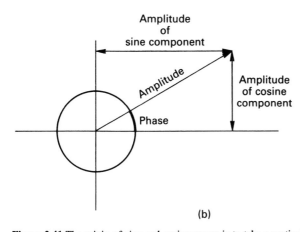

Amplitude
of
sine component

Amplitude

Amplitude
of cosine
component

Phase

(b)

Figure 2.41 The origin of sine and cosine waves is to take a particular viewpoint of a rotation. Any phase can be synthesized by adding proportions of sine and cosine waves.

the target frequency gives a non-zero integral when the input frequency is the same, whereas Figure 2.42(b) shows that with a different input frequency (in fact all other different frequencies) the integral is zero, showing that no component of the target frequency exists. Thus from a real waveform containing many frequencies all frequencies except the target frequency are excluded. The magnitude of the integral is proportional to the amplitude of the target component.

Figure 2.42(c) shows that the target frequency will not be detected if it is phase shifted 90° as the product of quadrature waveforms is always zero. Thus the discrete Fourier transform must make a further search for the target frequency using a cosine wave. It follows from the arguments above that the relative proportions of the sine and cosine integrals reveal the phase of the input

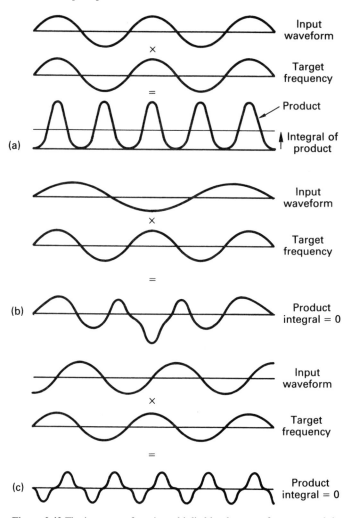

Figure 2.42 The input waveform is multiplied by the target frequency and the result is averaged or integrated. At (a) the target frequency is present and a large integral results. With another input frequency the integral is zero as at (b). The correct frequency will also result in a zero integral shown at (c) if it is at 90° to the phase of the search frequency. This is overcome by making two searches in quadrature.

component. Thus each discrete frequency in the spectrum must be the result of a pair of quadrature searches.

Searching for one frequency at a time as above will result in a DFT, but only after considerable computation. However, a lot of the calculations are repeated many times over in different searches. The fast Fourier transform gives the same result with less computation by logically gathering together all of the places where the same calculation is needed and making the calculation once.

The amount of computation can be reduced by performing the sine and cosine component searches together. Another saving is obtained by noting that every

180° the sine and cosine have the same magnitude but are simply inverted in sign. Instead of performing four multiplications on two samples 180 degrees apart and adding the pairs of products, it is more economical to subtract the sample values and multiply twice, once by a sine value and once by a cosine value.

The first coefficient is the geometric mean which is the sum of all of the sample values in the block divided by the number of samples. Figure 2.43 shows how the search for the lowest frequency in a block is performed. Pairs of samples are subtracted as shown, and each difference is then multiplied by the sine and the cosine of the search frequency. The process shifts one sample period, and a new sample pair are subtracted and multiplied by new sine and cosine factors.

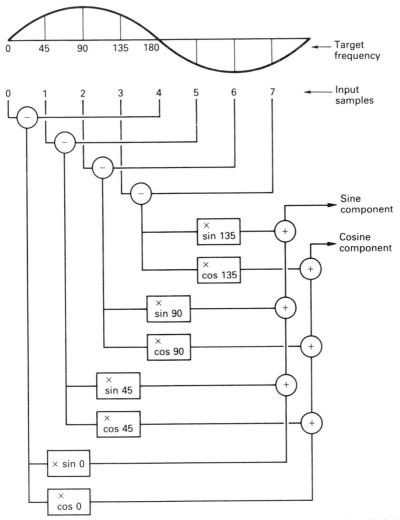

Figure 2.43 An example of a filtering search. Pairs of samples are subtracted and multiplied by sampled sine and cosine waves. The products are added to give the sine and cosine components of the search frequency.

This is repeated until all of the sample pairs have been multiplied. The sine and cosine products are then added to give the value of the sine and cosine coefficients respectively.

It is possible to combine the calculation of the DC component, which requires the sum of samples, and the calculation of the fundamental, which requires sample differences by combining the stages shown in Figure 2.44(a) which take a pair of samples and add and subtract them. Such a stage is called a butterfly because of the shape of the schematic. Figure 2.44(b) shows how the first two components are calculated. The phase rotation boxes attribute the input to the sine or cosine component outputs according to the phase angle. As shown the box

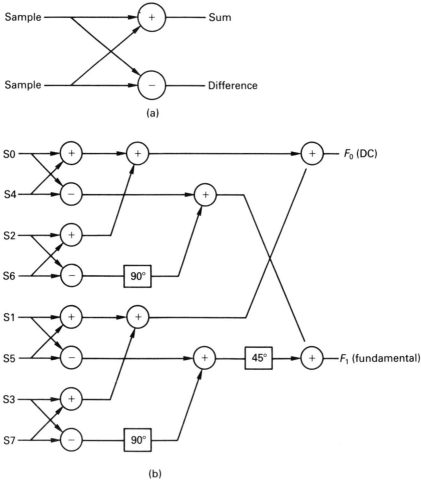

Figure 2.44 The basic element of an FFT is known as a butterfly as at (a) because of the shape of the signal paths in a sum and difference system. The use of butterflies to compute the first two coefficients is shown in (b). An actual example is given in (c) which should be compared with the result of (d) with a quadrature input. At (e) the butterflies for the first two coefficients form the basis of the computation of the third coefficient.

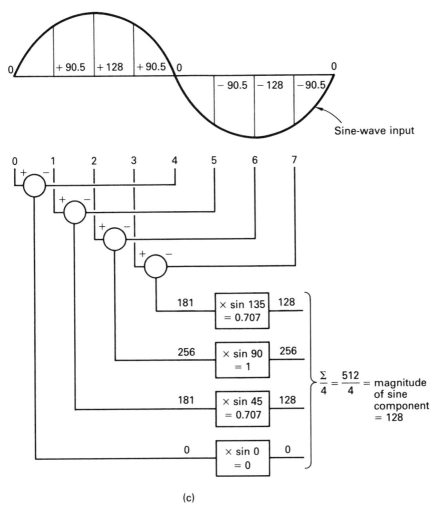

(c)

Figure 2.44(c)

labelled 90° attributes nothing to the sine output, but unity gain to the cosine output. The 45° box attributes the input equally to both components.

Figure 2.44(c) shows a numerical example. If a sine-wave input is considered where 0° coincides with the first sample, this will produce a zero sine coefficient and non-zero cosine coefficient. Figure 2.44(d) shows the same input waveform shifted by 90°. Note how the coefficients change over.

Figure 2.44(e) shows how the next frequency coefficient is computed. Note that exactly the same first stage butterfly outputs are used, reducing the computation needed.

A similar process may be followed to obtain the sine and cosine coefficients of the remaining frequencies. The full FFT diagram is shown in Figure 2.45(a). The spectrum this calculates is shown in Figure 2.45(b). Note that only half of the

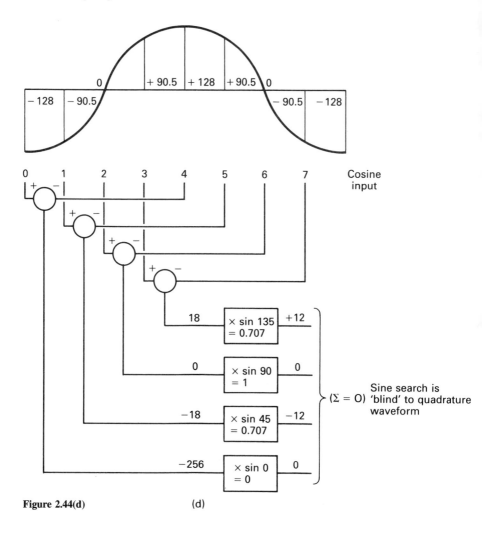

Figure 2.44(d)   (d)

coefficients are useful in a real band-limited system because the remaining coefficients represent frequencies above one half of the sampling rate.

The number of frequency coefficients resulting from a DFT is equal to the number of input samples. In the case of digital video, if the input consists of a larger number of samples it must cover a larger area of the screen, but its spectrum will be known more finely. Thus a fundamental characteristic of such transforms is that the more accurately the frequency and phase of a waveform is analysed, the less is known about where such frequencies exist on the screen axis.

2.22 The discrete cosine transform (DCT)

The DCT is a special case of a discrete Fourier transform in which the sine components of the coefficients have been eliminated leaving a single number.

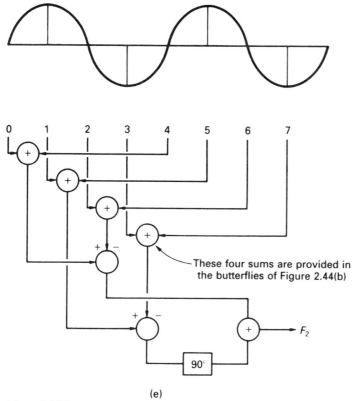

These four sums are provided in the butterflies of Figure 2.44(b)

90^{c}

F_2

(e)

Figure 2.44(e)

This is actually quite easy. Figure 2.46(a) shows the input samples to a transform process. By repeating the samples in a time-reversed order and performing a discrete Fourier transform on the double-length sample set a DCT is obtained. The effect of mirroring the input waveform is to turn it into an even function whose sine coefficients are all zero. The result can be understood by considering the effect of individually transforming the input block and the reversed block. Figure 2.46(b) shows that the phase of all the components of one block are in the opposite sense to those in the other. This means that when the components are added to give the transform of the double-length block all of the sine components cancel out, leaving only the cosine coefficients; hence the name of the transform[6]. In practice the sine component calculation is eliminated. Another advantage is that doubling the block length by mirroring doubles the frequency resolution, so that twice as many useful coefficients are produced. In fact a DCT produces as many useful coefficients as input samples.

For image processing two-dimensional transforms are needed. In this case for every horizontal frequency, a search is made for all possible vertical frequencies. A two-dimensional DCT is shown in Figure 2.47. The DCT is separable in that the two-dimensional DCT can be obtained by computing in each dimension separately. Fast DCT algorithms are available[7].

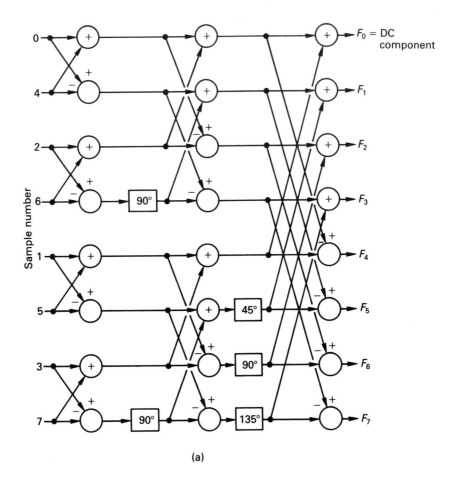

(a)

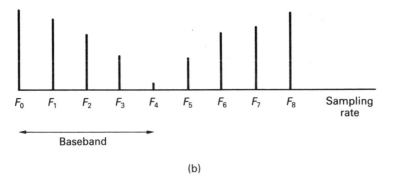

(b)

Figure 2.45 At (a) is the full butterfly diagram for an FFT. The spectrum this computes is shown at (b).

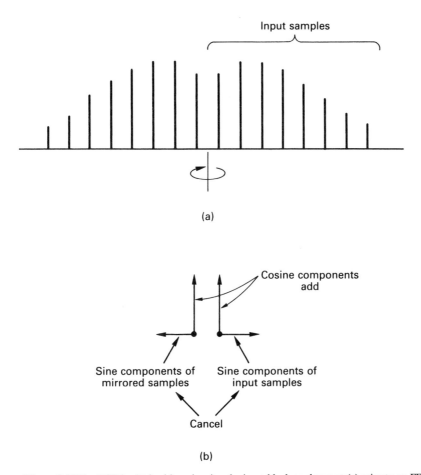

Figure 2.46 The DCT is obtained by mirroring the input block as shown at (a) prior to an FFT. The mirroring cancels out the sine components as at (b), leaving only cosine coefficients.

The DCT is primarily used in data reduction processing. The DCT itself does not result in any reduction, as there are as many coefficients as samples, but it converts the input video into a form where redundancy can be easily detected and removed.

2.23 Data reduction

The data rates resulting from conventional PCM video are quite high, and although recorders have been developed which store the signals in this form, they will remain exclusively in the professional domain for the foreseeable future. For production purposes, the simplicity of PCM video is attractive because it allows manipulations with the minimum of quality loss. The signals seldom need to travel long distances and the provision of sufficient data rate is not an issue. However, the increasing range of applications of digital video are taking it out of the studio and into the consumer domain. In this case transmission over long

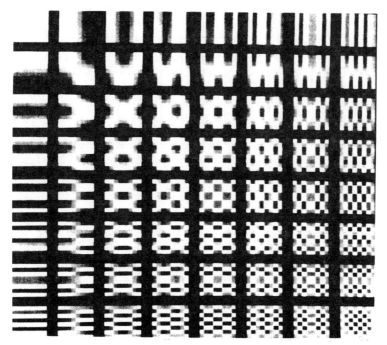

Figure 2.47 The discrete cosine transform breaks up an image area into discrete frequencies in two dimensions. The lowest frequency can be seen here at the top left corner. Horizontal frequency increases to the right and vertical frequency increases downwards.

distances is required, where the cost is generally proportional to the bit rate. There is then an obvious pressure to reduce the data rate. The running costs of a professional DVTR are reasonable in the context of the overall cost of a television production, but beyond the resources of the individual. If digital video recording is to be made available to the consumer, the running cost and tape consumption will need to be reduced considerably. Digital video recording in this context includes new developments such as interactive video (CD-I) which requires rapid random access to images on optical disk.

As PCM high definition requires about five times the data rate of normal definition then the use of data reduction will be mandatory to deliver the signal to the home and will be considered for production recorders.

The use of data reduction also allows the life of an existing transport and tape design to be extended by raising the apparent data rate. Ampex have used data reduction in order to record 4:2:2 component data on a D-2 type transport; 4:2:2 requires approximately twice the data rate as NTSC sampled at four times subcarrier.

The fundamentals of video data reduction are not new, but availability of equipment has been hampered until recently by the speed and complexity of the processing required. The cost of implementing coding techniques in VLSI circuitry has now fallen to a level where it is advantageous to use it. The large volume required for consumer applications further lowers the unit cost of such circuitry.

Data reduction is a flexible technology because the degree of coding complexity and the degree of compression used can be varied to suit the application. Video contains redundancy because typical images contain areas which are similar. The actual information in video is known as the entropy, which is the unpredictable or new part of the signal, and the remainder is redundancy, which is a part of the signal which is predictable. The sum of the two is the original data rate. The degree of compression cannot be so severe that the new data rate is less than the entropy, as information must then be lost. In theory, all of the redundancy could be removed, leaving only the entropy, but this would require a perfect algorithm which would be extremely complex. In practice the compression factor will be less than this so that some leeway is available. This allows simpler algorithms to be used and where necessary also permits multiple generations without artifacts being visible. Thus production DVTRs such as Sony's Digital Betacam and the Ampex DCT use only very mild compression of around 2:1.

For production recorders, only redundancy within the field is used, and no advantage is taken of the redundancy between fields as this would compromise editing. Clearly a consumer DVTR needs only single-generation operation and has simple editing requirements. A much greater degree of compression can then be used, which might also take advantage of redundancy between fields. The same is true for broadcasting, where bandwidth is at a premium. There is now no doubt that the future of television broadcasting (and radio for that matter) lies in data-reduced digital technology. Analog simply requires too much bandwidth.

There are thus a number of identifiable and different approaches to data reduction. For production purposes, *intrafield* data reduction is used with a mild compression factor in order to allow maximum editing freedom with negligible occurrence of artifacts. Compression algorithms intended for transmission of still images in other applications such as wirephotos can be adapted for intra-field video compression. The ISO JPEG (Joint Photographic Experts Group)[8,9] standard is such an algorithm. *Interfield* data reduction allows higher compression factors with infrequent artifacts for the delivery of post-produced material to the consumer. With even higher compression factors, leading to frequent artifacts, non-critical applications such as videophones and games are supported where the data rate has to be as low as possible. The ISO MPEG (Moving Picture Experts Group)[10] standards address these applications.

2.24 Intrafield data reduction

This type of data reduction takes each individual field (or frame in progressive scan standards) and treats it in isolation from any other field or frame. The most common algorithms are based on the discrete cosine transform described in Section 2.22.

Figure 2.47 showed an example of the different coefficients of a DCT for an 8 x 8 pixel block, and adding these together in different proportions will give any original pixel block. The top left coefficient conveys the DC component of the block. This one will be a unipolar (positive-only) value in the case of luminance and will typically be the largest value in the block as the spectrum of typical video signals is dominated by the DC component. Moving to the right the coefficients represent increasing horizontal spatial frequencies and moving downwards the coefficients represent increasing vertical spatial frequencies. The bottom right coefficient represents the highest diagonal frequencies in the block. All of these coefficients are bipolar, where the polarity indicates whether the original spatial waveform at that frequency was inverted.

In typical pictures, the coefficients representing the higher two-dimensional spatial frequencies will be zero or of small value in large areas of typical video, owing to motion blurring or simply plain undetailed areas before the camera. In general, the further from the top left corner the coefficient is, the smaller will be its magnitude on average. Coding gain (the technical term for reduction in the number of bits needed) is achieved by taking advantage of the zero and low-valued coefficients to cut down on the data necessary. Thus it is not the DCT which compresses the data, it is the subsequent processing. The DCT simply expresses the data in a form which makes the subsequent processing easier. Thus the correct terminology is to say that a compression algorithm is *DCT based*.

Once transformed, there are various techniques which can be used to reduce the data needed to carry the coefficients. These will be based on a knowledge of the signal statistics and the human vision mechanism and will often be combined in practical systems[11,12].

Possibly the simplest reduction method involves setting a threshold magnitude for coefficients. Only coefficients which exceed the threshold are transmitted, as it is assumed that smaller values make a negligible contribution to the picture block. Figure 2.48 shows the result, which is that most coefficients then have a value of zero.

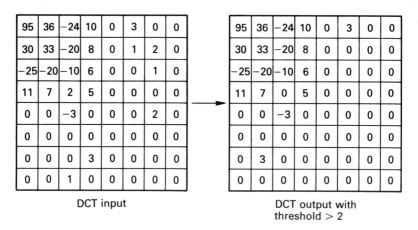

DCT input   DCT output with
                             threshold > 2

Figure 2.48 After the DCT, a simple way of compressing the data is to transmit only those coefficients which exceed a threshold.

Psycho-visual knowledge may also be used to process the coefficients. Omitting a coefficient means that the appropriate frequency component is missing from the reconstructed block. The difference between original and reconstructed blocks is regarded as noise added to the wanted data. The visibility of such noise is far from uniform. Figure 2.49 shows that the sensitivity of the eye to noise falls with frequency. The maximum sensitivity is at DC and as a result the top left coefficient is often treated as a special case and left unchanged. It may warrant more error protection than other coefficients.

Psycho-visual coding takes advantage of the falling sensitivity to noise by multiplying each coefficient by a different weighting constant as a function of its frequency. This has the effect of reducing the magnitude of each coefficient so that fewer bits are needed to represent it. Another way of looking at this process is that the coefficients are individually requantized with step sizes which increase with frequency. The larger step size increases the quantizing noise at frequencies where it is not visible.

Knowledge of the signal statistics gained from extensive analysis of real material can be used to describe the probability of a given coefficient having a given value. This is the basis of entropy coding, in which coefficients are described not by fixed wordlength numbers, but by variable-length codes. The shorter codes are allocated to the most probable values and the longer codes to the least probable values. This allows a coding gain on typical signals. One of the best known variable length codes is the Huffman code[13].

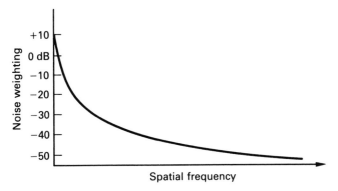

Figure 2.49 The sensitivity of the eye to noise is greatest at low frequencies and drops rapidly with increasing frequency. This can be used to mask quantizing noise caused by the compression process.

The main difficulty with variable-length codes is separating the symbols when they are serialized. With fixed wordlength, the bit clock is merely divided by the wordlength to obtain a word clock. With variable-length coding the bit stream coding must be such that the decoder can determine the boundaries between words unaided. Figure 2.50 shows an example of Huffman coding.

When serializing a coefficient block, it is normal to scan in a sequence where the largest coefficient values are scanned first. Clearly such a scan begins in the top left corner and ends in the bottom right corner. Statistical analysis of real program material can be used to determine an optimal scan, but in many cases a regular zig-zag scan shown in Figure 2.51 will be used with slight loss of performance. The advantage of such a scan is that on typical material the scan finishes with coefficients which are zero valued. Instead of transmitting these zeros, a unique 'end-of-block' symbol is transmitted instead. Just before the last finite coefficient and the EOB symbol it is likely that some zero-value coefficients

Coefficient	Code	Number of zeros	Code
1	1	1	11
2	001	2	101
3	0111	3	011
4	00001	4	0101
5	01101	5	0011
6	011001	etc.	etc.
7	0000001		
Run-length code	010		

Figure 2.50 In Huffman coding the most probable coefficient values are allocated to the shortest codes. All zero coefficients are coded with run-length coding which counts the number of zeros.

will be scanned. The coding enters a different mode whereby it simply transmits a unique prefix called a run-length prefix, followed by a code specifying the number of zeros which follow. This is also shown in Figure 2.50.

Figure 2.52(a) shows a block diagram of a representative image data reduction unit. The input image is blocked, and the DCT stage transforms the blocks into a form in which redundancy can be identified. Psycho-visual weighting then reduces coefficient values according to the human visual process. Block scanning and variable-length/run length coding finish the job. The receiver is shown in Figure 2.52(b). The input bit stream is deserialized into symbols, and the run-

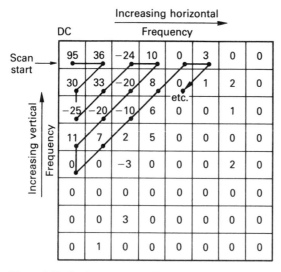

Figure 2.51 The zig-zag scan starting top left orders the coefficients in the best sequence for compression as the later ones will have smaller value.

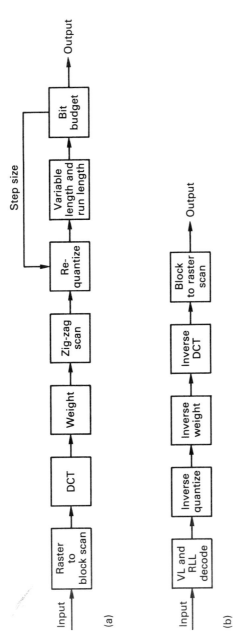

Figure 2.52 An intrafield DCT-based coder at (a) and the corresponding decoder at (b).

length decoder reassembles the runs of zeros. The variable-length decoder then converts back to constant wordlength coefficients. The psycho-visual weighting is reversed by a division which cancels the original multiplication. An inverse DCT then reconstructs the blocks.

The compression factor of the system of Figure 2.52 is a function of the input image. A detailed contrast image will result in more data than a soft image containing self-similar areas. This is not a problem for single-image applications like wirephotos, because the result is that on a fixed rate link the transmission time varies slightly from one image to the next, just as it does in a Fax machine.

In a recorder or a real-time transmission system the picture rate is constant and this variable compression is a nuisance because it demands a variable-rate link or recorder. The solution is to make the compression factor constant. This is done by using feedback from the output coder which is given a bit budget. If the bit budget is exceeded, the coefficients are requantized to larger steps. If the bit budget is underutilized, the quantization steps are made more accurate. This is an iterative process which converges on an optimally filled output block in a variable time. This variability is undesirable in real-time hardware and instead the coefficients may be requantized by all step sizes in turn. At the end of this fixed time process the best quantization step size is then picked.

Variable quantizing results in variable noise, and it is desirable to reduce the visibility of program-sensitive noise. One way in which this can be done is to combine a number of DCT blocks together into an entropy block. The entropy block is then given a bit budget. In this system, one DCT block having high entropy can use up the bit budget made available by other DCT blocks in the entropy block which have low entropy. Coarse quantization is not then necessary and an improvement in signal-to-noise ratio results. The chances of every DCT block in an entropy block having high entropy are not great, but can be reduced further by shuffling the DCT blocks so that an entropy block is made up from blocks which are distributed around the screen.

In practice entropy blocks cannot be made arbitrarily large because only an entire block can be properly decoded owing to the use of variable-length coding. In digital VTRs the entropy block length is restricted to the track length which can be recovered in shuttle (see Chapter 7), but a useful noise advantage is still obtained.

References

1. VANDERKOOY, J. and LIPSHITZ, S.P., Digital dither. Presented at the 81st Audio Engineering Society Convention (Los Angeles, 1986), preprint 2412 (C-8)
2. VAN DEN ENDEN, A.W.M. and VERHOECKX, N.A.M., Digital signal processing: theoretical background. *Philips Tech. Rev.*, **42**, 110–144, (1985)
3. MCCLELLAN, J.H., PARKS, T.W. and RABINER, L.R., A computer program for designing optimum FIR linear-phase digital filters. *IEEE Trans. Audio Electroacoust.* **AU-21**, 506–526 (1973)
4. CROCHIERE, R.E. and RABINER, L.R., Interpolation and decimation of digital signals – a tutorial review. *Proc. IEEE*, **69**, 300–331 (1981)
5. KRANIAUSKAS, P., 'Transforms in signals and systems', Ch. 6. Wokingham: Addison Wesley (1992)
6. AHMED, N., NATARAJAN, T. and RAO, K., Discrete cosine transform. *IEEE Trans. Comput.*, **C-23** 90–93 (1974)
7. DE WITH, P.H.N., Data compression techniques for digital video recording. PhD Thesis, Technical University of Delft (1992)

8. ISO Joint Photographic Experts Group standard JPEG-8-R8

9. WALLACE, G.K., Overview of the JPEG (ISO/CCITT) still image compression standard. ISO/JTC1/SC2/WG8 N932 (1989)

10. LE GALL, D., MPEG: a video compression standard for multimedia applications. *Commun. of the ACM*, **34**, No. 4, 46–58 (1991)

11. CLARKE, R.J. *Transform coding of images*. London: Academic Press, (1985)

12. NETRAVALI, A.N. and HASKELL, B.G., *Digital pictures - representation and compression*. Plenum Press, (1988)

13. HUFFMAN, D.A. A method for the construction of minimum redundancy codes. *Proc. IRE*. **40** 1098–1101 (1952)

Chapter 3

Video signals and conversion

The input to a DVTR may be a conventional analog component or composite signal requiring conversion, or a digital interface signal may be available, in which case the conversion can be bypassed. Current DVTRs make both analog and digital outputs available simultaneously. In this chapter both converters and digital interfaces are covered. Once in the digital domain, degradations can be controlled, and so the conversion processes to and from the digital domain become the main sources of degradation and warrant detailed treatment here.

3.1 The characteristics of video signals

Video signals are electrical waveforms which allow moving pictures to be conveyed from one place to another. Observing the real world with the human eye results in a two-dimensional image on the retina. This image changes with time and so the basic information is three dimensional. With two eyes a stereoscopic view can be obtained and stereoscopic television is possible with suitable equipment. However, this is restricted to specialist applications and has not been exploited in broadcasting.

An electrical waveform is two-dimensional in that it carries a voltage changing with respect to time. In order to convey three-dimensional picture information down a two-dimensional cable it is necessary to resort to scanning. Instead of attempting to convey the brightness of all parts of a picture at once, scanning conveys the brightness of a single point which moves with time.

The cathode ray tube is not a linear device, but produces light following a power law with an index of about 2.2. This non-linear characteristic is known as *gamma*. In practice an inverse law is applied in the camera so that no non-linear circuitry is needed in the television receiver. Thus recording and processing are performed on compressed signals. Perhaps surprisingly, the presence of the non-linearity makes little difference. One reason for this is the fact that the majority of the energy in a typical picture is concentrated at low frequencies.

In television systems the scan consists of rapid horizontal sweeps combined with a slower vertical sweep so that the image is scanned in lines. At the end of each vertical sweep, or frame, the process recommences. Computer monitors scan in this way, but in most broadcast systems the scanning process is 2:1 interlaced. In an interlaced system the vertical sweep speed is doubled so that spaces open up between the scanned lines. The vertical scan, or field, takes half as long and contains half as many lines. In the second field the areas which were missed in the first field are scanned. Figure 3.1(a) shows that this is readily

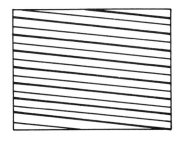

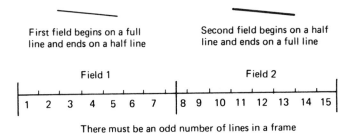

First field begins on a full
line and ends on a half line

Second field begins on a half
line and ends on a full line

| Field 1 | | | | | | | Field 2 | | | | | | | |
| 1 | 2 | 3 | 4 | 5 | 6 | 7 | 8 | 9 | 10 | 11 | 12 | 13 | 14 | 15 |

There must be an odd number of lines in a frame

Figure 3.1(a) 2:1 interlace.

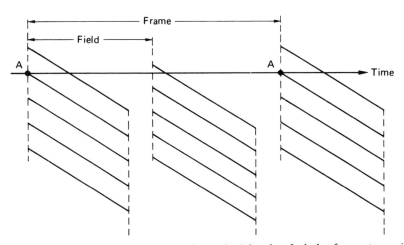

Figure 3.1(b) In an interlaced system, a given point A is only refreshed at frame rate, causing twitter on fine vertical detail.

achieved by having an odd number of lines (e.g. 525 or 625) in the frame so that the first field begins with a whole line and ends half-way along a line and the second field begins half-way through a line and ends on a whole line. The lines of the two fields then automatically mesh vertically.

The scanning process converts resolution on the image into the frequency domain. The higher the resolution of the image, the more lines are necessary to resolve the vertical detail. The line rate is increased along with the number of cycles of modulation which need to be carried in each line. If the frame rate remains constant, the bandwidth goes up as the square of the resolution. A 625 line system has a bandwidth of nearly 6 MHz, whereas a 1250 line HDTV system having twice the resolution needs about 30 MHz. The bandwidth required is more than four times higher because HDTV uses a 16:9 aspect ratio instead of 4:3, and so the lines are longer.

In interlaced systems, the field rate is intended to determine the flicker frequency, whereas the frame rate determines the bandwidth needed, which is thus halved along with the information rate. Information theory tells us that halving the information rate must reduce quality, and so the saving in bandwidth is accompanied by a variety of effects. Figure 3.1(b) shows the spatial/temporal sampling points in a 2:1 interlaced system. If an object has a sharp horizontal edge, it will be present in one field but not in the next. The refresh rate of the edge will be reduced to frame rate, 25 Hz or 30 Hz, and becomes visible as twitter.

Figure 3.2 shows some of the basic types of analog colour video. Each of these types can, of course, exist in a variety of line standards. Since practical colour cameras generally have three separate sensors, one for each primary colour, an

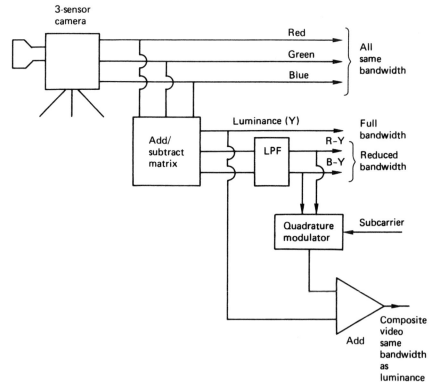

Figure 3.2 The major types of analog video. Red, green and blue signals emerge from the camera sensors, needing full bandwidth. If a luminance signal is obtained by a weighted sum of *R*, *G* and *B*, it will need full bandwidth, but the colour difference signals *R–Y* and *B–Y* need less bandwidth. Combining *R–Y* and *B–Y* into a subcarrier modulation scheme allows colour transmission in the same bandwidth as monochrome.

RGB system will exist at some stage in the internal workings of the camera, even if it does not emerge in that form. *RGB* consists of three parallel signals each having the same spectrum, and is used where the highest accuracy is needed, often for production of still pictures. Examples of this are paint systems and in computer-aided design (CAD) displays. *RGB* is seldom used for real-time video recording because of the high cost. As the red, green and blue signals directly represent part of the image, this approach is known as component video.

Some saving of bandwidth can be obtained by using colour difference working. The human eye relies on brightness to convey detail, and much less resolution is needed in the colour information. *R, G* and *B* are matrixed together to form a luminance (and monochrome-compatible) signal *Y* which has full bandwidth. The eye is not equally sensitive to the three primary colours, as can be seen in Figure 3.3(a), and so the luminance signal is a weighted sum.

The origin of the common colour bar test signal is shown in Figure 3.3(b). Binary *RGB* signals are produced, having one, two and four cycles per screen width. When these are added together, an eight-level luminance staircase results because of the unequal weighting. The matrix also produces two colour difference signals, *R−Y* and *B−Y*, and these are often displayed simultaneously on a vectorscope as shown in Figure 3.3(c). Note that the white bar and the black bar are not colours and so the colour difference signal is zero in those bars, resulting in a central spot. There are six remaining colours, each of which results in a spot on the perimeter of the vectorscope display.

Colour difference signals do not need the same bandwidth as *Y*, because the eye's acuity does not extend to colour vision. One-half or one-quarter of the bandwidth will do depending on the application. Chroma keying is more accurate with wide colour difference bandwidth, and so production systems use one-half of the luminance bandwidth for the colour difference signals. The overall bandwidth is then two-thirds that needed by *RGB*. Analog colour difference recorders such as Betacam and M-II record the luminance and colour difference signals separately. The D-1, D-5 and Digital Betacam formats record 525/60 or 625/50 colour difference signals digitally. In casual parlance, colour difference formats are often called component formats to distinguish them from composite formats.

For monochrome-compatible colour television broadcast in a single channel, the NTSC, PAL and SECAM systems interleave into the spectrum of a monochrome signal a subcarrier which carries two colour difference signals of restricted bandwidth. The subcarrier is intended to be invisible on the screen of a monochrome television set. A subcarrier-based colour system is generally referred to as composite video, and the modulated subcarrier is called chroma.

PAL and SECAM share the same scanning standard of 625/50, but the methods of conveying the colour are totally incompatible. NTSC scans at 525/59.94, but the colour system has a few things in common with PAL. All three standards use 2:1 interlace. Analog composite recorders include the B- and C-formats, and the D-2 and D-3 formats record PAL or NTSC digitally.

3.2 Introduction to conversion

There are a number of ways in which a video waveform can be digitally represented, but the most useful and therefore common is pulse code modulation or PCM which was introduced in Chapter 1. The input is a continuous-time,

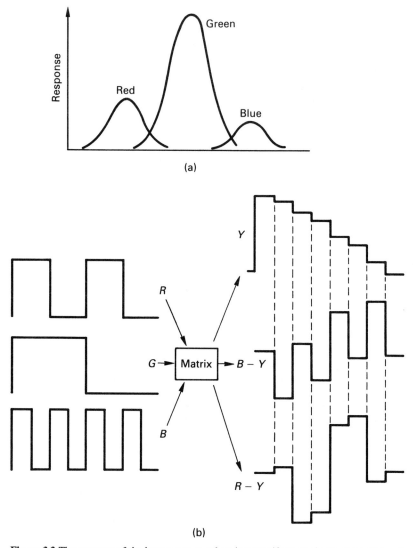

(a)

(b)

Figure 3.3 The response of the human eye to colour is not uniform as shown at (a). Colour bars originate as three square waves in *RGB*, but luminance obtained by weighted adding follows an irregular staircase shown at (b).

continuous-voltage video waveform, and this is converted into a discrete-time, discrete-voltage format by a combination of sampling and quantizing. As these two processes are orthogonal (a 64 dollar word for at right angles to one another) they are totally independent and can be performed in either order. Figure 3.4(a) shows an analog sampler preceding a quantizer, whereas (b) shows an asynchronous quantizer preceding a digital sampler. Ideally, both will give the same results; in practice each has different advantages and suffers from different deficiencies. Both approaches will be found in real equipment.

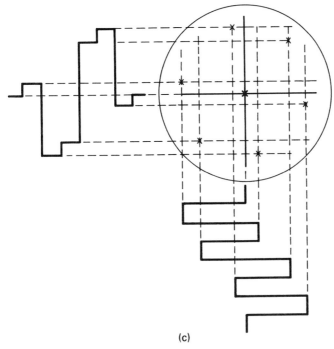

(c)

Figure 3.3 cont Colour difference signals can be shown two-dimensionally on a vectorscope as at (c).

The independence of sampling and quantizing allows each to be discussed quite separately in some detail, prior to combining the processes for a full understanding of conversion.

Whilst sampling an analog video waveform takes place in the time domain in an electrical ADC; this is because the analog waveform is the result of scanning an image. In reality the image has been spatially sampled in two dimensions (lines and pixels) and temporally sampled into fields along a third dimension. Sampling in a single dimension will be considered before moving on to more dimensions.

3.3 Sampling and aliasing

Sampling is no more than periodic measurement, and it will be shown here that there is no theoretical need for sampling to be detectable. Practical television equipment is, of course, less than ideal, particularly in the case of temporal sampling.

Video sampling must be regular, because the process of timebase correction prior to conversion back to a conventional analog waveform assumes a regular original process as was shown in Chapter 1. The sampling process originates with a pulse train which is shown in Figure 3.5(a) to be of constant amplitude and period. The video waveform amplitude-modulates the pulse train in much the same way as the carrier is modulated in an AM radio transmitter. One must be

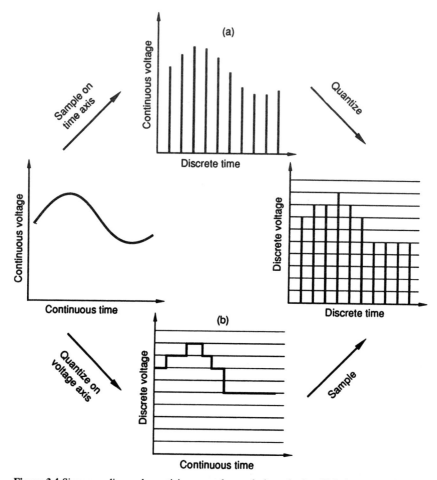

Figure 3.4 Since sampling and quantizing are orthogonal, the order in which they are performed is not important. In (a) sampling is performed first and the samples are quantized. This is common in audio converters. In (b) the analog input is quantized into an asynchronous binary code. Sampling takes place when this code is latched on sampling-clock edges. This approach is universal in video converters.

careful to avoid overmodulating the pulse train as shown in (b) and this is achieved by applying a DC offset to the analog waveform so that blanking corresponds to a level part-way up the pulses as at (c).

In the same way that AM radio produces sidebands or images above and below the carrier, sampling also produces sidebands, although the carrier is now a pulse train and has an infinite series of harmonics as shown in Figure 3.6(a). The sidebands repeat above and below each harmonic of the sampling rate as shown in (b).

The sampled signal can be returned to the continuous-time domain simply by passing it into a low-pass filter. This filter has a frequency response which prevents the images from passing, and only the baseband signal emerges,

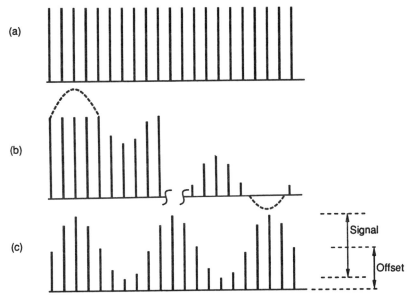

Figure 3.5 The sampling process requires a constant amplitude pulse train as shown in (a). This is amplitude modulated by the waveform to be sampled. If the input waveform has excessive amplitude or incorrect level, the pulse train clips as shown in (b). For a bipolar waveform, the greatest signal level is possible when an offset of half the pulse amplitude is used to centre the waveform as shown in (c).

completely unchanged. If considered in the frequency domain, this filter can be called an anti-image filter; if considered in the time domain it can be called a reconstruction filter. It can also be considered as a spatial filter if a sampled still image is being returned to a continuous image. Such a filter will be two dimensional.

If an input is supplied having an excessive bandwidth for the sampling rate in use, the sidebands will overlap (Figure 3.6(c)) and the result is aliasing, where certain output frequencies are not the same as their input frequencies but instead become difference frequencies (Figure 3.6(d)). It will be seen from Figure 3.6 that aliasing does not occur when the input frequency is equal to or less than half the sampling rate, and this derives the most fundamental rule of sampling, which is that the sampling rate must be at least twice the highest input frequency. Sampling theory is usually attributed to Shannon[1,2] who applied it to information theory at around the same time as Kotelnikov in Russia. These applications were pre-dated by Whittaker. Despite that it is often referred to as Nyquist's theorem.

Whilst aliasing has been described above in the frequency domain, it can be described equally well in the time domain. In Figure 3.7(a) the sampling rate is obviously adequate to describe the waveform, but at (b) it is inadequate and aliasing has occurred.

One often has no control over the spectrum of input signals and in practice it is necessary also to have a low-pass filter at the input to prevent aliasing. This anti-aliasing filter prevents frequencies of more than half the sampling rate from

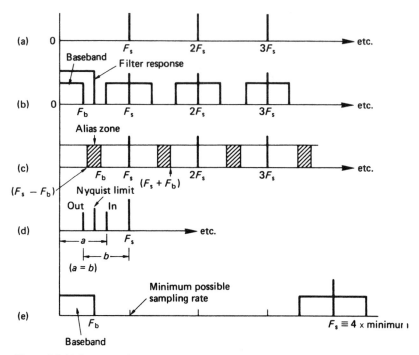

Figure 3.6 (a) Spectrum of sampling pulses. (b) Spectrum of samples. (c) Aliasing due to sideband overlap. (d) Beat-frequency production. (e) 4× oversampling.

reaching the sampling stage. The requirement for an anti-aliasing filter extends to two-dimensional sampling devices such as CCD sensors, as will be seen in Section 3.6.

Whilst electrical or optical anti-aliasing filters are quite feasible, there is no corresponding device which can precede the image sampling at frame or field rate in film or TV cameras and as a result aliasing is commonly seen on television and in the cinema, owing to the relatively low frame rates used. With a frame rate of 24 Hz, a film camera will alias on any object changing at more than 12 Hz. Such objects include the spokes of stagecoach wheels, especially when being chased by

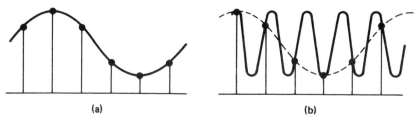

Figure 3.7 In (a), the sampling is adequate to reconstruct the original signal. In (b) the sampling rate is inadequate, and reconstruction produces the wrong waveform (dashed). Aliasing has taken place.

Indians. When the spoke-passing frequency reaches 24 Hz the wheels appear to stop. Temporal aliasing in television is less visible than might be thought because of the way in which the eye follows moving objects on the screen.

3.4 Reconstruction

If ideal low-pass anti-aliasing and anti-image filters are assumed, having a vertical cut-off slope at half the sampling rate, an ideal spectrum shown in Figure 3.8(a) is obtained. It was shown in Chapter 2 that the impulse response of a

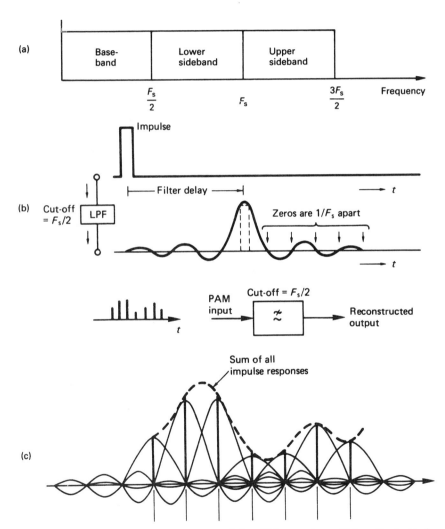

Figure 3.8 If ideal 'brick-wall' filters are assumed, the efficient spectrum of (a) results. An ideal low-pass filter has an impulse response shown in (b). The impulse passes through zero at intervals equal to the sampling period. When convolved with a pulse train at the sampling rate, as shown in (c), the voltage at each sample instant is due to that sample alone as the impulses from all other samples pass through zero there.

phase-linear ideal low-pass filter is a $\sin x/x$ waveform in the time domain, and this is repeated in Figure 3.8(b). Such a waveform passes through zero volts periodically. If the cut-off frequency of the filter is one-half of the sampling rate, the impulse passes through zero *at the sites of all other samples*. It can be seen from Figure 3.8(c) that at the output of such a filter, the voltage at the centre of a sample is due to that sample alone, since the value of *all* other samples is zero at that instant. In other words, the continuous-time output waveform must join up the tops of the input samples. In between the sample instants, the output of the filter is the sum of the contributions from many impulses, and the waveform smoothly joins the tops of the samples. If the time domain is being considered, the anti-image filter of the frequency domain can equally well be called the reconstruction filter. It is a consequence of the band-limiting of the original anti-aliasing filter that the filtered analog waveform could only travel between the sample points in one way. As the reconstruction filter has the same frequency response, the reconstructed output waveform must be identical to the original band limited waveform prior to sampling. A rigorous mathematical proof of reconstruction can be found in Betts.[3]

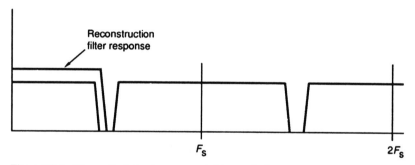

Figure 3.9 As filters with finite slope are needed in practical systems, the sampling rate is raised slightly beyond twice the highest frequency in the baseband.

The ideal filter with a vertical 'brick-wall' cut-off slope is difficult to implement. As the slope tends to vertical, the delay caused by the filter goes to infinity. In practice, a filter with a finite slope has to be accepted as shown in Figure 3.9. The cut-off slope begins at the edge of the required band, and consequently the sampling rate has to be raised a little to drive aliasing products to an acceptably low level. There is no absolute factor by which the sampling rate must be raised; it depends upon the filters which are available and the level of aliasing products which are acceptable. The latter will depend upon the wordlength to which the signal will be quantized.

3.5 Filter design

It is not easy to specify anti-aliasing and reconstruction filters, particularly the amount of stopband rejection needed. The amount of aliasing resulting would depend on, among other things, the amount of out-of-band energy in the input signal. Very little is known about the energy in typical source material outside the usual frequency range. As a further complication, an out-of-band signal will be attenuated by the response of the anti-aliasing filter to that frequency, but the residual signal will then alias, and the reconstruction filter will reject it according to its attenuation at the new frequency to which it has aliased. To take the opposite extreme, if a camera were used which had no response at all above the video band, no anti-aliasing filter would be needed.

It would also be acceptable to bypass one of the filters involved in a copy from one DVTR to another via the analog domain, although a digital transfer is of course to be preferred.

The nature of the filters used has a great bearing on the subjective quality of the system. Entire books have been written about analog filters, and they will only be treated briefly here.

Figure 3.10 shows the terminology used to describe the common elliptic low-pass filter. These are popular because they can be realized with fewer components than other filters of similar response. It is a characteristic of these

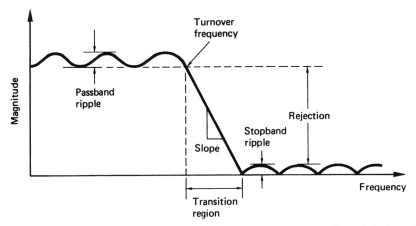

Figure 3.10 The important features and terminology of low-pass filters used for anti-aliasing and reconstruction.

elliptic filters that there are ripples in the passband and stopband. In much equipment the anti-aliasing filter and the reconstruction filter will have the same specification, so that the passband ripple is doubled. Sometimes slightly different filters are used to reduce the effect.

Active filters can simulate inductors using op-amp techniques, but they tend to suffer non-linearity at high frequencies where the falling open-loop gain reduces the effect of feedback. Active filters also can contribute noise, but this is not necessarily a bad thing in controlled amounts, since it can act as a dither source.

For video applications, the phase response of such filters must be linear (see Chapter 2). Since a sharp cut-off is generally achieved by cascading many filter sections which cut at a similar frequency, the phase responses of these sections will accumulate. The phase may start to leave linearity at only a half of the passband frequency, and near the cut-off frequency the phase error may be severe. Effective group-delay equalization is necessary.

It is possible to construct a ripple-free phase-linear filter with the required stopband rejection, but it may be expensive due to the amount of design effort needed and the component complexity, and it might drift out of specification as components age. The money may be better spent in avoiding the need for such a filter. Much effort can be saved in analog filter design by using oversampling. Chapter 2 showed that digital filters are inherently phase linear and, using LSI, can be inexpensive to construct. The technical superiority of oversampling converters along with economics means that they will be increasingly used in the future, which is why the subject is more prominent in this volume than the treatment of filter design.

3.6 Aperture effect

The reconstruction process of Figure 3.8 only operates exactly as shown if the impulses are of negligible duration. In many processes this is not the case, and many real devices keep the analog signal constant for a substantial part of or even all the period. The result is a waveform which is more like a staircase than a pulse train. The case where the pulses have been extended in width to become equal to the sample period is known as a zero-order hold system and has a 100% aperture ratio.

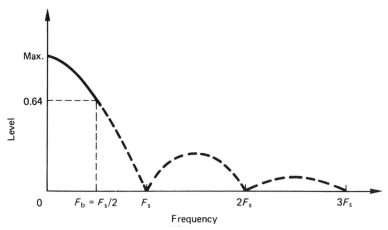

Figure 3.11 Frequency response with 100% aperture has nulls at multiples of sampling rate. Area of interest is up to half sampling rate.

It was shown in Chapter 2 that whereas pulses of negligible width have a uniform spectrum, which is flat within the baseband, pulses of 100% aperture ratio have a $\sin x/x$ spectrum which is shown in Figure 3.11. The frequency response falls to a null at the sampling rate, and as a result is about 4 dB down at the edge of the baseband. If the pulse width is stable, the reduction of high frequencies is constant and predictable, and an appropriate equalization circuit can render the overall response flat once more. An alternative is to use resampling which is shown in Figure 3.12. Resampling passes the zero-order hold waveform through a further synchronous sampling stage which consists of an analog switch which closes briefly in the centre of each sample period. The output of the switch will be pulses which are narrower than the original. If, for example, the aperture ratio is reduced to 50% of the sample period, the first frequency response null is now at twice the sampling rate, and the loss at the edge

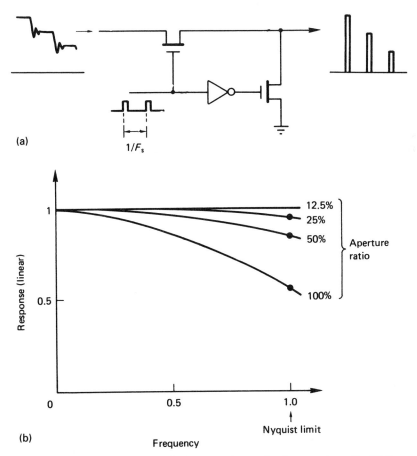

Figure 3.12 (a) Resampling circuit eliminates transients and reduces aperture ratio. (b) Response of various aperture ratios.

of the audio band is reduced. As the figure shows, the frequency response becomes flatter as the aperture ratio falls. The process should not be carried too far, as with very small aperture ratios there is little energy in the pulses and noise can be a problem. A practical limit is around 12.5% where the frequency response is virtually ideal.

The term resampling will also be found in descriptions of sampling-rate converters, where it refers to the process of finding samples at new locations to describe the original waveform. The context usually makes it clear which meaning is intended.

The aperture effect will show up in many aspects of television. Lenses have finite MTF (Modulation Transfer Function), such that a very small object becomes spread in the image. The image sensor will also have a finite aperture function. In tube cameras, the beam will have a finite radius, and will not necessarily have a uniform energy distribution across its diameter. In CCD cameras, the sensor is split into elements which may almost touch in some cases. The element integrates light falling on its surface, and so will have a rectangular aperture. In both cases there will be a roll-off of higher spatial frequencies.

The temporal aperture effect varies according to the equipment used. Tube cameras have a long integration time and thus a wide temporal aperture. Whilst this reduces temporal aliasing, it causes smear on moving objects. CCD cameras do not suffer from lag and as a result their temporal response is better.[4] Some CCD cameras deliberately have a short temporal aperture as the time axis is resampled by a mechanically driven revolving shutter. The intention is to reduce smear (hence the popularity of such devices for sporting events, but there will be more aliasing on certain subjects).

The eye has a temporal aperture effect which is known as persistence of vision, and the phosphors of CRTs continue to emit light after the electron beam has passed. These produce further temporal aperture effects in series with those in the camera.

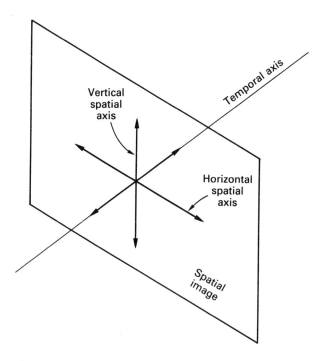

Figure 3.13 The three dimensions in which television signals are sampled. The time domain is the one which causes the greatest difficulty.

Current liquid crystal displays do not generate light, but act as a modulator to a separate light source. Their temporal response is rather slow, but there is a possibility to resample by pulsing the light source.

Figure 3.13 shows the three dimensions available to television signals and shows the possibilities for anti-aliasing, reconstruction and aperture effect in each.

3.7 Two-dimensional sampling spectra

Analog video samples in the time domain and vertically, whereas a two-dimensional still image such as a photograph must be sampled horizontally and vertically. In both cases a two-dimensional spectrum will result, one vertical/temporal and one vertical/horizontal.

Figure 3.14(a) shows a square matrix of sampling sites which has an identical spatial sampling frequency both vertically and horizontally. The corresponding spectrum is shown in Figure 3.14(b). The baseband spectrum is in the centre of the diagram, and the repeating sampling sideband spectrum extends vertically and horizontally. The star-shaped spectrum results from viewing an image of a man-made object such as a building containing primarily horizontal and vertical elements. A more natural scene such as foliage would result in a more circular or elliptical spectrum.

In order to return to the baseband image, the sidebands must be filtered out with a two-dimensional spatial filter. The shape of the two-dimensional frequency response shown in Figure 3.14(c) is known as a Brillouin zone.

Figure 3.14(d) shows an alternative sampling site matrix known as quincunx sampling because of the similarity to the pattern of five dots on a dice. The resultant spectrum has the same characteristic pattern as shown in Figure 3.14(e). The corresponding Brillouin zones are shown in Figure 3.14(f). Quincunx sampling offers a better compromise between diagonal and horizontal/vertical resolution but is complex to implement and is not used in any of the normal definition formats.

It is highly desirable to prevent spatial aliasing, since the result is visually irritating. In tube cameras the spatial aliasing will be in the vertical dimension only, since the horizontal dimension is continuously scanned. Such cameras seldom attempt to prevent vertical aliasing. CCD sensors can, however, alias in both horizontal and vertical dimensions, and so an anti-aliasing optical filter is generally fitted between the lens and the sensor. This takes the form of a plate which diffuses the image formed by the lens. Such a device can never have a sharp cut-off nor will the aperture be rectangular. The aperture of the anti-aliasing plate is in series with the aperture effect of the CCD elements, and the combination of the two effectively prevents spatial aliasing, and generally gives a good balance between horizontal and vertical resolution, allowing the picture a natural appearance.

With a conventional approach, there are effectively two choices. If aliasing is permitted, the theoretical information rate of the system can be approached. If aliasing is prevented, realizable anti-aliasing filters cannot sharp cut, and the information conveyed is below system capacity.

These considerations also apply at the television display. The display must filter out spatial frequencies above one-half the sampling rate. In a conventional CRT this means that a vertical optical filter should be fitted in front of the screen to

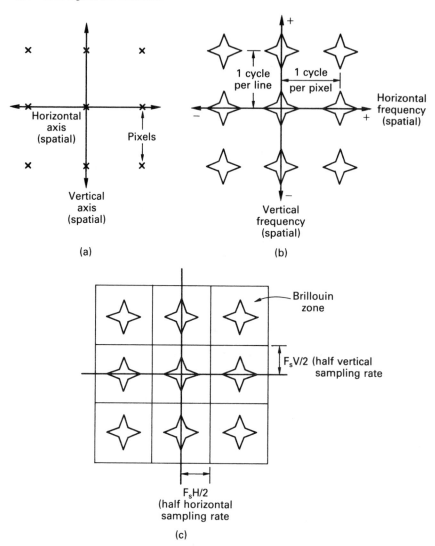

Figure 3.14 Image sampling spectra. The rectangular array of (a) has a spectrum shown at (b) having a rectangular repeating structure. Filtering to return to the baseband requires a two-dimensional filter whose response lies within the Brillouin zone shown at (c).

render the raster invisible. Again the aperture of a simply realizable filter would attenuate too much of the wanted spectrum, and so the technique is not used.

Figure 3.15 shows the spectrum of analog monochrome video (or of an analog component). The use of interlace has a similar effect on the vertical/temporal spectrum as the use of quincunx sampling on the vertical/horizontal spectrum. The concept of the Brillouin zone cannot really be applied to reconstruction in the spatial/temporal domains. This is partly due to there being two different units in which the sampling rates are measured and partly because the temporal sampling process cannot prevent aliasing in real systems.

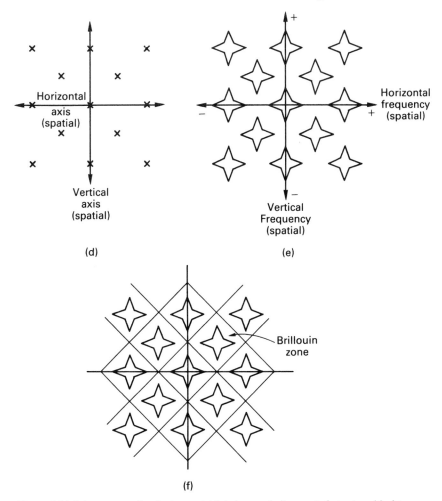

Figure 3.14 Quincunx sampling is shown at (d) to have a similar spectral structure (e). An appropriate Brillouin zone is required as at (f).

3.7.1 Three-dimensional Spectrum of NTSC

Analog composite video can only be fully described in three dimensions because of the presence of the subcarrier. Digital video samples in three dimensions and also has a three-dimensional (3-D) spectrum. As such spectra are difficult to illustrate, they are often portrayed in two dimensions at a time.

Figure 3.16 shows that the structure of the vertical/temporal spectrum of luminance is the same as that of the two colour difference signals because both have the same field and line rates. In NTSC (National Television Systems Committee), the three signals are encoded into a single channel having the same bandwidth as luminance by exploiting the periodic gaps in the spectrum. The two colour difference signals are used to generate reduced bandwidth signals which

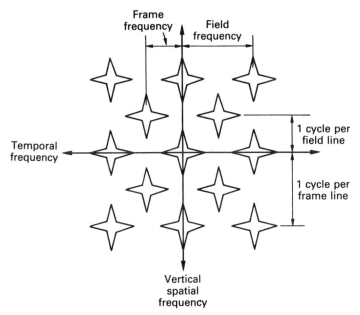

Figure 3.15 The vertical/temporal spectrum of monochrome video due to interlace.

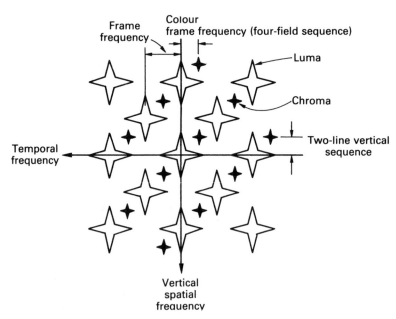

Figure 3.16 The vertical/temporal spectrum of NTSC. Note the one-quarter field-rate component responsible for the four-field sequence.

alternately phase modulate a subcarrier. The subcarrier is suppressed to produce a chroma signal.

In order to allow the maximum perceived resolution with minimum bandwidth, the chroma phase was shifted slightly with respect to horizontal, so that subcarrier phase demodulation would give a pair of signals known as I and Q (in phase and quadrature). This placed the Q signal on the colour diagram axis to which the eye is least sensitive.

The chroma is given by:

$$I \sin F_{sc} + Q \cos F_{sc}$$

such that at 90° intervals, the chroma waveform represents I, Q, $-I$, $-Q$ repeatedly. If the receiver samples the chroma at the same intervals, but with the same phase shift, the two baseband colour difference signals can be restored.

The chroma modulation process takes the spectrum of the colour difference signals and produces upper and lower sidebands around the frequency of subcarrier. Since both colour and luminance signals have gaps in their spectra at multiples of line rate, it follows that the two spectra can be made to interleave and share the same spectrum if an appropriate subcarrier frequency is selected. The subcarrier frequency of NTSC is an odd multiple of half line rate; 227.5 times to be precise. Figure 3.17 shows that this frequency means that on

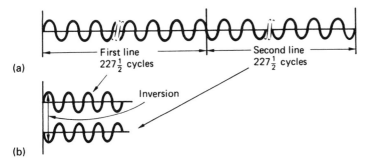

(a)

(b)

Figure 3.17 The half cycle offset in F_{sc} results in a two-line sequence (a) where the first line ends on a half cycle, and the second line chroma will be inverted with respect to the first as at (b).

successive lines the subcarrier will be phase inverted. There is thus a two-line sequence of subcarrier, responsible for a vertical frequency of half line frequency. The existence of line pairs means that two frames or four fields must elapse before the same relationship between line pairs and frame sync. repeats. This is responsible for a temporal frequency component of half the frame rate. These two frequency components can be seen in the vertical/temporal spectrum of Figure 3.16.

The effect of the chroma added to luminance is to make the luminance alternately too dark or too bright. The phase inversion causes this effect to cancel over pairs of lines, giving compatibility with monochrome receivers. The half frame rate component is responsible for the familiar four-field colour framing sequence. When editing NTSC recordings, this four field sequence must not be broken. If this rule is not followed, it is possible for a sudden inversion of subcarrier phase to occur at the edit point, which renders the signal unbroadcastable unless it undergoes additional processing.

As the chroma of NTSC is suppressed carrier, it is necessary for the receiver to regenerate the carrier frequency so that it knows when to sample the chroma. This is done by broadcasting a portion of subcarrier, known as the burst, between the sync pulse and the active line. A phase-locked loop in the receiver will freewheel between bursts. The half line offset of NTSC subcarrier means that if an oscilloscope is triggered from H-sync, normal and inverted bursts will appear superimposed on the trace.

Whilst the spectral interleaving of NTSC works fine for the video, there was a problem with the sound carrier. To prevent vision interference with the sound, the sound carrier of the 525/60 monochrome system had itself been placed at an odd multiple of half line rate, and so the addition of the chroma signal meant that chroma and sound could mutually interfere. The audio subcarrier frequency was standardized, and any change would have meant modification to every monochrome television set in the United States on the introduction of colour. The solution adopted was to contract the spectrum of the video slightly by reducing the frame rate to 29.97 Hz. This made the line rate 15 734.25 Hz and the subcarrier frequency 3.5795 MHz. The small disparity between field rate and 60 Hz was of little consequence when it was introduced, but the development of the video recorder revealed a difficulty in synchronizing NTSC recordings to real time, which was alleviated by the invention of drop-frame timecode. This allows a single count to count real-time seconds and NTSC rate frames at the same time by having dropped frames, which do not exist in the video, but which make the seconds count correct. The use of 29 February in the calendar has a similar effect.

The dependence of NTSC on the absolute phase of subcarrier to convey colour accurately led to some difficulties in multipath reception conditions in high-rise districts, and to the somewhat unfair redefinition of the system title as Never Twice the Same Colour. In fact NTSC works well in the majority of other locations.

3.7.2 Three-dimensional spectrum of PAL

When the PAL (Phase Alternating Line) system was being developed, it was decided that immunity to received phase errors should be a goal. Figure 3.18(a) shows how this was achieved. The two colour difference signals (U and V) are used to quadrature-modulate a subcarrier in a similar way as for NTSC, except that the phase of the V signal is reversed on alternate lines. The receiver must then reinvert the V signal in sympathy. If a phase error occurs in transmission, it will cause the phase of V alternately to lead and lag, as shown in Figure 3.18(b). If the colour difference signals are averaged over two lines, the phase error is eliminated and replaced with a small saturation error which is subjectively much less visible. The receiver needs to know whether or not to invert V on a particular line, and this information is conveyed by swinging the phase of the burst $\pm$ 135° on alternate lines. A damped PLL in the receiver will run at the average phase, i.e. subcarrier phase, but it will develop a half line rate phase error whose polarity determines the sense of V-switch.

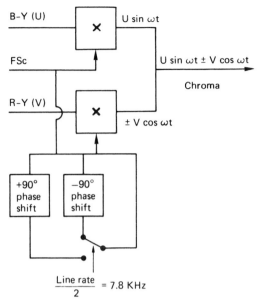

Figure 3.18(a) In PAL the phase of the feed to the V-modulator is reversed on alternate lines.

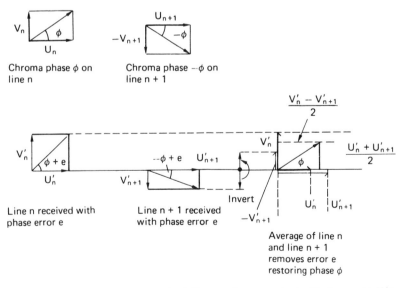

Figure 3.18(b) Top, chroma as transmitted. Bottom, chroma received with phase error. V is reversed on second line and the two lines are averaged, eliminating phase error, and giving instead a small saturation error.

Figure 3.19(a) shows the vertical temporal spectrum of the U signal, which is identical to that of luminance. However, the inversion of V on alternate lines causes a two-line sequence which is responsible for a vertical frequency component of half line rate. As the two-line sequence does not divide into 625 lines, two frames elapse before the same relationship between V-switch and the line number repeats. This is responsible for a half frame rate temporal frequency component. Figure 3.19(b) shows the resultant vertical/temporal spectrum after V-switch and illustrates that the V component has shifted diagonally so that its spectral entries lie half-way between the U component entries. Note that there is an area of the spectrum which appears not to contain signal energy in PAL. This

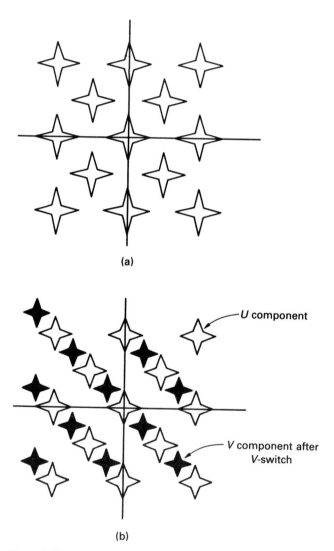

(a)

(b)

Figure 3.19 (a) The vertical/temporal spectrum of the U signal has the same structure as luminance. At (b) V-switch has the effect of shifting the spectrum diagonally with respect to U.

is known as the Fukinuki hole. Spectral interleaving with a half cycle offset of subcarrier frequency as in NTSC will not work, as Figure 3.19(c) shows. The solution is to adopt a subcarrier frequency with a quarter cycle per line offset. Multiplying the line rate by $283\frac{3}{4}$ allows the luminance and chrominance spectra to mesh as in Figure 3.19(d).

The quarter cycle offset is thus a fundamental consequence of elimination of phase errors in PAL but it does cause some other effects which raise the complexity of implementation, leading to the retaliatory name of Problems Are Lurking.

The quarter cycle offset means that there are now line quartets instead of line pairs, and this results in a vertical frequency component of one-quarter of line rate which can be seen in the figure. Furthermore four frames or eight fields have to

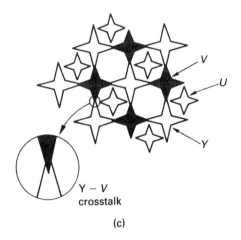

(c)

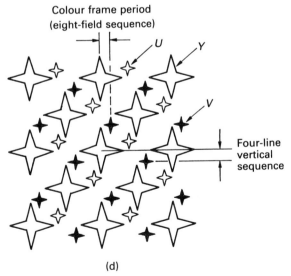

(d)

Figure 3.19 (contd.) A half cycle subcarrier offset will not work as (c) shows. Instead a quarter cycle offset is used as at (d).

elapse before the same relationship of subcarrier to frame timing repeats. This results in a temporal frequency component of one-quarter of frame rate which is also visible in the figure. This component restricts the way in which PAL recordings can be edited.

The three-quarter cycle offset of subcarrier also means that the line pair cancellation of NTSC is absent, and another means has to be found to achieve visibility reduction. This is done by adding half frame rate to subcarrier frequency, such that an inversion in subcarrier is caused from one field to the next. Since in an interlaced system lines one field apart are adjacent on the screen, cancellation is achieved. The penalty of this approach is that subcarrier phase creeps forward with respect to H-sync at one cycle per frame. The eight-field sequence contains 2500 unique lines all having the subcarrier in a slightly different position. Observing burst on an H-triggered oscilloscope shows a stable envelope with a blurred interior. Measuring the phase of subcarrier with respect to sync requires specialist equipment or a great deal of determination. This is of little consequence for broadcasting, but it does raise the complexity of recorders.

3.7.3 Three-dimensional spectrum of digital luminance

Sampling conventional video along the line to create pixels makes the horizontal axis of the 3-D spectrum repeat at multiples of the sampling rate. Thus combining the 3-D spectrum of analog luminance shown in Figure 3.16(a) with the sampling

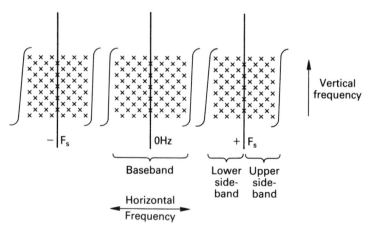

Figure 3.20 Spectrum of digital luminance is the baseband spectrum repeating around multiples of the sampling rate.

spectrum of Figure 3.6(b) gives the final spectrum shown in Figure 3.20. Colour difference signals will have a similar structure but often use a lower sampling rate and thereby have less horizontal resolution or bandwidth.

3.8 Kell effect

As noted, in conventional tube cameras and CRTs the horizontal dimension is continuous, whereas the vertical dimension is sampled. The aperture effect means that the vertical resolution in real systems will be less than sampling theory permits, and to obtain equal horizontal and vertical resolutions a greater number of lines is necessary. The magnitude of the increase is described by the so-called Kell factor,[5] although the term factor is a misnomer since it can have a range of values depending on the apertures in use and the methods used to measure resolution.[6] In digital video, sampling takes place in horizontal and vertical dimensions, and the Kell parameter becomes unnecessary. The outputs of digital systems will, however, be displayed on raster scan CRTs, and the Kell parameter of the display will then be effectively in series with the other system constraints.

3.9 Choice of sampling rate – component

If the reason for digitizing a video signal is simply to convey it from one place to another, then the choice of sampling frequency can be determined only by sampling theory and available filters. If, however, processing of the video in the digital domain is contemplated, the choice becomes smaller. In order to produce a two-dimensional array of samples which form rows and vertical columns, the sampling rate has to be an integer multiple of the line rate. This allows for the vertical picture processing necessary in special effects, telecine machines working on various aspect ratios, error concealment in recorders and standards conversion. Whilst the bandwidth needed by 525/59.94 video is less than that of 625/50, and a lower sampling rate might be used, practicality dictated that if a standard sampling rate for video components could be arrived at, then the design of standards converters would be simplified, and digital recorders would operate at a similar data rate even though the frame rates would differ in different standards. This was the goal of CCIR Recommendation 601, which combined the 625/50 input of EBU Docs Tech. 3246 and 3247 and the 525/59.94 input of SMPTE RP 125.

The result is not one sampling rate, but a family of rates based upon the magic frequency of 13.5 MHz.

Using this frequency as a sampling rate produces 858 samples in the line period of 525/59.94 and 864 samples in the line period of 625/50. For lower bandwidths, the rate can be divided by three-quarters, one-half or one-quarter to give sampling rates of 10.125, 6.75 and 3.375 MHz respectively. If the lowest frequency is considered to be 1, then the highest is 4. For maximum quality *RGB* working, three parallel, identical, sample streams would then be required, which would be denoted by 4:4:4. Colour difference signals intended for post production, where a wider colour difference bandwidth is needed, require 4:2:2 sampling for luminance, $R-Y$ and $B-Y$ respectively; 4:2:2 has the advantage that an integer number of colour difference samples also exist in both line standards. Figure 3.21 shows the spatial arrangement given by 4:2:2 sampling. Luminance samples appear at half the spacing of colour difference samples, and half of the luminance samples are in the same physical position as a pair of colour difference samples, these being called co-sited samples. The D-1, D-5 and Digital Betacam recording formats work with 4:2:2 sampling.

Figure 3.22(a) shows the one-dimensional spectrum which results from sampling 525/59.94 video at 13.5 MHz, and Figure 3.22(b) shows the result for 625/50 video. Further details of CCIR-601 sampling can be found in Section 3.22.

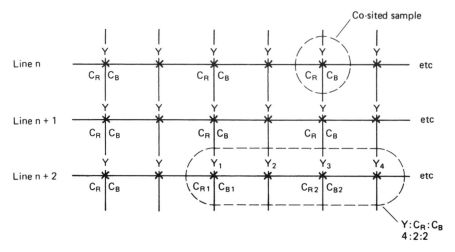

Figure 3.21 In CCIR-601 sampling mode 4:2:2, the line synchronous sampling rate of 13.5 MHz results in samples having the same position in successive lines, so that vertical columns are generated. The sampling rates of the colour difference signals C_R, C_B are one-half of that of luminance, i.e. 6.75 MHz, so that there are alternate Y-only samples and co-sited samples which describe Y, C_R and C_B. In a run of four samples, there will be four Y samples, two C_R samples and two C_B samples, hence 4:2:2

The conventional TV screen has an aspect ratio of 4:3, whereas in the future an aspect ratio of 16:9 may be adopted. Expressing 4:3 as 12:9 makes it clear that the 16:9 picture is 16/12 or 4/3 times as wide. There are two ways of handling 16:9 pictures in the digital domain. One is to retain the standard sampling rate of 13.5 MHz, which results in the horizontal resolution falling to three-quarters of its previous value, and the other is to increase the sampling rate in proportion to the screen width. This results in a luminance sampling rate of 13.5 × 4/3 MHz or 18.0 MHz.

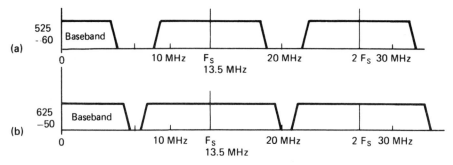

Figure 3.22 Spectra of video sampled at 13.5 MHz. At (a) the baseband 525/60 signal at left becomes the sidebands of the sampling rate and its harmonics. At (b) the same process for the 625/50 signal results in a smaller gap between baseband and sideband because of the wider bandwidth of the 625 system. The same sampling rate for both standards results in a great deal of commonality between 50 Hz and 60 Hz equipment.

3.10 Choice of sampling rate – composite

When composite video is to be digitized, the input will be a single waveform having spectrally interleaved luminance and chroma. Any sampling rate which allows sufficient bandwidth would convey composite video from one point to another; indeed 13.5 MHz has been successfully used to sample PAL and NTSC.

In many cases it will be necessary to decode the composite signal which will require some kind of digital filter. Whilst it is possible to construct filters with any desired response, it is a fact that a digital filter whose response is simply related to the sampling rate will be much less complex to implement. This is the reasoning which has led to the near universal use of four times subcarrier sampling rate. Figure 3.23 shows the spectra of PAL and NTSC sampled at $4 \times F_{sc}$. It will be evident that there is a considerable space between the edge of

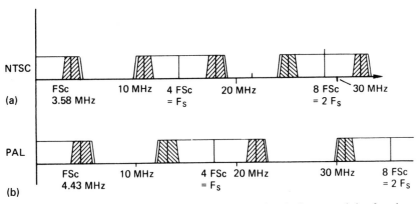

Figure 3.23 The spectra of NTSC at (a) and of PAL at (b) where both are sampled at four times the frequency of their respective subcarriers. This high sampling rate is unnecessary to satisfy sampling theory, and so both are oversampled systems. The advantages are in the large spectral gap between baseband and sideband which allows a more gentle filter slope to be employed, and in the relative ease of colour processing at a sampling rate related to subcarrier.

the baseband and the lower sideband. This allows the anti-aliasing and reconstruction filters to have a more gradual cut-off, so that ripple in the passband can be reduced. This is particularly important for C-format timebase correctors and for composite digital recorders, since both are digital devices in an analog environment, and signals may have been converted to and from the digital domain many times in the course of production.

3.11 Sampling-clock jitter

The instants at which samples are taken in an ADC and the instants at which DACs make conversions must be evenly spaced, otherwise unwanted signals can be added to the video. Figure 3.24 shows the effect of sampling-clock jitter on a sloping waveform. Samples are taken at the wrong times. When these samples have passed through a system, the timebase-correction stage prior to the DAC will remove the jitter, and the result is shown at (b). The magnitude of the

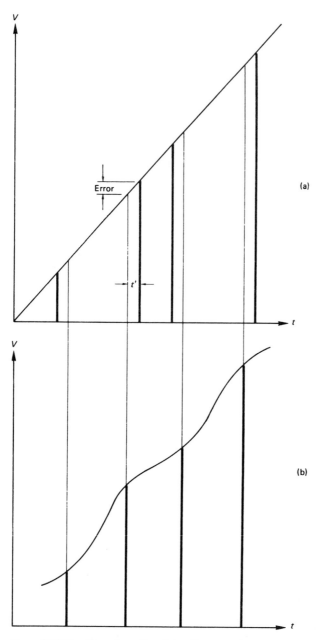

Figure 3.24 The effect of sampling timing jitter on noise. At (a) a sloping signal sampled with jitter has error proportional to the slope. When jitter is removed by reclocking, the result at (b) is noise.

unwanted signal is proportional to the slope of the audio waveform and so the amount of jitter which can be tolerated falls at 6 dB per octave. As the resolution of the system is increased by the use of longer sample wordlength, tolerance to jitter is further reduced. The nature of the unwanted signal depends on the spectrum of the jitter. If the jitter is random, the effect is noise-like and relatively benign unless the amplitude is excessive. Figure 3.25 shows the effect of differing amounts of random jitter with respect to the noise floor of various wordlengths. Note that even small amounts of jitter can degrade a 10 bit converter to the performance of a good 8 bit unit. There is thus no point in upgrading to higher-resolution converters if the clock stability of the system is insufficient to allow their performance to be realized.

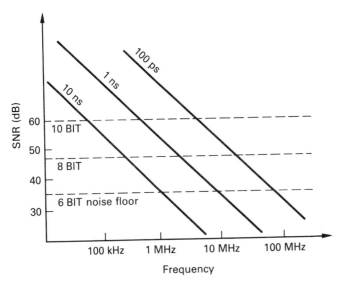

Figure 3.25 The effect of sampling-clock jitter on signal-to-noise ratio at various frequencies, compared with the theoretical noise floors with different wordlengths.

Clock jitter is not necessarily random. Figure 3.26 shows that one source of clock jitter is crosstalk or interference on the clock signal, although a balanced clock line will be more immune to such crosstalk. The unwanted additional signal changes the time at which the sloping clock signal appears to cross the threshold voltage of the clock receiver. This is simply the same phenomenon as that of Figure 3.24 but in reverse. The threshold itself may be changed by ripple on the clock receiver power supply. There is no reason why these effects should be random; they may be periodic and potentially visible.[7]

The allowable jitter is measured in picoseconds, as shown in Figure 3.25, and clearly steps must be taken to eliminate it by design. Converter clocks must be generated from clean power supplies which are well decoupled from the power used by the logic because a converter clock must have a signal-to-noise ratio of the same order as that of the signal. Otherwise noise on the clock causes jitter

(a)

(b)

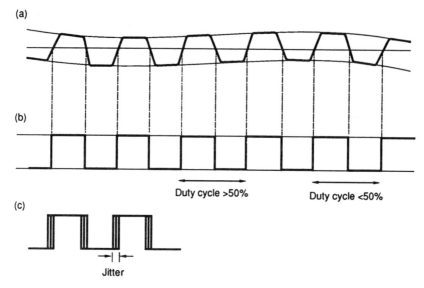

Duty cycle >50%   Duty cycle <50%

(c)

Jitter

Figure 3.26 Crosstalk in transmission can result in unwanted signals being added to the clock waveform. It can be seen here that a low-frequency interference signal affects the slicing of the clock and causes a periodic jitter.

which in turn causes noise in the video. The same effect will be found in digital audio signals, which are perhaps more critical.

3.12 Quantizing

Quantizing is the process of expressing some infinitely variable quantity by discrete or stepped values. Quantizing turns up in a remarkable number of everyday guises. Figure 3.27 shows that an inclined ramp enables infinitely variable height to be achieved, whereas a step-ladder allows only discrete heights to be had. A step-ladder quantizes height. When accountants round off sums of money to the nearest pound or dollar they are quantizing. Time passes continuously, but the display on a digital clock changes suddenly every minute because the clock is quantizing time.

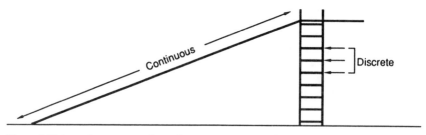

Continuous   Discrete

Figure 3.27 An analog parameter is continuous whereas a quantized parameter is restricted to certain values. Here the sloping side of a ramp can be used to obtain any height whereas a ladder only allows discrete heights.

In video and audio the values to be quantized are infinitely variable voltages from an analog source. Strict quantizing is a process which operates in the voltage domain only. For the purpose of studying the quantizing of a single sample, time is assumed to stand still. This is achieved in practice either by the use of a track–hold circuit or the adoption of a quantizer technology such as a flash converter which operates before the sampling stage.

Figure 3.28(a) shows that the process of quantizing divides the voltage range up into quantizing intervals Q, also referred to as steps S. In applications such as telephony these may advantageously be of differing size, but for digital video and audio the quantizing intervals are made as identical as possible. If this is done, the binary numbers which result are truly proportional to the original analog voltage, and the digital equivalents of mixing and gain changing can be performed by adding and multiplying sample values. If the quantizing intervals are unequal this cannot be done. When all quantizing intervals are the same, the term uniform quantizing is used. The term linear quantizing will be found, but this is a contradiction in terms.

The term LSB (Least Significant Bit) will also be found in place of quantizing interval in some treatments, but this is a poor term because quantizing works in the voltage domain. A bit is not a unit of voltage and can only have two values. In studying quantizing voltages within a quantizing interval will be discussed, but there is no such thing as a fraction of a bit.

Whatever the exact voltage of the input signal, the quantizer will locate the quantizing interval in which it lies. In what may be considered a separate step, the quantizing interval is then allocated a code value which is typically some form of binary number. The information sent is the number of the quantizing interval in which the input voltage lay. Whereabouts that voltage lay within the interval is not conveyed, and this mechanism puts a limit on the accuracy of the quantizer. When the number of the quantizing interval is converted back to the analog domain, it will result in a voltage at the centre of the quantizing interval as this minimizes the magnitude of the error between input and output. The number range is limited by the wordlength of the binary numbers used. In an 8 bit system, 256 different quantizing intervals exist, although in digital video the codes at the extreme ends of the range are reserved for synchronizing.

3.13 Quantizing error

It is possible to draw a transfer function for such an ideal quantizer followed by an ideal DAC, and this is also shown in Figure 3.28. A transfer function is simply a graph of the output with respect to the input. In audio, when the term linearity is used, this generally means the overall straightness of the transfer function. Linearity is a goal in video and audio, yet it will be seen that an ideal quantizer is anything but linear.

Figure 3.28(b) shows the transfer function is somewhat like a staircase, and blanking level is half-way up a quantizing interval, or on the centre of a tread. This is the so-called mid-tread quantizer which is universally used in video and audio. Figure 3.28(c) shows the alternative mid-riser transfer function which causes difficulty because it does not have a code value at blanking level and as a result the numerical code value is not proportional to the analog signal voltage.

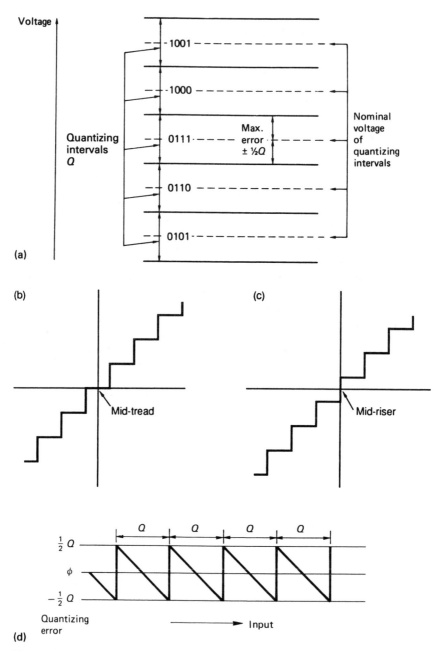

Figure 3.28 Quantizing assigns discrete numbers to variable voltages. All voltages within the same quantizing interval are assigned the same number which causes a DAC to produce the voltage at the centre of the intervals shown by the dashed lines in (a). This is the characteristic of the mid-tread quantizer shown in (b). An alternative system is the mid-riser system shown in (c). Here 0 volts analog falls between two codes and there is no code for zero. Such quantizing cannot be used prior to signal processing because the number is no longer proportional to the voltage. Quantizing error cannot exceed $\pm\frac{1}{2}Q$ as shown in (d).

Quantizing causes a voltage error in the audio sample which is given by the difference between the actual staircase transfer function and the ideal straight line. This is shown in Figure 3.28(d) to be a sawtooth-like function which is periodic in Q. The amplitude cannot exceed $\pm\frac{1}{2}Q$ peak-to-peak unless the input is so large that clipping occurs.

Quantizing error can also be studied in the time domain where it is better to avoid complicating matters with the aperture effect of the DAC. For this reason it is assumed here that output samples are of negligible duration. Then impulses from the DAC can be compared with the original analog waveform and the

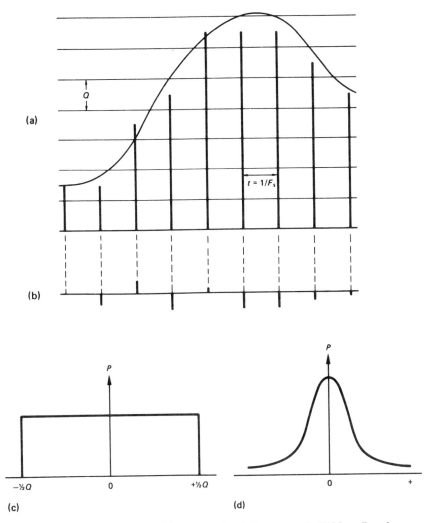

Figure 3.29 At (a) an arbitrary signal is represented to finite accuracy by PAM needles whose peaks are at the centre of the quantizing intervals. The errors caused can be thought of as an unwanted signal (b) added to the original. In (c) the amplitude of a quantizing error needle will be from $-\frac{1}{2}Q$ to $+\frac{1}{2}Q$ with equal probability. Note, however, that white noise in analog circuits generally has Gaussian amplitude distribution, shown in (d).

difference will be impulses representing the quantizing error waveform. This has been done in Figure 3.29. The horizontal lines in the drawing are the boundaries between the quantizing intervals, and the curve is the input waveform. The vertical bars are the quantized samples which reach to the centre of the quantizing interval. The quantizing error waveform shown at (b) can be thought of as an unwanted signal which the quantizing process adds to the perfect original. If a very small input signal remains within one quantizing interval, the quantizing error *is* the signal.

As the transfer function is non-linear, ideal quantizing can cause distortion. As a result practical digital video equipment deliberately uses non-ideal quantizers to achieve linearity. The quantizing error of an ideal quantizer is a complex function, and it has been researched in great depth.[8-11] It is not intended to go into such depth here. The characteristics of an ideal quantizer will only be pursued far enough to convince the reader that such a device cannot be used in quality video or audio applications.

As the magnitude of the quantizing error is limited, its effect can be minimized by making the signal larger. This will require more quantizing intervals and more bits to express them. The number of quantizing intervals multiplied by their size gives the quantizing range of the converter. A signal outside the range will be clipped. Provided that clipping is avoided, the larger the signal the less will be the effect of the quantizing error.

Where the input signal exercises the whole quantizing range and has a complex waveform (such as from a contrasty, detailed scene), successive samples will have widely varying numerical values and the quantizing error on a given sample will be independent of that on others. In this case the size of the quantizing error will be distributed with equal probability between the limits. Figure 3.29(c) shows the resultant uniform probability density. In this case the unwanted signal added by quantizing is an additive broadband noise uncorrelated with the signal, and it is appropriate in this case to call it quantizing noise. This is not quite the same as thermal noise which has a Gaussian probability shown in Figure 3.29(d) (see Chapter 2 for a treatment of statistics). The difference is of no consequence as in the large signal case the noise is masked by the signal. Under these conditions, a meaningful signal-to-noise ratio can be calculated as follows:

In a system using n bit words, there will be 2^n quantizing intervals. The largest sinusoid which can fit without clipping will have this peak-to-peak amplitude. The peak amplitude will be half as great, i.e. $2^{n-1} Q$ and the rms amplitude will be this value divided by $\sqrt{2}$.

The quantizing error has an amplitude of $\frac{1}{2} Q$ peak which is the equivalent of $Q/\sqrt{12}$ r.m.s. The signal-to-noise ratio for the large signal case is then given by:

$$20 \log_{10} \frac{\sqrt{12 \times 2^{n-1}}}{\sqrt{2}} \text{ dB}$$

$$= 20 \log_{10} (\sqrt{6} \times 2^{n-1}) \text{ dB}$$

$$= 20 \log \left(2^n \times \frac{\sqrt{6}}{2} \right) \text{ dB}$$

$$= 20n \log 2 + 20 \log \frac{\sqrt{6}}{2} \text{ dB}$$

$$= 6.02n + 1.76 \text{ dB}$$

By way of example, an 8 bit system will offer very nearly 50 dB SNR.

Whilst the above result is true for a large, complex, input waveform, treatments which then assume that quantizing error is *always* noise give results which are at variance with reality. The expression above is only valid if the probability density of the quantizing error is uniform. Unfortunately at low depths of modulations, and particularly with flat fields or simple pictures, this is not the case.

At low modulation depth, quantizing error ceases to be random and becomes a function of the input waveform and the quantizing structure as Figure 3.29 showed. Once an unwanted signal becomes a deterministic function of the wanted signal, it has to be classed as a distortion rather than a noise. Distortion can also be predicted from the non-linearity, or staircase nature, of the transfer function. With a large signal, there are so many steps involved that we must stand well back, and a staircase with 256 steps appears to be a slope. With a small signal there are few steps and they can no longer be ignored.

The effect can be visualized readily by considering a television camera viewing a uniformly painted wall. The geometry of the lighting and the coverage of the lens means that the brightness is not absolutely uniform, but falls slightly at the ends of the TV lines. After quantizing, the gently sloping waveform is replaced by one which stays at a constant quantizing level for many sampling periods and then suddenly jumps to the next quantizing level. The picture then consists of areas of constant brightness with steps between, resembling nothing more than a contour map; hence the use of the term *contouring* to describe the effect.

Needless to say the occurrence of contouring precludes the use of an ideal quantizer for high-quality work. There is little point in studying the adverse effects further as they should be and can be eliminated completely in practical equipment by the use of dither. The importance of correctly dithering a quantizer cannot be emphasized enough, since failure to dither irrevocably distorts the converted signal: there can be no process which will subsequently remove that distortion.

The signal-to-noise ratio derived above has no relevance to practical applications as it will be modified by the dither.

3.14 Introduction to dither

At high signal levels, quantizing error is effectively noise. As the depth of modulation falls, the quantizing error of an ideal quantizer becomes more strongly correlated with the signal and the result is distortion, visible as contouring. If the quantizing error can be decorrelated from the input in some way, the system can remain linear but noisy. Dither performs the job of decorrelation by making the action of the quantizer unpredictable and gives the system a noise floor like an analog system.[12,13]

In one approach, pseudo-random noise (see Chapter 2) with rectangular probability and a peak-to-peak amplitude of Q was added to the input signal prior to quantizing, but was subtracted after reconversion to analog. This is known as subtractive dither and was investigated by Schuchman[14] and much later by Sherwood.[15] Subtractive dither has the advantages that the dither amplitude is non-critical, the noise has full statistical independence from the signal[16] and has the same level as the quantizing error in the large-signal undithered case.[17] Unfortunately, it suffers from practical drawbacks, since the original noise waveform must accompany the samples or must be synchronously recreated at the DAC. This is virtually impossible in a system where the signal may have been edited or where its level has been changed by processing, as the noise needs to remain synchronous and be processed in the same way. All practical digital video systems use non-subtractive dither where the dither signal is added prior to quantization and no attempt is made to remove it at the DAC.[18] The introduction of dither prior to a conventional quantizer inevitably causes a slight reduction in the signal-to-noise ratio attainable, but this reduction is a small price to pay for the elimination of non-linearities.

The ideal (noiseless) quantizer of Figure 3.28 has fixed quantizing intervals and must always produce the same quantizing error from the same signal. In Figure 3.30 it can be seen that an ideal quantizer can be dithered by linearly

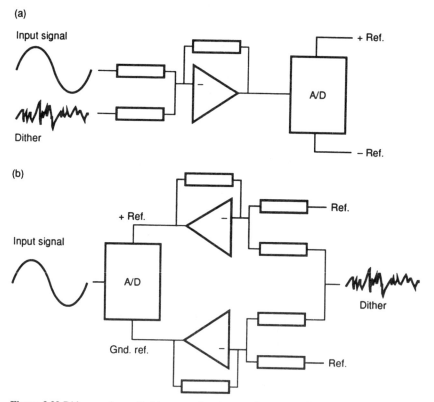

Figure 3.30 Dither can be applied to a quantizer in one of two ways. In (a) the dither is linearly added to the analog input signal, whereas in (b) it is added to the reference voltages of the quantizer.

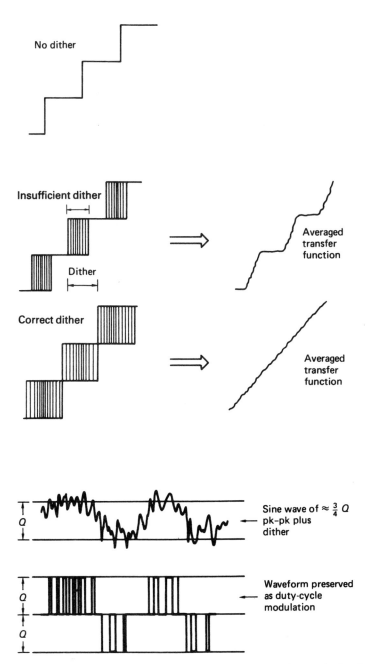

Figure 3.31 Wideband dither of the appropriate level linearizes the transfer function to produce noise instead of distortion. This can be confirmed by spectral analysis. In the voltage domain, dither causes frequent switching between codes and preserves resolution in the duty cycle of the switching.

adding a controlled level of noise either to the input signal or to the reference voltage which is used to derive the quantizing intervals. There are several ways of considering how dither works, all of which are equally valid.

The addition of dither means that successive samples effectively find the quantizing intervals in different places on the voltage scale. The quantizing error becomes a function of the dither, rather than a predictable function of the input signal. The quantizing error is not eliminated, but the subjectively unacceptable distortion is converted into a broadband noise which is more benign to the ear.

Some alternative ways of looking at dither are shown in Figure 3.31. Consider the situation where a low-level input signal is changing slowly within a quantizing interval. Without dither, the same numerical code is output for a number of sample periods, and the variations within the interval are lost. Dither has the effect of forcing the quantizer to switch between two or more states. The higher the voltage of the input signal within a given interval, the more probable it becomes that the output code will take on the next higher value. The lower the input voltage within the interval, the more probable it is that the output code will take the next lower value. The dither has resulted in a form of duty cycle modulation, and the resolution of the system has been extended indefinitely instead of being limited by the size of the steps.

Dither can also be understood by considering what it does to the transfer function of the quantizer. This is normally a perfect staircase, but in the presence of dither it is smeared horizontally until with a certain amplitude the average transfer function becomes straight.

3.15 Basic digital-to-analog conversion

This direction of conversion will be discussed first, since ADCs often use embedded DACs in feedback loops.

The purpose of a digital-to-analog converter is to take numerical values and reproduce the continuous waveform that they represent. Figure 3.32 shows the major elements of a conventional conversion subsystem, i.e. one in which oversampling is not employed. The jitter in the clock needs to be removed with a VCO or VCXO. Sample values are buffered in a latch and fed to the converter

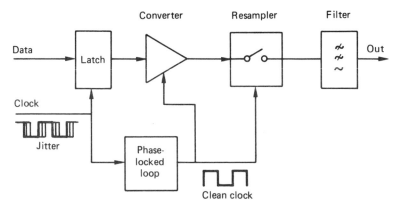

Figure 3.32 The components of a conventional converter. A jitter-free clock drives the voltage conversion, whose output may be resampled prior to reconstruction.

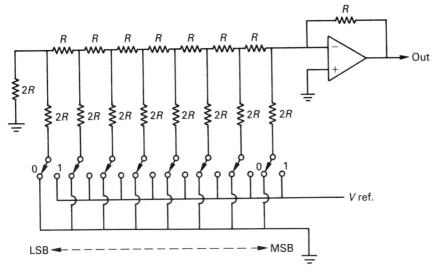

Figure 3.33 The classical *R–2R* DAC requires precise resistance values and 'perfect' switches.

element which operates on each cycle of the clean clock. The output is then a voltage proportional to the number for at least a part of the sample period. A resampling stage may be found next, in order to remove switching transients, reduce the aperture ratio or allow the use of a converter which takes a substantial part of the sample period to operate. The resampled waveform is then presented to a reconstruction filter which rejects frequencies above the audio band.

This section is primarily concerned with the implementation of the converter element. The most common way of achieving this conversion is to control binary-weighted currents and sum them in a virtual earth. Figure 3.33 shows the classical *R–2R* DAC structure. This is relatively simple to construct, but the resistors have to be extremely accurate. To see why this is so, consider the example of Figure 3.34. At (a) the binary code is about to have a major overflow, and all the low-order currents are flowing. At (b), the binary input has increased by one, and only the most significant current flows. This current must equal the sum of all the others plus one. The accuracy must be such that the step size is within the required limits.

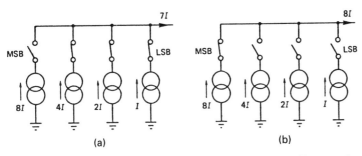

Figure 3.34 At (a) current flow with an input of 0111 is shown. At (b) current flow with input code one greater.

In this 8 bit example, if the step size needs to be a rather casual 10% accurate, the necessary accuracy is only one part in 2560, but for a 10 bit system it would become one part in 10 240. This degree of accuracy is difficult to achieve and maintain in the presence of ageing and temperature change.

3.16 Basic analog-to-digital conversion

The general principle of a quantizer is that different quantized voltages are compared with the unknown analog input until the closest quantized voltage is found. The code corresponding to this becomes the output. The comparisons can be made in turn with the minimal amount of hardware, or simultaneously with more hardware.

The flash converter is probably the simplest technique available for PCM video conversion. The principle is shown in Figure 3.35. The threshold voltage of every quantizing interval is provided by a resistor chain which is fed by a reference voltage. This reference voltage can be varied to determine the sensitivity of the input. There is one voltage comparator connected to every reference voltage, and the other input of all of the comparators is connected to the analog input. A comparator can be considered to be a 1-bit ADC. The input voltage determines how many of the comparators will have a true output. As one comparator is necessary for each quantizing interval, then, for example, in an 8 bit system there will be 255 binary comparator outputs, and it is necessary to use a priority encoder to convert these to a binary code. Note that the quantizing stage is asynchronous; comparators change state as and when the variations in the input waveform result in a reference voltage being crossed. Sampling takes place when the comparator outputs are clocked into a subsequent latch. This is an example of quantizing before sampling as was illustrated in Figure 3.4. Although the device is simple in principle, it contains a lot of circuitry and can only be practicably implemented on a chip. The analog signal has to drive a lot of inputs which results in a significant parallel capacitance, and a low-impedance driver is essential to avoid restricting the slewing rate of the input. The extreme speed of a flash converter is a distinct advantage in oversampling. Because computation of all bits is performed simultaneously, no track/hold circuit is required, and droop is eliminated. Figure 3.35(c) shows a flash converter chip. Note the resistor ladder and the comparators followed by the priority encoder. The MSB can be selectively inverted so that the device can be used either in offset binary or two's complement mode.

The flash converter is ubiquitous in digital video because of the high speed necessary. For audio purposes, many more conversion techniques are available and these are considered in Chapter 8.

3.17 Oversampling

Oversampling means using a sampling rate which is greater (generally substantially greater) than the Nyquist rate. Neither sampling theory nor quantizing theory *require* oversampling to be used to obtain a given signal quality, but Nyquist rate conversion places extremely high demands on component accuracy when a converter is implemented. Oversampling allows a given signal quality to be reached without requiring very close tolerance, and therefore expensive, components.

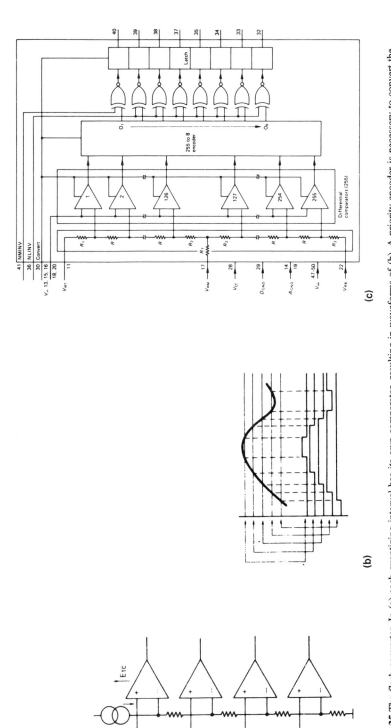

Figure 3.35 The flash converter. In (a) each quantizing interval has its own comparator, resulting in waveforms of (b). A priority encoder is necessary to convert the comparator outputs to a binary code. Shown in (c) is a typical 8 bit flash converter primarily intended for video applications. (Courtesy TRW).

Figure 3.36 shows the main advantages of oversampling. At (a) it will be seen that the use of a sampling rate considerably above the Nyquist rate allows the anti-aliasing and reconstruction filters to be realized with a much more gentle cut-off slope. There is then less likelihood of phase-linearity and ripple problems in the passband.

Figure 3.36(b) shows that information in an analog signal is two dimensional and can be depicted as an area which is the product of bandwidth and the linearly expressed signal-to-noise ratio. The figure also shows that the same amount of information can be conveyed down a channel with an SNR of half as much (6 dB less) if the bandwidth used is doubled, with 12 dB less SNR if bandwidth is quadrupled, and so on, provided that the modulation scheme used is perfect.

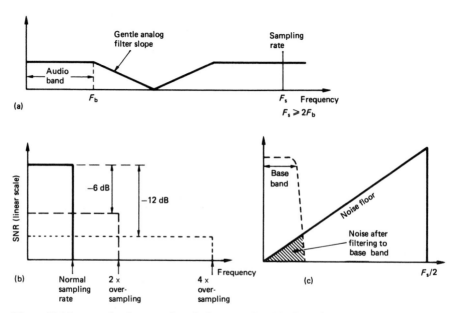

Figure 3.36 Oversampling has a number of advantages. In (a) it allows the slope of analog filters to be relaxed. In (b) it allows the resolution of converters to be extended. In (c) a *noise-shaped* converter allows a disproportionate improvement in resolution.

The information in an analog signal can be conveyed using some analog modulation scheme in any combination of bandwidth and SNR which yields the appropriate channel capacity. If bandwidth is replaced by sampling rate and SNR is replaced by a function of wordlength, the same must be true for a digital signal as it is no more than a numerical analog. Thus raising the sampling rate potentially allows the wordlength of each sample to be reduced without information loss.

Information theory predicts that if a signal is spread over a much wider bandwidth by some modulation technique, the SNR of the demodulated signal can be higher than that of the channel it passes through, and this is also the case in digital systems. The concept is illustrated in Figure 3.37. At (a) 4 bit samples are delivered at sampling rate F. As 4 bits have 16 combinations, the information

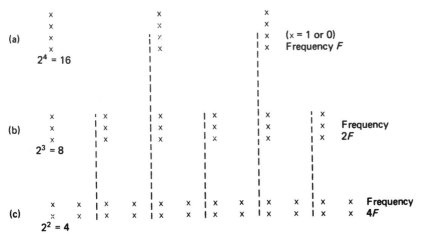

Figure 3.37 Information rate can be held constant when frequency doubles by removing 1 bit from each word. In all cases here it is 16F. Note bit rate of (c) is double that of (a). Data storage in oversampled form is inefficient.

rate is $16F$. At (b) the same information rate is obtained with 3 bit samples by raising the sampling rate to $2F$ and at (c) 2 bit samples having four combinations require to be delivered at a rate of $4F$. Whilst the information rate has been maintained, it will be noticed that the bit rate of (c) is twice that of (a). The reason for this is shown in Figure 3.38. A single binary digit can only have two states; thus it can only convey two pieces of information, perhaps 'yes' or 'no'. Two binary digits together can have four states, and can thus convey four pieces of information, perhaps 'spring summer autumn or winter', which is two pieces of information per bit. Three binary digits grouped together can have eight combinations, and convey eight pieces of information, perhaps 'doh re mi fah so lah te or doh', which is nearly three pieces of information per digit. Clearly the further this principle is taken, the greater the benefit. In a 16 bit system, each bit is worth 4K pieces of information. It is always more efficient, in information-capacity terms, to use the combinations of long binary words than to send single bits for every piece of information. The greatest efficiency is reached when the longest words are sent at the slowest rate which must be the Nyquist rate. This is one reason why PCM recording is more common than delta modulation, despite the simplicity of implementation of the latter type of converter. PCM simply makes more efficient use of the capacity of the binary channel.

As a result, oversampling is confined to converter technology where it gives specific advantages in implementation. The storage or transmission system will usually employ PCM, where the sampling rate is a little more than twice the input bandwidth. Figure 3.39 shows a digital VTR using oversampling converters. The ADC runs at n times the Nyquist rate, but once in the digital domain the rate needs to be reduced in a type of digital filter called a *decimator*. The output of this is conventional Nyquist rate PCM, according to the tape format, which is then recorded. On replay the sampling rate is raised once more in a further type of digital filter called an *interpolator*. The system now has the best of both worlds: using oversampling in the converters overcomes the shortcomings of

		00 = Spring 01 = Summer 10 = Autumn 11 = Winter	000 do 001 re 010 mi 011 fa 100 so 101 la 110 te 111 do	0000 0 0001 1 0010 2 0011 3 0100 4 0101 5 0110 6 0111 7 1000 8 1001 9 1010 A 1011 B 1100 C 1101 D 1110 E 1111 F		0000 FFFF	Digital audio sample values
	0 = No 1 = Yes						
No of bits	1	2	3	4		16	
Information per word	2	4	8	16		65536	
Information per bit	2	2	≈3	4		4096	

Figure 3.38 The amount of information per bit increases disproportionately as wordlength increases. It is always more efficient to use the longest words possible at the lowest word rate. It will be evident that 16 bit PCM is 2048 times as efficient as delta modulation. Oversampled data are also inefficient for storage.

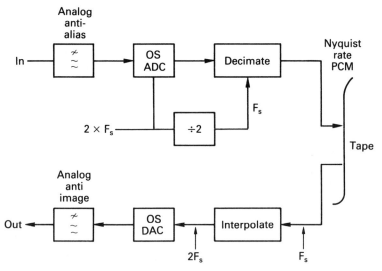

Figure 3.39 An oversampling DVTR. The converters run faster than sampling theory suggests to ease analog filter design. Sampling-rate reduction allows efficient PCM recording on tape.

analog anti-aliasing and reconstruction filters and the wordlength of the converter elements is reduced making them easier to construct; the recording is made with Nyquist rate PCM which minimizes tape consumption.

Oversampling is a method of overcoming practical implementation problems by replacing a single critical element or bottleneck by a number of elements whose overall performance is what counts. As Hauser[19] properly observed, oversampling tends to overlap the operations which are quite distinct in a conventional converter. In earlier sections of this chapter, the vital subjects of filtering, sampling, quantizing and dither have been treated almost independently. Figure 3.40(a) shows that it is possible to construct an ADC of predictable performance by taking a suitable anti-aliasing filter, a sampler, a dither source and a quantizer and assembling them like building bricks. The bricks are effectively in series and so the performance of each stage can only limit the overall performance. In contrast Figure 3.40(b) shows that with oversampling the overlap of operations allows different processes to augment one another, allowing a synergy which is absent in the conventional approach.

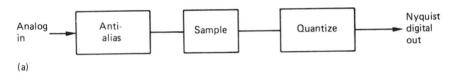

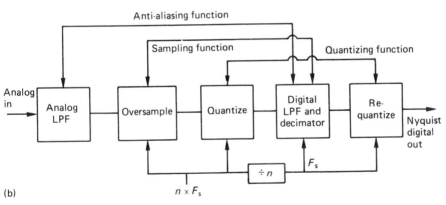

Figure 3.40 A conventional ADC performs each step in an identifiable location as in (a). With oversampling, many of the steps are distributed as shown in (b).

If the oversampling factor is n, the analog input must be bandwidth limited to $nF_s/2$ by the analog anti-aliasing filter. This unit need only have flat frequency response and phase linearity within the audio band. Analog dither of an amplitude compatible with the quantizing interval size is added prior to sampling at nF_s and quantizing.

Next, the anti-aliasing function is completed in the digital domain by a low-pass filter which cuts off at $F_s/2$. Using an appropriate architecture this filter can be absolutely phase linear and implemented to arbitrary accuracy. Such filters were discussed in Chapter 2. The filter can be considered to be the demodulator of Figure 3.36 where the SNR improves as the bandwidth is reduced. The wordlength can be expected to increase. As Chapter 2 illustrated, the multiplications taking place within the filter extend the wordlength considerably more than the bandwidth reduction alone would indicate. The analog filter serves only to prevent aliasing into the baseband at the oversampling rate; the signal spectrum is determined with greater precision by the digital filter.

With the information spectrum now Nyquist limited, the sampling process is completed when the rate is reduced in the decimator. One sample in n is retained.

The excess wordlength extension due to the anti-aliasing filter arithmetic must then be removed. Digital dither is added, completing the dither process, and the quantizing process is completed by requantizing the dithered samples to the appropriate wordlength which will be greater than the wordlength of the first quantizer. Alternatively noise shaping may be employed.

Figure 3.41(a) shows the building brick approach of a conventional DAC. The Nyquist rate samples are converted to analog voltages and then a steep-cut analog low-pass filter is needed to reject the sidebands of the sampled spectrum.

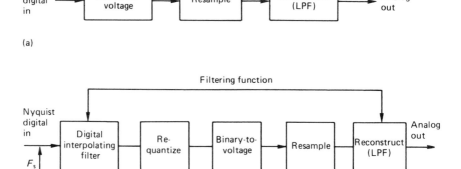

Figure 3.41 A conventional DAC in (a) is compared with the oversampling implementation in (b).

Figure 3.41(b) shows the oversampling approach. The sampling rate is raised in an interpolator which contains a low-pass filter which restricts the baseband spectrum to the audio bandwidth shown. A large frequency gap now exists between the baseband and the lower sideband. The multiplications in the interpolator extend the wordlength considerably and this must be reduced within the capacity of the DAC element by the addition of digital dither prior to requantizing.

Oversampling may also be used to considerable benefit in other dimensions. Figure 3.42 shows how vertical oversampling can be used to increase the resolution of a TV system. A 1250 line camera is used as the input device, but the 1250 line signal is fed to a standards converter which reduces the number of lines to 625. The standards converter must incorporate a vertical low pass spatial filter to prevent aliasing when the vertical sampling rate is effectively halved. Such a filter was described in Chapter 2. As it is a digital filter, it can have arbitrarily accurate performance, including a flat passband and steep cut-off slope. The combination of the vertical aperture effect of the 1250 line camera and the vertical LPF in the standards converter gives a better spatial frequency response than could be achieved with a 625 line camera. The improvement in subjective quality is quite noticeable in practice.

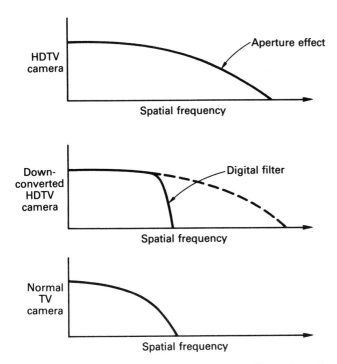

Figure 3.42 Using an HDTV camera with down conversion is a form of oversampling and gives better results than a normal camera because the aperture effect is overcome.

In the case of display technology, oversampling can also be used, this time to render the raster invisible and to improve the vertical aperture of the display. Once more a standards converter is required, but this now doubles the number of input lines using interpolation. Again the filter can have arbitrary accuracy. The vertical aperture of the 1250 line display does not affect the passband of the input signal because of the use of oversampling.

3.18 Factors affecting converter quality

In theory the quality of a digital audio system comprising an ideal ADC followed by an ideal DAC is determined at the ADC. The ADC parameters such as the sampling rate, the wordlength and any noise shaping used put limits on the quality which can be achieved. Conversely the DAC itself may be transparent, because it only converts data whose quality is already determined back to the analog domain. In other words, the ADC determines the system quality and the DAC does not make things any worse.

In practice both ADCs and DACs can fall short of the ideal, but with modern converter components and attention to detail the theoretical limits can be approached very closely and at reasonable cost. Shortcomings may be the result of an inadequacy in an individual component such as a converter chip, or due to incorporating a high-quality component in a poorly thought-out system. Poor

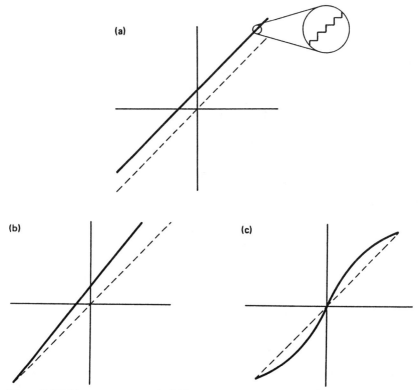

Figure 3.43 Main converter errors (solid line) compared with perfect transfer function (dotted line). These graphs hold for ADCs and DACs, and the axes are interchangeable; if one is chosen to be analog, the other will be digital.

system design can destroy the performance of a converter. Whilst oversampling is a powerful technique for realizing high-quality converters, its use depends on digital interpolators and decimators whose quality affects the overall conversion quality.

ADCs and DACs have the same transfer function, since they are only distinguished by the direction of operation, and therefore the same terminology can be used to classify the possible shortcomings of both.

Figure 3.43 shows the transfer functions resulting from the main types of converter error:

(1) *Offset error*. A constant appears to have been added to the digital signal. This has a serious effect in video systems because it alters the black level. Offset error is sometimes cancelled by digitally sampling the converter output during blanking and feeding it back to the analog input as a small control voltage.

(2) *Gain error*. The slope of the transfer function is incorrect. Since converters are often referred to one end of the range, gain error causes an offset error. Severe gain error causes clipping.

(3) *Integral linearity*. This is the deviation of the dithered transfer function from a straight line. It has exactly the same significance and consequences as linearity in analog circuits, since if it is inadequate, harmonic distortion will be caused.

(4) *Differential non-linearity* is the amount by which adjacent quantizing intervals differ in size. This is usually expressed as a fraction of a quantizing interval.

(5) *Monotonicity* is a special case of differential non-linearity. Non-monotonicity means that the output does not increase for an increase in input. Figure 3.34 showed how this can happen in a DAC. With a converter input code of 01111111 (127 decimal), the seven low-order current sources of the converter will be on. The next code is 10000000 (128 decimal), where only the eighth current source is operating. If the current it supplies is in error on the low side, the analog output for 128 may be less than that for 127. In an ADC non-monotonicity can result in missing codes. This means that certain binary combinations within the range cannot be generated by any analog voltage. If a device has better than $\frac{1}{2} Q$ linearity it must be monotonic.

(6) *Absolute accuracy*. This is the difference between actual and ideal output for a given input. For video and audio it is rather less important than linearity. For example, if all the current sources in a converter have good thermal tracking, linearity will be maintained, even though the absolute accuracy drifts.

3.19 Introduction to interfacing

Of all the advantages of digital video the most important of these for production work is the ability to record through multiple generations without quality loss. Effects machines perform transforms on images in the digital domain which remain impossible in the analog domain. For the highest-quality post production work, digital interconnection between such items as switchers, recorders and effects machines is highly desirable to avoid the degradation due to repeated conversion and filtering stages.

In 4:2:2 digital colour difference sampling according to CCIR-601, the luminance is sampled at 13.5 MHz, which is line synchronous to both broadcast line rates, and the two colour difference signals are sampled at one-half that frequency. Composite digital machines sample at four times subcarrier. All of the signals use 8 or 10 bit resolution. Video converters universally use parallel connection, where all bits of the pixel value are applied simultaneously to separate pins. Rotary head digital recorders lay data on the tape serially, but within the circuitry of the recorder, parallel presentation is in the majority, because it allows slower, and hence cheaper, memory chips to be used for interleaving and timebase correction. The Reed–Solomon error correction depends upon symbols assembled from several bits at once. Digital effects machines and switchers universally operate upon pixel values in parallel using fast multiplier chips.

Bearing all of this in mind, there is a strong argument for parallel connection, because the video naturally appears in the parallel format in typical machines. All that is necessary is a set of suitable driver chips, running at an appropriate sampling rate, to send video down cables having separate conductors for each bit of the sample, and clocks to tell the receiver when to sample the bit values. The cost in electronic components is very small, and for short distances this approach represents the optimum solution. An example would be where it is desired to dub a digital recording from one machine to another standing beside it.

Parallel connection has drawbacks too; these come into play when longer distances are contemplated. A multicore cable is expensive, and the connectors are physically large. It is difficult to provide good screening of a multicore cable without its becoming inflexible. More seriously, there are electronic problems with multicore cables. The propagation speeds of pulses down all of the cores in the cable will not be exactly the same, and so, at the end of a long cable, some bits may still be in transition when the clock arrives, while others may have begun to change to the value in the next pixel. In the presence of crosstalk between the conductors, and reflections due to suboptimal termination, the data integrity eventually becomes marginal.

Where it is proposed to interconnect a large number of units with a router, that device will be extremely complex because of the number of parallel signals to be handled.

The answer to these problems is the serial connection. All of the digital samples are multiplexed into a serial bit stream, and this is encoded to form a self-clocking channel code which can be sent down a single channel. Skew caused by differences in propagation speed cannot then occur. The bit rate necessary is in excess of 200 Mbits/s, but this is easily accommodated by coaxial cable. Provided suitable equalization and termination is used, it may be possible to send such a signal over cables intended for analog video. A similar approach was pioneered in digital audio by the AES/EBU serial interface, which allowed digital audio to be transmitted down existing twisted-pair analog cabling (see Chapter 8).

The cabling savings implicit in such a system are obvious, but the electronic complexity of a serial interconnect is much greater, as high-speed multiplexers or shift registers are necessary at the transmitting end, and a phase-locked loop, data separator and deserialiser are needed at the receiver to regenerate the parallel signal needed within the equipment. Although this increased complexity raises cost, it has to be offset against the saving in cabling. The availability of specialized chips is speeding the acceptance of serial transmission.

A distinct advantage of serial transmission is that a matrix distribution unit or router is more easily realized. Where numerous pieces of video equipment need to be interconnected in various ways for different purposes, a crosspoint matrix is an obvious solution. With serial signals, only one switching element per signal is needed, whereas in a parallel system, a matrix would be unwieldy. A serial system has a potential disadvantage that the time distribution of bits within the block has to be closely defined, and, once standardized, it is extremely difficult to increase the wordlength if this is found to be necessary. The CCIR 8 bit serial system suffered from this problem, and has been replaced by a new serial standard which incorporates two extension bits which can be transmitted as zero in 8 bit applications, but allows 10 bit use if necessary. In a parallel interconnect, the word extension can be achieved by adding extra conductors alongside the existing bits, which is much easier.

The third interconnect to be considered uses fibre optics. The advantages of this technology are numerous: the bandwidth of an optical fibre is staggering, as it is determined primarily by the response speed of the light source and sensor, and for this reason it has been adopted for a digital HDTV interface. The optical transmission is immune to electromagnetic interference from other sources, nor does it contribute any. This is advantageous for connections between cameras and control units, where a long cable run may be required in outside broadcast applications. The cable can be made completely from insulating materials, so that ground loops cannot occur, although many practical fibre-optic cables include electrical conductors for power and steel strands for mechanical strength.

Drawbacks of fibre optics are few. They do not like too many connectors in a given channel, as the losses at a connection are much greater than with an electrical plug and socket. It is preferable for the only breaks in the fibre to be at the transmitting and receiving points. For similar reasons, fibre optics are less suitable for distribution, where one source feeds many destinations. The familiar loop-through connection of analog video is just not possible. The bidirectional open-collector or tri-state buses of electronic systems cannot be implemented with fibre optics, nor is it easy to build a crosspoint matrix.

3.20 Digital video interfaces

At the time of writing standards or advanced proposals exist for both 4:2:2 component and $4F_{sc}$ composite digital in both 525/59.94 and 625/50 and in both parallel and serial forms. Interfaces also exist for widescreen and HDTV applications. All digital interfaces require to be standardized in the following areas: connectors, to ensure plugs mate with sockets; pinouts; electrical signal specification, to ensure that the correct voltages and timing are transferred; and protocol, to ensure that the meaning of the data words conveyed is the same to both devices. As digital video of any type is only data, it follows that the same physical and electrical standards can be used for a variety of protocols.

The parallel interface uses common connectors, pinouts and electrical levels for both line standards in both the component and composite versions. The same is true for the serial interfaces. Thus there are only two electrical interfaces: parallel and serial. The type of video being transferred is taken care of in the protocol diferences.

3.21 The parallel electrical interface

Composite signals use the same electrical and mechanical interface as is used for 4:2:2 component working.[20,21] This means that it is possible to plug erroneously a component signal into a composite machine. Whilst this cannot possibly work, no harm will be done because the signal levels and pinouts are the same.

Each signal in the interface is carried by a balanced pair using ECL drive levels with a nominal impedance of 110 ohms. As Figure 3.44 shows, there are eight signal pairs and two optional pairs, so that a 10 bit word can be accommodated. The optional signals are used to add bits at the least significant end of the word. Adding bits in this way extends resolution rather than increasing the magnitude. It will be seen from the figure that the optional bits are called Data −1 and Data −2 where the −1 and −2 refers to the power of two represented, i.e. 2^{-1} and 2^{-2}. The 8 bit word ends in a radix point and the extra bits below the radix point represent the half- and quarter quantizing intervals. In this way a degree of compatibility exists between 10 and 8 bit systems, as the correct magnitude will always be obtained when changing wordlength, and all that is lost is a degree of resolution in shortening the wordlength when the bits below the radix point are lost. The same numbering scheme can be used for both wordlengths; the longer wordlength simply has a radix point and an extra digit in any number base. Converting to the 8 bit equivalent is then simply a matter of deleting the extra digit and retaining the integer part.

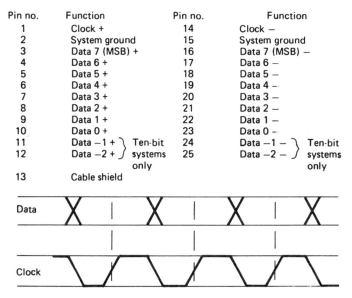

Pin no.	Function	Pin no.	Function
1	Clock +	14	Clock −
2	System ground	15	System ground
3	Data 7 (MSB) +	16	Data 7 (MSB) −
4	Data 6 +	17	Data 6 −
5	Data 5 +	18	Data 5 −
6	Data 4 +	19	Data 4 −
7	Data 3 +	20	Data 3 −
8	Data 2 +	21	Data 2 −
9	Data 1 +	22	Data 1 −
10	Data 0 +	23	Data 0 −
11	Data −1 + ⎫ Ten-bit	24	Data −1 − ⎫ Ten-bit
12	Data −2 + ⎭ systems only	25	Data −2 − ⎭ systems only
13	Cable shield		

Figure 3.44 In the parallel interface there is capacity for 10 bit words plus a clock where each signal is differential. In 8 bit systems 'Data −1' and 'Data −2' are not used. Clock transition takes place in the centre of a data bit cell as shown below.

A separate clock signal pair and a number of grounding and shielding pins complete the connection. A 25 pin D-type connector to ISO 2110–1989 is specified. Equipment always has female connectors, cables always have male connectors. Metal or metallized backshells are recommended for optimum shielding. Whilst equipment may produce or accept only 8 bit data, cables must be wired for all 10 bits.

Connector latching is by a pair of 4–40 (an American thread) screws, with suitable posts provided on the female connector. It is important that the screws are used as the multicore cable is quite stiff and can eventually unseat the plug if it is not secured. Some early equipment had slidelocks instead of screw pillars, but these proved to be too flimsy.

Figure 3.44 also shows the relationship between the clock and the data. A positive-going clock edge is used to sample the signal lines after the level has settled between transitions. In 4:2:2, the clock will be line-locked 27 MHz irrespective of the line standard, whereas in composite digital the clock will be four times the frequency of PAL or NTSC subcarrier.

The parallel interface is suitable for distances of up to 50 metres. Beyond this distance equalization is likely to be necessary and skew or differential delay between signals may become a problem. For longer distances a serial interface is a better option.

3.22 The 4:2:2 parallel interface

It is not necessary to digitize sync in component systems, since the sampling rate is derived from sync. The only useful video data are those sampled during the active line. All other parts of the video waveform can be recreated at a later time. It is only necessary to standardize the size and position of a digital active line. The position is specified as a given number of sampling-clock periods from the leading edge of sync, and the length is simply a standard number of samples. The component digital active line is 720 luminance samples long. This is slightly

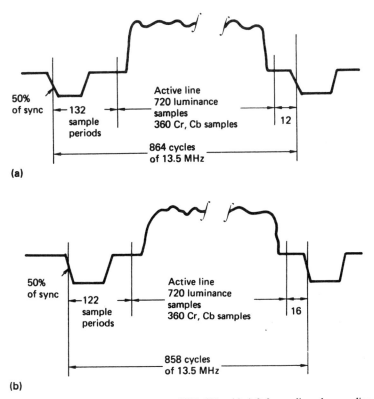

Figure 3.45 (a) In 625 line systems to CCIR-601, with 4:2:2 sampling, the sampling rate is exactly 864 times line rate, but only the active line is sampled, 132 sample periods after sync. (b) In 525 line systems to CCIR-601, with 4:2:2 sampling, the sampling rate is exactly 858 times line rate, but only the active line is sampled, 122 sample periods after sync. Note active line contains exactly the same quantity of data as for 50 Hz systems.

longer than the analog active line and allows for some drift in the analog input. Ideally the first and last samples of the digital active line should be at blanking level.

Figure 3.45 shows that in 625 line systems[22] the control system waits for 132 sample periods before commencing sampling the line. Then 720 luminance samples and 360 of each type of colour difference sample are taken, 1440 samples in all. A further 12 sample periods will elapse before the next sync edge, making 132 + 720 + 12 = 864 sample periods. In 525 line systems,[21] the analog active line is in a slightly different place and so the controller waits 122 sample periods before taking the same digital active line samples as before. There will then be 16 sample periods before the next sync edge, making 122 + 720 + 16 = 858 sample periods.

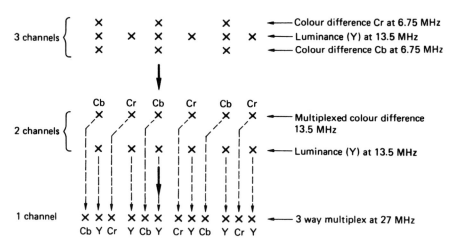

Figure 3.46 The colour difference sampling rate is one-half that of luminance, but there are *two* colour difference signals, C_r and C_b; hence the colour difference data rate is equal to the luminance data rate, and a 27 MHz interleaved format is possible in a single channel.

Figure 3.46 shows the luminance signal sampled at 13.5 MHz and two colour difference signals sampled at 6.75 MHz. Three separate signals with different clock rates are inconvenient and so multiplexing can be used. If the colour difference signals are multiplexed into one channel, then two 13.5 MHz channels will be required. If these channels are multiplexed into one, a 27 MHz clock will be required. The word order will be:

C_b, Y, C_r, Y, etc.

In order unambiguously to deserialize the samples, the first sample in the line is always C_b.

In addition to specifying the location of the samples, it is also necessary to standardize the relationship between the absolute analog voltage of the waveform and the digital code value used to express it so that all machines will interpret the numerical data in the same way. These relationships are in the voltage domain and are independent of the line standard used.

Figure 3.47 shows how the luminance signal fits into the quantizing range of an 8 bit system. Black is at a level of 16_{10} and peak white is at 235_{10} so that there is some tolerance of imperfect analog signals. The sync pulse will clearly go outside the quantizing range, but this is of no consequence as conventional syncs are not transmitted. The visible voltage range fills the quantizing range and this gives the best possible resolution.

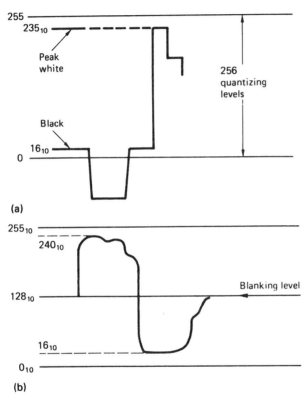

(a)

(b)

Figure 3.47 (a) The luminance signal fits into the quantizing range with a little allowance for excessive gain. Here black is at 16_{10} and peak white is at 235_{10}. The sync pulse goes outside the quantizing range but this is of no consequence as it is not transmitted. (b) The colour difference signals use offset binary where blanking level is at 128_{10}, and the peaks occur at 16_{10} and 240_{10} respectively.

The colour difference signals use offset binary, where 128_{10} is the equivalent of blanking voltage. The peak analog limits are reached at 16_{10} and 240_{10} respectively, allowing once more some latitude for maladjusted analog inputs.

Note that the code values corresponding to all ones and all zeros, i.e. the two extreme ends of the quantizing range are not allowed to occur in the active line as they are reserved for synchronizing. Converters must be followed by circuitry which catches these values and forces the LSB to a different value if out-of-range analog inputs are applied.

The peak-to-peak amplitude of Y is 220 quantizing intervals, whereas for the colour difference signals it is 225 intervals. There is thus a small gain difference between the signals. This will be cancelled out by the opposing gain difference at any future DAC, but must be borne in mind when digitally converting to other standards.

As conventional syncs are not sent, horizontal and vertical synchronizing is achieved by special bit patterns sent with each line. Immediately before the digital active line location is the *SAV* (Start of Active Video) pattern, and immediately after is the *EAV* (End of Active Video) pattern. These unique patterns occur on every line and continue throughout the vertical interval.

Each sync pattern consists of four symbols. The first is all ones and the next two are all zeros. As these cannot occur in active video, their detection reliably indicates a sync pattern. The fourth symbol is a data byte which contains three data bits, *H*, *F* and *V*. These bits are protected by four redundancy bits which form a seven bit Hamming codeword for the purpose of detecting and correcting errors.

Figure 3.48(a) shows the structure of the sync pattern. The sync bits have the following meanings:

H is used to distinguish between *SAV*, where it is set to 0, and *EAV*, where it is set to 1.

F defines the state of interlace and is 0 during the first field and 1 during the second field. *F* is only allowed to change at *EAV*. In interlaced systems, one field begins at the centre of a line, but there is no sync pattern at that location so the field bit changes at the end of the line in which the change took place.

V is 1 during vertical blanking and 0 during the active part of the field. It can only change at *EAV*. Figure 3.48(b) (top) shows the relationship between the sync pattern bits and 625 line analog timing, whilst below is the relationship for 525 lines. Only the active line is transmitted and this leaves a good deal of spare capacity. The two line standards differ on how this capacity is used. In 625 lines, only the active line period may be used on lines 20 to 22 and 333 to 335.[22] Lines 20 and 333 are reserved for equipment self-testing.

In 525 lines there is considerably more freedom and ancillary data may be inserted anywhere there is no active video, either during horizontal blanking or during, vertical blanking, or both.[21] The all-zeros and all-ones codes are reserved for synchronizing and cannot be allowed to appear in ancillary data. In practice

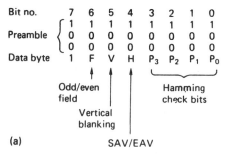

(a)   SAV/EAV

Figure 3.48(a) The 4 byte synchronizing pattern which precedes and follows every active line sample block has this structure.

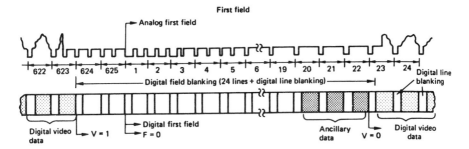

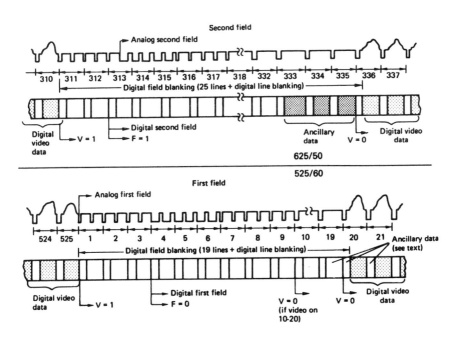

625/50

525/60

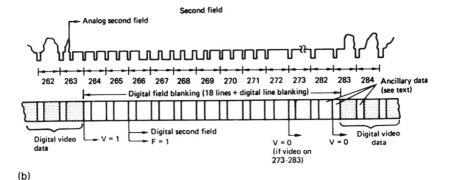

(b)

Figure 3.48(b) The relationships between analog video timing and the information in the digital timing reference signals for 625/50 (above) and 525/60 (below).

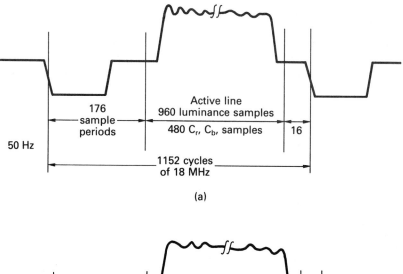

(a)

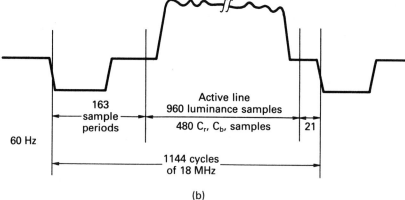

(b)

Figure 3.49 In 16:9 working with an 18 MHz sampling rate the sampling structure shown here results.

only 7 bits of the 8 bit word can be used as data; the eighth bit is redundant and gives the byte odd parity. As all ones and all zeros are even parity, the sync pattern cannot then be generated accidentally.

For 16:9 aspect ratio working, the line and the field rate remain the same, but the luminance sampling rate may be raised to 18 Mhz and the colour difference sampling rates are raised to 9 MHz. This results in the sampling structure shown for 50 Hz in Figure 3.49. There are now 960 luminance pixels and 2 x 480 colour difference pixels. The parallel interface remains the same except that the clock rate rises to 36 MHz.

3.23 The composite digital parallel interface

Composite digital samples at four times subcarrier frequency, and so there will be major differences between the standards.

Whilst the 4:2:2 interface transmits only active lines and special sync patterns, the composite interfaces carry the entire composite waveform; syncs, burst and all. Although ancillary data may be placed in sync tip, the sync edges must be present. In the absence of ancillary data, the data on the parallel interface are essentially the continuous stream of samples from a converter which is digitizing a normal analog composite signal. Virtually all that is necessary to return to the analog domain is a DAC and a filter. One of the reasons for this different approach is that the sampling clock in composite video is subcarrier based. The sample values during sync can change with ScH phase in NTSC and PAL and change with the position in the frame in PAL due to the 25 Hz component. It is simpler to convey sync sample values on the interface than to go to the trouble of recreating them later.

The instantaneous voltage of composite video can go below blanking on dark saturated colours, and above peak white on bright colours. As a result the quantizing ranges need to be stretched in comparison with 4:2:2 in order to accommodate all possible voltage excursions. Sync tip can be accommodated at the low end and peak white is some way below the end of the scale. It is not so easy to determine when overload clipping will take place in composite as the sample sites are locked to subcarrier. The degree of clipping depends on the chroma phase. When samples are taken either side of a chroma peak, clipping will be less likely to occur than when the sample is taken at the peak. Advantage is taken of this phenomenon in PAL as the peak analog voltage of a 100% yellow bar goes outside the quantizing range. The sampling phase is such that samples are sited either side of the chroma peak and remain within the range.

The PAL and NTSC versions of the composite digital interface will be described separately. The electrical interface is the same for both, and was described in Section 3.21.

3.24 PAL interface

The quantizing range of digital PAL is shown in Figure 3.50.[23] Blanking level is at 64_{10} or 40 hex and sync tip is the lowest allowable code of 1 as 0 is reserved for digital synchronizing along with 255. Peak white is 211_{10} or D3 hex. As with 4:2:2, two optional bits can be added below the LSB to extend the resolution. In 10 bit working blanking becomes 40.0 hex and peak white becomes D3.0 hex, although some documents will be found which confusingly shift the radix point down in 10 bit mode and denote blanking by 100 hex and peak white by 34C hex.

In PAL, the composite digital interface samples at $4 \times F_{sc}$ with sample phase aligned with burst phase. PAL burst swing results in burst phases of $\pm 135°$ and samples are taken at these phases and at $\pm 45°$, precisely half-way between the U and V axes. This sampling phase is easy to generate from burst and avoids premature clipping of chroma. It is most important that samples are taken exactly at the points specified, since any residual phase error in the sampling clock will cause the equivalent of a chroma phase error when samples from one source are added to samples from a different source in a switcher. A digital switcher can only add together pairs of samples from different inputs, but if these samples were not taken at the same instants with respect to their subcarriers, the samples represent different vectors and cannot be added.

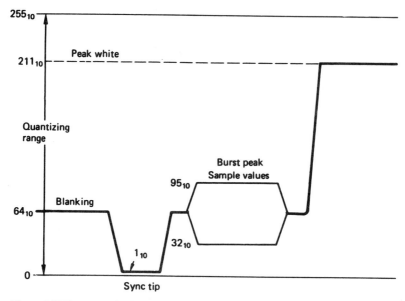

Figure 3.50 The composite PAL signal fits into the quantizing range as shown here. Note that there is sufficient range to allow the instantaneous voltage to exceed that of peak white in the presence of saturated bright colours. Values shown are decimal equivalents in a 10 or 8 bit system. In a 10 bit system the additional 2 bits increase resolution, not magnitude, so they are below the radix point and the decimal equivalent is unchanged. PAL samples in phase with burst, so that values shown are on the burst peaks and are thus also the values of the envelope.

Figure 3.51 shows how the sampling clock may be derived. The incoming sync is used to derive a burst gate, during which the samples of burst are analysed. If the clock is correctly phased, the sampled burst will give values of 95_{10}, 64_{10}, 32_{10}, 64_{10}, repeated, whereas if a phase error exists, the values at the burst crossings will be above or below 64_{10}. The difference between the sample values and blanking level can be used to drive a DAC which controls the sampling VCO. In this way any phase errors in the ADC are eliminated, because the sampling clock will automatically servo its phase to be identical to digital burst. Burst swing causes the burst peak and burst crossing samples to change places, so a phase comparison is always possible during burst. DC level shifts can be removed by using both positive and negative burst crossings and averaging the results. This also has the effect of reducing the effect of noise.

In PAL, the subcarrier frequency contains a 25 Hz offset, and so $4 \times F_{sc}$ will contain a 100 Hz offset. The sampling rate is not h-coherent, and the sampling structure is not quite orthogonal. As subcarrier is given by:

$$F_{sc} = 283\tfrac{3}{4} \times F_h + F_v/2$$

The sampling rate will be given by:

$$F_s = 1135 F_h + 2F_v$$

This results in 709 379 samples per frame, and there will not be a whole number of samples in a line. In practice, 1135 sample periods, numbered 0 to 1134, are defined as one digital line, with an additional four sample periods per

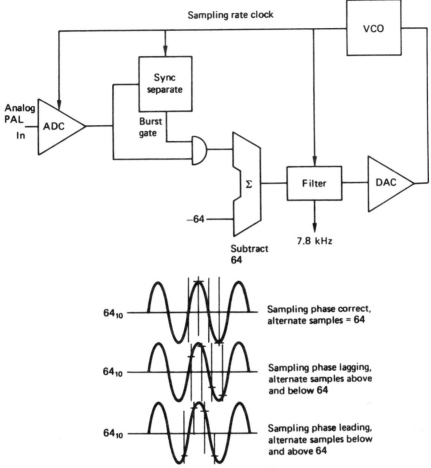

Figure 3.51 Obtaining the sample clock in PAL. The values obtained by sampling burst are analysed. When phase is correct, burst will be sampled at zero crossing and sample value will be 64_{10} or blanking level. If phase is wrong, sample will be above or below blanking. Filter must ignore alternate samples at burst peaks and shift one sample every line to allow for burst swing. It also averages over several burst crossings to reduce jitter. Filter output drives DAC and thus controls sampling clock VCO.

frame which are included by having 1137 samples, numbered 0 to 1136, in lines 313 and 625. Figure 3.52(a) shows the sample numbering scheme for an entire line. Note that the sample numbering begins at 0 at the start of the digital active line so that the horizontal blanking area is near the end of the digital line and the sample numbers will be large. The digital active line is 948 samples long and is longer than the analog active line. This allows the digital active line to move with 25 Hz whilst ensuring the entire analog active line is still conveyed.

Since sampling is not h-coherent, the position of sync pulses will change relative to the sampling points from line to line. The relationship can also be changed by the ScH phase of the analog input. Zero ScH is defined as coincidence between sync and zero degrees of subcarrier phase at line 1 of field

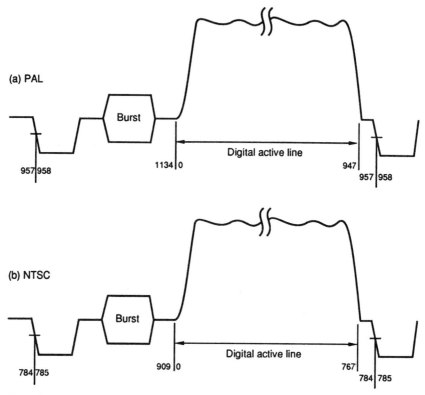

Figure 3.52 (a) Sample numbering in digital PAL. There are defined to be 1135 sample periods per line of which 948 are the digital active line. This is longer than the analog active line. Two lines per frame have two extra samples to compensate for the 25 Hz offset in subcarrier. NTSC is shown at (b). Here there are 910 samples per line of which 768 are the digital active line.

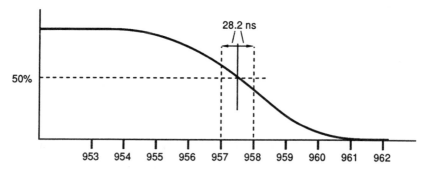

Figure 3.53 As PAL is sampled half-way between the colour axes, sample sites will fall either side of 50% sync at the zero ScH measurement line.

1. Since composite digital samples on burst phase, not on subcarrier phase, the definition of zero ScH will be as shown in Figure 3.53, where it will be seen that two samples occur at exactly equal distances either side of the 50% sync point. If the input is not zero ScH, the samples conveying sync will have different values. Measurement of these values will allow ScH phase to be computed. In a DVTR installation, non-standard ScH is only a problem on the initial conversion from analog because composite DVTRs do not record sync, and will regenerate zero ScH syncs on replay.

3.25 NTSC interface

Although they have some similarities, PAL and NTSC are quite different when analyzed at the digital sample level.

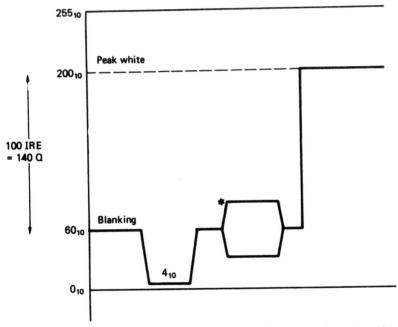

Figure 3.54 The composite NTSC signal fits into the quantizing range as shown here. Note that there is sufficient range to allow the instantaneous voltage to exceed peak white in the presence of saturated, bright colours. Values shown are decimal equivalents in an 8 or 10 bit system. In a 10 bit system the additional 2 bits increase resolution, not magnitude, so they are below the radix point and the decimal equivalent is unchanged. *Note that, unlike PAL, NTSC does not sample on burst phase and so values during burst are not shown here. See Fig. 3.55 for burst sample details.

Figure 3.54 shows how the NTSC waveform fits into the quantizing structure.[24] Blanking is at 60_{10} in an 8 bit system, and peak white is at 200_{10}, so that 1 IRE unit is the equivalent of $1.4\,Q$. These different values are due to the different sync/vision ratio of NTSC. PAL is 7:3 whereas NTSC is 10:4. As with 4:2:2 and PAL, two optional extra bits at the LSB end of the sample can extend the resolution.

Subcarrier in NTSC has an exact half-line offset, so there will be an integer number of cycles of subcarrier in two lines. F_{sc} is simply $227.5 \times F_h$, and as sampling is at $4 \times F_{sc}$, there will be $227.5 \times 4 = 910$ samples per line period, and the sampling will be orthogonal. Figure 3.52(b) shows that the digital active line consists of 768 samples numbered 0 to 767. Horizontal blanking follows the digital active line in sample numbers 768 to 909.

The sampling phase is chosen to facilitate encoding and decoding in the digital domain. In NTSC there is a phase shift of 123° between subcarrier and the I axis. As burst is an inverted piece of the subcarrier waveform, there is a phase shift of 57° between burst and the I axis. Composite digital NTSC does not sample in phase with burst, but on the I and Q axes at 57°, 147°, 237° and 327° with respect to burst.

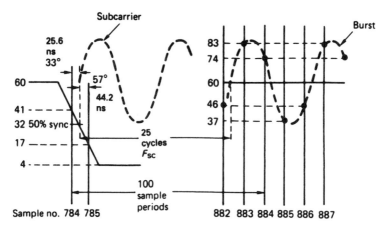

Figure 3.55 NTSC ScH phase. Sampling is not performed in phase with burst as in PAL, but on the I and Q axes. Since in NTSC there is a phase angle of 57° between burst and I, this will also be the phase at which burst samples should be taken. If ScH phase is zero, then phase of subcarrier taken at 50% sync will be zero, and the samples will be taken 33° before and 57° after sync; 25 cycles of subcarrier or 100 samples later, during burst, the sample values will be obtained. Note that if NTSC burst is inverted subcarrier, so sample 785 is positive, but sample 885 is negative.

Figure 3.55 shows how this approach works in relation to sync and burst. Zero ScH is defined as zero degrees of subcarrier at the 50% point on sync, but the 57 degree sampling phase means that the sync edge is actually sampled 25.6 nsec ahead of, and 44.2 nsec after the 50% point. Similarly, when the burst is reached, the phase shift means that burst sample values will be 46_{10}, 83_{10}, 74_{10} and 37_{10} repeating. The phase locked loop which produces the sampling clock will digitally compare the samples of burst with the values given here. Since it is not sampling burst at a zero crossing, the slope will be slightly less, so the gain of the phase error detector will also be less, and more prone to burst noise than in the PAL process. The phase error can, however, be averaged over several burst samples to overcome this problem.

As in PAL, if the analog input does not have zero ScH phase, the sync pulse values will change, but burst values will not. As in PAL, NTSC DVTRs do not record sync, and will regenerate zero ScH syncs on replay.

3.26 Serial digital interface (SDI)

The interface described here has been developed to allow up to 10 bit samples of component or composite digital video to be communicated serially.[25] 16:9 format component signals with 18 MHz sampling rate can also be handled. The interface allows ancillary data including transparent conveyance of AES/EBU digital audio channels (see Chapter 8).

Scrambling, or pseudo-random coding, uses concepts which will be introduced in Chapter 4. The serial interface uses convolutional coding, which is simpler to implement in a cable installation because no separate synchronizing of the randomizing is needed.

The components necessary for a composite serial link are shown in Figure 3.56. Parallel component or composite data having a wordlength of up to 10 bits form the input. These are fed to a 10 bit shift register which is clocked at ten times the input rate, which will be 270 MHz or $40 \times F_{sc}$. If there are only 8 bits in the input words, the missing bits are forced to zero for transmission except for the all-ones condition which will be forced to ten ones. The serial data from the shift register are then passed through the scrambler, in which a given bit is converted to the exclusive–OR of itself and two bits which are five and nine clocks ahead. This is followed by another stage, which converts channel ones into transitions. The resulting signal can be fed down 75 Ω coaxial cable using BNC connectors.

The scrambling process at the transmitter spreads the signal spectrum and makes that spectrum reasonably constant and independent of the picture content. It is possible to assess the degree of equalization necessary by comparing the energy in a low frequency band with that in higher frequencies. The greater the disparity, the more equalization is needed. Thus fully automatic cable equalization is easily achieved. The receiver must generate a bit clock at 270 MHz or $40 \times F_{sc}$ from the input signal, and this clock drives the input sampler and slicer which converts the cable waveform back to serial binary. The local bit clock also drives a circuit which simply reverses the scrambling at the transmitter. The first stage returns transitions to ones, and the second stage is a mirror image of the encoder which reverses the exclusive–OR calculation to output the original data. Since transmission is serial, it is necessary to obtain word synchronization, so that correct deserialization can take place.

In the component parallel input, the *SAV* and *EAV* sync patterns are present and the all-ones and all-zeros bit patterns these contain can be detected in the shift register and used to reset the deserializer.

In the composite parallel interface signal, there are no equivalents of the 4:2:2 sync patterns and it is necessary to create an equivalent. The timing reference and identification signal (TRS-ID) is added during blanking, and the receiver can detect the patterns which it contains. TRS-ID consists of five words which are inserted just after the leading edge of video sync. Figure 3.57(a) shows the location of TRS-ID at samples 967–971 in PAL and Figure 3.57(b) shows the location at samples 790–794 in NTSC.

Out of the five words in TRS-ID, the first four are for synchronizing, and consist of a single word of all ones, followed by three words of all zeros. The fifth word is for identification, and carries the line and field numbering information shown in Figure 3.58. The field numbering is colour framing

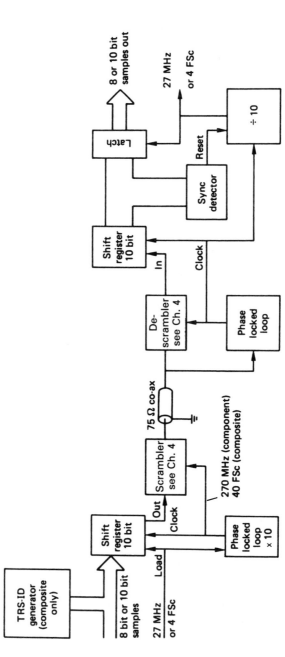

Figure 3.56 Major components of a serial scrambled link. Input samples are converted to serial form in a shift register clocked at ten times the sample rate. The serial data are then scrambled for transmission. On reception, a phase-locked loop recreates the bit-rate clock and drives the de-scrambler and serial-to-parallel conversion. On detection of the sync pattern, the divide-by-ten counter is rephased to load parallel samples correctly into the latch. For composite working the bit rate will be 40 times subcarrier, and a sync pattern generator (top left) is needed to inject TRS-ID into the composite data stream. See Figure 3.58 for TRS-ID detail.

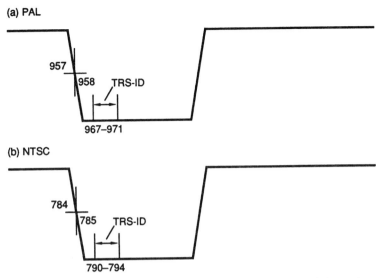

Figure 3.57 In composite digital it is necessary to insert a sync pattern during analog sync tip to ensure correct deserialization. The location of TRS-ID is shown at (a) for PAL and at (b) for NTSC.

information which is useful for editing. In PAL the field numbering will go from zero to seven, whereas in NTSC it will only reach three.

On detection of the synchronizing symbols, a divide-by-ten circuit is reset, and the output of this will clock words out of the shift register at the correct times. This output will also become the output word clock.

It is a characteristic of all randomizing techniques that certain data patterns will interact badly with the randomizing algorithm to produce a channel waveform which is low in clock content. These so-called pathological data patterns[26] are extremely rare in real program material, but can be generated in test equipment and used to check the adjustment of the phase-locked loop in a receiver.

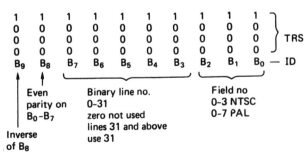

Figure 3.58 The contents of the TRS-ID pattern which is added to the transmission during the horizontal sync pulse just after the leading edge. The field number conveys the composite colour framing field count, and the line number carries a restricted line count intended to give vertical positioning information during the vertical interval. This count saturates at 31 for lines of that number and above.

References:

1. SHANNON, C.E., A mathematical theory of communication. *Bell Syst. Tech. J.*, **27**, 379 (1948)
2. JERRI, A.J., The Shannon sampling theorem – its various extensions and applications: a tutorial review. *Proc. IEEE*, **65**, 1565–1596 (1977)
3. BETTS, J.A., *Signal Processing Modulation and Noise*, Ch.6. Sevenoaks: Hodder and Stoughton (1970).
4. GURLEY, T. and HASLETT, C., Resolution considerations in using CCD imagers in broadcast quality cameras. *SMPTE J.*, **94**, 882–895 (1985)
5. KELL, R., BEDFORD, A. and TRAINER, M.A., An experimental television system, Part 2 *Proc. IRE*, **22**, 1246–1265 (1934)
6. HSU, S., The Kell factor: past and present. *SMPTE J*, **95**, 206–214 (1986)
7. HARRIS, S., The effects of sampling clock jitter on Nyquist sampling analog to digital converters and on oversampling delta-sigma ADCs. *J. Audio Eng. Soc.*, **38**, 537–542 (1990)
8. BENNETT, W. R., Spectra of quantized signals. *Bell Syst. Tech. J.*, **27** 446–472 (1948)
9. WIDROW, B., Statistical analysis of amplitude quantized sampled-data systems. *Trans. AIEE*, Part II, **79**, 555–568 (1961)
10. LIPSHITZ, S.P., WANNAMAKER, R.A. AND VANDERKOOY, J., Quantization and dither: a theoretical survey. *J. Audio Eng. Soc.*, **40**, 355–375 (1992)
11. MAHER, R.C., On the nature of granulation noise in uniform quantization systems. *J. Audio Eng. Soc.*, **40**, 12–20 (1992)
12. GOODALL, W. M., Television by pulse code modulation. *Bell System Tech. J.*, **30**, 33–49 (1951)
13. ROBERTS, L. G., Picture coding using pseudo-random noise. *IRE Trans. Inform. Theory*, **IT-8**, 145–154 (1962)
14. SCHUCHMAN, L., Dither signals and their effect on quantizing noise. *Trans. Commun. Technol.*, **COM-12**, 162–165 (1964)
15. SHERWOOD D.T., Some theorems on quantization and an example using dither. In *Conf. Rec., 19th Asilomar Conf. on circuits, systems and computers*, (Pacific Grove, CA 1985)
16. LIPSHITZ, S.P., Wannamaker, R.A. and Vanderkooy, J., Quantization and dither: a theoretical survey. *J. Audio Eng. Soc.* , **40**, 355–375 (1992)
17. GERZON, M. and CRAVEN, P.G., Optimal noise shaping and dither of digital signals. Presented at 87th Audio Engineering Society Convention (New York, 1989), Preprint No. 2822 (J-1)
18. VANDERKOOY, J. and LIPSHITZ, S.P., Resolution below the least significant bit in digital systems with dither. *J. Audio Eng. Soc.*, **32**, 106–113 (1984)
19. HAUSER, M.W., Principles of oversampling A/D conversion. *J. Audio Eng. Soc.*, **39**, 3–26 (1991)
20. CCIR Recommendation 656
21. SMPTE 125M, Television – Bit Parallel Digital Interface – Component Video Signal 4:2:2
22. EBU Doc. Tech. 3246
23. SMPTE Proposed Standard – Bit parallel digital interface for 625/50 system PAL composite digital video signals
24. SMPTE 244M, Television – System M/NTSC Composite Video Signals - Bit-Parallel Digital Interface.
25. SMPTE Proposed Standard – 10-bit 4:2:2 Component and 4FSc NTSC Composite Digital Signals – Serial Digital Interface
26. EGUCHI, T., Pathological check codes for serial digital interface systems. Presented at SMPTE Conf., Los Angeles, Oct. 1991.

Chapter 4

Channel coding

Digital recording on tape and transmission along interface cables are quite different tasks, but they have a great deal in common and have always been regarded as being different applications of the same art. In both cases channel coding is needed to convert data into a waveform suitable for the path along which it is to be sent. Although the physics of the recording media or cable propagation are unaffected by the meaning attributed to signals, digital techniques are rather different from those used with analog signals, although often the same phenomenon shows up in a different guise. In this chapter the fundamentals of digital recording and transmission are introduced along with descriptions of the coding techniques used in practical applications. The parallel subject of error correction is dealt with in the next chapter.

4.1 Introduction to the channel

Data can be recorded on many different media and conveyed using many forms of transmission. The generic term for the path down which the information is sent is the *channel*. In a transmission application, the channel may be no more than a length of cable or an optical fibre. In a recorder the channel will include the record head, the tape and the replay head. In analog systems, the characteristics of the channel affect the signal directly. It is a fundamental strength of digital video that by using pulse code modulation the quality can be made independent of the channel. The dynamic range required by the program material no longer directly decides the dynamic range of the channel.

In digital circuitry there is a great deal of noise immunity because the signal has only two states, which are widely separated compared with the amplitude of noise. In both digital recording and transmission this is not always the case. In magnetic recording, noise immunity is a function of track width and reduction of the working SNR of a digital track allows the same information to be carried in a smaller area of the medium, improving economy of operation. In broadcasting, the noise immunity is a function of the transmitter power and reduction of working SNR allows lower power to be used with consequent economy. These reductions also increase the random error rate, but, as was seen in Chapter 1, an error-correction system may already be necessary in a practical system and it is simply made to work harder.

In real channels, the signal may *originate* with discrete states which change at discrete times, but the channel will treat it as an analog waveform and so it will not be *received* in the same form. Various loss mechanisms will reduce the amplitude of the signal. These attenuations will not be the same at all frequencies. Noise will be picked up in the channel as a result of stray electric fields or magnetic induction. As a result the voltage received at the end of the channel will have an infinitely varying state along with a degree of uncertainty due to the noise. Different frequencies can propagate at different speeds in the channel; this is the phenomenon of group delay. An alternative way of considering group delay is that there will be frequency-dependent phase shifts in the signal and these will result in uncertainty in the timing of pulses.

In digital circuitry, the signals are generally accompanied by a separate clock signal which reclocks the data to remove jitter as was shown in Chapter 1. In contrast, it is generally not feasible to provide a separate clock in recording and transmission applications. In the transmission case, a separate clock line not only would raise cost, but is impractical because at high frequency it is virtually impossible to ensure that the clock cable propagates signals at the same speed as the data cable except over short distances. In the recording case, provision of a separate clock track is impractical at high density because mechanical tolerances cause phase errors between the tracks. The result is the same: timing differences between parallel channels which are known as skew.

The solution is to use a self-clocking waveform and the generation of this is a further essential function of the coding process. Clearly if data bits are simply clocked serially from a shift register in so-called direct recording or transmission this characteristic will not be obtained. If all the data bits are the same, for example all zeros, there is no clock when they are serialized.

It is not the channel which is digital; instead the term describes the way in which the received signals are *interpreted*. When the receiver makes discrete decisions from the input waveform it attempts to reject the uncertainties in voltage and time. The technique of channel coding is one where transmitted waveforms are restricted to those which still allow the receiver to make discrete decisions despite the degradations caused by the analog nature of the channel.

4.2 Transmission principles

Electromagnetic energy propagates in a manner which is a function of frequency, and our partial understanding requires it to be considered as electrons, waves or photons so that we can predict its behaviour in given circumstances.

At DC and at the low frequencies used for power distribution, electromagnetic energy is called electricity and it is remarkably aimless stuff which needs to be transported completely inside conductors. It has to have a complete circuit to flow in, and the resistance to current flow is determined by the cross-sectional area of the conductor. The insulation around the conductor and the spacing between the conductors has no effect on the ability of the conductor to pass current. At DC an inductor appears to be a short circuit, and a capacitor appears to be an open circuit.

As frequency rises, resistance is exchanged for impedance. Inductors display increasing impedance with frequency, capacitors show falling impedance. Electromagnetic energy becomes increasingly desperate to leave the conductor. The first symptom is that the current flows only in the outside layer of the conductor effectively causing the resistance to rise. This is the skin effect and gives rise to such techniques as Litz wire, which has as much surface area as possible per unit cross-section, and to silver-plated conductors in which the surface has lower resistivity than the interior.

As the energy is starting to leave the conductors, the characteristics of the space between them become important. This determines the impedance. A change of impedance causes reflections in the energy flow and some of it heads back towards the source. Constant impedance cables with fixed conductor spacing are necessary, and these must be suitably terminated to prevent reflections. The most important characteristic of the insulation is its thickness as this determines the spacing between the conductors.

As frequency rises still further, the energy travels less in the conductors and more in the insulation between them, and their composition becomes important and they begin to be called dielectrics. A poor dielectric like PVC absorbs high-frequency energy and attenuates the signal. So-called low-loss dielectrics such as PTFE are used, and one way of achieving low loss is to incorporate as much air in the dielectric as possible by making it in the form of a foam or extruding it with voids.

This frequency-dependent behaviour is the most important factor in deciding how best to harness electromagnetic energy flow for information transmission. It is obvious that the higher the frequency, the greater the possible information rate, but in general, losses increase with frequency, and flat frequency response is elusive. The best that can be managed is that over a narrow band of frequencies, the response can be made reasonably constant with the help of equalization. Unfortunately raw data when serialized have an unconstrained spectrum. Runs of identical bits can produce frequencies much lower than the bit rate would suggest. One of the essential steps in a transmission system is to modify the spectrum of the data into something more suitable.

At moderate bit rates, say a few megabits per second, and with moderate cable lengths, say a few metres, the dominant effect will be the capacitance of the cable due to the geometry of the space between the conductors and the dielectric between. The capacitance behaves under these conditions as if it were a single capacitor connected across the signal. Figure 4.1 shows the equivalent circuit.

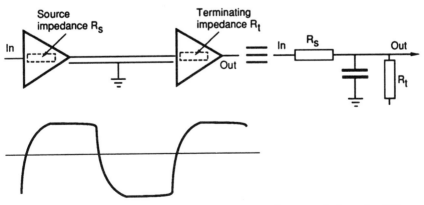

Figure 4.1 With a short cable, the capacitance between the conductors can be lumped as if it were a discrete component. The effect of the parallel capacitor is to slope off the edges of the signal.

The effect of the series source resistance and the parallel capacitance is that signal edges or transitions are turned into exponential curves as the capacitance is effectively being charged and discharged through the source impedance. This effect can be observed on the AES/EBU interface with short cables. Although the position where the edges cross the centreline is displaced, the signal eventually reaches the same amplitude as it would at DC.

As cable length increases, the capacitance can no longer be lumped as if it were a single unit; it has to be regarded as being distributed along the cable. With rising frequency, the cable inductance also becomes significant, and it too is distributed.

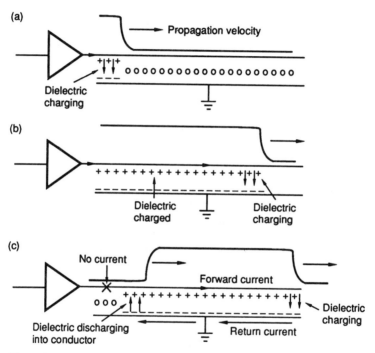

Figure 4.2 A transmission line conveys energy packets which appear to alternate with respect to the dielectric. In (a) the driver launches a pulse which charges the dielectric at the beginning of the line. As it propagates the dielectric is charged further along as in (b). When the driver ends the pulse, the charged dielectric discharges into the line. A current loop is formed where the current in the return loop flows in the opposite direction to the current in the 'hot' wire.

The cable is now a transmission line and pulses travel down it as current loops which roll along as shown in Figure 4.2. If the pulse is positive, as it is launched along the line, it will charge the dielectric locally as at (a). As the pulse moves along, it will continue to charge the local dielectric as at (b). When the driver finishes the pulse, the trailing edge of the pulse follows the leading edge along the line. The voltage of the dielectric charged by the leading edge of the pulse is now higher than the voltage on the line, and so the dielectric discharges into the line as at (c). The current flows forward as it is in fact the same current which is flowing into the dielectric at the leading edge. There is thus a loop of current rolling down the line flowing forwards in the 'hot' wire and backwards in the return. The analogy with the tracks of a Caterpillar tractor is quite good. Individual plates in the track find themselves being lowered to the ground at the front and raised again at the back.

The constant to-ing and fro-ing of charge in the dielectric results in the dielectric loss of signal energy. Dielectric loss increases with frequency and so a long transmission line acts as a filter. Thus the term 'low-loss' cable refers primarily to the kind of dielectric used.

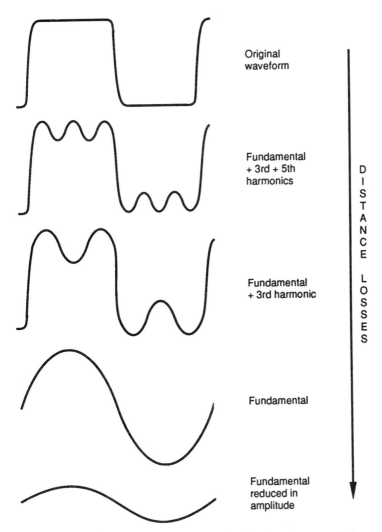

Figure 4.3 A signal may be square at the transmitter, but losses increase with frequency, and as the signal propagates, more of the harmonics are lost until only the fundamental remains. The amplitude of the fundamental then falls with further distance.

Transmission lines which transport energy in this way have a characteristic impedance caused by the interplay of the inductance along the conductors with the parallel capacitance. One consequence of that transmission mode is that correct termination or matching is required between the line and both the driver and the receiver. When a line is correctly matched, the rolling energy rolls straight out of the line into the load and the maximum energy is available. If the impedance presented by the load is incorrect, there will be reflections from the mismatch. An open circuit will reflect all of the energy back in the same polarity as the original, whereas a short circuit will reflect all of the energy back in the opposite polarity. Thus impedances above or below the correct value will have a tendency towards reflections whose magnitude depends upon the degree of mismatch and whose polarity depends upon whether the load is too high or too low. In practice it is the need to avoid reflections which is the most important reason to terminate correctly.

Reflections at impedance mismatches have practical applications; electricity companies inject high-frequency pulses into faulty cables and the time taken until the reflection from the break or short returns can be used to locate the source of damage. The same technique can be used to find wiring breaks in large studio complexes.

A perfectly square pulse contains an indefinite series of harmonics, but the higher ones suffer progressively more loss. A square pulse at the driver becomes less and less square with distance as Figure 4.3 shows. The harmonics are progressively lost until in the extreme case all that is left is the fundamental. A transmitted square wave is received as a sine wave. Fortunately data can still be recovered from the fundamental signal component.

Once all the harmonics have been lost, further losses cause the amplitude of the fundamental to fall. The effect worsens with distance and it is necessary to ensure that data recovery is still possible from a signal of unpredictable level.

4.3 Magnetic recording

Magnetic recording relies on the hysteresis of certain magnetic materials. After an applied magnetic field is removed, the material remains magnetized in the same direction. By definition the process is non-linear, and analog magnetic recorders have to use bias to linearize it. Digital recorders are not concerned with the non-linearity, and HF bias is unnecessary.

Figure 4.4 shows the construction of a typical digital record head, which is not dissimilar to an analog record head. A magnetic circuit carries a coil through which the record current passes and generates flux. A non-magnetic gap forces the flux to leave the magnetic circuit of the head and penetrate the medium. The current through the head must be set to suit the coercivity of the tape, and is arranged almost to saturate the track. Clearly the larger the amplitude of the recorded waveform the better will be the signal-to-noise ratio on replay, but when saturation is approached distortion of the waveform negates the noise advantage. The amplitude of the record current is constant, and recording is performed by reversing the direction of the current with respect to time. As the track passes the head, this is converted to the reversal of the magnetic field left on the tape with respect to distance. The magnetic recording is therefore bipolar. Figure 4.5 shows that the recording is actually made just after the trailing pole of the record head where the flux strength from the gap is falling. As in analog recorders, the width

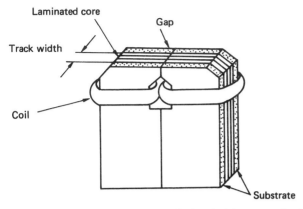

Figure 4.4 A digital record head is similar in principle to an analog head but uses much narrower tracks.

of the gap is generally made quite large to ensure that the full thickness of the magnetic coating is recorded, although this cannot be done if the same head is intended to replay.

Figure 4.6 shows what happens when a conventional inductive head, i.e. one having a normal winding, is used to replay the bipolar track made by reversing the record current. The head output is proportional to the rate of change of flux and so only occurs at flux reversals. In other words, the replay head differentiates the flux on the track. The polarity of the resultant pulses alternates as the flux changes and changes back. A circuit is necessary which locates the peaks of the pulses and outputs a signal corresponding to the original record current waveform. There are two ways in which this can be done.

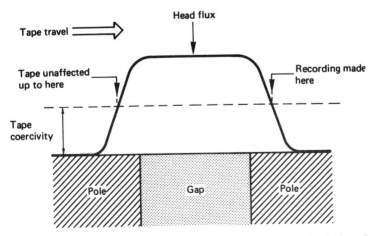

Figure 4.5 The recording is actually made near the trailing pole of the head where the head flux falls below the coercivity of the tape.

The amplitude of the replay signal is of no consequence and often an AGC system is used to keep the replay signal constant in amplitude. What matters is the time at which the write current, and hence the flux stored on the medium, reverses. This can be determined by locating the peaks of the replay impulses, which can conveniently be done by differentiating the signal and looking for zero crossings. Figure 4.7 shows that this results in noise between the peaks. This problem is overcome by the gated peak detector, where only zero crossings from a pulse which exceeds the threshold will be counted. The AGC system allows the thresholds to be fixed. As an alternative, the record waveform can also be restored by integration, which opposes the differentiation of the head as in Figure 4.8[1].

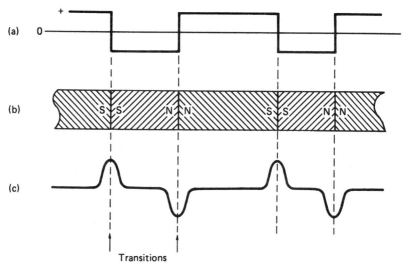

Figure 4.6 Basic digital recording. At (a) the write current in the head is reversed from time to time, leaving a binary magnetization pattern shown at (b). When replayed, the waveform at (c) results because an output is only produced when flux in the head changes. Changes are referred to as transitions.

The head shown in Figure 4.4 has a frequency response shown in Figure 4.9. At DC there is no change of flux and no output. As a result inductive heads are at a disadvantage at very low speeds. The output rises with frequency until the rise is halted by the onset of thickness loss. As the frequency rises, the recorded wavelength falls and flux from the shorter magnetic patterns cannot be picked up so far away. At some point, the wavelength becomes so short that flux from the back of the tape coating cannot reach the head and a decreasing thickness of tape contributes to the replay signal[2]. In digital recorders using short wavelengths to obtain high density, there is no point in using thick coatings. As wavelength further reduces, the familiar gap loss occurs, where the head gap is too big to resolve detail on the track. The construction of the head results in the same action as that of a two-point transversal filter, as the two poles of the head see the tape with a small delay interposed due to the finite gap. As expected, the head response is like a comb filter with the well-known nulls where flux cancellation

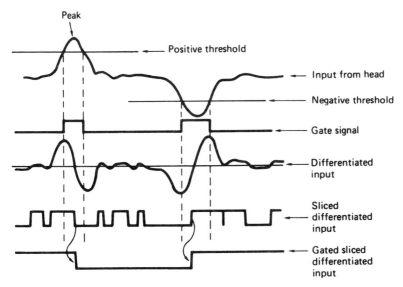

Figure 4.7 Gated peak detection rejects noise by disabling the differentiated output between transitions.

takes place across the gap. Clearly the smaller the gap the shorter the wavelength of the first null. This contradicts the requirement of the record head to have a large gap. In quality analog audio recorders, it is the norm to have different record and replay heads for this reason, and the same will be true in digital machines which have separate record and playback heads. Clearly where the same pair of heads are used for record and play, the head gap size will be determined by the playback requirement.

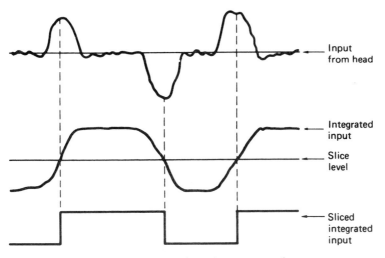

Figure 4.8 Integration method for re-creating write-current waveform.

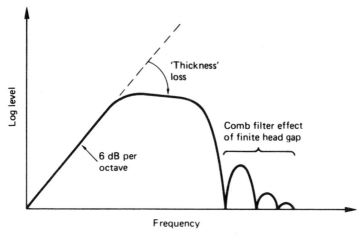

Figure 4.9 The major mechanism defining magnetic channel bandwidth

As can be seen, the frequency response is far from ideal, and steps must be taken to ensure that recorded data waveforms do not contain frequencies which suffer excessive losses.

Digital video recorders must operate at high density in order to offer a reasonable playing time. This implies that the shortest possible wavelengths will be used. Figure 4.10 shows that when two flux changes, or transitions, are recorded close together, they affect each other on replay. The amplitude of the composite signal is reduced, and the position of the peaks is pushed outwards. This is known as inter symbol interference, or peak shift distortion, and it occurs in all magnetic media.

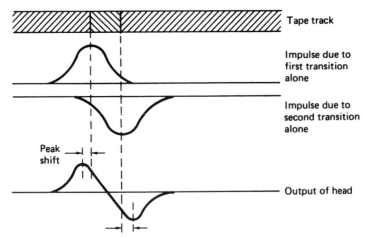

Figure 4.10 Readout pulses from two closely recorded transitions are summed in the head and the effect is that the peaks of the waveform are moved outwards. This is known as peak shift distortion and equalization is necessary to reduce the effect.

The effect is primarily due to high-frequency loss and it can be reduced by equalization on replay, as is done in most tapes, or by precompensation on record as is done in hard disks.

Excessive record current will increase peak shift distortion and with it the error rate. There is thus an optimum record current which is a compromise between noise and distortion.

4.4 Azimuth recording and rotary heads

Figure 4.11(a) shows that in azimuth recording, the transitions are laid down at an angle to the track by using a head which is tilted. Machines using azimuth recording must always have an even number of heads, so that adjacent tracks can be recorded with opposite azimuth angle. The two track types are usually referred to as A and B. Figure 4.11(b) shows the effect of playing a track with the wrong

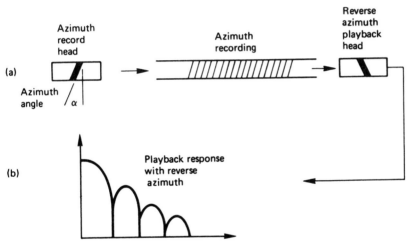

Figure 4.11 In azimuth recording (a), the head gap is tilted. If the track is played with the same head, playback is normal, but the response of the reverse azimuth head is attenuated (b).

type of head. The playback process suffers from an enormous azimuth error. The effect of azimuth error can be understood by imagining the tape track to be made from many identical parallel strips. In the presence of azimuth error, the strips at one edge of the track are played back with a phase shift relative to strips at the other side. At some wavelengths, the phase shift will be 180°, and there will be no output; at other wavelengths, especially long wavelengths, some output will reappear. The effect is rather like that of a comb filter and serves to attenuate crosstalk due to adjacent tracks so that no guard bands are required. Since no tape is wasted between the tracks, more efficient use is made of the tape. The term guard-band-less recording is often used instead of, or in addition to, the term azimuth recording. The failure of the azimuth effect at long wavelengths is a characteristic of azimuth recording, and it is necessary to ensure that the spectrum of the signal to be recorded has a small low-frequency content. The signal will need to pass through a rotary transformer to reach the heads, and cannot therefore contain a DC component.

In machines such as early D-2 recorders and some digital camcorders there is no separate erase process, and erasure is achieved by overwriting with a new waveform. Overwriting is only successful when there are no long wavelengths in the earlier recording, since these penetrate deeper into the tape, and the short wavelengths in a new recording will not be able to erase them. In this case the ratio between the shortest and longest wavelengths recorded on tape should be limited.

Restricting the spectrum of the code to allow erasure by overwrite also eases the design of the rotary transformer.

4.5 DVTR head construction

Design of a head for DVTRs is not easy, since there are a number of conflicting requirements. The high coercivity of the tape used requires that the head should be able to pass high flux densities into the tape without saturating. The bit rate of digital video is such that eddy current losses in the head are significant.

Ferrite is attractive as a head material because it is a non-conductor and this limits losses. Unfortunately currently available ferrites saturate before 1500 Oe tape can be fully modulated. Metals are available which will carry the required flux density, but they suffer from eddy current losses. One solution to the problem is to make a composite head, where the bulk of the head is made from ferrite, but metal poles are fitted which concentrate the flux from a large cross-section of ferrite into a small track width.

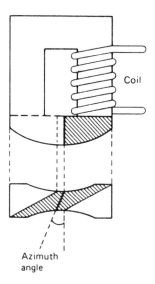

Figure 4.12 As ferrite will saturate before high coercivity tape, it cannot be used for head poles, but as shown here, it can be used for the bulk of the head, with metal tips to focus the flux to the tip. Eddy current losses in the metal are minimized. Alternatives are laminated or amorphous metal heads.

Another approach to limiting eddy current losses is lamination. Laminated metal heads have been used in stationary-head recorders for many years, but it is difficult to fabricate laminated heads for digital recorders because of the small dimensions involved. Developments in plating technology mean that it is now possible to fabricate laminated heads on an extremely small scale by plating layers of magnetic material alternately with thinly deposited insulating layers. The construction of such a head is shown in Figure 4.4.

In the amorphous head, particles of metal are sintered under pressure to form the magnetic circuit. The metal allows high flux density, but the magnetic circuit has much higher electrical resistance than solid metal because the metal particles are only joined at their corners. In this way eddy current losses are reduced.

4.6 Equalization

The characteristics of most channels are that signal loss occurs which increases with frequency. This has the effect of slowing down rise times and thereby sloping off edges. If a signal with sloping edges is sliced, the time at which the waveform crosses the slicing level will be changed, and this causes jitter. Figure 4.13 shows that slicing a sloping waveform in the presence of baseline wander causes more jitter.

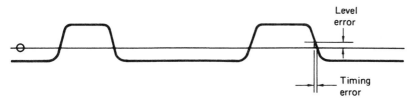

Figure 4.13 A DC offset can cause timing errors.

On a long cable, high-frequency roll-off can cause sufficient jitter to move a transition into an adjacent bit period. This is called intersymbol interference and the effect becomes worse in signals which have greater asymmetry, i.e. short pulses alternating with long ones. The effect can be reduced by the application of equalization, which is typically a high-frequency boost, and by choosing a channel code which has restricted asymmetry.

Compensation for peak shift distortion in recording requires equalization of the channel,[3] and this can be done by a network after the replay head, termed an equalizer or pulse sharpener,[4] as in Figure 4.14(a). This technique uses transversal filtering to oppose the inherent transversal effect of the head. As an alternative, precompensation in the record stage can be used as shown in Figure 4.14(b). Transitions are written in such a way that the anticipated peak shift will move the readout peaks to the desired timing.

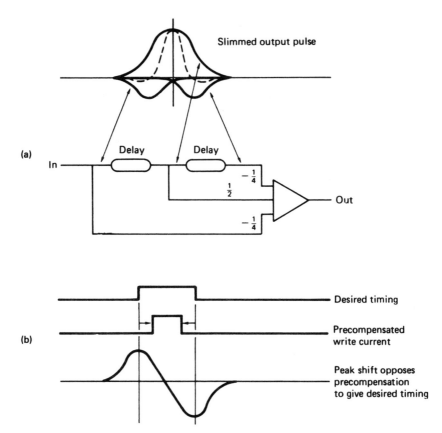

Figure 4.14 Peak shift distortion is due to the finite width of replay pulses. The effect can be reduced by the pulse slimmer shown in (a) which is basically a transversal filter. The use of a linear operational amplifier emphasizes the analog nature of channels. Instead of replay pulse slimming, transitions can be written with a displacement equal and opposite to the anticipated peak shift as shown in (b).

4.7 Data separation

The important step of information recovery at the receiver or replay circuit is known as data separation. The data separator is rather like an analog-to-digital converter because the two processes of sampling and quantizing are both present. In the time domain, the sampling clock is derived from the clock content of the channel waveform. In the voltage domain, the process of *slicing* converts the analog waveform from the channel back into a binary representation. The slicer is thus a form of quantizer which has only 1 bit resolution. The slicing process makes a discrete decision about the voltage of the incoming signal in order to reject noise. The sampler makes discrete decisions along the time axis in order to reject jitter. These two processes will be described in detail.

4.8 Slicing

The slicer is implemented with a comparator which has analog inputs but a binary output. In a cable receiver, the input waveform can be sliced directly. In an inductive magnetic replay system, the replay waveform is differentiated and must first pass through a peak detector (Figure 4.7) or an integrator (Figure 4.8). The signal voltage is compared with the midway voltage, known as the threshold, baseline or slicing level, by the comparator. If the signal voltage is above the threshold, the comparator outputs a high level; if below, a low level results.

Figure 4.15 shows some waveforms associated with a slicer. At (a) the transmitted waveform has an uneven duty cycle. The DC component, or average level, of the signal is received with high amplitude, but the pulse amplitude falls as the pulse gets shorter. Eventually the waveform cannot be sliced.

At (b) the opposite duty cycle is shown. The signal level drifts to the opposite polarity and once more slicing is impossible. The phenomenon is called baseline

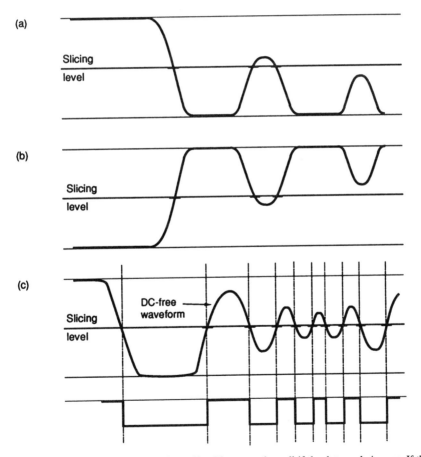

Figure 4.15 Slicing a signal which has suffered losses works well if the duty cycle is even. If the duty cycle is uneven, as at (a), timing errors will become worse until slicing fails. With the opposite duty cycle, the slicing fails in the opposite direction as at (b). If, however, the signal is DC free, correct slicing can continue even in the presence of serious losses, as (c) shows.

wander and will be observed with any signal whose average voltage is not the same as the slicing level.

At (c) it will be seen that if the transmitted waveform has a relatively constant average voltage, slicing remains possible up to high frequencies even in the presence of serious amplitude loss, because the received waveform remains symmetrical about the baseline.

It is clearly not possible simply to serialize data in a shift register for so-called direct transmission, because successful slicing can only be obtained if the number of ones is equal to the number of zeros; there is little chance of this happening consistently with real data. Instead, a modulation code or channel code is necessary. This converts the data into a waveform which is DC free or nearly so for the purpose of transmission.

The slicing threshold level is naturally zero in a bipolar system such as magnetic inductive replay or a cable. When the amplitude falls it does so

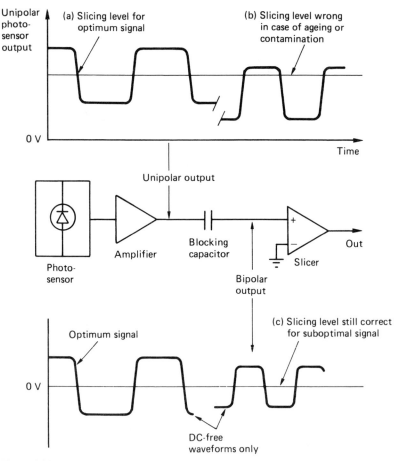

Figure 4.16 (a) Slicing a unipolar signal requires a non-zero threshold. (b) If the signal amplitude changes, the threshold will then be incorrect. (c) If a DC-free code is used, a unipolar waveform can be converted to a bipolar waveform using a series capacitor. A zero threshold can be used and slicing continues with amplitude variations.

symmetrically and slicing continues. The same is not true of M-R heads and optical pickups, which both respond to intensity and therefore produce a unipolar output. If the replay signal is sliced directly, the threshold cannot be zero, but must be some level approximately half the amplitude of the signal as shown in Figure 4.16(a). Unfortunately when the signal level falls it falls towards zero and not towards the slicing level. The threshold will no longer be appropriate for the signal as can be seen at (b). This can be overcome by using a DC-free coded waveform. If a series capacitor is connected to the unipolar signal from an optical pickup, the waveform is rendered bipolar because the capacitor blocks any DC component in the signal. The DC-free channel waveform passes through unaltered. If an amplitude loss is suffered, Figure 4.16(c) shows that the resultant bipolar signal now reduces in amplitude about the slicing level and slicing can continue.

Whilst cables and optical recording channels need to be DC free, some channel waveforms used in magnetic recording have a reduced DC component, but are not completely DC free. As a result the received waveform will suffer from baseline wander. If this is moderate, an adaptive slicer which can move its

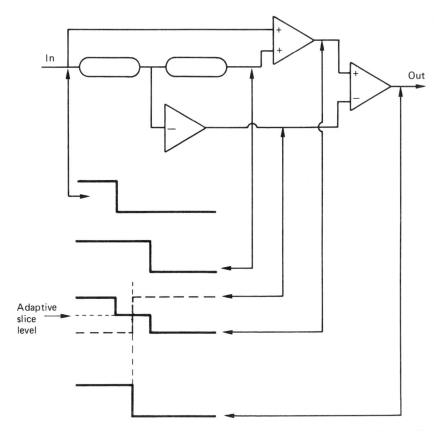

Figure 4.17 An adaptive slicer uses delay lines to produce a threshold from the waveform itself. Correct slicing will then be possible in the presence of baseline wander. Such a slicer can be used with codes which are not DC free.

threshold can be used. As Figure 4.17 shows, the adaptive slicer consists of a pair of delays. If the input and output signals are linearly added together with equal weighting, when a transition passes, the resultant waveform has a plateau which is at the half-amplitude level of the signal and can be used as a threshold voltage for the slicer.

4.9 Jitter rejection

The binary waveform at the output of the slicer will be a replica of the transmitted waveform, except for the addition of jitter or time uncertainty in the position of the edges due to noise, baseline wander, intersymbol interference and imperfect equalization.

Binary circuits reject noise by using discrete voltage levels which are spaced further apart than the uncertainty due to noise. In a similar manner, digital coding combats time uncertainty by making the time axis discrete using events, known as transitions, spaced apart at integer multiples of some basic time period, called a detent, which is larger than the typical time uncertainty. Figure 4.18 shows how this jitter rejection mechanism works. All that matters is to identify the detent in which the transition occurred. Exactly where it occurred within the detent is of no consequence.

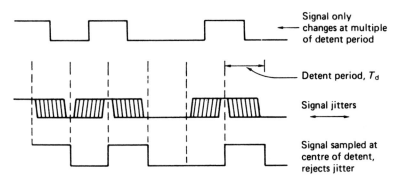

Figure 4.18 A certain amount of jitter can be rejected by changing the signal at multiples of the basic detent period T_d.

As ideal transitions occur at multiples of a basic period, an oscilloscope, which is repeatedly triggered on a channel-coded signal carrying random data, will show an eye pattern if connected to the output of the equalizer. Study of the eye pattern reveals how well the coding used suits the channel. In the case of transmission, with a short cable, the losses will be small, and the eye opening will be virtually square except for some edge sloping due to cable capacitance. As cable length increases, the harmonics are lost and the remaining fundamental gives the eyes a diamond shape. The same eye pattern will be obtained with a recording channel where it is uneconomic to provide bandwidth much beyond the fundamental.

Noise closes the eyes in a vertical direction, and jitter closes the eyes in a horizontal direction, as in Figure 4.19. If the eyes remain sensibly open, data separation will be possible. Clearly more jitter can be tolerated if there is less noise, and vice versa. If the equalizer is adjustable, the optimum setting will be where the greatest eye opening is obtained.

In the centre of the eyes, the receiver must make binary decisions at the channel bit rate about the state of the signal, high or low, using the slicer output. As stated, the receiver is sampling the output of the slicer, and it needs to have a sampling clock in order to do that. In order to give the best rejection of noise and jitter, the clock edges which operate the sampler must be in the centre of the eyes.

As has been stated, a separate clock is not practicable in recording or transmission. A fixed frequency clock at the receiver is of no use as even if it was sufficiently stable, it would not know what phase to run at.

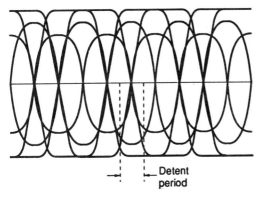

Figure 4.19 A transmitted waveform which is generated according to the principle of Figure 4.17 will appear like this on an oscilloscope as successive parts of the waveform are superimposed on the tube. When the waveform is rounded off by losses, diamond-shaped eyes are left in the centre, spaced apart by the detent period.

The only way in which the sampling clock can be obtained is to use a phase-locked loop to regenerate it from the clock content of the self-clocking channel-coded waveform. In phase-locked loops, the voltage-controlled oscillator is driven by a phase error measured between the output and some reference, as described in Chapter 2, such that the output eventually has the same frequency as the reference. If a divider is placed between the VCO and the phase comparator, the VCO frequency can be made to be a multiple of the reference. This also has the effect of making the loop more heavily damped. If a channel-coded waveform is used as a reference to a PLL, the loop will be able to make a phase comparison whenever a transition arrives and will run at the channel bit rate. When there are several detents between transitions, the loop will *flywheel* at the last known frequency and phase until it can rephase at a subsequent transition. Thus a continuous clock is recreated from the clock content of the channel waveform. In a recorder, if the speed of the medium should change, the PLL will change frequency to follow. Once the loop is locked, clock edges will be phased with the average phase of the jittering edges of the input waveform. If, for example, rising edges of the clock are phased to input transitions, then falling edges will be in the centre of the eyes. If these edges are used to clock the sampling process, the maximum jitter and noise can be rejected. The output of the slicer when sampled by the PLL edge at the centre of an eye is the value of a channel bit. Figure 4.20 shows the complete clocking system of a channel code from encoder to data separator. Clearly data cannot be separated if the PLL is not locked, but it cannot be locked until it has seen transitions for a reasonable period. In recorders, which have discontinuous recorded blocks to allow editing, the solution is to precede each data block with a pattern of transitions whose sole purpose is to provide a timing reference for synchronizing the phase-locked loop. This pattern is known as a preamble. In interfaces, the transmission can be continuous and there is no difficulty remaining in lock indefinitely. There will simply be a short delay on first applying the signal before the receiver locks to it.

One potential problem area which is frequently overlooked is to ensure that the VCO in the receiving PLL is correctly centred. If it is not, it will be running with a static phase error and will not sample the received waveform at the centre of the eyes. The sampled bits will be more prone to noise and jitter errors. VCO centring can simply be checked by displaying the control voltage. This should not change significantly when the input is momentarily interrupted.

4.10 Channel coding

In summary, it is not practicable simply to serialize raw data in a shift register for the purpose of recording or for transmission except over relatively short distances. Practical systems require the use of a modulation scheme, known as a channel code, which expresses the data as waveforms which are self-clocking in order to reject jitter, to separate the received bits and to avoid skew on separate clock lines. The coded waveforms should further be DC free or nearly so to enable slicing in the presence of losses and have a narrower spectrum than the raw data to make equalization possible.

Jitter causes uncertainty about the time at which a particular event occurred. The frequency response of the channel then places an overall limit on the spacing of events in the channel. Particular emphasis must be placed on the interplay of bandwidth, jitter and noise, which will be shown here to be the key to the design of a successful channel code.

Figure 4.21 shows that a channel coder is necessary prior to the record stage, and that a decoder, known as a data separator, is necessary after the replay stage. The output of the channel coder is generally a logic level signal which contains a 'high' state when a transition is to be generated. The waveform generator produces the transitions in a signal whose level and impedance is suitable for driving the medium or channel. The signal may be bipolar or unipolar as appropriate.

Some codes eliminate DC entirely, which is advantageous for optical media and for rotary-head recording. Some codes can reduce the channel bandwidth needed by lowering the upper spectral limit. This permits higher linear density, usually at the expense of jitter rejection. Other codes narrow the spectrum by raising the lower limit. A code with a narrow spectrum has a number of advantages. The reduction in asymmetry will reduce peak shift and data separators can lock more readily because the range of frequencies in the code is smaller. In theory the narrower the spectrum the less noise will be suffered, but

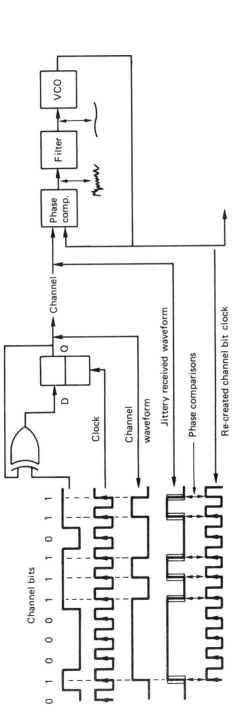

Figure 4.20 The clocking system when channel coding is used. The encoder clock runs at the channel bit rate, and any transitions in the channel must coincide with encoder clock edges. The reason for doing this is that, at the data separator, the PLL can lock to the edges of the channel signal, which represent an intermittent clock, and turn it into a continuous clock. The jitter in the edges of the channel signal causes noise in the phase error of the PLL, but the damping acts as a filter and the PLL runs at the average phase of the channel bits, rejecting the jitter.

this is only achieved if filtering is employed. Filters can easily cause phase errors which will nullify any gain.

A convenient definition of a channel code (for there are certainly others) is: 'A method of modulating real data such that they can be reliably received despite the shortcomings of a real channel, while making maximum economic use of the channel capacity'.

The basic time periods of a channel-coded waveform are called positions or detents, in which the transmitted voltage will be reversed or stay the same. The symbol used for the units of channel time is T_d.

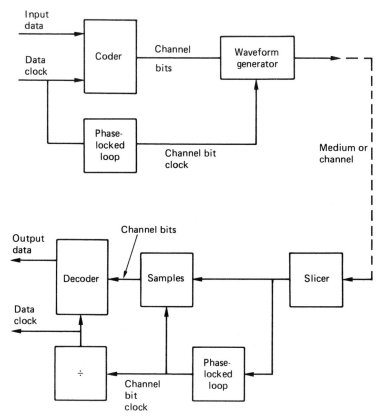

Figure 4.21 The major components of a channel coding system. See text for details.

There are many ways of creating such a waveform, but the most convenient is to convert the raw data bits to a larger number of *channel bits* which are output from a shift register to the waveform generator at the detent rate. The coded waveform will then be high or low according to the state of a channel bit which describes the detent.

Channel coding is the art of converting real data into channel bits. Figure 4.22 shows that there are two conventions in use relating channel bits to the recorded waveform. The most commonly used convention is one in which a channel bit one represents a voltage (or flux) change, whereas a zero represents no change. This convention is used because it is possible to assemble sequential groups of channel bits together without worrying about whether the polarity of the end of the last group matches the beginning of the next. The polarity is unimportant in most codes and all that matters is the length of time between transitions. Less common is the convention where the channel bit state directly represents the direction of the recording current. Clearly steps then need to be taken to ensure that the boundary between two groups is properly handled. Such an approach is used in the D-3/D-5 formats and will be explained in Section 5.20.

It should be stressed that channel bits are not recorded. They exist only in a circuit technique used to control the waveform generator. In many media, for example D-3/D-5, the channel bit rate is beyond the frequency response of the channel and so it *cannot* be recorded.

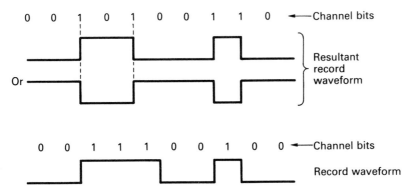

Figure 4.22 The two conventions for channel bit notation. A channel bit one most commonly represents a transition, but some codes use the bit status to describe the direction of the record current.

One of the fundamental parameters of a channel code is the density ratio (DR). One definition of density ratio is that it is the worst-case ratio of the number of data bits recorded to the number of transitions in the channel. It can also be thought of as the ratio between the Nyquist rate of the data (one-half the bit rate) and the frequency response required in the channel. The storage density of data recorders has steadily increased due to improvements in medium and transducer technology, but modern storage densities are also a function of improvements in channel coding. Figure 4.23(a) shows how the density ratio has improved as more sophisticated codes have been developed.

As jitter is such an important issue in digital recording and transmission, a parameter has been introduced to quantify the ability of a channel code to reject time instability. This parameter, the jitter margin, also known as the window margin or phase margin (T_w), is defined as the permitted range of time over which a transition can still be received correctly, divided by the data bit-cell period (T).

Since equalization is often difficult in practice, a code which has a large jitter margin will sometimes be used because it resists the effects of intersymbol

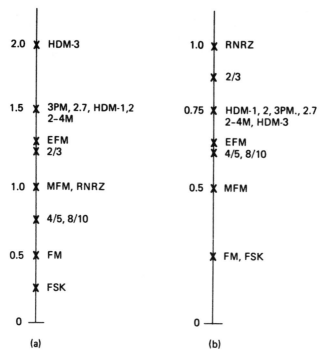

Figure 4.23 (a) Comparison of codes by density ratio; (b) comparison of codes by figure of merit. Note how 4/5, 2/3, 8/10 + RNRZ move up because of good jitter performance; HDM-3 moves down because of jitter sensitivity.

interference well. Such a code may achieve a better performance in practice than a code with a higher density ratio but poor jitter performance.

A more realistic comparison of code performance will be obtained by taking into account both density ratio and jitter margin. This is the purpose of the figure of merit (FoM), which is defined as DR x T_w. Figure 4.23(b) shows a number of codes compared by FoM.

4.11 Recording-oriented codes

Many channel codes are sufficiently versatile that they have been used in recording, electrical or optical cable transmission and radio transmission. Others are more specialized and are intended for only one of these categories. Channel coding has roots in computers, in telemetry and in telex services, but has for some time been considered a single subject. These starting points will be considered here.

In magnetic recording, the first digital recordings were developed for early computers and used very simple techniques. Figure 4.24(a) shows that in return-to-zero (RZ) recording, the record current has a zero state between bits and flows in one direction to record a one and in the opposite direction to record a zero. Thus every bit contains two flux changes which replay as a pair of pulses, one positive and one negative. The signal is self-clocking because pulses always occur. The order in which they occur determines the state of the bit. RZ recording cannot erase by overwrite because there are times when no record current flows. Additionally the signal amplitude is only one-half of what is possible. These problems were overcome in the non-return-to-zero (NRZ) code shown in Figure 4.24(b). As the name suggests, the record current does not cease between bits, but flows at all times in one direction or the other dependent on the state of the bit to be recorded. This results in a replay pulse only when the data bits change from one state to another. As a result if one pulse was missed, the subsequent bits would be inverted. This was avoided by adapting the coding such that the record current would change state or invert whenever a data one occurred, leading to the term non-return-to-zero-invert or (NRZI) shown in Figure 4.24(c). In NRZI a

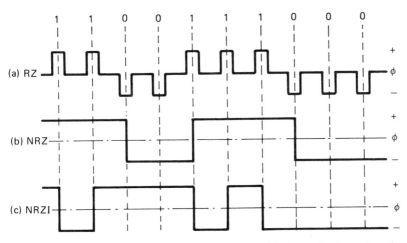

Figure 4.24 Early magnetic recording codes. RZ shown at (a) had poor signal-to-noise ratio and poor overwrite capability. NRZ at (b) overcame these problems but suffered error propagation. NRZI at (c) was the final result where a transition represented a one. NRZI is not self-clocking.

replay pulse occurs whenever there is a data one. Clearly neither NRZ nor NRZI are self-clocking, but require a separate clock track. Skew between tracks can only be avoided by working at low density and so the system cannot be used for digital audio. However, virtually all of the codes used for magnetic recording are based on the principle of reversing the record current to produce a transition.

4.12 Transmission oriented codes

In cable transmission, also known as line signalling, and in telemetry, the starting point was often the speech bandwidth available in existing telephone lines and radio links. There was no DC response, just a range of frequencies available. Figure 4.25(a) shows that a pair of frequencies can be used, one for each state of a data bit. The result is frequency shift keying (FSK) which is the same as would be obtained from an analog frequency modulator fed with a two-level signal. Clearly FSK is DC free and self-clocking.

Instead of modulating the frequency of the signal, the phase can be modulated or shifted instead, leading to the generic term of phase shift keying or PSK. This method is highly suited to broadcast as it is easily applied to a radio frequency carrier. The simplest technique is selectively to invert the carrier phase according to the data bit as in Figure 4.25(b). There can be many cycles of carrier in each bit period. This technique is known as phase encoding (PE) and is used in GPS (Global Positioning System) broadcasts. The receiver in a PE system is a well-

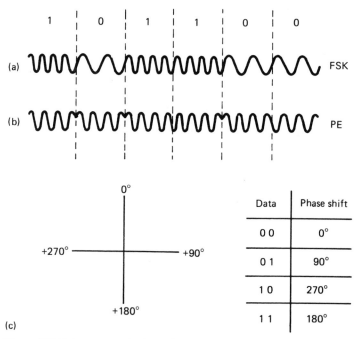

Figure 4.25 Various communications-oriented codes are shown here: at (a) frequency shift keying (FSK), at (b) phase encoding and at (c) differential quadrature phase shift keying (DQPSK).

damped phase-locked loop which runs at the average phase of the transmission. Phase changes will then result in phase errors in the loop and so the phase error is the demodulated signal.

4.13 General purpose codes

Despite the different origins of codes, there are many similarities between them.

If the two frequencies in an FSK system are one octave apart, the limiting case in which the highest data rate is obtained is when there is one half cycle of the lower frequency or a whole cycle of the high frequency in one bit period. This gives rise to the term frequency modulation (FM). In the same way, the limiting case of phase encoding is where there is only one cycle of carrier per bit. In recording, this technique is what is meant by the same term. These can be contrasted in Figure 4.26.

The FM code, also known as Manchester code or bi-phase mark code, shown in Figure 4.26(a), was the first practical self-clocking binary code and it is suitable for both transmission and recording. It is DC free and very easy to encode and decode. It is the code specified for the AES/EBU digital audio interconnect standard which will be described in Chapter 8. In the field of recording it remains in use today only where density is not of prime importance, for example in SMPTE/EBU timecode for professional audio and video recorders and in floppy disks.

In FM there is always a transition at the bit-cell boundary which acts as a clock. For a data one, there is an additional transition at the bit-cell centre. Figure 4.26(a) shows that each data bit can be represented by two channel bits. For a data zero, they will be 10, and for a data one they will be 11. Since the first bit is always one, it conveys no information, and is responsible for the density ratio of only one-half. Since there can be two transitions for each data bit, the jitter margin can only be half a bit, and the resulting FoM is only 0.25. The high clock content of FM does, however, mean that data recovery is possible over a wide range of speeds; hence the use for timecode. The lowest frequency in FM is due to a stream of zeros and is equal to half the bit rate. The highest frequency is due to a stream of ones and is equal to the bit rate. Thus the fundamentals of FM are within a band of one octave. Effective equalization is generally possible over such a band. FM is not polarity conscious and can be inverted without changing the data.

Figure 4.26(b) shows how an FM coder works. Data words are loaded into the input shift register which is clocked at the data bit rate. Each data bit is converted to two channel bits in the codebook or lookup table. These channel bits are loaded into the output register. The output register is clocked twice as fast as the input register because there are twice as many channel bits as data bits. The ratio of the two clocks is called the code rate; in this case it is a rate one-half code. Ones in the serial channel bit output represent transitions whereas zeros represent no change. The channel bits are fed to the waveform generator which is a 1 bit delay, clocked at the channel bit rate, and an exclusive OR gate. This changes state when a channel bit one is input. The result is a coded FM waveform where there is always a transition at the beginning of the data bit period, and a second optional transition whose presence indicates a one.

In PE there is always a transition in the centre of the bit but Figure 4.26(c) shows that the transition between bits is dependent on the data values. Although its origins were in line coding, PE can be used for optical and magnetic recording as it is DC free and self-clocking. It has the same DR and T_w as FM, and the waveform can also be described using channel bits, but with a different notation. As PE is polarity sensitive, the channel bits determine the level of the encoded signal rather than causing a transition. Figure 4.26(d) shows that the allowable channel bit patterns are now 10 and 01.

In modified frequency modulation (MFM) also known as Miller code,[5] the highly redundant clock content of FM was reduced by the use of a phase-locked loop in the receiver which could flywheel over missing clock transitions. This technique is implicit in all the more advanced codes. Figure 4.27(a) shows that the bit-cell centre transition on a data one was retained, but the bit-cell boundary transition was now only required between successive zeros. There are still two

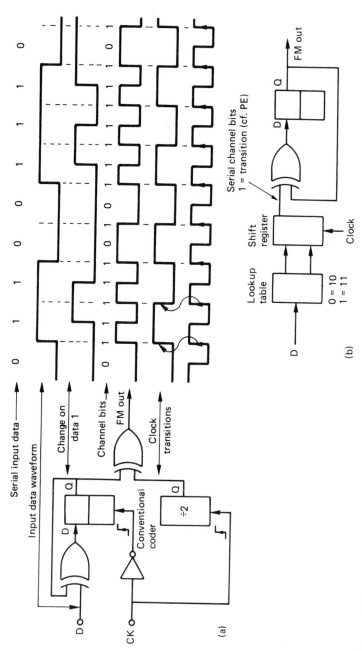

Figure 4.26 FM and PE contrasted. At (a) are the FM waveform and the channel bits which may be used to describe transitions in it. The FM coder is shown at (b). The PE waveform is shown at (c). As PE is polarity conscious, the channel bits must describe the signal level rather than the transitions. The coder is shown at (d).

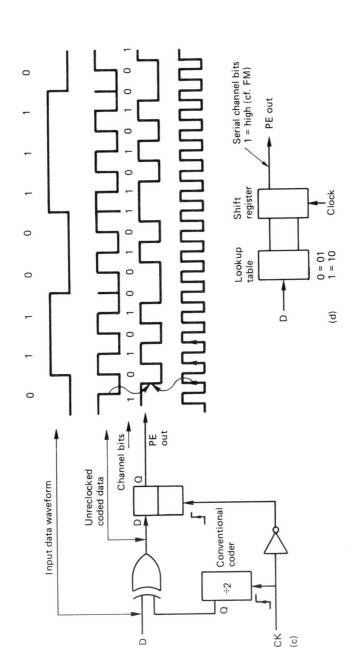

Figure 4.26 (continued).

channel bits for every data bit, but adjacent channel bits will never be one, doubling the minimum time between transitions and giving a DR of 1. Clearly the coding of the current bit is now influenced by the preceding bit. The maximum number of prior bits which affect the current bit is known as the constraint length L_c, measured in data bit periods. For MFM $L_c = T$. Another way of considering the constraint length is that it assesses the number of data bits which may be corrupted if the receiver misplaces one transition. If L_c is long, all errors will be burst errors.

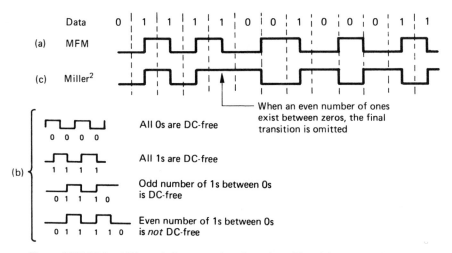

Figure 4.27 MFM or Miller code is generated as shown here. The minimum transition spacing is twice that of FM or PE. MFM is not always DC free as shown at (b). This can be overcome by the modification of (c) which results in the Miller^2 code.

MFM doubled the density ratio compared with FM and PE without changing the jitter performance; thus the FoM also doubles, becoming 0.5. It was adopted for many rigid disks at the time of its development, and remains in use on double-density floppy disks. It is not, however, DC free. Figure 4.27(b) shows how MFM can have DC content under certain conditions.

4.14 Miller^2 code

The Miller^2 code is derived from MFM, and Figure 4.27(c) shows that the DC content is eliminated by a slight increase in complexity[6,7]. Wherever an even number of ones occurs between zeros, the transition at the last one is omitted. This creates two additional, longer run lengths and increases the T_{max} of the code. The decoder can detect these longer run lengths in order to reinsert the suppressed ones. The FoM of Miller^2 is 0.5 as for MFM. Miller^2 is used in high-rate instrumentation recorders and in the D-2 and DCT DVTR formats.

4.15 Group codes

Further improvements in coding rely on converting patterns of real data to patterns of channel bits with more desirable characteristics using a conversion table known as a codebook. If a data symbol of m bits is considered, it can have 2^m different combinations. As it is intended to discard undesirable patterns to improve the code, it follows that the number of channel bits n must be greater than m. The number of patterns which can be discarded is:

$$2^n - 2^m$$

One name for the principle is group code recording (GCR), and an important parameter is the code rate, defined as:

$$R = \frac{m}{n}$$

It will be evident that the jitter margin T_w is numerically equal to the code rate, and so a code rate near to unity is desirable. The choice of patterns which are used in the codebook will be those which give the desired balance between clock content, bandwidth and DC content. Figure 4.28 shows that the upper spectral

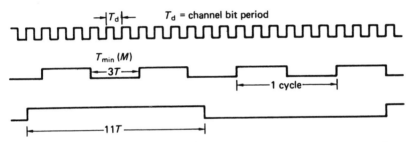

Figure 4.28 A channel code can control its spectrum by placing limits on T_{min} (M) and T_{max} which define upper and lower frequencies. The ratio of T_{max}/T_{min} determines the asymmetry of waveform and predicts DC content and peak shift. Example shown is EFM.

limit can be made to be some fraction of the channel bit rate according to the minimum distance between ones in the channel bits. This is known as T_{min}, also referred to as the minimum transition parameter M, and in both cases is measured in data bits T. It can be obtained by multiplying the number of channel detent periods between transitions by the code rate. Unfortunately, codes are measured by the number of consecutive zeros in the channel bits, given the symbol d, which is always one less than the number of detent periods. In fact T_{min} is numerically equal to the density ratio:

$$T_{min} = M = DR = \frac{(d + 1) \times m}{n}$$

It will be evident that choosing a low code rate could increase the density ratio, but it will impair the jitter margin. The figure of merit is:

$$FoM = DR \times T_w = \frac{(d + 1) \times m^2}{n^2}$$

since:

$$T_{w} = m/n$$

Figure 4.28 also shows that the lower spectral limit is influenced by the maximum distance between transitions T_{max}. This is also obtained by multiplying the maximum number of detent periods between transitions by the code rate. Again, codes are measured by the maximum number of zeros between channel ones, k, and so:

$$T_{max} = \frac{(k + 1) \times m}{n}$$

and the maximum/minimum ratio P is:

$$P = \frac{(k + 1)}{(d + 1)}$$

The length of time between channel transitions is known as the *run length*. Another name for this class is the run-length-limited (RLL) codes.[8] Since m data bits are considered as one symbol, the constraint length L_c will be increased in RLL codes to at least m. It is, however, possible for a code to have run-length limits without it being a group code.

In practice, the junction of two adjacent channel symbols may violate run-length limits, and it may be necessary to create a further codebook of symbol size $2n$ which converts violating code pairs to acceptable patterns. This is known as merging and follows the golden rule that the substitute $2n$ symbol must finish with a pattern which eliminates the possibility of a subsequent violation. These patterns must also differ from all other symbols.

Substitution may also be used to different degrees in the same nominal code in order to allow a choice of maximum run length, e.g. 3PM.[9] The maximum number of symbols involved in a substitution is denoted by r.[10,11] There are many RLL codes and the parameters $d, k, m, n,$ and r are a way of comparing them.

Sometimes the code rate forms the name of the code, as in 2/3, 8/10 and EFM; at other times the code may be named after the d, k parameters, as in 2,7 code. Various examples of group codes will be given to illustrate the principles involved.

4.16 2/3 code

Figure 4.29(a) shows the codebook of an optimized code which illustrates one merging technique. This is a 1,7,2,3,2 code known as 2/3. It is designed to have a good jitter window in order to resist peak shift distortion in disk drives, but it also has a good density ratio.[12] In 2/3 code, pairs of data bits create symbols of three channel bits. For bandwidth reduction, codes having adjacent ones are eliminated so that $d = 1$. This halves the upper spectral limit and the DR is improved accordingly:

$$DR = \frac{(d + 1) \times m}{n} = \frac{2 \times 2}{3} = 1.33$$

Data	Code
0 0	1 0 1
0 1	1 0 0
1 0	0 0 1
1 1	0 1 0

(a)

Data	Illegal code	Substitution
0 0 0 0	1 0 1 1 0 1	1 0 1 0 0 0
0 0 0 1	1 0 1 1 0 0	1 0 0 0 0 0
1 0 0 0	0 0 1 1 0 1	0 0 1 0 0 0
1 0 0 1	0 0 1 1 0 0	0 1 0 0 0 0

(b)

Figure 4.29 2/3 code. At (a) two data bits (m) are expressed as three channel bits (n) without adjacent transitions (d = 1). Violations are dealt with by substitution.

$$DR = \frac{(d+1)m}{n} = \frac{2 \times 2}{3} = 1.33$$

Adjacent data pairs can break the encoding rule; in these cases substitutions are made, as shown in (b).

In Figure 4.29(b) it will be seen that some group combinations cause violations. To avoid this, pairs of three channel bit symbols are replaced with a new six channel bit symbol. L_c is thus $4T$, the same as for the 4/5 code. The jitter window is given by:

$$T_w = \frac{m}{n} = \frac{2}{3} T$$

and the FoM is:

$$\frac{2}{2} \times \frac{4}{3} = \frac{8}{9}$$

This is an extremely good figure for an RLL code, and is some 10% better than the FoM of 3PM[13] and 2,7, and as a result 2/3 has been highly successful in Winchester disk drives.

4.17 EFM code in D-3/D-5

The $\frac{1}{2}$ inch D-3 and D-5 formats use a group code in which m = 8 and n = 14, so the code rate is 0.57. The code is called 8,14 after the main parameters. It will be evident that the jitter margin T_w is numerically equal to the code rate, and so for jitter resistance a code rate close to unity is preferable. The choice of patterns which are used in the codebook will be those which give the desired balance between clock content, bandwidth and DC content.

The code used in D-3/D-5 uses the convention in which a channel bit one represents a high in the recorded waveform. In this convention a flux reversal or transition will be written when the channel bits change.

In Figure 4.30 it is shown that the upper spectral limit can be made to be some fraction of the channel bit rate according to the minimum distance between transitions in the channel bits, which in 8,14 is two channel bits. This is known as T_{min}, also referred to as the minimum transition parameter M, and in both cases is measured in data bits T. It can be obtained by multiplying the number of channel detent periods between transitions by the code rate. In fact T_{min} is numerically equal to the density ratio:

$$T_{min} = M = DR = \frac{2 \times 8}{14} = 1.14$$

This DR is a little better than the figure of 1 for the codes used in D-1 and D-2.

The figure of merit is:

$$FoM = DR \times T_w = \frac{2 \times 8^2}{14^2} = 0.65$$

since:

$$T_w = \frac{m}{n} = \frac{8}{14}$$

Figure 4.30 also shows that the lower spectral limit is influenced by the maximum distance between transitions T_{max}, which also determines the minimum clock content. This is also obtained by multiplying the maximum number of detent periods between transitions by the code rate. In 8,14 code this is seven channel bits, and so:

$$T_{max} = \frac{7 \times 8}{14} = 4$$

and the maximum/minimum ratio P is:

$$P = \frac{4}{1.14} = 3.51$$

The length of time between channel transitions is known as the run length. Another name for this class is the run-length-limited (RLL) codes.[14] Since eight data bits are considered as one symbol, the constraint length L_c will be increased in this code to at least eight bits.

In practice, the junction of some adjacent channel symbols may violate coding rules, and it is necessary to extend the codebook so that the original data can be represented by a number of alternative codes at least one of which will be acceptable. This is known as substitution. Owing to the coding convention used, which generates a transition when the channel bits change, transitions will also be generated at the junction of two channel symbols if the adjacent bits are different. It will be seen in Figure 4.30 that the presence of a junction transition can be controlled by selectively inverting all of the bits in the second channel symbol. Thus for every channel bit pattern in the code, an inverted version also

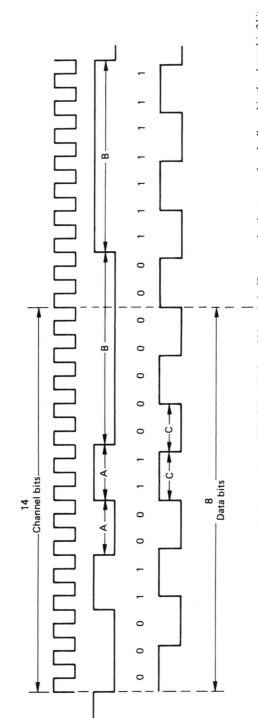

Figure 4.30 In the 8,14 code of D-3, eight data bit periods are divided into 14 channel bit periods. However, the shortest run length allowed in the channel is 2 bits, shown at A. This restriction is obtained by selecting 14 bit patterns from those available. The longest run length in the code is seven channel bits. Note that the shortest run length A is 14% longer than the shortest run length in the raw data C. Thus density ratio DR is 1.14. Using this code 14% more data can be recorded with the same wavelength on tape as a simple code.

Data	Code A (begins with 0)	CDS	Code B (begins with 1)	CDS	Code C (begins with 0)	CDS	Code D (begins with 1)	CDS
00								
↑								
42	0110001000111	0	1001110011000	0	0110001100111	0	1001110011000	0
43	0110000111100	0	1001111000011	0	0110000111100	0	1001111000011	0
44	0110000111001	0	1001111000110	0	0110000111001	0	1001111000010	0
45	0110001110011	0	1001111001100	0	0110000111011	0	1001111001100	0
46	0110001100111	0	1001110011000	0	0110000100111	0	1001110011000	0
47	0110000111110	0	1001111000001	0	0110000011110	0	1001111100001	0
48	0110000011111	0	1001111100000	0	0110000001111	0	1001111111000	0
49	0111110000001	-2	1000000110011	-2	0111111001100	-4	1000001111110	2
50	0111001100000	-2	1000000111001	-2	0111111000010	-4	1000011001111	2
51	0111000010000	-2	1000000111100	-2	0111111000011	-4	1000011001111	2
52	0111000011000	-2	1000001100011	-2	0111110011100	-4	1000011100111	2
53	0111000001100	-2	1000001100110	-2	0111110011001	-4	1000011111001	2
54	0111100000110	-2	1000001100001	-2	0111110001001	-4	1000011111001	2
55	0111000000011	-2	1000000111000	-2	0111110000111	-4	1000011111100	2
56	0110011100000	-2	1000011000011	-2	0111100111100	-4	1000011100111	2
57	0110011000001	-2	1000011000110	-2	0111100111001	-4	1000011001110	2
↓								
255								

Figure 4.31 Part of the codebook for D-3 EFM code. For every 8 bit data word (left) there are four possible channel bit patterns, two of which begin with 0 and two of which begin with 1. This allows successive symbols to avoid violating the minimum run-length limit (A in Figure 4.30) at the junction of the two symbols. See Figures 4.32 and 4.33 for further details.

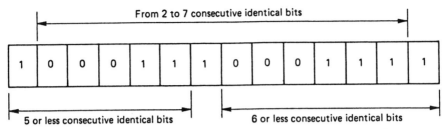

Figure 4.32 The selected 14 bit patterns follow the rules that there cannot be more than five consecutive identical bits at the beginning or more than six at the end. In addition the code digital sum (CDS) cannot exceed 4. See Figure 4.33 for derivation of CDS.

exists. Figure 4.31 shows part of the 8,14 code (EFM) used in the D-3 format. As stated, 8 bit data symbols are represented by 14 bit channel symbols. There are 256 combinations of eight data bits, whereas 14 bits have 2^{14} or 16 384 combinations. The initial range of possible codes is reduced by the requirements of the maximum and minimum run length limits and by a requirement that there shall not be more than five identical bits in the first six bits of the code and not more than 6 in the last 7 bits as shown in Figure 4.32.

One of the most important parameters of a channel pattern is the code digital sum (CDS) shown in Figure 4.33. This is the number of channel ones minus the

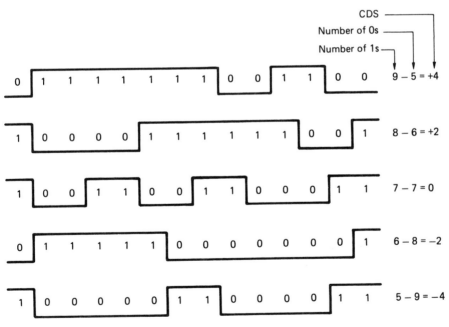

Figure 4.33 Code digital sum (CDS) is the measure of the DC content of a given channel symbol. It is obtained by subtracting the number of zeros in the symbol from the number of ones. Shown above are five actual 14 bit symbols from the D-3 code showing the range of CDS allowed from −4 to +4. Although CDS of zero is optimum, there are not enough patterns with zero CDS to represent all combinations of eight data bits.

number of channel zeros. As the CDS represents the DC content or average voltage of the channel pattern it is to be kept to a minimum.

There are only 118 codes (and 118 inverse codes) which are DC free (CDS = 0) as well as meeting the other constraints. In order to obtain 256 data combinations, codes with non-zero CDS have to be accepted. The actual codes used in 8,14 have a CDS of 0, ±2 or ±4.

The CDS is a special case of a more general parameter called the digital sum value (DSV). DSV is a useful way of predicting how an analog channel such as a tape/head system will handle a binary waveform. In a stream of bits, a one causes one to be added to the DSV whereas a zero causes one to be subtracted. Thus DSV is a form of running discrete integration. Figure 4.34(a) shows how the DSV varies along the time axis. The end DSV is the DSV at the end of a string of channel symbols. Clearly CDS is the end DSV of one code pattern in isolation. The next end DSV is the current one plus the CDS of the next symbol as shown in Figure 4.34(b).

The absolute DSV of a symbol is shown in Figure 4.34(c). This is obtained by finding the peak DSV. Large absolute DSVs are associated with low frequencies and low clock content. When encoding is performed, each 8 bit data symbol selects four locations in the lookup table each of which contains a 14 bit pattern. The recording is made by selecting the most appropriate one of four candidate channel bit patterns. The decoding process is such that any of the four channel patterns will decode to the same data.

The four possible channel symbols for each data byte are classified according to Figure 4.31 into types A, B, C or D. Since 8,14 coding requires alternative inverse symbols, two of the candidates are simply bit inversions of the other two. Where codes are not DC free there may be a pair of +2 CDS candidates and their −2 CDS inverses or a +2 CDS and a +4 CDS candidate and their inverses which will of course have −2 and −4 CDS. In the case of all but two of the DC-free codes the two candidates are one and the same code and the four lookup table locations contain two identical codes and two identical inverse codes. As a result of some of the codes being identical, although there are 1024 locations in the table, only 770 different 14 bit patterns are used, representing 4.7% of the total.

Code classes are further subdivided into class numbers, which go from 1 to 5 and specify the number of identical channel bits at the beginning of the symbol, and a priority number, which only applies to codes of CDS ±2 and is obtained from the channel bit pattern at the end of the code according to Figure 4.35.

Clearly the junction of two channel patterns cannot be allowed to violate the run-length limits. As the next code cannot have more than five consecutive identical bits at the beginning, the previous code could end with up to 2 bits in the same state without exceeding the maximum run length of seven. If this limit would be exceeded by one of the four candidate codes, it will be rejected and one of those having an earlier transition would be chosen instead. Similarly if the previous code ends in 01 or 10, the first bit of the next code must be the same as the last bit of the previous code or the minimum run-length limit will be violated. The run-length limits can always be met because every code has an inverse, so out of the four possible channel symbols available for a given data byte two of them will begin with 0 and two begin with 1. In some cases, such as where the first code ends in 1100, up to four of the candidates for the next code could meet the run-length limits. In this case the best candidate will be chosen to optimize some other parameter.

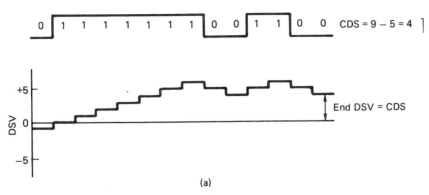

(a)

Figure 4.34(a) DSV is obtained by subtracting one for every zero, and adding one for every one which passes during the integration time. Thus DSV changes every channel bit. Note that end DSV = CDS.

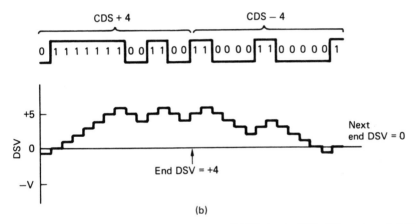

(b)

Figure 4.34(b) The next end DSV is the current end DSV plus the CDS of the next symbol. Note how the choice of a CDS −4 symbol after a +4 symbol brings DSV back to zero.

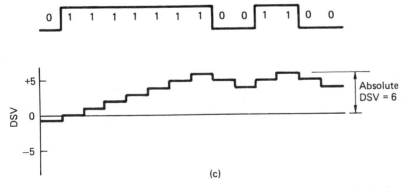

(c)

Figure 4.34(c) The absolute or peak DSV is the greatest value the DSV can have during the symbol. As shown here, it can be greater than CDS.

In order to follow how the encoder selects the best channel pattern it is necessary to discuss the criteria that are used. There are a number of these, some of which are compulsory, such as the run-length limits, and others which will be met if possible on a decreasing scale of importance. If a higher criterion cannot be met the decision will still attempt to meet as many of the lower ones as possible.

+2 end DSV end pattern of channel bits	−2 end DSV end pattern of channel bits	Priority
. . . xxxxx110	. . . xxxxx001	4
. . . xxxx1100	. . . xxxx0011	1
. . . xxx11000	. . . xxx00111	2
. . . xx110000	. . . xx001111	3
. . . x1100000	. . . x0011111	8
. . . xxxxx001	. . . xxxxx110	10
. . . xxxx0011	. . . xxxx1100	5
. . . xxx00111	. . . xxx11000	6
. . . xx001111	. . . xx110000	7
. . . x0011111	. . . x1100000	9
. . . 00111111	. . . 11000000	11

x: Don't care bit

Figure 4.35 Codes having end DSV of ±2 are prioritized according to the above table as part of the selection process.

The overall goal is to meet the run-length limits with a sequence of symbols which has the highest clock content, lowest LF and DC content and the least asymmetry to reduce peak shift. Some channel symbols will be better than others, a phenomenon known as pattern sensitivity. The least optimal patterns are not so bad that they will *cause* errors, but they will be more prone to errors due to other causes. Minimizing the use of sensitive waveforms will enhance the data reliability and is as good as an improvement in the signal-to-noise ratio.

As there are 2^{10} different patterns, there will be 2^{20} different combinations of two patterns. Clearly it is out of the question to create a lookup table to determine how best to merge two patterns. It has to be done algorithmically. The flowchart of the algorithm is shown in Figure 4.36.

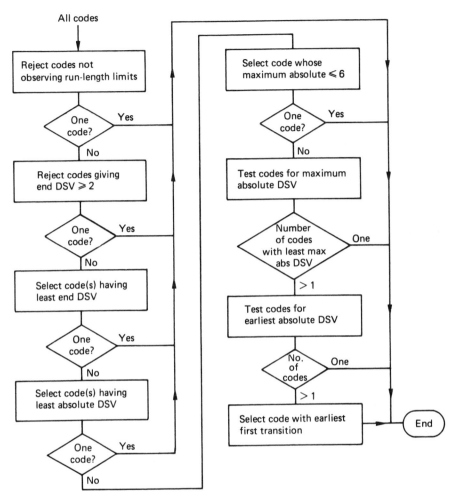

Figure 4.36 The four candidate codes, A,B,C,D, of Figure 4.31 are compared according to this flow chart to locate the single best code which will represent the data byte. Any of the codes will result in the same decode on replay.

The process begins when a data byte selects four candidate channel symbols. Initially tests are made to eliminate unsuitable patterns, and on some occasions, only one code will emerge from these tests. There are so many combinations, however, that it is possible for several candidate codes to pass the initial tests, and so the flowchart continues to select the best code by further criteria.

The first selection is based on maintaining the run-length limits at the junction between the previous code and the current one and keeping the end DSV as small as possible. If two or more codes give an equal minimum end DSV, the code with the smallest absolute DSV will be selected. If this criterion still results in more than one code being available, a further selection is made to optimize the spectrum due to the junction of the previous and current symbols. The codes are tested to see if any give six or fewer identical channel bits across the junction. If none of the codes has this characteristic there will be a large run length at the junction and the best code will be one that has a run length of less than 6 bits later. This criterion will also be applied if more than one code passes the junction run-length test.

If a decision still cannot be made, the remaining candidates could have ± 2 end DSV or 0 end DSV. In the former case the priority tables are invoked, and the code(s) with the highest priority is selected. In the latter case, or if two codes emerge equal from the priority test, any code(s) which has a run length of less than 6 bits at the end is selected. This makes merging with the next symbol easier. It is possible that no code will pass the end run-length test, or that two or more codes are still equal. In this case some of the criteria cannot be met or are equally met, and the final choice reverts to a further selection of the code with minimum absolute DSV. This test was made much earlier, but some codes with equal minimum values could have been rejected in intermediate tests. If two codes still remain, the one whose Absolute DSV appears earliest in the bit stream will be selected. If two codes still remain, the one with the earliest transition is selected.

The complexity of the coding rules in 8,14 is such that it could not have been economically implemented until recently. This illustrates the dependence of advanced recorders on LSI technology.

4.18 Error detection in group codes

In the 8,14 code only 4.7% of the 14 bit patterns are actually recorded, since the others have undesirable characteristics such as excessive DC content or insufficient clock content. In practice reading errors will occur which can corrupt some or all of the channel bits in a symbol. Random noise effects or peak shift could result in a tape transition being shifted along the time axis, or in the wrong number of transitions being detected in a symbol. This will change the channel bit pattern determined by the data separator.

As there are many more channel bit combinations than those which are actually used, it is probable that a random error will convert a channel symbol into one of the patterns which are not used. Thus it is possible for the lookup table which decodes 14 channel bits back to eight data bits to perform an error detecting function. When an illegal 14 bit code is detected, the lookup table will output an error flag. Clearly this method is not infallible, as it is possible for an error to convert one valid code into a different valid code, which this scheme would not detect. However, the additional detection capability can be used to enhance the power of the error-correction systems which can make use of the error flags produced by the 14,8 decoder. This subject will be discussed in more detail in Chapter 6.

4.19 Tracking signals

Many recorders use track-following systems to help keep the head(s) aligned with the narrow tracks used in digital media. These can operate by sensing low-frequency tones which are recorded along with the data. Whilst this can be done by linearly adding the tones to the coder output, this requires a linear record amplifier. An alternative is to use the DC content group codes. A code is devised where for each data pattern, several code patterns exist having a range of DC components. By choosing groups with a suitable sequence of DC offsets, a low frequency can be added to the coded signal. This can be filtered from the data waveform on replay.

4.20 Randomizing

Randomizing is not a channel code, but a technique which can be used in conjunction with a channel code. Randomizing with NRZI (RNRZI) is used in the D-1 format and in conjunction with partial response (see Section 4.21) in Digital Betacam. It is also used in conjunction with the 8,14 code of D-3/D-5. Figure 4.37 shows that the randomizing system is arranged outside the channel coder.

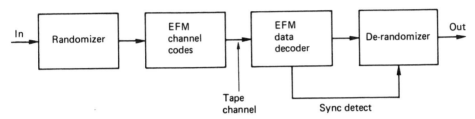

Figure 4.37 The randomizing system of D-3 is arranged outside the EFM channel coder. The pseudo-random sequence added during recording must be generated in a synchronized manner during replay so it can be subtracted. This is done by the EFM sync detector. Note that the sync pattern is not randomized!

NRZ has a DR of 1 and a jitter window of 1 and so has an FoM of 1 which is better than the group codes. It does, however, suffer from an unconstrained spectrum and poor clock content. This can be overcome using randomizing. Figure 4.38 shows that, at the encoder, a pseudo-random sequence (see Chapter 2) is added modulo-2 to the serial data and the resulting ones generate transitions in the channel. This process drastically reduces T_{max} and reduces DC content. At the receiver the transitions are converted back to a serial bit stream to which the same pseudo-random sequence is again added modulo-2. As a result the random signal cancels itself out to leave only the serial data, provided that the two pseudo-random sequences are synchronized to bit accuracy.

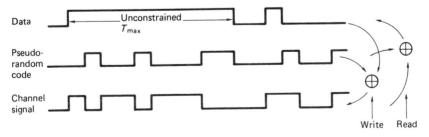

Figure 4.38 Modulo-2 addition with a pseudo-random code removes unconstrained runs in real data. Identical process must be provided on replay.

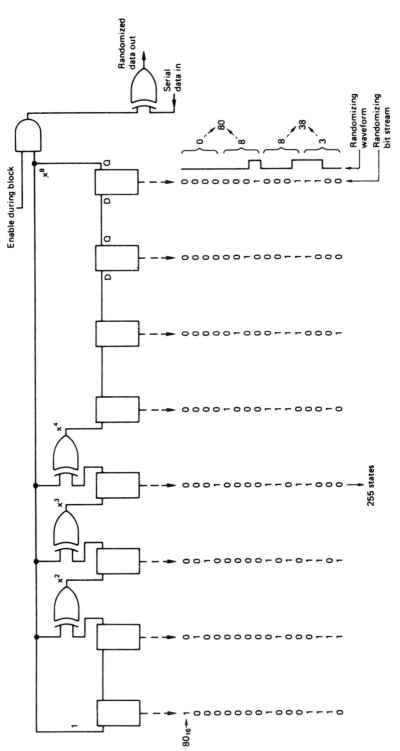

Figure 4.39 The polynomial generator circuit shown here calculates $x^8 + x^4 + x^3 + x^2 + 1$ and is preset to 80_{16} at the beginning of every sync block. When the generator is clocked it will produce a Galois field having 255 states (see Chapter 2). The right-hand bit of each field element becomes the randomizing bit stream and is fed to an exclusive OR gate in the data stream. Randomizing is disabled during preambles and sync patterns. It is also possible to randomize using a counter working at byte rate which addresses a PROM. Eight exclusive OR gates will then be needed to randomize 1 byte at a time.

The 8,14 code displays pattern sensitivity because some waveforms are more sensitive to peak shift distortion than others. Pattern sensitivity is only a problem if a sustained series of sensitive symbols needs to be recorded. Randomizing ensures that this cannot happen because it breaks up any regularity or repetition in the data. The data randomizing is performed by using the exclusive OR function of the data and a pseudo-random sequence as the input to the channel coder. On replay the same sequence is generated, synchronized to bit accuracy, and the exclusive OR of the replay bit stream and the sequence is the original data.

The randomizing polynomial and one way in which it can be implemented are shown in Figure 4.39. As the polynomial generates a maximum length sequence from an 8 bit wordlength, the sequence length is given by $2^8 - 1 = 255$. The sequence would repeat endlessly but for the fact that it is preset to 80_{16} at the beginning of each sync block immediately after the sync pattern is detected. Figure 4.40 shows the randomizing sequence starting from 80_{16}.

80	38	D2	81	49	76	82	DA	9A	86	6F	AF	8B	B0	F1	9C
D1	12	A5	72	37	EF	97	59	31	B8	EA	53	C8	3F	F4	58
40	1C	E9	C0	24	38	41	6D	4D	C3	B7	D7	45	D8	78	CE
68	89	52	B9	9B	F7	CB	AC	18	5C	F5	29	E4	1F	7A	2C
20	8E	74	60	92	9D	A0	B6	A6	E1	DB	EB	22	6C	3C	67
B4	44	A9	DC	CD	FB	65	56	0C	AE	FA	14	F2	0F	3D	16
10	47	3A	30	C9	4E	50	5B	D3	F0	ED	75	11	36	9E	33
5A	A2	54	EE	E6	FD	32	2B	06	57	7D	0A	F9	87	1E	0B
88	23	1D	98	64	27	A8	AD	69	F8	F6	BA	08	1B	CF	19
2D	51	2A	77	F3	7E	99	15	83	AB	3E	85	FC	43	8F	05
C4	91	0E	4C	B2	13	D4	D6	34	7C	7B	5D	84	8D	E7	8C
96	28	95	BB	79	BF	CC	8A	C1	55	9F	42	FE	A1	C7	02
E2	48	07	26	D9	09	6A	6B	1A	BE	BD	2E	C2	C6	73	46
4B	94	CA	DD	BC	5F	66	C5	E0	AA	4F	21	FF	D0	63	01
71	A4	03	93	EC	04	B5	35	0D	DF	5E	17	61	E3	39	A3
25	4A	E5	6E	DE	2F	B3	62	70	D5	A7	90	7F	E8	B1	

Figure 4.40 The sequence which results when the randomizer of Figure 4.39 is allowed to run.

Clearly the sync pattern cannot be randomized, since this causes a Catch-22 situation where it is not possible to synchronize the sequence for replay until the sync pattern is read, but it is not possible to read the sync pattern until the sequence is synchronized!

The randomizing in D-3 is clearly block based, since this matches the block structure on tape. Where there is no obvious block structure, convolutional or endless randomizing can be used. This is the approach used in the scrambled serial digital video interconnect described in Section 3.26, which allows composite or component video of up to 10 bit wordlength to be sent serially.

4.21 Partial response

It has been stated that a magnetic head acts as a transversal filter, because it has two poles. In addition the output is differentiated, so that the head may be thought of as a $(1-D)$ impulse response system, where D is the delay which is a function of the tape speed and gap size. It is this delay which results in intersymbol interference. Conventional equalizers attempt to oppose this effect, and succeed in raising the noise level in the process of making the frequency response linear.

Figure 4.41 shows that the frequency response necessary to pass data with insignificant peak shift is a bandwidth of half the bit rate, which is the Nyquist rate. In Class IV partial response, the frequency response of the system is made to have nulls at DC and at the Nyquist rate. Such a frequency response is particularly advantageous for rotary head recorders as it is DC free and the low-frequency content is minimal; hence the use in Digital Betacam. The required response is achieved by an overall impulse response of $(1 - D^2)$ where D is now the bit period. There are a number of ways in which this can be done.

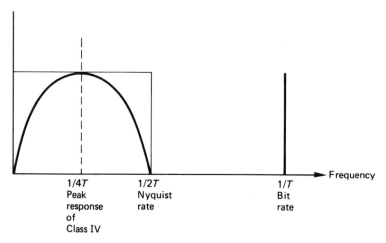

Figure 4.41 Class IV response has spectral nulls at DC and the Nyquist rate, giving a noise advantage, since magnetic replay signal is weak at both frequencies in a high-density channel.

If the head gap is made equal to 1 bit, the $(1 - D)$ head response may be converted to the desired response by the use of a $(1 + D)$ filter, as in Figure 4.42(a).[15] Alternatively, a head of unspecified gapwidth may be connected to an integrator, and equalized flat to reproduce the record current waveform before being fed to a $(1 - D^2)$ filter as in Figure 4.42(b).[16]

The result of both of these techniques is a ternary signal. The eye pattern has two sets of eyes as in Figure 4.42(c).[17] When slicing such a signal, a smaller amount of noise will cause an error than in the binary case.

The treatment of the signal thus far represents an equalization technique, and not a channel code. However, to take full advantage of Class IV partial response, suitable precoding is necessary prior to recording, which does then constitute a channel coding technique. This precoding is shown in Figure 4.43(a). Data are added modulo-2 to themselves with a 2 bit delay. The effect of this precoding is that the outer levels of the ternary signals, which represent data ones, alternate in polarity on all odd bits and on all even bits. This is because the precoder acts like two interleaved 1 bit delay circuits, as in Figure 4.43(b). As this alternation of polarity is a form of redundancy, it can be used to recover the 3 dB SNR loss encountered in slicing a ternary eye pattern. Viterbi decoding [18] can be used for this purpose. In Viterbi decoding, each channel bit is not sliced individually; the slicing decision is made in the context of adjacent decisions. Figure 4.44 shows a replay waveform which is so noisy that, at the decision point, the signal voltage crosses the centre of the eye, and the slicer alone cannot tell whether the correct decision is an inner or an outer level. In this case, the decoder essentially allows both decisions to stand, in order to see what happens. A symbol representing indecision is output. It will be seen from the figure that as subsequent bits are received, one of these decisions will result in an absurd situation, which indicates that the other decision was the right one. The decoder can then locate the undecided symbol and set it to the correct value.

Viterbi decoding requires more information about the signal voltage than a simple binary slicer can discern. Figure 4.45 shows that the replay waveform is sampled and quantized so that it can be processed in digital logic. The sampling rate is obtained from the embedded clock content of the replay waveform. The digital Viterbi processing logic must be able to operate at high speed to handle

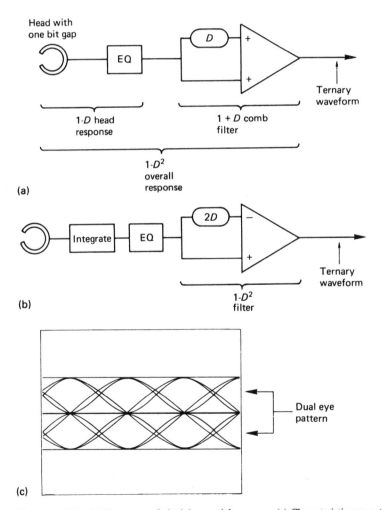

Figure 4.42 (a), (b) Two ways of obtaining partial response. (c) Characteristic eye pattern of ternary signal.

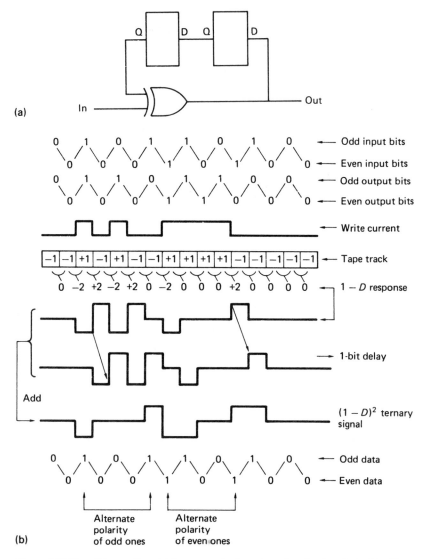

Figure 4.43 Class IV precoding at (a) causes redundancy in replay signal as derived in (b).

serial signals from a DVTR head. Its application in Digital Betacam is eased somewhat by the adoption of data reduction which reduces the data rate at the heads by a factor of two.

Clearly a ternary signal having a dual eye pattern is more sensitive than a binary signal, and it is important to keep the maximum run length T_{max} small in order to have accurate AGC. The use of pseudo-random coding along with partial response equalization and precoding is a logical combination.[19] There is then considerable overlap between the channel code and the error-correction system. Viterbi decoding is primarily applicable to channels with random errors due to

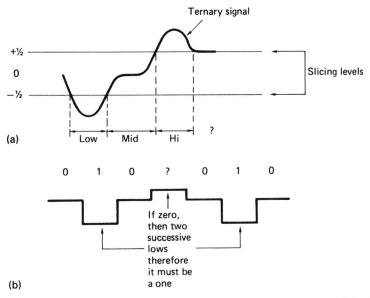

Ternary signal

+½
0
−½

Slicing levels

(a)   Low   Mid   Hi   ?

0   1   0   ?   0   1   0

If zero,
then two
successive
lows
therefore
it must be
(b)   a one

Figure 4.44 (a) A ternary signal suffers a noise penalty because there are two slicing levels. (b) The redundancy is used to determine the bit value in the presence of noise. Here the pulse height has been reduced to make it ambiguous 1/0, but only 1 is valid as zero violates the redundancy rules.

Gaussian statistics, and they cannot cope with burst errors. In a head-noise-limited system, however, the use of a Viterbi detector could increase the power of an separate burst error-correction system by relieving it of the need to correct random errors due to noise. The error-correction system could then concentrate on correcting burst errors unimpaired. This point will become clearer upon referring to Chapter 5.

4.22 Convolutional randomising

The randomizing in DVTRs is block based, since this matches the block structure of the recording. Where there is no obvious block structure, convolutional or

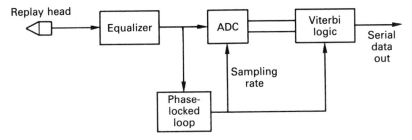

Replay head

Equalizer   ADC   Viterbi
                             logic   Serial
                                        data
                                        out

Sampling
rate

Phase-
locked
loop

Figure 4.45 A Viterbi decoder is implemented in the digital domain by sampling the replay waveform with a clock locked to the embedded clock of the channel code.

endless randomizing can be used. This is the approach used in the scrambled serial interface described in Chapter 3, which allows composite or component video of up to 10 bit wordlength to be sent serially along with digital audio channels.

In convolutional randomizing, the signal sent down the channel is the serial data waveform which has been convolved with the impulse response of a digital filter. On reception the signal is deconvolved to restore the original data. Figure 4.46(a) shows that the filter is an infinite-impulse response (IIR) filter which has recursive paths from the output back to the input. As it is a 1 bit filter its output cannot decay, and, once excited, it runs indefinitely. The filter is followed by a transition generator which consists of a 1 bit delay and an exclusive OR gate. An input 1 results in an output transition on the next clock edge. An input 0 results in no transition.

A result of the infinite-impulse response of the filter is that frequent transitions are generated in the channel which result in sufficient clock content for the phase-locked loop in the receiver.

Transitions are converted back to ones by a differentiator in the receiver. This consists of a 1 bit delay with an exclusive OR gate comparing the input and the output. When a transition passes through the delay, the input and the output will be different and the gate outputs a one which enters the deconvolution circuit. Figure 4.46(b) shows that in the deconvolution circuit a data bit is simply the exclusive OR of a number of channel bits at a fixed spacing. The deconvolution is implemented with a shift register having the exclusive OR gates connected in a reverse pattern to that in the encoder. The same effect as block randomizing is obtained, in that long runs are broken up and the DC content is reduced, but it has the advantage over block randomizing that no synchronizing is required to remove the randomizing, although it will still be necessary for deserialization. Clearly the system will take a few clock periods to produce valid data after commencement of transmission; this is no problem on a permanent-wired connection where the transmission is continuous.

4.23 Synchronizing

Once the PLL in the data separator has locked to the clock content of the transmission, a serial channel bit stream and a channel bit clock will emerge from the sampler. In a group code, it is essential to know where a group of channel bits begins in order to assemble groups for decoding to data bit groups. In a randomizing system it is equally vital to know at what point in the serial data stream the words or samples commence. In serial transmission and in recording, channel bit groups or randomized data words are sent one after the other, 1 bit at a time, with no spaces in between, so that although the designer knows that a data block contains, say, 128 bytes, the receiver simply finds 1024 bits in a row. If the exact position of the first bit is not known, then it is not possible to put all the bits in the right places in the right bytes, a process known as deserializing. The effect of sync slippage is devastating, because a one-bit disparity between the bit count and the bit stream will corrupt every symbol in the block.[20]

The synchronization of the data separator and the synchronization to the block format are two distinct problems which are often solved by the same sync pattern. Deserializing requires a shift register which is fed with serial data and read out once per word. The sync detector is simply a set of logic gates which are arranged to recognize a specific pattern in the register. The sync pattern is either

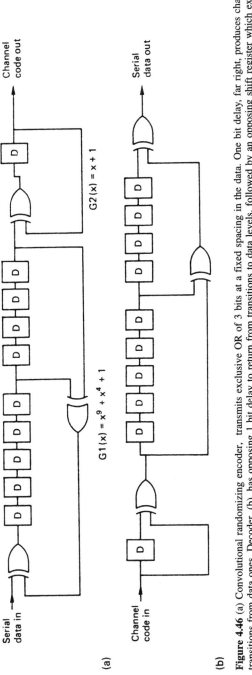

Figure 4.46 (a) Convolutional randomizing encoder, transmits exclusive OR of 3 bits at a fixed spacing in the data. One bit delay, far right, produces channel transitions from data ones. Decoder, (b), has opposing 1 bit delay to return from transitions to data levels, followed by an opposing shift register which exactly reverses the coding process.

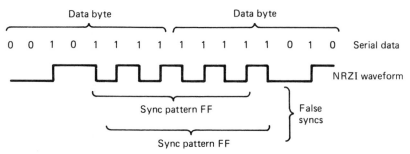

Figure 4.47 Concatenation of two words can result in the accidental generation of a word which is reserved for synchronizing.

identical for every block or has a restricted number of versions and it will be recognized by the replay circuitry and used to reset the bit count through the block. Then by counting channel bits and dividing by the group size, groups can be deserialized and decoded to data groups. In a randomized system, the pseudorandom sequence generator is also reset. Then by counting derandomized bits from the sync pattern and dividing by the wordlength enables the replay circuitry to deserialize the data words.

In digital audio the two's complement coding scheme is universal and traditionally no codes have been reserved for synchronizing; they are all available for sample values. It would in any case be impossible to reserve all ones or all zeros as these are in the centre of the range in twos complement. Even if a specific code were excluded from the recorded data so it could be used for synchronising, this cannot ensure that the same pattern cannot be falsely created at the junction between two allowable data words. Figure 4.47 shows how false synchronizing can occur due to concatenation. It is thus not practical to use a bit pattern which is a data code value in a simple synchronizing recognizer.

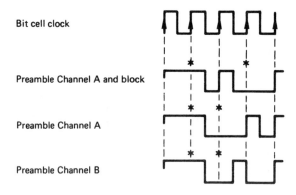

Figure 4.48 The sync patterns of the AES/EBU operate by violating the run-length circuits.

In run-length-limited codes this is not a problem. The sync pattern is no longer a data bit pattern but is a specific waveform. If the sync waveform contains run lengths which violate the normal coding limits, there is no way that these run lengths can occur in encoded data, nor any possibility that they will be interpreted as data. They can, however, be readily detected by the replay circuitry. The sync patterns of the AES/EBU interface are shown in Figure 4.48. It will be seen from Figure 4.26 that the maximum run length in FM coded data is 1 bit. The sync pattern begins with a run length of $1\frac{1}{2}$ bits which is unique. There are three types of sync pattern in the AES/EBU interface, as will be seen in Chapter 18. These are distinguished by the position of a second pulse after the run-length violation. Note that the sync patterns are also DC free like the FM code.

In a group code there are many more combinations of channel bits than there are combinations of data bits. Thus after all data bit patterns have been allocated group patterns, there are still many unused group patterns which cannot occur in the data. With care, group patterns can be found which cannot occur due to the concatenation of any pair of groups representing data. These are then unique and can be used for synchronizing.

References

1. DEELEY, E.M., Integrating and differentiating channels in digital tape recording. *Radio Electron. Eng.*, **56**, 169–173 (1986)
2. MEE, C.D., *The Physics of Magnetic Recording*. Amsterdam and New York: Elsevier–North Holland Publishing (1978)
3. JACOBY, G.V., Signal equalization in digital magnetic recording. *IEEE Trans. Magn.*, **MAG-11**, 302–305 (1975)
4. SCHNEIDER, R.C., An improved pulse-slimming method for magnetic recording. *IEEE Trans. Magn.*, **MAG-11**, 1240–1241 (1975)
5. MILLER, A., US Patent 3,108,261 (1960)
6. MALLINSON, J.C. and MILLER, J.W., Optimum codes for digital magnetic recording. *Radio Electron. Eng.*, **47**, 172–176 (1977)
7. MILLER, J.W., DC-free encoding for data transmission system. US Patent 4 027,335 (1977)
8. TANG, D.T., Run-length-limited codes. IEEE Int. Symp. on Information Theory (1969)
9. COHN, M. and JACOBY, G., Run-length reduction of 3PM code via lookahead technique. *IEEE Trans. Magn.*, **18**, 1253–1255 (1982)
10. HORIGUCHI, T. and MORITA, K., On optimization of modulation codes in digital recording *IEEE Trans. Magn.,* **12**, 740–742 (1976)
11. FRANASZEK, P.A., Sequence state methods for run-length linited coding. *IBM J. Res. Dev.* **14**, 376–383 (1970)
12. JACOBY, G.V. and KOST, R., Binary two-thirds-rate code with full word lookahead. *IEEE Trans. Magn.*, **20**, 709–714 (1984)
13. JACOBY, G.V., A new lookahead code for increased data density. *IEEE Trans. Magn.*, **13**, 1202–1204 (1977)
14. UEHARA, T., NAKAYAMA, T., MINAGUCHI, H., SHIBAYA, H., SEKIGUCHI, T. and OBA, Y., A new 8–14 modulation and its application to small format VTR. SMPTE Tech. Conf. (1989)
15. YOKOYAMA, K., Digital video tape recorder. *NHK Technical Monograph*, No 31 (March 1982)
16. COLEMAN, C.H., *et al.*, High data rate magnetic recording in a single channel. *J. IERE*, **55**, 229–236 (1985)
17. KOBAYASHI, H., Application of partial response channel coding to magnetic recording systems. *IBM J. Res. Dev.*, **14**, 368–375 (1970)
18. FORNEY, G.D. JR., The Viterbi algorithm, *Proc. IEEE*, **61**, 268–278 (1973)
19. WOOD, R.W. and PETERSEN, D.A., Viterbi detection of Class IV partial response on a magnetic recording channel. *IEEE Trans. Commun.*, **34**, 454–461 (1968)
20. GRIFFITHS, F.A., A digital audio recording system. Presented at the 65th Audio Engineering Society Convention (London, 1980), preprint 1580(C1)

Chapter 5

Error correction

The subject of error correction is almost always described in mathematical terms by specialists for the benefit of other specialists. Such mathematical approaches are quite inappropriate for a proper understanding of the concepts of error correction and only become necessary to analyse the quantitative behaviour of a system. The description below will use the minimum possible amount of mathematics, and it will then be seen that error correction is, in fact, quite straightforward.

5.1 Sensitivity of message to error

Before attempting to specify any piece of equipment, it is necessary to quantify the problems to be overcome and how effectively they need to be overcome. For a digital recording system the causes of errors must be studied to quantify the problem, and the sensitivity of the destination to errors must be assessed. In video and audio the sensitivity to errors must be subjective. In PCM, the effect of a single bit in error depends upon the significance of the bit. If the least significant bit of a sample is wrong, the chances are that the effect will be lost in the noise. Conversely, if a high-order bit is in error, a massive transient will be added to the waveform. The use of data reduction complicates the subject. In theory, if redundancy has been removed from a signal, it becomes less tolerant of errors.

Whilst the exact BER (Bit Error Rate) which can be tolerated will depend on the application, digital video is much more tolerant of residual bit errors than audio which in turn is more tolerant than computer data.

In all of these cases, if the maximum error rate which the destination can tolerate is likely to be exceeded by the unaided channel, some form of error handling will be necessary.

There are a number of terms which have idiomatic meanings in error-correction. The raw BER is the error rate of the medium, whereas the residual or uncorrected BER is the rate at which the error-correction system fails to detect or miscorrects errors. In practical digital systems, the residual BER is negligibly small. If the error correction is turned off, the two figures become the same. Many DVTRs have a maintenance feature which allows the error correction to be turned 'off'. In practice it means that errors are still detected but are output as mid-grey pixels instead of their actual incorrect off tape value. This is not quite the same thing as having the correction truly disabled.

5.2 Error mechanisms

There are many different types of recording and transmission channel and consequently there will be many different mechanisms which may result in errors. As was the case for channel coding, although there are many different applications, the basic principles remain the same.

In magnetic recording, data can be corrupted by mechanical problems such as media dropout and poor tracking or head contact, or Gaussian thermal noise in replay circuits and heads. Inside equipment, data are conveyed on short wires and the noise environment is under the designer's control. With suitable design techniques, errors can be made effectively negligible. In communication systems, there is considerably less control of the electromagnetic environment. In cables, crosstalk and electromagnetic interference occur and can corrupt data, although optical fibres are resistant to interference of this kind. In long-distance cable transmission the effects of lightning and exchange switching noise must be considered.

In Chapter 4 it was seen that when group codes are used, a single defect in a group changes the group symbol and may cause errors up to the size of the group. Single-bit errors are therefore less common in group-coded channels.

Irrespective of the cause, all of these mechanisms cause one of two effects. There are large isolated corruptions, called error bursts, where numerous bits are corrupted all together in an area which is otherwise error free, and there are random errors affecting single bits or symbols. Whatever the mechanism, the result will be that the received data will not be exactly the same as those sent. It is a tremendous advantage of digital recording that the discrete data bits will be each either right or wrong. A bit cannot be off-colour as it can only be interpreted as 0 or 1. Thus the subtle degradations of analog systems are absent from digital recording and transmission channels and will only be found in converters. Equally if a binary digit is known to be wrong, it is only necessary to invert its state and then it must be right and indistinguishable from its original value! Thus error correction itself is trivial; the hard part is working out *which* bits need correcting.

In chapter 2 the Gaussian nature of noise probability was discussed. Some conclusions can be drawn from the Gaussian distribution of noise.[1] Firstly, it is not possible to make error-free digital recordings, because however high the signal-to-noise ratio of the recording, there is still a small but finite chance that the noise can exceed the signal. Measuring the signal-to-noise ratio of a channel establishes the noise power, which determines the width of the noise distribution curve relative to the signal amplitude. When in a binary system the noise amplitude exceeds the signal amplitude, but with the opposite polarity, a bit error will occur. Knowledge of the shape of the Gaussian curve allows the conversion of signal-to-noise ratio into bit error rate (BER). It can be predicted how many bits will fail due to noise in a given recording, but it is not possible to say *which* bits will be affected. Increasing the SNR of the channel will not eliminate errors; it just reduces their probability. The logical solution is to incorporate an error-correction system.

5.3 Basic error correction

Error correction works by adding some bits to the data which are calculated from the data. This creates an entity called a codeword which spans a greater length of time (or distance along a tape track) than 1 bit alone. The statistics of noise means that whilst 1 bit may be lost in a codeword, the loss of the rest of the codeword because of noise is highly improbable. As will be described later in this chapter, codewords are designed to be able to correct totally a finite number of corrupted bits. The greater the timespan over which the coding is performed, or, on a recording medium, the greater area over which the coding is performed, the greater will be the reliability achieved, although this does mean that an encoding delay will be experienced on recording, and a similar or greater decoding delay on reproduction.

Shannon [2] disclosed that a message can have any desired degree of accuracy provided that it is spread over a sufficient time or area. Engineers have to compromise, because an infinite coding delay in the recovery of an error-free signal is not acceptable. Most short-distance digital interfaces do not employ error correction because the build-up of coding delays in large systems is unacceptable. On the other hand a short delay in the reproduction of a tape is seldom a source of difficulty.

If error correction is necessary as a practical matter, it is then only a small step to put it to maximum use. All error correction depends on adding bits to the original message, and this of course increases the number of bits to be recorded, although it does not increase the information recorded. It might be imagined that error correction is going to reduce storage capacity, because space has to be found for all the extra bits. Nothing could be further from the truth. Once an error-correction system is used, the signal-to-noise ratio of the channel can be reduced, because the raised BER of the channel will be overcome by the error-correction system. Reduction of the SNR by 3 dB in a magnetic tape track can be achieved by halving the track width, provided that the system is not dominated by head or preamplifier noise. This doubles the recording density, making the storage of the additional bits needed for error correction a trivial matter. In short, error correction is not a nuisance to be tolerated; it is a vital tool needed to maximize the efficiency of recorders. The DVTR would not be economically viable without it.

5.4 Error handling

Figure 5.1 shows the broad subdivisions of error handling. The first stage might be called error avoidance and includes such measures as placing the audio blocks near to the centre of the tape. The data pass through the channel, which causes whatever corruptions it feels like. On receipt of the data the occurrence of errors is first detected, and this process must be extremely reliable, as it does not matter how effective the correction or how good the concealment algorithm, if it is not

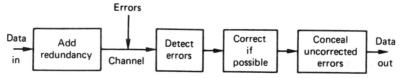

Figure 5.1 The basic stages of an error-correction system. Of these the most critical is the detection stage, since this controls the subsequent actions.

known that they are necessary! The detection of an error then results in a course of action being decided.

In most cases of VTR replay a retry is not possible because the data are required in real time. Many magnetic tape data recorders have *read after write*. During recording, offtape data are immediately checked for errors. If an error is detected, the tape will abort the recording, reverse to the beginning of the current block and erase it. The data from that block are then recorded further down the tape. This is the recording equivalent of a retransmission in a communications system. Such processes are not practicable in DVTRs, again because of the real-time operating environment.

5.5 Concealment by interpolation

There are some practical differences between data recording for video and the computer data recording application. Although video or audio recorders seldom have time for retries, they have the advantage that there is a certain amount of redundancy in the information conveyed. Thus if an error cannot be corrected, then it can be concealed. If a sample is lost, it is possible to obtain an approximation to it by interpolating between the samples before and after the missing one. Clearly concealment of any kind cannot be used with computer data.

If there is too much corruption for concealment, the only course in video is to repeat the previous field or frame in a freeze as it is unlikely that the corrupt picture is watchable.

In general, if use is to be made of concealment on replay, the data must generally be reordered or shuffled prior to recording. To take a simple example, odd-numbered samples are recorded in a different area of the medium from even-numbered samples. On playback, if a gross error occurs on the tape, depending on its position, the result will be either corrupted odd samples or corrupted even samples, but it is most unlikely that both will be lost. Interpolation is then possible if the power of the correction system is exceeded. In practice the shuffle employed in digital video recorders is two dimensional and rather more complex. Further details can be found in Section 7.8. The concealment technique described here is only suitable for PCM recording. If data reduction has been employed, different concealment techniques will be needed. In the case of DCT-based systems, an entire coefficient block may be lost, requiring estimation of, typically, 32 pixel values.

It should be stressed that corrected data are indistinguishable from the original and thus there can be no visible or audible artifacts. In contrast, concealment is only an approximation to the original information and could be detectable. In practical DVTRs, concealment occurs infrequently unless there is a defect requiring attention, and its presence is difficult to see or hear.

5.6 Parity

The error-detection and error-correction processes are closely related and will be dealt with together here. The actual correction of an error is simplified tremendously by the adoption of binary. As there are only two symbols, 0 and 1, it is enough to know that a symbol is wrong, and the correct value is obvious. Figure 5.2 shows a minimal circuit required for correction once the bit in error

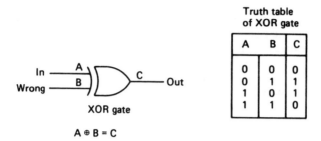

Figure 5.2 Once the position of the error is identified, the correction process in binary is easy.

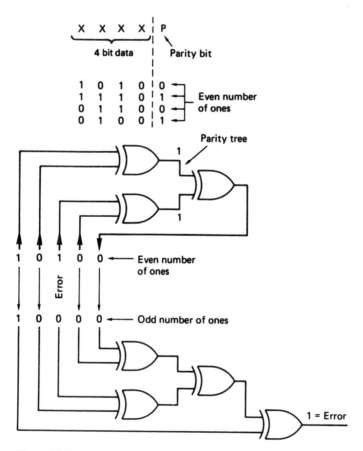

Figure 5.3 Parity checking adds up the number of ones in a word using, in this example, parity trees. One error bit and odd numbers of errors are detected. Even numbers of errors cannot be detected.

has been identified. The XOR (exclusive OR) gate shows up extensively in error correction and the figure also shows the truth table. One way of remembering the characteristics of this useful device is that there will be an output when the inputs are different. Inspection of the truth table will show that there is an even number of ones in each row (zero is an even number) and so the device could also be called an even parity gate. The XOR gate is also an adder in modulo-2 (see Chapter 2).

Parity is a fundamental concept in error detection. In Figure 5.3, the example is given of a 4 bit data word which is to be protected. If an extra bit is added to the word which is calculated in such a way that the total number of ones in the 5 bit word is even, this property can be tested on receipt. The generation of the parity bit in Figure 5.3 can be performed by a number of the ubiquitous XOR gates configured into what is known as a parity tree. In the figure, if a bit is corrupted, the received message will be seen no longer to have an even number of ones. If 2 bits are corrupted, the failure will be undetected. This example can be used to introduce much of the terminology of error correction. The extra bit added to the message carries no information of its own, since it is calculated from the other bits. It is therefore called a *redundant* bit. The addition of the redundant bit gives the message a special property, i.e. the number of ones is even. A message having some special property *irrespective of the actual data content* is called a *codeword*. All error correction relies on adding redundancy to real data to form codewords for transmission. If any corruption occurs, the intention is that the received message will not have the special property; in other words if the received message is not a codeword there has definitely been an error. The receiver can check for the special property without any prior knowledge of the data content. Thus the same check can be made on all received data. If the received message is a codeword, there probably has not been an error. The word 'probably' must be used because the figure shows that 2 bits in error will cause the received message to be a codeword, which cannot be discerned from an error-free message. If it is known that generally the only failure mechanism in the channel in question is loss of a single bit, it is *assumed* that receipt of a codeword

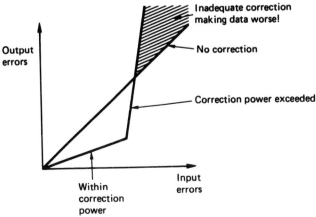

Figure 5.4 An error-correction system can only reduce errors at normal error rates at the expense of increasing errors at higher rates. It is most important to keep a system working to the left of the knee in the graph.

means that there has been no error. If there is a probability of two error bits, that becomes very nearly the probability of failing to detect an error, since all odd numbers of errors will be detected, and a 4 bit error is much less likely. It is paramount in all error-correction systems that the protection used should be appropriate for the probability of errors to be encountered. An inadequate error-correction system is actually worse than not having any correction. Error-correction works by trading probabilities. Error-free performance with a certain error rate is achieved at the expense of performance at higher error rates. Figure 5.4 shows the effect of an error correction system on the residual BER for a given raw BER. It will be seen that there is a characteristic knee in the graph. If the expected raw BER has been misjudged, the consequences can be disastrous. Another result demonstrated by the example is that we can only guarantee to detect the same number of bits in error as there are redundant bits.

5.7 Block and convolutional codes

Figure 5.5(a) shows a strategy known as a crossword code, or product code. The data are formed into a two-dimensional array, in which each location can be a single bit or a multibit symbol. Parity is then generated on both rows and columns. If a single bit or symbol fails, one row parity check and one column parity check will fail, and the failure can be located at the intersection of the two failing checks. Although two symbols in error confuse this simple scheme, using more complex coding in a two-dimensional structure is very powerful, and further examples will be given throughout this chapter.

The example of Figure 5.5(a) assembles the data to be coded into a block of finite size and then each codeword is calculated by taking a different set of

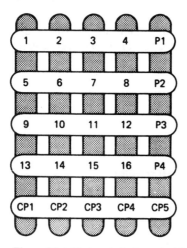

(a)

Figure 5.5 A block code is shown in (a). Each location in the block can be a bit or a word. Horizontal parity checks are made by adding P1, P2, etc., and cross-parity or vertical checks are made by adding CP1, CP2, etc. Any symbol in error will be at the intersection of the two failing codewords. In (b) a convolutional coder is shown. Symbols entering are subject to different delays which result in the codewords in (c) being calculated. These have a vertical part and a diagonal part. A symbol in error will be at the intersection of the diagonal part of one code and the vertical part of another.

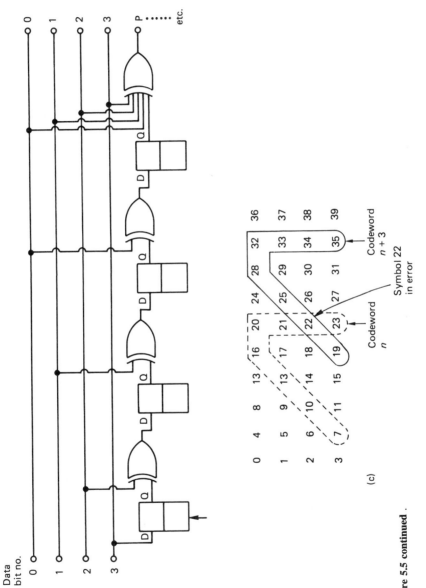

Figure 5.5 continued .

symbols. This should be contrasted with the operation of the circuit of Figure 5.5(b). Here the data are not in a block, but form an endless stream. A shift register allows four symbols to be available simultaneously to the encoder. The action of the encoder depends upon the delays. When symbol 3 emerges from the first delay, it will be added (modulo 2) to symbol 6. When this sum emerges from the second delay, it will be added to symbol 9 and so on. The codeword produced is shown in Figure 5.5(c) where it will be seen to be bent such that it has a vertical section and a diagonal section. Four symbols later the next codeword will be created one column further over in the data.

This is a convolutional code because the coder always takes parity on the same pattern of symbols which is convolved with the data stream on an endless basis. Figure 5.5(c) also shows that if an error occurs, it can be located because it will cause parity errors in two codewords. The error will be on the diagonal part of one codeword and on the vertical part of the other so that it can be located uniquely at the intersection and corrected by parity.

Comparison with the block code of Figure 5.5(a) will show that the convolutional code needs less redundancy for the same single-symbol location and correction performance as only a single redundant symbol is required for every four data symbols. Convolutional codes are computed on an endless basis which makes them inconvenient in recording applications where editing is anticipated. Here the block code is more appropriate as it allows edit gaps to be created between codes. In the case of uncorrectable errors, the convolutional principle causes the syndromes to be affected for some time afterwards and results in miscorrections of symbols which were not actually in error. This is called error propagation and is a characteristic of convolutional codes. Recording media tend to produce somewhat variant error statistics because media defects and mechanical problems cause errors which do not fit the classical additive noise channel. Convolutional codes can easily be taken beyond their correcting power if used with real recording media. In transmission and broadcasting, the error statistics are more stable and the editing requirement is absent. As a result convolutional codes are used in digital broadcasting whereas block codes are used in recording.

5.8 Hamming code

In a one-dimensional code, the position of the failing bit can be determined by using more parity checks. In Figure 5.6, the four data bits have been used to compute three redundancy bits, making a 7 bit codeword. The four data bits are examined in turn, and each bit which is a one will cause the corresponding row of a generator matrix to be added to an exclusive OR sum. For example, if the data were 1001, the top and bottom rows of the matrix would be XORed. The matrix used is known as an identity matrix, because the data bits in the codeword are identical to the data bits to be conveyed. This is useful because the original data can be stored unmodified, and the check bits are simply attached to the end to make a so-called systematic codeword. Almost all digital recording equipment uses systematic codes. The way in which the redundancy bits are calculated is simply that they do not all use every data bit. If a data bit has not been included in a parity check, it can fail without affecting the outcome of that check. The position of the error is deduced from the pattern of successful and unsuccessful checks in the check matrix. This pattern is known as a syndrome.

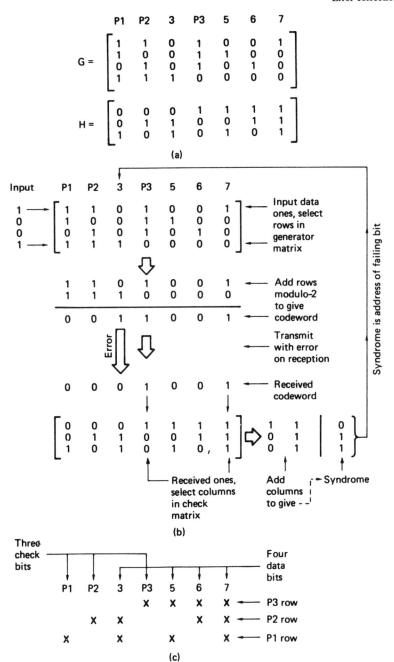

Figure 5.6 (a) The generator and check matrices of a Hamming code. The data and check bits are arranged as shown because this causes the syndrome to be the binary address of the failing bit. (b) An example of Hamming code generation and error correction. (c) Another way of looking at Hamming code is to say that the rows of crosses in this chart are calculated to have even parity. If bit 3 fails, parity check P3 is not affected, but parity checks P1 and P2 both include bit 3 and will fail.

In the figure the example of a failing bit is given. Bit 3 fails, and because this bit is included in only two of the checks, there are two ones in the failure pattern, 011. As some care was taken in designing the matrix pattern for the generation of the check bits, the syndrome, 011, is the address of the failing bit. This is the fundamental feature of the Hamming codes due to Richard Hamming.[3] The performance of this 7 bit codeword can be assessed. In 7 bits there can be 128 combinations, but in four data bits there are only 16 combinations. Thus out of 128 possible received messages, only 16 will be codewords, so if the message is completely trashed by a gross corruption, it will still be possible to detect that this has happened 112 times out of 127, as in these cases the syndrome will be non-zero (the 128th case is the correct data). There is thus only a probability of detecting that all of the message is corrupt. In an idle moment it is possible to work out, in a similar way, the number of false codewords which can result from different numbers of bits being assumed to have failed. For less than 3 bits, the failure will always be detected, because there are three check bits. Returning to the example, if 2 bits fail, there will be a non-zero syndrome, but if this is used to point to a bit in error, a miscorrection will result. From these results can be deduced another important feature of error codes. The power of detection is always greater than the power of correction, which is also fortunate, since if the correcting power is exceeded by an error it will at least be a known problem, and steps can be taken to prevent any undesirable consequences.

The efficiency of the example given is not very high because three check bits are needed for every four data bits. Since the failing bit is located with a binary-split mechanism, it is possible to double the code length by adding a single extra check bit. Thus with 4 bit syndromes there are 15 non-zero codes and so the codeword will be 15 bits long: 4 bits are redundant and 11 are data. Using 5 bits of redundancy, the code can be 31 bits long and contain 26 data bits. Thus provided that the number of errors to be detected stays the same, it is more efficient to use long codewords. Error-correcting memories use typically four or

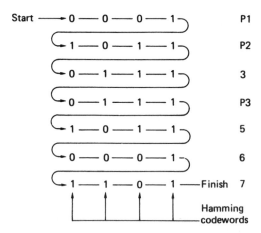

Figure 5.7 The vertical columns of this diagram are all codewords generated by the matrix of Figure 5.6, which can correct a single-bit error. If these words are recorded in the order shown, a burst error of up to 4 bits will result in one single-bit error in each codeword, which is correctable. Interleave and de-interleave require memory, and causes delay.

eight data bytes plus redundancy. A drawback of long codes is that if it is desired to change a single memory byte it is necessary to read the entire codeword, modify the desired data byte and re-encode – the so-called read–modify–write process.

The Hamming code shown is limited to single-bit correction, but with the addition of another bit of redundancy can be made to correct 1 bit and detect 2 bit errors. This is ideal for error-correcting MOS memories where the SECDED (Single Error-Correcting Double-Error Detecting) characteristic matches the type of failures experienced.

The correction of 1 bit is of little use in the presence of burst errors, but a Hamming code can be made to correct burst errors by using interleaving. Figure 5.7 shows that if several codewords are calculated beforehand and woven together as shown before they are sent down the channel, then a burst of errors which corrupts several bits will become a number of single-bit errors in separate codewords upon de-interleaving.

Interleaving is used extensively in digital recording, and will be discussed in greater detail later in this chapter.

5.9 Hamming distance

It is useful at this point to introduce the concept of Hamming distance. It is not a physical distance but a specific measure of the difference between two binary numbers. Hamming distance is defined in the general case as the number of bit positions in which a pair of words differ. The Hamming distance of a code is defined as the minimum number of bits that must be changed in any codeword in order to turn it into another codeword. This is an important yardstick because if errors convert one codeword into another, it will have the special characteristic of the code and so the corruption will not even be detected.

Figure 5.8 shows Hamming distance diagrammatically. A 3 bit codeword is used with two data bits and one parity bit. With 3 bits, a received code could have eight combinations, but only four of these will be codewords. The valid codewords are shown in the centre of each of the disks, and these will be seen to be identical to the rows of the truth table in Figure 5.2. At the perimeter of the disks are shown the received words which would result from a single-bit error, i.e. they have a Hamming distance of one from codewords. It will be seen that the same received word (on the vertical bars) can be obtained from a different single-bit corruption of any three codewords. It is thus not possible to tell which codeword was corrupted, so although all single-bit errors can be detected, correction is not possible. This diagram should be compared with that of Figure 5.9, which is a Venn diagram where there is a set in which the MSB is 1 (upper circle), a set in which the middle bit is 1 (lower left circle) and a set in which the LSB is 1 (lower right circle). Note that in crossing any boundary only 1 bit changes, and so each boundary represents a Hamming distance change of one. The four codewords of Figure 5.8 are repeated here, and it will be seen that single-bit errors in any codeword produce a non-codeword, and so single-bit errors are always detectable.

Correction is possible if the number of non-codewords is increased by increasing the number of redundant bits. This means that it is possible to spread out the actual codewords in Hamming distance terms.

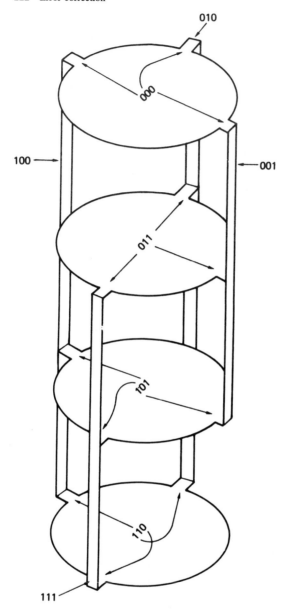

Figure 5.8 Hamming distance of two. The disk centres contain codewords. Corrupting each bit in turn produces the distance 1 values on the vertical members. In order to change one codeword to another, 2 bits must be changed, so the code has a Hamming distance of two.

Figure 5.10(a) shows a distance 2 code, where there is only one redundancy bit, and so half of the possible words will be codewords. There will be non-codewords at distance 1 which can be produced by altering a single bit in either of two codewords. In this case it is not possible to tell what the original codeword was in the case of a single-bit error.

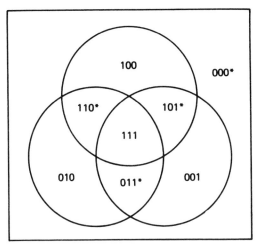

Figure 5.9 Venn diagram shows a 1 bit change crossing any boundary which is a Hamming distance of one. Compare with Figure 5.8. Codewords marked *.

Figure 5.10(b) shows a distance 3 code, where there will now be at least two non-codewords between codewords. If a single-bit error occurs in a codeword, the resulting non-codeword will be at distance 1 from the original codeword. This same non-codeword could also have been produced by changing 2 bits in a different codeword. If it is known that the failure mechanism is a single bit, it can be *assumed* that the original codeword was the one which is closest in Hamming distance to the received bit pattern, and so correction is possible. If, however, our assumption about the error mechanism proved to be wrong, and in fact a 2 bit error had occurred, this assumption would take us to the wrong codeword, turning the event into a 3 bit error. This is an illustration of the knee in the graph of Figure 5.4, where if the power of the code is exceeded it makes things worse.

Figure 5.10(c) shows a distance 4 code. There are now three non-codewords between codewords, and clearly single-bit errors can still be corrected by choosing the nearest codeword. Double-bit errors will be detected, because they result in non-codewords equidistant in Hamming terms from codewords, but it is not possible uniquely to determine what the original codeword was.

5.10 Cyclic codes

The parallel implementation of a Hamming code can be made very fast using parity trees, which is ideal for memory applications where access time is increased by the correction process. However, in digital recording applications, the data are stored serially on a track, and it is desirable to use relatively large data blocks to reduce the amount of the medium devoted to preambles, addressing and synchronizing. Where large data blocks are to be handled, the use of a lookup table or tree has to be abandoned because it would become impossibly large. The principle of codewords having a special characteristic will still be employed, but they will be generated and checked algorithmically by

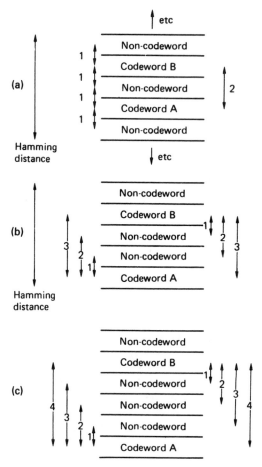

Figure 5.10 (a) Distance 2 code; non-codewords are at distance 1 from two possible codewords so it cannot be deduced what the correct one is. (b) Distance 3 code; non-codewords which have *single-bit errors* can be attributed to the nearest codeword. Breaks down in presence of double-bit errors. (c) Distance 4 code; non-codewords which have single-bit errors can be attributed to the nearest codeword, AND double-bit errors form *different* non-codewords, and can thus be detected but not corrected.

equations. The syndrome will then be converted to the bit(s) in error not by looking them up, but by solving an equation.

Where data can be accessed serially, simpler circuitry can be used because the same gate will be used for many XOR operations. Unfortunately the reduction in component count is only paralleled by an increase in the difficulty of explaining what takes place.

The circuit of Figure 5.11 is a kind of shift register, but with a particular feedback arrangement which leads it to be known as a twisted-ring counter. If seven message bits A–G are applied serially to this circuit, and each one of them is clocked, the outcome can be followed in the diagram. As bit A is presented and the system is clocked, bit A will enter the left-hand latch. When bits B and C are presented, A moves across to the right. Both XOR gates will have A on the upper input from the right-hand latch, the left one has D on the lower input and the right one has B on the lower input. When clocked, the left latch will thus be loaded with the XOR of A and D, and the right one with the XOR of A and B. The remainder of the sequence can be followed, bearing in mind that when the same term appears on both inputs of an XOR gate, it goes out, as the exclusive OR of something with itself is nothing. At the end of the process, the latches contain three different expressions. Essentially, the circuit makes three parity checks through the message, leaving the result of each in the three stages of the register. In the figure, these expressions have been used to draw up a check matrix. The significance of

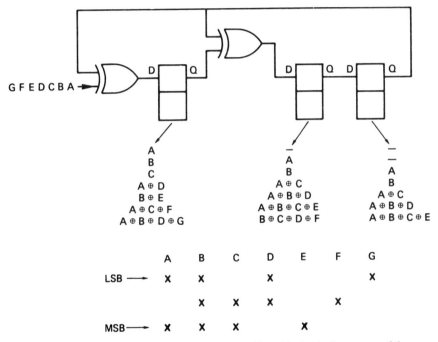

Figure 5.11 When seven successive bits A–G are clocked into this circuit, the contents of the three latches are shown for each clock. The final result is a parity-check matrix.

these steps can now be explained. The bits A B C and D are four data bits, and the bits E F and G are redundancy. When the redundancy is calculated, bit E is chosen so that there are an even number of ones in bits A B C and E; bit F is chosen such that the same applies to bits B C D and F, and similarly for bit G. Thus the four data bits and the three check bits form a 7bit codeword. If there is no error in the codeword, when it is fed into the circuit shown, the result of each of the three parity checks will be zero and every stage of the shift register will be cleared. As the register has eight possible states, and one of them is the error-free condition, then there are seven remaining states; hence the 7 bit codeword. If a bit in the codeword is corrupted, there will be a non-zero result. For example, if bit D fails, the check on bits A B D and G will fail, and a one will appear in the left-hand latch. The check on bits B C D F will also fail, and the centre latch will set. The check on bits A B C E will not fail, because D is not involved in it, making the right-hand bit zero. There will be a syndrome of 110 in the register, and this will be seen from the check matrix to correspond to an error in bit D. Whichever bit fails, there will be a different 3 bit syndrome which uniquely identifies the failed bit. As there are only three latches, there can be eight different syndromes. One of these is zero, which is the error-free condition, and so there are seven remaining error syndromes. The length of the codeword cannot exceed 7 bits, or there would not be enough syndromes to correct all of the bits. This can also be made to tie in with the generation of the check matrix. If 14 bits, A to N, were fed into the circuit shown, the result would be that the check matrix repeated twice, and if a syndrome of 101 were to result, it could not be determined whether bit D or bit K failed. Because the check repeats every 7 bits, the code is said to be a cyclic redundancy check (CRC) code.

In Figure 5.6 an example of a Hamming code was given. Comparison of the check matrix of Figure 5.11 with that of Figure 5.6 will show that the only difference is the order of the matrix columns. The two different processes have thus achieved exactly the same results, and the performance of both must be identical. This is not true in general, but a very small cyclic code has been used for simplicity and to allow parallels to be seen. In practice CRC code blocks will be much longer than the blocks used in Hamming codes.

It has been seen that the circuit shown makes a matrix check on a received word to determine if there has been an error, but the same circuit can also be used to generate the check bits. To visualize how this is done, examine what happens if only the data bits A B C and D are known, and the check bits E F and G are set to zero. If this message, ABCD000, is fed into the circuit, the left-hand latch will afterwards contain the XOR of A B C and zero, which is of course what E should be. The centre latch will contain the XOR of B C D and zero, which is what F should be and so on. This process is not quite ideal, however, because it is necessary to wait for three clock periods after entering the data before the check bits are available. Where the data are simultaneously being recorded and fed into the encoder, the delay would prevent the check bits being easily added to the end of the data stream. This problem can be overcome by slightly

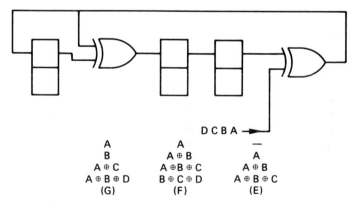

D C B A ⟶

A	A	—
B	A ⊕ B	A
A ⊕ C	A ⊕ B ⊕ C	A ⊕ B
A ⊕ B ⊕ D	B ⊕ C ⊕ D	A ⊕ B ⊕ C
(G)	(F)	(E)

Figure 5.12 By moving the insertion point three places to the right, the calculation of the check bits is completed in only four clock periods and they can follow the data immediately. This is equivalent to premultiplying the data by x^3.

modifying the encoder circuit as shown in Figure 5.12. By moving the position of the input to the right, the operation of the circuit is advanced so that the check bits are ready after only four clocks. The process can be followed in the diagram for the four data bits A B C and D. On the first clock, bit A enters the left two latches, whereas on the second clock, bit B will appear on the upper input of the left XOR gate, with bit A on the lower input, causing the centre latch to load the XOR of A and B and so on.

The way in which the cyclic codes work has been described in engineering terms, but it can be described mathematically if analysis is contemplated.

Just as the position of a decimal digit in a number determines the power of 10 (whether that digit means one, ten or a hundred), the position of a binary digit determines the power of 2 (whether it means one, two or four). It is possible to rewrite a binary number so that it is expressed as a list of powers of 2. For example, the binary number 1101 means $8 + 4 + 1$, and can be written:

$$2^3 + 2^2 + 2^0$$

In fact, much of the theory of error correction applies to symbols in number bases other than 2, so that the number can also be written more generally as:

$$x^3 + x^2 + 1 \; (2^0 = 1)$$

which also looks much more impressive. This expression, containing as it does various powers, is of course a polynomial, and the circuit of Figure 5.11 which has been seen to construct a parity-check matrix on a codeword can also be described as calculating the remainder due to dividing the input by a polynomial using modulo-2 arithmetic. In modulo-2 there are no borrows or carries, and addition and subtraction are replaced by the XOR function, which makes hardware implementation very easy. In Figure 5.13 it will be seen that the circuit of Figure 5.11 actually divides the codeword by a polynomial which is:

$$x^3 + x + 1 \text{ or } 1011$$

This can be deduced from the fact that the right-hand bit is fed into two lower-order stages of the register at once. Once all the bits of the message have been clocked in, the circuit contains the remainder. In mathematical terms, the special property of a codeword is that it is a polynomial which yields a remainder of zero when divided by the generating polynomial. The receiver will make this division, and the result should be zero in the error-free case. Thus the codeword itself disappears from the division. If an error has occurred it is considered that this is due to an error polynomial which has been added to the codeword polynomial. If a codeword divided by the check polynomial is zero, a non-zero syndrome must represent the error polynomial divided by the check polynomial. Thus if the syndrome is multiplied by the check polynomial, the latter will be cancelled out and the result will be the error polynomial. If this is added modulo-2 to the received word, it will cancel out the error and leave the corrected data.

Some examples of modulo-2 division are given in Figure 5.13 which can be compared with the parallel computation of parity checks according to the matrix of Figure 5.11.

The process of generating the codeword from the original data can also be described mathematically. If a codeword has to give zero remainder when divided, it follows that the data can be converted to a codeword by adding the remainder when the data are divided. Generally speaking the remainder would

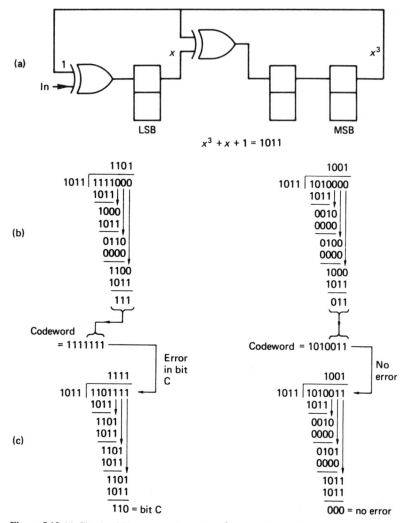

Figure 5.13 (a) Circuit of Figure 5.11 divides by $x^3 + x + 1$ to find remainder. At (b) this is used to calculate check bits. At (c) right, zero syndrome, no error.

have to be subtracted, but in modulo-2 there is no distinction. This process is also illustrated in Figure 5.13. The four data bits have three zeros placed on the right-hand end, to make the wordlength equal to that of a codeword, and this word is then divided by the polynomial to calculate the remainder. The remainder is added to the zero-extended data to form a codeword. The modified circuit of Figure 5.12 can be described as premultiplying the data by x^3 before dividing.

CRC codes are of primary importance for detecting errors, and several have been standardized for use in digital communications. The most common of these are:

$$x^{16} + x^{15} + x^2 + 1 \text{ (CRC-16)}$$
$$x^{16} + x^{12} + x^5 + 1 \text{ (CRC-CCITT)}$$

5.11 Punctured codes

The 16 bit cyclic codes have codewords of length $2^{16}-1$ or 65 535 bits long. This may be too long for the application. Another problem with very long codes is that with a given raw BER, the longer the code, the more errors will occur in it. There may be enough errors to exceed the power of the code. The solution in both cases is to shorten or *puncture* the code. Figure 5.14 shows that in a punctured code, only the end of the codeword is used, and the data and redundancy are preceded by a string of zeros. It is not necessary to record these zeros, and of course, errors cannot occur in them. Implementing a punctured code is easy. If a CRC generator starts with the register cleared and is fed with serial zeros, it will not change its state. Thus it is not necessary to provide the zeros; encoding can begin with the first data bit. In the same way, the leading zeros need not be provided during

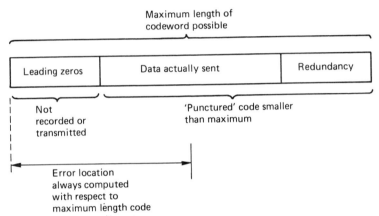

Figure 5.14 Codewords are often shortened, or punctured, which means that only the end of the codeword is actually transmitted. The only precaution to be taken when puncturing codes is that the computed position of an error will be from the beginning of the codeword, not from the beginning of the message.

playback. The only precaution needed is that if a syndrome calculates the location of an error, this will be from the beginning of the codeword, not from the beginning of the data. Where codes are used for detection only, this is of no consequence.

5.12 Applications of cyclic codes

The AES/EBU digital audio interface described in Chapter 8 uses an 8 bit cyclic code to protect the channel-status data. The polynomial used and a typical circuit for generating it can be seen in Figure 5.15. The full codeword length is 255 bits but it is punctured to 192 bits, or 24 bytes, which is the length of the AES/EBU channel-status block. The CRCC is placed in the last byte.

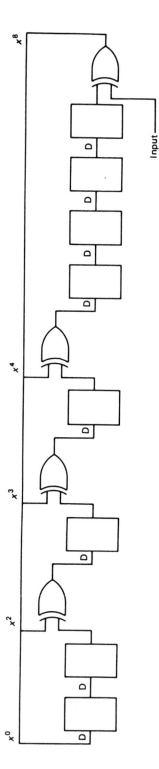

Figure 5.15 The CRCC in the AES/EBU interface is generated by premultiplying the data by x^8 and dividing by $x^8 + x^4 + x^3 + x^2 + 1$. The process can be performed on a serial input by the circuit shown. Premultiplication is achieved by connecting the input at the most significant end of the system. If the output of the right-hand XOR gate is 1 then a 1 is fed back to all of the powers shown, and the polynomial process required is performed. At the end of 23 data bytes, the CRCC will be in the eight latches. At the end of an error-free 24 byte message, the latches will be all zero.

5.13 Burst correction

Figure 5.16 lists all of the possible codewords in the code of Figure 5.11. Examination will show that it is necessary to change at least 3 bits in one codeword before it can be made into another. Thus the code has a Hamming distance of three and cannot detect 3 bit errors. The single-bit error-correction limit can also be deduced from the figure. In the example given, the codeword 0101100 suffers a single-bit error marked * which converts it to a non-codeword at a Hamming distance of one. No other codeword can be turned into this word by a single-bit error; therefore the codeword which is the shortest Hamming distance away must be the correct one. The code can thus reliably correct single-bit errors. However, the codeword 0100111 can be made into the same failure word by a 2 bit error, also marked *, and in this case the original codeword cannot be found by selecting the one which is nearest in Hamming distance. A 2 bit error cannot be corrected and the system will miscorrect if it is attempted.

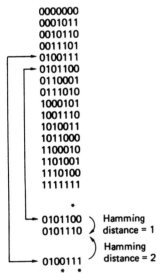

Figure 5.16 All possible codewords of $x^3 + x + 1$ are shown, and the fact that a double error in one codeword can produce the same pattern as a single error in another. Thus double errors cannot be corrected.

The concept of Hamming distance can be extended to explain how more than 1 bit can be corrected. In Figure 5.17 the example of 2 bits in error is given. If a codeword four bits long suffers a single-bit error, it could produce one of 4 different words. If it suffers a two-bit error, it could produce one of 3 + 2 + 1 different words as shown in the figure (the error bits are underlined). The total number of possible words of Hamming distance 1 or 2 from a four bit codeword is thus:

$$4 + 3 + 2 + 1 = 10$$

If the 2 bit error is to be correctable, no other codeword can be allowed to become one of this number of error patterns because of a 2 bit error of its own. Thus every codeword requires space for itself plus all possible error patterns of Hamming distance 2 or 1, which is 11 patterns in this example. Clearly there are only 16 patterns available in a 4 bit code, and thus no data can be conveyed if 2 bit protection is necessary. The number of different patterns possible in a word of n bits is:

$$1 + n + (n-1) + (n-2) + (n-3) + \ldots$$

and this pattern range has to be shared between the ranges of each codeword without overlap. For example, an 8 bit codeword could result in $1 + 8 + 7 + 6 + 5 + 4 + 3 + 2 + 1 = 37$ patterns. As there are only 256 patterns in 8 bits, it follows that only 256/37 pieces of information can be conveyed. The nearest integer

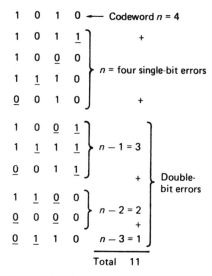

Figure 5.17 Where double-bit errors occur, the number of patterns necessary is $(n - 1) + (n - 2) + (n - 3) + \ldots$. Total necessary is $1 + n + (n - 1) + (n - 2) + (n - 3) + \ldots$ etc. Example here is of 4 bits, and all possible patterns up to a Hamming distance of two are shown (errors underlined).

below is six, and the nearest power of 2 below is four, which corresponds to two data bits and six check bits in the 8 bit word. The amount of redundancy necessary to correct *any* 2 bits in error is large, and as the number of bits to be corrected grows, the redundancy necessary becomes enormous and impractical. A further problem is that the more redundancy is added, the greater the probability of an error in a codeword. Fortunately, in practice errors occur in bursts, as has already been described, and it is a happy consequence that the number of patterns that result from the corruption of a codeword by *adjacent* 2 bit errors is much smaller.

It can be deduced that the number of redundant bits necessary to correct a burst error is twice the number of bits in the burst for a perfect code. This is done by working out the number of received messages which could result from corruption of the codeword by bursts of from 1 bit up to the largest burst size allowed, and then making sure that there are enough redundant bits to allow that number of combinations in the received message.

Some codes, such as the Fire code due to Philip Fire[4], are designed to correct single bursts, whereas later codes such as the B-adjacent code due to Bossen[5] could correct two bursts. The Reed–Solomon codes (Irving Reed and Gustave Solomon[6]) have the advantage that an arbitrary number of bursts can be corrected by choosing the appropriate amount of redundancy at the design stage.

Whilst the Fire code was discovered at about the same time as the superior Reed–Solomon codes, it was dominant in disk drives for a long time because it was so much easier to implement. Now that LSI technology has advanced, the complexity of Reed–Solomon codes is no longer an issue and Fire code is seldom used.

5.14 Introduction to the Reed–Solomon codes

The Reed–Solomon codes (Irving Reed and Gustave Solomon) are inherently burst correcting[6] because they work on multibit symbols rather than individual bits. The R–S codes are also extremely flexible in use. One code may be used both to detect and correct errors and the number of bursts which are correctable can be chosen at the design stage by the amount of redundancy. A further advantage of the R–S codes is that they can be used in conjunction with a separate error-detection mechanism in which case they perform only the correction by erasure. R–S codes operate at the theoretical limit of correcting efficiency. In other words, no more efficient code can be found.

In the simple CRC system described in Section 5.10, the effect of the error is detected by ensuring that the codeword can be divided by a polynomial. The CRC codeword was created by adding a redundant symbol to the data. In the Reed–Solomon codes, several errors can be isolated by ensuring that the codeword will divide by a number of polynomials. Clearly if the codeword must divide by, say, two polynomials, it must have two redundant symbols. This is the minimum case of an R–S code. On receiving an R–S coded message there will be two syndromes following the division. In the error free case, these will both be zero. If both are not zero, there is an error.

It has been stated that the effect of an error is to add an error polynomial to the message polynomial. The number of terms in the error polynomial is the same as the number of errors in the codeword. The codeword divides to zero and the syndromes are a function of the error only. There are two syndromes and two equations. By solving these simultaneous equations it is possible to obtain two unknowns. One of these is the position of the error, known as the *locator*, and the other is the error bit pattern, known as the *corrector*. As the locator is the same size as the code symbol, the length of the codeword is determined by the size of the symbol. A symbol size of 8 bits is commonly used because it fits in conveniently with both 16 bit audio samples and byte-oriented computers. An 8 bit syndrome results in a locator of the same wordlength. Eight bits have 2^8 combinations, but one of these is the error-free condition, and so the locator can specify one of only 255 symbols. As each symbol contains 8 bits, the codeword will be 255 x 8 = 2040 bits long.

As further examples, 5 bit symbols could be used to form a codeword 31 symbols long, and 3 bit symbols would form a codeword seven symbols long. This latter size is small enough to permit some worked examples, and will be used further here. Figure 5.18 shows that in the seven-symbol codeword, five symbols of three bits each, A–E, are the data, and P and Q are the two redundant symbols. This simple example will locate and correct a single symbol in error. It does not matter, however, how many bits in the symbol are in error.

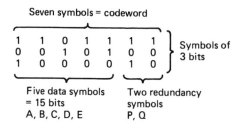

Figure 5.18 A Reed–Solomon codeword. As the symbols are of 3 bits, there can only be eight possible syndrome values. One of these is all zeros, the error-free case, and so it is only possible to point to seven errors; hence the codeword length of seven symbols. Two of these are redundant, leaving five data symbols.

The two check symbols are solutions to the following equations:

$$A \oplus B \oplus C \oplus D \oplus E \oplus P \oplus Q = 0$$

$$a^7A \oplus a^6B \oplus a^5C \oplus a^4D \oplus a^3E \oplus a^2P \oplus aQ = 0$$

where a is a constant. The original data A – E followed by the redundancy P and Q pass through the channel.

The receiver makes two checks on the message to see if it is a codeword. This is done by calculating syndromes using the following expressions, where the prime (') implies the received symbol which is not necessarily correct:

$$S_0 = A' \oplus B' \oplus C' \oplus D' \oplus E' \oplus P' \oplus Q'$$

(This is in fact a simple parity check.)

$$S_1 = a^7A' \oplus a^6B' \oplus a^5C' \oplus a^4D' \oplus a^3E' \oplus a^2P' \oplus aQ'$$

If two syndromes of all zeros are not obtained, there has been an error. The information carried in the syndromes will be used to correct the error. For the purpose of illustration, let it be considered that D' has been corrupted before moving to the general case. D' can be considered to be the result of adding an error of value E to the original value D such that $D' = D + E$:

As:

$$A \oplus B \oplus C \oplus D \oplus E \oplus P \oplus Q = 0$$

then:

$$A \oplus B \oplus C \oplus (D \oplus E) \oplus E \oplus P \oplus Q = E = S_0$$

As:

$$D' = D \oplus E$$

then:

$$D = D' \oplus E = D' \oplus S_0$$

Thus the value of the corrector is known immediately because it is the same as the parity syndrome S_0. The corrected data symbol is obtained simply by adding S_0 to the incorrect symbol.

At this stage, however, the corrupted symbol has not yet been identified, but this is equally straightforward.

As:

$$a^7A \oplus a^6B \oplus a^5C \oplus a^4D \oplus a^3E \oplus a^2P \oplus aQ = 0$$

Then:

$$a^7A \oplus a^6B \oplus a^5C \oplus a^4(D \oplus E) \oplus a^3E \oplus a^2P \oplus aQ = a^4E = S_1$$

Thus the syndrome S_1 is the error bit pattern E, but it has been raised to a power of a which is a function of the position of the error symbol in the block. If the position of the error is in symbol k, then k is the locator value and:

$$S_0 \times a^k = S_1$$

Hence:

$$a^k = \frac{S_1}{S^0}$$

The value of k can be found by multiplying S_0 by various powers of a until the product is the same as S_1. Then the power of a necessary is equal to k. The use of the descending powers of a in the codeword calculation is now clear because the error is then multiplied by a different power of a dependent upon its position. S_1 is known as the locator, because it gives the position of the error. The process of finding the error position by experiment is known as a Chien search.[7]

5.15 R–S Calculations

Whilst the expressions above show that the values of P and Q are such that the two syndrome expressions sum to zero, it is not yet clear how P and Q are calculated from the data. Expressions for P and Q can be found by solving the two R–S equations simultaneously. This has been done in Appendix 5.1. The following expressions must be used to calculate P and Q from the data in order to satisfy the codeword equations. These are:

$$P = a^6A \oplus aB \oplus a^2C \oplus a^5D \oplus a^3E$$

$$Q = a^2A \oplus a^3B \oplus a^6C \oplus a^4D \oplus aE$$

In both the calculation of the redundancy shown here and the calculation of the corrector and the locator it is necessary to perform numerous multiplications and raising to powers. This appears to present a formidable calculation problem at both the encoder and the decoder. This would be the case if the calculations involved were conventionally executed. However, the calculations can be simplified by using logarithms. Instead of multiplying two numbers, their logarithms are added. In order to find the cube of a number, its logarithm is added three times. Division is performed by subtracting the logarithms. Thus all of the manipulations necessary can be achieved with addition or subtraction, which is straightforward in logic circuits.

The success of this approach depends upon the simple implementation of log tables. As was seen in Chapter 2, raising a constant, a, known as the *primitive element*, to successively higher powers in modulo-2 gives rise to a Galois field. Each element of the field represents a different power n of a. It is a fundamental of the R–S codes that all of the symbols used for data, redundancy and syndromes are considered to be elements of a Galois field. The number of bits in the symbol determines the size of the Galois field, and hence the number of symbols in the codeword.

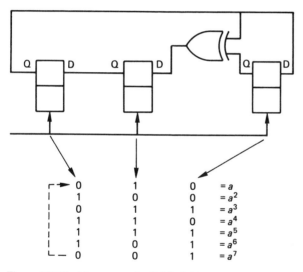

Figure 5.19 The bit patterns of a Galois field expressed as powers of the primitive element a. This diagram can be used as a form of log table in order to multiply binary numbers. Instead of an actual multiplication, the appropriate powers of a are simply added.

Figure 5.19 repeats a Galois field deduced in Chapter 2. The binary values of the elements are shown alongside the power of a they represent. In the R–S codes, symbols are no longer considered simply as binary numbers, but also as equivalent powers of a. In Reed–Solomon coding and decoding, each symbol will be multiplied by some power of a. Thus if the symbol is also known as a power of a it is only necessary to add the two powers. For example, if it is necessary to multiply the data symbol 100 by a^3, the calculation proceeds as follows, referring to Figure 5.19.

$100 = a^2$ so $100 \times a^3 = a^{(2 + 3)} = a^5 = 111$

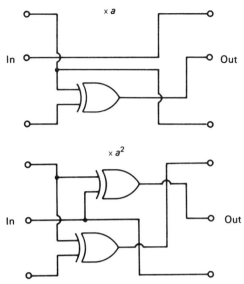

Figure 5.20 Some examples of GF multiplier circuits.

Note that the results of a Galois multiplication are quite different from binary multiplication. Because all products must be elements of the field, sums of powers which exceed seven wrap around by having seven subtracted. For example:

$$a^5 \times a^6 = a^{11} = a^4 = 110$$

Figure 5.20 shows some examples of circuits which will perform this kind of multiplication. Note that they require a minimum amount of logic.

Input data	A	101	$a^6 A = 111$	$a^2 A = 010$
	B	100	$a\ B = 011$	$a^3 B = 111$
	C	010	$a^2 C = 011$	$a^6 C = 001$
	D	100	$a^5 D = 001$	$a^4 D = 101$
	E	111	$a^3 E = 010$	$a\ E = 101$
Check symbols	P	100 ←	———— 100	╱ 100
	Q	100 ←		

Codeword	A	101	$a^7 A = 101$
	B	100	$a^6 B = 010$
	C	010	$a^5 C = 101$
	D	100	$a^4 D = 101$
	E	111	$a^3 E = 010$
	P	100	$a^2 P = 110$
	Q	100	$a\ Q = 011$
	$S_0 = \overline{000}$		$S_1 = \overline{000}$ ← Both syndromes zero

Figure 5.21 Five data symbols A–E are used as terms in the generator polynomials derived in Appendix 5.1 to calculate two redundant symbols P and Q. An example is shown at the top. Below is the result of using the codeword symbols A–Q as terms in the checking polynomials. As there is no error, both syndromes are zero.

A, B, C, D, E

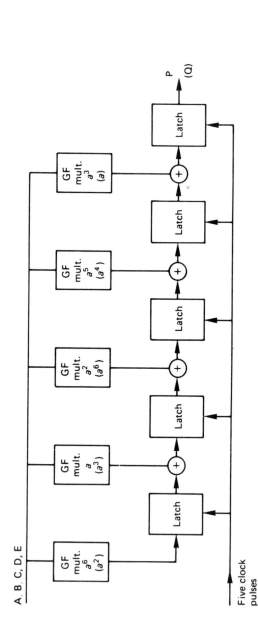

Figure 5.22 If the five data symbols of Figure 5.21 are supplied to this circuit in sequence, after five clocks, one of the check symbols will appear at the output. Terms without brackets will calculate P, bracketed terms calculate Q.

Figure 5.21 shows an example of the Reed–Solomon encoding process. The Galois field shown in Figure 5.19 has been used, having the primitive element a = 010. At the beginning of the calculation of P, the symbol A is multiplied by a.[6] This is done by converting A to a power of a. According to Figure 5.19, 101 = a^6 and so the product will be $a^{(6+6)} = a^{12} = a^5 = 111$. In the same way, B is multiplied by a, and so on, and the products are added modulo-2. A similar process is used to calculate Q.

Figure 5.22 shows a circuit which can calculate P or Q. The symbols A – E are presented in succession, and the circuit is clocked for each one. On the first clock, a^6A is stored in the left-hand latch. If B is now provided at the input, the second GF multiplier produces aB and this is added to the output of the first latch and when clocked will be stored in the second latch which now contains a^6A + aB. The process continues in this fashion until the complete expression for P is available in the right-hand latch. The intermediate contents of the right-hand latch are ignored.

The entire codeword now exists, and can be recorded or transmitted. Figure 5.21 also demonstrates that the codeword satisfies the checking equations. The modulo-2 sum of the seven symbols, S_0, is 000 because each column has an even number of ones. The calculation of S_1 requires multiplication by descending powers of a. The modulo-2 sum of the products is again zero. These calculations confirm that the redundancy calculation was properly carried out.

Figure 5.23 gives three examples of error correction based on this codeword. The erroneous symbol is marked with a dash. As there has been an error, the syndromes S_0 and S_1 will not be zero.

7	A	101	a^7A = 101	$\frac{S_1}{S_0} = \frac{a^4}{1} = a^4$
6	B	100	a^6B = 010	
5	C	010	a^5C = 101	
4	D′	101	a^4D′ = 011 ←	$k = 4$
3	E	111	a^3E = 010	
2	P	100	a^2P = 110	D′ + S_0 = 101 + 001
1	Q	100	a Q = 011	D = 100
	S_0 =	001	S_1 = 110	

7	A	101	a^7A = 101	$\frac{S_1}{S_0} = \frac{1}{a^2} = \frac{1}{a^2} \times \frac{a^5}{a^5} = a^5$
6	B	100	a^6B = 010	
5	C′	110	a^5C = 100 ←	$k = 5$
4	D	100	a^4D = 101	
3	E	111	a^3E = 010	
2	P	100	a^2P = 110	C′ + S_0 = 110 + 100
1	Q	100	a Q = 011	C = 010
	S_0 =	100	S_1 = 001	

7	A′	111	a^7A = 111 ←	$\frac{S_1}{S_0} = \frac{a}{a} = 001 = a^7$
6	B	100	a^6B = 010	
5	C	010	a^5C = 101	
4	D	100	a^4D = 101	$k = 7$
3	E	111	a^3E = 010	
2	P	100	a^2P = 110	A′ + S_0 = 111 + 010
1	Q	100	a Q = 011	A = 101
	S_0 =	010	S_1 = 010	

Figure 5.23 Three examples of error location and correction. The number of bits in error in a symbol is irrelevant; if all three were wrong, S_0 would be 111, but correction is still possible.

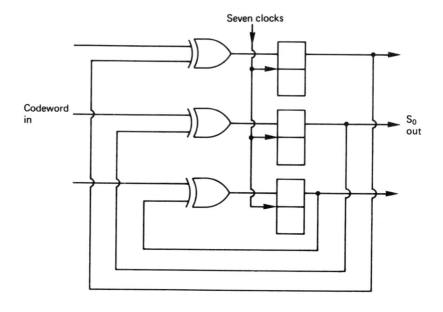

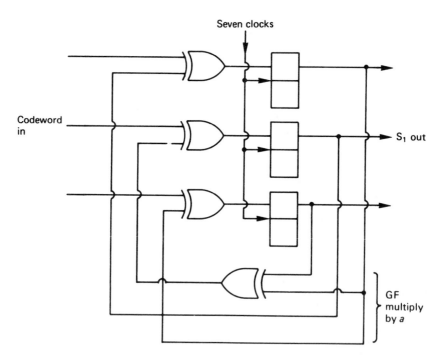

Figure 5.24 Circuits for parallel calculation of syndromes S_0, S_1. S_0 is a simple parity check. S_1 has a GF multiplication by a in the feedback, so that A is multiplied by a^7, B is multiplied by a^6, etc., and all are summed to give S_1.

Figure 5.24 shows circuits suitable for parallel calculation of the two syndromes at the receiver. The S_0 circuit is a simple parity checker which accumulates the modulo-2 sum of all symbols fed to it. The S_1 circuit is more subtle, because it contains a Galois field (GF) multiplier in a feedback loop, such that early symbols fed in are raised to higher powers than later symbols because they have been recirculated through the GF multiplier more often. It is possible to compare the operation of these circuits with the example of Figure 5.23 and with subsequent examples to confirm that the same results are obtained.

5.16 Correction by erasure

In the examples of Figure 5.23, two redundant symbols P and Q have been used to locate and correct one error symbol. If the positions of errors are known by some separate mechanism (see product codes, Section 5.18) the locator need not be calculated. The simultaneous equations may instead be solved for two correctors. In this case the number of symbols which can be corrected is equal to the number of redundant symbols. In Figure 5.25(a) two errors have taken place, and it is known that they are in symbols C and D. Since S_0 is a simple parity check, it will reflect the modulo-2 sum of the two errors. Hence:

$$S_0 = E_C \oplus E_D$$

The two errors will have been multiplied by different powers in S_1, such that:

$$S_1 = a^5 E_C + a^4 E_D$$

These two equations can be solved, as shown in the figure, to find E_C and E_D, and the correct value of the symbols will be obtained by adding these correctors to the erroneous values. It is, however, easier to set the values of the symbols in error to zero. In this way the nature of the error is rendered irrelevant and it does not enter the calculation. Thas setting of symbols to zero gives rise to the term erasure. In this case:

$$S_0 = C \oplus D$$
$$S_1 = a^5 C + a^4 D$$

Erasing the symbols in error makes the errors equal to the correct symbol values and these are found more simply as shown in Figure 5.25(b)

Practical systems will be designed to correct more symbols in error than in the simple examples given here. If it is proposed to correct by erasure an arbitrary number of symbols in error given by t, the codeword must be divisible by t different polynomials. Alternatively if the errors must be located and corrected, $2t$ polynomials will be needed. These will be of the form $(x + a^x)$ where n takes all values up to t or $2t$. a is the primitive element discussed in Chapter 2.

Where four symbols are to be corrected by erasure, or two symbols are to be located and corrected, four redundant symbols are necessary, and the codeword polynomial must then be divisible by:

$$(x + a^0)(x + a^1)(x + a^2)(x + a^3)$$

Upon receipt of the message, four syndromes must be calculated, and the four correctors or the two error patterns and their positions are determined by solving

$$
\begin{array}{llll}
A & 1\dot{0}1 & a^7A = & 101 \\
B & 100 & a^6B = & 010 \\
(C \oplus E_C) & 001 & a^5 (C \oplus E_C) & \dot{1}11 \\
(D \oplus E_D) & 0\dot{1}0 & a^4 (D \oplus E_D) & 111 \\
E & 111 & a^3E = & 010 \\
P & \dot{1}00 & a^2P = & 110 \\
Q & 1\dot{0}\dot{0} & a\,Q = & 011 \\
S_1 & = \overline{1\dot{0}\dot{1}} & S_1 = & \overline{000}
\end{array}
$$

$S_0 = E_C \oplus E_D \qquad S_1 = a^5E_C \oplus a^4E_D$

$S_1 = a^5E_C \oplus a^4 (S_0 \oplus E_C)$

$\quad = a^5E_C \oplus a^4S_0 \oplus a^4E_C$

$\therefore E_C = \dfrac{S_1 \oplus a^4S_0}{a^5 \oplus a^4} = \dfrac{000 \oplus 011}{001} = 011$

$C = (C \oplus E_C) \oplus E_C = 001 \oplus 011 = \underline{010}$

$S_1 = a^5 (S_0 \ominus E_D) \oplus a^4E_D$

$\quad = a^5S_0 \oplus a^5E_D \oplus a^4E_D$

$\therefore E_D = \dfrac{S_1 \oplus a^5S_0}{a^5 \oplus a^4} = \dfrac{000 \oplus 110}{001} = 110$

$D = (D \oplus E_D) + E_D = 010 \oplus 110 = \underline{100} \qquad$ **(a)**

$$
\begin{array}{lll}
A & 101 & a^7A = 101 \\
B & 100 & a^6B = 010 \quad S_0 = C \oplus D \\
C & \underline{000} & a^5C = \underline{000} \\
D & \underline{000} & a^4D = \underline{000} \quad S_1 = a^5C \oplus a^4D \\
E & 111 & a^3E = 010 \\
P & 100 & a^2P = 110 \\
Q & 100 & a\,Q = 011 \\
S_0 & =\underline{100} & S_1 = 000
\end{array}
$$

$S_1 = a^5S_0 \oplus a^5D \oplus a^4D = a^5S_0 \oplus D$

$\therefore D = S_1 \oplus a^5S_0 = 000 \oplus 100 = \underline{100}$

$S_1 = a^5C \oplus a^4C \oplus a^4S_0 = C \oplus a^4S_0$

$\therefore C = S_1 \oplus a^4S_0 = 000 \oplus 010 = \underline{010}$

(b)

Figure 5.25 If the location of errors is known, then the syndromes are a known function of the two errors as shown in (a). It is, however, much simpler to set the incorrect symbols to zero, i.e. to *erase* them as in (b). Then the syndromes are a function of the wanted symbols and correction is easier.

four simultaneous equations. This generally requires an iterative procedure, and a number of algorithms have been developed for the purpose.[8-10] Modern DVTR formats use 8 bit R–S codes and erasure extensively. The primitive polynomial commonly used with GF(256) is:

$$x^8 + x^4 + x^3 + x^2 + 1$$

The codeword will be 255 bytes long but will often be shortened by puncturing. The larger Galois fields require less redundancy, but the computational problem increases. LSI chips have been developed specifically for R–S decoding in many high volume formats.[11]

5.17 Interleaving

The concept of bit interleaving was introduced in connection with a single-bit correcting code to allow it to correct small bursts. With burst-correcting codes such as Reed–Solomon, bit interleave is unnecessary. In most channels, particularly high-density recording channels used for digital video or audio, the burst size may be many bytes rather than bits, and to rely on a code alone to correct such errors would require a lot of redundancy. The solution in this case is to employ symbol interleaving, as shown in Figure 5.26. Several codewords

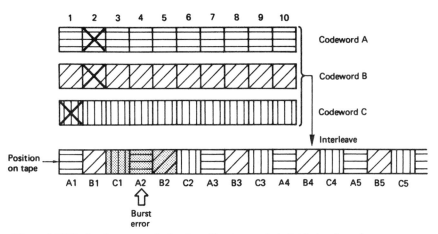

Figure 5.26 The interleave controls the size of burst errors in individual codewords.

are encoded from input data, but these are not recorded in the order they were input, but are physically reordered in the channel, so that a real burst error is split into smaller bursts in several codewords. The size of the burst seen by each codeword is now determined primarily by the parameters of the interleave, and Figure 5.27 shows that the probability of occurrence of bursts with respect to the burst length in a given codeword is modified. The number of bits in the interleave word can be made equal to the burst-correcting ability of the code in the knowledge that it will be exceeded only very infrequently.

There are a number of different ways in which interleaving can be performed. Figure 5.28 shows that in block interleaving, words are reordered within blocks which are themselves in the correct order. This approach is attractive for rotary-head recorders, because the scanning process naturally divides the tape up into blocks. The block interleave is achieved by writing samples into a memory in sequential address locations from a counter, and reading the memory with non-sequential addresses from a sequencer. The effect is to convert a one-dimensional sequence of samples into a two-dimensional structure having rows and columns.

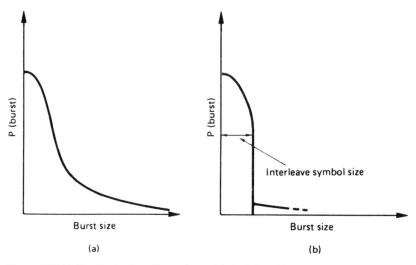

Figure 5.27 (a) The distribution of burst sizes might look like this. (b) Following interleave, the burst size within a codeword is controlled to that of the interleave symbol size, except for gross errors which have low probability.

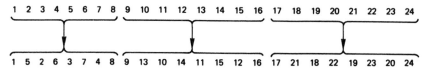

Figure 5.28 In block interleaving, data are scrambled within blocks which are themselves in the correct order.

Rotary-head recorders naturally interleave spatially on the tape. Figure 5.29 shows that a single, large tape defect becomes a series of small defects owing to the geometry of helical scanning.

The alternative to block interleaving is convolutional interleaving where the interleave process is endless. In Figure 5.30 symbols are assembled into short blocks and then delayed by an amount proportional to the position in the block.

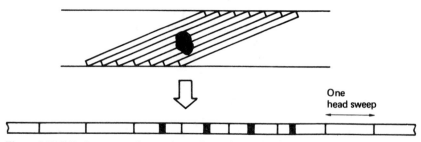

Figure 5.29 Helical-scan recorders produce a form of mechanical interleaving, because one large defect on the medium becomes distributed over several head sweeps.

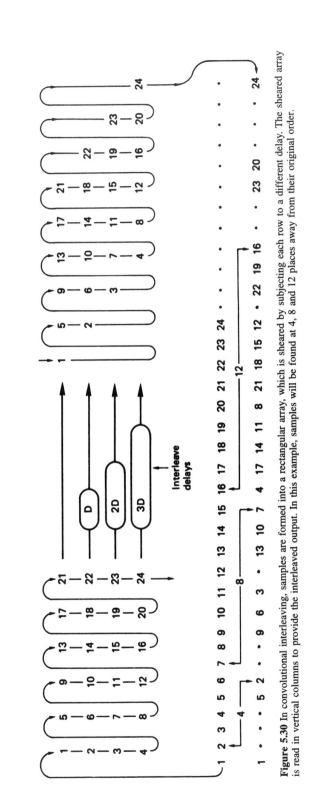

Figure 5.30 In convolutional interleaving, samples are formed into a rectangular array, which is sheared by subjecting each row to a different delay. The sheared array is read in vertical columns to provide the interleaved output. In this example, samples will be found at 4, 8 and 12 places away from their original order.

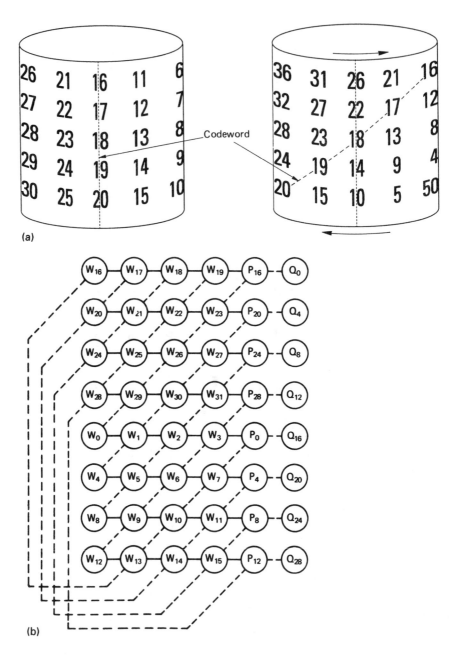

Figure 5.31 A block-completed convolutional interleave can be considered to be the result of shearing a cylinder as in (a). This results in horizontal and diagonal codewords as shown in (b).

It will be seen from the figure that the delays have the effect of shearing the symbols so that columns on the left side of the diagram become diagonals on the right. When the columns on the right are read, the convolutional interleave will be obtained. Convolutional interleave works well in transmission applications where there is no natural track break. Convolutional interleave has the advantage of requiring less memory to implement than a block code. This is because a block code requires the entire block to be written into the memory before it can be read, whereas a convolutional code requires only enough memory to cause the required delays. Now that RAM is relatively inexpensive, convolutional interleave is less popular.

It is possible to make a convolutional code of finite size by making a loop. Figure 5.31(a) shows that symbols are written in columns on the outside of a cylinder. The cylinder is then sheared or twisted, and the columns are read. The result is a block-completed convolutional interleave shown at (b). This technique is used in the audio blocks of the Video-8 format.

5.18 Product codes

In the presence of burst errors alone, the system of interleaving works very well, but it is known that in most practical channels there are also uncorrelated errors of a few bits due to noise. Figure 5.32 shows an interleaving system where a dropout-induced burst error has occurred which is at the maximum correctable size. All three codewords involved are working at their limit of one symbol. A random error due to noise in the vicinity of a burst error will cause the correction power of the code to be exceeded. Thus a random error of a single bit causes a further entire symbol to fail. This is a weakness of an interleave solely designed to handle dropout-induced bursts. Practical high-density equipment must address the problem of noise-induced or random errors and burst errors occurring at the same time. This is done by forming codewords both before and after the interleave process. In block interleaving, this results in a *product code*, whereas in the case of convolutional interleave the result is called *cross-interleaving*.

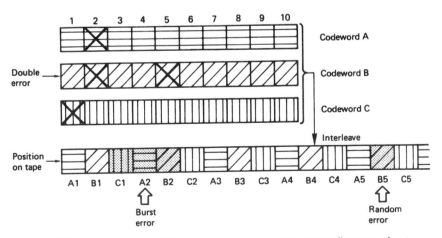

Figure 5.32 The interleave system falls down when a random error occurs adjacent to a burst.

Figure 5.33 shows that in a product code the redundancy calculated first and checked last is called the outer code, and the redundancy calculated second and checked first is called the inner code. The inner code is formed along tracks on the medium. Random errors due to noise are corrected by the inner code and do not impair the burst-correcting power of the outer code. Burst errors are declared uncorrectable by the inner code which flags the bad samples on the way into the de-interleave memory. The outer code reads the error flags in order to correct the flagged symbols by erasure. The error flags are also known as erasure flags. As it does not have to compute the error locations, the outer code needs half as much redundancy for the same correction power. Thus the inner code redundancy does

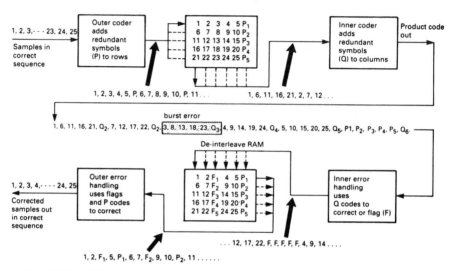

Figure 5.33 In addition to the redundancy P on rows, inner redundancy Q is also generated on columns. On replay, the Q code checker will pass on flags F if it finds an error too large to handle itself. The flags pass through the de-interleave process and are used by the outer error correction to identify which symbol in the row needs correcting with P redundancy. The concept of crossing two codes in this way is called a product code.

not raise the code overhead. The combination of codewords with interleaving in several dimensions yields an error-protection strategy which is truly synergistic, in that the end result is more powerful than the sum of the parts. Needless to say, the technique is used extensively in modern DVTR formats.

5.19 Introduction to error correction in DVTR

The interleave and error-correction systems of D-3 will now be discussed by way of a representative example. Details of other formats will be found in Chapter 9. Figure 5.34 shows a conceptual block diagram of the system which shows that D-3 uses a product code formed by producing Reed–Solomon codewords at right angles across an array. The array is formed in a memory which contains an entire field (after two-way distribution) of data, and the layout used in PAL can be seen in Figure 5.35. Incoming samples (bytes) are written into the array in columns.

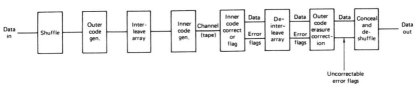

Figure 5.34 Block diagram of error-correction strategy of D-3 DVTR.

Each column is then made into a codeword by the addition of 8 bytes of redundancy. These are the outer codewords. Each row of the array is then formed into eight inner code words by the addition of eight bytes of redundancy to each. In order to make a recording, the memory is read in rows, and one inner codeword fits into one sync block along the track. Every sync block in an eight-field sequence is given a unique header address. This process continues until the entire contents of the array have been laid on tape. Owing to the use of segmentation this will require three segments in NTSC and four in PAL.

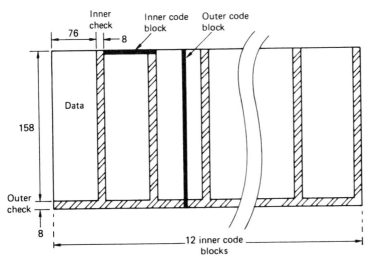

Figure 5.35 The field array of PAL D-3. Incoming data are written in columns and eight R–S bytes are added to make outer codes. The array is split into 12 equal parts, and one row of each part has eight R–S bytes added to make an inner code. There are thus 12 inner code blocks across the array. One inner code is held in one sync block and in practice the codeword is extended to protect the ID pattern.

Writing the memory in columns and reading in rows achieves the necessary interleave.

On replay, a combination of random errors and burst errors will occur. Data will come from tape in the sequence of the inner codewords. The 8,14 channel decoder may provide error flags to assist the inner decoder. In D-3 each inner code has 8 bytes of redundancy, so it would be possible to locate and correct up to 4 bytes in error or correct up to eight flagged errors in the codeword. This, however is not done, because it is better to limit the correction power and use the remaining redundancy to decrease the probability of miscorrection. In this way, a smaller number of random errors are corrected with a high degree of confidence. Larger errors cause the entire inner codeword to be declared corrupt, and it is written into the appropriate row of the de-interleave array as all zeros, with error flags set. When all of the rows of the array are completed, it is possible to begin processing the columns. A burst error on tape which destroys one or more inner codewords will result in single-byte errors with flags in many different outer codewords. The presence of the error flags means that the outer code does not need to compute the position of the errors, so the full power of the outer code redundancy is available for correction. The eight redundancy bytes of D-3 can correct eight error bytes. The process of using error flags to assist a code is called erasure. It will be evident that enormous damage must be done to the tape track before 4 bytes are corrupted in a single outer codeword, which gives high resistance to dropouts and tape scratches.

5.20 Concealment and shuffle

In the event of a gross error, correction may not be possible, and some bytes may be declared uncorrectable. In this case the errors must be concealed by interpolation. In a full-bit-rate format, the distribution of alternate samples into different tracks means that an uncorrectable tape track error causes half of the samples in a certain area of the image to be lost, but the remainder give a good impression of the image to the interpolator. However, because of the regular structure of the product code block, uncorrectable burst errors would show up on the screen as a rectangular area containing interpolations. This would appear slightly softer than the rest of the picture. The eye is extremely good at finding such regularity, so the visibility is higher than might be expected. The solution to this problem is to perform a two-dimensional pseudo-random shuffle on the position of video samples before generating the product code. The reverse shuffle is performed on replay. This has the effect of breaking up the regular block of errors into individual errors located over a considerable area. The positions of interpolated samples due to an uncorrected error now form a pseudo-random pattern with much decreased visibility.

The shuffle is also necessary to allow a reasonable picture to be obtained in shuttle. In this mode, only part of the data can be replayed, and the shuffle ensures that samples are updated over as wide a screen area as possible. The shuffle parameters are a compromise between the requirements of concealment and shuttle picture.

In a format using data reduction, uncorrectable errors cause more difficulty. There is an obvious problem that the data reduction process is designed to reduce natural redundancy in the source data, and this must make concealment more difficult. Generally, data-reduced formats must use a larger amount of error-correction redundancy in order to reduce the incidence of concealment. For example, Digital Betacam uses 20% redundancy compared with 16% for D-3, although D-3 has a recording density about 35% higher. There are further less obvious problems. In a DCT-based system, it is coefficients which are recorded, not pixel values. A coefficient in error will affect the reproduction of typically 32 pixels. In order to obtain picture-in-shuttle, and to keep deserialization reasonably simple, all of the coefficients for one DCT block must be recorded together in the same sync block. In the case of an uncorrectable error, the entire DCT block will be lost. Unfortunately the block-based data reduction cannot be preceded by a pixel shuffle as this destroys the natural redundancy of the image by raising the high frequency content. A shuffle can and should still be used, but it must shuffle entire DCT blocks. The block based shuffle is easily visible in shuttle, where the picture will be noticeably mosaiced. In fact this is an easy way to establish the block size of any format. The block based shuffle means that uncorrectable errors result in single DCT blocks spread about the screen. Concealment of an entire block is more difficult than concealment of a single pixel, but in most DVTR formats the compression factor is relatively mild and there is still some redundancy left. The DC coefficient of the missing block is the most visible, but this can be obtained by spatially averaging the DC coefficients of the surrounding blocks. This technique cannot, however, give reliable results for higher spatial frequencies. A better technique is to rely upon data from a previous field which, because of interlace, describe lines in between the missing lines. An entire missing block can then be concealed by interpolation. Changing the shuffle from field to field ensures that a tape scratch cannot destroy data from the same place in every field. Further details of shuffle mechanisms will be found in Chapter 7.

5.21 Editing interleaved recordings

The interleave, de-interleave, time compression and timebase-correction processes cause delay and any data reduction stages will further increase that delay. Confidence replay takes place later than the distance between record and replay heads would indicate.

In analog recording, there is a direct relationship between the distance down the track and the time through the recording. A further consequence of interleaving in digital recorders is that the reordering of samples means that this relationship is lost.

Editing must be undertaken with care. In a block-based interleave, edits can be made at block boundaries so that coded blocks are not damaged, but these blocks may be as big as a field. This is adequate for normal editing using vision cuts, but such blocks are usually too large for accurate audio editing, and editing within the video field (so-called vertical editing) to perform dissolves or wipes is impossible.

The only way in which accurate editing can be performed in the presence of interleave is to use a read–modify–write approach, where an entire field is read into memory and de-interleaved to the real-time sample sequence. Any desired part of the field can be replaced with new material before it is re-interleaved and re-recorded. In recorders which can only record or play at one time, an edit of this kind would take a long time because of all of the tape repositioning needed. With extra heads read–modify–write editing can be performed dynamically. The replay head plays back the existing recording, and this is de-interleaved to the normal sample sequence, a process which introduces a delay. The sample stream now passes through a signal processor which can insert external material. The output of the processor is then fed to the record interleave stage which introduces further delay. This signal passes to the record heads which must be positioned so that the original recording on the tape reaches them at the same time that the re-encoded signal arrives, despite the encode and decode delays. In a rotary-head recorder this can be done by positioning the record heads at a different height to the replay heads so that they reach the same tracks on different revolutions.

The process will be detailed in chapter 7.

Appendix 5.1 Calculation of Reed–Solomon generator polynomials

For a Reed–Solomon codeword over $GF(2^3)$, there will be seven 3 bit symbols. For the location and correction of one symbol, there must be two redundant symbols P and Q, leaving A–E for data.

The following expressions must be true, where a is the primitive element of $x^3 \oplus x \oplus 1$ and $\oplus$ is XOR throughout:

$$A \oplus B \oplus C \oplus D \oplus E \oplus P \oplus Q = 0 \qquad (1)$$

$$a^7A \oplus a^6B \oplus a^5C \oplus a^4D \oplus a^3E \oplus a^2P \oplus aQ = 0 \qquad (2)$$

Dividing Eqn (2) by a:

$$a^6A \oplus a^5B \oplus a^4C \oplus a^3D \oplus a^2E \oplus aP \oplus Q = 0$$
$$= A \oplus B \oplus C \oplus D \oplus E \oplus P \oplus Q$$

Cancelling Q, and collecting terms:

$$(a^6 \oplus 1)A \oplus (a^5 \oplus 1)B \oplus (a^4 \oplus 1)C \oplus (a^3 \oplus 1)D \oplus (a^2 \oplus 1)E = (a \oplus 1)P$$

Using Figure 5.19 to calculate $(a^n \oplus 1)$, e.g. $a^6 \oplus 1 = 101 \oplus 001 = 100 = a^2$:

$$a^2A \oplus a^4B \oplus a^5C \oplus aD \oplus a^6E = a^3P$$
$$a^6A \oplus aB \oplus a^2C \oplus a^5D \oplus a^3E = P$$

Multiply Eqn (1) by a^2 and equating to (2):

$$a^2A \oplus a^2B \oplus a^2C \oplus a^2D \oplus a^2E \oplus a^2P \oplus a^2Q = 0$$
$$= a^7A \oplus a^6B \oplus a^5C \oplus a^4D \oplus a^3E \oplus a^2P \oplus aQ$$

Cancelling terms a^2P and collecting terms (remember $a^2 \oplus a^2 = 0$):

$$(a^7 \oplus a^2)A \oplus (a^6 \oplus a^2)B \oplus (a^5 \oplus a^2)C \oplus (a^4 \oplus a^2)D \oplus (a^3 \oplus a^2)E = (a^2 \oplus a)Q$$

Adding powers according to Figure 5.19, e.g. $a^7 \oplus a^2 = 001 \oplus 100 = 101 = a^6$:

$$a^6A \oplus B \oplus a^3C \oplus aD \oplus a^5E = a^4Q$$
$$a^2A \oplus a^3B \oplus a^6C \oplus a^4D \oplus aE = Q$$

References

1. MICHAELS, S.R., Is it Gaussian? *Electron. World Wireless World*, January, 1993 72–73
2. SHANNON, C.E., A mathematical theory of communication. *Bell System Tech. J.* **27** 379 (1948)
3. HAMMING, R.W., Error-detecting and error-correcting codes. *Bell Syst. Tech. J.*, **26**, 147–160 (1950).
4. FIRE, P., A class of multiple-error correcting codes for non-independent errors. *Sylvania Reconnaissance Systems Lab. Rep.*, RSL-E-2 (1959)
5. BOSSEN, D.C., B-adjacent error correction. *IBM J. Res. Dev.*, **14**, 402–408 (1970)
6. REED, I.S. and SOLOMON, G., Polynomial codes over certain finite fields. *J. Soc. Ind. Appl. Math.*, **8**, 300–304 (1960)

7. CHIEN, R.T., CUNNINGHAM, B.D. and OLDHAM, I.B., Hybrid methods for finding roots of a polynomial – with application to BCH decoding. *IEEE Trans. Inf. Theory.*, **IT-15**, 329–334 (1969)

8. BERLEKAMP, E.R., *Algebraic Coding Theory*. New York: McGraw-Hill (1967). Reprint edition: Laguna Hills CA: Aegean Park Press (1983)

9. SUGIYAMA, Y. *et al.*, An erasures and errors decoding algorithm for Goppa codes. *IEEE Trans. Inf. Theory*, **IT-22**, (1976)

10. PETERSON, W.W. and WELDON, E.J., *Error Correcting Codes* 2nd.edn., Cambridge MA: MIT Press (1972).

10. ONISHI, K., SUGIYAMA, K., ISHIDA, Y., KUSONOKI, Y. and YAMAGUCHI, T., An LSI for Reed–Solomon encoder/decoder. Presented at the 80th Audio Engineering Society Convention (Montreux, 1986), preprint 2316(A-4).

Chapter 6

Rotary-head tape transports

There is more to digital video recording than electronics. It depends heavily on mechanical engineering of the highest quality, and several extraordinarily accurate servo systems. This chapter looks at the techniques necessary to build and control a rotary-head transport.

6.1 Why rotary heads?

The helical-scan tape deck has more in common with the helicopter than just the geometrical terminology. The rotary-head recorder is to the fixed-head recorder what the rotary-winged flying machine is to the fixed-wing machine.

In both cases the rotary machine is more complex, more expensive, consumes more power, needs more maintenance and adjustment, and makes more noise than its fixed counterpart. If these were our only criteria, this comparison would amount to a condemnation. The truth of the matter is that all of these characteristics have to be accepted in order to obtain one particular attribute which cannot be obtained in any other way. In the case of the helicopter, the ability to stop dead in mid-air is vital for many applications. In the case of the helical recorder, the attribute obtained is the ability to record exceptional bandwidths with high density and to be able to replay at varying speed. If these are the requirements, there is no competition from simpler hardware. The problems have to be overcome by matching each one with the appropriate mechanical design, materials and control systems.

The attractions of the helical recorder are that the head-to-tape speed and hence bandwidth are high, whereas the linear tape speed is not. The space between tracks is determined by the linear tape speed, not by multitrack head technology. Chapter 4 showed how rotary-head machines make better use of the tape area, particularly if azimuth recording is used. The high head speed raises the frequency of offtape signals, and since output is proportional to frequency, playback signals are raised above head noise even with very narrow tracks.

With stationary heads, the offtape frequency is proportional to the linear tape speed and this makes recovery of data at other than the correct speed extremely difficult as data separators tend to work well only over a narrow speed range. In contrast, with rotary heads the scanning speed dominates head-to-tape speed and variations in the linear speed of the tape have a smaller effect, especially if the rotational speed is modulated by the linear speed. Thus picture-in-shuttle and slow motion are readily accommodated in a rotary-head machine.

6.2 Helical geometry

Figure 6.1 shows the general arrangement of the two major categories of rotary-head recorder. In transverse-scan recorders, relatively short tracks are recorded almost at right angles to the direction of tape motion by a rotating headwheel containing four or six heads. The transverse-scan approach allows for a compact construction and the signals replayed from the short tracks suffer relatively little timebase error. In helical-scan recorders, the tape is wrapped around the drum in such a way that it enters and leaves in two different positions along the drum axis. This causes the rotating heads to record long slanting tracks, with the penalty that the mechanism is rather larger. Timebase error is increased because of the longer tracks. In both approaches, the pitch of the tracks (defined as the

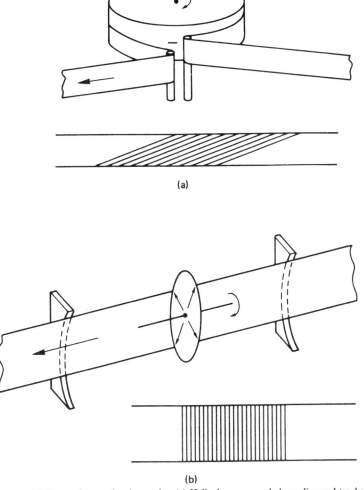

(a)

(b)

Figure 6.1 Types of rotary-head recorder. (a) Helical scan records long diagonal tracks. (b) Transverse scan records short tracks across the tape.

spacing between the same feature on successive tracks) is determined by the linear tape speed rather than by head design. The space between tracks can easily be made much smaller than in stationary-head recorders; in fact it can be zero or even negative.

The use of rotary heads was instrumental in the development of the first (analog) video recorders. As video signals consist of discrete lines and frames, it was possible to conceal the interruptions in the tracks of a rotary-head machine by making them coincident with the time when the CRT was blanked during flyback. The first video recorders developed by Ampex used the transverse-scan approach, with four evenly spaced heads on the rotor; hence the name quadruplex which was given to this system. The tracks were a little shorter than the 2 inch width of the tape, and several sweeps were necessary to build up a video frame. The geometry of the scanning was arranged so that one head would reach the end of a track just as the next head reached the beginning of the next track. The changeovers between the heads were made during the horizontal synchronizing pulses.

Variable-speed operation in rotary-head machines is obtained by deflecting the playback heads along the drum axis to follow the tape tracks. Periodically the heads will need to jump in order to omit or repeat a field. In transverse scan the number of tracks needed to accommodate one field is high, and the head deflection required to jump fields was virtually impossible to achieve.

In helical scanning, the tracks become longer, so fewer of them are needed to accommodate a field. Figure 6.2 shows that the head displacement needed for field jumping is then reduced.

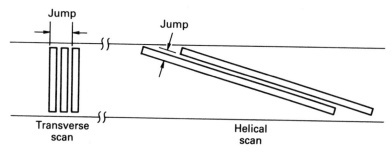

Figure 6.2 Helical scan results in longer tracks so a shorter distance needs to be jumped to miss out or repeat a field.

For professional use, the quadruplex format gave way to 1 inch analog C-format, which used helical scan and an almost total wrap to fit an entire field into a slant track about 15 in (380 mm) long. The changeover between tracks was then made in the vertical interval. Field jumps could then be made with a head displacement of single track.

In digital recorders the analog-to-digital conversion process represents the video signal in a form which requires a much smaller signal-to-noise ratio but with a much higher bandwidth. As a result, tracks on the tape are required to be narrower but longer. A single track containing an entire digital field would be impractically long and in practice fields are inevitably segmented into between

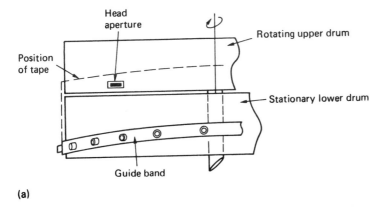

(a)

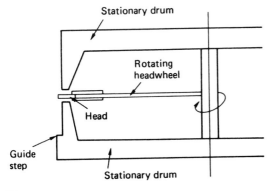

(b)

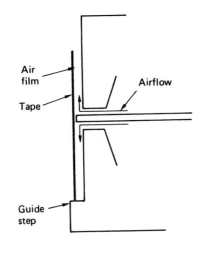

(c)

Figure 6.3 (a) Rotating-top-type scanner. The upper drum is slightly smaller than the lower drum due to the air film it develops. Helical band guides lower edge of tape. (b) Stationary-top scanner, where headwheel rotates in a slot between upper and lower drums. (c) Airflow in stationary-top scanner. Headwheel acts as a centrifugal pump, producing air film between tape and drums.

six (NTSC D-2, Digital Betacam) and 16 (D-5) tracks, but as the tracks are so much narrower in digital recorders the head displacement required is of the same order as on analog machines.

Figure 6.3 shows the two fundamental approaches to drum design. In the rotating upper drum system, one or more heads are mounted on the periphery of a revolving drum (also known as the scanner). The fixed base of the drum carries a helical ramp in the form of a step (see inset) or, for greater wear resistance, a hardened band which is suitably attached. Alternatively, both top and bottom of the drum are fixed, and the headwheel turns in a slot between them. Both approaches have advantages and disadvantages. The rotating upper drum approach is simpler to manufacture than the fixed upper drum, because the latter requires to be rigidly and accurately cantilevered out over the headwheel. The rotating part of the drum will produce an air film which raises its effective diameter. The rotor will thus need to be made a slightly different diameter to the lower drum, so that the tape sees a constant diameter as it rises up the drum. There will be plenty of space inside the rotor to install individually replaceable heads.

The fixed upper drum approach requires less power, since there is less air resistance. The headwheel acts as a centrifugal pump, and supplies air to the periphery of the slot where it lubricates both upper and lower drums, which are of the same diameter. It is claimed that this approach gives head contact which is more consistent over the length of the track, but it makes the provision of replaceable heads more difficult, and it is generally necessary to replace the entire headwheel as an assembly.

The presence of the air film means that the tape surface is not normally in contact with the cylindrical surface of the drum. Many drums have a matt etched finish, which does not become polished in service because there is no contact. The thickness of the air film is that where the pumping effect of the rotating drum reaches equilibrium with the tape tension. Figure 6.4 shows that the heads project

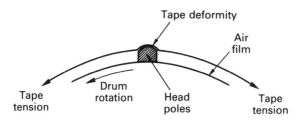

Figure 6.4 The tape is supported on an air film and the heads must project by a greater distance to achieve contact pressure.

out of the drum by a distance which must exceed the air film thickness in order to deform the tape slightly. In the absence of such a deformation there would be no contact pressure. It will be clear that the tape tension must be maintained accurately if the desired head contact pressure is to be obtained.

The creation and collapse of the deformities in the tape results in appreciable acoustic output, in the form of an irritating buzz. The production of a deformity in the tape due to head impact results in the propagation of a wave motion down

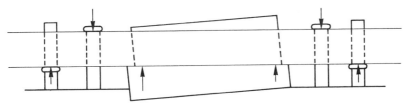

Figure 6.5 The head drum is shown here as if it had been unrolled to make the tape straight. It can then be seen that the drum step acts as a single flanged guide. The entry and exit guides work in conjunction with the drum step to locate the tape accurately.

the tape. This has a finite velocity and the velocity of the head must always be slower or it will produce a shock wave resulting in tremendous contact forces and rapid wear.

The presence of the air film means that the tape is only located around the drum by one edge. It must be arranged to follow the helical step without drifting away from it. Two sets of fixed guides, known as the entry and exit guides, lead the tape to and from the ramp. Figure 6.5 shows the tape path around the drum as if it had been unrolled into a plane. It will be seen that the step on the drum acts as a single flanged guide. The two fixed guides are arranged to contact only one edge of the tape each. The height and angle of the tape is set by the drum step and the lower flange of the outer guide. The tape is prevented from leaving that path by the upper flange of the inner guide. The reference flanges are fixed and will be made of some wear-resistant material such as ceramic. The other flanges may be spring loaded to accommodate slight variations in tape width.

The tape may wrap around the drum by various amounts. Some early analog machines used a complete circuit around the drum which led the tape to cross itself in the so-called Alpha wrap. The C-format used almost a complete circuit of the drum where the tape turns sharply around the entrance and exit guides in the shape of an Omega. These techniques were necessary to allow the use of a single head, which avoided banding in analog recording, but the result is a machine which is difficult to lace and cannot use a cassette. In DVTRs the tape

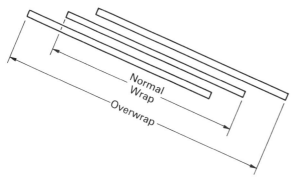

Figure 6.6 In helical scan recordings, successive tracks start at a different distance along the tape. These appear displaced around the drum and so an overwrap is needed to allow the whole track to be read by a deflected head.

passes between half-way and three-quarters of the way around the drum. The total angle of drum rotation for which the heads touch the tape is called the *mechanical wrap angle* or the *head contact angle*. The angle over which a useful recorded track is laid down is always somewhat shorter than the mechanical wrap angle. This is not only to allow the head/tape contact to settle after the initial impact, but also to allow the entire track to be read when the track-following heads are deflected. Figure 6.6 shows that successive tracks start at a different distance along the tape. Deflecting a head to follow a different track results in that track being read earlier or later than normal, and an extended wrap is necessary to guarantee head contact with a deflected head.

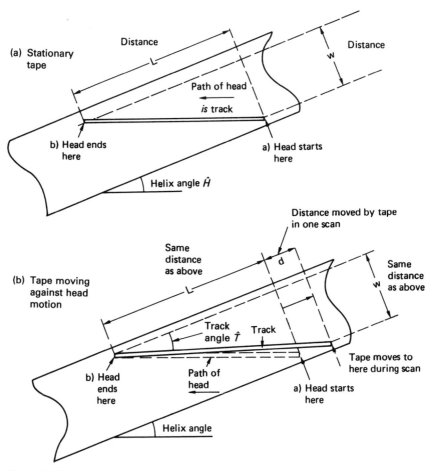

Figure 6.7 When the tape is moving the track laid down will be at an angle which is different from the helix angle, because the tape is in a different place at the end of the scan than at the beginning. Track length can be considered as two components L and w for stationary case, and L, d and w for moving case. Hence:.

$$\frac{w}{L} = \tan \hat{H} \text{ (part (a)) and } \frac{w}{L + d} = \tan \hat{T} \text{ (part (b)) or } \frac{w}{L - d} = \tan \hat{T} \text{ (part (c)).}$$

It will be evident that as the tape is caused to travel along the drum axis by the ramp, it actually takes on the path of a helix. The head rotates in a circular path, and so will record diagonal tracks across the width of the tape. So it is not really the scanning which is helical, it is the tape path.

In practical machines the tape may, in normal forward motion, travel up the ramp (e.g. D-2) or down the ramp (e.g. D-3). This reverses the slant angle of the tracks as will be seen in Figure 6.15. In addition, the drum can rotate either with (e.g. D-3) or against (e.g. D-2) the direction of linear tape motion.

If the tape is stationary, as in Figure 6.7(a), the head will constantly retrace the same track, and the angle of the track can be calculated by measuring the rise of the tape along the drum axis, and the circumferential distance over which this rise takes place. The latter can be obtained from the diameter of the drum and the wrap angle. The tangent of the *helix angle* is given by the rise over the distance. It can also be obtained by measuring the distance along the ramp corresponding to the wrap angle. In conjunction with the rise, this dimension will give the sine of the helix angle.

However, when the tape moves, the angle between the tracks and the edge of the tape will not be the helix angle. Figure 6.7(b) shows an example in which tape climbs up the drum which rotates against the direction of tape travel (e.g. D-2). When the head contact commences, the tape will be at a given location, but when the head contact ceases, the tape will have moved a certain linear distance and the resultant track will be longer.

Figure 6.7(c) shows what happens when the tape moves down the drum in the same direction as head rotation. In this case the track is shorter.

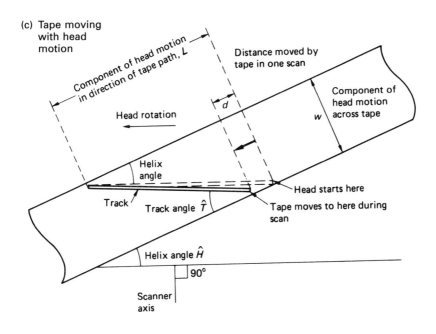

(c) Tape moving with head motion

Component of head motion in direction of tape path, *L*

Distance moved by tape in one scan

Head rotation

Component of head motion across tape

d

w

Helix angle

Head starts here

Track

Track angle $\hat{T}$

Tape moves to here during scan

Helix angle $\hat{H}$

90°

Scanner axis

In order to obtain the *track angle* it is necessary to take into account the tape motion. The length of the track resulting from scanning a stationary tape, which will be at the helix angle, can be resolved into two distances at right angles as shown in Figure 6.8. One of these is across the tape width, the other is along the length of the tape. The tangent of the helix angle will be the ratio of these lengths. If the length along the tape is corrected by adding or subtracting the distance the tape moves during one scan, depending upon whether tape motion aids or opposes drum rotation, the new ratio of the lengths will be the tangent of the track angle. In practice this process will often be reversed, because it is the track angle which is standardized in a given format, and the transport designer has to find a helix angle which will produce it.

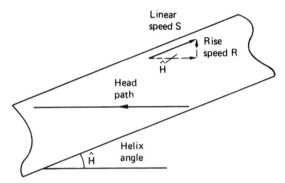

Figure 6.8 The linear speed of the tape S can be resolved into the speed of the tape along the scanner axis which is the rise speed R. $R = S \sin H$. Dividing the rise speed by the head passing frequency gives the track pitch. Head passing frequency is simply the number of heads multiplied by the scanner rotational frequency. Thus track pitch is proportional to tape speed.

It can also be seen from Figure 6.8 that when a normally recorded tape is stopped, the head must be deflected by a triangular waveform or ramp in order to follow the track. A further consequence of the track angle being different to the helix angle is that when azimuth recording is used, the azimuth angles at which the heads are mounted in the drum are not the same as the angles between the transitions and the edge of the track. One of the angles is slightly increased and one is slightly reduced. In D-3, for example, the difference is 0.017°.

The relative direction of drum and tape motion is unimportant, as both configurations work equally well. Often the direction is left undefined until many other parameters have been settled. If the segmentation and coding scheme proposed results in the wavelengths on tape being on the short side, opposite rotation will be chosen, as this lengthens the tracks and with it the wavelength. Sometimes the direction of rotation is a given; in Digital Betacam, playback of analog tapes was a requirement, so the rotation direction had to be the same as in analog Betacam.

Provided that the tape linear speed and drum speed remain the same, the theoretical track angle will remain the same. In practice this will only be the case if the tape tension is constant. Figure 6.9 shows that if the back tension changes, the effective length of the tape will also change, and with it the track angle. It will be evident that the result is a tracking error which increases towards the ends of the track. In addition the changed track length will alter the signal timing, advancing it at one end of the track whilst delaying it at the other, a phenomenon known as *skew*. As shown above, tension errors also affect the air film thickness and head contact pressure. All digital rotary-head recorders need some form of tape tension servo to maintain the tape tension around the drum constant irrespective of the size of the pack on the supply hub. In practice tension servos can only control the tension of the tape entering the drum. Since there will be friction between the edge of tape and the drum step, the tape tension will gradually increase between the entrance and exit guides, and so the tape will be extended more towards the exit guide. When the tape subsequently relaxes, it will be found that the track is actually curved. The ramp can be made to deviate from a theoretical helix to counteract this effect, or all drums can be built to the same design, so that effectively the track curvature becomes part of the format. Another possibility is to use some form of embedded track-following system, or a system like azimuth recording which tolerates residual tracking errors.

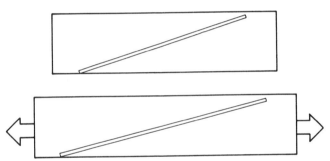

Figure 6.9 Tape is flexible, so change of tension will result in change of length. This causes a change in track angle known as skew shown exaggerated here.

When the tape direction reverses, the sense of the friction in the drum will also reverse, so the back tension has to increase to keep the mid-span tension the same as when going forward.

When verifying the track angle produced by a new design, it is usual to develop a tape which it has recorded with magnetic fluid, and take measurements under a travelling microscope. With the very small track widths of digital recorders, it is usually necessary to compensate for skew by applying standard tension to the tape when it is being measured, or by computing a correction factor for the track angle from the modulus of elasticity of the tape.

6.3 Track and head geometry

The *track pitch* is the distance, measured at right angles to the tracks, from a given place on one track to the same place on the next. The track pitch is a function of the linear tape speed, the head-passing frequency and the helix angle. It can be seen in Figure 6.8 that the linear speed and the helix angle determine the rise rate (or fall rate) with respect to the drum axis, and knowledge of the

(a)

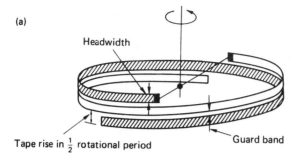

Headwidth

Tape rise in $\frac{1}{2}$ rotational period

Guard band

(b)

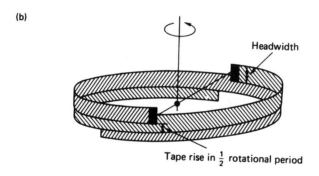

Headwidth

Tape rise in $\frac{1}{2}$ rotational period

(c)

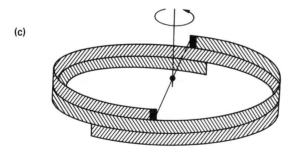

Figure 6.10 In the absence of azimuth recording, guard bands (a) must be left between the tracks. With azimuth recording, the record head may be wider than (b) or of the same width as (c) the track.

rotational period of the drum will allow the travel in one revolution to be calculated. If the travel is divided by the number of active heads on the drum, the result will be the track pitch. If everything else remains equal, the track pitch is proportional to the linear tape speed. Note that the track angle will also change with tape speed.

Figure 6.10(a) shows that in guard-band recording, the track pitch is equal to the width of the track plus the width of the guard band. The track width is determined by the width of the head poles, and the linear tape speed will be high enough so that the desired guard band is obtained. In guard band recording, the erase head is wider than the record head, which in turn is wider than the replay head, as shown in Figure 6.11(a). This ensures that despite inevitable

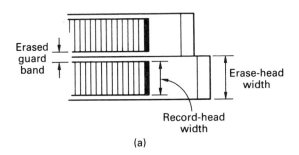

(a)

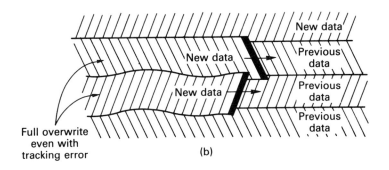

(b)

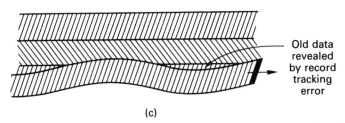

(c)

Figure 6.11 (a) The erase head is wider than the record head in guard-band recording. At (b) If the azimuth record head is wider than the track, full overwrite is obtained even with misalignment. At (c) if the azimuth record head is the same width as the track, misalignment results in failure to overwrite and an erase head becomes necessary.

misalignments, the entire area to be recorded is erased and the playback head is entirely over a recorded track.

In azimuth recording the situation is different, depending upon whether it is proposed to use flying erase heads. In Figure 6.10(b) the head width is greater than the track pitch, so that the tape does not rise far enough for one track to clear the previous one. Part of the previous track will be overwritten, so that the track width and the track pitch become identical. As Figure 6.11(b) shows, this approach guarantees that, when re-recording, previous tracks are fully over-written as the overlapping heads cover the entire tape area at least once, in places twice. For some purposes, flying erase heads are not then necessary.

The alternative shown in Figure 6.10(c) is for the track width to be exactly the same as the track pitch so there is no overlapping. In this case misalignment during re-recording can allow a thin strip of a previous track to survive unless a flying erase head is used. This is shown in Figure 6.11(c).

6.4 Head configurations

There is some freedom in the positioning of heads in the drum. Figure 6.12(a) shows a drum which carries four heads spaced evenly around the periphery. All of the heads are at the same height on the drum axis, which means that they would all pass the same point in space as the drum rotates.

One revolution of such a drum would lay down four evenly spaced tracks on the tape, and would play them back equally well. With a wrap angle of 180°, two heads would be in contact with the tape at any one time, and so the data rate of an individual head will be half the total.

If it is necessary to play back at variable speed, each of the heads will need to deflect on its own actuator, and will need to be individually controlled, so the cost of implementation will be rather high. An alternative approach is shown in Figure 6.12(b) where the heads are mounted in pairs at 180°. The same tape format can be recorded, provided that the heads in each pair are mounted in different planes. The separation between the head planes depends on the track pitch and the angular separation betwen the heads. If this geometry is correct, the same format will result, but the time at which the various tracks are laid down will be different, as the figure shows. The tracks are effectively written in pairs, known as *segments*. No problem will arise provided that the record and reproduce electronics are designed to expect to transfer data at the appropriate time. The main advantage of this approach is that there is now only a requirement for two head positioners, which is a great simplification of the drum.

The physical stagger between the heads is necessary whether the heads are intended for azimuth recording or guard-band recording. In both cases the head is larger than the track it writes, due to the poles being milled away in the area of the gap. It is not possible to put the heads side by side without a large guard band resulting. Figure 6.13 shows that staggering the heads allows the guard band to be any size, even negative in azimuth applications.

The heads in the segment are staggered and if the recording waveforms in the two heads are synchronous, diagonal tracks will begin in slightly different places along the tape as is evident in the D-2 format. Alternatively it is possible to delay the record signal to one of the heads so that both tracks begin and end in the same place. This is done, for example, in D-3/D-5 and as a result the edit gaps between sectors line up in adjacent tracks allowing the use of a single flying erase head

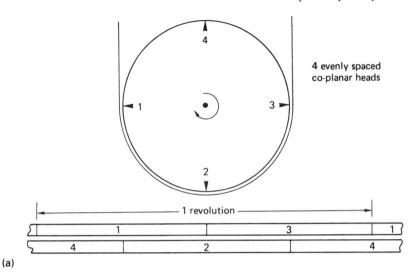

(a)

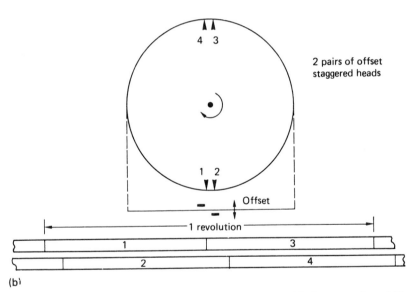

(b)

Figure 6.12 (a) Evenly spaced heads in a single plane require individual actuators for variable speed. (b) Two of the heads are slid along the tape track to give pairs of offset-staggered heads. Same tape format results if signal timing to heads is suitably modified.

shared between the tracks. The bit error rate from the trailing head of a staggered head pair is generally slightly worse than that of the leading head because it is working in the shock-wave pattern set up by the first head, and flies over any particles of debris which the first head loosens.

The stagger is necessary to allow the two heads physically to overlap, but it also means that the transverse displacement between the two heads is not equal to the track pitch. Figure 6.14 shows that the longitudinal offset between the

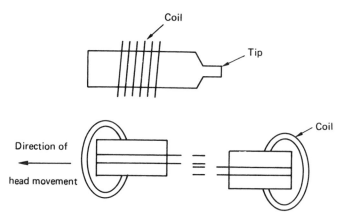

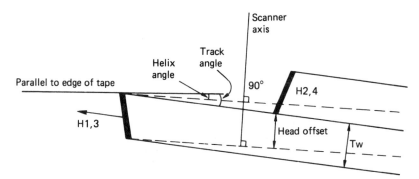

Figure 6.13 Staggering the heads allows any relative track spacing to be used.

heads must take into account the fact that the tape is moving down the drum as the heads pass. By the time the trailing head has reached a given point on a track made by the leading head, that track will be lower on the drum than it was when it was written, and so the trailing head must be positioned lower on the drum to put the next track in the correct place.

Figure 6.14 The movement of the tape causes the track angle to be different from the helix angle of the scanner. Thus the track width T_w is not the same as the head offset. The necessary adjustment to the head spacing along the scanner axis is derived in the text.

It is easy to calculate the adjustment necessary, and an example is given here using the D-3 format. In both PAL and NTSC versions, the tape falls by two track widths in half a rotation of the drum. The correction is obtained by calculating the fall which takes place between the passing of the two heads, or in 6.789° of rotation, which is as follows:

(1) for PAL

$$\text{tape rise} = \frac{18 \times 2 \times 6.789}{180}\ \mu m = 1.36\ \mu m$$

(2) for NTSC

$$\text{tape rise} = \frac{20 \times 2 \times 6.789}{180} \,\mu\text{m} = 1.51 \,\mu\text{m}$$

Subtracting these correction factors from the track pitch results in the head displacement along the drum axis which is necessary to produce the standard format. The displacement is 16.7 µm for PAL and 18.5 µm for NTSC. DVTRs vary considerably in the number of heads installed in the drum. Chapter 5 introduced the concept of read–modify–write or pre-read in which the tape tracks are read by heads prior to the record heads for editing purposes. In many cases, such as D-2 and D-3, the pre-read function is obtained by deflecting the track-following playback heads so that they precede the record heads. Clearly there is then no confidence replay in this editing mode.

In formats which use data reduction, the compression and expansion processes introduce significant additional delay into the read–modify–write loop and the pre-read head must then be physically further advanced. The additional distance required may be beyond the deflection range of the track-following actuator and extra heads will be necessary. Extra heads do, however, mean that confidence replay is always available.

Figure 6.15(a) shows an early D-2 drum in which two pairs of record heads are mounted opposite one another so that they function alternately with a 180° wrap. The replay-head pairs are mounted at 90° on track-following actuators.

Figure 6.15(b) shows a D-3 drum which has a pair of flying erase heads in addition to the record and play heads. In D-3 the two tracks in the segment are aligned by delaying the record signals, so one flying erase head functions for two tracks.

The D-5 format is backward compatible with D-3 tapes, but can also record the higher data rate of component digital video by doubling the data throughput of the drum. This is done by having four parallel tracks per segment, requiring four heads on each base. To play a D-3 tape, only two of the heads are used. In order to work in components, the drum speed is unchanged, but the tape linear speed is doubled. Figure 6.15(c) shows a D-5 drum in which the general arrangement is the same as for D-3, but each base is fitted with four heads.

Figure 6.15(d) shows the drum of an analog-compatible Digital Betacam. The two tracks in each segment are aligned by delays so that double-width flying erase heads can be used. The erase, record A and record B heads corresponding to one segment can be seen to the bottom right of the diagram, with the same configuration diametrically opposite. Fixed confidence replay heads are arranged nearly at right angles to the record heads. These heads trace the tracks which have just been recorded. At the top and bottom of the diagram can be seen the advanced playback heads which are also used for track following. Finally there are two more track-following actuators which carry pairs of heads which are the width of tracks on analog Betacam tapes.

High-definition recording requires extremely high data rates and this is accommodated by using many heads in parallel. Figure 6.15(e) shows the head arrangement of a DVTR built by BTS[1] in which eight heads are required in one segment. Although the heads are distributed around the perimeter of the drum, the record signals are subject to differing delays such that all tracks in a segment start in the same place and a single erase head a little over eight tracks wide can be used. The resultant track pattern is shown in Figure 6.15(f)

6.5 Time compression

The length of the track laid on the tape is a function of the drum diameter and the wrap angle. Figure 6.16 shows a number of ways in which the same length of track can be put on the tape.

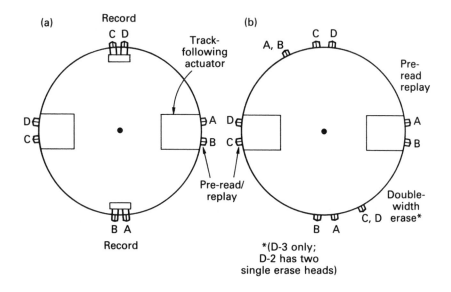

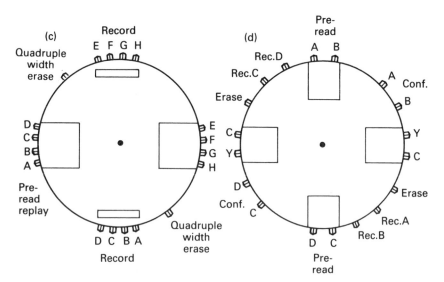

Figure 6.15 Various drum configurations contrasted. At (a) early D-2 recorders had no flying erase. At (b) later D-2 and D-3 drums have flying erase. At (c) D-5 uses four tracks per segment. Two heads of D-5 head base will register with D-3 segments. At (d) analog-compatible Digital Betacam has separate confidence replay heads as well as track-following analog heads.

A small drum with a large wrap angle works just as well as a large drum with a small wrap angle. If the tape speed, and hence the track rate, is constant, and for the purposes of this comparison the number of heads on the drum remains constant, the heads on the smaller drum will take a longer time to traverse the track than the heads on the larger drum. This has the effect of lowering the

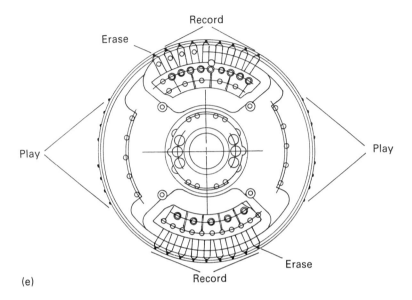

(e)

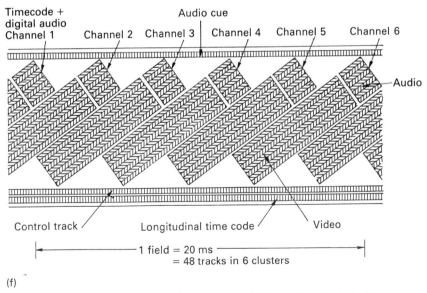

(f)

Figure 6.15 (e) the head configuration of an eight channel HD recorder with single flying erase. (f) the track pattern of the drum in (e). Delays are used to line up the tracks written by the staggered heads.

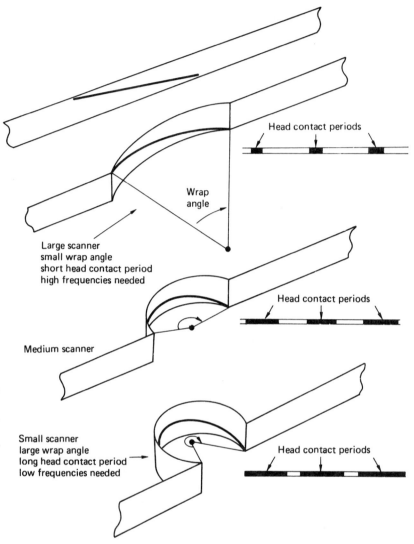

Figure 6.16 A standard track can be put on tape with a variety of scanners. A large wrap allows the lowest frequencies at the head but increases complexity of threading mechanism and increases tape path friction. The helix angle will be different in each case in order to match the tape rise speed to the head peripheral speed thus giving the same track angle.

frequencies seen by the heads, and is responsible for the 270 degree wrap of the Sony D-1 recorders.

Changing the wrap angle also means that the helix angle will need to be different so that the same track angle is achieved in all cases. In practice, a larger drum can be used to mount more heads which work in turn, so that the drum speed will then be less than before. Alternatively the space inside the larger drum may be used to incorporate track-following heads. Another advantage of the large drum is that the reduced wrap angle is easier to thread up. A small drum is attractive for a portable machine since it is compact and requires less power. The greater wrap angle has to be accepted.

The different drum sizes in the example of Figure 6.16 traced standard tracks in different periods of time, as shown in the diagram. In analog recorders such as the C-format and U-matic, the time period had to be one television field so that the television waveform could be directly fed to the heads, and design of the drum was extremely inflexible.

In the digital domain there is even more freedom. The video field is expressed by a given number of samples, and as long as these appear on replay in the right sequence, their actual position in the recording or the exact time at which they were recorded is of no consequence. Clearly the record and replay processes must complement one another.

Time compression is used in Digital Betacam in order to play analog tapes. The drum diameter needed for Digital Betacam was larger than for the analog format in order to accommodate the high bit rate with the segmentation chosen. However, the helix angle of a DB transport is such that when analog Betacam tapes are played at the correct linear speed, the track angle matches the head path. Thus the analog heads follow the tracks. As the drum is larger than the original, the head-to-tape speed is too high and the analog Betacam signal is time compressed as it replays. It is expanded in the TBC. The Digital Betacam format has to take the analog-compatible helix angle as a given.

6.6 Segmentation

The number of bits to be recorded for one field will be a direct result of the sampling scheme chosen. The minimum wavelength which can be reliably recorded will then determine the length of track that is necessary.

With 4:2:2 sampling, and allowing for redundancy and the presence of the digital audio, there will be about 4.5 Mbits in one field for 50 Hz, and about 3.75 Mbits for 60 Hz. These figures will be reduced in proportion to the compression factor if data reduction is used. For example, Ampex DCT and Digital Betacam use 2:1 reduction. With $4 \times F_{sc}$ composite sampling, the figures will be about 3 Mbits and 2 Mbits per field respectively.

Since current wavelengths are restricted to about 0.6–0.9 μm (which records 2 bits) then the total track lengths needed will be between about 1 and 2 metres. Clearly no-one in their right mind is going to design a drum large enough to put the whole of one field on one track. A further consideration is that it is not a good idea to pass all the data through one head. Eddy current losses in the head get worse at high frequencies, and should the single head clog or fail, all of the data are lost.

The solution to both problems is *segmentation* where the data for one field are recorded in a number of head sweeps. With segmentation it is easy to share the data between more than one head, a technique known as distribution. In the D-1 and D-5 formats four heads are necessary, whereas in D-2, D-3 and Digital Betacam, two heads are necessary, and the formats, reflect these restrictions.

With segmentation, the contents of a field can be divided into convenient-sized pieces for recording. This allows the width of the tape to be chosen. If the tape is wide, then tracks of a given length can be placed at a greater angle to the edge of the tape, and so the tape will move more slowly for a given track rate. This means that the effective rewinding time will be reduced because a given

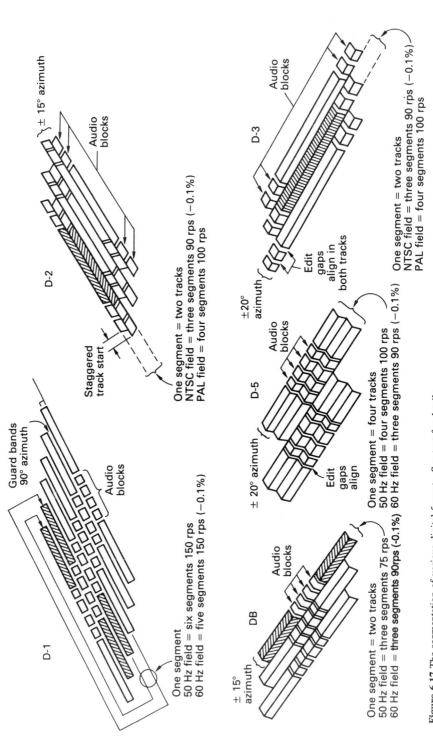

Figure 6.17 The segmentation of various digital formats. See text for details.

recording will occupy a shorter length of tape. Taken to extremes, this would result in very wide tape on small reels.

This is not the only criterion, however. A wide tape needs a physically larger drum assembly, and requires greater precision in guidance. It is seldom possible to engineer a tape transport with total precision, so the tape will always be expected to accommodate small inaccuracies by flexing. The stiffness of the tape against bending in its own plane is proportional to the moment of inertia of its cross-section. This rises disproportionately with tape width. The selection of a narrower tape will ease transport accuracy requirements slightly. The final factor to be considered is the recording density. A high-density recording requires less tape area per unit time, and so the effective rewinding speed will be proportional to the recording density. Consideration of these factors led to the choice of $\frac{3}{4}$ inch or $\frac{1}{2}$ inch wide tape for the digital video cassettes. The choice was basically between those widths and 1 inch tape, since choice of a non-standard width would have unnecessarily raised the cost of the medium as existing slitters could not have been used.

Having chosen the tape width, the number of segments per field can be established. A large number of short steep tracks will give the same overall track length as a smaller number of long shallow tracks. For normal speed operation, there is little difference between the two approaches, but for variable speed, the smaller the number of segments the better, since the magnitude of head jumps will be reduced.

The actual segmentation techiques used in the various formats are compared in Figure 6.17. Composite digital formats use subcarrier-locked sampling rates, so the data rate is substantially higher in PAL than in NTSC and the segmentation changes to reflect the data rate. In component formats the data rate stays the same whether 50 Hz or 60 Hz field rate is used as the same sampling rate is used in both line standards. In this case the segmentation is used to simplify supporting two field rates with as much common hardware as possible.

For these reasons D-2 and D-3, which are both composite digital, use the same segmentation approach. In PAL, data for each field are divided into four segments, each of which requires two tracks, one of each azimuth type. There are thus eight tape tracks per field. In NTSC the data rate is less and three segments suffice, so the field is accommodated in six tracks.

D-1 has a constant segment rate of 300 segments per second. In the case of 50 Hz fields, each contains six segments, whereas 60 Hz fields contain five segments. Once more each segment consists of two tracks.

The Ampex DCT and Sony Digital Betacam formats have a similar data rate to digital NTSC after the reduction process and also require three segments or six tracks per field in the 60 Hz version. However, the 50 Hz version uses four segments or eight tracks per field, so a common segment rate cannot be used because there is no common factor at these lower rates.

6.7 The basic rotary-head transport

Figure 6.18 shows the important components of a rotary-head helical-scan tape transport. There are four servo systems which must correctly interact to obtain all modes of operation: two reel servos, the drum servo and the capstan servo. The capstan and reel servos together move and tension the tape, and the drum servo moves the heads. For variable-speed operation a further servo system will be necessary to deflect the heads.

There are two approaches to capstan drive: those which use a pinch roller and those which do not. In a pinch roller drive, the tape is held against the capstan by pressure from a resilient roller which is normally pulled towards the capstan by a solenoid. The capstan only drives the tape over a narrow speed range, generally the range in which broadcastable pictures are required. Outside this range, the pinch roller retracts, the tape will be driven by reel motors alone, and the reel motors will need to change their operating mode; one becomes a velocity servo whilst the other remains a tension servo.

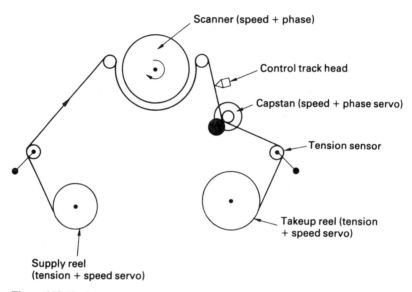

Figure 6.18 The four servos essential for proper operation of a helical-scan DVTR. Cassette-based units will also require loading and threading servos, and for variable speed a track-following servo will be necessary.

In a pinch-roller-less transport, the tape is wrapped some way around a relatively large capstan, to give a good area of contact. A drilled capstan connected to a suction pump can also be used to obtain extra adhesion. The tape is always in contact with the capstan, irrespective of operating mode, and so the reel servos never need to change mode. A large capstan has to be used to give sufficient contact area, and to permit high shuttle speed without excessive motor rpm. This means that at play speed it will be turning slowly, and must be accurately controlled and free from cogging. A multipole ironless-rotor pancake-type brush motor is often used, or a sinusoidal drive brushless motor.

The simplest operating mode to consider is the first recording on a blank tape. In this mode, the capstan will rotate at constant speed and drive the tape at the linear speed specified for the format. The drum must rotate at a precisely determined speed, so that the correct number of tracks per unit distance will be laid down on the tape. Since in a segmented recording each track will be a constant fraction of a television field, the drum speed must ultimately be determined by the incoming video signal to be recorded. To take the example of a PAL D-2 or D-3 recorder having two record-head pairs, eight tracks or four segments will be necessary to record one field, and so the drum must make exactly two complete revolutions in one field period, requiring it to run at 100 Hz. In the case of NTSC D-2 or D-3, there are six tracks or three segments per field, and so the drum must turn at one and a half times field rate, or a little under 90 Hz. The phase of the drum rotation with respect to input video timing depends upon the time delay necessary to shuffle and interleave the video samples. This time will vary from a minimum of about one segment to more than a field depending on the format.

6.8 Controlling motor speed

In various modes of operation, the capstan and/or the drum will need to have accurate control of their rotational speed. During crash record (a mode in which no attempt is made to lock to a previous recording on the tape) the capstan must run at an exact and constant speed. When the drum is first started, it must be brought to the correct speed before phase lock can be attempted. The principle of speed control commonly used will be examined here.

Figure 6.19(a) shows that the motor whose speed is to be controlled is fitted with a toothed wheel or slotted disk. For convenience, the number of slots will usually be some power of 2. A sensor, magnetic or optical, will produce one pulse per slot, and these will be counted by a binary divider. A similar counter is driven by a reference frequency. This may often be derived by multiplying the input video field rate in a phase-locked loop. The operation of a phase-locked loop was described in Chapter 2.

The outputs of the two counters are taken to a full adder, whose output drives a DAC which in turn drives the motor. The bias of the motor amplifier is arranged so that a DAC code of one-half of the quantizing range results in zero drive to the motor, and smaller or larger codes will result in forward or reverse drive.

If the count in the tacho divider lags behind the count in the reference divider, the motor will receive increased power, whereas if the count in the tacho divider leads the count in the reference divider, the motor will experience reverse drive, which slows it down. The result is that the speed of the motor is exactly proportional to the reference frequency. In principle the system is a phase-locked loop, where the voltage-controlled oscillator has been replaced by a motor and a frequency-generating wheel.

6.9 Phase locked servos

In a DVTR the rotational phase of the drum and capstan must be accurately controlled. In the case of the drum, the phase must be controlled so that the heads reach the beginning of a track at a time which is appropriate to the station reference video fed to the machine.

A slightly more complex version of the speed control system of Figure 6.19(a) is required, as will be seen in Figure 6.19(b). In addition to a toothed wheel or slotted disk, the motor carries a reference slot which produces a rotational phase reference commonly called *once-round tach*. This reference presets the tach

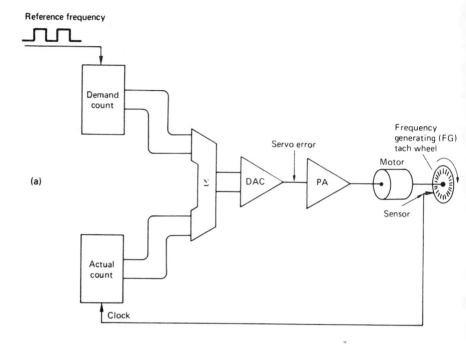

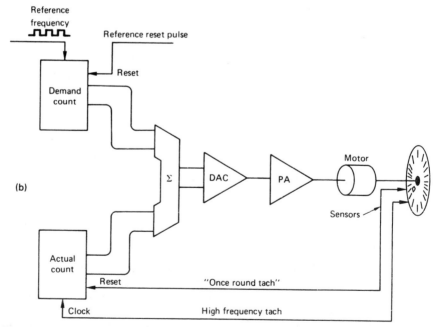

Figure 6.19 (a) Motor speed control using frequency generator on motor shaft. Pulses from FG are compared with pulses from reference to derive servo error. (b) An additional sensor resets the actual count once per revolution, so it counts motor phase angle. Demand count is reset by reference timing. Thus motor phase is locked to reference.

divider, so that the tach count becomes an accurate binary representation of the actual angle of rotation.

A similar divider is fed by a reference clock as before, and preset at appropriate intervals. The reference clock has the same frequency as the tooth-passing frequency of the tacho at normal speed. In a PAL D-2 machine which needs two drum rotations per field, the counter will need to be preset twice per field, or, more elegantly, the counter will have an additional high-order bit which does not go to the adder, and then it can be preset once per field, since neglect of the upper bit will cause two repeated counts of half a field duration each, with an overflow between.

The adder output will increase or decrease the motor drive until the once-round tach occurs exactly opposite the reference preset pulse, because in this condition the sum of the two inputs to the adder is always zero.

The binary count of the tach counter can be used to address a rotation phase PROM. This will be programmed to generate signals which enable the different sectors of the recorded format to be put in the correct place on the track. For example, if it is desired to edit one audio channel without changing any other part of a recording, the record head must be enabled for a short period at precisely the correct drum angle. The drum phase PROM will provide the timing information needed.

When the tape is playing, the phase of the control track must be locked to reference segment phase in order to achieve accurate tracking.

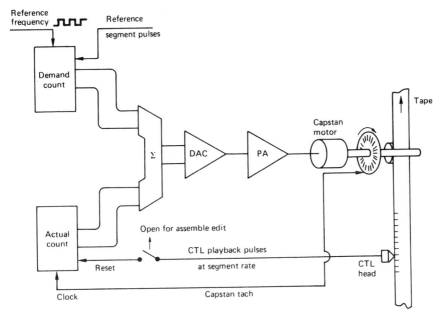

Figure 6.20 If the encoded counter is reset by CTL pulses, it will count linear tape phase, i.e. distance between CTL pulses. Controlling demand counter from reference segment pulses phase-locks tape CTL track to segment rate resulting in correct tracking. At an assemble edit the reset is disabled and the capstan servo makes a smooth transition to the velocity control mode of Figure 6.19(a).

Figure 6.20 shows that a similar configuration to the drum servo is used, but there is no once-round tach on the capstan wheel. Instead, the tach counter is reset by the segment pulses obtained by replaying the control track. Since the speed of the control track is proportional to the capstan speed, resetting the tach count in this way results in a count of control track phase. The reference counter is reset by segment rate pulses, which can be obtained from the drum, and so the capstan motor will be driven in such a way that the phase error between control track pulses and reference pulses is minimized. In this way the rotary heads will accurately track the diagonal tracks.

During an assemble edit, the capstan will phase lock to control track during the preroll, but must revert to constant speed mode at the in-point, since the control track will be recorded from that point. This transition can be obtained by simply disabling the capstan tach counter reset, which causes the system to revert to the speed control servo of Figure 6.19.

6.10 Tension servos

It has been shown that tape tension control is critical in helical-scan machines, primarily to ensure interchange and the correct head contact. Tension control will also be necessary for shuttle to ensure correct tape packing.

Figure 6.21 shows a typical back tension control system. A swinging guide called a tension arm is mounted on a position sensor which can be optical or magnetic. A spring applies a force to the tension arm in a direction which would make the tape path longer. The position sensor output is connected to the supply reel motor amplifier which is biased in such a way that when the sensor is in the centre of its travel the motor will receive no drive. The polarity of the system is arranged so that the reel motor will be driven in reverse when the spring contracts. The result is that the reel motor will apply a reverse torque which will

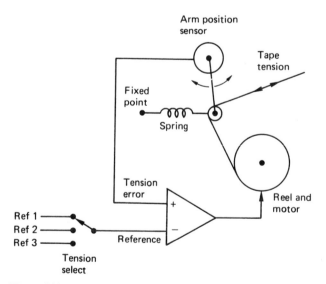

Figure 6.21 Tension servo controls reel motor current so that motor extends sprung arm. Sensor determines extension of spring and thus tape tension.

extend the spring as it attempts to return the tension arm to the neutral position. If the system is given adequate loop gain, a minute deflection of the arm will result in full motor torque, so the arm will be kept in an essentially constant position. This means that the spring will have a constant length, and so the tape tension will be constant. Different tensions can be obtained by switching offsets into the feedback loop, which result in the system null being at a different extension of the spring.

The error in the servo will only be small if the reel can accelerate fast enough to follow tape motion. In a machine with permanent capstan engagement, the capstan can accelerate much faster than the reels can. If not controlled, this would lead to the tension arm moving to one or other end of its travel, resulting in tape stretch, or a slack loop which will subsequently snatch tight with the same results. A fixed acceleration limit on the capstan servo would prevent the problem, but it would have to be set to allow a full reel on a large-size cassette to keep up. The motion of a small cassette with vastly reduced inertia would be made artificially ponderous. The solution is to feed back the displacement of the tension sensors to the capstan servo. If the magnitude of the tension error from either tension arm is excessive, the capstan acceleration is cut back. In this way the reels are accelerated as fast as possible without the tension becoming incorrect.

In a cassette-based recorder, the tension arms usually need to be motorized so that they can fit into the mouth of the cassette for loading, and pull tape out into the threaded position. It is possible to replace the spring which provides tape tension with a steady current through the arm motor. By controlling this current, the tape tension can be programmed.

6.11 Tape remaining sensing

It is most important in a cassette to prevent the tape running out at speed. The tape is spliced to a heavy leader at each end, and this leader is firmly attached to the reel hub. In an audio cassette, there is sufficient length of this leader to reach to the other reel, and so the impact of a run-off can be withstood. This approach cannot be used with a video cassette, because the heavy leader cannot be allowed to enter the drum, as it would damage the rotating heads.

The transport must compute the tape remaining in order to prevent running off at speed. This may be done by measuring the linear speed of the tape and comparing it with the rotational speed of the reel. The linear speed will be the capstan speed in a permanent capstan drive transport, a timer roller will be necessary in a pinch-roller-type transport. Alternatively, tape remaining may be computed by comparing the speed of the two reels. The rotational speed of the reels will be obtained from a frequency generator (FG) on the reel motors. Figure 6.22 shows a simple method of computing the tape remaining. Pulses from the capstan FG cause a counter to increment. When a reel FG pulse occurs, the count will be transferred to a latch, and the counter will be reset. When the reel is full, there will be many capstan FG pulses between reel FG pulses, but as the radius of the tape pack falls, the count transferred to the latch will also fall. It will be possible to determine the limit count from a knowledge of the capstan and reel hub diameters, and the number of teeth on their generators. The latch count is not quite the pack radius, because if the tension arm is moving due to an acceleration, the linear speed of the tape at the capstan will not be the same as the linear speed

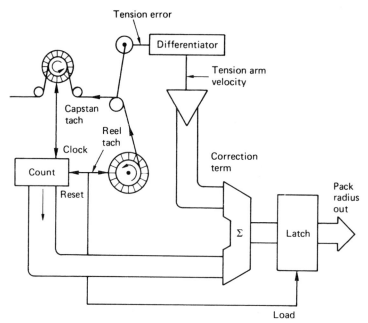

Figure 6.22 Tape remaining is calculated by comparing capstan tach with reel tach. If tension arm is moving, tape speed at reel and capstan will be different, so correction term from tension arm sensor is added. Pinch-roller-type transports disengage the capstan in shuttle, and so the timer roller tacho would be used instead.

at the reel. To prevent false shutdowns when accelerating near the end of the tape, the tension arm signal may be differentiated to give an arm velocity signal, and this can be digitized and used to produce a correction factor for the radius parameter.

To prevent run-offs, the reel pack radius of the reel which is unwinding profiles the allowable shuttle speed, so that as the pack radius falls, the tape speed falls with it. Thus when the tape finally runs out, it will be travelling at very low speed, and the photoelectric sensor which detects the leader will be able to halt the transport without damage.

6.12 Brushless DC motors

The reliability of digital circuitry is of little consequence if a breakdown is caused by the failure of an associated mechanical component. Video recorders, including digital video recorders, are a complex alliance of mechanical, magnetic and electronic technology, and the electronic wizardry has to be matched by some pretty good mechanical engineering. As the cost of electronics falls, it becomes possible to replace certain mechanical devices cost effectively, and there is an impetus to do this if a wear mechanism can be eliminated. The brushless motor is one such device. The conventional DC brush motor is ubiquitous, and life would be infinitely less convenient without it, for it allows reasonable efficiency, a wide speed range, reversing and relatively compact size. The weak point of all motors of this kind is the brush/commutator system, which serves to distribute current to the windings which are in the best position relative to the field to generate torque. There is a physical wear mechanism, and the best brush material developed will still produce a conductive powder which will be distributed far and wide by the need to have airflow through the motor for cooling. The interruption of current in an inductive circuit results in sparking, which can cause electrical interference and erosion of the brushes and commutator. The brushless motor allows all of the benefits of the DC motor, without the drawbacks of commutation.

Figure 6.23 shows that a brushless motor is not unlike a normal motor turned inside out. In a normal motor, the field magnet is stationary, and the windings rotate. In a brushless motor, the windings are stationary, and the magnet rotates. The stationary windings eliminate the need to supply current to the rotor, and

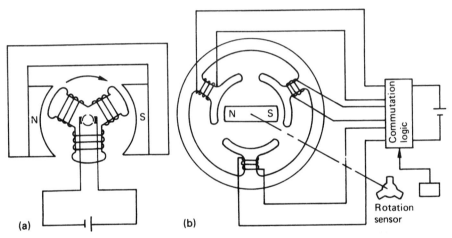

Figure 6.23 At (a) a conventional brush motor has rotating windings. Current is fed through stationary bushes and commutation is automatic. At (b) the motor has been turned inside out, the magnet revolves and the windings are now stationary, so they can be directly connected to an electronic commutating circuit. The rotation sensor on the magnet shaft tells the commutator when to switch.

with it the need for brushes. The commutating action is replaced by electronic switches. These need to be told the rotational angle of the shaft, a function which is intrinsic in the conventional commutator. A rotation sensor performs this function.

Figure 6.24 shows the circuit of a typical brushless motor. The three-phase winding is driven by six switching devices, usually power FETs. By switching these on in various combinations, it is possible to produce six resultant field directions in the windings. The switching is synchronized to the rotation of the magnet, such that the magnetic field of the rotor always finds itself at right angles to the field from the windings, and so produces the most torque. In this condition the motor will produce the most back EMF, and the normal way of adjusting the rotation sensor is to allow the motor to run on no load and to adjust the angular sensor position mechanically until the motor consumes minimum current.

The rotating magnet has to be sufficiently powerful to provide the necessary field, and in early brushless motors was heavy, which gave the motor a high inertial time constant. Whilst this was of no consequence in steady speed applications, it caused problems in servos. The brushless servo motor was basically waiting for high-energy permanent magnets, which could produce the necessary field without excessive mass. These rare earth magnets are currently more expensive than the common ferrite magnet, and so the first applications of brushless motors have been in machines where the motor cost is a relatively small proportion of the high overall cost, and where reliability is paramount. Professional recorders come into this category. Down time for brush replacement

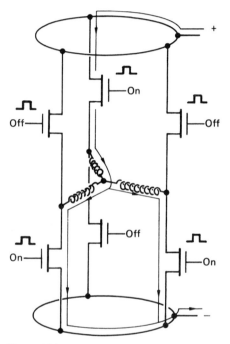

Figure 6.24 Circuit of a brushless DC motor is basically a three-phase bridge. Six different flux directions can be obtained by switching combinations of FETs. One example is shown.

and labour costs eclipse the cost of the brushes. The drum motor of a video recorder in a modern post production suite has to run at speed hour after hour, day after day, and is a natural application of a brushless motor.

The development of the power FET also facilitated brushless motors, since all DC motors regenerate, which is to say that when the torque opposes the direction of rotation, the current reverses. FETs are not perturbed by current direction, whereas bipolar devices were at best inefficient or would at worst fail in the presence of reverse current. Power FETs can handle currents which would destroy brush gear, and so large transient accelerations are easily obtained, overcoming the inertia of the rotating magnet.

A typical brushless motor appears to the drive amplifier just like a normal DC motor. It has only two power terminals, has back EMF, and will regenerate. The only major difference is the way that reversing is achieved. Brush motors reverse by reversing drive polarity, whereas brushless motors reverse by changing the phase of the commutation.

The number of motor poles directly influences the complexity of the switching circuitry, and brushless motors tend to have relatively few poles. Conventional motors suffer from cogging, or a cyclic variation in torque, and those with few poles suffer most. Whilst it is of little consequence in a drum motor, which runs at high speed and has the inertia of the drum to smooth out rotation, it can be important in direct drive capstan motors, which turn at low speed and have low inertia.

Many transports retain multipole brush motors for the capstan, but it is possible to construct a cogging-free motor. The commutation circuit is no longer switching, but consists of a number of analog amplifiers which will feed the motor with sinusoidal waveforms in fixed phase relationships. In the case of a two-phase motor, this will be two waveforms at 90°; for a three-phase motor, it will be three waveforms at 120°.

The drive signals for the amplifiers are produced by a number of rotation sensors, which directly produce analog sinusoids. These can conveniently be Hall effect sensors which detect the fields from rotating magnets.

6.13 Switched-mode motor amplifiers

The switched-mode motor amplifier has much in common with the switched-mode power supply, since both have the same objectives, namely an increase in electrical efficiency through reduced dissipation, and a reduction in size and weight. In studio based machines reduced dissipation will help to increase reliability, whereas in portable machines the efficiency is paramount since existing battery technology is still a handicap.

The linear amplifier must act as a variable resistance, and so current flowing through it will cause heat to be developed. Linear amplifiers are particularly inefficient for driving tape reel motors, since to obtain fast shuttle speed, the supply voltage must be high, and this means that when the machine plays, the reels are turning slowly and the motor voltage will be very small, so that most of the power supply voltage has to be dropped by the amplifier, which is extremely inefficient. Some transports using linear motor amplifiers will program a switched-mode power supply to provide just enough voltage for the instantaneous requirements, helping to raise efficiency.

The principle of a switched-mode amplifier is quite simple. The current is controlled by an electronic switch which is either fully on or fully off. In both cases dissipation in the switch is minimal. The only difficulty consists of providing a variable output despite the binary switching. This will be done by a combination of duty cycle contol and filtering.

Figure 6.25 shows a typical switched-mode motor amplifier. It consists of a normal bridge configuration with a number of additional components, a pair of inductors and a current sense resistor in series with the motor, and a number of reverse connected flywheel diodes.

If it is desired to make current flow through the motor from left to right, then field-effect transistors T_1 and T_4 will be turned fully on. Owing to the presence of the inductors, the current through the motor increases gradually, and when the desired current is reached, transistor T_1 is switched off. The current flowing in

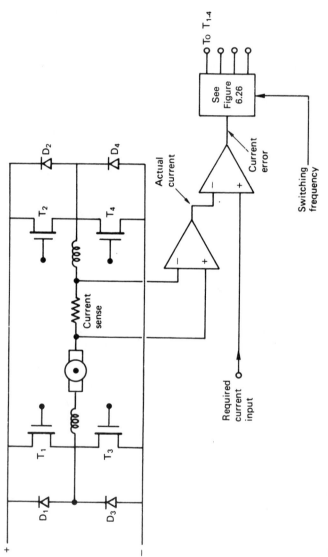

Figure 6.25 General arrangement of switched-mode power amplifier. Devices T_1–T_4 are power FETs which are on or off. Inductors in series with motor inductance limit rate of change of current.

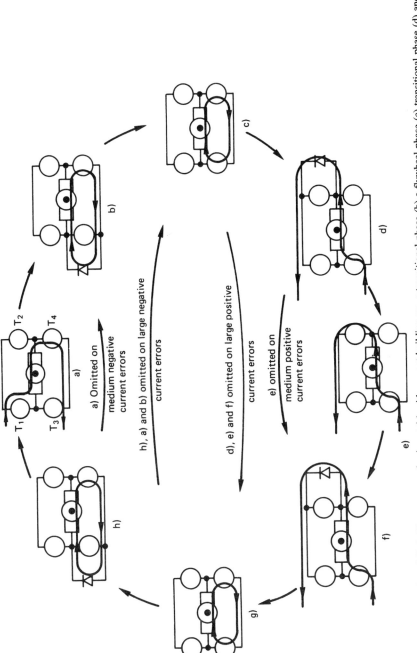

Figure 6.25 continued Switching sequence begins at (a) with current building up, a transitional phase (b) a flywheel phase (c) transitional phase (d) and at (e) the system regenerates, or opposes the power supply. This causes current to fall. System then passes through remaining phases back to (a). To increase current, system spends more time in phase (a), whereas to reduce current, system spends more time in phase (e). Figure 6.26 shows how this is done.

the inductive circuit must continue flowing, and it will do so through D_3, as shown in (b). Greater efficiency will be obtained if T_3 is then switched on, as the forward drop of the diode is then bypassed. Transistor T_4 is then switched off, and the current loop will be blocked, causing the flux in the inductors to decay, and raising their terminal voltage. This will result in current flowing through D_2 back to the power supply. Greater efficiency will be obtained if T_2 is turned on. The current is now being opposed by the power supply and will decay, and after a short time, transistor T_2 must be switched off and transistor T_4 will be switched on again. In this way, the current rises and falls about the desired value. If the switching rate is made high, the variations in current will be small with respect to the average current. The inertia of the motor will in any case prevent any mechanical response at the switching frequency. It will be noted that during this process current flowed in reverse through two of the transistors, requiring the use of field-effect devices.

Clearly if current flowing from right to left is required, the bridge switching will change over, but the principle remains the same.

The torque generated by the motor is proportional to the current, and torque can be applied with or against rotation. For example, when the transport is in play mode, the take-up motor is turning in the same direction as its torque, whereas the supply motor is providing back tension, and is turning against its torque. In this case, the motor EMF will cause current to flow in the flywheel circuit, and the switching will take energy out of the current flywheel back to the power supply. This is the principle of regenerative braking. If the motor is being turned by the tape, it will generate, and a current will flow as shown in (c). The current will rise gradually owing to the presence of the inductors. When the current reaches the value needed to give the correct back tension, T_3 will be switched off and the flywheel current will find itself blocked. The result will be a flux collapse causing the inductors to raise their terminal voltage until a current path is found. When the voltage exceeds the power supply voltage, current will flow in D_1, back to the supply. Again greater efficiency will be obtained if T_1 is switched on, since the diode drop is bypassed. Since the power supply voltage is opposing the motor EMF, the current will fall, and when it has fallen sufficiently, T_1 will be switched off, and T_3 will be switched on again.

The switching sequence of the transistors is important, since turning on the wrong pair will short out the power supply! One method of controlling the switching is to produce a current error by comparing the current sensed with the desired current. The current error then changes the DC level of a triangle wave, which is compared with four thresholds, each of which controls one of the transistors. Figure 6.26 shows the switching sequence which results. Note that when the current error is zero, the system alternates equally between opposing and assisting the current, so there is no change.

A motor which is producing back tension will return power to the supply, which will be used by the motor which is taking up and by the drum motor. If the machine is braking from a high shuttle speed, both reel motors may together produce more power than the rest of the machine can use, and the power supply voltage will rise. In AC-powered machines, it is necessary to shunt the supply with a resistor in this condition, whereas in battery-powered machines, the regenerative current simply recharges the battery. Clearly a power failure in shuttle is no problem, for as long as the reels are being decelerated, power is generated. This can be augmented if necessary by decelerating the drum.

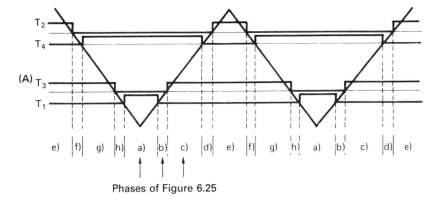

Phases of Figure 6.25

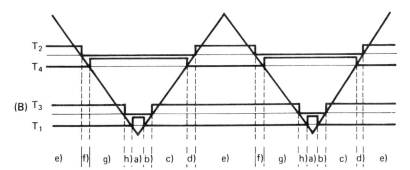

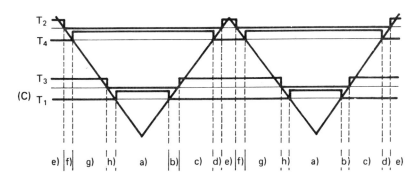

Figure 6.26 The power FETs of Figure 6.25 are switched by comparing the current error with a sawtooth signal produced from the switching frequency. Four offset voltages are added to the current error, and four comparators are used, one for each power device. The offsets are constant, so all four current errors move together.

At (A) above, the current error is zero, so the switching is symmetrical because time period (a) has the same length as time period (e) and the current is neither increased nor reduced. At (B) the current error is negative, and phase (a) is very short whereas phase (e) is much longer; thus current reduces because the motor is regenerating. At (C) the current error is positive and phase (a) is now longer than phase (e), so current increases. If the current error increases further, some phases will no longer take place. An inverse of the error in (C) will result in phase (e) disappearing since (d) and (f) are identical. Further increase will cause (d), (e) and (f) to disappear giving the sequence a, b, c, g, h, ...

6.14 Digital video cassettes

The D-1 and D-2 formats use the same mechanical parts and dimensions in their respective $\frac{3}{4}$ inch cassettes, even though the kind of tape and the track pattern are completely different. The Ampex DCT cassette is the same as a D-2 cassette. D-3 and D-5 use the same $\frac{1}{2}$ inch cassette, and Digital Betacam uses a $\frac{1}{2}$ inch cassette which is identical mechanically to the analog Betacam cassette, but contains different tape.

The main advantages of a cassette are that the medium is better protected from contamination whilst out of the transport, and that an unskilled operator or a mechanical elevator can load the tape.

It is not true that cassettes offer any advantage for storage except for the ease of handling. In fact a cassette takes up more space than a tape reel, because it must contain two such reels, only one of which will be full at any one time. In some cases it is possible to reduce the space needed by using flangeless hubs and guiding liner sheets, as is done in the Compact Cassette and RDAT, or pairs of hubs with flanges on opposite sides, as in U-matic. Whilst such approaches are acceptable for consumer and industrial products, they are inappropriate for the digital video cassette, because as a professional unit it will be expected to wind at high speeds in automation and editing systems. Accordingly the digital cassette contains two fully flanged reels side by side. The centre of each hub is fitted with a thrust pad and when the cassette is not in the drive a spring acts on this pad and presses the lower flange of each reel firmly against the body of the cassette to exclude dust. When the cassette is in the machine the relative heights of the reel turntables and the cassette supports are such that the reels seat on the turntables before the cassette comes to rest. This opens a clearance space between the reel flanges and the cassette body by compressing the springs. This should be borne in mind if a machine is being tested without the cassette elevator as a suitable weight must be placed on the cassette in order to compress the springs.

		D-1	D-2	D-3	D-5	DCT	Digital Betacam
Track pitch (μm)		45	35	18	18	35	26
Tape speed (mm/s)		286·9	131·7	83·2	167·2	131·7	96·7
	S	14/11	32	64/50	32/25	32	40
Play time (min)	M	50/37	104	125/95	62/47	104	–
	L	101/75	208	245/185	123/92	208	124
Data rate (mbits/s)		216	142	142	288	113	126
Density (mbits/cm²)		4	5·8	13	13	5·8	10

Figure 6.27 The D-1/D-2, D-3/D-5, DCT and Digital Betacam tape sizes and playing times contrasted.

The use of a cassette means that it is not as easy to provide a range of sizes as it is with open reels. Simply putting smaller reels in a cassette with the same hub spacing does not produce a significantly smaller cassette. The only solution is to specify different hub spacings for different sizes of cassette. This gives the best volumetric efficiency for storage, but it does mean that the transport must be able to reposition the reel drive motors if it is to play more than one size of cassette.

Digital Betacam offers two cassette sizes, whereas the other formats offer three. If the small, medium and large digital video cassettes are placed in a stack with their throats and tape guides in a vertical line, the centres of the hubs will be seen to fall on a pair of diagonal lines going outwards and backwards. This arrangement was chosen to allow the reel motors to travel along a linear track in machines which accept more than one size. The D-1 format has very low recording density by modern standards and is somewhat pushed to get long playing time. The large-size cassette was the largest size which could be accommodated in a transport which would still fit in a 19 inch rack. Figure 6.27 compares the sizes and capacities of the various digital cassettes.

6.15 The D-1/D-2/DCT cassette

All three sizes of cassette have basically the same structure, and detail differences will be noted. The cassette has a double-door arrangement shown in Figure 6.28. When the cassette is removed, both sides of the tape in the throat are covered. The inner door is guided by a curved track. The door extends to the edges of the small and medium cassettes, but this is unnecessary on the large cassette. The door has a lock which prevents accidental opening, and this is released by a pin when the cassette enters the transport. The lock release mechanism is as near the edge of the small cassette as possible, but it cannot be in the same place on the medium cassette, as it would foul the tape path to the larger reel. Three lock release pins are needed, one for each size, and the larger cassettes need dummy slots which clear the pins used by the smaller sizes.

The cassettes also have hub locks which prevent unwanted rotation in storage or transit. On the larger two sizes, the lock is released by a lever operated by the act of opening the door. There is insufficient room for this mechanism on the small cassette, and so the brake is released by the central post in the transport.

The cassettes are designed for front or side loading, and so have guiding slots running at right angles. Most studio recorders are front loading, whereas most automated machines use side loading. The front-loading guide groove is centrally positioned and the threading throat forms a lead-in to it, helping to centralize the smaller cassettes in a loading slot which will accept a large cassette.

A number of identification holes are provided in the cassettes which are sensed by switches on the transport. Four of these are coding holes which are in the form of break-off tabs which will be set when the cassette is made, and four of them are resettable user holes, which can be controlled with a screwdriver. Table 6.1 shows the significance of the coding and user holes.

Areas are specified for the positioning of labels, and these are recessed to prevent fouling of elevators or guides. Automated machines will use the end location for a bar code which can be read by the elevator while the cassette is stacked.

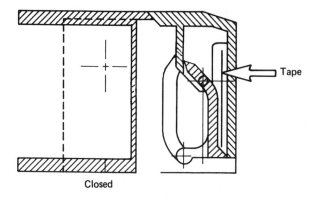

Closed

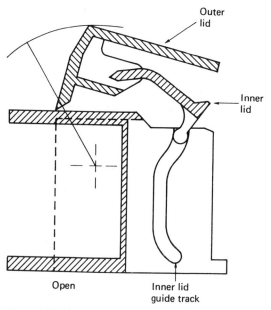

Open   Inner lid
              guide track

Figure 6.28 When the cassette lid is closed, both sides of the tape are protected by covers. As the outer lid swings up on a pivot, the inner lid is guided around the back of the tape by a curved track.

6.16 The D-3/D-5 cassette

All three sizes of cassette have basically the same structure, and detail differences will be noted. The cassette has a double-door arrangement shown in Figure 6.29. The inner door hinges in the top of the outer door. When the cassette is removed, both sides of the tape in the throat are covered. The inner door is guided by a curved track. The door extends to the edges of the S and M cassettes only. The door has a lock which prevents accidental opening, and this is released by a pin when the cassette enters the transport. The lock release mechanism is at the edge of the S and M cassettes, and slightly inset on the L cassette. Three lock release

Table 6.1 (a) Manufacturers' coding holes (0 = tab removed). (b) User holes (0 = tab removed)

(a) Holes 1 and 2 shall be used in combination to indicate tape thickness according to the following logic table:	Holes 3 and 4 shall be used to indicate the coercivity of the magnetic recording tape.

Hole Number: 1 2

          0 0 = 16 μm tape
          0 1 = 13 μm tape
          1 0 = Undefined/reserved
          1 1 = Undefined/reserved

Hole number: 3 4

          0 0 = Class 850
          0 1 = Undefined/reserved
          1 0 = Undefined/reserved
          1 1 = Undefined/reserved

(b) When a '0' state exists, the user holes shall
    identify the following conditions:

    1. Total record lockout
       (audio/video/cue/time code/control track)
    2. Reserved and undefined
    3. Reserved and undefined
    4. Reserved and undefined

pins are needed, one for each size, and the larger cassettes need dummy slots which clear the release pins used by the smaller sizes.

The cassettes also have hub locks which prevent unwanted rotation in storage or transit. On all sizes, the lock is released by a rounded post on the deckplate which enters the cassette as it is lowered. This post contains a light source for the BOT/EOT sensors. Light from the post travels across the cassette on a path nearly parallel to the door and if allowed to pass the transparent leader tape emerges through a hole in each end of the cassette which is only revealed when the cassette door is open.

The cassettes are designed for front- or side-loading, and so have guiding slots running at right angles. The front-loading groove is centrally positioned, whereas the side-loading groove runs across the cassette on the opposite side to the door.

A number of identification holes are provided in the cassettes which are sensed by switches on the transport. Three of these are coding holes which are in the

Open

Tape

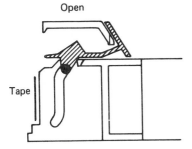

Closed

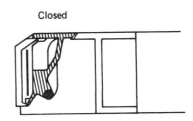

Figure 6.29 The D-3 cassette has a double door which protects both sides of the front tape run when closed. The inner door (shaded) carries guide pins which run in serpentine tracks in the ends of the cassette. These guide the door around the back of the tape as the cassette closes.

Table 6.2 The cassette has two sets of coding holes. The first of these, labelled 1,2,3 is for cassette recognition. The second, labelled a,b,c is for user record lockout. Hole significance is shown in the tables. Holes 1, 2 and 3 shall be used in combination to indicate tape thickness and diameter of hub.

Hole numbers:

(1) = 0 low coercivity
(1) = 1 high coercivity

(2)	(3)	
0	0	11 µm tape, small-diameter hub
0	1	11 µm tape, large-diameter hub
1	0	14 µm tape, small-diameter hub
1	1	14 µm tape, large-diameter hub

A '1' in the above table indicates that the indicator tab is removed or open, an undetected state by the record/player sensor mechanism.

When a '0' state exists, the user holes shall identify the following conditions:

(a) Total record lockout (audio/video/cue/timecode/control track)
(b) Video and control-track record lockout
(c) Reserved and undefined

---

form of break-off tabs which will be set when the cassette is made, and three of them are resettable user holes, which can be controlled with a screwdriver. Table 6.2 shows the significance of the coding and user holes. It will be seen that the hub diameter of the cassette can be conveyed in the coding holes. The hub of the L cassette is larger in diameter than that of the other sizes. The tape-remaining computation needs to know the hub diameter as well as the tape thickness to work out the remaining time from the reel FGs. It is possible to mix hub sizes and cassette sizes. A large-size hub may be used in a small cassette to increase shuttle speed, reducing access time with the penalty of reduced playing time.

The first user hole is a total record lockout, whereas the second only prevents video and control track recording, and thus allows audio editing. The third user hole is undefined. Two of the user holes are used to align the cassette in the transport. The transport registration pins are fitted with switches.

6.17 Loading the cassette

The sequence of operations when a cassette is inserted in the machine will be followed.

In a studio machine, all cassette sizes can be used without any adjustment. The operator simply pushes the cassette into the aperture in the machine and the cassette is lowered onto the transport by an elevator. The smaller sizes are located at the centre of the aperture by sprung guides which are pushed aside when a large-size cassette is used. The presence of the cassette is sensed optically, or by switches, and by the same means the machine can decide which size of cassette has been inserted. The cassette fits into a cage or compartment which is driven by a toothed rack so that it can move inwards and down. Alternatively the cassette may be driven by rubber belts. In portable machines and camcorders only the small cassette will be accommodated and the cassette compartment will be closed by hand.

As the hub spacing differs between cassette sizes, the transport automatically moves the sliding reel motors to the correct position. The final part of horizontal travel unlocks the cassette door. The cassette elevator is then driven downwards and the door is opened. The opened cassette is then lowered onto the reel motors, and locating dowels on the transport register the cassette body. The hub brakes are released either by a post entering the cassette as it is lowered or by the act of opening the door. The identification tabs on the cassette operate the sensor switches on the deckplate. The several guides and tension arms and the pinch roller, where applicable, are positioned so that the throat of the cassette drops over them with the front run of tape between them and the head drum.

In some transports the elevator can be manually operated by turning a slotted socket on the motor shaft with a screwdiver inserted through an aperture in the front of the machine below the control panel. This is useful in the case of a power failure if the cassette must be retrieved. In some designs, the transport can still operate with the elevator removed. This allows a great deal more space to work on the transport. The cassette must be loaded by hand with the door already opened. In the absence of the sensors on the elevator it will be necessary to move the reel motors to the correct spacing by entering an appropriate software routine. The system software will also have to be told the elevator is missing or it will interpret the condition as an error.

6.18 Threading the tape

It is inherent in helical-scan recorders that the tape enters and leaves the head drum at different heights. In open-reel recorders, the reels are simply mounted at different heights, but in a cassette this is not practicable. The tape must be geometrically manipulated in some way. There are several approaches to the geometrical problem:

(1) The drum can be inclined so that the height of the tape is the same at entry and exit.

(2) The drum can be vertical and the tape is manipulated out of the plane of the cassette on both entry and exit sides.

(3) The tape enters the drum in the plane of the cassette and is manipulated on the exit side only.

(4) The tape leaves the drum in the plane of the cassette and is manipulated on the entry side only.

In the Sony D-2 transports, the first approach is taken for tape guidance. Figure 6.30(a) shows tape wrapping a drum, with the usual elevation difference between entrance and exit. In (b) the drum has been tilted so that entrance and exit guides are at the same height. The tape now approaches in the wrong plane. It will be found that if the wrap angle on the entry and exit guides is reduced, an angle can be found where the edge of the tape enters and leaves in the plane of the cassette, as shown in (c). At this stage the tape edge is in the cassette plane, but its surface is not at right angles to that plane, it is leaning over. The entry and exit guides are now tilted in the plane of the tape tangential to the drum until the tape feeding them is at right angles to the cassette plane, as in (d). In this way, the tape is not subjected to any twisting as it always remains planar. The same approach is used in the RDAT transports built by Sony. The coplanar approach allows a very shallow transport construction which is highly suitable for portable operation.

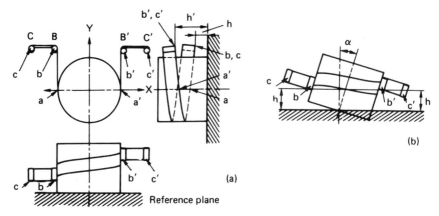

Figure 6.30 At (a) the scanner has a vertical axis which results in a height difference and a twist between the entrance plane BC and the exit plane B′C′.

At (b) the scanner has been tilted through an angle α such that points b and b′ are both at height h.

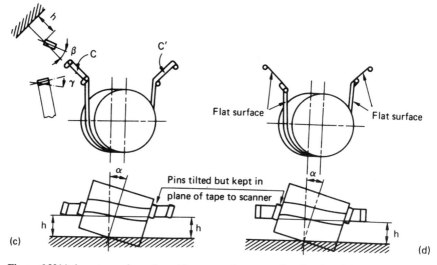

Figure 6.30(c) the wrap angle on the guides nearest the scanner is reduced until the edge of the tape lies in the reference plane. The tape in planes C and C′ remains flat. The pins now incline at angle β to the reference surface.

At (d) the outer pins can be made vertical if the plane of C and C′ is brought perpendicular to the reference surface. This is done by tilting the inner pins but keeping them in the plane of the tape from inner pin to scanner. Tape entry and exit is now coplanar. (Based on drawings courtesy of Sony Broadcast).

Figure 6.31 shows the second approach used in the Sony D-1 transport. This uses an extended wrap angle in order to reduce the frequencies at the heads. The previous approach is difficult to use with an extended wrap. The drum axis is vertical and tape is led down from the supply reel to the drum entrance. Tape then climbs up the drum ramp, and is led down once more to the cassette plane.

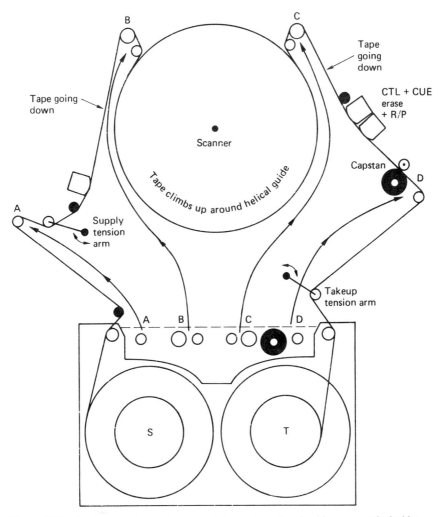

Figure 6.31 In the Sony D-1 transport an extended wrap is used, and guides move on both sides of the scanner to create the wrap. Tape begins the helix below the cassette plane and ends the scan above it. This contrasts with the Ampex approach where the tape begins the helix far below the cassette plane and ends in the cassette plane.

Figure 6.32 shows the arrangement of the Panasonic D-3 and D-5 machines which use the third method. Digital Betacam adopts the same technique. Tape stays in the plane of the cassette on the supply side and the drum is angled to receive it. Tape leaving the drum is manipulated back to the cassette plane.

Figure 6.33 shows arrangement (4) which is used in Ampex D-2 and DCT transports. Here the drum is angled so that tape leaves it in the plane of the take-up reel. All manipulation is then done between the supply reel and the drum entry.

Various methods exist to achieve the helical displacement of the tape. Some VTR transports have used conical posts, but these have the disadvantages that there is a considerable lateral force against the edge of the tape, and that they cannot be allowed to revolve or the tape would climb off them. Angled pins do not suffer side force, but again cannot be allowed to revolve. The friction caused by non-rotating pins can be reduced by air lubrication from a compressor, as used in Ampex transports, or by vibrating them ultrasonically with a piezo electric actuator, as is done in certain Sony transports.

In the Ampex D-2 and DCT transports, the tape in the plane of the cassette is slightly twisted on a long run, and then passes around a conventional guide which causes it to leave the cassette plane at an angle. The twist is too small to approach

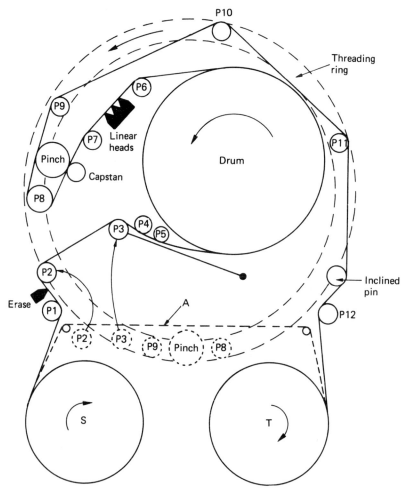

Figure 6.32 Threading sequence of Panasonic D-3 transport. When cassette is first loaded, tape runs straight between the cassette pins (dashed line shown at A) in front of the moving guide pins P2, P3, P9, P8 and the pinch roller. Guides P2 and P3 wrap the entry side by swinging on arms. P3 is in fact the tension arm. The pinch roller and its guides travel anticlockwise on the large threading ring. As the ring rotates P10 and P11 guide the return loop. The inclined pin hinges over the edge of the tape and does not need to be in the cassette mouth at threading start.

the elastic limit of the tape, which is quite unharmed. A second guide set at the same angle as the drum axis passes the tape to the drum[2]. Figure 6.34 contrasts the tape twist and angled guide methods.

The threading process will be considered using two different transports as examples.

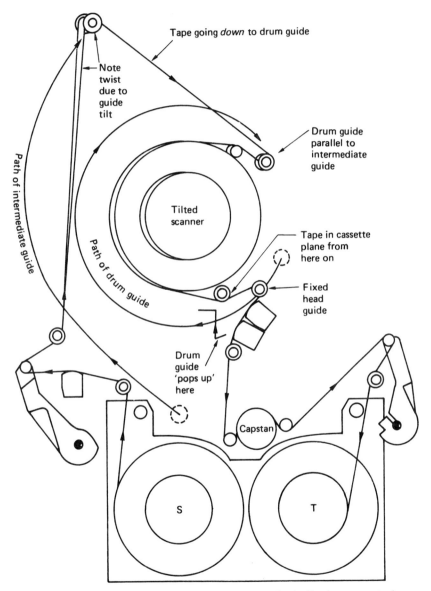

Figure 6.33 Fixed head guide swings out, and capstan guides swing in. Tension arms extend. Then drum and intermediate guides complete scanner wrap.

If the scanner guides are not operated, tape can be transported past stationary heads for timecode striping or prepositioning tape without scanner wear.

In the Panasonic D-3/D-5 transports, as with any VCR, the guides start inside the cassette and move to various positions as threading proceeds. The sequence can be followed in Figure 6.32. The entry side threading is performed by guide P2 which swings anticlockwise on an arm to wrap the tape onto fixed guide P1 and the full-width erase head and by the tension arm guide P3 which swings clockwise to bring the tape across the drum entry guides P4 and P5. The drum

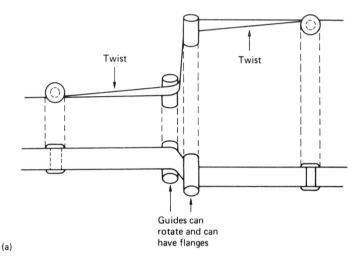

(a)

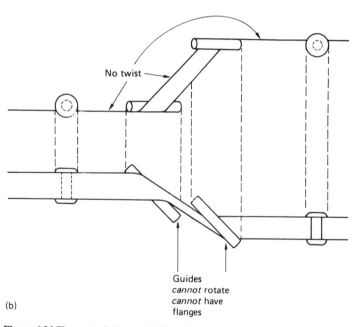

(b)

Figure 6.34 The contradictions of shifting the tape plane in helical scan. If the tape is twisted, the guides can rotate. If it is not, they cannot. Long gentle twist is good, but not compact enough for portable use.

wrapping and exit side threading is performed by guides which move in a circular path on a threading ring, which rotates around the drum and capstan. When the cassete is initially lowered, guide P8, the pinch roller and guide P9 are inside the front run of tape. As the threading ring turns anticlockwise, these guides take a loop of tape from the cassette and begin to wrap it around the drum. As the threading ring proceeds further, guide P10 and then guide P11 come into contact with the return loop, and the leading guide completes the wrap of the drum and wraps fixed exit guide P6, the fixed heads, fixed capstan guide P7 and the capstan. The pinch roller completes its travel by locating in a cage which is operated by the pinch solenoid. It is no longer supported by the threading ring.

The Ampex $\frac{3}{4}$ inch transport is designed for rapid threading and unthreading without tape damage, and particular care was taken to ensure that the tape path geometry is perfect not just when threaded, but at all times during the threading process. The threading sequence can be followed in Figures 6.35 and 6.31.

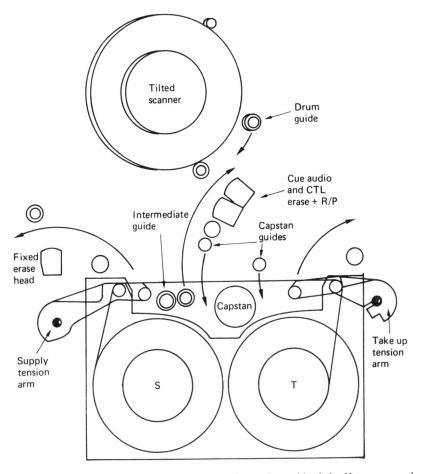

Figure 6.35 Ampex D-2 transport with cassette just lowered onto drive hubs. Note permanently engaged capstan in cassette throat.

The permanently engaged capstan fits inside the cassette throat. A short movement of the tape guides allows the tape to wrap the capstan and the stationary timecode/erase head. This is known as coplanar mode, which means that the tape path is still entirely in the plane of the tape reels. In this mode tape can be shuttled at high speed, and it is possible to erase and timecode-stripe without causing wear to the rotary-head assembly. Timecode can also be read to position a tape without rotary-head wear.

For functions involving the rotary heads, the threading process proceeds further. There are two guides which primarily control threading the tape around the drum. The drum guide moves in a circular path on a threading ring, which rotates concentric with the drum. This guide begins its motion on the wrong side of the tape, but as the threading ring turns, the guide pops up and engages the back of the tape. Then as the threading ring rotates further, the guide is slowly lowered along the drum axis at the correct rate by a cam, such that the tape is laid onto the drum at the helix angle. When the drum guide reaches the end of its travel, its supporting shaft comes up against a fixed vee-block which positions it repeatably. It is held in contact with the block by a solenoid.

The intermediate guide is designed to move away from the cassette as the drum guide proceeds around the threading ring, and the tilt angle of this guide, which imparts the tape twist, is changed as it moves so that a cylindrical wrap is always maintained. This guide is mounted on three vee-shaped rollers which are preloaded outwards and ride in a matching slot in the deckplate. The tilt of the guide is controlled by a spherical roller on an extension of the guide shaft, which bears against a cam profile below the guide track. The principle is shown in Figure 6.36. All of the cam profiles which achieve these operations were computer generated.

Since the total guide wrap angle of cassette transports inevitably amounts to several revolutions, tension build-up is often a problem. In this transport, all tape guides are lubricated by compressed air, except for the tilting threading guide,

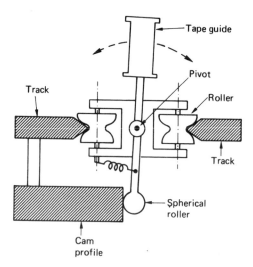

Figure 6.36 The spherical roller and cam profile tilt the tape guide axis to the correct angle as threading proceeds. Tape geometry can then be perfect at all points in the threading.

which is a roller. The drum guide has to travel a long distance, and it is difficult to provide a permanent air supply. The air feed is through the solenoid locking arm, so that air supply becomes available when the tape is fully threaded.

6.19 Operating modes of a digital recorder

The digital video recorder is expected to do much more than record and replay in a modern installation. The main operating modes will be examined here, followed by the more obscure modes.

In *crash record* the tape is either blank or considered to be blank, and no reference will be made to any previous information on the tape. As with analog video recorders, if a crash recording is made in the middle of an existing recording, the playback will lose lock at the transition.

In this mode the full-width erase head will be active, and the entire tape format will be laid down, including audio blocks and control track.

There are a fixed number of segments in a field, and so the drum speed will be locked to incoming video. The drum phase will be determined by the delay needed to shuffle and encode the data in a segment. Owing to the encoding delay, the recording heads on the drum will begin tracing a segment some time after the beginning of the input field. The capstan will simply rotate at constant speed, driving the tape at the speed specified in the format. As the rotating heads begin a diagonal track, a segment pulse will be recorded in the control track. Once per field, the segment pulse will be accompanied by a field pulse. There will also be a colour frame pulse recorded at appropriate intervals.

6.20 Colour-framed playback

Ordinary framing in component recorders only requires that the segmentation on tape is properly undone, so that all of the segments in one field are assembled together, and that the interlace sequence is synchronous with reference, so that an odd field comes from tape when there is an odd field in the station reference. Composite recorders require colour framing, where the off-tape field must also be the same type of field in the four- or eight-field sequence as exists in the reference. Many component formats support colour framing which is useful in case they need to record decoded composite signals which may later be re-encoded. If the component replay is colour framed, artifacts due to residual chroma in luminance can be minimized.

The error-correction and de-interleaving processes on replay require a finite time in which to operate, and so the transport must play back segments ahead of real time, in the same way that analog machines play back ahead of real time for timebase-correction purposes. The drum speed will be synchronous with reference, and the drum phase will be determined by the decoding delay.

The capstan system will be responsible for tracking and framing, and will need to vary the speed of the tape until framing is achieved. It will then vary the phase of the tape to optimize tracking.

The capstan and tape form part of a phase-locked loop where the phase of the control track pulses is compared with reference pulses. In order to achieve colour framing, the phase comparison must be between reference colour frame pulses and offtape colour frame pulses. In this way the linear motion of the tape is phased such that reference and offtape framing are the same. The capstan speed must vary during this part of the lock-up sequence, and the picture may be temporarily degraded unless the machine has provision for operating at non-normal speed.

Once framing or colour framing is achieved, the capstan will switch to a different mode in order to obtain accurate tracking. The phase comparison will now be made more often using all of the control track pulses. If the phase error is used to modify the capstan drive, the error can be eliminated, since the capstan drives the tape which produces the control track segment pulses. Eliminating this timing error results in the rotating heads following the tape tracks properly. Artificially delaying or advancing the reference pulses from the drum will result in a tracking adjustment.

6.21 Assembly editing

In an assemble edit, new material is appended to an existing recording in such a way that the video timing structure continues unbroken over the edit point. In a component recording, only the syncs need to be unbroken, whereas in a composite recording, the subcarrier phase will also need to be continuous.

The recording will begin at a vertical interval, and it will be necessary to have a preroll in order to synchronize tape and drum motion to the signal to be recorded. The procedure during the preroll is similar to that of framed playback, except that the input video timing is used. The goal of the preroll process is to ensure that the record head is at the beginning of the first segment in a field exactly one encode delay after the beginning of the desired field in the input video signal. At this point the record head will be turned on. After the assemble point, there will not necessarily be a control track, and the capstan must smoothly enter constant speed mode without a disturbance to tape motion. The control track will begin to record in a continuation of the phase of the existing control track. This process will then continue indefinitely until halted.

6.22 Insert editing

An insert differs from an assemble in that a short part of a recording is replaced by new material somewhere in the centre. An insert can only be made on a tape which has a continuous control track and timecode to allow edit control, because the in- and out-point edits must both be synchronous. The preroll will be exactly as for an assemble edit, and the video record process will be exactly the same, but the capstan control will be achieved by playing back the control track at all times, so that the new video tracks are laid down in exactly the same place as the previous recording. At the out-point, the record heads will be turned off at the end of the last segment in a field.

As the tracks used in DVTRs are so narrow, some thought has to be given to the results of mechanical tolerances when edits are performed. In transports with no flying erase, the record-head width is typically 10% larger than the track width, to ensure full overwrite. As a result a correctly aligned insert edit leaves a track which is slightly narrower than normal at the out-point. This is not a serious problem as the result of a narrow track is that the signal-to-noise ratio is a little less, so the error-correction system works harder.

There is, however, a potential problem if repeated edits are made in the same area of a recording. Figure 6.37(a) shows the effect of making a second insert edit on top of an earlier edit at the same frame addresses. The second edit is performed with a small tracking error. At the beginning of the insert, the effect is to make the last track of the previous recording slightly less than its normal width, but this is not a problem. However, at the end of the insert, the previous last track is not completely overwritten, and an unwanted *sliver track* of the same azimuth type as the wanted track is left. This will cause a serious reduction in signal quality on playback. The problem is overcome in studio transports by making the record heads the same width as the track pitch and using a flying erase head which is slightly wider than the recorded segment. Figure 6.37(b) shows that in D-3 the flying erase head is physically positioned in advance of the record heads by virtue of a higher elevation in the scanner and an angular advance of about 210°. Thus the erase head for a particular record head pair is on the opposite side of the scanner. The timing of the erase current must be shifted by the 210° advance angle so that erasing begins in the correct place on the tape.

The use of the erase head results in a guard band being created before the first segment of the insert and after the last segment, as in Figure 6.37(c), but not between segments as would happen if the erase head were immediately in front of the record head. The erase head is slightly wider than the width of two tracks or one segment.

The result of the guard bands is that slight mispositioning during an edit now results in the slight noise from an erased guard band being read instead of a coherent signal. Mispositioning during a repeat insert edit merely increases the width of the guard band at one end of the insert.

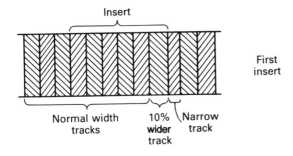

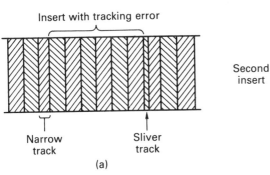

(a)

Figure 6.37 (a) Inaccurate insert edit leaves sliver of previous track which causes errors.

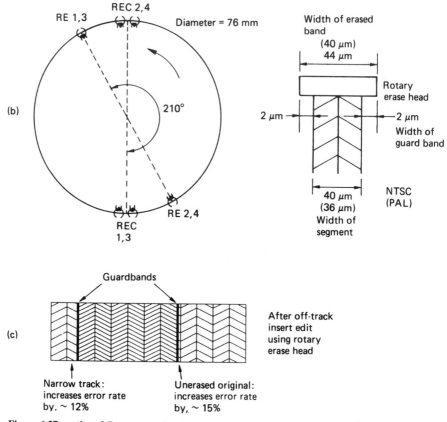

Figure 6.37 continued Rotary erase head at (b) is positioned to leave 2 µm guard band at beginning and end of insert as shown at (c). Guard band partially erases sliver track, reducing error rate.

The flying erase heads will also be used for a short period at the beginning of an assemble edit until the tape erased by the full-width stationary erase head has reached the scanner.

6.23 Fast striping

Many machines have a mode in which the control track and timecode tracks can be written or *striped* at high speed. The tape is driven at typically three times normal speed and artificially higher-frequency signals are generated and supplied to the stationary heads which record these linear tracks. In some machines this fast striping can be done in coplanar mode, where the tape does not contact the drum and rotary-head wear is avoided. In others the drum is still wrapped and must rotate in order to develop an air film, but clearly no slant tracks can be recorded at such a linear speed.

Fast striping records only the control and timecode tracks, which is sufficient reference to allow insert editing to be used. However, when the inserts are made, it is important that the entire slant track is recorded by recording video *and* all of the audio channels. If this is not done, the tape format is violated by recording, say, the video but no audio. On replay the machine will find blank lengths of track where it is expecting ID codes and an error condition may occur.

6.24 Edit optimize

When an edit is made, it is important that the new slant tracks are laid down in exactly the correct place along the tape so that a change of track phase does not occur at the edit point. On a perfectly adjusted machine editing a tape which it has itself recorded, this will not happen, but when the tape being edited was recorded elsewhere, there may be a discrepancy between the locations of the control track heads on the two machines concerned.

Edit optimize is an operating mode in which the edit is not made by recording tracks in the *correct* place, but by recording tracks having the *same tracking error* as those already on the tape. As a result the edited tape will require the same tracking adjustment everywhere. This is particularly useful when it is required to edit only the audio blocks as a tracking error during an audio edit results in sectors having an offset as shown in Figure 6.38. Such a track cannot be played properly at any setting of the tracking control.

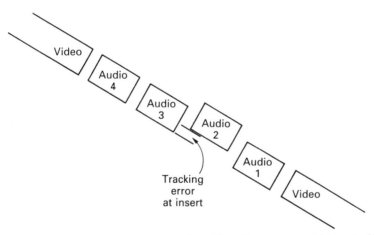

Figure 6.38 If an insert edit of one audio channel is made on a tape containing a tracking error the resultant track has no optimum tracking position. Edit optimize matches the tracking error so that the same tracking can be used for all sectors.

In edit optimize, prior to an edit, the machine plays the tape with the record heads and varies the capstan phase in order to locate the tracking setting where the maximum signal level, or the minimum error rate, is obtained. This tracking will then be employed during the edit so that new tracks have the same or nearly the same alignment as the old tracks.

Whilst edit optimize is a useful feature, it should not be used to excess or when it is not essential. A series of assembly edits, in which each one is optimized to the end of the last recording, may result in tolerance build-up where the tracking slowly changes at each edit as a result of residual error in the optimize system.

6.25 Tape speed override

One of the most useful features of a production recorder is the ability to operate at variable speed. The variable-speed modes variously available are TSO (Tape Speed Override), slow motion/jog and shuttle.

In TSO, the speed is only changed by a maximum of about 15% from normal in order to trim a program to fit a broadcast time slot. Clearly the audio must be fully recovered, and so no replay-head jumping is permissible. The speed of the entire transport is changed by changing the transport timing reference with respect to station reference. The drum and the capstan change speed in proportion so that the heads still follow all of the slant tracks properly. All of the audio blocks are recovered, and full-quality digital audio is output. Owing to the speed change, the audio sampling rate will not be exactly 48 kHz, and a digital pitch changer or sampling-rate converter can be used if necessary. Clearly the offtape field rate will no longer match reference, and the difference is accommodated by a frame store/timebase corrector, which is written at offtape speed and read at reference speed. Fields will occasionally be skipped or repeated as TBC addresses lap one another.

In slow motion or jog, it is not normal to recover the audio fully, since it will only be needed for cueing, and so the track-following head system comes into operation. Where audio is recovered, it will contain discontinuities.

6.26 Variable-speed replay

The variable-speed range first achieved by the C-format analog machines has essentially become the yardstick by which later formats are measured. It is important for the success of a DVTR that at least an equal speed range is available and the means to obtain this will be discussed here. Although the problem of variable speed is defined by the format, the solutions adopted by various manufacturers are quite different and will be contrasted.

It was seen in Section 6.3 that the movement of the tape results in the tracks having an angle different from the helix angle. The rotary head will only be able to follow the track properly if the tape travels at the correct speed. At all other speeds, the head will move at an angle to the tracks. If the head is able to move along the drum axis as it turns, it will be possible to follow whole tracks at certain tape speeds by moving the head as a function of the rotational angle of the drum. The necessary function can be appreciated by considering the situation when the tape is stopped. The tape track will, of course, be at the track angle, but the head will rotate at the helix angle. The head can be made to follow a stationary track by deflecting it at constant rate by one segment pitch per sweep. In other words, a ramp or triangle waveform is necessary to deflect the head. The slope of the ramp is proportional to the speed *difference*, since at normal speed the difference is zero and no deflection is needed. Clearly the deflection cannot continue to grow for ever, because the head will run out of travel, and it must then jump to miss out some tracks and reduce the deflection.

There are a number of issues to be addressed in providing a track-following system. The use of segmented formats means that head jumps necessary to omit or repeat one or more fields must jump over several segments. This requires a mechanical head-positioning system which has the necessary travel and will work reliably despite the enormous acceleration experienced at the perimeter of the drum. As there are generally two head bases, two such systems are needed, and they must be independently controlled since they are mounted in opposition on the drum and contact the tape alternately. In addition a control system is required which will ensure that jumps only take place at the end of a field to prevent a picture from two different fields being displayed.

The degree of accuracy required is much higher than in analog formats because the tracks are much narrower.

When the tape speed is close to three times normal, most of the time a two-field jump will be necessary at the end of every field. Figure 6.39 shows the resulting ramp deflection waveform (for one head pair only). Since the control

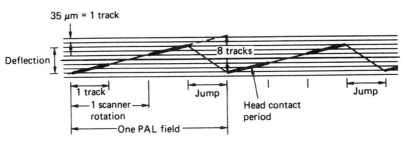

Figure 6.39 Head deflection waveform for PAL D-3 at +3× normal speed. This requires a jump of two fields between every field played, and this corresponds to eight tracks. Since head pairs trace the tape alternately, the head has half a revolution in which to jump, so the actual jump is only six tracks. However, the vertical position of the above waveform is subject to an uncertainty of plus or minus two tracks because capstan phase is random during variable speed.

track phase is random, an offset of up to $\pm\frac{1}{2}$ field will be superimposed on the deflection, so that if a two-field jump must always be possible, a total deflection of three fields must be available. This, along with the segmentation employed, determines the mechanical travel of the heads.

6.27 The actuator

In Sony and Panasonic machines, the actuator used for head deflection is based on piezoelectric elements as used in numerous previous products. Figure 6.40 shows the construction of the Sony dynamic tracking head. A pair of parallel piezoelectric bimorphs is used, to ensure that head zenith is affected as little as possible by deflection. The basic principle of the actuator is that an applied voltage causes the barium titanate crystal to shrink. If two thin plates are bonded together to create a bimorph, the shrinkage of one of them will result in bending. A stale sandwich displays the same effect. Application of a voltage to one or other of the elements allows deflection in either direction, although care must be taken to prevent reverse voltage being applied to an element since this will destroy the inherent electric field. In view of the high-g environment, which attempts to restore the actuator to the neutral position, high deflection voltages are necessary. The deflection amplifiers are usually static, and feed the drum via slip rings which are often fitted on the top of the drum. When worn, these can spark and increase the error rate. Piezoelectric actuators display hysteresis, and some form of position feedback is necessary to allow a linear system. This is obtained by strain gauges which are attached to one of the bimorphs, and can be seen in the figure. When power is first applied to the transport, the actuator is supplied with a gradually decaying sinusoidal drive signal, which removes any unwanted set from the bimorph.

In Ampex D-2 and DCT machines, the piezoelectric actuator was not considered adequate for the larger travel demanded in a segmented format,[3] and a moving-coil actuator has been developed. These had been used experimentally in certain analog recorders, but gave way to piezoelectric actuators in the

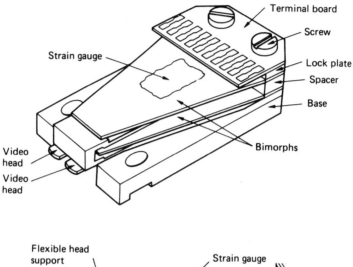

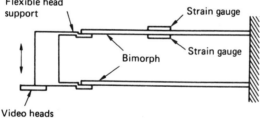

Figure 6.40 The dynamic tracking head of a Sony D-2 transport uses a pair of parallel bimorphs to maintain head zenith angle. Note use of strain gauges for feedback. (Courtesy Sony Broadcast).

C-format. Now that rare earth magnets are available, which offer high field strength with low mass, the moving-coil actuator becomes attractive again, because it allows a low-mass cantilever which has higher resonant frequencies and requires less force to deflect. The moving coil is inherently a low-impedance device requiring a current drive which is easier to provide than the high voltages needed by piezoelectric devices.

Figure 6.41(a) shows the concept of the moving-coil head and Figure 6.41(b) shows the appearance of the actual unit used in D-2. The cantilever is folded from thin sheet metal which is perforated to assist the folding process. The resulting structure is basically a torsion box supported on a wide flexural pivot. This means that it can bend up and down, but it cannot twist, since twisting would introduce unwanted azimuth errors. The cantilever carries the actuator coil, and is supported in a metal shoe which carries the magnet.

Positional feedback of the cantilever deflection is obtained by a photoelectric system. This has one light source and two sensors between which moves a blade which is integral with the cantilever. When the cantilever deflects, a differential signal results from the sensors. The photoelectric sensor is mounted inside the top of the drum, and automatically aligns with the moving blade when the top is fitted.

For the DCT format a similar actuator was developed, but having a parallel action to maintain constant head zenith angle.

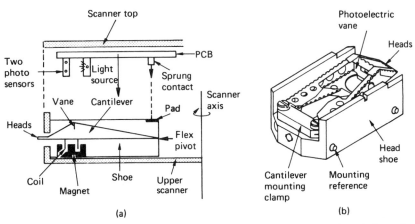

Figure 6.41 (a) Showing the concept of moving-coil head deflection. The cantilever is flexurally pivoted at the opposite end to the heads, and position feedback is obtained from a vane on the cantilever which differentially varies the light falling on two photosensors. (b) The appearance of an actual replaceable AST head assembly. (Courtesy Ampex).

Whichever of these actuators is used, the combination of actuator, drive amplifier and position feedback gives a subassembly which will deflect the head in proportion to an applied voltage. It is then necessary to provide suitable drive signals to ensure that the deflection makes the head follow the track.

6.28 Detecting the tracking error

Track following is a means of actively controlling the relationship between the replay head and the track so that the track is traced more accurately than it would be by purely mechanical means.

This can be applied to systems operating at normal speed, in order to allow interchange in adverse conditions as is done in Digital Betacam, but in many formats track following is an option, and satisfactory interchange can be achieved without it. The tracking error will be used on two different levels. Firstly, the DC component of the tracking error will be used to set the average elevation of the head about which the ramp deflection will take place. Secondly,

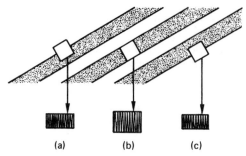

(a)   (b)   (c)

Figure 6.42 Effect of tracking error on playback signal. Signal amplitude in (a) and (c) is identical, despite sense of tracking error. Maximum signal occurs with correct alignment as in (b).

variations of tracking error during the track can be used to compensate for tracks which are not straight, due to some relative misalignment between the machine which recorded the tape and the player. The tracking-error-detection systems differ between manufacturers and these differences will be noted.

Figure 6.42 shows three relationships of the head to the track, and corresponding signal output. The waveforms in Figure 6.42 correspond to the RF envelope of the channel-coded signal. Case (a) and case (c) display the same output, although the tracking error has the opposite sense. Simple processing of the RF level only gives the magnitude of the error, not the sense.

In order to extract the sense of the tracking error, it is necessary to move the tracking head, to see if the error becomes greater or smaller. The process of manually tuning an AM radio is very similar.

In Sony D-2 machines, the head elevation is changed by small steps between segments, and if the steps cause the average RF level to fall, the direction of the steps is reversed. This process is known colloquially as 'bump and look', and was originally developed for the Betacam products.

In the Ampex machines, the head is subject to a sinusoidal oscillation or dither, as was done in C-format machines. One field scan contains many cycles of dither. The effect on the RF envelope, as shown in Figure 6.43, is an amplitude modulation of the carrier, which has little effect on the video, owing to the insensitivity of the digital recording system to amplitude effects. Figure 6.43(a) shows that the effect of dither on a correctly aligned head is a frequency doubling in the RF envelope. Figures.6.43(b) and (c) show the effect of the head off track. Both cases appear similar, but the phase of the envelope modulation is different, and can be used to extract the sense of the tracking error.

Each cantilever carries two heads, one of each azimuth type, and the RF levels from the two heads are averaged together. This gives a 3 dB improvement in signal-to-noise ratio, as well as accommodating manufacturing tolerances in the elevation of the video tips. Only one detector or synchronous rectifier is then required per cantilever.

Dither cannot be used with analog VTRs employing azimuth recording because the transverse head motion interacts with the azimuth angle to give the effect of rising and falling head-to-tape speed. In FM recording, this introduces an unwanted signal into the video, which is why Sony developed the bump and look system for Betacam. The effect is still present in a digital recorder, but the

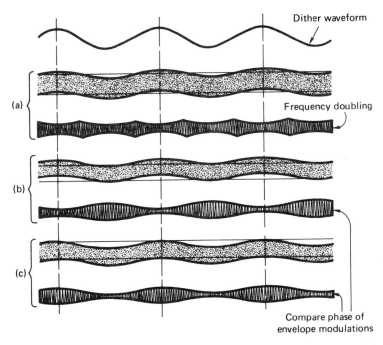

Figure 6.43 Top, dither waveform which causes head to oscillate across track. At (a) is optimum alignment, showing frequency doubling in RF envelope. With head above track centre, as in (b), RF amplitude increases as head reaches lowest point, whereas reverse applies in case (c).

result is that the instantaneous offtape data rate rises and falls slightly. This is accommodated by the phase-locked loop in the data separator, and has no effect on the data. A harmless dither component will be observed in the VCO control voltage, and the speed variation in the discrete data is completely removed in the timebase correction.

In Figure 6.44 the RF is detected to obtain a level, which is fed to a phase-sensitive rectifier, whose reference is the dither drive signal. The output of the phase-sensitive rectifier is a tracking error signal which contains both magnitude and sense and rather a lot of harmonics of dither. Careful choice of the dither frequency allows easier cancelling of the dither harmonics. In the VPR-300, there are five and a half cycles of dither per segment, or 11 cycles per revolution. Both heads are dithered by the same waveform, which means that the dither on odd segments will be phase reversed with respect to even segments. A dither frequency of 1100 Hz results in PAL, whereas in NTSC it is 990 Hz.

The tracking error is averaged over a pair of segments to cancel the harmonics and to produce an elevation error. The tracking error will also be sampled at several points down the track to see if there is a consistent curvature in the tracking. This can be reduced by adding a correction curve to the deflection waveform which will adjust itself until the best envelope is obtained over the whole track length.

A different approach to measuring track curvature is used in Sony D-2 and Panasonic transports. As has been stated, deflecting a head which uses azimuth

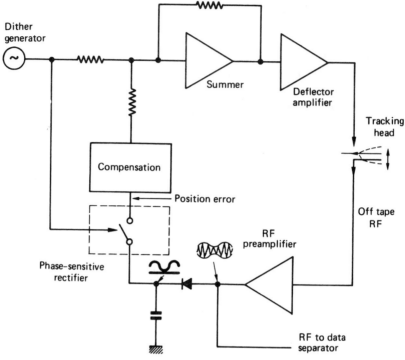

Figure 6.44 The tracking error is extracted from the RF envelope by a phase-sensitive rectifier.

recording causes timing changes. If a pair of heads of opposite azimuth are tracing the appropriate tracks, tracking error will result in differential timing changes. This can be measured by comparing the time at which sync patterns are detected in the two channels. Figure 6.45 illustrates the principle. This system will detect tracking errors due to track distortion. Unfortunately, manufacturing tolerances in the physical stagger between the heads on both the machine which made the recording and the player will combine to put a permanent offset in the

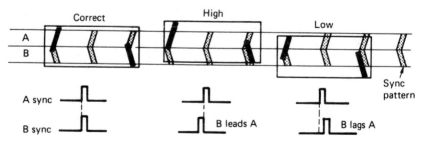

Figure 6.45 In the Sony D-2 DT system the tracking error is detected by comparing the times at which sync patterns are detected by the two heads on each arm. Owing to the use of azimuth recording a component of transverse movement results in a movement of the effective position of the head along the track.

tracking error derived using this principle. It is necessary to calibrate the system each time it is used. The bump and look system maximizes the RF level at the beginning of the track, and the control system then inserts a changing offset into the sync timing comparator until it too gives zero tracking error at the beginning of the track. The offset is then held at that value. This process removes the static deflection and allows the tracking error to be used to deflect the heads within the track.

The Digital Betacam format is unique in that it contains tracking tones in the slant tracks which are part of the format. These tracking tones are intended to eliminate manual tracking adjustments in normal play and cannot measure tracking errors which change along the track.

6.29 The ramp generator

The positional feedback generated by the observation of the dithered RF envelope or the sync pattern phase is not sufficiently accurate to follow the tracks unassisted except at normal speed where it can be used as an interchange aid. In variable speed the deflection of the head is predicted to produce a feedforward signal which adds to the head deflection. The feedback then only has to correct for the difference between the feedforward and the actuality. When the tape travels at the wrong speed, the track angle changes, and so the head needs to deflect by a distance proportional to the angle it has rotated in order to follow the track. The deflection signal will be in the form of a ramp, which becomes steeper as the tape speed deviates more from normal. The actual speed of the capstan can be used to generate the slope of the ramp. One possible implementation of this is shown in Figure 6.46. A counter has count-up and count-down inputs. The first of these is driven by the capstan tacho disk, and the second is driven by a clock whose frequency is exactly equal to that generated by the capstan tacho at normal speed. When the capstan runs at normal speed, the counter receives as many up

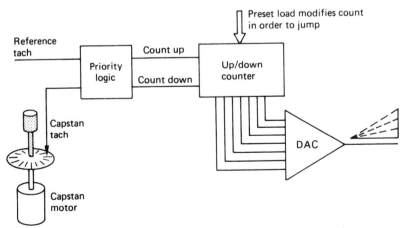

Figure 6.46 An up/down counter is fed with pulses from the capstan tach and from a reference whose frequency is precisely that of capstan tach at normal speed. The counter will thus integrate speed deviation from unity, and the DAC will produce a ramp whose slope is proportional to speed difference. This is the feedforward signal which drives the head deflection system.

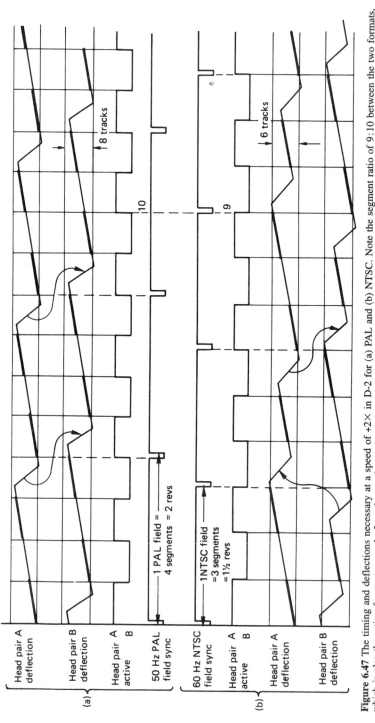

Figure 6.47 The timing and deflections necessary at a speed of +2× in D-2 for (a) PAL and (b) NTSC. Note the segment ratio of 9:10 between the two formats, which is also the ratio of scanner speeds. In order to play entire fields, jumps must take place about the field boundary, so that if one head pair jumps, the other must follow (serpentine arrow). In NTSC there are three segments per field, so the jumping follows a two-field sequence, where the head fails to jump in one field, but jumps twice in the next.

clocks as down clocks, and remains unchanged. However, if the capstan speed is raised, the counter will begin to count up at a rate proportional to the speed difference. The counter drives a DAC which produces the deflection ramp. The RF amplitude detector will generate pulses which are also fed into the counter so that the elevation correction can be made. It is also possible to predict the average or static deflection of the heads from the control track phase. The capstan frequency generator can be used to measure control track phase. The capstan FG wheel will be designed so that a known number of FG pulses are generated when the capstan transports the tape by the distance between control track segment pulses. The FG pulses are fed to a counter which is reset by segment pulses from the control track head. The counter then produces control track phase which can be used to establish head elevation.

The same deflection ramp slope will be fed to both head pairs so that they will read alternate segments for an entire field. At some point it will be necessary to jump the heads to reduce the deflection, and this requires some care. The heads are 180° opposed, and contact the tape alternately. The jump takes place while the head is out of contact with the tape. The two head pairs will have to jump at different times, half a drum revolution apart. Clearly if one head jumps, the second head must also jump, otherwise the resulting picture will have come from two fields. As the jumps are half a revolution apart, it follows that the decision to jump must be made half a drum revolution *before* the end of the current field. The decision is made by extrapolating the deflection ramp forward to see what the deflection *will be* when the end of the field is reached. If the deflection will exceed half a field, it can be reduced by jumping one field. If the deflection will exceed one field, it can be reduced by jumping two fields. The jump can be executed by adding or subtracting a number of pulses in the ramp counter.

Tape tension changes can cause the track width to vary minutely. This is normally of no consequence, but when taken over all of the tracks in a segment the error may be significant. It is possible to compare the tracking error before and after a jump, and if the error becomes greater, the jump distance was inappropriate for the tape being played. It is possible to modify the distance jumped simply by changing the number of pulses fed to the ramp counter during the jump command. In this way the jump distance can optimize itself for the tape being played.

Figure 6.47(a) shows the ramping action for the two moving heads in PAL D-2 or D-3 with the tape moving at twice normal speed. It will be seen that when one head jumps, the other one will also jump, so both heads always play the same field. The timing shift due to the heads being separated by half a revolution can be seen. As there are four segments per field in PAL, corresponding to two drum revolutions, all fields will contain the same sequence. Figure 6.47(b) shows the equivalent sequence of events for NTSC. As there are three segments per field and two moving heads, the action differs between odd fields and even fields. During one field, a given head may jump twice, but in the next field it will not jump at all.

6.30 Track-following block diagram

Figure 6.48 shows an Ampex D-2/DCT track-following system. There is an inner feedback loop which consists of the head actuator, the position feedback sensor and an amplifier. This loop is a position servo which makes the head deflection

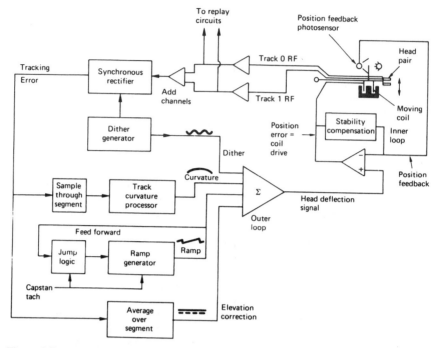

Figure 6.48 Ampex D-2 track-following system. Position feedback in an inner loop around the head positioner linearizes and damps positioner so that mechanical deflection is proportional to head deflection signal from outer loop. Dither generator wobbles the head and drives synchronous receiver to obtain tracking error which is used to correct the head elevation and to compensate for track curvature. Feedforward system generates ramps.

proportional to the input voltage. Like any position servo it is provided with compensation to prevent oscillation and maximize frequency response. The inner loop is driven by the sum of four signals. These are:

(1) The dither signal, which is a sinusoid designed to wobble the head either side of its average elevation.

(2) The elevation correction obtained by averaging the tracking error over the entire track.

(3) The track curvature compensation, which is a segment rate curve obtained by sampling the tracking error at several points along the track.

(4) The feedforward ramp and jump signal. The slope is obtained from capstan speed difference and the jumps are initiated by analysing the deflection.

Figure 6.49 shows the track-following system used by Sony and Panasonic. The capstan FG and control track are used together for elevation prediction, and capstan FG is used alone for ramp slope prediction. The bump and look system is controlled by the RF detector, which is also used to calibrate the differential sync pattern timing detector.

In both types of machine, there are two moving heads and so two of these systems are necessary. They are largely independent except for a common jump

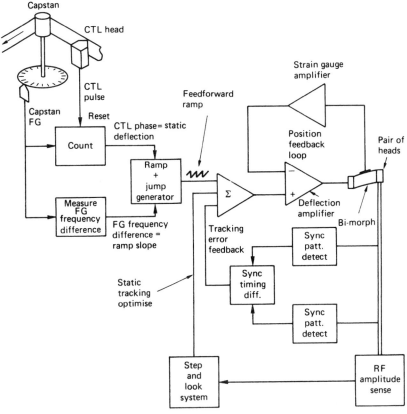

Figure 6.49 The DT system used by Sony D-2 machines combines ramp feedforward from the capstan speed and control track with tracking feedback from the differential sync detection of Figure 6.45. In addition the bump and look system slightly offsets the heads by a different amount each scan and assesses the RF amplitude to find an optimum static deflection. This is really a slow dither process. Note that this is a conceptual diagram. In practice many of these stages are carried out by microprocessor.

control system which ensures that when one head jumps during the last segment of a field the other head will follow once it has played that segment.

When a head jumps, it will move to a track which began at a different place along the tape, and so the timing in that track will not be the same as in the track which the head left. In a segmented format, the effect is magnified by the number of tracks in a field. To support a speed range from $-1 \times$ to $+3 \times$, it has been seen that an overall head travel of three fields is necessary. From the start of a given segment to the start of the same segment three fields away is nearly 8 mm in PAL D-2, and over 6.5 mm in NTSC D-2. The wrap of the scanner must be extended to allow tape contact over a greater angle, and the replay circuitry must be able to accommodate the timing uncertainty which amounts to about 5% of the segment period. Clearly the timing error can be eliminated by the timebase-correction processes within the playback system.

6.31 Camcorder transports

One of the greatest difficulties in designing a digital camcorder is obtaining sufficient battery life without excessive weight. A camcorder is impracticable with $\frac{3}{4}$ inch tape, but quite possible with the $\frac{1}{2}$ inch formats. Most camcorders will be designed to accept only the smallest, or perhaps the two smaller, sizes of cassette, as this reduces the size of the transport and sufficient battery life is unlikely to be available to record the longest tape.

Compressed-air lubricated or ultrasonic guides are impractical and extensive use will be made of rolling element bearings, where possible, and fixed slant posts. Shuttle speed will be restricted in order to save power and to reduce tape tension.

As the main purpose of a camcorder is signal acquisition, features not essential to this function can be omitted. Simple backspace assembly editing is adequate, and flying erase heads can be dispensed with, reducing noise and power consumption.

6.32 Aligning for interchange

One of the most important aspects of DVTR maintenance is to ensure that tapes made on a particular machine meet the specifications laid down in the format. If they do, then it will be possible to play those tapes on any other properly aligned machine. In this section the important steps necessary to achieve interchange between transports will be outlined. Regular cleaning, particularly of the drum step, is necessary to maintain interchange and no interchange adjustment should be attempted until it has been verified that the machine is clean.

When the cassette is lowered into the transport it seats on pillars which hold it level. The tape hubs seat on the reel turntables. The first step in aligning the transport is to ensure that the reel hubs and all of the guides the tape runs past on its way to and from the drum are at the correct height. The guides are generally threaded so that they can be screwed up and down. In the correct position, the tape will stay in the cassette plane and distortion will be avoided. The height of the cassette pillars can be adjusted to ensure that the spools inside the cassette are lifted free of the cassette body at the end of the elevator travel. If this is not done the spools will rub against the cassette body, causing debris and tension errors.

Once the tape can be passed through the machine without damage, the basic transport functions can be checked. Since tape tension affects the track angle and the head contact pressure, verifying the correct tension is essential before attempting any adjustments at the drum. This is done with a tape tension gauge. Many tension gauges change their reading as a result of tape motion and it may be necessary to calibrate the gauge whilst moving the tape and calibration weight at approximately the correct speed for the format. The tension can then be checked in various transport and shuttle modes. Since the drum friction is in the opposite sense when the tape is reversed, the back tension must be higher than for forward mode to keep the average drum tension constant. In some transports the tension-sensing arm is not statically balanced, and the tape tension becomes a function of the orientation of the machine. In this case the adjustment must be made with the machine in the attitude in which it is to be used.

The track spacing on record is determined by the capstan speed, which must be checked. As the capstan speed will be controlled by a frequency-generating wheel on the capstan shaft, it is generally only necessary to check that the capstan FG frequency is correct in record mode. A scratch tape will be used for this check.

Helical interchange can now be considered. Tape passing around the drum is guided in three ways. On the approach, the tape is steered by the entrance guides, which continue to affect the first part of the drum wrap. The centre part of the drum wrap is guided by the machined step on the drum base. Finally the last part of the wrap is steered by the exit guides. Helical interchange is obtained by adjusting the entrance and exit guide heights so that the tape passes smoothly between the three regions.

As tape is flexible, it will distort as it passes around the drum if the entrance and exit guides are not correctly set. The state of alignment can be assessed by working out the effect of misalignments on the ability of the replay head to follow tape tracks. Figure 6.50(a) shows an example of the entrance guide being too low. The tape is forced to climb up to reach the drum step, and then it has to

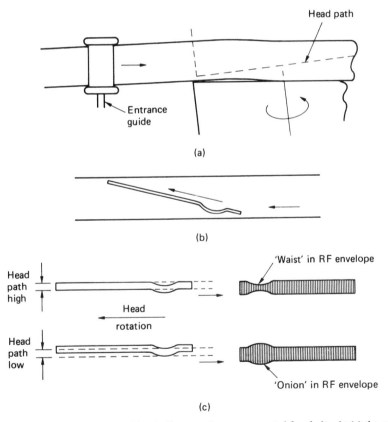

Figure 6.50 The effects of guide misalignment shown exaggerated for clarity. At (a) the entrance guide is too low and forces the tape to flex as it enters the scanner. At (b) the tape relaxes to produce a bent track. At (c) an alignment tape is being played and the transport has bent the tracks. The RF envelope will show different disturbances as the tracking is offset above or below optimum. A correctly aligned transport has an envelope which collapses uniformly as the tracking is offset.

bend down again to run along the step. If straight tracks were originally recorded on the tape, they will no longer be straight when the tape is distorted in this way. Figure 6.50(b) shows what happens to the track. Since in an azimuth recording machine the head is larger than the track, small distortions of this kind will be undetectable. It is necessary to offset the tracking deliberately so that the effect of the misalignment can be seen. If the head is offset upwards, then the effect will be that the RF signal grows in level briefly at the beginning of the track, giving the envelope an onion-like appearance on an oscilloscope. If the head is offset downwards, the distortion will take the track away from the head path and the RF envelope will be waisted. If the misalignment is in the exit guide, then the envelope disturbances will appear at the right-hand end of the RF envelope. The height of both the entrance and exit guides is adjusted until no disturbance of the RF envelope rectangularity is apparent whatever tracking error is applied. A rough alignment can be performed with a tape previously recorded on a trustworthy machine, but final alignment requires the use of a reference tape.

Once the mechanical geometry of the drum is set up, straight tracks on tape will appear straight to the drum, and it is then possible to set up the tracking. This requires adjustment of the position of the control track head along the tape path. This is done by observing the RF level of a test tape on playback. If the machine has a front panel tracking adjustment, it should be set to zero whilst the mechanical adjustment is made.

The final interchange adjustment is to ensure that the drum timing is correct. Even with correct geometry, the tracks can be laid down at the correct angle and spacing, but at the wrong height on the tape, as Figure 6.51 shows. A recording made with this adjustment incorrect may still play, but would cause serious difficulty if insert editing is attempted, particularly of the audio blocks.

The point where recording commences is determined by the sensor which generates a pulse once per revolution of the drum. The correct timing can be obtained either by physically moving the sensor around the drum axis, or by adjusting a variable delay in series with an artificially early fixed sensor. A

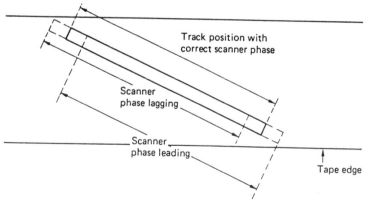

Figure 6.51 Even with correct tape path geometry, a machine can record data in the wrong place along the track if the scanner phase is misadjusted. The scanner pulse generator signal is rephased or delayed in order to make the adjustment.

timing reference tape is necessary that has an observable event in the RF waveform. The tape is played, and the sensor or delay is adjusted to give the specified relative timing between the event on the reference tape and the sensor pulse. When this is correct, the machine will record tracks in the right place along the helical sweep.

6.33 Head replacement

In modern DVTRs, head replacement generally requires the replacement of the entire rotating disk or wafer, which contains factory-adjusted heads. The exception is the Ampex approach where individual head bases are replaceable. These are prealigned and no mechanical adjustment is necessary. When heads are replaced, certain electronic adjustments are necessary. Replay heads require equalization to compensate for high-frequency loss, and this varies with head wear. When a head is replaced the equalization will no longer be correct. Equalization is adjusted manually by playing a test tape and minimizing the error rate. Some machines are able to adjust their own replay equalization in service. Record heads need to have the record current set. If this is too low then the replay error rate will be excessive due to noise, whereas if it is too high peak shift distortion will result and difficulties may be experienced in overwriting recordings. Some machines can automatically optimize the record current by analysing the error rate from the confidence replay heads.

Track-following heads mounted on actuators will display some spread in their resonant frequency and mechanical damping factor, and it will be necessary to adjust the drive circuitry to suit.

6.34 Cart. machines

The cart. machine began life as a device which was designed to assemble commercial breaks automatically from a library of cassettes. Improvements in storage density have led the concept to be extended to a point where the entire playout of a TV station comes from a mechanized library.

A cart. machine consists of a storage area for cassettes, a number of transports and a simple signal switcher, a robotic arm which moves cassettes, and a computerized control system running from a real time clock.

The storage area consists of compartments to hold cassettes in the library. This is often modular so that different sizes can be constructed. Most libraries store cassettes on a rectangular grid, but as an alternative the library may be a large cylinder which can rotate as part of the access mechanism.

The robotic arm is capable of traversing the entire area of the library and the transports with an X–Y motion. The arm is equipped with a bar code reader so that it can identify cassettes, and a gripper which can move forward to grasp the selected cassette. The control of the robot must be extremely accurate as damage can be caused if a cassette is pushed into a transport or a library compartment when there is a misalignment. In addition to high accuracy, the robot must move at high speed so that the machine can assemble programs from short spots on different cassettes. The robot will be driven by powerful motors through toothed belts or steel cables so that a library several metres long can be traversed in a second or so. Interlocks are necessary to cut the power if someone opens the machine, as a traversing robot can cause injury. The motion of the robot is controlled by velocity and position feedback so that a traverse can begin and end with smooth acceleration. In large libraries it is impossible to assemble the modules accurately, and the library will not be an exact rectangular grid. Before use, the robot learns the position of every compartment by successively accessing each one and locating its precise position from a reference point.

Early cart. machines were analog and were restricted to storing one spot or *event* on each cassette. This allows any sequence of playout to be obtained. As storage density improved, it became wasteful to have only one event per cassette, and control systems were developed which could handle multiple events on each. A problem arises where a playlist requires two events in different places on the same cassette to be assembled. This is overcome by dubbing one of the events to a spare caching cassette which is kept in the library for that purpose. In the digital domain such dubbing causes no loss of quality, whereas an analog machine would have suffered generation loss. Long programs such as feature films can be automatically split into several cassettes for playout.

Many cart. machines can store hundreds of hours of material and are designed to work unattended for long periods. Often there are more tape transports fitted than necessary so that in the case of a failure one can be deassigned and the work reallocated to the remainder. Transports can usually be withdrawn on rails for servicing whilst the remainder of the machine continues to operate. Some machines have two robots. If one fails it will be deactivated and the remaining robot will push it out of the way.

References

1. LÜTZELER, J., An experimental HDTV cassette recorder. *18th ITS Symp. Rec.*, 302–316 (Montreux 1993)
2. RYAN, D.M., Mechanical considerations in the design of a digital video cassette recorder. Presented at International Broadcasting Convention, (Brighton, 1988) *IEE Conf. Publ. No. 293*, 387–390 (1988)
3. OLDERSHAW, R., Design of an automatic scan tracking system for a D-2 recorder. *IEE Conf. Publ. No. 293*, 395–398 (1988)

The DVTR signal system

The transport simply guides the heads repeatably along tape tracks so that waveforms can be recorded and replayed. The head/tape system is imperfect and introduces timebase and data errors. The signal system adapts the characteristics of the tape transport to the requirements of digital video recording.

7.1 Introduction

The signal system of a DVTR lies between the signal input/output connectors and the heads, and in production machines is divided into separate record and replay sections so that both processes can take place at the same time. Simultaneous record and replay capability is necessary not only for confidence replay, but also for pre-read editing modes. The input may be composite or component, and data reduction may or may not be employed. The various DVTR formats largely employ the same processing stages, but there are considerable differences in the order in which these are applied. It is proposed to define here the processes and then to contrast the formats by the way in which they are applied in Chapter 9.

Although the recording technique used in composite formats is digital, it is vital to remember at all times that the data which are recorded are no more than a numerical representation of a composite video waveform. All of the characteristics of composite video remain, including the requirement for a colour framing system to synchronize the four- or eight-field sequences embedded in the subcarrier.

No description of a composite digital VTR can be complete without a discussion of the techniques necessary to handle colour framing and the intimately related ScH phase, and colour processing needed for variable-speed replay. There are considerable differences between the subcarriers of PAL and NTSC, and so there will be corresponding differences between the approaches to colour framing and between the data rates which result from digitizing the two standards. As a result both D-2 and D-3 are really formats which leave different tape footprints in PAL and NTSC, but which nevertheless have a lot in common in order to use the same circuitry and mechanical parts as much as possible. Since colour framing has such a far reaching effect on composite recording, it will be necessary to treat the subject first so that the implications for following topics become clear.

7.2 Colour framing in PAL

In PAL, the eight-field sequence comes about because of the quarter cycle offset of subcarrier against line rate. There are 283 ¾ cycles of subcarrier in one line, which means that four lines must pass before the same relationship occurs between subcarrier and horizontal sync. The odd number of lines in a frame necessary for interlace mean that four frames must elapse before the four-line sequence assumes the same relationship with vertical. Unlike NTSC which has a half cycle offset, PAL does not naturally have good cancellation of chroma on the screen. This is achieved by the addition of 25 Hz to the subcarrier frequency, which causes chroma on a given line to be antiphase with chroma on the line in the next field which will be physically adjacent on the interlaced display. Although this 25 Hz component achieves its goal, it also complicates the colour framer because instead of having four different relationships of subcarrier to horizontal there are now 2500!

Since composite digital samples using burst as a phase reference, it is necessary to follow what the burst does with respect to horizontal. Owing to the

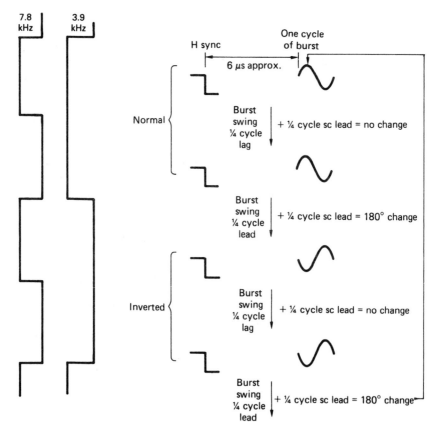

Figure 7.1 Quarter cycle subcarrier H relationship and burst swing combine to give four-line sequence.

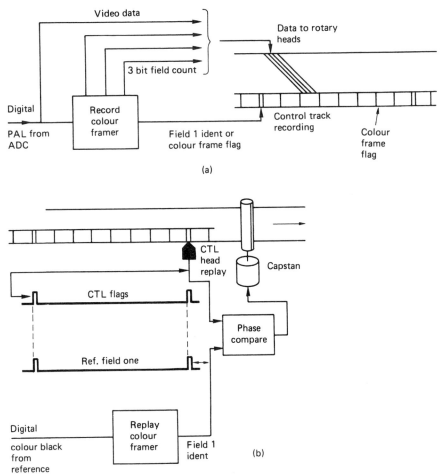

Figure 7.2 At (a) the presence of field 1 on the imput is denoted by a colour frame flag on the control track. The field sequence is also written in the rotary tracks.

At (b), on replay the capstan speed will be changed until offtape colour frame flags coincide with reference field 1 identification. Replay video will then be colour framed to reference.

quarter cycle offset, subcarrier phase advances by 90° from line to line, but the burst swings forward 90° on one line and back 90° on the next to convey the state of V-switch. This means that the burst swing will alternately cancel or double the subcarrier phase advance, giving two lines with the same burst to sync relationship followed by two lines with an inverted burst to sync relationship. Figure 7.1 shows that these four lines repeat at 3.9 kHz and contain two complete cycles of V-switch which run at 7.8 kHz. Once every four frames, line 1 of the frame will be the first of the four line types, and this fact will be indicated by the colour framing flag on the control track. It is the job of the record colour framer to determine when to produce that colour framing flag. Figure 7.2(a) shows the record colour framing process.

On replay, a second colour framer examines the reference input to determine when the start of the colour framing sequence occurs. Figure 7.2(b) shows that the phase difference between the reference colour frame flag and the replay colour frame pulse from the control track controls the capstan speed until the pulse and the flag coincide. When this is achieved, the tape playback is said to be colour framed, and the lines from the tape will be of exactly the same type as the lines in the reference signal. The offtape samples can be fed directly to the machine output. In all other replay modes, a colour processor will be necessary to convert the offtape line type to the reference line type. Since the control track phase is meaningless at anything other than the correct speed, composite digital machines also record identification codes on the helical tracks which uniquely locate a segment within the eight-field sequence. In some machines there is only one colour framing circuit, and it is simply switched to the input or the reference according to whether the machine is recording or playing back.

As was seen in Chapter 3, the sampling clock in PAL uses burst as a phase reference. The colour framer must use sample values obtained by digitizing the leading edge of sync with a burst-phased sampling clock.

The first stage in colour framing is to determine the phase of burst swing. This process is integral with the operation of the sampling-clock phase-locked loop. The phase-locked loop includes the video ADC so that chroma phase errors are minimized. The ADC runs constantly, and digitizes the entire video signal. Control of the VCO is achieved by examining the numerical value of samples taken during the burst.

Figure 7.3 shows one possible implementation. Owing to PAL burst swing, burst phase can have one of two values, 90° apart, so both of them will have the same phase relationship to $4 \times F_{sc}$. A two-phase divider running from the VCO produces a pair of quadrature square waves at subcarrier frequency. These are

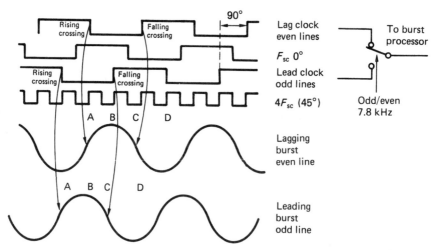

Figure 7.3 Two quadrature clocks are derived from $4F_{sc}$ whose crossings are at 45° phase in PAL. These two clocks are used on alternate lines, where they predict the position and direction of a burst crossing. If it is a downward crossing, the phase error needs to be inverted. If the odd/even sequence gets out of step, the clock moves forward a quadrant when an incoming burst moves back a quadrant, so the burst is perceived as inverted. The phase error alternates at half line rate and can be used to reset the 7.8 kHz divider.

used on alternate lines to synchronize the numerical processing of sampled burst. In the first quadrant, A, there should be a positive burst crossing, and blanking level, or 64 is subtracted from the sample value to give a phase error measurement. In the next quadrant, B, a positive burst value, above 64, should be obtained. In the third quadrant, C, there should be a negative burst crossing; 64 will be subtracted from the sample value, and the result inverted to give a phase error value. The phase error values for several cycles of burst are numerically averaged and fed to a DAC which produces the VCO control voltage. Upon first applying an input, the alternate selection of the quadrature control signals will have a random phase which may be right or wrong. If by chance it is correct, the above sequence of events will hold true for all lines. However, if the selection is in the wrong phase, the timing will lag by a quadrant when burst leads by a quadrant and vice versa. This will make the burst invert with respect to the measurement timing on alternate lines, and a negative peak value, below 64, will be obtained instead of a positive peak value, above 64, in quadrant B. This condition is easily detected, and is used to reset the phase of the line frequency divider. This divider will now be truly reflecting the input burst swing, and an accurate phase comparison can be made between burst and sampling clock on every line. The line frequency divider is now producing 7.8 kHz.

By numerically analysing the ADC output, it is easy to detect the sync pulses, and using programmable counters it is possible to detect both vertical and horizontal syncs from their duration. In this way a gate can be opened during the first line of each frame. During the gate, the state of 7.8 kHz is examined, and this will only be true on alternate frames, and allows four-field colour framing to be achieved. The burst swing (7.8 kHz) derived colour framing cannot tell whether it has found field 1 or field 5, and this can only be resolved by looking at the 3.9 kHz relationship between burst and sync. The problems involved in determining the colour frame are summarized below, prior to the somewhat involved solutions.

Since sampling is subcarrier locked, it is necessary to consider how sync pulses move with respect to subcarrier rather than the other way round. The quarter cycle offset means that the position of a sync edge will move forward by one quadrant of subcarrier per line.

The presence of the 25 Hz offset causes sync edges to slide back constantly with respect to the sampling clock by four cycles or 225 nanoseconds per frame. The absolute position of the sync edge depends on ScH phase of the input signal which can drift.

Assessment of ScH phase according to the definition can only be made once every eight fields, and reliance on a single measurement is prone to noise. Techniques must be found to allow a colour framer to make a continuous assessment of framing so that a faster, more reliable lock is achieved.

Figure 7.4(a) shows how the phase of sync with respect to subcarrier can be found for any line in the eight-field sequence. The presence of the 25 Hz component is responsible for the diagonal slippage. Since phase only has meaning with respect to a cycle, it is possible to redraw Figure 7.4(a) to produce (b). The timing of sync with respect to subcarrier now takes on the appearance of a frame rate sawtooth. The sync edge has a finite slope, and so several samples will be taken during the transition. Figure 7.4(c) shows how the phase of the instant when the 50% level of sync is crossed can be computed to a fraction of a subcarrier cycle. Since this position moves by a fixed amount per line

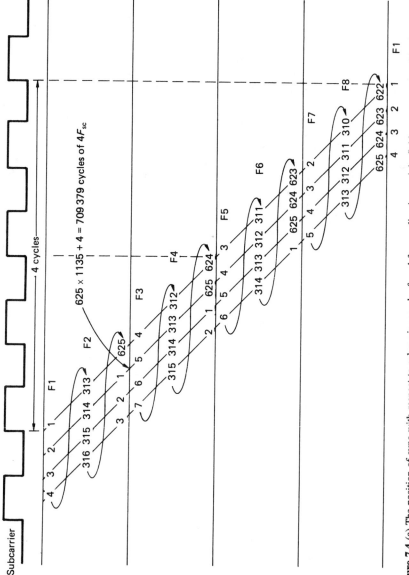

Figure 7.4 (a) The position of sync with respect to subcarrier can be found for any line in an eight-field sequence using this chart. The quarter cycle offset causes sync to move forward one quadrant per line over a four-line sequence, but the addition of 25 Hz causes sync to slip back towards subcarrier by one cycle per frame.

(a)

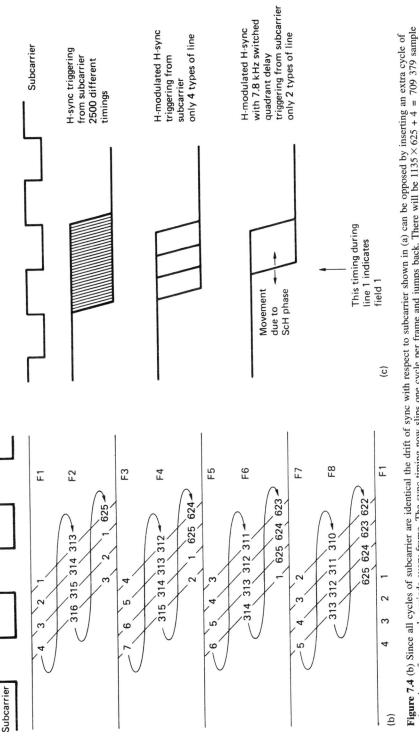

Figure 7.4 (b) Since all cycles of subcarrier are identical the drift of sync with respect to subcarrier are identical. The sync timing now slips one cycle per frame. The sync timing now slips one cycle per frame and jumps back. There will be $1135 \times 625 + 4 = 709\,379$ sample subcarrier or four sample periods every frame. By modulating the position of sync by 0.36 ns per line, it can be made to have a constant relationship to subcarrier over a four-line period. periods in a frame exactly. By modulating the position of sync by 0.36 ns per line, it can be made to have a constant relationship to subcarrier over a four-line period. (c) Horizontal modulation gives four types of line by cancelling the effect of 25 Hz. Using 7.8 Hz from Figure 7.3 to insert or remove delays of one sample period results in two relationships. Sampling during line 1 will determine whether field 1 or field 5 is present.

(0.36 nanoseconds) it is possible to subtract a time which is obtained by multiplying the line number in the frame by 0.36 nanoseconds. This process is called horizontal modulation, and results in a modulated sync edge which appears to have four phases which are stationary with respect to subcarrier. The four phases are due to the quarter cycle offset. A further offset of one sample period is subtracted on alternate lines according to the state of 7.8 kHz, giving modulated sync edges which now have two phases. During the colour frame, the sync edge will be in phase with subcarrier, and during frame 3 it will be antiphase. The colour frame is thus uniquely identified. If the input is not exactly EBU ScH phase, there will be a fixed phase error in the sync timing, and the system must pick the sync edge which is most nearly in phase with subcarrier to identify frame 1.

7.3 Colour framing in NTSC

The four-field sequence of NTSC arises because of the half cycle offset of subcarrier with respect to line frequency. The phase-locked loop which produces the sampling clock synchronizes to burst, but with a 57° offset so that samples are taken on the $R-Y$ and $B-Y$ axes. The standard ScH phase relationship will occur on the first line of the four-field sequence, and on every other line. On the lines between, the sync edge will be located two sample periods away. These lines are easily detected and so the colour frame flag is readily produced.

7.4 The data to be recorded

The input data rate of a component digital machine can be directly deduced from the CCIR-601 standard. In every active line, 720 luminance samples and 360 of each type of colour difference sample are produced, making a total of 1440 samples per line (see Chapter 3). In 625/50, lines 11–310 and lines 324–623 are recorded, making 300 lines per field, or 1500 lines per second. The D-1 and D-5 formats record these data directly. In 525/60, lines 14–263 and lines 276–525 are recorded, making 250 lines per field, which results in the same data rate of 1500 lines per second. In both cases the video data rate will be 1500 × 1440 samples per second, or 2.16 megasamples per second.

If 16:9 format data with a luminance sampling rate of 18 MHz is to be recorded, these rates will be increased by $\frac{4}{3}$.

In composite formats the situation becomes more complex as the sampling clock is precisely derived from subcarrier. The very existence of the samples indicates the phase of subcarrier, and so it is not necessary to record the burst. The subcarrier has a mathematical relationship with sync, which can readily be reconstructed on replay, and so it is not necessary to record syncs either. Accordingly, D-2 and D-3 only record the active line, along with sufficient positioning information so that syncs and burst can be regenerated on replay. If a non-standard ScH signal is fed into a composite recorder, standard ScH will be automatically generated on playback.

Both D-2 and D-3 in PAL record 948 samples symmetrically disposed around the unblanked active line, and in NTSC record 768 samples similarly. In each case, sample 0 is defined as the first sample in the active line; this is a different approach to analog video which considers the line to start at the sync edge. Since not all of the line period is recorded, it then becomes important to ensure that sampling commences in a consistent place on each line of each frame, and that the first sample has a consistent relationship to subcarrier. Clearly the position of the first sample in a line must be on one cycle or another of the sampling clock, and, as has been seen, this is derived from input burst. The edge of the picture is, however, defined by the sync pulse leading edge, and the input stage has to resolve the conflict of sampling at a fixed relationship to H-sync in order to keep the edge of the picture straight with the need to sample coherently with subcarrier. In NTSC this is relatively easy, owing to the simple relationship between subcarrier and sync. It is only necessary to wait a fixed number of sample periods after sync, and the first sample of the active line will be consistently located.

In the PAL system it becomes more complex because of the 25 Hz component of subcarrier. In the absence of 25 Hz, there would be exactly $283\frac{3}{4}$ cycles per line and exactly 1135 sample clocks per line. Instead, there will be an additional four sample clocks in one frame period.

The H-modulator in the colour framer allows the ScH phase of the input to be established, and this can be used to ensure that the first sample period of line 1 of the eight-field sequence is identified. From then on, the beginning of subsequent lines is deemed to occur 1135 sample periods later. This means that at the end of the field, the virtual beginning of a line will be a half cycle of subcarrier early. During the vertical interval, the line count of one line is modified to 1137, and the error is removed for the beginning of the next field. The first sample of the active line is obtained by counting a whole number of cycles of sampling clock from the virtual beginning of the line.

Using the above mechanisms, samples can be put into memory in a consistent way. Because H-sync was displaced to align it with subcarrier, the picture on tape will be slightly rhombic, but this is of no consequence, because identical circuitry, including an H-modulator, is necessary on the replay side of the machine to generate a read clock from reference subcarrier and to generate a subcarrier coherent read start pulse from reference sync. The picture distortion caused by H-modulating the input sync is cancelled by H-modulating output sync. Figure 7.5 shows that the unblanked picture lies within the rhombic outline of the recorded area.

In either standard, if the ScH phase of the input changes, the sync pulse will move with respect to the sampling structure, but the system will continue to select the same cycle of subcarrier with which to start the sampling by adapting the measured ScH phase value. If subcarrier phase drifts so much that it inverts, the colour framer cannot reframe if the machine is recording, since this would result in a discontinuous control track. It will be necessary to stay with the same subcarrier cycle which results in a drift of the picture position. If drift continues for an entire cycle, the input stage will need to dump four samples to prevent the picture winding across the screen. This will cause a picture shift.

Not all lines of the field are recorded, and in fact the lines which are recorded vary from one field to the next. This is necessary to allow picture-in-shuttle. The recording is composite and contains an embedded chroma signal. Colour processing is necessary in shuttle to change the phase of the offtape signal to that of reference. When tracks are crossed in shuttle, sync blocks are picked up at random, and a frame store is updated by information which has come from several different fields. This is only possible if samples off tape can be colour processed. The necessary interleave and shuffle processes in a DVTR mean that

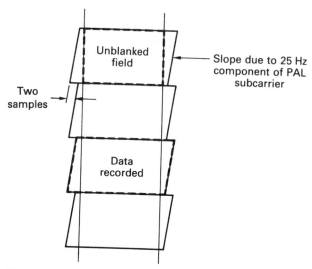

Figure 7.5 In PAL, the data to be recorded are subcarrier locked and result in a rhombic field. The sloping sides are in video blanking and have no ill effect.

each sync block contains samples which have come from various places within a field segment. When a frame store is updated in shuttle, successive samples in a given line could have come from a different colour line type, and they would no longer represent the modulation of a continuous subcarrier. The colour processor would not be able to operate.

The solution adopted in D-2 is to record more lines than necessary, so that the first line of each field recorded can change over a four- or eight-field sequence as shown in Figure 7.6. The choice of the first line to be recorded is made by the input colour framer. This ensures that all fields on tape have the same chroma phase at the same line number.

At normal speed and in slow motion, the recorded lines are put back into the correct position in the reference fields, and the normal chroma sequences result, but in shuttle, the colour processor now only needs to know the line number of recovered pixels and they can be correctly processed without knowing the number of the field from which they came. The offset of the line start causes a loss of vertical resolution in shuttle (four lines in PAL, two in NTSC).

D-3 uses the same technique in NTSC, but achieves the same goal in a slightly different way in PAL. Instead of moving the starting line over four lines vertically, a range of two lines is used to handle changes in V-switch in conjunction with a two-pixel horizontal shift which opposes the subcarrier inversion between line pairs. Figure 7.7(a) shows how the sampling structure results in every field beginning with a $(U-V)$ sample. The sample numbers in Figure 7.7(a) require some explanation. As the first sample in the active line is defined as sample 0 and there are 1135 samples per line, the samples will be numbered 0–1134. Thus samples 1133 and 0 are actually two samples apart, and selecting one or the other results in an inversion.

The offset of the line start causes a loss of vertical resolution in shuttle of two lines in NTSC and PAL along with a loss of horizontal resolution of two pixels in PAL only, but this is acceptable since resolution falls in shuttle in any case due to movement in the picture.

The raw video data rate which must be sustained by a composite digital recorder can now be derived. For PAL, 948 samples in 304 lines at 50 Hz result in 14 409 600 samples per second, whereas for NTSC, 768 samples in 255 lines at 59.94 Hz result in 11 738 649.6 samples per second. Each sample is of 8 bit resolution in both D-2 and D-3.

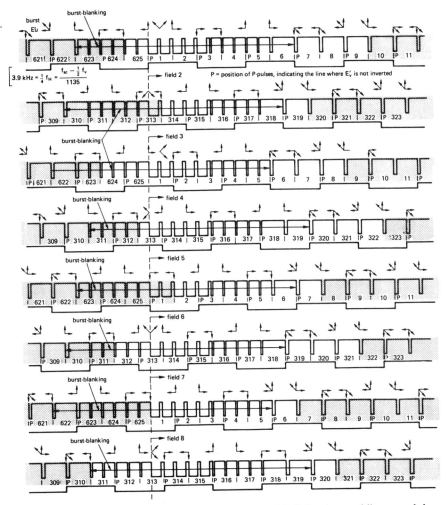

Figure 7.6(a) Each field recorded contains 304 lines in PAL D-2, but the actual lines recorded change from field to field so that the fields always begin with the same line type in the PAL sequence. This eases the production of a picture in shuttle since the colour processor then only needs to know the position in the field, since all fields offtape appear identical.

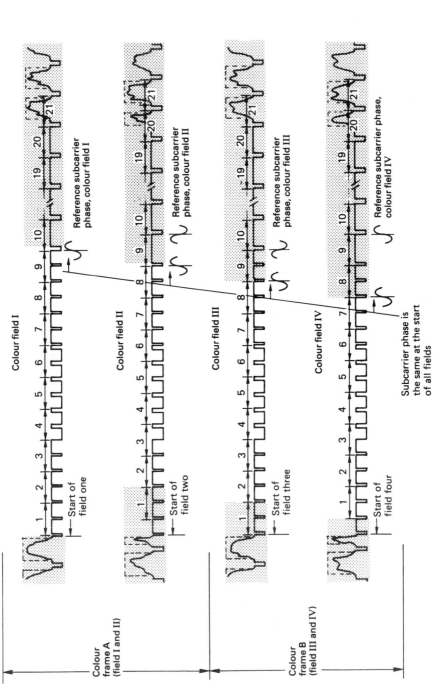

Figure 7.6(b) The recorded lines in NTSC D-2 are shown shaded here. The starting point in each field is chosen so that the subcarrier phase is the same at the beginning of all fields on tape.

Field number	(a) PAL	(b) NTSC
1	Line 8 Sample 1133	Line 9 Sample 0
2	Line 320 Sample 0	Line 8 Sample 0
3	Line 7 Sample 1133	Line 9 Sample 2
4	Line 321 Sample 1133	Line 8 Sample 2
5	Line 8 Sample 0	
6	Line 320 Sample 1133	
7	Line 7 Sample 0	
8	Line 321 Sample 0	

Figure 7.7 Composite sampling requires the first recorded sample to move from field to field to enable picture-in-shuttle with constant colour framing offtape.

At (a) combinations of two sample shifts to invert chroma and one line shift to reverse V-switch allow every field on tape to begin with $U - V$ sample in PAL.

At (b) NTSC requires only two sample shifts to compensate for inversion of subcarrier from line to line.

In practice, these figures will need to be increased somewhat to allow for an error-correction overhead, the presence of addressing or identification codes and for the recording of four audio channels. Additionally, a proportion of each track will be used up with the preambles and sync patterns necessary to the operation of the channel coding, and tolerance gaps needed to allow independent editing of audio and video.

7.5 Distribution and concealment

Distribution is shown in Figure 7.8. This is a process of sharing the data rate over two or more signal paths or channels so that the bit rate and head-to-tape speed in each is reduced and concealment is possible if one signal path fails. The data are subsequently recombined on playback. In full-bit-rate formats distribution is performed immediately after the input stage as shown in Figure 7.8(a). The channels are recombined immediately before the concealment stage. Each channel requires its own tape track and head. The parallel tracks which result form a *segment*.

Component formats require three signal components to be recorded in parallel. These components must be distributed between the number of signal channels used. In D-1 and D-5 no data reduction is employed and four signal channels are required. The distribution strategy is based on the requirement for concealment of uncorrected errors. This requires samples from all three video components to be distributed evenly over all four recording channels. If this is done the loss of a channel causes an equal loss to each video component rather than a greater loss concentrated in one component.

(a)   0 1 0 1 0 1 0 1
      1 0 1 0 1 0 1 0 → etc.
      0 1 0 1 0 1 0 1
      1 0 1 0 1 0 1 0
            ↓
          etc.

(b)   0 0 0 0 0 0 0 0 │ 1 1 1 1 1 1 1 1 │ 0 0 0 0 0 0 0 0
      0 0 0 0 0 0 0 0 │ 1 1 1 1 1 1 1 1 │ 0 0 0 0 0 0 0 0
      0 0 0 0 0 0 0 0 │ 1 1 1 1 1 1 1 1 │ 0 0 0 0 0 0 0 0
      0 0 0 0 0 0 0 0 │ 1 1 1 1 1 1 1 1 │ 0 0 0 0 0 0 0 0
      ───
      1 1 1 1 1 1 1 1 │ 0 0 0 0 0 0 0 0 │ 1 1 1 1 1 1 1 1
      1 1 1 1 1 1 1 1 │ 0 0 0 0 0 0 0 0 │ 1 1 1 1 1 1 1 1
      1 1 1 1 1 1 1 1 │ 0 0 0 0 0 0 0 0 │ 1 1 1 1 1 1 1 1
      1 1 1 1 1 1 1 1 │ 0 0 0 0 0 0 0 0 │ 1 1 1 1 1 1 1 1

Figure 7.8 In full-bit formats, distribution is on a pixel basis as shown at (a). If data reduction is used, distribution can be on a DCT block basis or an entropy block basis as shown at (b).

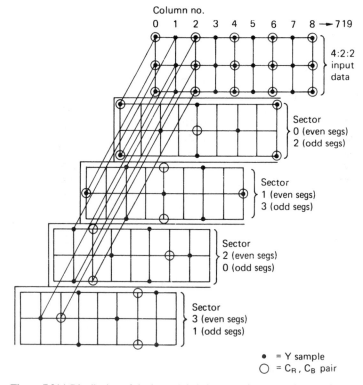

Figure 7.9(a) Distribution of the input 4:2:2 data over four parallel channels is performed as shown here. The criterion is the best concealment ability in case of the loss of one or more channels.

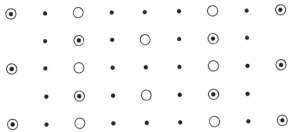

Figure 7.9(b) The result of combining the channels when data from sector 1 are lost. Spatial interpolation can be used to restore picture content.

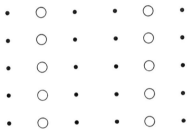

Figure 7.9(c) When sectors 0 and 1 are both lost both Y and C_R, C_B are still available at half the normal sampling rate and so effective concealment is still possible.

Figure 7.9(a) shows the distribution strategy of D-1 in which the data are distributed over four channels.[1] The distribution is complicated by the fact that the video data consist of pixels which are alternately co-sited Y, C_R, C_B samples and Y only samples. The goal of the distribution strategy is to permit the best concealment possible in the case of lost sectors, and Figure 7.9(b) also shows the samples which will be lost if one sector is unrecoverable. Horizontal or vertical interpolation is possible to conceal the missing samples. Figure 7.9(c) shows the result if two sectors are lost. Samples of both luminance and colour difference are still available at one-half of the original sampling rates of each, and so a reduced-bandwidth picture can still be produced.

Where data reduction is employed, the reduction process takes place directly on the input signal and produces blocks of coefficients. The contents of the DCT blocks cannot be divided because of the requirement of picture-in-shuttle. Owing to the use of variable-length coding DCT blocks have a range of sizes after compression making distribution on a block basis impossible. Thus if distribution takes place after data reduction it must be based on entropy blocks since these are of constant size. When a single entropy block is recovered in shuttle, it must contain all of the coefficients of the DCT blocks it contains otherwise the pixel data cannot be recreated in that screen area. Alternatively the distribution process may take place prior to data reduction in which case the pixel block becomes the minimum unit of data. See Figure 7.8(b).

In composite digital formats, data to be recorded are distributed between the two heads which are active at any one time. Figure 7.10 shows the segmented

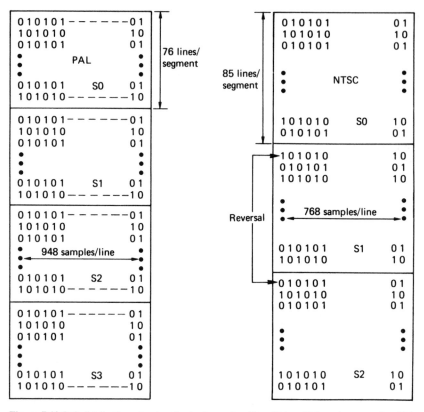

Figure 7.10 D-2 distribution, showing the track number (0 or 1) in which a given sample will be recorded. In PAL (left) there is an even number of lines in the segment so they are all the same. In NTSC there is an odd number, so the distribution reverses from segment to segment in order to maintain the pattern across segment boundaries.

distribution scheme for D-2 and Figure 7.11 shows the same scheme applied to D-3 but over entire fields. In both cases the distribution ensures that in both rows and columns of a field, alternate samples are recorded by a different head. If samples from a given head are lost for any reason, each lost sample is surrounded on four sides by samples from the other head. In the case of complete loss of signal from one head, due perhaps to clogging, it is still possible to produce a picture of reasonable quality from the remaining head because the quality will be as if the picture had originally been sampled at $2 \times F_{sc}$.

7.6 Video mapping

In binary PCM systems, the samples consist of a number of bits, in this case eight, which each determine whether a particular power of 2 should be present in the output level. An 8 bit system has 256 quantizing intervals, and an error in the least significant bit of a sample results in an error of one of these levels, whereas an error in the most significant bit results in an error of 128 levels, or half of the

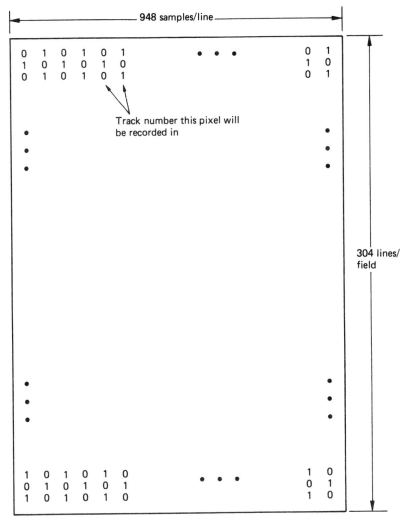

Figure 7.11 Distribution scheme for PAL D-3 (NTSC similar) shows that alternate pixels in two dimensions are recorded by alternate heads. Loss of one head signal allows interpolation from the remaining data.

signal range. If the two most significant bits are considered, the maximum possible error will be 192 levels, but the largest errors will result if the sample value is near the end of the range, as shown in Figure 7.12(a).

Essentially some bits are more important than others in PCM systems. An uncorrected least significant bit would probably go unnoticed on real program material, whereas an uncorrected most significant bit would result in an obvious dot contrasting with the surrounding picture area. The eye is most sensitive to such errors where the background is dark, i.e. the numerical values of the samples involved are small, and yet it is in exactly this region that the double bit error is the greatest.[2]

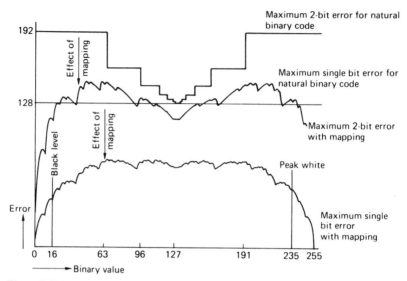

Figure 7.12(a) A single-bit error will cause a maximum deviation of 128Q in natural binary, but this is reduced to the lower line by mapping. A double-bit error will cause a maximum deviation of 128 + 64 = 192Q, and the effect of mapping on this magnitude of error is also shown.

Least significant four bits

Input	0	1	2	3	4	5	6	7	8	9	A	B	C	D	E	F
0	00	80	40	20	10	08	04	02	01	C0	A0	90	88	84	82	81
1	60	50	48	44	42	41	30	28	24	22	21	18	14	12	11	0C
2	0A	09	06	05	03	E0	D0	C8	C4	C2	C1	B0	A8	A4	A2	A1
3	98	94	92	91	8C	8A	89	86	85	83	70	68	64	62	61	58
4	54	52	51	4C	4A	49	46	45	43	38	34	32	31	2C	2A	29
5	26	25	23	1C	1A	19	16	15	13	0E	0D	0B	07	F0	E8	E4
6	E2	E1	D8	D4	D2	D1	CC	CA	C9	C6	C5	C3	B8	B4	B2	B1
7	AC	AA	A9	A6	A5	A3	9C	9A	99	96	95	93	8E	8D	8B	87
8	78	74	72	71	6C	6A	69	66	65	63	5C	5A	59	56	55	53
9	4E	4D	4B	47	3C	3A	39	36	35	33	2E	2D	2B	27	1E	1D
A	1B	17	0F	F8	F4	F2	F1	EC	EA	E9	E6	E5	E3	DC	DA	D9
B	D6	D5	D3	CE	CD	CB	C7	BC	BA	B9	B6	B5	B3	AE	AD	AB
C	A7	9E	9D	9B	97	8F	7C	7A	79	76	75	73	6E	6D	6B	67
D	5E	5D	5B	57	4F	3E	3D	3B	37	2F	1F	FC	FA	F9	F6	F5
E	F3	EE	ED	EB	E7	DE	DD	DB	D7	CF	BE	BD	BB	B7	AF	9F
F	7E	7D	7B	77	6F	5F	3F	FE	FD	FB	F7	EF	DF	BF	7F	FF

Most significant four bits

Figure 7.12(b) The mapping table. This will need to be reversed on playback.

Mapping is a process which is designed to reduce the dominance of the most significant bits. Incoming video samples to be recorded are fed to a lookup table which translates each 8 bit value to a different 8 bit value. The reverse process takes place on replay, and in the absence of errors, the original data are restored perfectly. However, if 1 or 2 bits of the mapped sample are wrong, the incorrect value which results from the reverse mapping process will have an error which is considerably smaller.

Figure 7.12(a) shows the result of mapping is to reduce the actual error magnitude when bit errors occur. If the error-correction system is working properly, this is of no consequence, but it was included in D-1 because it was felt that portable machines might be made which had full record circuitry, but which had confidence replay without error-correction to reduce power consumption and size. In this case, mapping would result in a real improvement in subjective quality. Developments in LSI technology mean that full error correction is now possible even in portable machines, so this feature is in fact unnecessary, and it has no parallel in later formats.

The mapping table is shown in Figure 7.12(b). This is most commonly implemented in a PROM. An example is shown to illustrate the reduction in error magnitude achieved. Only active line video samples are mapped.

7.7 Segmentation techniques

Segmentation is shown in Figure 7.13. This is the process of dividing the data resulting from one video field over several segments in order to obtain tape tracks of reasonable length. The replay system must have some means to ensure that associated segments are correctly reassembled into the original field. This is generally a function of the control track. There are several approaches to segmentation in practical formats as the division can take place at various points within the encoding process.

In D-1 and D-2, the approach shown in Figure 7.13(a) is used. Here segmentation takes place immediately after distribution. The segmented data are then independently shuffled prior to the addition of redundancy. Each track on the tape is recorded with an independent product code. This requires less RAM to implement, but it means that from an error-correction standpoint each tape track is self-contained and must deal alone with any errors encountered.

The D-3 and D-5 formats use the approach shown in Figure 7.13(b). Here, following distribution, the entire field is used to produce one large shuffled product code in each channel. The product code is then segmented for recording on tape. Although more RAM is required to assemble the large product code, the benefit is that outer codewords on tape spread across several tracks and redundancy in one track can compensate for errors in another. The result is that the size of a single burst error which can be fully corrected is increased. As RAM is now cheaper than when the first formats were designed, there is little penalty in adopting this approach.

The approach of Digital Betacam is somewhere between the previous systems. Figure 7.13(c) shows that the input field is converted to blocks of pixels to suit the data reduction process. These blocks are shuffled over the entire field, but segmentation takes place before the generation of product codes.

The segmentation process can be tailored to allow mechanical commonality between different line standards. In component video the sampling rate and data

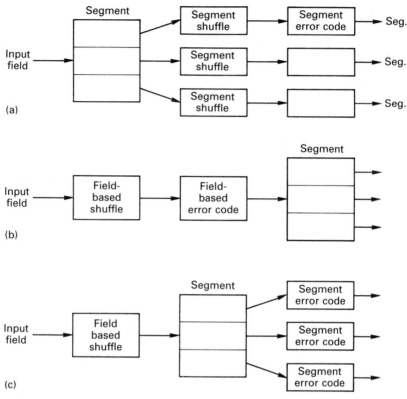

Figure 7.13 Segmentation of data can take three forms. At (a) each segment is independently shuffled and coded. At (b) segmentation takes place after shuffling and coding the whole field. At (c) segmentation occurs between the shuffle and the coding.

rate are the same in both standards. As the fields in the two line standards contain 300 and 250 lines, it makes a good deal of sense for each segment or track pair to record the highest common multiple, 50 lines, such that a field will comprise either six or five segments. The segment rate will then be 300 Hz in both standards, and since the scanner in a typical transport has two head assemblies, it will turn at 150 revolutions per second. The transport can be mechanically identical in the two line standards. It should be appreciated that in fact the field rate of the 525 line system is 59.94 Hz, and so the scanner speed (and hence the capstan speed) will be 0.1% slower in the 525 line version; this is of no real consequence to the format, except for some very small dimensional changes.

In composite digital, the disparity of subcarrier frequencies results in different data rates and a common drum speed is impracticable.

7.8 The shuffle strategy

Error correction in DVTRs is more complex than in other forms of recording because of the number of conflicting requirements. Chapter 5 showed that interleave is necessary to break up burst errors, and that a product code gives an efficient and reliable system.

Unfortunately the product code produces a regular structure of rows and columns, and if such a system is overwhelmed, regular patterns of uncorrected errors are produced, and the effectiveness of concealment is reduced because the eye can still perceive the regular structure.

An irregular data rearrangement or *shuffle* can be designed to take errors which are contiguous on the tape track and disperse them over two dimensions on the screen, making the concealment more effective. For the best concealment, the shuffle should work over the entire field and this will also help the provision of picture-in-shuttle.

In shuttle the track-following process breaks down and the recovery of entire segments is impossible. Figure 7.14 shows that the path of the head crosses tape tracks obliquely. The use of azimuth recording allows the replay head to be about 50% wider than the track, and so a useful replay signal results for a reasonable proportion of the head path, at the times where the head is near the centreline of a track of the same azimuth type, interrupted by noise when the heads cross tracks of the wrong azimuth type.

A picture of some sort is still needed in shuttle, in order to assist in the location of wanted material, but the quality does not need to be as high as in other modes. The format must be designed from the outset with the provision of shuttle pictures in mind.

The sectors are broken into short elements called *sync blocks* which are smaller than the length of track which can be recovered at typical shuttle speeds. Each sync block contains one or two inner codewords, and so it is possible to tell if the sync block was correctly recovered or not, without reference to any other part of the recording.

If a sync block is read properly or is correctable, it is used to update a frame store which refreshes the picture monitor. Sync blocks which are uncorrectable will not update the framestore, and so data from an earlier field will remain there

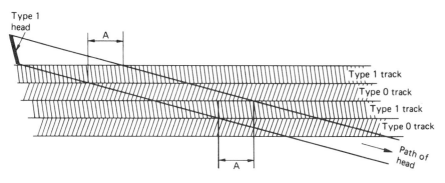

Figure 7.14 During shuttle, the heads cross tracks randomly as shown here (exaggerated). Owing to the use of azimuth recording, a head can only play a track of its own type (0 or 1) but as the head is typically 50% wider than the track (see Section 4.4) it is possible to recover normal signal for the periods above marked A. If sync blocks are shorter than this period, they can be picked up intact. In fact a slightly longer pickup will be possible because the replay system may tolerate a less-than-perfect signal. In any case the final decision is made by checking that the sync block recovered contains valid or correctable codewords.

to refresh the display. The contents of sync blocks must be designed to allow the recovery of meaningful picture information when recovered singly. For example, there is little point in recovering a sync block filled with luminance samples if the colour data are elsewhere. In practice sync blocks must contain all components of the pixels therein. Similarly in data-reduced formats sync blocks must contain all coefficients of the DCT blocks.

Using this mechanism, picture-in-shuttle is composed of data from different segments of many offtape fields. A field-based shuffle is complex to implement and D-3 was the first format to use it. In the earlier D-1 and D-2 formats the shuffle was restricted to operate only over one segment of the field.

A problem with segmented recordings is that at certain tape speeds beating occurs between the passage of tracks and the drum rotation so that some parts of the segments are never recovered and the picture has to be refreshed with stale data which are no longer representative of the recording. There are two solutions to the problem. The use of a field-based shuffle helps because one offtape sync block then contains samples from all over the screen.

The beating effect is mechanical and results in certain parts of a track being inaccessible. If the data within successive tracks are shuffled differently, beating will cause loss from all over the picture once more. Thus in a segment-based shuffle, each track in the field will use a different shuffle. The use of distribution leads to two or more tracks working in parallel. A tape scratch would damage all tracks in a segment in the same place. If the channels in the segment use different shuffles, uncorrectable errors due to scratches will be dispersed across the screen. In composite formats the shuffle in successive fields of the colour frame sequence may be different.

Obtaining a shuttle picture is easier if the shuffle is random, but a random shuffle is less effective for concealment, because it can result in variable density of uncorrected errors, which are harder to conceal than the constant error density resulting from a maximum distance shuffle.

Essentially the field of data to be shuffled is considered to be a two-dimensional memory, and the shuffle is achieved by address mapping in each dimension. The address generator used should not be unnecessarily complicated. Clearly the shuffle process on recording has to be exactly reversed on replay.

In address mapping, samples in each channel of a segment are at addresses which are initially sequential. The samples are selected non-sequentially by generating a suitable address sequence. When data reduction is used, individual pixels cannot be shuffled, but instead it is the addresses of DCT blocks which are mapped.

In principle, the address sequence could be arbitrarily generated from a lookup table, but the memory arrays are large, and this approach would be extremely expensive to implement. It is desirable that the address generation should be algorithmic to reduce cost, but an algorithm must be found which gives irregular results.

The solution adopted in DVTR formats is to obtain a pseudo-random address sequence by using address multiplication by a prime number in modulo arithmetic for one of the mapping axes. This is easier than it sounds, as the simple example of Figure 7.15(a) shows. In this example, 16 pixels are to be shuffled. The pixel addresses are multiplied by 11, which is relatively prime to 16, and the result is expressed modulo-16, which is to say that if the product exceeds an integer multiple of 16, that integer multiple is subtracted. It

Address A	A x 11		A x 11 mod 16
0	0		0
1	11		11
2	22	(−16)	6
3	33	(−32)	1
4	44	(−32)	12
5	55	(−48)	7
6	66	(−64)	2
7	77	(−64)	13
8	88	(−80)	8
9	99	(−96)	3
10	110	(−96)	14
11	121	(−112)	9
12	132	(−128)	4
13	143	(−128)	15
14	154	(−144)	10
15	165	(−160)	5

Figure 7.15(a) The permuted addresses for a shuffle can be obtained by multiplication of the addresses by a number relatively prime to the modulo base.

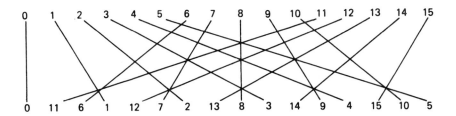

Figure 7.15(b) The shuffle which results from the calculation in Figure 7.15(a).

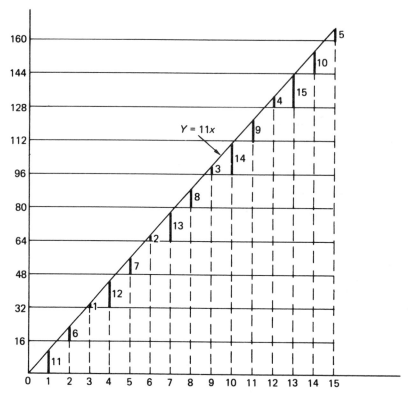

Figure 7.15(c) Modulo arithmetic is rather similar to quantizing. The results of Figure 7.15(a) can be obtained by quantizing the graph of $y = 11x$ with the quantizing intervals of 16 units.

will be seen from Figure 7.15(b) that an effective shuffle is created. Modulo arithmetic has a similar effect to quantizing, in fact a number expressed modulo is the quantizing error due to quantizing in steps equal to the modulo base as Figure 7.15(c) shows. When the input has a large range, the quantizing error becomes random.

Generating a randomizing effect with modulo arithmetic depends upon the terms in the expression being relatively prime so that repeats are not found in the resulting shuffle, and this constrains the dimensions which can be used for the codewords.

A calculation of the type described will shuffle samples or DCT blocks in a pseudo-random manner in one dimension, but in the other dimension of the memory a pseudo-random shuffle is undesirable as this would result in a variable-distance shuffle. A straightforward rotation or barrel shift is used in the other dimension to give a maximum distance shuffle. Figure 7.16 shows a conceptual example. When samples are read in rows for recording they retain the same horizontal sequence but there is an offset in the starting address which is a simple function of the row number. This turns a column into a series of diagonals. The combination of these two processes results in the two-dimensional shuffle.

Input column

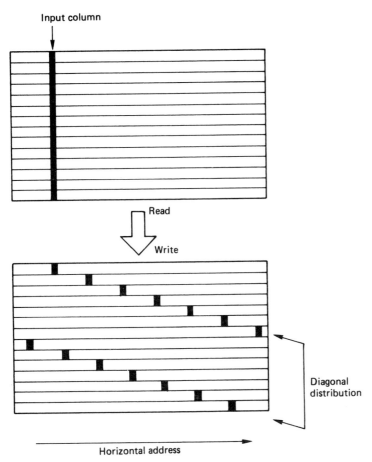

Read

Write

Diagonal
distribution

Horizontal address

Figure 7.16 The second dimension of the shuffle is obtained by offsetting the horizontal address during transfer from one array to another. This results in a diagonal shuffle if the offset increases by a constant from one line to the next.

The effect of the shuffle can be seen by turning off the correction and concealment circuits on a machine and searching for a large dropout with the jog control. This will reveal the irregular diagonal structure.

In machines using data reduction the shuffle serves an additional purpose. In this case it is DCT blocks which are shuffled. As variable-length coding is used, the DCT blocks cannot be shuffled after data reduction, but the shuffle must be performed on blocks of pixels prior to data reduction. The data reduction unit assembles fixed-size entropy blocks from several variable-length DCT blocks. If all of the DCT blocks in an entropy block contain a lot of detail and produce a correspondingly large amount of data, the compression factor will have to be increased. The block shuffle helps to prevent this happening by making the relative proportion of high- and low-detail blocks more uniform over the field data. For example, an undetailed area of the picture would be converted into undetailed DCT blocks scattered through the field data. These result in few coefficients on data reduction, making space in each entropy block for more highly detailed DCT blocks.

7.9 Error correction

The product code of a DVTR may extend over a track, as in D-1, D-2 and Digital Betacam, or over the entire field, as in D-3 and D-5. A two-channel distribution is used in D-3 in which data from one field are distributed to become two field arrays. Figure 7.17 shows one field array of D-3 PAL in which outer codes are vertical columns. Data are recorded on tape by passing horizontally across the array to form inner codewords which are placed sequentially along the track. The length of the inner codeword is important. The inner codeword will correct random errors, but if its correction power is exceeded the inner code declares the entire block bad, and the outer code must correct by erasure. If the inner code were too large, this would effectively magnify burst errors to the size of the codeword. On the other hand making an inner code too short needlessly increases the amount of redundancy to be recorded.

In D-3 one row of the segment array is made into 12 inner code blocks in PAL and nine in NTSC, and this reduces error magnification due to small bursts. Each array will be recorded on four different tracks for PAL, three for NTSC. Two arrays are needed to record one field. Each array is recorded in tracks of the same azimuth type. The outer redundancy is distributed evenly over the tracks. Since the outer codes contain eight redundancy symbols, each can correct eight symbols by erasure. This corresponds to 8 bytes per column of the field array. The largest data loss which can be handled will be when this damage is experienced in every column of the array, so the maximum correctable burst-error size is given by multiplying the number of columns in the sector array by eight. The resulting figures are $912 \times 8 = 7296$ data bytes for PAL and $765 \times 8 = 6120$ data bytes for NTSC. These figures are for video data only; the actual size of the burst will be larger because the length of the track involved also contains sync and ID patterns and inner redundancy.

As the field array is spread over several tracks, the length of a correctable tape defect along the track depends upon the number of tracks over which the defect spreads. Figure 7.18 shows that if the error is due to a helical scratch or a particle of debris passing under the head, it will be restricted to one track only and the correctable track length will be a maximum. If the defect is a linear tape scratch affecting all tracks, the correctable length of the defect is given by dividing the field array correction power by the number of tracks in which the array is recorded (three or four).

The maximum correctable single-track burst corresponds to about 19 mm of track length, or a longitudinal tape scratch of about 1.6 mm width.

If these conditions are exceeded, total correction is no longer possible, and rows of flagged erroneous data will appear in the field array. Concealment will become necessary and the concealment patterns are made irregular by using shuffling.

In shuttle, sync blocks will be recovered at random, and the shuffle means that when a sync block is successfully read, the pixels it contains are spread over the field, so the frame store will be updated all over instead of just in certain areas.

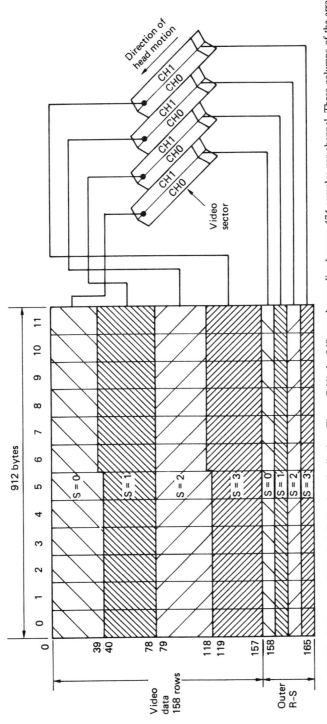

Figure 7.17 The field array of PAL D-3. Following distribution (Figure 7.11) the 948 samples per line become 474 samples per channel. Three columns of the array shown here hold 474 samples. Eight redundancy bytes are added to each column to form outer codes. The rows of the array are split into 12 parts and each has an ID pattern and redundancy added to make an inner code which occupies one sync block. The array is recorded on one of the tracks of four segments. The second array is recorded on the other tracks. Outer redundancy is recorded first in each track.

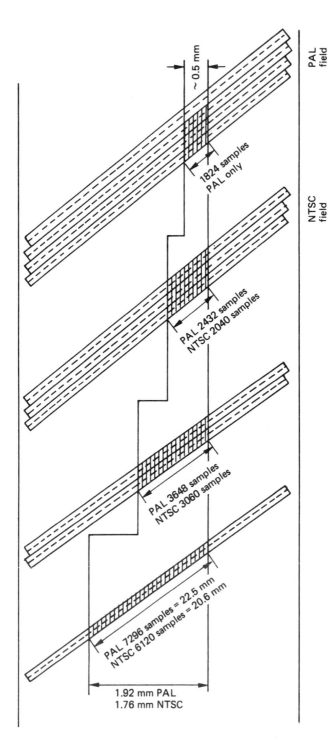

Figure 7.18 Error-correcting performance of D-3. For a single-segment helical scratch, reference to Figure 7.17 shows that eight rows can be corrected in each track by outer codes. This corresponds to 8 × 912 = 7296 samples (PAL) or 8 × 765 = 6120 samples (NTSC). In the case of a scratch along the tape, the maximum correction per field array must be divided by the number of tracks affected. In NTSC there are six tracks per field so a sustained scratch of 2040 samples can be corrected. In PAL there are eight tracks per field so a sustained scratch of 1824 samples can be corrected. This could be up to about 0.5 mm wide.

The twinkling effect on the picture in shuttle is caused by the shuffle. When data reduction is used, it is DCT blocks which are shuffled and the shuttle picture reveals a mosaiced structure.

7.10 The sync block

The recording density in DVTRs is such that it is not possible mechanically to position the heads with sufficient accuracy to locate an individual bit. The heads are rotated with reasonable accuracy, and the replay signal is accepted as and when it arrives.

In a serial recording, data can only be recovered if it is possible correctly to deserialize the replay waveform into multibit symbols once more. Error correction is only possible if the set of symbols making up a codeword can be reassembled, and the distribution, shuffle and segmentation processes can only be reversed if the position of data blocks along the track can be uniquely identified. The synchronizing system is specifically designed to achieve these tasks.

The sync block gets its name because it always begins with a synchronizing pattern which serves to phase the data separator and the deserializer. If randomizing is used, as in D-1, D-3/5 and Digital Betacam, sync detection will also be used to preset the derandomizer to the correct starting value. The sync pattern should differ from itself shifted by as many bits as possible to reduce the possibility of errors causing false sync detection. Within a sector, sync patterns occur at regular spacing, so it is possible for the replay circuitry to predict the arrival of the sync pattern in a time window.

Following the sync pattern is a 2 byte ID code which uniquely identifies this sync block in an eight-field sequence.

Once the data separator is locked and the deserializer is correctly phased, the clock content of the channel code employed will maintain the locked condition. However, the presence of dropouts or head tenting will cause momentary interruptions in the offtape signal, and this may be sufficient to cause the phase-locked loop in the data separator to lose lock. If this happens, all data after the dropout will be lost because they are unsynchronized. Correct deserialization and error correction are impossible.

The solution is to provide sync patterns (strictly speaking they are resynchronizing patterns) on a periodic basis along the track by breaking it up into a series of sync blocks. If lock is lost due to a dropout, it can then be recovered at the next sync pattern. Thus the size of the sync block determines the maximum amount of data which can be corrupted due to sync loss. There is an optimum spacing for sync patterns. If they are too far apart, the data lost through sync loss are excessive; if they are too close together, too much of the track is wasted recording patterns. In practice dropouts have a characteristic size distribution and the sync block can be made a little larger than a typical dropout so that sync is regained shortly after the dropout ends.

A further constraint on sync block size is the requirement to recover short sections of track in shuttle. If sync patterns are too far apart the proportion of data recovered in shuttle will be impaired. Samples from any sync block properly recovered can be put in the correct place in a frame store by reference to the ID code.

The size of a sync block is determined by synchronizing criteria, whereas the size of inner codewords is determined by data reliability criteria. Thus the two are not necessarily the same size, and in practice sync blocks will be found containing one or two inner codewords. Only one ID is needed per sync block, and this may be included in one of the codewords.

Figure 7.19(a) shows a PAL D-3 sync block beginning with a 2 byte sync pattern. The data block of 76 bytes then follows, and the 8 bytes of inner redundancy are calculated over the ID code as well as the data, so a random error in the ID can be corrected. The codeword is thus 86 bytes long. The entire sync block occupies about a quarter millimetre of track.

Figure 7.19(b) shows a PAL D-2 sync block. A 2 byte synchronizing pattern serves to phase the data separator and the deserializer. Following this is a 2 byte ID code which uniquely identifies this sync block in an eight-field sequence. The first data block of 76 bytes then follows, and the 8 bytes of inner redundancy are calculated over the ID code as well as the data, so a random error in the ID can be corrected. The first codeword is thus 86 bytes long. The second inner code block is 2 bytes shorter because it contains no ID. The entire sync block occupies just over half a millimetre of track.

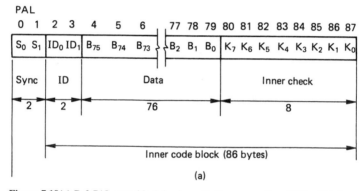

Figure 7.19(a) D-3 PAL sync block begins with the sync pattern 97F1 which is not randomized. The 2-byte ID, the data and the 8 bytes of inner check symbols are all randomized prior to EFM coding. The same block structure is used in both audio and video sectors.

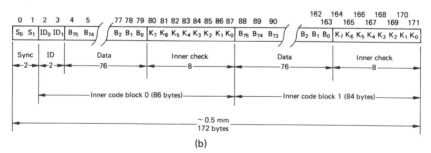

Figure 7.19(b) The sync blocks of D-2 contain two codewords but only one ID code which forms part of the first codeword. As a result, the first code block is 2 bytes longer than the second.

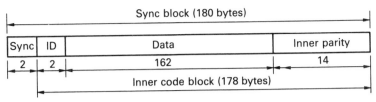

Figure 7.19(c) To obtain coding gain in compressed formats the sync blocks have to be large and require a correspondingly large number of check bytes.

Figure 7.19(c) shows a Digital Betacam sync block. As data reduction is used, the recorded data consist of entropy blocks. There is no point in having small inner codewords and so these are twice the size of D-2 and D-3 blocks minimum. Note that almost twice as many check bytes are used in each inner code to maintain the required proportion of redundancy.

Figure 7.20(a) shows the ID structure of D-3 which is very similar to that of D-2. The information recorded in the ID code is split into two parts. The first byte and bit 0 of the second is the 9 bit sync block number in the track; the remaining 7 bits of the second byte identify the sector. The V/A bit specifies whether the block is audio or video. The segment bits determine which segment out of four for PAL and three for NTSC is present, and the field bits specify the position in the eight- or four-field sequences to help colour framing.

Figure 7.20(b) shows the sync block numbering within the segment for PAL, and Figure 7.20(c) shows the equivalent for NTSC.

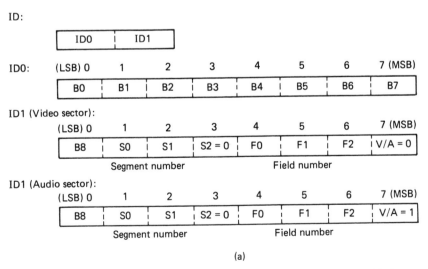

(a)

Figure 7.20(a) D-3 ID pattern consists of 2 bytes. ID0 and bit 0 of ID1 form a 9 bit block address. Bit 7 of ID1 is the video/audio flag and determines the type of sector. Remainder of the data carries field number (0–3 NTSC, 0–7 PAL) and segment number (0–2 NTSC, 0–PAL). Segment number requires only 2 bit code; thus S2 = 0.

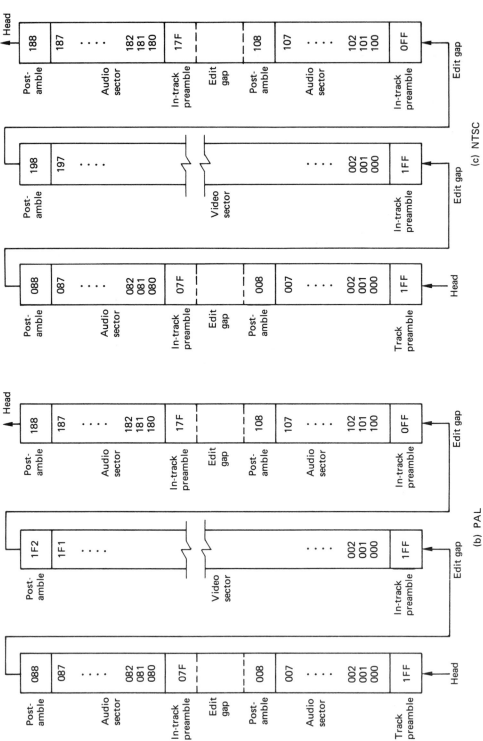

Figure 7.20(b) Showing ID code numberings to identify individually every sync block in the track. PAL video sector has more sync blocks and reaches higher count.

7.11 Gaps, preambles and postambles

Each slant track is subdivided into sectors. In D-1, D-5, DCT and Digital Betacam there is a video sector at each end and four audio sectors in the middle. In D-2 and D-3 there are two audio sectors at each end, and one video sector in the centre. It is necessary to be able to edit any or all of the audio channels independently of the video. For this reason short spaces known as edit gaps are left between the sectors to allow the write current to turn on and off away from wanted data. Since the write current can only turn off at the end of a sector, it follows that the smallest quantum of data which can be written in the track at one time is a whole sector, although the smallest quantum which can be read is a sync block.

During a dropout the phase-locked loop frequency will not have time to drift very far, but achieving sync at the beginning of a track is more difficult. A preamble is provided before the first sync block in a sector to allow the phase-locked loop in the data separator to lock. The preamble also contains a sync pattern and ID code so that the machine can confirm the position of the head before entering the sector proper. At the end of the sector a postamble containing an ID code is written before the write current is turned off. The pre- and postamble details of D-3 can be seen in Figure 7.21.

The space between two adjacent sectors is known as an edit gap, and it will be seen in Figure 7.21 to begin with the postamble of the previous sector and end with the preamble of the next sector. Editing may result in a discontinuity nominally in the middle of the gap. There is some latitude, but the new recording must not begin so early that the postamble at the end of the previous sector is damaged, and at least 20 bytes of preamble must be written before the sync pattern at the beginning of the next sector, because it will not be possible to maintain continuity of bit phase at an edit, and the PLL must resynchronize.

In practice the length of the postamble, gap and preamble combined will be made exactly equal to the length of one or two sync blocks according to the format. This simplifies the design of the sequencer which controls the track recording.

7.12 Colour processing

When variable speed is used, the transport cannot change its drum speed by very much because this affects the head/tape dynamics. If the tape speed is too low, some fields on tape have to be repeated to maintain field rate, whereas if tape speed is too high, some will need to be skipped. The effect of a head jump on a composite recording is that the subcarrier sequence is randomly broken. If variable speed is to be used, then it is necessary to decode the discontinuous incoming subcarrier, and re-encode it to continuous reference phase. The unit which does this job is called the colour processor. A digital filter is necessary to separate the chroma from the luminance. In NTSC there are only two line types, and the colour processor simply has to invert the chroma selectively before adding it back to the luminance.

In PAL, as usual, the solution is more complex because of the use of *V*-switch. Chroma is filtered from luminance as before, but then the chroma signal will

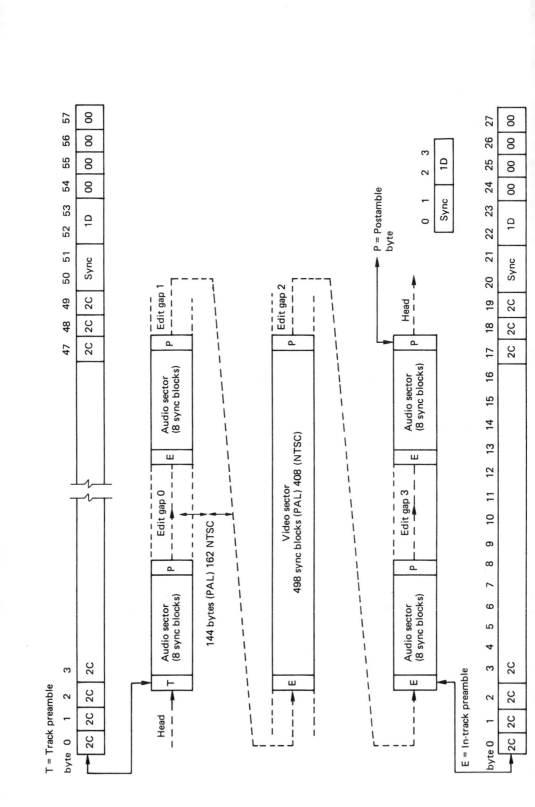

T = Track preamble

byte 0 1 2 3
2C 2C 2C 2C

Head

Audio sector (8 sync blocks) | T

Edit gap 0 | P

144 bytes (PAL) 162 NTSC

Video sector 498 sync blocks (PAL) 408 (NTSC) | E

Edit gap 2 | P

P = Postamble byte

E = In-track preamble

byte 0 1 2 3
2C 2C 2C 2C

Audio sector (8 sync blocks) | E

Edit gap 3 | P

Audio sector (8 sync blocks) | E

Head

Audio sector (8 sync blocks) | P

Edit gap 1 | P

47 48 49 50 51 52 53 54 55 56 57
2C 2C 2C Sync 1D 00 00 00 00 00

0 1 2 3
Sync 1D

17 18 19 20 21 22 23 24 25 26 27
2C 2C 2C Sync 1D 00 00 00 00 00

have to be re-encoded not just with the correct phase, but also with the correct sense of V-switch.

Composite video interleaves the basically similar spectra of chroma and luminance by shifting the chroma spectrum by half a line with respect to luminance as was seen in Chapter 3. They can only be fully separated by using a comb filter or a spatio-temporal filter. There are various requirements for luminance/chrominance separation at different levels of cost and complexity, each appropriate to a given application.

A bandpass filter will be used for minimum cost and complexity, and can be readily described because operation is directly parallel to that of an analog filter. Figure 7.22(a) shows that an input signal enters an operational amplifier both

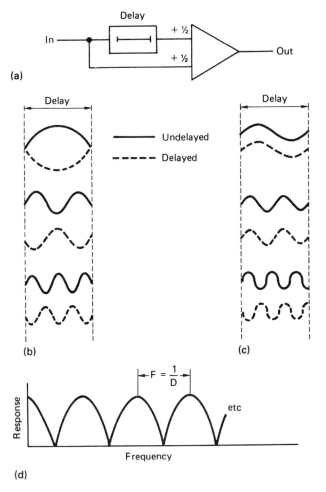

Figure 7.22 Simple comb filter at (a) has delay in one input of adder. At some frequencies (b), delay causes cancellation, whereas at others (c) delayed and undelayed signals are in phase. Frequency response shown at (d).

directly and through a delay. The phase difference between the ends of the delay is a function of the input frequency, and will be given by:

$$\frac{\text{delay period}}{\text{signal period}} \times 360°$$

The op-amp output is the vector sum of the two inputs:

$$\tfrac{1}{2}V_{in} + \tfrac{1}{2}V_{in}\sin T$$

where T is the phase angle between the inputs. When the delay period exceeds the signal period, the phase shift exceeds 360°, and clearly subtracting 360° or multiples thereof does not change the vector sum. There will thus be a series of signal periods all of which will have the same gain. The frequency response becomes repetitive; hence the term comb filter.

Figure 7.22(b) shows several frequencies, all of which suffer complete cancellation due to effective inversion by the delay, and Figure 7.22(c) shows frequencies which give unity gain because the delay is an integer multiple of the signal period. Figure 7.22(d) shows the overall frequency response, which has a

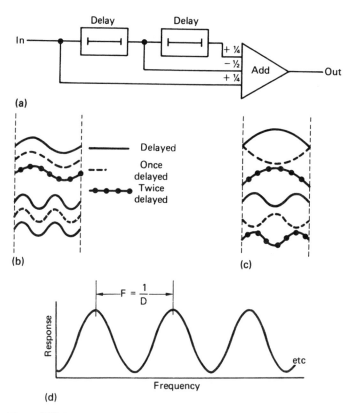

Figure 7.23 Two-delay comb filter at (a). In (b) certain frequencies suffer 360° shift in one delay, but since once-delayed signal has twice the weighting there is cancellation. At (c) is 180° resultant phase shift in one delay, removed by inverting input, permitting unity gain. Response at (d) is cosinusoid.

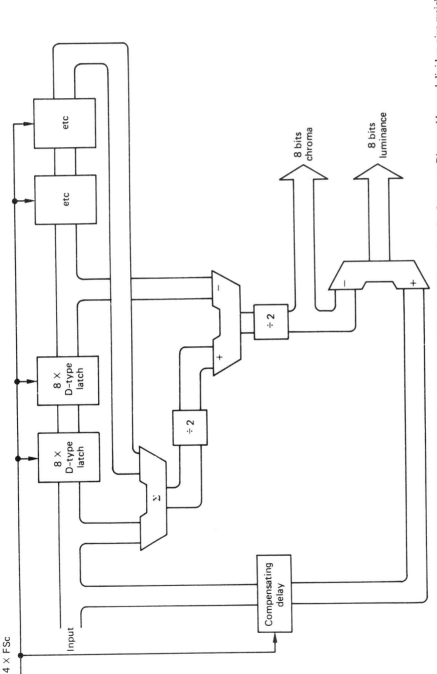

Figure 7.24 Digital *Y/C* separation at $4 \times F_{sc}$ uses pairs of latches to give 180° phase shift at subcarrier frequency. Binary adders and dividers give weighting of $+\frac{1}{4}$, $-\frac{1}{2}$, $+\frac{1}{4}$ to three samples. Chroma output is subtracted from the input to give luminance. There is only one response peak at F_{sc} since Nyquist limit for $4 \times F_{sc}$ sampling is reached at $2 \times F_{sc}$.

rectified cosine shape. Note that the peak spacing is at the reciprocal of the delay period.

A sharper response peak can be obtained by using two delays, as in Figure 7.23(a). The op-amp now has three inputs. Figure 7.23(b) shows the situation where a frequency which suffers a 180° shift in each delay is applied. Since the twice-delayed signal and the input signal will add, they must be given half as much gain as the signal from the centre tap. The op-amp thus has weighted gains of $+\frac{1}{4}$, $-\frac{1}{2}$ and $+\frac{1}{4}$. The frequency response shown in Figure 7.23(d) is a cosinusoid, again with the peaks spaced at the reciprocal of the delay.

Transferring to the digital domain, signal voltage is represented by a binary number, delay is achieved using latches or RAM. and the operational amplifier is replaced by an adder. Figure 7.24 shows the digital equivalent of Figure 7.23. A phase shift of 180° is readily achieved in a $4 \times F_{sc}$ system by using two sample periods of delay.

The $4 \times F_{sc}$ filter of Figure 7.24 has a gain peak at subcarrier frequency, and the output will be chroma. To obtain luminance, output values are subtracted from input values, with a compensating delay.

The above filters do not offer very good performance and their use is restricted to economy applications. In many broadcast and facility operations, the highest quality is required. Section 3.7 evolved the spectra of NTSC and PAL in some detail. Since the spectral interleave of a composite signal is primarily on multiples of line rate, it follows that delays of one line can be used in a comb filter, so that the frequency response peaks will be at multiples of F_h.

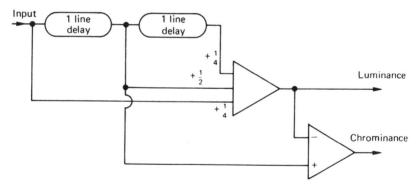

Figure 7.25 Simple line comb filter. Frequency response is ideal, but there are practical shortcomings explained in the text.

Figure 7.25 shows a simple line comb filter. The vertical/horizontal frequency response is shown in Figure 7.26. Although the horizontal spectral response appears ideal for NTSC applications, in fact there are some snags. Firstly the summing junction which is designed to reject chroma is adding together adjacent points on different lines, and is actually reducing the vertical resolution of the picture. Secondly, the filter is working with real chroma,

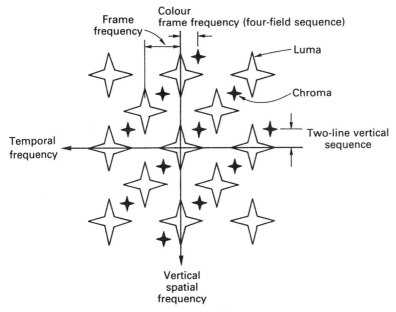

Figure 7.26 The vertical/temporal spectrum of NTSC.

whose phase can change according to picture content, whereas perfect comb response is only achieved when the chroma phase remains consistent over the three points feeding the summing junction. Vertical changes in chroma phase will cause the comb to fail to cancel or *mesh*, and residual chroma will appear in the luminance as a series of white dots at horizontal boundaries between colours.

Some of the vertical resolution can be restored by using a bandpass filter in conjunction with the line comb. Figure 7.27 shows that incoming video passes through two filters in parallel. One is a low-pass filter which cuts just below chroma frequencies, the other is a band-limiting filter. The outputs of the two filters are subtracted to give a bandpass response, which contains chroma and high-frequency luminance. This signal is applied to the line comb, which rejects chroma without impairing vertical resolution at frequencies below the bandpass. The high-frequency luminance can then be added back to the low-pass-filtered signal to give full-bandwidth luminance. The vertical/horizontal frequency response is curtailed in the horizontal direction so that only the horizontal frequencies where subcarrier is found are affected. Comb mesh failure can be detected by analyzing the chroma signals at the ends of the comb, and if chroma will not be cancelled, the high-frequency luminance is not added back to the main channel, and a low-pass response results.

The line comb gives quite good results in NTSC, as horizontal and vertical resolution are good, but the loss of vertical resolution at high frequency means that diagonal resolution is poor.

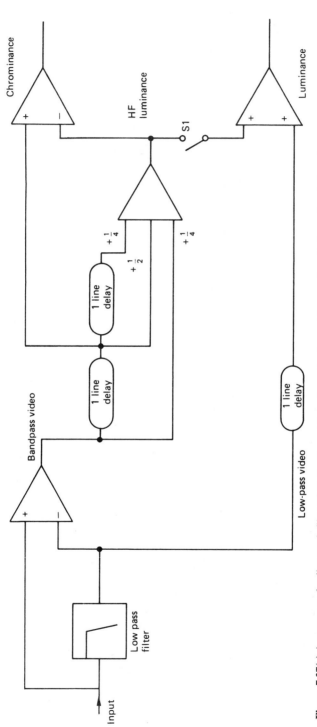

Figure 7.27(a) A more complex line comb filter where the line comb works on bandpass video to reduce the loss of vertical resolution. HF luminance is added back to low-pass signal to restore luminance bandwidth. If comb fails to mesh due to vertical chroma phase change, switch S1 opens to prevent chroma breaking through. Luminance bandwidth is reduced.

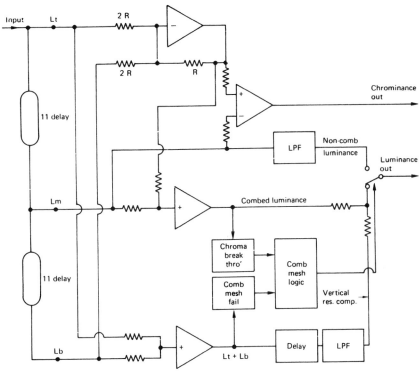

Figure 7.27(b) Rearranging the filter of Figure 7.27(a) in this way eliminates a delay line by restoring vertical resolution a different way. Vertical resolution compensation is achieved by taking signals from the top and bottom of the delays and adding them back to luminance via a low-pass filter shown bottom right. In the digital domain, replace operational amplifiers with adders, delays with RAM. Low-pass filters will be FIR types as described.

A line comb filter is at a disadvantage in PAL because of the spreading between U and V components. What is needed is a comb filter having delays of two lines, but this will have an even more severe effect on diagonal frequencies, so PAL comb filters are often found with only single-line delays, a choice influenced by commonality with an NTSC product.

Once the chroma has been separated, it can be processed to make it synchronous with reference.

Figure 7.28(a) shows that from line to line, the phase of U advances 90° due to the quarter cycle offset, and the phase of V alternately leads and lags U. Figure 7.28(b) shows that if chroma is sampled on the U and V axes the result of these two effects is that from one line to the next, the chroma samples represent different sequences of U and V. The shift to the right of the U sample due to the quarter cycle offset can be seen. It is not immediately obvious how one line of chroma could be made into another with this approach.

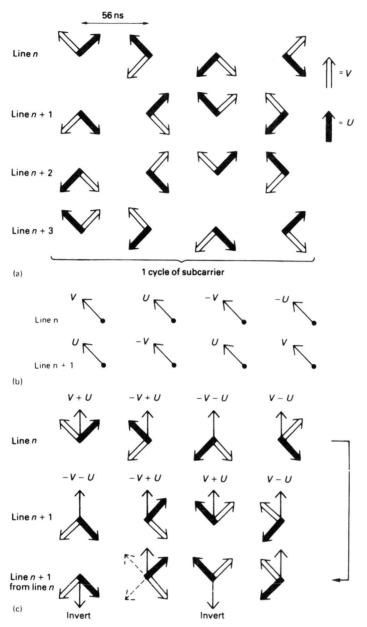

Figure 7.28 (a) The combined effects of V-switch and quarter cycle offset in PAL cause the above relative phases of U and V from line to line in a four-line sequence which only repeats after four frames. (b) If a sampling system takes samples on the U and V axes, it results in the samples having the values shown here. It is not then possible to convert from one line type to the next because, for example, V cannot be processed to become U and so on. (c) If sampling is performed with sample phase between U and V axes (thin arrow) the samples represent sums and differences of the two signals (cosine term neglected). It will be seen that line n can be made into line n + 1 by inverting the samples when U and V have the same sign. When the sample is made, phase information is lost and only amplitude is known. For this reason, the non-inverted samples phase-mirror (dotted arrow) because the phase is determined in the context of adjacent samples.

The solution adopted in composite digital is to sample at 45° to the U and V axes, i.e. in phase with the burst. Figure 7.28(c) shows that when this is done, the samples represent $U \times \cos 45 + V \times \cos 45$ etc. If everything is normalized by dividing by $\cos 45$, the samples become $U + V, -U + V$, etc.

If it is required to convert a line into the next line type, having the opposite sense of V-switch, this can be done by inverting the samples where U and V have different polarities, but not where they have the same polarity.

If the difference is two lines, the only requirement is to invert the whole chroma waveform, as V-switch is the same after two lines, and there have been two quarter cycle offsets of subcarrier making 180°.

If the difference is three lines, an inversion combined with V-switch reversal and a quadrature shift is needed, and this can simply be done by inverting samples where U and V have the same polarity and not where the polarity is different.

The type of line required on the output is available from the reference colour framer, and the type of line played back is determined from the ID codes in variable speed and from the line address in shuttle. By comparing the two line types, the conversion to be performed by the colour processor can be determined.

7.13 Field interpolators

Owing to the use of interlace, the head jumps may result in an odd field being played when an even field is needed, and vice versa. The vertical picture

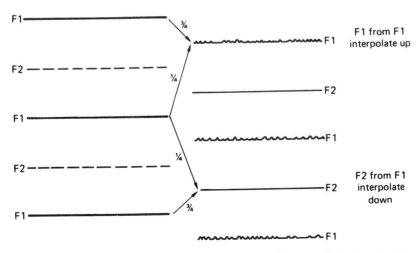

Figure 7.29 Vertical interpolation of either output field from either input field using a half line shift means that output resolution is not changed whether the VTR is interlaced or not, and vertical movement is eliminated.

movement which results from outputting the wrong field can be completely removed by vertical interpolation.

The output raster and the input raster are shifted slightly so that neither input field aligns with either output field. By using memory to produce three delays of one line each, samples representing four points in a vertical line on the input field are simultaneously available to a four point FIR filter. If the output field is to be the same as the input field, the phase of the interpolator will be such that the sample value for a line one-quarter of the way down from an input line will be computed. If the opposite type of field is required, the order of the coefficients to the FIR filter will be reversed such that a line three-quarters of the way down from an input line will be computed. Figure 7.29 illustrates how this process results in the image staying at the same vertical position on the screen irrespective of the relation of input and output fields.

The luminance conveys the subjective resolution, and so the vertical chroma interpolation can be done with a simpler filter having only one line of delay to give two points.

If field interpolation is combined with comb filter decoding in a composite DVTR, the output picture in slow motion has the same bandwidth as in colour-framed operation, and there are no other artifacts to show that the picture has been processed.

7.14 Editing

The term editing covers a multitude of possibilities in video production. Simple video editors work in two basic ways, by assembling or by inserting sections of material comprising a whole number of frames to build the finished work.

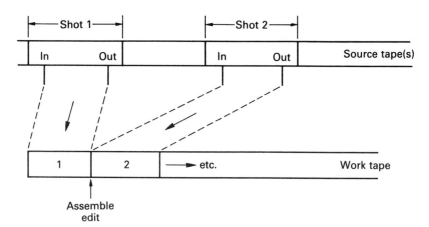

Figure 7.30 Assembly is the most basic form of editing where source clips are sequentially added to the end of a recording.

Assembly begins with a blank master recording. The beginning of the work is copied from the source, and new material is successively appended to the end of the previous material. Figure 7.30 shows how a master recording is made up by assembly from source recordings. Insert editing begins with an existing recording in which a section is replaced by the edit process.

At its most general, editing is subdivided into horizontal editing, which refers to any changes with respect to the time axis, and vertical editing,[3] which is the generic term for processes which take place on an imaginary z-axis running back into the screen. These include keying, dissolves, wipes, layering and so on.[4] DVEs may also be used for editing, where a page turn or rotate effect reveals a new take.

In all types of editing the goal is the appropriate sequence of material at the appropriate time. The first type of picture editing was by physically cutting and splicing film, in order mechanically to assemble the finished work. This approach was copied on early quadruplex video recorders, a difficult and laborious process. This gave way to electronic editing on VTRs where lengths of source tape were copied to the master.

Timecode is essential to editing, as many different processes occur during an edit, and each one is programmed beforehand to take place at a given timecode value. Provision of a timecode reference effectively synchronizes the processes.

SMPTE standard timecode for 525/60 use is shown in Figure 7.31. EBU timecode is basically similar to SMPTE except that the frame count will reach a lower value in each second. These store hours, minutes, seconds and frames as binary-coded decimal (BCD) numbers, which are serially encoded along with user bits into an FM channel code (see Chapter 4) which is recorded on one of the linear audio tracks of the tape. The user bits are not specified in the standard, but a common use is to record the take or session number.

VTRs vary in their detailed operation, but all have in common the use of error correction. This requires an interleave, or reordering, of samples to reduce the impact of large errors, and the assembling of many samples into an error-correcting codeword. Codewords are recorded in constant-sized blocks on the medium. In DVTRs this will be a segment or even a field. When data reduction is used, pixels are not recorded at all. Instead the data are in the form of coefficients which describe areas of the picture.

Vertical editing requires the modification of source material within the field to pixel accuracy. This contradicts the large interleaved block-based codes of real media. Editing to pixel accuracy simply cannot be performed directly on real media.

The solution is to ensure that the medium itself is only edited at block boundaries so that entire error-correction codewords are written down. In order to obtain greater editing accuracy, blocks must be read from the medium and de-interleaved into RAM, modified there and re-interleaved for writing back on the medium, the so called *read–modify–write* process.

The digital tape editor consists of three main areas. Firstly, the various contributory recordings must enter the processing stage at the right time with respect to the master recording. This will be achieved using a combination of timecode, transport synchronization and RAM timebase correction. The synchronizer will take control of the various transports during an edit so that one section reaches its out-point just as another reaches its in-point.

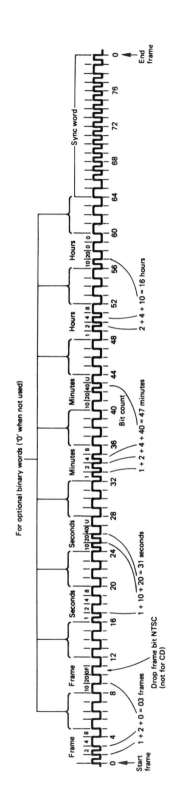

Figure 7.31 In SMPTE standard timecode, the frame number and time are stored as eight BCD symbols. There is also space for 32 user-defined bits. The code repeats every frame. Note the asymmetrical sync word which allows the direction of tape movement to be determined.

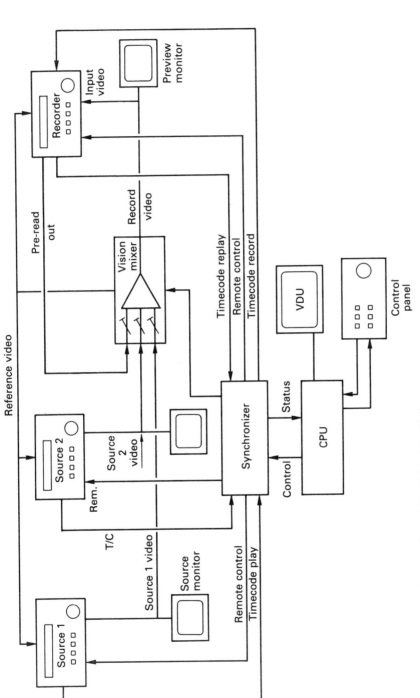

Figure 7.32 Block diagram of a tape edit controller. See text for details.

Secondly the video signal path of the editor must take the appropriate action, under timecode control, such as a dissolve or wipe, at the edit point. This requires some digital processing circuitry except in the case of the simplest editor which merely switches sources during the vertical interval.

Thirdly the editing operation must be supervised by a control system which coordinates the operation of the transports and the signal processing to achieve the desired result.

Figure 7.32 shows a block diagram of an editor. Each source transport must produce timecode locked to the data. The synchronizer section of the control system uses the timecode to determine the relative timing of sources and sends remote control signals to the transport(s) to make the timing correct. The

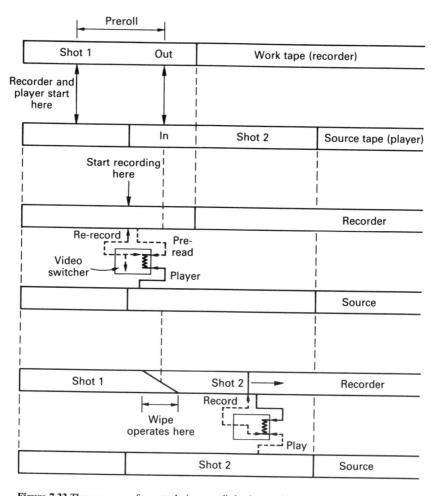

Figure 7.33 The sequence of events during an edit having a wipe between the clips.

master recorder is also fed with timecode in such a way that it can make a contiguous timecode track when performing assembly edits. The control system also generates a master video reference to which contributing devices must genlock in order to feed data into the edit process.

If vertical edits such as dissolves or wipes are contemplated, the master recorder must be a DVTR which has a pre-read function. Data from the pre-read heads are routed to the vision mixer and the mixer output is fed to the record input of the master recorder. The signal processor takes contributing sources and mixes or vertically edits them as instructed by the control system. The mix is then routed to the recorder.

Figure 7.33 shows the sequence of events during an edit where there is a wipe transition from the end of the previous clip on the master to the beginning of the next. Both the master recorder and the source machine will reverse away from their respective edit points by the same number of frames, typically a few seconds. Both transports then roll and lock to reference video. If the correct timecode relationship is not obtained, the source machine will be frame slipped faster or slower until both will reach their edit points simultaneously. Initially the master recorder is simply playing back with the pre-read heads, and sending data to the vision mixer. The vision mixer is switched to the master recorder input and so the end of the first clip is seen on the monitor. When the appropriate timecode is reached, the master recorder begins recording at a field boundary. As the record input is simply the pre-read output, the tape is re-recorded with the existing data. However, once recording has commenced, the vision mixer transitions from the master pre-read signal to the source machine signal. This transition may take as long as required. In the middle of the transition the output fields will contain data from both tapes. At the end of the transition the vision mixer is outputting data from the source machine only, and the two machines are now dubbing. This will continue for as long as required.

A preview of the edit can be obtained by performing all of the above steps with the exception of the master recorder entering record mode. The preview can be repeated as often as required and the edit points and the transition period can be changed until the desired effect is obtained without committing anything to tape.

In component DVTRs, any frame relationship betwen the two tapes may be used, but in the case of composite working, the edit must be constrained by the requirement for colour framing.

If a DVTR with three sets of heads and two playback signal paths is used, the edit can be monitored off tape on the master recorder confidence replay channel. This is shown dotted in Figure 7.33. The confidence replay signal may not be decoded to video, as this would effectively require two complete replay channels for use with pre-read. Instead the confidence channel may consist of an inner code error-detection circuit which monitors the error rate of the recorded tracks.

References

1. BRUSH, R.,Video data shuffling for the 4:2:2 DVTR. Presented at 20th SMPTE Television Conf. (Chicago, 1986), *SMPTE J.*., **95**, 1009–1016 (1985)

2. SLAVIN, K.R., and WELLS, N.D., The effect of random bit errors on YUV component video signals – II. *BBC Res. Dep. Tech. Memo.,* ER-1526 (1985)
3. RUBIN, M., The emergence of the desktop: Implications to offline editing. *Record of 18th ITS.* 384–389 (Montreux, 1993)
4. TROTTIER, L., Digital video compositing on the desktop. *Record of 18th ITS,* 564–570 (Montreux, 1993)

Chapter 8

Digital audio in DVTRs

Digital technology made inroads into audio a little before it transformed video, and much of that technology has been adopted in DVTRs to obtain exceptional sound quality.

8.1 Introduction

Once audio has been converted to the digital domain, it becomes data which do not differ in principle from any other. The major difference is that a high-quality digital audio channel will require only 1 megabit per second, which is considerably less than the data rates which are necessary for video. Although the frequency range of audio is much less than that of video, the dynamic range is much greater, and sample wordlengths between 14 and 20 bits will be found. Whilst the sampling and quantizing theory discussed in Chapter 3 is just as valid for audio signals, video converter technology is insufficiently accurate for use with the wordlengths needed in audio and different techniques have evolved.

As has been seen, DVTRs have rotary heads in order to support the substantial data rate. The presence of several channels of digital audio causes an increase in data rate of only a few percent, and it is universal to record the audio with the same heads as the video by allocating small audio blocks at specified places along the main recorded tracks. This simplifies the construction of the machine tremendously, since there are no separate audio heads, and the same RF and coding circuitry is timeshared between audio and video, along with part of the error-correction circuitry.

Standards exist for the interconnection of audio machines in the digital domain, not the least important being the AES/EBU interface which has found wide acceptance and is fully detailed here.

8.2 What can we hear?

The acuity of the human ear is astonishing. It can detect tiny amounts of distortion, and will accept an enormous dynamic range. The only criterion for quality that we have is that if the ear cannot detect impairments in properly conducted tests, we must say that the reproduced sound is perfect. Thus quality is completely subjective and can only be checked by listening tests. However, any characteristic of a signal which can be heard can also be measured by a suitable instrument. The subjective tests can tell us how sensitive the instrument should be. Then the objective readings from the instrument give an indication of how acceptable a signal is in respect of that characteristic. Fielder[1] has properly suggested that audio converter design should be based on psycho-acoustics.

The sense we call hearing results from acoustic, mechanical, nervous and mental processes in the ear/brain combination, leading to the term psychoacoustics. It is only possible briefly to introduce the subject here, but the interested reader is also referred to Moore[2] for an excellent treatment.

Usually, people's ears are at their most sensitive between about 2 kHz and 5 kHz, and although some people can detect 20 kHz at high level, there is much evidence to suggest that most listeners cannot tell if the upper frequency limit of sound is 20 kHz or 16 kHz.[3,4] For a long time it was thought that frequencies below about 40 Hz were unimportant, but it is becoming clear that reproduction of frequencies down to 20 Hz improves reality and ambience.[5] A digital system can deliver a response down to DC and although this is not necessary for audio, it may be advantageous for instrumentation applications. The dynamic range of the ear is obtained by a logarithmic response, and certainly exceeds 100 dB. At the extremes of this range, the ear is either straining to hear or in pain. Neither of these cases can be described as pleasurable or entertaining, and it is hardly necessary to produce recordings of this dynamic range for the consumer since, among other things, he or she is unlikely to have anywhere sufficiently quiet to listen to them. On the other hand extended listening to music which has been excessively compressed is fatiguing.

Before digital techniques were used for high-quality audio, it was thought that the principles of digitizing were adequately understood, but the disappointing results of some early digital audio machines showed that this was not so. The ear could detect the minute imperfections of filters and converters, which could be neglected in, for example, instrumentation applications. The distortions due to quantizing without dither were found to be subjectively unacceptable. A more rigorous study of digitization was soon applied, and the essentials of it can be found here along with a treatment of the essential dithering techniques. The important topic of oversampling is also shown here to be soundly based on information theory, and its significant inherent advantages for audio, particularly when used with noise shaping, are discussed.

8.3 Choice of sampling rate for audio

Sampling theory is only the beginning of the process which must be followed to arrive at a suitable sampling rate. The finite slope of realizable filters will compel designers to raise the sampling rate. For consumer products, the lower the sampling rate the better, since the cost of the medium is directly proportional to the sampling rate: thus sampling rates near to twice 20 kHz are to be expected. For professional products, there is a need to operate at variable speed for pitch correction. When the speed of a digital recorder is reduced, the offtape sampling rate falls, and Figure 8.1 shows that with a minimal sampling rate the first image frequency can become low enough to pass the reconstruction filter. If the sampling frequency is raised without changing the response of the filters, the speed can be reduced without this problem. Thus 48 kHz became the professional sampling rate.

Although in a perfect world the adoption of a single sampling rate might have had virtues, for practical and economic reasons digital audio has essentially three

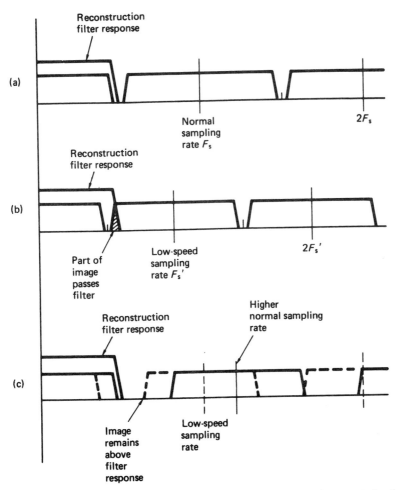

Figure 8.1 At normal speed, the reconstruction filter correctly prevents images entering the baseband, as at (a). When speed is reduced, the sampling rate falls, and a fixed filter will allow part of the lower sideband of the sampling frequency to pass. If the sampling rate of the machine is raised, but the filter characteristic remains the same, the problem can be avoided, as at (c).

rates to support: 32 kHz for broadcast, 44.1 kHz for CD and its mastering equipment, and 48 kHz for 'professional' use.[6] The currently available DVTR formats offer only 48 kHz audio sampling.

8.4 Basic digital-to-analog conversion

This direction of conversion will be discussed first, since ADCs often use embedded DACs in feedback loops.

The purpose of a digital-to-analog converter is to take numerical values and reproduce the continuous waveform that they represent. Figure 8.2 shows the

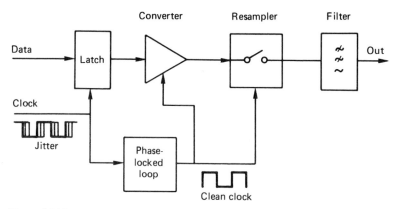

Figure 8.2 The components of a conventional converter. A jitter-free clock drives the voltage conversion, whose output may be resampled prior to reconstruction.

major elements of a conventional conversion subsystem, i.e. one in which oversampling is not employed. The jitter in the clock needs to be removed with a VCO or VCXO. Sample values are buffered in a latch and fed to the converter element which operates on each cycle of the clean clock. The output is then a voltage proportional to the number for at least a part of the sample period. A resampling stage may be found next, in order to remove switching transients, reduce the aperture ratio or allow the use of a converter which takes a substantial part of the sample period to operate. The resampled waveform is then presented to a reconstruction filter which rejects frequencies above the audio band.

This section is primarily concerned with the implementation of the converter element. There are two main ways of obtaining an analog signal from PCM data. One is to control binary-weighted currents and sum them; the other is to control the length of time a fixed current flows into an integrator. The two methods are contrasted in Figure 8.3. They appear simple, but are of no use for audio in these forms because of practical limitations. In Figure 8.3(c), the binary code is about to have a major overflow, and all the low-order currents are flowing. In Figure 8.3(d), the binary input has increased by one, and only the most significant current flows. This current must equal the sum of all the others plus one. The accuracy must be such that the step size is within the required limits. In this simple 4 bit example, if the step size needs to be a rather casual 10% accurate, the necessary accuracy is only one part in 160, but for a 16 bit system it would become one part in 655 360, or about 2 ppm. This degree of accuracy is almost impossible to achieve, let alone maintain in the presence of ageing and temperature change.

The integrator-type converter in this 4 bit example is shown in Figure 8.3(e); it requires a clock for the counter which allows it to count up to the maximum in less than one sample period. This will be more than 16 times the sampling rate. However, in a 16 bit system, the clock rate would need to be 65 536 times the sampling rate, or about 3 GHz.

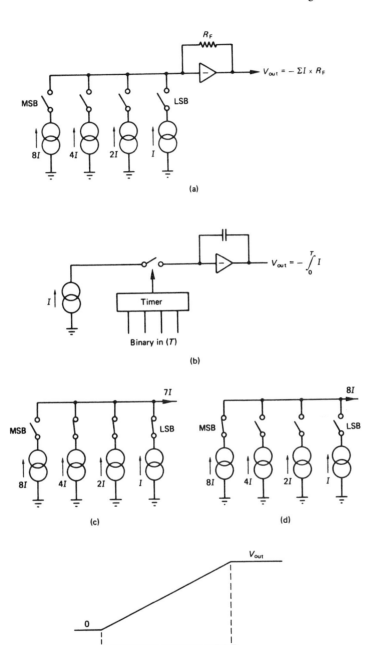

Figure 8.3 Elementary conversion: (a) weighted current DAC; (b) timed integrator DAC; (c) current flow with 0111 input; (d) current flow with 1000 input; (e) integrator ramps up for 15 cycles of clock for input 1111.

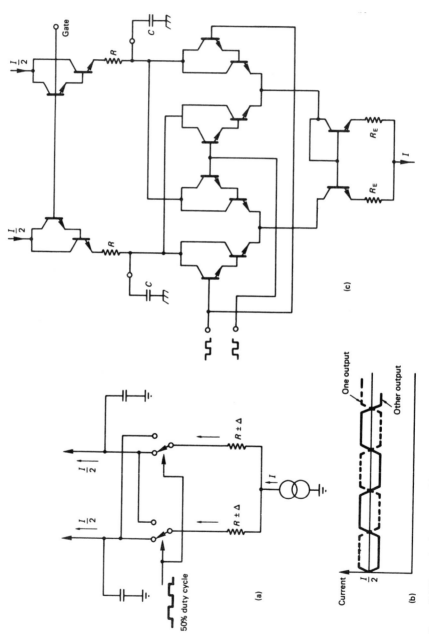

Figure 8.4 Dynamic element matching. (a) Each resistor spends half its time in each current path. (b) Average current of both paths will be identical if duty cycle is accurately 50%. (c) Typical monolithic implementation. Note clock frequency is arbitrary.

One method of producing currents of high relative accuracy is *dynamic element matching*.[7,8] Figure 8.4 shows a current source feeding a pair of nominally equal resistors. The two will not be the same owing to manufacturing tolerances and drift, and thus the current is only approximately divided between them. A pair of changeover switches places each resistor in series with each output. The average current in each output will then be identical, provided that the duty cycle of the switches is exactly 50%. This is readily achieved in a divide-by-two circuit. The accuracy criterion has been transferred from the resistors to the time domain in which accuracy is more readily achieved. Current averaging is performed by a pair of capacitors which do not need to be of any special quality. By cascading these divide-by-two stages, a binary-weighted series of currents can be obtained, as in Figure 8.5. In practice, a reduction in the number of stages can be obtained by using a more complex switching arrangement. This generates currents of ratio 1:1:2 by dividing the current into four paths and feeding two of them to one output, as shown in Figure 8.6. A major advantage of this approach is that no trimming is needed in manufacture, making it attractive for mass production. Freedom from drift is a further advantage.

To prevent interaction between the stages in weighted-current converters, the currents must be switched to ground or into the virtual earth by changeover switches. The on-resistance of these switches is a source of error, particularly the MSB, which passes most current. A solution in monolithic converters is to fabricate switches whose area is proportional to the weighted current, so that the voltage drops of all the switches are the same. The error can then be removed with a suitable offset. The layout of such a device is

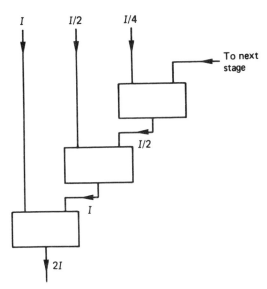

Figure 8.5 Cascading the current dividers of Figure 8.4 produces a binary-weighted series of currents.

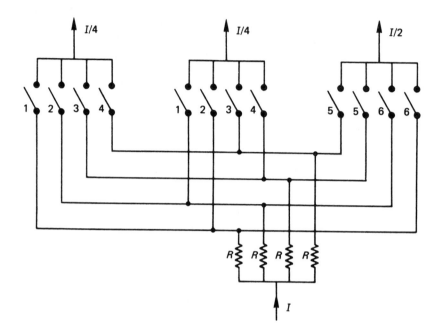

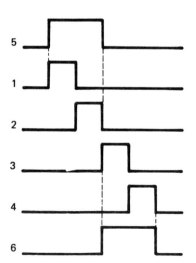

Figure 8.6 More complex dynamic element-matching system. Four drive signals (1, 2, 3, 4) of 25% duty cycle close switches of corresponding number. Two signals (5, 6) have 50% duty cycle, resulting in two current shares going to right-hand output. Division is thus into 1:1:2.

dominated by the MSB switch since, by definition, it is as big as all the others put together.

The practical approach to the integrator converter is shown in Figures 8.7 and 8.8 where two current sources whose ratio is 256:1 are used; the larger is timed by the high byte of the sample and the smaller is timed by the low byte. The necessary clock frequency is reduced by a factor of 256. Any inaccuracy in the current ratio will cause one quantizing step in every 256 to be of the wrong size as shown in Figure 8.9, but current tracking is easier to achieve in a monolithic device. The integrator capacitor must have low dielectric leakage and relaxation, and the operational amplifier must have low bias current as this will have the same effect as leakage.

The output of the integrator will remain constant once the current sources are turned off, and the resampling switch will be closed during the voltage plateau

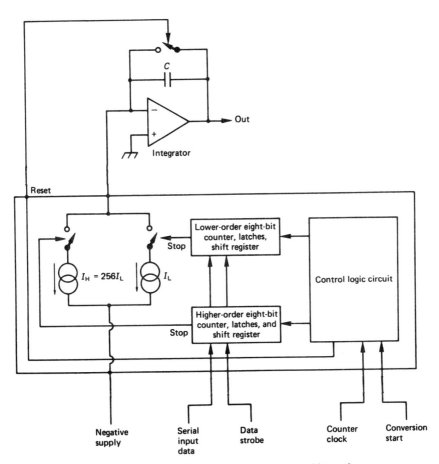

Figure 8.7 Simplified diagram of Sony CX-20017. The high-order and low-order current sources (I_H and I_L) and associated timing circuits can be seen. The necessary integrator is external.

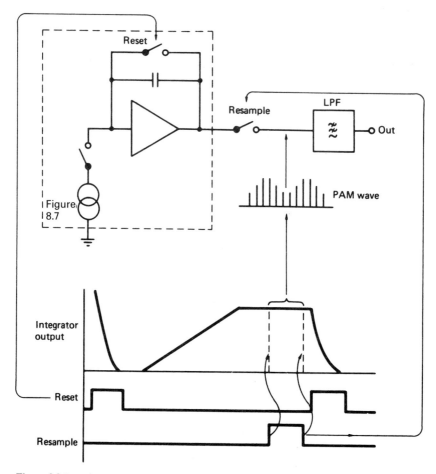

Figure 8.8 In an integrator converter, the output level is only stable when the ramp finishes. An analog switch is necessary to isolate the ramp from subsequent circuits. The switch can also be used to produce a PAM (Pulse Amplitude Modulated) signal which has a flatter frequency response than a zero-order hold (staircase) signal.

to produce the pulse-amplitude-modulated output. Clearly this device cannot produce a zero-order hold output without an additional sample–hold stage, so it is naturally complemented by resampling. Once the output pulse has been gated to the reconstruction filter, the capacitor is discharged with a further switch in preparation for the next conversion. The conversion count must take place in rather less than one sample period to permit the resampling and discharge phases. A clock frequency of about 20 MHz is adequate for a 16 bit 48 kHz unit, which permits the ramp to complete in 12.8 ms, leaving 8 ms for resampling and reset.

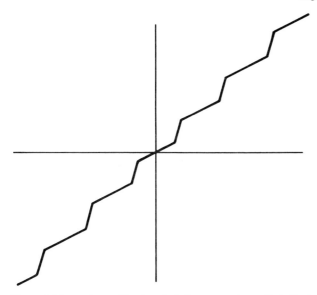

Figure 8.9 Imprecise tracking in a dual-slope converter results in the transfer function shown here.

8.5 Basic analog-to-digital conversion

A conventional analog-to-digital subsystem is shown in Figure 8.10. Following the anti-aliasing filter there will be a sampling process. Many of the ADCs described here will need a finite time to operate, whereas an instantaneous sample must be taken from the input. The solution is to use a track/hold circuit. Following sampling the sample voltage is quantized. The number of the quantized level is then converted to a binary code, typically two's complement. This section is concerned primarily with the implementation of the quantizing step.

The flash converter is probably the simplest technique available for PCM and DPCM conversion. The principle was shown in Chapter 3. Although the device is simple in principle, it contains a lot of circuitry and can only be practicably implemented on a chip. A 16 bit device would need a ridiculous 65 535 comparators, and thus these converters are not practicable for direct audio conversion, although they will be used to advantage in the DPCM and oversampling converters described later in this chapter. The analog signal has to drive a lot of inputs, which results in a significant parallel capacitance, and a low-impedance driver is essential to avoid restricting the slewing rate of the input. The extreme speed of a flash converter is a distinct advantage in oversampling. Because computation of all bits is performed simultaneously, no track/hold circuit is required, and droop is eliminated.

Reduction in component complexity can be achieved by quantizing serially. The most primitive method of generating different quantized voltages is to connect a counter to a DAC as in Figure 8.11. The resulting staircase voltage

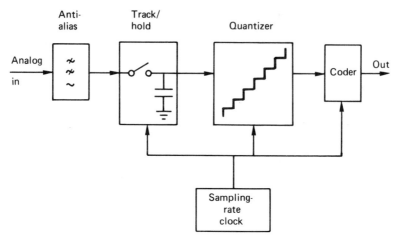

Figure 8.10 A conventional analog-to-digital subsystem. Following the anti-aliasing filter there will be a sampling process, which may include a track–hold circuit. Following quantizing, the number of the quantized level is then converted to a binary code, typically two's complement.

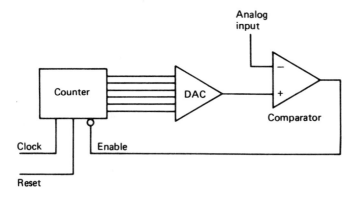

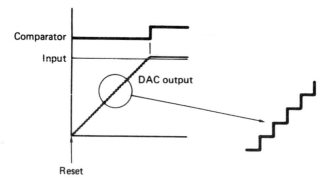

Figure 8.11 Simple ramp ADC compares output of DAC with input. Count is stopped when DAC output just exceeds input. This method, although potentially accurate, is much too slow for digital audio.

is compared with the input and used to stop the clock to the counter when the DAC output has just exceeded the input. This method is painfully slow and is not used in practice as a much faster method exists which is only slightly more complex. Using successive approximation, each bit is tested in turn, starting with the MSB. If the input is greater than half range, the MSB will be retained and used as a base to test the next bit, which will be retained if the input exceeds three-quarters range and so on. The number of decisions is equal to the number of bits in the word, in contrast to the number of quantizing intervals which was the case in the previous example. A drawback of the successive approximation converter is that the least significant bits are computed last, when droop is at its worst. Figures 8.12 and 8.13 show that droop can cause a successive approximation converter to make a significant error under certain circumstances.

Analog-to-digital conversion can also be performed using the dual-current-source-type DAC principle in a feedback system; the major difference is that the two current sources must work sequentially rather than concurrently. Figure 8.14 shows a 16 bit application in which the capacitor of the track/hold circuit is also used as the ramp integrator. The system operates as follows. When the track/hold FET switches off, the capacitor C will be holding the sample voltage. Two

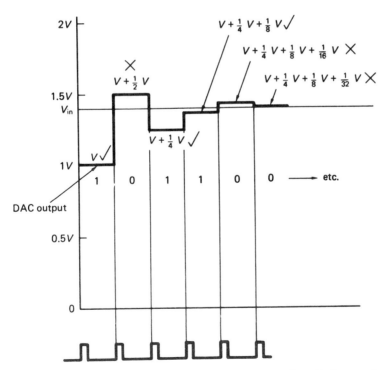

Figure 8.12 Successive approximation tests each bit in turn, starting with the most significant. The DAC output is compared with the input. If the DAC output is below the input ($\checkmark$) the bit is made 1; if the DAC output is above the input ($\times$) the bit is made 0.

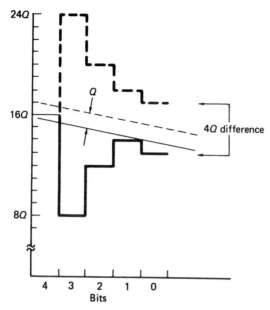

Figure 8.13 Two drooping track–hold signals (solid and dashed lines) which differ by one quantizing interval Q are shown here to result in conversions which are $4Q$ apart. Thus droop can destroy the monotonicity of a converter. Low-level signals (near the midrange of the number system) are especially vulnerable.

currents of ratio 128:1 are capable of discharging the capacitor. Owing to this ratio, the smaller current will be used to determine the seven least significant bits, and the larger current will determine the nine most significant bits. The currents are provided by current sources of ratio 127:1. When both run together, the current produced is 128 times that from the smaller source alone. This approach means that the current can be changed simply by turning off the larger source, rather than by attempting a changeover.

With both current sources enabled, the high-order counter counts up until the capacitor voltage has fallen below the reference of $-128Q$ supplied to comparator 1. At the next clock edge, the larger current source is turned off. Waiting for the next clock edge is important, because it ensures that the larger source can only run for entire clock periods, which will discharge the integrator by integer multiples of $128Q$. The integrator voltage will overshoot the $128Q$ reference, and the remaining voltage on the integrator will be less than $128Q$ and will be measured by counting the number of clocks for which the smaller current source runs before the integrator voltage reaches zero. This process is termed residual expansion. The break in the slope of the integrator voltage gives rise to the alternative title of gear-change converter. Following ramping to ground in the conversion process, the track/hold circuit must settle in time for the next conversion. In this 16 bit example, the high-order conversion needs a maximum count of 512, and the low-order needs 128, a total of 640. Allowing 25% of the sample period for the track/hold circuit to

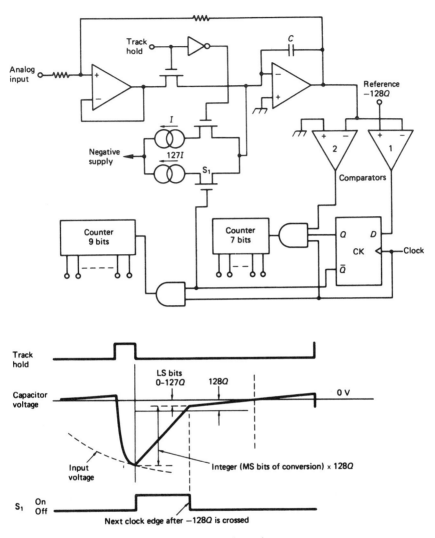

Figure 8.14 Dual-ramp ADC using track–hold capacitor as integrator.

operate, a 48 kHz converter would need to be clocked at some 40 MHz. This is rather faster than the clock needed for the DAC using the same technology.

8.6 Alternative converters

Although PCM audio is universal because of the ease with which it can be recorded and processed numerically, there are several alternative related methods of converting an analog waveform to a bit stream. The output of these converter types is not Nyquist rate PCM, but this can be obtained from them by appropriate digital processing. In advanced conversion systems it is possible to adopt an alternative converter technique specifically to take advantage of a particular characteristic. The output is then digitally converted to Nyquist rate PCM in order to obtain the advantages of both.

Conventional PCM has already been introduced. In PCM, the amplitude of the signal only depends on the number range of the quantizer, and is independent of the frequency of the input. Similarly, the amplitude of the unwanted signals introduced by the quantizing process is also largely independent of input frequency.

Figure 8.15 introduces the alternative converter structures. The top half of the diagram shows converters which are differential. In differential coding the value of the output code represents the difference between the current sample voltage and that of the previous sample. The lower half of the diagram shows converters which are PCM. In addition, the left side of the diagram shows single bit converters, whereas the right side shows multi-bit converters.

In differential pulse code modulation (DPCM), shown at top right, the difference between the previous absolute sample value and the current one is quantized into a multibit binary code. It is possible to produce a DPCM signal from a PCM signal simply by subtracting successive samples; this is digital differentiation. Similarly the reverse process is possible by using an accumulator or digital integrator (see Chapter 2) to compute sample values from the differences received. The problem with this approach is that it is very easy to lose the baseline of the signal if it commences at some arbitrary time. A digital high-pass filter can be used to prevent unwanted offsets.

Differential converters do not have an absolute amplitude limit. Instead there is a limit to the maximum rate at which the input signal voltage can change. They are said to be slew rate limited, and thus the permissible signal amplitude falls at 6 dB per octave. As the quantizing steps are still uniform, the quantizing error amplitude has the same limits as PCM. As input frequency rises, ultimately the signal amplitude available will fall down to it.

If DPCM is taken to the extreme case where only a binary output signal is available then the process is described as delta modulation (top left in Figure 8.15). The meaning of the binary output signal is that the current analog input is above or below the accumulation of all previous bits. The characteristics of the system show the same trends as DPCM, except that there is severe limiting of the rate of change of the input signal. A DPCM decoder must accumulate all the difference bits to provide a PCM output for conversion to analog, but with a 1 bit signal the function of the accumulator can be performed by an analog integrator.

If an integrator is placed in the input to a delta modulator, the integrator's amplitude response loss of 6 dB per octave parallels the converter's amplitude limit of 6 dB per octave; thus the system amplitude limit becomes independent of frequency. This integration is responsible for the term sigma-delta modulation, since in mathematics sigma is used to denote summation. The input integrator can be combined with the integrator already present in a delta modulator by a slight rearrangement of the components (bottom left in Figure 8.15). The transmitted signal is now the amplitude of the input, not the slope; thus the receiving integrator can be dispensed with, and all that is necessary to after the DAC is an LPF to smooth the bits. The removal of the integration stage at the

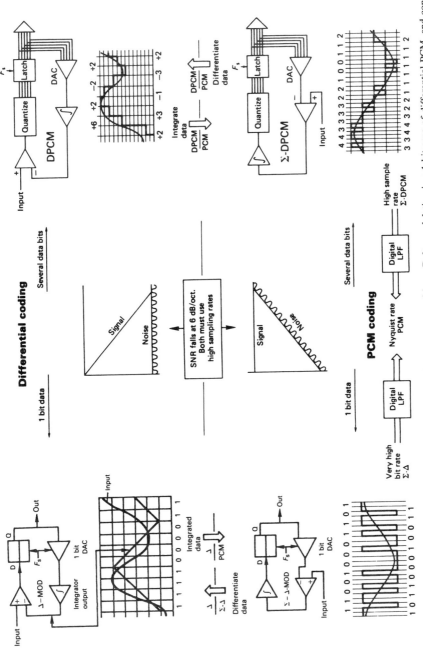

Figure 8.15 The four main alternatives to simple PCM conversion are compared here. Delta modulation is a 1 bit case of differential PCM, and conveys the slope of the signal. The digital output of both can be integrated to give PCM. Σ–Δ (sigma-delta) is a 1 bit case of Σ-DPCM. The application of integrator before differentiator makes the output true PCM, but tilts the noise floor; hence these can be referred to as 'noise-shaping' converters.

decoder now means that the quantizing error amplitude rises at 6 dB per octave, ultimately meeting the level of the wanted signal.

The principle of using an input integrator can also be applied to a true DPCM system and the result should perhaps be called sigma DPCM (bottom right in Figure 8.15). The dynamic range improvement over delta-sigma modulation is 6 dB for every extra bit in the code. Because the level of the quantizing error signal rises at 6 dB per octave in both delta-sigma modulation and sigma DPCM, these systems are sometimes referred to as 'noise-shaping' converters, although the word 'noise' must be used with some caution. The output of a sigma DPCM system is again PCM, and a DAC will be needed to receive it, because it is a binary code.

As the differential group of systems suffer from a wanted signal that converges with the unwanted signal as frequency rises, they must all use very high sampling rates.[9] It is possible to convert from sigma DPCM to conventional PCM by reducing the sampling rate digitally. When the sampling rate is reduced in this way, the reduction of bandwidth excludes a disproportionate amount of noise because the noise shaping concentrated it at frequencies beyond the audio band. The use of noise shaping and oversampling is the key to the high resolution obtained in advanced converters.

8.7 Oversampling

Oversampling means using a sampling rate which is greater (generally substantially greater) than the Nyquist rate. Neither sampling theory nor quantizing theory *require* oversampling to be used to obtain a given signal quality, but Nyquist rate conversion places extremely high demands on component accuracy when a converter is implemented. Oversampling allows a given signal quality to be reached without requiring very close tolerance, and therefore expensive, components. Although it can be used alone, the advantages of oversampling are better realized when it is used in conjunction with noise shaping. Thus in practice the two processes are generally used together and the terms are often seen used in the loose sense as if they were synonymous. For a detailed and quantitative analysis of oversampling having exhaustive references the serious reader is referred to Hauser.[10]

In Section 8.4, where dynamic element matching was described, it was seen that component accuracy was traded for accuracy in the time domain. Oversampling is another example of the same principle.

The advantages of oversampling were introduced in Chapter 3 in connection with video conversion, but the theory applies to audio just as well. Oversampling permits the use of a converter element of shorter wordlength, making it possible to use a flash converter in audio applications. The flash converter is capable of working at very high frequency and so large oversampling factors are easily realized. The flash converter needs no track/hold system as it works instantaneously. The drawbacks of track/hold are thus eliminated. If the sigma DPCM converter structure of Figure 8.15 is realized with a flash converter element, it can be used with a high oversampling factor. Figure 8.16(c) shows that this class of converter has a rising noise floor. If the highly oversampled output is fed to a digital low-pass filter which has the

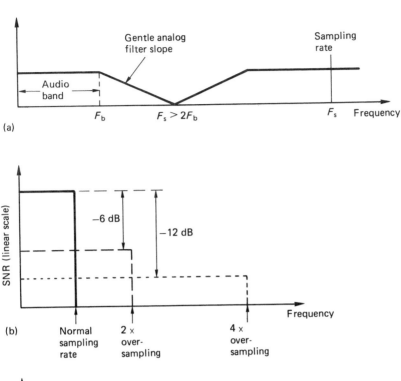

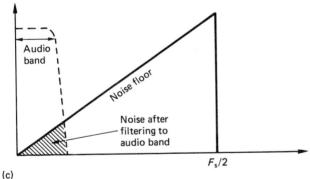

Figure 8.16 Oversampling has a number of advantages. In (a) it allows the slope of analog filters to be relaxed. In (b) it allows the resolution of converters to be extended. In (c) a *noise-shaped* converter allows a disproportionate improvement in resolution.

same frequency response as an analog anti-aliasing filter used for Nyquist rate sampling, the result is a disproportionate reduction in noise because the majority of the noise was outside the audio band. A high-resolution converter can be obtained using this technology without requiring unattainable component tolerances.

8.8 Oversampling without noise shaping

If an oversampling converter is considered which makes no attempt to shape the noise spectrum, it will be clear that if it contains a perfect quantizer, no amount of oversampling will increase the resolution of the system, since a perfect quantizer is blind to all changes of input within one quantizing interval, and looking more often is of no help. It was shown earlier that the use of dither would linearize a quantizer, so that input changes much smaller than the quantizing interval would be reflected in the output, and this remains true for this class of converter.

Figure 8.17 shows the example of a white-noise-dithered quantizer, oversampled by a factor of four. Since dither is correctly employed, it is valid to speak of the unwanted signal as noise. The noise power extends over the whole baseband up to the Nyquist limit. If the basebandwidth is reduced by the oversampling factor of four back to the bandwidth of the original analog input, the noise bandwidth will also be reduced by a factor of four, and the noise power will be one-quarter of that produced at the quantizer. One-quarter noise power implies one-half the noise voltage, so the SNR of this example has been increased by 6 dB, the equivalent of one extra bit in the quantizer. Information theory predicts that an oversampling factor of four would allow an extension by 2 bits. This method is suboptimal in that very large oversampling factors would be needed to obtain useful resolution extension, but it would still realize some advantages, particularly the elimination of the steep-cut analog filter.

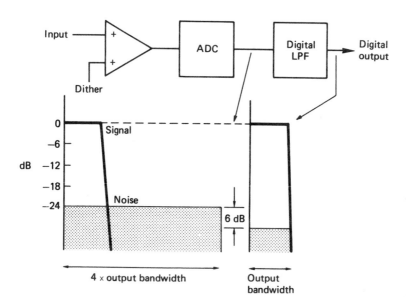

Figure 8.17 In this simple oversampled converter, 4× oversampling is used. When the converter output is low-pass filtered, the noise power is reduced to one-quarter, which in voltage terms is 6 dB. This is a suboptimal method and is not used.

The division of the noise by a larger factor is the only route left open, since all the other parameters are fixed by the signal bandwidth required. The reduction of noise power resulting from a reduction in bandwidth is only proportional if the noise is white, i.e. it has uniform power spectral density (PSD). If the noise from the quantizer is made spectrally non-uniform, the oversampling factor will no longer be the factor by which the noise power is reduced. The goal is to concentrate noise power at high frequencies, so that after low-pass filtering in the digital domain down to the audio input bandwidth, the noise power will be reduced by more than the oversampling factor.

8.9 Noise shaping

Noise shaping dates from the work of Cutler[11] in the 1950s. It is a feedback technique applicable to quantizers and requantizers in which the quantizing process of the current sample is modified in some way by the quantizing error of the previous sample.

When used with requantizing, noise shaping is an entirely digital process which is used, for example, following word extension due to the arithmetic in digital mixers or filters in order to return to the required wordlength. It will be found in this form in oversampling DACs. When used with quantizing, part of the noise-shaping circuitry will be analog. As the feedback loop is placed around an ADC it must contain a DAC. When used in converters, noise-shaping is primarily an implementation technology. It allows processes which are conveniently available in integrated circuits to be put to use in audio conversion. Once integrated circuits can be employed, complexity ceases to be a drawback and low cost mass production is possible.

The term 'noise shaping' is idiomatic and in some respects unsatisfactory because not all devices which are called noise shapers produce true noise. The caution which was given when treating quantizing error as noise is also relevant in this context. Whilst 'quantizing-error-spectrum shaping' is a bit of a mouthful, it is useful to keep in mind that noise-shaping means just that in order to avoid some pitfalls. Some noise shaper architectures do not produce a signal decorrelated quantizing error and need to be dithered.

Figure 8.18(a) shows a requantizer using a simple form of noise shaping. The low-order bits which are lost in requantizing are the quantizing error. If the value of these bits is added to the next sample before it is requantized, the quantizing error will be reduced. The process is somewhat like the use of negative feedback in an operational amplifier except that it is not instantaneous, but encounters a one sample delay. With a constant input, the mean or average quantizing error will be brought to zero over a number of samples, achieving one of the goals of additive dither. The more rapidly the input changes, the greater the effect of the delay and the less effective the error feedback will be. Figure 8.18(b) shows the equivalent circuit seen by the quantizing error, which is created at the requantizer and subtracted from itself one sample period later. As a result the quantizing error spectrum is not uniform, but has the shape of a raised sine wave shown at (c); hence the term noise shaping. The noise is very small at DC and rises with frequency, peaking at the Nyquist frequency at a level determined by the size of the quantizing step. If used with oversampling, the noise peak can be moved outside the audio band.

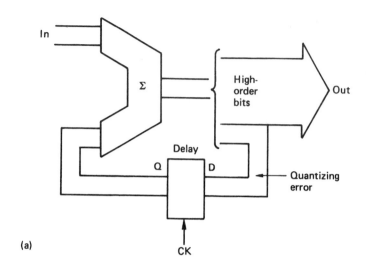

(a)

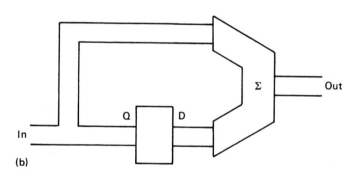

(b)

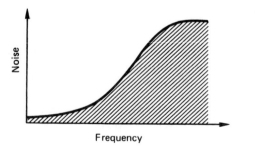

(c)

Figure 8.18 (a) A simple requantizer which feeds back the quantizing error to reduce the error of subsequent samples. The one-sample delay causes the quantizing error to see the equivalent circuit shown in (b) which results in a sinusoidal quantizing error spectrum shown in (c).

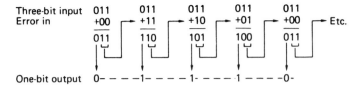

Figure 8.19 By adding the error caused by truncation to the next value, the resolution of the lost bits is maintained in the duty cycle of the output. Here, truncation of 011 by 2 bits would give continuous zeros, but the system repeats 0111, 0111, which, after filtering, will produce a level of three-quarters of a bit.

Figure 8.19 shows a simple example in which two low-order bits need to be removed from each sample. The accumulated error is controlled by using the bits which were neglected in the truncation, and adding them to the next sample. In this example, with a steady input, the roundoff mechanism will produce an output of 01110111 . . . . If this is low-pass filtered, the three ones and one zero result in a level of three-quarters of a quantizing interval, which is precisely the level which would have been obtained by direct conversion of the full digital input. Thus the resolution is maintained even though two bits have been removed.

The noise-shaping technique was used in the first-generation Philips CD players which oversampled by a factor of four. Starting with 16 bit PCM from the disk, the 4 X oversampling will in theory permit the use of an ideal 14 bit converter, but only if the wordlength is reduced optimally. The oversampling DAC system used is shown in Figure 8.20.[12] The interpolator arithmetic extends the wordlength to 28 bits, and this is reduced to 14 bits using the error feedback loop of Figure 8.18. The noise floor rises slightly towards the edge of the audio band, but remains below the noise level of a conventional 16 bit DAC which is shown for comparison.

The 14 bit samples then drive a DAC using dynamic element matching. The aperture effect in the DAC is used as part of the reconstruction filter response, in conjunction with a third-order Bessel filter which has a response 3 dB down at

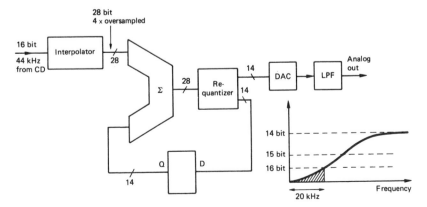

Figure 8.20 The noise-shaping system of the first generation of Philips CD players.

30 kHz. Equalization of the aperture effect within the audio passband is achieved by giving the digital filter which produces the oversampled data a rising response. The use of a digital interpolator as part of the reconstruction filter results in extremely good phase linearity.

Noise shaping can also be used without oversampling. In this case the noise cannot be pushed outside the audio band. Instead the noise floor is shaped or weighted to complement the unequal spectral sensitivity of the ear to noise.[1,13,14] Unless we wish to violate Shannon's theory, this psycho-acoustically optimal noise shaping can only reduce the noise power at certain frequencies by increasing it at others. Thus the average log PSD over the audio band remains the same, although it may be raised slightly by noise induced by imperfect processing.

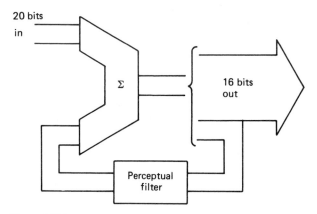

Figure 8.21 Perceptual filtering in a requantizer gives a subjectively improved SNR.

Figure 8.21 shows noise shaping applied to a digitally dithered requantizer. Such a device might be used when, for example, making a CD master from a 20 bit recording format. The input to the dithered requantizer is subtracted from the output to give the error due to requantizing. This error is filtered (and inevitably delayed) before being subtracted from the system input. The filter is not designed to be the exact inverse of the perceptual weighting curve because this would cause extreme noise levels at the ends of the band. Instead the perceptual curve is levelled off[15] such that it cannot fall more than, for example, 40 dB below the peak.

Psycho-acoustically optimal noise shaping can offer nearly 3 bits of increased dynamic range when compared with optimal, spectrally flat dither.

8.10 Noise-shaping ADCs

The sigma DPCM converter introduced in Figure 8.15 has a natural application here and is shown in more detail in Figure 8.22. The current digital sample from the quantizer is converted back to analog in the embedded DAC. The DAC output differs from the ADC input by the quantizing error. The DAC

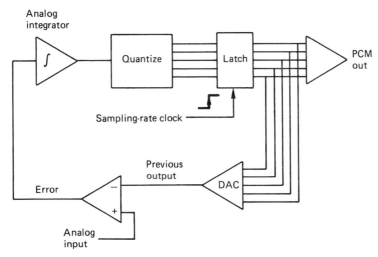

Figure 8.22 The sigma DPCM converter of Figure 8.15 is shown here in more detail.

output is subtracted from the analog input to produce an error which is integrated to drive the quantizer in such a way that the error is reduced. With a constant input voltage the average error will be zero because the loop gain is infinite at DC. If the average error is zero, the mean or average of the DAC outputs must be equal to the analog input. The instantaneous output will deviate from the average in what is called an idling pattern. The presence of the integrator in the error feedback loop makes the loop gain fall with rising frequency. With the feedback falling at 6 dB per octave, the noise floor will rise at the same rate.

Figure 8.23 shows a simple oversampling system using a sigma DPCM converter and an oversampling factor of only four. The sampling spectrum shows that the noise is concentrated at frequencies outside the audio part of the oversampling baseband. Since the scale used here means that noise power is represented by the area under the graph, the area left under the graph after the filter shows the noise-power reduction. Using the relative areas of similar triangles shows that the reduction has been by a factor of 16. The corresponding noise-voltage reduction would be a factor of four, or 12 dB, which corresponds to an additional 2 bits in wordlength. These bits will be available in the wordlength extension which takes place in the decimating filter. Owing to the rise of 6 dB per octave in the PSD of the noise, the SNR will be 3 dB worse at the edge of the audio band.

One way in which the operation of the system can be understood is to consider that the coarse DAC in the loop defines fixed points in the audio transfer function. The time averaging which takes place in the decimator then allows the transfer function to be interpolated between the fixed points. True signal-independent noise of sufficient amplitude will allow this to be done to infinite resolution, but by making the noise primarily outside the audio band the resolution is maintained but the audio band SNR can be extended. A first-order noise-shaping ADC of the kind shown can produce signal-dependent quantizing

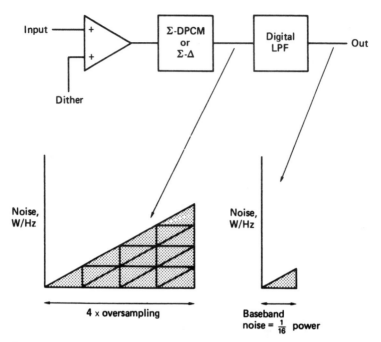

Figure 8.23 In a sigma-DPCM or Σ–Δ converter, noise amplitude increases by 6 dB/octave, noise power by 12dB/octave. In this 4$\times$ oversampling converter, the digital filter reduces bandwidth by four, but noise power is reduced by a factor of 16. Noise voltage falls by a factor of four or 12 dB.

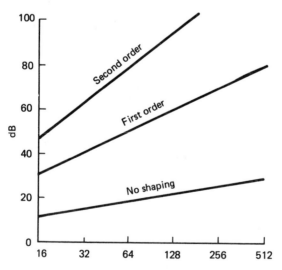

Figure 8.24 The enhancement of SNR possible with various filter orders and oversampling factors in noise-shaping converters.

error and requires analog dither. However, this can be outside the audio band and so need not reduce the SNR achieved.

A greater improvement in dynamic range can be obtained if the integrator is supplanted to realize a higher-order filter.[16] The filter is in the feedback loop and so the noise will have the opposite response to the filter and will therefore rise more steeply to allow a greater SNR enhancement after decimation. Figure 8.24 shows the theoretical SNR enhancement possible for various loop filter orders and oversampling factors. A further advantage of high-order loop filters is that the quantizing noise can be decorrelated from the signal making dither unnecessary. High-order loop filters were at one time thought to be impossible to stabilize, but this is no longer the case, although care is necessary. One technique which may be used is to include some feedforward paths as shown in Figure 8.25.

An ADC with high-order noise shaping was disclosed by Adams[17] and a simplified diagram is shown in Figure 8.26. The comparator outputs of the 128 times oversampled 4 bit flash ADC are directly fed to the DAC which consists of 15 equal resistors fed by CMOS switches. As with all feedback loops, the transfer characteristic cannot be more accurate than the feedback, and in this case the feedback accuracy is determined by the precision of the DAC.[18] Driving the

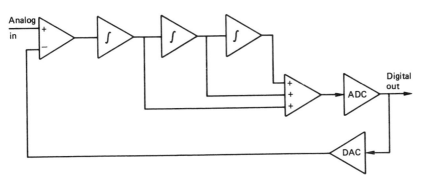

Figure 8.25 Stabilizing the loop filter in a noise-shaping converter can be assisted by the incorporation of feedforward paths as shown here.

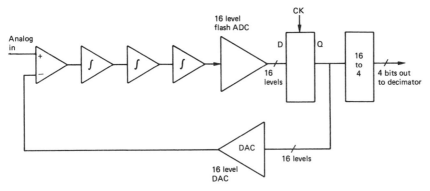

Figure 8.26 An example of a high-order noise-shaping ADC. See text for details.

DAC directly from the ADC comparators is more accurate because each input has equal weighting. The stringent MSB tolerance of the conventional binary-weighted DAC is then avoided. The comparators also drive a 16 to 4 priority encoder to provide the 4 bit PCM output to the decimator. The DAC output is subtracted from the analog input at the integrator. The integrator is followed by a pair of conventional analog operational amplifiers having frequency-dependent feedback and a passive network which gives the loop a fourth-order response overall. The noise floor is thus shaped to rise at 24 dB per octave beyond the audio band. The time constants of the loop filter are optimized to minimize the amplitude of the idling pattern as this is an indicator of the loop stability. The 4 bit PCM output is low-pass filtered and decimated to the Nyquist frequency. The high oversampling factor and high-order noise shaping extend the dynamic range of the 4 bit flash ADC to 108 dB at the output.

8.11 A 1 bit DAC

It might be thought that the waveform from a 1 bit DAC is simply the same as the digital input waveform. In practice this is not the case. The input signal is a logic signal which need only be above or below a threshold for its binary value to be correctly received. It may have a variety of waveform distortions and a duty cycle offset. The area under the pulses can vary enormously. In the DAC output

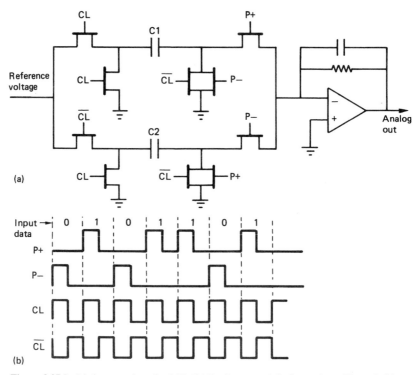

Figure 8.27 In (a) the operation of a 1 bit DAC relies on switched capacitors. The switching waveforms are shown in (b).

the amplitude needs to be extremely accurate. A 1 bit DAC uses only the binary information from the input, but reclocks to produce accurate timing and uses a reference voltage to produce accurate levels. The area of pulses produced is then constant. Thus 1 bit DACs will be found in noise-shaping ADCs as well as in the more obvious application of producing analog audio.

Figure 8.27(a) shows a 1 bit DAC which is implemented with MOS field-effect switches and a pair of capacitors. Quanta of charge are driven into or out of a virtual earth amplifier configured as an integrator by the switched capacitor action. Figure 8.27(b) shows the associated waveforms. Each data bit period is divided into two equal portions: that for which the clock is high, and that for which it is low. During the first half of the bit period, pulse P + is generated if the data bit is a 1, or pulse P− is generated if the data bit is a 0. The reference input is a clean voltage corresponding to the gain required.

C1 is *discharged* during the second half of every cycle by the switches driven from the complemented clock. If the next bit is a 1, during the next high period of the clock the capacitor will be connected between the reference and the virtual earth. Current will flow into the virtual earth until the capacitor is charged. If the next bit is not a 1, the current through C1 will flow to ground.

C2 is *charged* to reference voltage during the second half of every cycle by the switches driven from the complemented clock. On the next high period of the clock, the reference end of C2 will be grounded, and so the op-amp end will assume a negative reference voltage. If the next bit is a 0, this negative reference will be switched into the virtual earth; if not the capacitor will be discharged.

Thus on every cycle of the clock, a quantum of charge is either pumped into the integrator by C1 or pumped out by C2. The analog output therefore precisely reflects the ratio of ones to zeros.

8.12 One bit noise-shaping ADCs

In order to overcome the DAC accuracy constraint of the sigma DPCM converter, the sigma-delta converter can be used as it has only 1 bit internal resolution. A 1 bit DAC cannot be non-linear by definition as it defines only two points on a transfer function. It can, however, suffer from other deficiencies such as DC offset and gain error although these are less offensive in audio. The 1 bit ADC is a comparator.

As the sigma-delta converter is only a 1 bit device, clearly it must use a high oversampling factor and high order noise shaping in order to have sufficiently good SNR for audio.[19] In practice the oversampling factor is limited not so much by the converter technology as by the difficulty of computation in the decimator. A sigma-delta converter has the advantage that the filter input 'words' are 1 bit long and this simplifies the filter design as multiplications can be replaced by selection of constants.

Conventional analysis of loops falls down heavily in the 1 bit case. In particular the gain of a comparator is difficult to quantify, and the loop is highly non-linear so that considering the quantizing error as additive white noise in order to use a linear loop model gives rather optimistic results. In the absence of an accurate mathematical model, progress has been made empirically, with listening tests and by using simulation.

Single-bit sigma-delta converters are prone to long idling patterns because the low resolution in the voltage domain requires more bits in the time domain to be

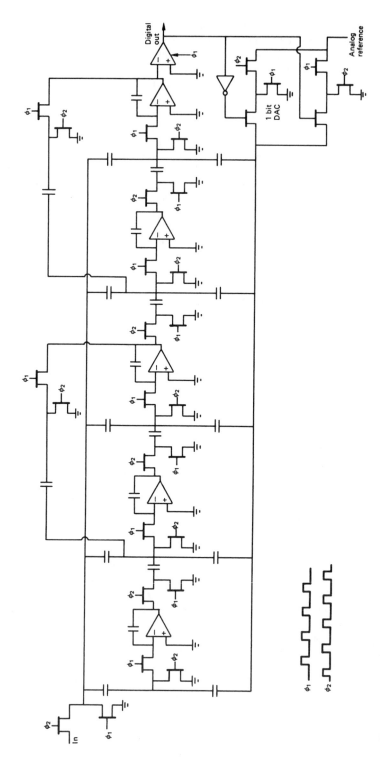

Figure 8.28 A third-order sigma–delta modulator using a switched capacitor loop filter.

integrated to cancel the error. Clearly the longer the period of an idling pattern the more likely it is to enter the audio band as an objectional whistle or 'birdie'. They also exhibit threshold effects or deadbands where the output fails to react to an input change at certain levels. The problem is reduced by the order of the filter and the wordlength of the embedded DAC. Second- and third-order feedback loops are still prone to audible idling patterns and threshold effect.[20] The traditional approach to linearising sigma delta converters is to use dither. Unlike conventional quantizers, the dither used was of a frequency outside the audio band and of considerable level. Square-wave dither has been used and it is advantageous to choose a frequency which is a multiple of the final output sampling rate as then the harmonics will coincide with the troughs in the stopband ripple of the decimator. Unfortunately the level of dither needed to linearize the converter is high enough to cause premature clipping of high-level signals, reducing the dynamic range. This problem is overcome by using in-band white-noise dither at low level.[21]

An advantage of the 1 bit approach is that in the 1 bit DAC, precision components are replaced by precise timing in switched capacitor networks. The same approach can be used to implement the loop filter in an ADC. Figure 8.28 shows a third-order sigma-delta modulator incorporating a DAC based on the principle of Figure 8.27. The loop filter is also implemented with switched capacitors.

8.13 Factors affecting converter quality

In theory the quality of a digital audio system comprising an ideal ADC followed by an ideal DAC is determined at the ADC. The ADC parameters such as the sampling rate, the wordlength and any noise shaping used put limits on the quality which can be achieved. Conversely the DAC itself may be transparent, because it only converts data whose quality are already determined back to the analog domain. In other words, the ADC determines the system quality and the DAC does not make things any worse.

In practice both ADCs and DACs can fall short of the ideal, but with modern converter components and attention to detail the theoretical limits can be approached very closely and at reasonable cost. Shortcomings may be the result of an inadequacy in an individual component such as a converter chip, or due to incorporating a high-quality component in a poorly thought-out system. Poor system design can destroy the performance of a converter. Whilst oversampling is a powerful technique for realizing high-quality converters, its use depends on digital interpolators and decimators whose quality affects the overall conversion quality.[22]

The shortcomings of converters were considered in Chapter 3 in connection with video. The same considerations hold for audio except that greater accuracy is needed.

Clocks which are free of jitter are a critical requirement in converters as was shown in Section 3.11. The effects of clock jitter are proportional to the slewing rate of the audio signal rather than depending on the sampling rate, and as a result oversampling converters are no more prone to jitter than conventional converters.[23] Clock jitter is a form of frequency modulation with a small modulation index. Sinusoidal jitter produces sidebands which may be audible. Random jitter raises the noise floor which is more benign but still undesirable. As clock jitter produces artifacts proportional to the audio slew rate, it is quite easy to detect. A spectrum analyser is connected to the converter output and a low audio frequency signal is input. The test is then repeated with a high audio frequency. If the noise floor changes, there is clock jitter. If the noise floor rises but remains substantially flat, the jitter is random. If there are discrete frequencies in the spectrum, the jitter is periodic. The spacing of the discrete frequencies from the input frequency will reveal the frequencies in the jitter.

Aliasing of audio frequencies is not generally a problem, especially if oversampling is used. However, the nature of aliasing is such that it works in the frequency domain only and translates frequencies to new values without changing amplitudes. Aliasing can occur for any frequency above one-half the sampling rate. The frequency to which it aliases will be the difference frequency between the input and the nearest sampling-rate multiple. Thus in a non-oversampling converter, *all* frequencies above half the sampling rate alias into the audio band. This includes radio frequencies which have entered via audio or power wiring or directly. RF can leapfrog an analog anti-aliasing filter capacitively. Thus good RF screening is necessary around ADCs, and the manner of entry of cables to equipment must be such that the RF energy on them is directed to earth.

Oversampling converters respond to RF on the input in a different manner. Although all frequencies above half the sampling rate are folded into the baseband, only those which fold into the audio band will be audible. Thus an unscreened oversampling converter will be sensitive to RF energy on the input at frequencies within $\pm 20\,\text{kHz}$ of integer multiples of the sampling rate. Fortunately interference from the digital circuitry at exactly the sampling rate will alias to DC and be inaudible.

Converters are also sensitive to unwanted signals superimposed on the references. In fact the multiplicative nature of a converter means that reference noise amplitude-modulates the audio to create sidebands. Power supply ripple on the reference due to inadequate regulation or decoupling causes sidebands 50, 60, 100 or 120 Hz away from the audio frequencies, yet do not raise the noise floor when the input is quiescent. The multiplicative effect reveals how to test for it. Once more a spectrum analyser is connected to the converter output. An audio frequency tone is input, and the level is changed. If the noise floor changes with the input signal level, there is reference noise. RF interference on a converter reference is more insidious, particularly in the case of noise-shaped devices. Noise-shaped converters operate with signals which must contain a great deal of high-frequency noise just beyond the audio band. RF on the reference amplitude-modulates this noise and the sidebands can enter the audio band, raising the noise floor or causing discrete tones depending on the nature of the pickup.

Noise-shaped converters are particularly sensitive to a signal of half the sampling rate on the reference. When a small DC offset is present on the input, the bit density at the quantizer must change slightly from 50%. This results in idle patterns whose spectrum may contain discrete frequencies. Ordinarily these are designed to occur near half the sampling rate so that they are beyond the audio band. In the presence of half-sampling-rate interference on the reference, these tones may be demodulated into the audio band.

Although the faithful reproduction of the audio band is the goal, the nature of sampling is such that converter design must respect RF engineering principles if quality is not to be lost. Clean references, analog inputs, outputs and clocks are all required, despite the potential radiation from digital circuitry within the equipment and uncontrolled electromagnetic interference outside.

Unwanted signals may be induced directly by ground currents, or indirectly by capacitive or magnetic coupling. It is good practice to separate grounds for analog and digital circuitry, connecting them in one place only.

Capacitive coupling uses stray capacitance between the signal source and the point where the interference is picked up. Increasing the distance or conductive screening helps. Coupling is proportional to frequency and the impedance of the receiving point. Lowering the impedance at the interfering frequency will reduce the pickup. If this is done with capacitors to ground, it need not reduce the impedance at the frequency of wanted signals.

Magnetic or inductive coupling relies upon a magnetic field due to the source current flow inducing voltages in a loop. A reduction in inductive coupling requires the size of any loops to be minimized. Digital circuitry should always have ground planes in which return currents for the logic signals can flow. At high frequency, return currents flow in the ground plane directly below the signal tracks and this minimizes the area of the transmiting loop. Similarly ground planes in the analog circuitry minimize the receiving loop whilst having no effect on baseband audio. A further weapon against inductive coupling is to use ground fill between all traces on the circuit board. Ground fill will act like a shorted turn to alternating magnetic fields. Ferrous screening material will also reduce inductive coupling as well as capacitive coupling.

The reference of a converter should be decoupled to ground as near to the integrated circuit as possible. This does not prevent inductive coupling to the lead frame and the wire to the chip itself. In the future converters with on-chip references may be developed to overcome this problem.

In summary, the spectral analysis of converters gives a useful insight into design weaknesses. If the noise floor is affected by the signal level, reference noise is a possibility. If the noise floor is affected by signal frequency, clock jitter is likely. Should the noise floor be unaffected by both, the noise may be inherent in the signal or in analog circuit stages.

8.14 Operating levels in digital audio

Analog tape recorders use operating levels which are some way below saturation. The range between the operating level and saturation is called the headroom. In this range, distortion becomes progressively worse and sustained recording in the headroom is avoided. However, transients may be recorded in the headroom as the ear cannot respond to distortion products unless they are sustained. The PPM level meter has an attack time constant which simulates the temporal distortion sensitivity of the ear. If a transient is too brief to deflect a PPM into the headroom, it will not be heard either.

Operating levels are used in two ways. On making a recording from a microphone, the gain is increased until distortion is just avoided, thereby obtaining a recording having the best SNR. In post production the gain will be set to whatever level is required to obtain the desired subjective effect in the context of the program material. This is particularly important to broadcasters who require the relative loudness of different material to be controlled so that the listener does not need to make continuous adjustments to the volume control.

In order to maintain level accuracy, analog recordings are traditionally preceded by line-up tones at standard operating level. These are used to adjust the gain in various stages of dubbing and transfer along landlines so that no level changes occur to the program material.

Unlike analog recorders, digital recorders do not have headroom, as there is no progressive onset of distortion until converter clipping, the equivalent of saturation, occurs at 0dBFs. Accordingly many digital recorders have level meters which read in dBFs. The scales are marked with 0 at the clipping level and all operating levels are below that. This causes no difficulty provided the user is aware of the consequences.

However, in the situation where a digital copy of an analog tape is to be made, it is very easy to set the input gain of the digital recorder so that line-up tone from the analog tape reads 0dB. This lines up digital clipping with the analog operating level. When the tape is dubbed, all signals in the headroom suffer converter clipping.

In order to prevent such problems, manufacturers and broadcasters have introduced artificial headroom on digital level meters, simply by calibrating the scale and changing the analog input sensitivity so that 0 dB analog is some way below clipping. Unfortunately there has been little agreement on how much artificial headroom should be provided, and machines which have it are seldom labelled with the amount. There is an argument which suggests that the amount of headroom should be a function of the sample wordlength, but this causes difficulties when transferring from one wordlength to another. The EBU[24] concluded that a single relationship between analog and digital level was desirable. In 16 bit working, 12 dB of headroom is a useful figure, but now that 18 and 20 bit converters are available, the new EBU draft recommendation specifies 18 dB.

8.15 Introduction to the AES/EBU interface

In all the above interconnects, there is enough similarity due to the common purpose to make interfacing possible with a little extra hardware, but enough difference to be irritating.

The AES/EBU digital audio interface, originally published in 1985,[25] was proposed to embrace all the functions of existing formats in one standard. The goal was to ensure interconnection of professional digital audio equipment irrespective of origin. The EBU ratified the AES proposal with the proviso that the optional transformer coupling was made mandatory and led to the term AES/EBU interface, also called EBU/AES by some Europeans. The contribution of the BBC to the development of the interface must be mentioned here. Alongside the professional format, Sony and Philips developed a similar format now known as SPDIF (Sony Philips Digital Interface) intended for consumer use. This offers different facilities to suit the application, yet retains sufficient compatibility with the professional interface so that, for many purposes, consumer and professional machines can be connected together.[26,27]

The AES concerns itself with professional audio and accordingly has had little to do with the consumer interface. Thus the recommendations to standards bodies such as the IEC (International Electrotechnical Commission) regarding the professional interface came primarily through the AES whereas the consumer interface input was primarily from industry, although based on AES, professional proposals. The IEC and various national standards bodies naturally tended to combine the two into one standard such as IEC 958[28] which refers to the professional interface and the consumer interface. This process has been charted by Finger.[29]

Understandably, with so many standards relating to the same subject differences in interpretation arise leading to confusion in what should or should not be implemented, and indeed what the interface should be called. This chapter will refer generically to the professional interface as the AES/EBU interface and the consumer interface as SPDIF.

8.16 The electrical interface

Many of the older interconnects have separate lines for bit clocks and sampling-rate clocks, which is acceptable for the short distances required for simple dubbing, but causes problems in the broadcast environment where long lines might be needed in a studio complex. It was desired to use the existing analog audio cabling in such installations, which would be 600 ohm balanced line screened, with one cable per audio channel, or in some cases one twisted pair per channel with a common screen. At audio frequency the impedance of cable is high and the 600 ohm figure is that of the source and termination.

If a single serial channel is to be used, the interconnect has to be self-clocking and self-synchronizing, i.e. the single signal must carry enough information to allow the boundaries between individual bits, words and blocks to be detected reliably. To fulfil these requirements, the AES/EBU and SPDIF interfaces use FM channel code (see Chapter 4) which is DC free, strongly self-clocking and capable of working with a changing sampling rate. Synchronization of deserialization is achieved by violating the usual encoding rules.

The use of FM means that the channel frequency is the same as the bit rate when sending data ones. Tests showed that in typical analog audio-cabling installations, sufficient bandwidth was available to convey two digital audio channels in one twisted pair. The standard driver and receiver chips for RS-422A[30] data communication (or the equivalent CCITT-V.11) are employed for professional use, but work by the BBC[31] suggested that equalization and transformer coupling are desirable for longer cable runs, particularly if several twisted pairs occupy a common shield. Successful transmission up to 350 m has been achieved with these techniques.[32] Figure 8.29 shows the standard

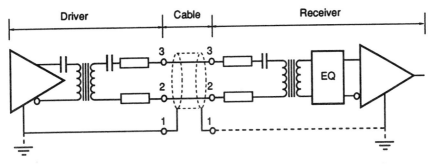

Figure 8.29 Recommended electrical circuit for use with the standard two-channel interface.

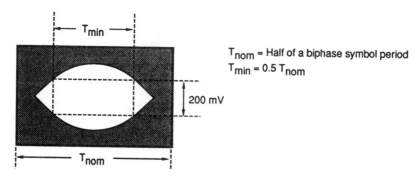

Figure 8.30 The minimum eye pattern acceptable for correct decoding of standard two-channel data.

configuration. The output impedance of the drivers will be about 110 ohms, and the impedance of the cable used should be similar at the frequencies of interest. The driver was specified in AES3–1985 to produce between 3 and 10 V peak-to-peak into such an impedance but this was changed to between 2 and 7V in AES3–1992 to reflect better the characteristics of actual RS-422 driver chips.

The original receiver impedance was set at a high 250 ohms, with the intention that up to four receivers could be driven from one source. This has been found to be inadvisable because of reflections caused by impedance mismatches and AES3–1992 is now a point-to-point interface with source, cable and load impedance all set at 110 ohms.

In Figure 8.30, the specification of the receiver is shown in terms of the minimum eye pattern (see Chapter 4) which can be detected without error. It will be noted that the voltage of 200 mV specifies the height of the eye opening at a width of half a channel bit period. The actual signal amplitude will need to be larger than this, and even larger if the signal contains noise. Figure 8.31 shows the recommended equalization characteristic which can be applied to signals received over long lines.

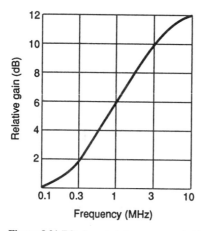

Figure 8.31 EQ characteristic recommended by the AES to improve reception in the case of long lines.

The purpose of the standard is to allow the use of existing analog cabling, and as an adequate connector in the shape of the XLR is already in wide service, the connector made to IEC 268 Part 12 has been adopted for digital audio use. Effectively, existing analog audio cables having XLR connectors can be used without alteration for digital connections. The AES/EBU standard does, however, require that suitable labelling should be used so that it is clear that the connections on a particular unit are digital. Whilst the XLR connector was never designed to have constant impedance in the megahertz range, it is capable of towing an outside broadcast vehicle without unlatching.

The need to drive long cables does not generally arise in the domestic environment, and so a low-impedance balanced signal is not necessary. The electrical interface of the consumer format uses a 0.5 V peak single-ended signal, which can be conveyed down conventional audio-grade coaxial cable connected with RCA 'phono' plugs. Figure 8.32 shows the resulting consumer interface as specified by IEC 958.

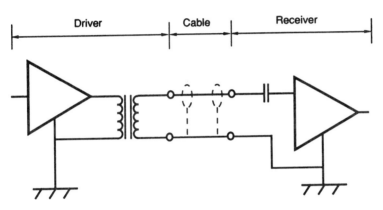

Figure 8.32 The consumer electrical interface.

It is common knowledge from practice and from the original proposals and standards that professional audio devices use balanced signals on XLR connectors and consumer devices use unbalanced signals on RCA connectors. Unfortunately there is nothing in IEC 958 to require it. This is a grave omission because it is possible to build equipment having the professional signal structure yet outputting an unbalanced signal. Although this conforms to IEC 958 the resultant device is as much use as the proverbial chocolate teapot because it is no use to either type of user. Consumers cannot use it because the professional channel-status information is meaningless to consumer equipment, and professionals cannot use it because it will not drive long cables and reject interference. It is to be hoped that this matter will be rectified in the next revision.

There is a separate proposal[33] for a professional interface using coaxial cable for distances of around 1000 m. This is simply the AES/EBU protocol but with a 75 ohm coaxial cable carrying a 1 volt signal so that it can be handled by analog video distribution amplifiers. Impedance-converting transformers are already on sale to allow balanced 110 ohm to unbalanced 75 ohm matching.

8.17 Frame structure

In Figure 8.33 the basic structure of the professional and consumer formats can be seen. One subframe consists of 32 bit cells, of which four will be used by a synchronizing pattern. Subframes from the two audio channels, A and B, alternate on a time division basis. Up to 24 bit sample wordlength can be used, which should cater for all conceivable future developments, but normally 20 bit maximum length samples will be available with four auxiliary data bits, which can be used for a voice-grade channel in a professional application. In a consumer RDAT machine, subcode can be transmitted in bits 4–11, and the 16 bit audio in bits 12–27.

Preceding formats sent the most significant bit first. Since this was the order in which bits were available in successive approximation converters it has become a *de-facto* standard for interchip transmission inside equipment. In contrast, this format sends the least significant bit first. One advantage of this approach is that simple serial arithmetic is then possible on the samples because the carries produced by the operation on a given bit can be delayed by one bit period and then included in the operation on the next higher-order bit. There is additional complication, however, if it is proposed to build adaptors from one of the manufacturers' formats to the new format because of the word reversal. This problem is a temporary issue, as new machines are designed from the outset to have the standard connections.

The format specifies that audio data must be in two's complement coding. Whilst pure binary could accept various alignments of different wordlengths with only a level change, this is not true of two's complement. If different wordlengths are used, the MSBs must always be in the same bit position otherwise the polarity will be misinterpreted. Thus the MSB has to be in bit 27 irrespective of wordlength. Shorter words are leading zero filled up to the 20 bit capacity. The channel-status data included from AES3–1992 signalling of the actual audio wordlength used so that receiving devices could adjust the digital dithering level needed to shorten a received word which is too long or pack samples onto a disk more efficiently.

Four status bits accompany each subframe. The validity flag will be reset if the associated sample is reliable. Whilst there have been many aspirations regarding what the V bit could be used for, in practice a single bit cannot specify much, and

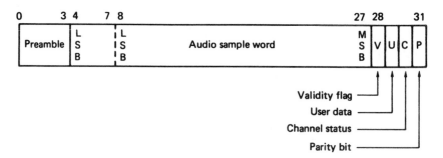

Figure 8.33 The basic subframe structure of the AES/EBU format. Sample can be 20 bits with four auxiliary bits, or 24 bits. LSB is transmitted first.

if combined with other V bits to make a word, the time resolution is lost. AES3–1992 described the V bit as indicating that the information in the associated subframe is 'suitable for conversion to an analog signal'. Thus it might be reset if the interface was being used for non-audio data as is done, for example, in CD-I players.

The parity bit produces even parity over the subframe, such that the total number of ones in the subframe is even. This allows for simple detection of an odd number of bits in error, but its main purpose is that it makes successive sync patterns have the same polarity, which can be used to improve the probability of detection of sync. The user and channel-status bits are discussed later.

Two of the subframes described above make one frame, which repeats at the sampling rate in use. The first subframe will contain the sample from channel A, or from the left channel in stereo working. The second subframe will contain the sample from channel B, or the right channel in stereo. At 48 kHz, the bit rate will be 3.072 MHz, but as the sampling rate can vary, the clock rate will vary in proportion.

In order to separate the audio channels on receipt the synchronizing patterns for the two subframes are different as Figure 8.34 shows. These sync patterns begin with a run length of 1.5 bits which violates the FM channel coding rules and so cannot occur due to any data combination. The type of sync pattern is denoted by the position of the second transition which can be 0.5, 1.0 or 1.5 bits away from the first. The third transition is designed to make the sync patterns DC free.

The channel-status and user bits in each subframe form serial data streams with 1 bit of each per audio channel per frame. The channel-status bits are given a block structure and synchronized every 192 frames, which at 48 kHz gives a block rate of 250 Hz, corresponding to a period of 4 milliseconds. In order to synchronize the channel-status blocks, the channel A sync pattern is replaced for

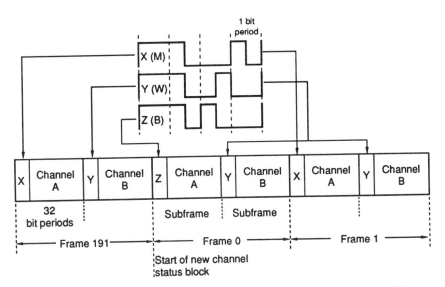

Figure 8.34 Three different preambles (X, Y and Z) are used to synchronize a receiver at the starts of subframes.

one frame only by a third sync pattern which is also shown in Figure 8.34. The AES standard refers to these as X, Y and Z whereas IEC 958 calls them M, W and B. As stated, there is a parity bit in each subframe, which means that the binary level at the end of a subframe will always be the same as at the beginning. Since the sync patterns have the same characteristic, the effect is that sync patterns always have the same polarity and the receiver can use that information to reject noise. The polarity of transmission is not specified, and indeed an accidental inversion in a twisted pair is of no consequence, since it is only the transition that is of importance, not the direction.

8.18 Talkback in auxiliary data

When 24 bit resolution is not required, which is most of the time, the four auxiliary bits can be used to provide talkback.

This was proposed by broadcasters[34] to allow voice coordination between studios as well as program exchange on the same cables. Here 12 bit samples of the talkback signal are taken at one-third the main sampling rate. Each 12 bit sample is then split into three nibbles (half a byte, for gastronomers) which can

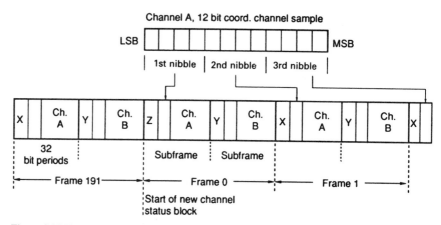

Figure 8.35 The coordination signal is of a lower bit rate to the main audio and thus may be inserted in the auxiliary nibble of the interface subframe, taking three subframes per coordination sample.

be sent in the auxiliary data slot of three successive samples in the same audio channel. As there are 192 nibbles per channel status block period, there will be exactly 64 talkback samples in that period. The reassembly of the nibbles can be synchronized by the channel-status sync pattern as shown in Figure 8.35. Channel-status byte 2 reflects the use of auxiliary data in this way.

8.19 Professional channel status

In both the professional and consumer formats, the sequence of channel-status bits over 192 subframes builds up a 24 byte channel-status block. However, the contents of the channel-status data are completely different between the two applications. The professional channel-status structure is shown in Figure 8.36. Byte 0 determines the use of emphasis and the sampling rate, with details in Figure 8.37. Byte 1 determines the channel usage mode, i.e. whether the data transmitted are a stereo pair, two unrelated mono signals or a single mono signal, and details the user bit handling. Figure 8.38 gives details. Byte 2 determines wordlength as in Figure 8.39. This was made more comprehensive in AES3–1992. Byte 3 is applicable only to multichannel applications. Byte 4 indicates the suitability of the signal as a sampling-rate reference and will be discussed in more detail later in this chapter.

There are two slots of 4 bytes each which are used for alphanumeric source and destination codes. These can be used for routing. The bytes contain 7 bit ASCII characters (printable characters only) sent LSB first with the eighth bit set to zero acording to AES3–1992. The destination code can be used to operate an automatic router, and the source code will allow the origin of the audio and other remarks to be displayed at the destination.

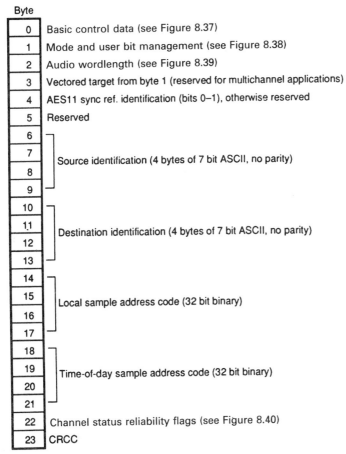

Byte

0	Basic control data (see Figure 8.37)
1	Mode and user bit management (see Figure 8.38)
2	Audio wordlength (see Figure 8.39)
3	Vectored target from byte 1 (reserved for multichannel applications)
4	AES11 sync ref. identification (bits 0–1), otherwise reserved
5	Reserved
6	
7	Source identification (4 bytes of 7 bit ASCII, no parity)
8	
9	
10	
11	Destination identification (4 bytes of 7 bit ASCII, no parity)
12	
13	
14	
15	Local sample address code (32 bit binary)
16	
17	
18	
19	Time-of-day sample address code (32 bit binary)
20	
21	
22	Channel status reliability flags (see Figure 8.40)
23	CRCC

Figure 8.36 Overall format of the professional channel-status block.

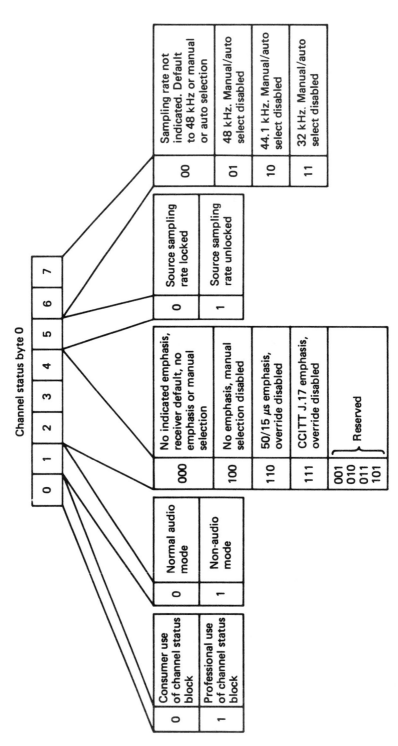

Figure 8.37 The first byte of the channel-status information in the AES/EBU standard deals primarily with emphasis and sampling-rate control.

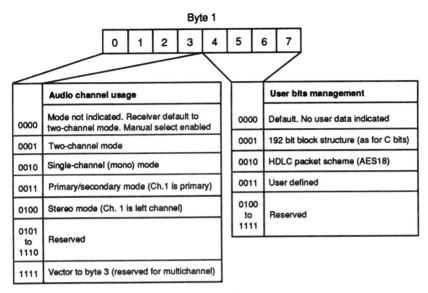

Figure 8.38 Format of byte 1 of professional channel status.

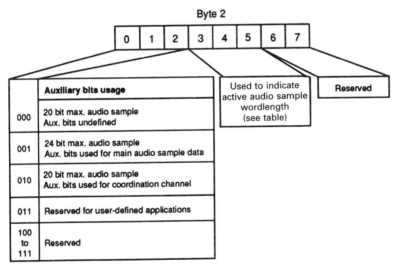

Bits states 3 4 5	Audio wordlength (24 bit mode)	Audio wordlength (20 bit mode)
0 0 0	Not indicated	Not indicated
0 0 1	23 bits	19 bits
0 1 0	22 bits	18 bits
0 1 1	21 bits	17 bits
1 0 0	20 bits	16 bits
1 0 1	24 bits	20 bits

Figure 8.39 Format of byte 2 of professional channel status.

Bytes 14–17 convey a 32 bit sample address which increments every channel-status frame. It effectively numbers the samples in a relative manner from an arbitrary starting point. Bytes 18–21 convey a similar number, but this is a time-of-day count, which starts from zero at midnight. As many digital audio devices do not have real-time clocks built in, this cannot be relied upon. AES3–92 specified that the time-of-day bytes should convey the real time at which a recording was made, making it rather like timecode. There are enough combinations in 32 bits to allow a sample count over 24 hours at 48 kHz. The sample count has the advantage that it is universal and independent of local supply frequency. In theory if the sampling rate is known, conventional hours, minutes, seconds, frames timecode can be calculated from the sample count, but in practice it is a lengthy computation and users have proposed alternative formats in which the data from EBU or SMPTE timecode are transmitted directly in these bytes. Some of these proposals are in service as *de facto* standards.

The penultimate byte contains four flags which indicate that certain sections of the channel-status information are unreliable (see Figure 8.40). This allows the transmission of an incomplete channel-status block where the entire structure is not needed or where the information is not available. For example, setting bit 5 to a logical one would mean that no origin or destination data would be interpreted by the receiver, and so they need not be sent.

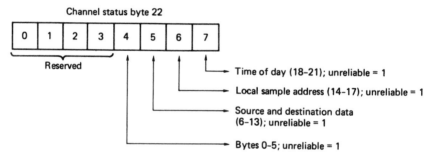

Figure 8.40 Byte 22 of channel status indicates if some of the information in the block is unreliable.

The final byte in the message is a CRCC which converts the entire channel-status block into a codeword (see Chapter 5). The channel-status message takes 4 ms at 48 kHz and in this time a router could have switched to another signal source. This would damage the transmission, but will also result in a CRCC failure, so the corrupt block is not used. Error correction is not necessary, as the channel-status data are either stationary, i.e. they stay the same, or change at a predictable rate, e.g. timecode. Stationary data will only change at the receiver if a good CRCC is obtained.

8.20 User bits

The user channel consists of 1 bit per audio channel per sample period. Unlike channel status, which only has a 192 bit frame structure, the user channel can have a flexible frame length. Figure 8.38 showed how byte 1 of the channel-status frame describes the state of the user channel. Many professional devices do not use the user channel at all and would set the all-zeros code. If the user channel frame has the same length as the channel-status frame then code 0001 can be set. One user channel format which is standardized is the data packet scheme of AES18–1992[35,36] This was developed from proposals to employ the user channel for labelling in an asynchronous format.[37] A computer industry standard protocol known as HDLC (High-level Data Link Control)[38] is employed in order to take advantage of readily available integrated circuits.

The frame length of the user channel can be conveniently made equal to the frame period of an associated device. For example, it may be locked to film, TV or RDAT frames. The frame length may vary in NTSC as there are not an integer number of samples in a frame.

8.21 Synchronizing

When digital audio signals are to be assembled from a variety of sources, either for mixing down or for transmission through a TDM (Time Division Multiplexing) system, the samples from each source must be synchronized to one another in both frequency and phase. The source of samples must be fed with a reference sampling rate from some central generator, and will return samples at that rate. The same will be true if digital audio is being used in conjunction with VTRs. As the scanner speed and hence the audio block rate is locked to video, it follows that the audio sampling rate must be locked to video. Such a technique has been used since the earliest days of television in order to allow vision mixing, but now that audio is conveyed in discrete samples, these too must be genlocked to a reference for most production purposes.

AES11–1991[39] documented standards for digital audio synchronization and requires professional equipment to be able to genlock either to a separate reference input or to the sampling rate of an AES/EBU input.

As the interface uses serial transmission, a shift register is required in order to return the samples to parallel format within equipment. The shift register is generally buffered with a parallel loading latch which allows some freedom in the exact time at which the latch is read with respect to the serial input timing. Accordingly the standard defines synchronism as an identical sampling rate, but with no requirement for a precise phase relationship. Figure 8.41 shows the timing tolerances allowed. The beginning of a frame (the frame edge) is defined as the leading edge of the X preamble. A device which is genlocked must correctly decode an input whose frame edges are within ±25% of the sample period. This is quite a generous margin, and corresponds to the timing shift due to putting about a kilometre of cable in series with a signal. In order to prevent tolerance build-up when passing through several devices in series, the output timing must be held within ±5% of the sample period.

The reference signal may be an AES/EBU signal carrying program material, or it may carry muted audio samples, the so-called digital audio silence signal. Alternatively it may just contain the sync patterns. The accuracy of the reference is specified in bits 0 and 1 of byte 4 of channel status (see Figure 8.36). Two zeros indicate the signal is not reference grade (but some equipment may still be able to lock to it); 01 indicates a Grade 1 reference signal which is ±1 ppm

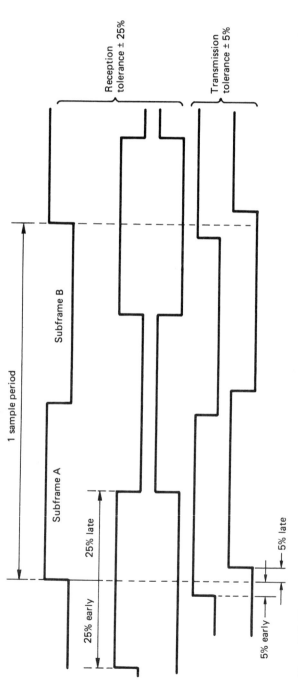

Figure 8.41 The timing accuracy required in AES/EBU signals with respect to a reference (a). Inputs over the range shown at (b) must be accepted, whereas outputs must be closer in timing to the reference as shown at (c).

accurate, whereas 10 indicates a Grade 2 reference signal which is ±10 ppm accurate. Clearly devices which are intended to lock to one of these references must have an appropriate phase-locked-loop capture range.

Modern digital audio devices may also have a video input for synchronizing purposes. Video syncs (with or without picture) may be input, and a phase-locked loop will multiply the video frequency by an appropriate factor to produce a synchronous audio sampling clock.

8.22 Timing tolerance of serial interfaces

There are three parameters of interest when conveying audio down a serial interface, and these have quite different importance depending on the application. The parameters are:

(1) The jitter tolerance of the serial FM data separator.
(2) The jitter tolerance of the audio samples at the point of conversion back to analog.
(3) The timing accuracy of the serial signal with respect to other signals.

The serial interface is a digital interface, in that it is designed to convey discrete numerical values from one place to another. If those samples are correctly received with no numerical change, the interface is perfect. The serial interface carries clocking information, in the form of the transitions of the FM channel code and the sync patterns, and this information is designed to enable the data separator to determine the correct data values in the presence of jitter. It was shown in Chapter 4 that the jitter window of the FM code is half a data bit period in the absence of noise. This becomes a quarter of a data bit when the eye opening has reached the minimum allowable in the professional specification as can be seen from Figure 8.30. If jitter is within this limit, which corresponds to about 80 nanoseconds peak-to-peak, the serial digital interface perfectly reproduces the sample data, irrespective of the intended use of the data. The data separator of an AES/EBU receiver requires a phase-locked loop in order to decode the serial message. This phase-locked loop will have jitter of its own, particularly if it is a digital phase-locked loop where the phase steps are of finite size. Digital phase-locked loops are easier to implement along with other logic in integrated circuits. There is no point in making the jitter of the phase-locked loop vanishingly small as the jitter tolerance of the channel code will absorb it. In fact the digital phase locked loop is simpler to implement and locks up quicker if it has larger phase steps and therefore more jitter.

This has no effect on the ability of the interface to convey discrete values, and if the data transfer is simply an input to a digital recorder no other parameter is of consequence as the data values will be faithfully recorded. However, it is a further requirement in some applications that a sampling clock for a converter is derived from a serial interface signal.

The jitter tolerance of converter clocks is measured in hundreds of picoseconds. Thus a phase-locked loop in the FM data separator of a serial receiver chip is quite unable to drive a converter directly as the jitter it contains will be as much as a thousand times too great.

Figure 8.42 shows how an outboard converter should be configured. The serial data separator has its own phase-locked loop which is less jittery than the serial waveform and so recovers the audio data. The serial data are presented to a shift register which is read in parallel to a latch when an entire sample is present by a clock edge from the data separator. The data separator has done its job of correctly returning a sample value to parallel format. A quite separate phase-locked loop with extremely high damping and low jitter is used to regenerate the sampling clock. This may use a crystal oscillator or it may be a number of loops in series to increase the order of the jitter filtering. In the professional channel status, bit 5 of byte 0 indicates whether the source is locked or unlocked. This bit can be used to change the damping factor of the phase-locked loop or to switch from a crystal to a varicap oscillator. When the source is unlocked, perhaps because a recorder is in varispeed, the capture range of the phase locked loop can be widened and the increased jitter is accepted. When the source is locked, the capture range is reduced and the jitter is rejected.

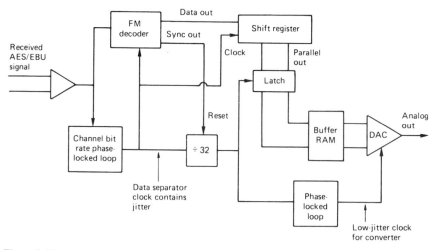

Figure 8.42 In an outboard converter, the clock from the data separator is not sufficiently free of jitter and additional clock regeneration is necessary to drive the DAC.

The third timing criterion is only relevant when more than one signal is involved as it affects the ability of, for example, a mixer to combine two inputs.

In order to decide which criterion is most important, the following may be helpful. A single signal which is involved in a data transfer to a recording medium is concerned only with eye pattern jitter as this affects the data reliability.

A signal which is to be converted to analog is concerned primarily with the jitter at the converter clock. Signals which are to be mixed are concerned with the eye pattern jitter and the relative timing. If the mix is to be monitored, all three parameters become important.

8.23 Asynchronous operation

In practical situations, genlocking is not always possible. In a satellite transmission, it is not really practicable to genlock a studio complex half-way round the world to another. Outside broadcasts may be required to generate their own master timing for the same reason. When genlock is not achieved, there will be a slow slippage of sample phase between source and destination due to such factors as drift in timing generators. This phase slippage will be corrected by a synchronizer, which is intended to work with frequencies which are nominally the same. It should be contrasted with the sampling-rate converter which can work at arbitrary but generally greater frequency relationships. Although a sampling-rate converter can act as a synchronizer, it is a very expensive way of doing the job. A synchronizer can be thought of as a lower-cost version of a sampling-rate converter which is constrained in the rate difference it can accept.

In one implementation of a digital audio synchronizer,[40] memory is used as a timebase corrector as was illustrated in Chapter 2. Samples are written into the memory with the frequency and phase of the source and, when the memory is half-full, samples are read out with the frequency and phase of the destination. Clearly if there is a net rate difference, the memory will either fill up or empty over a period of time, and in order to recentre the address relationship, it will be necessary to jump the read address. This will cause samples to be omitted or repeated, depending on the relationship of source rate to destination rate, and would be audible on program material. The solution is to detect pauses or low-level passages and permit jumping only at such times. The process is illustrated in Figure 8.43. Such synchronizers must have sufficient memory capacity to absorb timing differences between quiet passages where jumping is possible, and

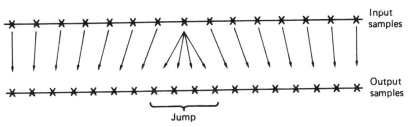

Figure 8.43 In jump synchronizing, input samples are subjected to a varying delay to align them with output timing. Eventually the sample relationship is forced to jump to prevent delay building up. As shown here, this results in several samples being repeated, and can only be undertaken during program pauses, or at very low audio levels. If the input rate exceeds the output rate, some samples will be lost.

so the average delay introduced by them is quite large, typically 128 samples. They are, however, relatively inexpensive. An alternative to address jumping is to undertake sampling-rate conversion for a short period (Figure 8.44) in order to slip the input/output relationship by one sample.[41] If this is done when the signal level is low, short word-length logic can be used.

The difficulty of synchronizing unlocked sources is eased when the frequency difference is small. This is one reason behind the clock accuracy standards for AES/EBU timing generators.[42]

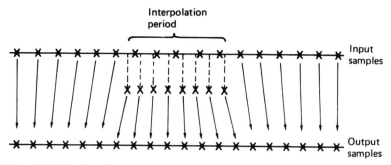

Figure 8.44 An alternative synchronizing process is to use a short period of interpolation in order to regulate the delay in the synchronizer.

8.24 Audio in the scrambled serial video interconnect

In this interconnect, which was described in Chapter 3, there is provision for auxiliary data to be sent during vertical and horizontal sync pulses.[43,44] Figure 8.45 shows that following the usual TRS-ID, there will be an auxiliary data flag whose value must be $3FC_{16}$. Following this is a code which identifies the kind of data which are being sent. In the case of digital audio, it will be all ones. Next, a symbol count parameter specifies how many symbols of user data are being sent in this packet. The audio data proper follow, and at the end of the packet a checksum is calculated.

Figure 8.46 shows that the system wordlength is 9 bits, and that three 9 bit symbols are used to convey all of the essential bits of the 32 used in the AES/EBU subframe. Since DVTRs have four audio channels, there are two channel bits which specify the channel number to which the subframe belongs. A further bit, Z, specifies the beginning of the 192 sample channel-status message. V, U and C have the same significance as in the normal AES/EBU standard, but the P bit 7 reflects parity on the three 9 bit symbols.

In component systems the audio is placed according to the ancillary data specified for the parallel standard. Figure 8.47(a) shows the position of ancillary data for PAL and (b) shows the location for NTSC. The exact positions of the packets in the video structure are not specified, but it is only necessary to provide a little RAM buffering at both ends of the link, and this becomes unimportant, as the receiver can determine the sampling rate from the video timing and demultiplex the channels according to the symbol labelling.

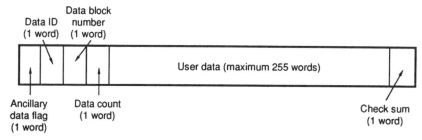

Figure 8.45 Ancillary data format (see text).

Address \ Bit	x3	x3 + 1	x3 + 2
B9	$\overline{B8}$	$\overline{B8}$	$\overline{\overline{B8}}$
B8	A (2^5)	A (2^{14})	P
B7	A (2^4)	A (2^{13})	C
B6	A (2^3)	A (2^{12})	U
B5	A (2^2)	A (2^{11})	V
B4	A (2^1)	A (2^{10})	A MSB (2^{19})
B3	A LSB (2^0)	A (2^9)	A (2^{18})
B2	CH (MSB)	A (2^8)	A (2^{17})
B1	CH (LSB)	A (2^7)	A (2^{16})
B0	Z	A (2^6)	A (2^{15})

Figure 8.46 AES/EBU data for one audio sample is sent as three 9 bit symbols. A = audio sample. Bit Z = AES/EBU channel-status block start bit.

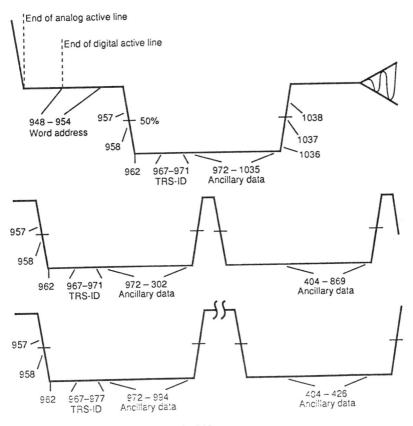

Figure 8.47(a) Ancillary data locations for PAL.

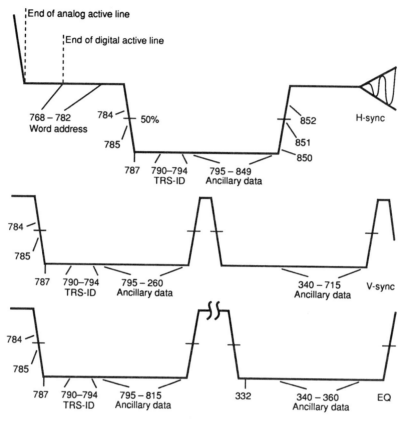

Figure 8.47(b) Ancillary data locations for NTSC.

8.25 Digital audio in VTRs

The audio performance of video recorders has traditionally lagged behind that of audio-only recorders. In video recorders, the use of rotary heads to obtain sufficient bandwidth results in a wide tape whose longitudinal audio tracks travel relatively slowly by professional audio standards. In all rotary-head recorders, the intermittent head contact causes shock-wave patterns to propagate down the tape, making low-flutter figures difficult to achieve. This is compounded by the action of the capstan servo which has to change tape speed to maintain control track phase if the video heads are to track properly.

The requirements of lip-sync dictate that the same head must be used for both recording and playback, when the optimum head design for these two functions is different. When dubbing from one track to the next, one head gap will be recording the signal played back by the adjacent magnetic circuit in the head, and mutual inductance can cause an oscillatory loop if extensive antiphase crosstalk cancelling is not employed. Placing the tracks on opposite sides of the tape would help this problem, but phase errors between the channels can then be introduced by tape weave. This can mean the difference between a two-channel recorder and a stereo recorder. Crosstalk between the timecode and audio tracks can also restrict performance.

The adoption of digital techniques essentially removes these problems for the audio in a DVTR. Once the audio is in numerical form, wow, flutter and channel-phase errors can be eliminated by timebase correction; crosstalk ceases to occur and, provided a suitable error-correction strategy is employed, the only degradation of the signal will be due to quantizing. The most significant advantages of digital recording are that there is essentially no restriction on the number of generations of re-recording which can be used and that proper crossfades can be made in the audio at edit points, following a rehearsal if necessary.

Digital audio recording with video is rather more difficult than in an audio-only environment. The special requirements of professional video recording have determined many of the parameters of the format, and have resulted in techniques not found in audio-only recorders.

The audio samples are carried by the same channel as the video samples. The audio could have used separate stationary heads, but this would have increased tape consumption and machine complexity. In order to permit independent audio and video editing, the tape tracks are given a block structure. Editing will require the heads momentarily to go into record as the appropriate audio block is reached. Accurate synchronization is necessary if the other parts of the recording are to remain uncorrupted. The sync block structure of the video sector continues in the audio sectors because the same read/write circuitry is used for audio and video data. Clearly the ID code structure must also continue through the audio. In order to prevent audio samples from arriving in the frame store in shuttle, the audio addresses are different from the video addresses. Despite the additional complexity of sharing the medium with video, the professional DVTR must support such functions as track bouncing, synchronous recording and split audio edits with variable crossfade times.

The audio samples in a DVTR are binary numbers just like the video samples, and although there is an obvious difference in sampling rate and wordlength, the use of time compression means that this only affects the relative areas of tape devoted to the audio and video samples. The most important difference between audio and video samples is the tolerance to errors. The acuity of the ear means that uncorrected audio samples must not occur more than once every few hours. There is little redundancy in sound when compared with video, and concealment of errors is not desirable on a routine basis. In video, the samples are highly redundant, and concealment can be effected using samples from previous or subsequent lines or, with care, from the previous frame.

Whilst subjective considerations require greater data reliability in the audio samples, audio data form a small fraction of the overall data and it is difficult to protect them with an extensive interleave whilst still permitting independent editing. For these reasons major differences can be expected between the ways that audio and video samples are handled in a digital video recorder. One such difference is that the error-correction strategy for audio samples uses a greater amount of redundancy. Whilst this would cause a serious playing-time penalty in an audio recorder, even doubling the audio data rate in a video recorder only raises the overall data rate by a few per cent. The arrangement of the audio blocks is also designed to maximize data integrity in the presence of tape defects and head clogs. Chapter 6 showed that the audio blocks are at the ends of the head

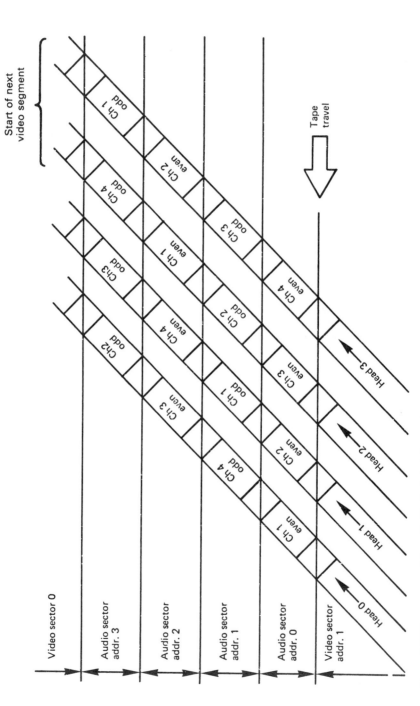

Figure 8.48 The structure of the audio blocks in D-1 format showing the double recording, the odd/even interleave, the sector addresses, and the distribution of audio channels over all heads. The audio samples recorded in this area represent a 6.666 ms time slot in the audio recording.

sweeps in D-2 and D-3, but are placed in the middle of the segment in D-1, D-5, Digital Betacam and DCT.

The audio sample interleave varies in complexity between the various formats. It will be seen from Figure 8.48 that the physical location of a given audio channel rotates from segment to segment. In this way a tape scratch will cause slight damage to all channels instead of serious damage to one. Data are also distributed between the heads, and so if one (or sometimes two) of the four heads clogs the audio is still fully recovered. The D-2 and D-3 formats differ considerably between PAL and NTSC versions owing to the difference between the subcarrier frequencies of the two standards. In PAL one field requires eight tracks, and so the track rate will be 400 Hz, and since there are four audio blocks in each track, the audio block rate will be 1600 Hz. In NTSC one field requires six tracks, so the track rate will be 360 Hz (minus 0.1%) and the audio block rate will be 1440 Hz (minus 0.1%). Since the audio sampling rate is unchanged by the video format, the number of samples in each audio block will be different in the two versions of D-2 and D-3.

8.26 Audio strategy of D-1

The actual mechanism of video editing is simply to start recording the new data at a field boundary, the result appearing as a cut in the picture. This is also the most basic way of editing the audio; at an interleave block boundary the new recording is substituted for the old. It is to be expected that this will result in step discontinuities of the audio waveform, audible as clicks, but this may well be acceptable in a portable machine whose tapes will be the raw material for post production. In order to allow click free editing without read–modify–write D-1 simply records all audio data twice.[45] Thus the same audio data appear in two versions which are physically separate on tape. Double recording is much less error resistant than using the same space for error-correcting codes, but this arrangement allows a more satisfactory edit to be performed by initially updating only half of the blocks with new data. During this overlap period, the end of the previous recording and the beginning of the new will both be present, and the DVTR can perform a crossfade in the digital domain between the two sample streams on replay. At the end of an insert, the reverse crossfade would take place. The overlap period is flexible, because the best crossfade time varies subjectively with the material recorded. Clearly, on performing the edit, the crossfade period is simply the time for which only half of the sample blocks are recorded. On replay, the crossfader needs to know how its coefficients should vary with time to match what has been recorded. This is neatly solved by incorporating a gain parameter in the audio blocks, which will change during the overlap period and control the replay crossfader. The format is such that machines which do not support this mode record zeros in the parameter position, and this code results in no action in any player. There is a flaw in this simple crossfading approach because the 100% redundancy is absent during the overlap period, and dropouts or mistracking during crossfades cause the machine to interpolate using the odd/even interleave. The problem can of course be overcome by using read–modify–write.

The error-correction system of D-1 uses product codes as described in Chapter 5. Codewords are formed prior to interleaving – the so-called outer code – and further codewords are formed after interleaving, known as the inner code. The inner code is optimized to correct random errors, so that these will not be seen by the outer code. Burst errors will overwhelm the inner code; it will simply declare all data in the codeword as bad, and attach error flags to them. Following de-interleave, the outer code can use the error flags to perform erasure correction, which will not be impaired by random errors. The product coding is done by writing data into an array in columns, and adding column redundancy to form the outer code. The array is then read in rows, which interleaves the data, and row redundancy is added to form the inner code. Figure 8.49 shows the details of the audio product code generation. The inner code is the same as for video, because

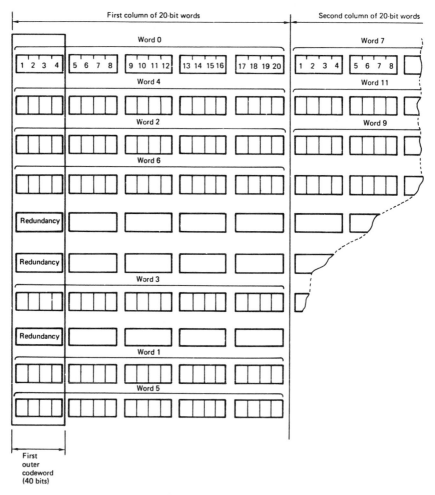

Figure 8.49(a) Data are written into an array as 20 bit columns, and read out as rows. The column redundancy is produced in 4 bit wide columns, and forms the outer codewords of 40 bits each.

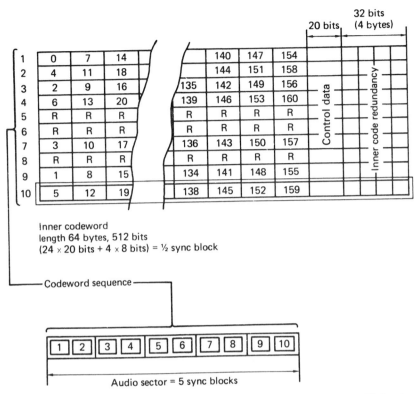

Figure 8.49(b) The row redundancy forms the inner code, as four check bytes are added to the data to produce ten codewords of 64 bytes each. The relationship to the tape track is such that two inner codewords occupy one sync block. Five sync blocks can hold the entire interleave block.

common circuitry can then be used, but the outer code is different from the video outer code which is not discussed here. The audio data are contained in 20 bit words, and 168 of these form one audio-write block. Most of these are audio samples, but there are also control words and housekeeping data which will be detailed later. The data are written into columns which are seven words high. The columns are written non-sequentially to produce the maximum distance between adjacent samples after interleave; 24 columns are necessary. Each column is then treated as five columns of 4 bits each, and 3 nibbles of redundancy are added to each column, so that there are now ten rows. Redundancy is now produced along each row, and 4 bytes are added, making the total length of a row 64 bytes. One sync block holds 128 bytes; thus the rows are written sequentially, and can be accommodated in five sync blocks, which is one audio-write block. Although it is common to use a further interleave between the inner code and the actual recording stage in digital audio-only recording, this is not practicable in the DVTR because it contradicts the requirement for blocks to be read randomly in shuttle.

8.27 Audio strategy of D-2

In D-2 the double audio recording of D-1 was retained, although the odd/even separation was no longer employed. In order to prevent the increase in concealments when editing, D-2 did not update one copy of the audio and then the other, but updated both copies at once. This made a crossfade impossible, and a Vee-edit (a brief fadeout followed by a fadein) is employed instead to avoid clicks. A Vee-edit is of no use for editing in music as it is audible. Read−modify−write was therefore essential for quality work. With no provision to update the audio copies individually, there is then no reason to use double recording. Unfortunately the opportunity to use the doubled recording area for proper error correction coding was not taken. This left D-2 with a flawed audio error-correction strategy, which combined with the lack of flying erase on early machines to cause difficulties.

A product code is used, and the interleave is generated by the usual memory array, as Figure 8.50 illustrates. The 20 bit audio samples are written into the array in rows, where $2\frac{1}{2}$ rows of bytes are needed for one row of samples. Each

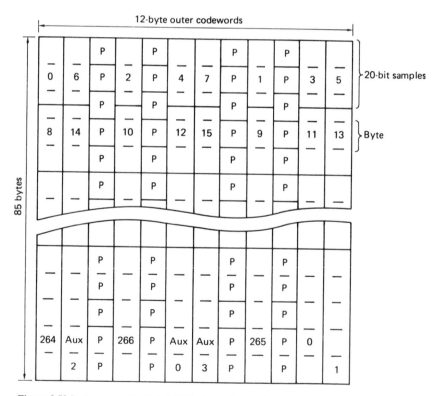

Figure 8.50 In the composite digital VCR, the audio samples are written into the interleave array in rows to produce outer codewords, and read out in 85 byte columns to form sync blocks as shown in Figure 8.51.

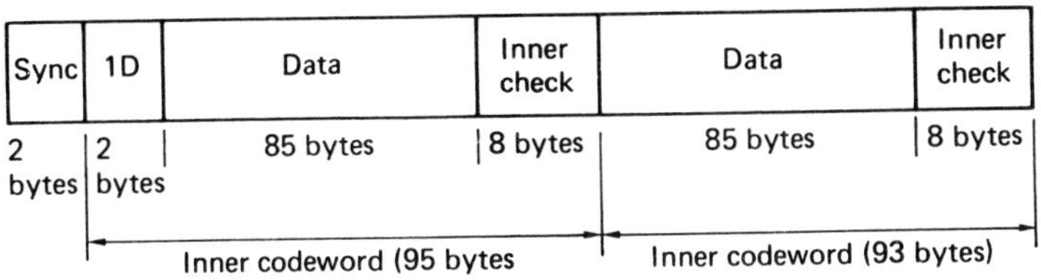

Sync	1D	Data	Inner check	Data	Inner check
2 bytes	2 bytes	85 bytes	8 bytes	85 bytes	8 bytes

Inner codeword (95 bytes)   Inner codeword (93 bytes)

Figure 8.51 One sync block of the composite digital format contains two inner codewords formed from columns of Figure 8.50. Six sync blocks are necessary to hold the entire interleave block, and form one audio sector (NTSC).

row of the array is loaded with eight samples, and then 4 bytes of Reed–Solomon redundancy are added to form an outer code. Reading the array in rows and adding 8 bytes of R–S redundancy produces inner codewords. Two of these inner codewords can be accommodated in one sync block as shown in Figure 8.51. Accordingly six sync blocks are necessary to record one audio block.[45,46]

8.28 Audio strategy of D-3

D-3 is probably the first DVTR format properly to address the problem of audio recording in the company of video data. D-3 uses 100% redundancy, but double recording is not used. Instead, for every data byte there is a byte of Reed–Solomon code redundancy.

As in other formats, each audio channel is recorded independently. A product code is used, but in D-3 the interleave is generated over a period of one complete field by a memory array, as Figure 8.52 illustrates for PAL. The 20 bit audio samples are written into the array in rows, where $2\frac{1}{2}$ bytes are needed for one sample. A block of 30 samples requires 75 bytes to which 1 byte of auxiliary data is added to make the 76 byte data content of a sync block. It will be seen from the figure that four of these are formed across each row, and eight rows are necessary to contain the 960 samples required in a field period. The interleave process alters the sequence of samples in the block as shown. Reading the array in byte-sized columns and adding 8 bytes of R–S redundancy produces outer codewords. The inner coding is then performed by adding eight R–S redundancy bytes to each 76 byte data symbol to make a sync block. Accordingly 64 sync blocks are necessary to record one audio block (eight sectors/field × eight sync blocks/sector).

In NTSC, the audio sector rate is lower, so each sector contains more samples. The field interleave block remains the same except that the rows contain only three sync blocks of 85 bytes; 48 sync blocks are necessary to record one audio block (six sectors/field × eight sync blocks/sector).

In both line standards, the sync blocks associated with one audio product code are distributed over all of the tracks in the field. As there is as much outer redundancy as data, full error-correction performance is maintained up to the point where half of the audio recording area in a field is lost. A clogged replay head only loses one-quarter of the audio and is not a problem. Two clogged heads are fully correctable except that tape dropouts will now be concealed. Insert edits with mistracking only damage the first or last track in a field, and this represents only one sixth (NTSC) or one-eighth (PAL) of the product code even if the whole

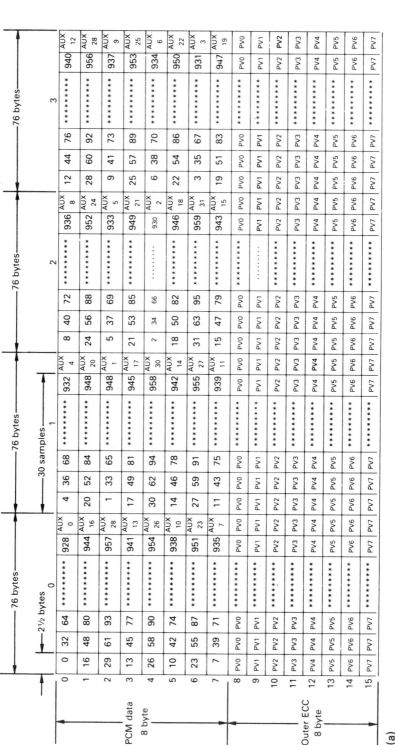

Figure 8.52(a) D-3 audio block (PAL). Audio samples of 20 bit length are written non-sequentially along rows of an array as shown here; 30 samples and one auxiliary data byte can be accommodated in one 76 byte block. Outer codes are formed vertically.

(a)

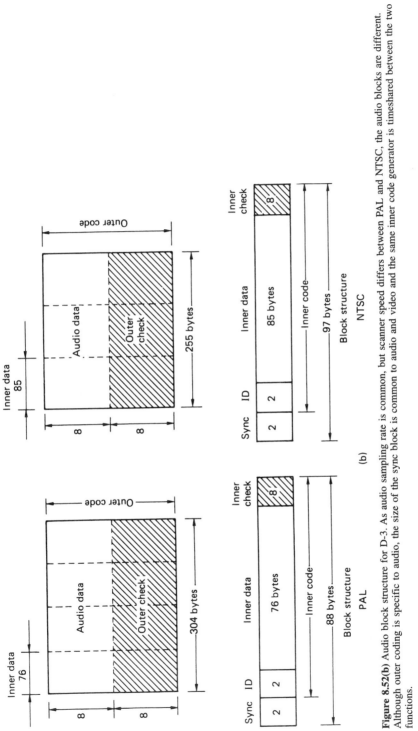

Figure 8.52(b) Audio block structure for D-3. As audio sampling rate is common, but scanner speed differs between PAL and NTSC, the audio blocks are different. Although outer coding is specific to audio, the size of the sync block is common to audio and video and the same inner code generator is timeshared between the two functions.

track is unreadable. D-1 and D-2 do not have this ability because the product blocks are restricted to individual segments.

D-3 supports simple editing whereby a new recording is commenced and a Vee-edit is used to conceal the click. The field-sized product block means that this type of edit is only field accurate. This is adequate for ENG cameras and cart. machines which can be built to perform assemble edits without using flying erase. This cuts complexity and scanner noise.

The simple crossfade mode of D-1 is not supported as there is no double recording. Thus all production editing is performed by read–modify–write. Edits can then have any crossfade period and can be sample accurate.

8.29 Writing audio sectors

In each sector, the track commences with a preamble to synchronize the phase-locked loop in the data separator on replay. Each of the sync blocks begins, as the name suggests, with a synchronizing pattern which allows the read sequencer to deserialize the block correctly. At the end of a sector, it is not possible simply to turn off the write current after the last bit, as the turnoff transient would cause data corruption. It is necessary to provide a postamble such that current can be turned off away from the data. It should now be evident that any editing has to take place a sector at a time. Any attempt to rewrite one sync block would result in damage to the previous block owing to the physical inaccuracy of replacement, damage to the next block due to the turnoff transient, and inability to synchronize to the replaced block because of the random phase jump at the point where it began. The sector in a DVTR is analogous to the cluster in a disk drive. Owing

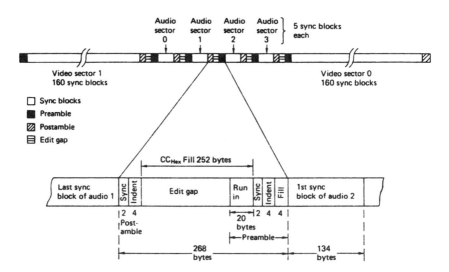

Figure 8.53 The position of preambles and postambles with respect to each sector is shown along with the gaps necessary to allow individual sectors to be written without corrupting others. When the whole track is recorded, 252 bytes of CC hex fill are recorded after the postamble before the next sync pattern. If a subsequent recording commences in this gap, it must do so at least 20 bytes before the end in order to write a new run-in pattern for the new recording.

to the difficulty of writing in exactly the same place as a previous recording, it is necessary to leave tolerance gaps between sectors where the write current can turn on and off to edit individual write blocks. For convenience, the tolerance gaps are made the same length as a whole number of sync blocks. Figure 8.53 shows that in D-1 the edit gap is two sync blocks long, as it is in D-3, whereas in D-2 it is only one sync block long. The first half of the tolerance gap is the postamble of the previous block, and the second half of the tolerance gap acts as the preamble for the next block. The tolerance gap following editing will contain, somewhere in the centre, an arbitrary jump in bit phase, and a certain amount of corruption due to turnoff transients. Provided that the postamble and preamble remain intact, this is of no consequence.

8.30 Synchronization between audio sampling rate and video field rate

Clearly the number of audio sync blocks in a given time is determined by the number of video fields in that time. It is only possible to have a fixed tape structure if the audio sampling rate is locked to video. With 625/50 machines, the sampling rate of 48 kHz results in exactly 960 audio samples in every field.

For use on 525/60, it must be recalled that the 60 Hz is actually 59.94 Hz. As this is slightly slow, it will be found that in 60 fields, exactly 48 048 audio samples will be necessary. Unfortunately 60 will not divide into 48 048 without a remainder. The largest number which will divide 60 and 48 048 is 12; thus in $60/12 = 5$ fields there will be $48\,048/12 = 4004$ samples. Over a five-field sequence the fields contain 801, 801, 801, 801 and 800 samples respectively, adding up to 4004 samples.

8.31 AES/EBU compatibility

In order to comply with the AES/EBU digital audio interconnect, wordlengths between 16 and 20 bits can be supported, but it is necessary to record a code in the sync block to specify the wordlength in use. Pre-emphasis may have been used prior to conversion, and this status is also to be conveyed, along with the four channel-use bits. The AES/EBU digital interconnect uses a block-sync pattern which repeats after 192 sample periods corresponding to 4 ms at 48 kHz. Since the block size is different to that of the DVTR interleave-block, there can be any phase relationship between interleave-block boundaries and the AES/EBU block-sync pattern. In order to recreate the same phase relationship between block sync and sample data on replay, it is necessary to record the position of block sync within the interleave block. It is the function of the interface control word in the audio data to convey these parameters. There is no guarantee that the 192 sample block-sync sequence will remain intact after audio editing; most likely there will be an arbitrary jump in block-sync phase. Strictly speaking a DVTR playing back an edited tape would have to ignore the block-sync positions on the tape, and create new block sync at the standard 192 sample spacing. Unfortunately the DVTR formats are not totally transparent to the whole of the AES/EBU data stream, as certain information is not recorded.

As a DVTR can individually edit audio channels, it does not require a great leap of the imagination to see that a multitrack audio-only machine could be made by filling the tape tracks with audio sectors. The number of channels this would permit is staggering and it may be more useful to incorporate a reduced-resolution or monochrome video channel. It should be pointed out that such a machine is outside the intentions of the formats described here.

References

1. FIELDER, L.D., Human auditory capabilities and their consequences in digital audio converter design. In *Audio in Digital Times*, New York: AES (1989)
2. MOORE, B.C.J., *An introduction to the psychology of hearing*, London: Academic Press (1989)
3. MURAOKA, T., IWAHARA, M. and YAMADA, Y., Examination of audio bandwidth requirements for optimum sound signal transmission. *J. Audio Eng. Soc.*, **29**, 2–9 (1982)
4. MURAOKA, T., YAMADA, Y. and YAMAZAKI, M., Sampling frequency considerations in digital audio. *J. Audio Eng. Soc.*, **26**, 252–256 (1978)
5. FINCHAM, L.R., The subjective importance of uniform group delay at low frequencies. Presented at the 74th Audio Engineering Society Convention (New York, 1983), preprint 2056(H-1)
6. ANON., AES recommended practice for professional digital audio applications employing pulse code modulation: preferred sampling frequencies. AES5–1984 (ANSI S4.28–1984). *J. Audio Eng. Soc.*, **32**, 781–785 (1984)
7. v.d. PLASSCHE, R.J., Dynamic element matching puts trimless converters on chip. *Electronics*, 16 June (1983)
8. v.d. PLASSCHE, R.J. AND GOEDHART, D., A monolithic 14 bit D/A converter. *IEEE J. Solid-State Circuits*, **SC-14**, 552–556 (1979)
9. ADAMS, R.W., Companded predictive delta modulation: a low-cost technique for digital recording. *J. Audio Eng. Soc.*, **32**, 659–672 (1984)
10. HAUSER, M.W., Principles of oversampling A/D conversion. *J. Audio Eng. Soc.*, **39**, 3–26 (1991)
11. CUTLER, C.C., Transmission systems employing quantization. US Patent 2, 927, 962 (1960)
12. v.d. PLASSCHE, R.J. AND DIJKMANS, E.C., A monolithic 16 bit D/A conversion system for digital audio. In *Digital Audio*, ed. B.A. Blesser, B. Locanthi and T.G. Stockham Jr, pp.54–60. New York: AES (1983)
13. GERZON, M. and CRAVEN, P.G., Optimal noise shaping and dither of digital signals. Presented at the 87th Audio Engineering Society Convention (New York, 1989), preprint 2822(J-1)
14. WANNAMAKER, R.A., Psychoacoustically optimal noise shaping. *J. Audio Eng. Soc.*, **40**, 611–620 (1992)
15. LIPSHITZ, S.P., WANNAMAKER, R.A. and VANDERKOOY, J., Minimally audible noise shaping. *J. Audio Eng. Soc.*, **39**, 836–852 (1991)
16. ADAMS, R.W., Design and implementation of an audio 18-bit A/D converter using oversampling techniques. Presented at the 77th Audio Engineering Society Convention (Hamburg, 1985), preprint 2182
17. ADAMS, R.W., An IC chip set for 20 bit A/D conversion. In *Audio in Digital Times*, New York: AES (1989)
18. RICHARDS, M., Improvements in oversampling analogue to digital converters. Presented at the 84th Audio Engineering Society Convention (Paris, 1988), preprint 2588(D-8)
19. INOSE, H. and YASUDA, Y., A unity bit coding method by negative feedback. *Proc. IEEE*, **51**, 1524–1535 (1963)
20. NAUS, P.J. *et al.*, Low signal level distortion in sigma-delta modulators. Presented at the 84th Audio Engineering Society Convention., (Paris, 1988), preprint 2584
21. STIKVOORT, E., High order one bit coder for audio applications. Presented at the 84th. Audio Engineering Society Convention, (Paris, 1988), preprint 2583(D-3)
22. LIPSHITZ, S.P. and VANDERKOOY, J., Are D/A converters getting worse? Presented at the 84th Audio Engineering Society Convention (Paris, 1988), preprint 2586 (D-6)
23. HARRIS, S., The effects of sampling clock jitter on Nyquist sampling analog to digital converters and on oversampling delta-sigma ADCs. *J. Audio Eng. Soc.*, **38**, 537–542 (1990)
24. MOLLER, L., Signal levels across the EBU/AES digital audio interface. In *Proc. 1st NAB Radio Montreux Symp.*, Montreux, pp. 16–28 (1992).
25. Audio Engineering Society, AES recommended practice for digital audio engineering – serial transmission format for linearly represented digital audio data. *J. Audio Eng. Soc.*, **33**, 975–984 (1985)
26. EIAJ CP-340 *A digital audio interface*. EIAJ, Tokyo (1987)

27. EIAJ CP-1201 *Digital audio interface* (revised). EIAJ, Tokyo (1992)
28. IEC 958 *Digital audio interface, first edition*. IEC, Geneva (1989)
29. FINGER, R., AES3–1992: the revised two channel digital audio interface. *J. Audio Eng. Soc.*, **40**, 107–116 (1992)
30. EIA RS-422A. Electronic Industries Association, 2001 Eye St NW, Washington, DC 20006, USA
31. SMART, D.L., Transmission performance of digital audio serial interface on audio tie lines. *BBC Des. Dep. Tech. Memo.*, 3.296/84
32. European Broadcasting Union, Specification of the digital audio interface. *EBU Doc. Tech.*, 3250
33. RORDEN, B. and GRAHAM, M., A proposal for integrating digital audio distribution into TV production. *J. SMPTE*, 606–608, September (1992)
34. GILCHRIST, N., Co-ordination signals in the professional digital audio interface. In *Proc. AES/EBU Interface Conf.* pp. 13–15. Burnham: AES (1989)
35. AES18–1992, Format for the user data channel of the AES digital audio interface. *J. Audio Eng. Soc.*, **40**, 167–183 (1992)
36. NUNN, J.P., Ancillary data in the AES/EBU digital audio interface. In *Proc. 1st NAB Radio Montreux Symp.* pp. 29–41 (1992)
37. KOMLY, A. and VIALLEVIEILLE, A., Programme labelling in the user channel. In *Proc. AES/EBU Interface Conf.* pp. 28–51. Burnham: AES (1989)
38. ISO 3309 *Information processing systems – Data communications – High level data link frame structure*. (1984)
39. DUNN, J., Considerations for interfacing digital audio equipment to the standards AES3, AES5 and AES11. In *Proc. AES 10th Int. Conf.*, pp. 122 New York: AES (1991)
40. GILCHRIST, N.H.C., Digital sound: sampling-rate synchronization by variable delay. *BBC Res. Dep. Rep.*, 1979/17
41. LAGADEC, R., A new approach to sampling rate synchronization. Presented at the 76th Audio Engineering Society Convention (New York, 1984), preprint 2168
42. SHELTON, W.T., Progress towards a system of synchronization in a digital studio. Presented at the 82nd Audio Engineering Society Convention (London, 1986), preprint 2484(K7)
43. SMPTE Proposed Standard – 10-bit 4:2:2 Component and 4FSc NTSC Composite Digital Signals – Serial Digital Interface
44. WILKINSON, J.H., Digital audio in the digital video studio – a disappearing act? Presented at 9th Int. AES Conf., Detroit (1991)
45. GREGORY, S., *Introduction to the 4:2:2 Digital Video Tape Recorder*. London: Pentech Press (1988)
46. Ampex Corporation, Ampex digital format for video and audio tape recording of composite video signals using 19mm type D-2 cassette. Redwood City, CA (1988)

Chapter 9

The DVTR formats

Elsewhere in this book DVTRs have been discussed primarily in principle. In this chapter available details of actual formats are included for reference.

9.1 The D-1 format

D-1 was the first production DVTR format and records 4:2:2 component data using ¾ inch 850 oersted tape. Figure 9.1(a) shows the track layout. Azimuth recording is not used; instead guard bands are placed between the tracks. These tracks consist of pairs of sectors containing the video data, and the four audio channels are carried in smaller sectors between them. The audio is then in the centre of the tape, where the better data reliability compensates for the fact that the audio blocks must be interleaved over a smaller area than the video. As a further measure, all audio sectors are recorded twice with a different head and in a different sector location for each version. Figure 9.1(a) also shows that there are three linear tracks in addition to the slant tracks.

A control track is used to drive the capstan in replay and in the various edit modes as was explained in Chapters 6 and 7. As this is a segmented format, the control track contains pulses which occur every two segments as in Figure 9.1(b). This is the equivalent of once per scanner rotation and so these will be at 150 Hz at normal speed. The segment is considered to begin after the audio blocks at the centre of the track; in fact the servo pulse coincides with the end of the preamble on the video sector.

Once per frame, a second pulse is recorded. The frame pulse accompanies every sixth servo pulse for 625 lines and every fifth servo pulse for 525 lines. There is no field pulse, since in 525 line working it would have to occur in between the servo pulses.

It was shown in chapter 8 that interaction between the audio sampling rate and the 525 line frame rate produces a five-frame sequence, and this is recorded using a third control track pulse. Finally, if the component input has come from a decoded composite signal, the colour framing flag of that composite signal can optionally be recorded. If a residual subcarrier footprint exists in the component recording, it can be cancelled out if the coder/decoder combination is reversible and if the recording is colour framed to a subsequent composite modulator. Most component formats have such a flag for this purpose.

The cue audio track is designed to permit audio to be heard over a wide speed range, when the slant tracks are not accessible. The recording is analog with conventional bias, and is not intended to be of high quality. The timecode track is essentially identical to the existing EBU/SMPTE timecodes used on other video products.

The segment begins after the audio blocks, with sectors 0 and 1, and continues on the next pair of tracks with sectors 2 and 3. This arrangement was used because it ensures that in a four-headed machine data from each segment are

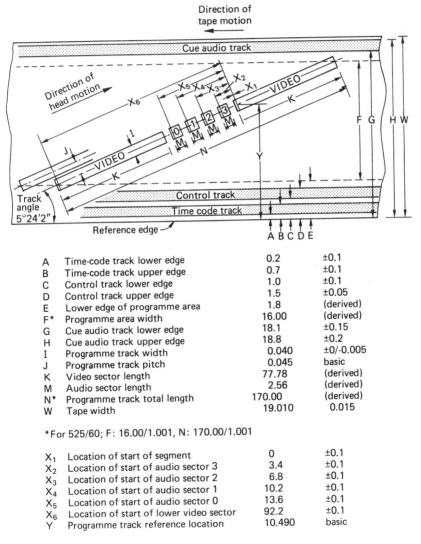

A	Time-code track lower edge	0.2	±0.1
B	Time-code track upper edge	0.7	±0.1
C	Control track lower edge	1.0	±0.1
D	Control track upper edge	1.5	±0.05
E	Lower edge of programme area	1.8	(derived)
F*	Programme area width	16.00	(derived)
G	Cue audio track lower edge	18.1	±0.15
H	Cue audio track upper edge	18.8	±0.2
I	Programme track width	0.040	±0/-0.005
J	Programme track pitch	0.045	basic
K	Video sector length	77.78	(derived)
M	Audio sector length	2.56	(derived)
N*	Programme track total length	170.00	(derived)
W	Tape width	19.010	0.015

*For 525/60; F: 16.00/1.001, N: 170.00/1.001

X_1	Location of start of segment	0	±0.1
X_2	Location of start of audio sector 3	3.4	±0.1
X_3	Location of start of audio sector 2	6.8	±0.1
X_4	Location of start of audio sector 1	10.2	±0.1
X_5	Location of start of audio sector 0	13.6	±0.1
X_6	Location of start of lower video sector	92.2	±0.1
Y	Programme track reference location	10.490	basic

All dimensions in mm

Figure 9.1(a) The track dimensions of D-1. Note that the segment begins at X_1 after the audio blocks.

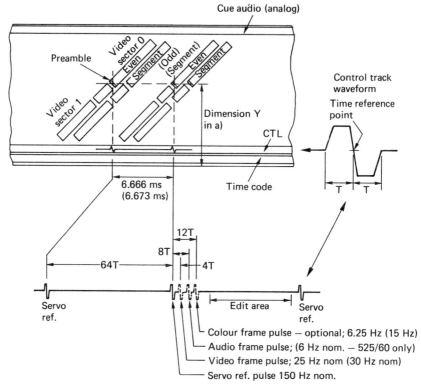

Figure 9.1(b) The arrangement of the D-1 control track. Servo pulses coincide with the beginning of an even segment after the audio blocks. The next segment has no control track pulse, and so the pulses repeat at drum rotation rate for a four-headed machine. Additional pulses locate the top segment in a frame and record optional colour framing (see text). The value T is $\frac{1}{64}$ the time taken for four tracks to pass. Values shown are for 625/50, with 525/60 values in brackets. 525/50 also has audio frame pulse described in Chapter 8.

distributed over all four heads, allowing maximum potential for concealment in the case of uncorrectable errors. Figure 9.2 shows the relationship between sector number and head number. Heads 0 and 1 begin the track by playing sectors 2 and 3 of an odd segment, and continue through the audio sectors to play sectors 0 and 1 of the next segment. If head 1 should clog, sector 1 will be lost in even numbered segments, whereas sector 3 will be lost in odd numbered segments. Similarly if head 2 clogs, sector 2 in even-numbered segments and sector 0 in odd-numbered segments will be lost. It will be seen that this alternation between odd and even segments is reflected in the data distribution over the four sectors.

Beginning the video field part-way down the track assists the concealment strategy as explained, but it does, however, make the provision of variable-speed playback very difficult. This is because field repeating or omission has to be done by track jumping as was seen in chapter 6. In D-1 if a track jump is to be performed, it must take place within the length of the audio blocks. This is an extremely short time and in practice cannot be done. Early machines had

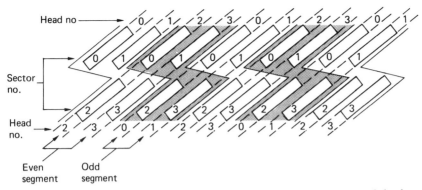

Figure 9.2 Sector distribution within a segment. In even segments, sector number equals head number, whereas in odd segments (shown shaded) head 0 exchanges with head 2 and head 1 exchanges with head 3. If, for example, head 1 were to clog, sector 1 would be lost in even segments whereas sector 3 would be lost in odd segments. In the absence of this arrangement, a clogged head would lose half of every other segment, which would be harder to conceal.

fixed heads and a narrow speed range. Later, Sony developed a machine with a large number of moving heads and duplicated replay channels where the picture could be assembled by channel selection; a complex approach is detailed in Section 9.8.

The distribution strategy of D-1 was detailed in Section 7.5. Following distribution the sample values are mapped according to the techniques described in section 7.6.

9.2 Outer code generation

Figure 9.3(a) shows the sample sequence from the sector distributor. If samples in this sequence were made into an outer code and written in the sector array as a column, the effect would be as shown in Figure 9.3(b). Samples relating to one pixel would appear in three different inner codewords, and so it would not be possible to update pixels properly in the case where a single sync block is recovered in shuttle. The sector array has done an excellent job of interleaving the samples. Unfortunately it has done too well, and it is necessary to oppose some of the sector array interleave with a reverse interleave prior to the generation of outer codewords in order to get all samples relating to a pixel into one sync block.

Figure 9.3(c) shows that the samples from the distributor are split into three blocks of one-third of a line which each contain 120 samples. These blocks are then subjected to a four-way interleave which produces four 30 byte blocks to which 2 bytes of Reed–Solomon redundancy are added to produce outer codewords. It will be seen from Figure 9.3(c) that each codeword is formed entirely from the same type of sample. When these outer codewords become adjacent columns of the sector array, it will be seen from Figure 9.3(d) that all three samples relating to a given pixel will be in the same row of the array, and so will be recorded in the same sync block, permitting frame store updating in shuttle.[1]

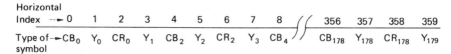

Figure 9.3(a) The output of the four channel distributor is a sequence of this kind in each channel. There will be 360 bytes in each line.

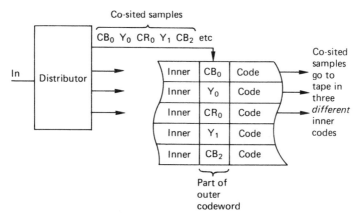

Figure 9.3(b) The result of interleaving the sample sequence of (a) is that co-sited samples appear in different inner codes and cannot be recovered in shuttle.

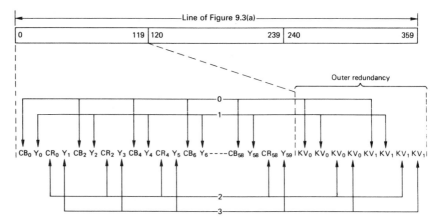

Figure 9.3(c) The line of (a) is split into three parts. Each is then made into four interleaved codewords as shown here. Each outer code has 30 data bytes and two redundancy bytes. Twelve such outer codes are needed to complete the line. Each code is formed from the same type of sample.

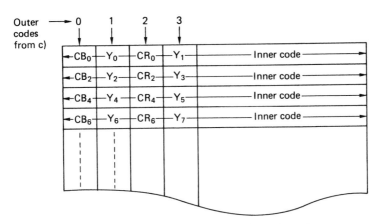

Figure 9.3(d) When the outer codes of (c) are used to form columns in a sector array as shown here, the inner codes will contain co-sited pixels due to the reverse interleave which was performed prior to generating the outer codes. Inner codes picked up at random in shuttle now can be used to update a frame store.

The process must be repeated three times to deal with the whole line, and this will result in 12 outer code blocks which occupy 12 adjacent columns in the sector array. As there are 50 lines in the segment, the sector array will need 12 x 50 = 600 columns.

9.3 Shuffle in D-1

Figure 9.4(a) shows the address generator which is used in the D-1 shuffle.[1] On recording, this device generates the read addresses to shuffle the sector array before it is written to tape. On playback, the same configuration determines the write addresses, so that offtape data are automatically subjected to a reverse shuffle as the sector array is written.

The column counter is cleared at the beginning of the sector, and produces a column count from 0 to 599. The columns in the sector array are arranged into groups of four, so that the co-sited samples will still be in the same inner codewords after group permutation. There are thus 150 group addresses, and these are shuffled by multiplying them by 41, which is relatively prime to 150, and expressing the product modulo-150. This is performed by the column map PROM, and it will be seen that the two least significant bits of the column address bypass the PROM so that groups of four columns are permuted together. This process results in the horizontal dimension of the shuffle.

The vertical dimension of the shuffle is obtained by performing a vertical address permutation on each column in the sector array, where the starting address of the process is also permuted.

Considering a horizontal row through a group of four columns, the left-hand three samples are the components of a co-sited pixel. The right-hand sample is a luminance-only sample. The row permutations must be the same for the first three columns of the group, again to maintain the presence of all components of a co-sited pixel in an inner codeword, but the luminance-only pixel in the fourth column is physically near on the screen, and concealment would be better if it were in a different inner codeword. Accordingly, the row start count permutation stays the same for columns 0, 1 and 2, but an AND gate detects a column value of 3 which adds a constant to the row start address in the fourth column of the group. The column count is multiplied by 30 and expressed modulo-32 to give the starting address except when the last column of the group is encountered, when five is added to the product before being expressed modulo-32.

The row start count is loaded into the row counter which is clocked at sample rate. The row count runs from 0 to 31 since there are 32 symbols in an outer

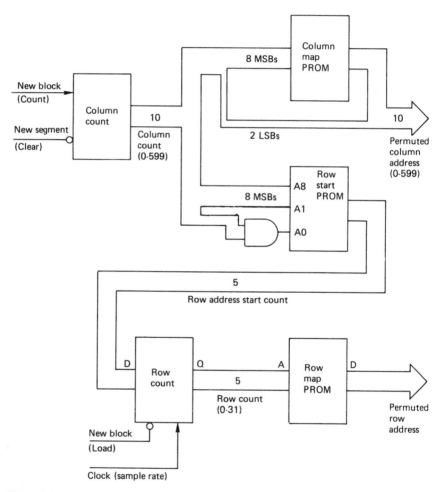

Figure 9.4(a) Shuffle address generator of D-1. The two least significant bits of the column count bypass the column map PROM so that sets of four columns are permuted to keep co-sited samples adjacent. The row counter is loaded with a starting count from the Row Start PROM. When the two least significant bits of the column count are one, this corresponds to the last column of the set of four. This condition is detected by the AND gate which modifies the Row Start PROM address to shuffle the luminance only pixel in the last column relative to the co-sited samples in the other three columns.

Row address

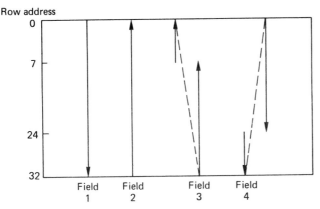

Figure 9.4(b) Modification of the row sequence from field to field improves randomness of shuffle for better shuttle picture. Field 1 reads forward from 0, Field 2 reads reverse from 32. Field 3 reads reverse from 7 and Field 4 reads forwards from 24.

codeword and hence 32 rows in the sector array. The row count is multiplied by seven, which is relatively prime to 32, and the product is expressed modulo-32 to produce a permuted row address.

The pixels within a sector are now shuffled, but all sectors are not shuffled in the same way. The shuttle picture is improved by changing the shuffle over a four-field sequence, and this is shown in Figure 9.4(b).

Since two heads work in parallel, a linear tape scratch could cause damage at the same place in two sector arrays, and could therefore damage the concealment distribution strategy. This is prevented by rotating the row address by 16 between sectors written by adjacent heads, and is simply implemented by inverting the MSB of the row address. Then in different fields, the row address is rotated by differing amounts.

9.4 Sync blocks

If an inner codeword were made from a complete row of the sector array, it would contain 600 bytes of data, but this is far too large, for the reasons stated in Section 7.9. Instead, the sector array is divided horizontally into ten product blocks, so

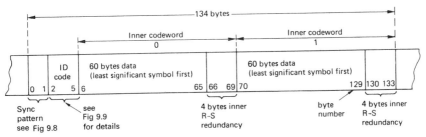

Figure 9.5 The D-1 block begins with synchronizing and identification, and contains two inner codewords each having 4 bytes of redunduncy.

that each inner codeword contains only 60 bytes of data. Then 4 bytes of Reed–Solomon redundancy are added to form a 64 byte codeword. Making each codeword into a sync block would introduce an excessive synchronizing overhead. Instead two codewords form a sync block, and 160 sync blocks will be necessary to contain the entire sector array.

Figure 9.5 shows the details of a sync block. The two 64 byte inner codewords are preceded by a synchronizing pattern and a 4 byte identification code. This code uniquely labels every sync block over a four-field sequence, and is especially useful in shuttle when tracks are crossed randomly. Each sync block represents a track length of just less than half a millimetre.

9.5 RNRZI channel coding

The principles of channel coding were detailed in chapter 4 and so this section will confine itself to those details specific to the implementation in D-1.

D-1 uses randomizing to break up uncontrolled run lengths in the raw data. Randomizing does not, however, result in run-length limiting, it only reduces the probability of longer run lengths. DC content is eliminated by randomizing, but low frequencies will still be present resulting in long wavelengths on tape which cannot be fully erased by overwrite. The presence of low frequencies in the channel makes the system less suitable for azimuth recording, which is not used, and requires the presence of guard bands between the tracks. Residual tracking errors are prevented from modulating the replay signal by making the replay head a little narrower than the record head, as is done in stationary-head recorders. The lack of azimuth recording means that in shuttle either head of the parallel pair can pick up sync blocks from either track of the segment. This is an advantage for machines which have no track-following mechanism.

The possibility of long wavelengths on tape means that a separate erase process is necessary before recording, and, as with all helical-scan video recorders, a stationary erase head cannot be used for editing, and erase heads must be mounted on the scanner. In order to reduce mechanical complexity in the scanner and the number of connections which must be brought to the rotating assembly, a combined erase and record head has been developed.[2] Figure 9.6 shows that the erase and write gaps share a common centre polepiece. The record and erase drive circuits are both in the scanner, and can be enabled by the same signal. Only two signal connections are now needed to each record head. Erase

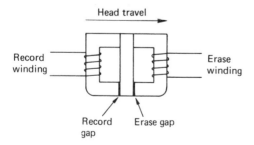

Figure 9.6 A separate erase head is necessary with RNRZ recording, and this shares a common pole with the record head. Gaps between sectors must be large enough to accommodate the displacement between erase and record functions.

is enabled whenever the record amplifier is activated by a third signal. This does, however, mean that writing and erasing begin and end at the same time, rather than in the same place on the tape. For example, at the end of writing a sector, the write head will be turned off, but at that time the erase gap will have erased ahead of the write gap, leaving a short length of erased track. Spaces between sectors have been deliberately left in the tracks so that editing of individual sectors can take place, for example when performing a frame insert, or where only one channel of audio is being recorded.

The tape used is an oxide type with a coercivity of only 850 Oe, since at the time D-1 was standardized the heads necessary to take full advantage of higher-coercivity metal-powder tapes were not fully developed. It was found at the time of design that the best available heads could not saturate metal-powder tape at the frequencies involved. The use of guard bands combined with tape of moderate

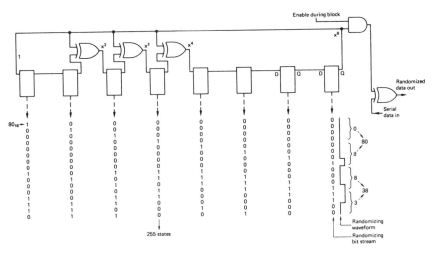

Figure 9.7(a) The polynomial generator (top) calculates $x^8 + x^4 + x^3 + x^1$ and is preset to 80_{16} every five sync blocks at the addresses shown in (b). When the generator is clocked, it will produce a Galois field having 255 states (see Chapter 2). The right-hand bit of each field element becomes the randomizing bit stream, and is fed to an exclusive OR gate in the data stream. Randomizing is disabled during the sync and ID patterns, but the generator continues to run.

It is also possible to randomize using a counter working at byte rate which addresses PROM. Eight exclusive OR gates will then be needed to randomize the byte in one clock period.

03	19	31	47	5D	75	8B	A3
08	20	36	4C	64	7A	92	A8
0D	25	3B	53	69	81	97	AD
14	2A	42	58	70	86	9C	B4

Figure 9.7(b) The above list shows the sync block ID codes at which the randomizer is reset. This is every five blocks for a sector length of 160 blocks (video sector). Note that the ID addresses are base 14 (see Figure 9.9(a)), and so it is possible to calculate the next address by adding 5 but treating the sum as a base 14 number. For example, the third ID shown above is 0D which is 13 decimal. Adding 5 makes 18 decimal which is 14 in base 14. The audio sectors are five sync blocks long, and so the reset will take place at the first block, which is C3 or D3. Some of the above IDs can be seen marked * in Figure 9.9(b).

Sequence A

```
|80   38   D2   81   49   76
 82   DA   9A   86   6F   AF   8B   B0   F1   9C   D1   12   A5   72   37   EF
 97   59   31   B8   EA   53   C8   3F   F4   58   40   1C   E9   C0   24   3B
 41   6D   4D   C3   B7   D7   45   D8   78   CE   68   89   52   B9   9B   F7
 CB   AC   18   5C   F5   29   E4   1F   7A   2C   20   8E   74   60   92   9D
 A0   B6   A6   E1   DB   EB   22   6C   3C   67   B4   44   A9   DC   CD   FB
 65   56   0C   AE   FA   14   F2   0F   3D   16   10   47   3A   30   C9   4E
 50   5B   D3   F0   ED   75   11   36   9E   33   5A   A2   54   EE   E6   FD
 32   2B   06   57   7D   0A   F9   87   1E   0B   88   23   1D   98   64   27
```

Sequence B

```
 A8   AD   69   F8   F6   BA
 08   1B   CF   19   2D   51   2A   77   F3   7E   99   15   83   AB   3E   85
 FC   43   8F   05   C4   91   0E   4C   B2   13   D4   D6   34   7C   7B   5D
 84   8D   E7   8C   96   28   95   BB   79   BF   CC   8A   C1   55   9F   42
 FE   A1   C7   02   E2   48   07   26   D9   09   6A   6B   1A   BE   BD   2E
 C2   C6   73   46   4B   94   CA   DD   BC   5F   66   C5   E0   AA   4F   21
 FF   D0   63   01   71   A4   03   93   EC   04   B5   35   0D   DF   5E   17
 61   E3   39   A3   25   4A   E5   6E   DE   2F   B3   62   70   D5   A7   90
 7F   E8   B1  |80   38   D2   81   49   76   82   DA   9A   86   6F   AF   8B
                        ╲— Sequence repeat
```

Sequence C

```
 B0   F1   9C   D1   12   A5
 72   37   EF   97   59   31   B8   EA   53   C8   3F   F4   58   40   1C   E9
 C0   24   3B   41   6D   4D   C3   B7   D7   45   D8   78   CE   68   89   52
 B9   9B   F7   CB   AC   18   5C   F5   29   E4   1F   7A   2C   20   8E   74
 60   92   9D   A0   B6   A6   E1   DB   EB   22   6C   3C   67   B4   44   A9
 DC   CD   FB   65   56   0C   AE   FA   14   F2   0F   3D   16   10   47   3A
 30   C9   4E   50   5B   D3   F0   ED   75   11   36   9E   33   5A   A2   54
 EE   E6   FD   32   2B   06   57   7D   0A   F9   87   1E   0B   88   23   1D
 98   64   27   A8   AD   69   F8   F6   BA   08   1B   CF   19   2D   51   2A
```

Sequence D

```
 77   F3   7E   99   15   83
 AB   3E   85   FC   43   8F   05   C4   91   0E   4C   B2   13   D4   D6   34
 7C   7B   5D   84   8D   E7   8C   96   28   95   BB   79   BF   CC   8A   C1
 55   9F   42   FE   A1   C7   02   E2   48   07   26   D9   09   6A   6B   1A
 BE   BD   2E   C2   C6   73   46   4B   94   CA   DD   BC   5F   66   C5   E0
 AA   4F   21   FF   D0   63   01   71   A4   03   93   EC   04   B5   35   0D
 DF   5E   17   61   E3   39   A3   25   4A   E5   6E   DE   2F   B3   62   70
 D5   A7   90   7F   E8   B1  |80   38   D2   81   49   76   82   DA   9A   86
 6F   AF   8B   B0   F1   9C   D1   12   A5   72   37   EF   97   59   31   B8
```

Sequence E   ┌— During sync + 1D — not used

```
|EA   53   C8   3F   F4   58|
 40   1C   E9   C0   24   3B   41   6D   4D   C3   B7   D7   45   D8   78   CE
 68   89   52   B9   9B   F7   CB   AC   18   5C   F5   29   E4   1F   7A   2C
 20   8E   74   60   92   9D   A0   B6   A6   E1   DB   EB   22   6C   3C   67
 B4   44   A9   DC   CD   FB   65   56   0C   AE   FA   14   F2   0F   3D   16
 10   47   3A   30   C9   4E   50   5B   D3   F0   ED   75   11   36   9E   33
 5A   A2   54   EE   E6   FD   32   2B   06   57   7D   0A   F9   87   1E   0B
 88   23   1D   98   64   27   A8   AD   69   F8   F6   BA   08   1B   CF   19
 2D   51   2A   77   F3   7E   99   15   83   AB   3E   85   FC   43   8F   05
```

Figure 9.7(c) The sequence which results when the randomizer of (a) is allowed to run for five sync blocks. The first six symbols are not used, since they are generated when the sync pattern and ID patterns are being recorded. Five sync blocks exceed the sequence length of 255 ($2^8 - 1$) and repeats of the sequence can be seen underlined.

coercivity means that the recording density achieved gives a tape consumption which is no better than that of an analog machine. The picture quality is, of course, above criticism.

The data randomizing is performed by recording the exclusive OR function of the data and a Galois field. These were described in chapter 2. The randomizing polynomial and one way in which it can be implemented are shown in Figure 9.7(a). The polynomial is in fact the same one as is used for the generation of the inner and outer Reed–Solomon codes.

As the polynomial generates a maximum length sequence from an eight-bit wordlength, the sequence length is given by $2^8 - 1 = 255$. The sequence will repeat endlessly over this period, and could have been allowed to run over the entire length of a sector were it not for the requirement to have picture-in-shuttle. In order to recover the data from a randomized sync block, the sequence has to be recreated in the same relative phase as existed when the block was written. As the number of bytes in a sync block is not the same as the number of states in the sequence, each sync block would begin with a different state. This is of no consequence if the sector is played from end to end, but in shuttle only certain sync blocks will be recovered, and the correct starting state of the sequence will need to be preset into the sequence generator for each block. All of the starting values would have to be stored, raising the complexity of implementation. On the other hand, a sequence which is too short could raise the possibility of false sync detection.

A compromise is obtained by allowing the sequence to run for five sync blocks before resetting it. Since the audio sectors consist of five sync blocks, the sequence does indeed continue throughout audio sectors. However, in the video sectors there are 160 sync blocks, and this is conveniently a multiple of five, such that there are 32 repeated sequences in each sector. If a sync block is picked up at random in shuttle, it is only necessary to decide which of five starting states is necessary. Figure 9.7(b) shows the sync block numbers at which the sequence is reset, and Figure 9.7(c) shows the randomizing sequence. The repeat after 255 states is marked. At the very beginning of each of these sync blocks, coincident with the first bit of the sync pattern, the cyclic circuit is preset to 80_{16} and generates the sequence shown. The first 6 bytes of the sync block are the sync pattern and the ID. Clearly these cannot be randomized, since this causes a Catch-22 situation where it is not possible to synchronize the sequence for replay until the ID is read, but it is not possible to read the ID until the sequence is synchronized!

To avoid this situation, the sequence is allowed to run, but it is not used until the first genuine data byte in the sync block. The sync pattern and the ID code have to be rendered DC free in a way which does not require randomizing. Clearly the sync/ID information also has to be provided with its own error-correction mechanism, since it is excluded from the main codewords in the sync block.

9.6 Synchronization and identification

Each sync block contains two inner codewords, as was shown in Figure 9.5. It is called a sync block because it is the smallest quantum of data on the track with which the playback channel can synchronize independently. Synchronizing occurs on three levels; to the bit, to the symbol, and to the sync block.

The recording density used in DVTRs is such that mechanical measurement of scanner phase is not sufficiently accurate to locate a given bit. Synchronization on playback is achieved by letting the heads rotate to a reasonable standard of accuracy and accepting the signals at the exact time they are replayed. A phase-locked loop in the replay circuitry must lock to the actual bit rate of the offtape signal so that the individual bits in the recording can be separated. At the beginning of a track a reference for the phase-locked loop, called a preamble, is recorded. This contains no data, but serves to set the frequency of the PLL to be the same as the offtape bit rate, and thus achieve bit synchronism. Once the loop is locked, it can stay in lock by phase comparing the location of data transitions with its own. In this way bit synchronism can be achieved at the beginning of the track, maintained throughout it, and even regained if it is lost due to a severe dropout, since the PLL can relock to data transitions.

Once bit synchronization is achieved, the serial bit stream has to be correctly divided up into 8 bit symbols to restore the original samples. This is word synchronization, and it is achieved with the help of a unique bit pattern which always occurs at the start of the sync block. The purpose of this sync pattern is to reset the divide-by-eight counter which deserializes the data into symbols. The correct detection of the sync pattern is extremely important. For example, detecting it 1 bit early or late would corrupt every symbol in the sync block, since the LSB of one sample would become the MSB of the next. The sync pattern of D-1 is a 16 bit code shown in Figure 9.8 which carries a range of run lengths so that it differs from itself shifted by as many bits as possible. Random errors are then less likely to produce a mistimed sync detection, and an accurate detection is still possible in the case of a random bit error. The sync pattern is DC free because it contains as many ones as zeros. In the body of a sector, sync patterns occur regularly every 134 bytes, so it is desirable for the replay circuitry to predict the position of a window in which the next sync pattern will be seen. This flywheel mechanism reduces the possibility of false sync detection.

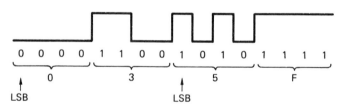

Figure 9.8 The sync pattern of D-1 carries a variety of run lengths so that it is very difficult to detect sync with a bit shift in thed presence of noise. Serialization is least significant bit (LSB) first, so sync pattern is written 3OF5.

Once symbol synchronizing is achieved, it is possible to read the sync block, and it remains to determine *which* sync block has been found. In normal play it will be the one after the previous one, but in shuttle the sequence is unpredictable. This is the third level of synchronization, and is the function of the ID pattern which occupies 4 bytes.

The correct identification of the sync block address is crucial, because a number of processes depend on it:

(1) It must be possible to distinguish reliably between audio and video sectors, so that audio does not end up on the screen in shuttle.

(2) There are five different states to which the pseudo random sequence generator could be preset, only one of which is right.

(3) The shuffle permutation changes over a four-field sequence. The position in the sequence must be known, or the sync block cannot be de-shuffled.

(4) There are four parallel channels of data and the picture cannot be demultiplexed correctly if the channel number of a sync block is not known.

The ID system carries the following parameters to meet the above requirements:

(1) A 2 bit field ID which repeats over a four-field sequence to reveal the shuffle permutation to be used. This sequence can become discontinuous at edits.

(2) A 3 bit segment ID which counts segments through a field. It will count 0–5 in 625 line systems and 0–4 in 525 line systems.

(3) The sector ID LSB which specifies which track of the two parallel tracks in a segment is being read.

(4) The sector ID MSB which alternates between audio and video sectors and between the first and second halves of the track.

(5) An 8 bit sync block number specifying the sync block address within a sector for video, within a sector pair for audio.

Using the above information, if the ID pattern is correctly recovered, it is possible to position the sync block precisely over a four-field sequence. All of the mechanisms which depend on sync block position will then operate with a high degree of reliability even in shuttle.

As the sync block ID is so important, it is protected against random errors by coding each 4 bits of ID address into an 8 bit codeword. This redundancy also allows the codewords generated to be DC free, since they cannot be randomized. The coding scheme used is a distance 4 BCH code and is implemented with lookup tables as shown in Figure 9.9(a). Only 14 of the codes out of the 16 possible are DC free, and so the ID numbering system is base 14, so that the 8 bit sync block numbering has a range of 196_{10} (14^2) which is more than enough for the video sectors. The segment number never exceeds 5, and so the segment/ field ID can also be expressed base 14.

Input ID	ID code	Input ID	ID code
0	1B	8	96
1	2E	9	A3
2	35	A	B8
3	47	B	CA
4	5C	C	D1
5	69	D	E4
6	72	(E) ⎱ Invalid code	
7	8D	(F) ⎰ Not dc free	

Figure 9.9(a) ID cannot be protected by codewords in the sync block due to use of RNRZ coding. Thus ID must have its own redundancy, and each 4 bits of Input ID is expressed as an 8 bit word which is a distance 4 BCH codeword. Codewords for E and F are not DC free and are not used, so ID code is base 14.

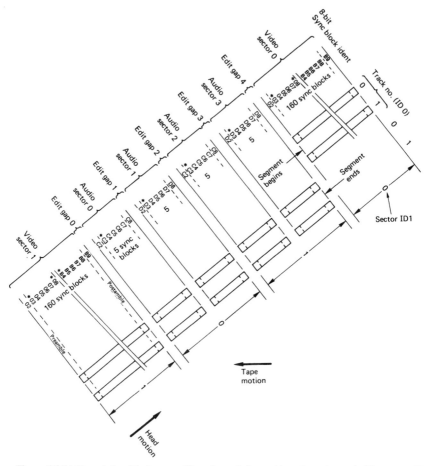

Figure 9.9(b) The relationship between ID codes and the position along the track. The sector ID is a 2 bit value comprising ID0 and ID1 shown here. These are combined with the segment and field ID to form the following:

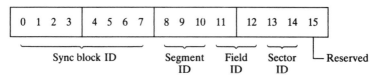

0 1 2 3	4 5 6 7	8 9 10 11	12 13 14 15

| Sync block ID | Segment ID | Field ID | Sector ID | Reserved |

This is then mapped according to (a) from 4 bit symbols to 8 bit symbols, to make a 4 byte ID pattern shown in Figure 9.5. The * symbol indicates IDs of sync blocks at which the randomizer of Figure 9.7 is reset.

With 4 bits of redundancy, correction of single-bit errors and detection of double-bit errors is possible using a 256 location PROM.

Figure 9.9(b) shows the relationship between ID codes and sync block position over a complete segment.

In normal speed playback, sync blocks are played in sequence, and the player can predict what the next ID code will be and compare it with the value read to reduce further the probability of incorrect synchronization. In shuttle this is not possible, but it is quite likely in shuttle that if a complete sync block is recovered, the ID of the next sync block can also be read, and so a pair of inner codewords straddled by a pair of contiguous ID codes should be observed.[3]

9.7 D-1 Block diagram

Figure 9.10(a) shows a typical block diagram of the record section of a D-1 machine, where the inputs will be component video and four audio channels. Audio and video inputs can be either analog or digital, and machines can incorporate converters which will be bypassed if a direct digital input is available. Whichever input form is used, the input video will always control the timing of the recording circuitry. In the case of a digital video input, the 27 MHz clock accompanying parallel data or the 270 MHz clock of SDI will be used to derive the symbol clock for much of the recorder. In the case of an analog input, the sync pulses will be fed to a phase-locked loop which produces a line locked sampling rate which then will be used for the symbol clock.

The video data are distributed over four logical channels as was shown in Figure 7.9. Only one of these is shown in full since they differ only in detail.

Following distribution, the mapping process of Figure 7.12 is performed. The reverse interleave of Figure 9.3 then takes place, and these data blocks then have two redundancy bytes added to make outer codes which are written into a sector array in columns. When the sector array is full, it is transferred to a second array memory, but the read addresses are sequential, whereas the write addresses are generated by the shuffler of Figure 9.4, so that the second array is then shuffled. While this is taking place input outer codes will be written into a second pair of arrays which work alternately.

The audio processing takes place in parallel with the video, using a distribution scheme which spreads samples from all channels over all four heads. Since audio is not two dimensional, no video-style shuffle is necessary, and a regular array is used to form a product block.

The audio samples have longer wordlength than video samples, and there are no details such as co-sited samples to handle, so the outer coding of the audio is somewhat different to that of the video, but the dimensions of the product block are designed so that the audio inner codes are identical in size to video inner codes. In this way, the inner code generation, randomizing, ID generation and serializing are common to both audio and video, which effectively share the same circuitry, heads and tracks in a time multiplex.

At the beginning of a track, the audio and video data to be recorded have been interleaved and shuffled and are held in RAM so they can be made available at the appropriate time.

Input to the serializer will be from the ID generator which produces the preamble and the sync/ID pattern of the first sync block. The serializer input is then switched to the data path.

Reading along a row of the shuffled video sector array then produces two inner blocks, and 4 bytes of redundancy are added to each to make inner codewords which are randomized and recorded in the sync block. The ID generator then produces the next sync/ID pattern, and the process repeats 160 times until the sector is completed.

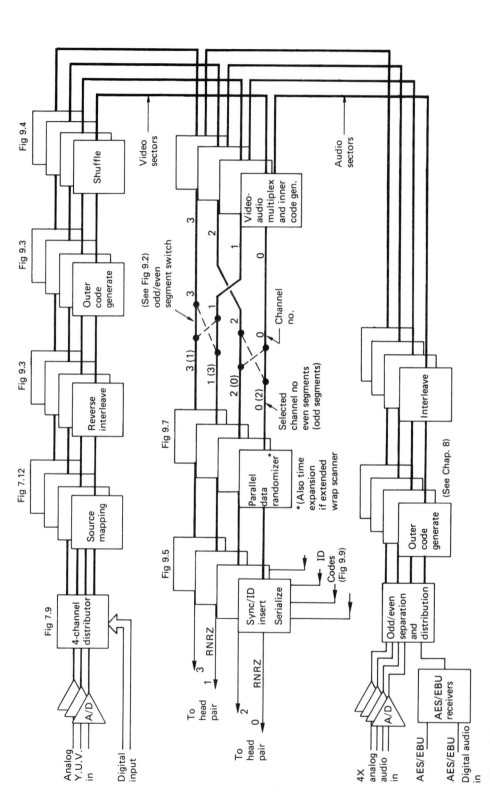

Figure 9.10(a) The essential stages in a D-1 record system described in the text. Note that the odd/even segment switching can be performed using a more complex multiplexer on the input to the inner code generator. Shown separately for clarity. The parallel data randomizer shown here could be implemented as a serial randomizer *after* the serializer.

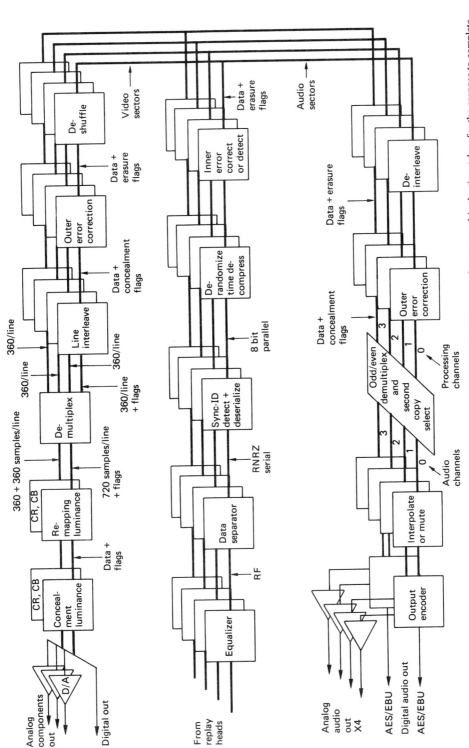

Figure 9.10(b) D-1 replay system. Note time decompression stage to allow data read in one head sweep to be processed in the time taken for the scanner to complete one revolution.

At the end of the sector the postamble is written followed by the edit gap and the preamble and sync/ID for the audio sector. The multiplexer on the input to the inner coder switched to the audio RAM during the gap, and now audio inner blocks are turned into inner codewords, randomized and recorded as before.

Five sync blocks are needed to record one audio sector; then another gap is generated. This process continues until the track is completed at the end of the second video sector with a postamble. Since the logical segment begins after the audio blocks, the inner coder must switch to a different distribution channel for the second half of the track, as shown in Figure 9.2. There are four logical processing channels, but only two tracks in a segment, so the need to select one of two channels for each track is clear.

Figure 9.10(b) shows the replay system. The offtape signal is equalized and fed to the data separator, which contains a phase-locked loop. This will synchronize to the bit clock. Sync patterns and IDs are recognized and used to synchronize the derandomizer and the shift register needed to deserialize the data stream.

The inner code processor corrects single-symbol errors with high reliability since four R–S equations agree on the single error.[3] Two symbols or more in error are used to generate erasure flags for the outer codes. Every symbol in the inner code is flagged bad. Inner blocks are then written into a sector array, audio or video as determined by the ID code, and when it is full, the contents are transferred to a second array. This time the read address comes from the shuffle generator, and the write address is sequential. The data are thus de-shuffled, and any burst errors are now dotted around the sector array.

The outer correction now uses the erasure flags which have come from the inner detection system. Two error symbols in each outer code can be corrected. If there are more, correction is not possible, and uncorrectable flags accompany the samples forward. Since there are 600 columns in the sector array, and thus the same number of outer codewords, then a maximum 1 200 bytes of data can be lost from a sector and still corrected. This corresponds to 20 inner codewords, ten sync blocks or a track length of about 4.8 mm.

The reverse interleave is then opposed, and the four channels are combined. The recombination must reflect the changing relationship between head number and sector number. The video mapping is then reversed to restore the original sample values. Samples and uncorrectable flags now pass to the concealment system which can interpolate over different distances and in different directions dependent on the nature of the errors to be concealed.

The samples are now in their original sequence, and can be output digitally or fed to converters.

The audio samples are corrected by inner and outer codes in the same way, and as there are two copies of all audio data, any error-free data will be used to reassemble the output samples. The distribution of audio samples over all channels makes the audio demultiplexer more complex because it has to select any audio channel from any processing channel, and in the case of an uncorrectable error, it must select the second copy from a different channel.

9.8 Variable speed in D-1

Track following in variable speed is difficult in D-1 because of the high rotational speed and the short distance in which the heads can jump. It is possible to obtain a small range of speeds around normal by changing the drum and capstan speeds by the same amount so that full tracking is still obtained. There are limits to the range possible because offtape frequencies change and the replay PLLs find it hard to lock. The dynamics of the head/tape interface also change with speed and the bit error rate will deteriorate. The disparity between drum speed and reference is resolved by repeating or skipping fields in a frame store.

Beyond this limited speed range the machine has no option but to unlock the capstan and drum servos and cross tracks. The head-to-tape speed can be made constant by programming the drum speed from the tape speed. The track crossing causes guard-band noise which makes a proportion of sync blocks unreadable. There will, however, be short lengths of track where the replay signal is unimpaired. Azimuth recording is not used, so any head can play any track. Reading will also be possible with a certain amount of mistracking until the SNR becomes inadequate. It is possible to compute the proportion of data which will be available from the system geometry and noise tolerance. In fact this does not change with tape speed, and remains constant at 40–50% as Figure 9.11 shows.

With the tape moving very slowly, the scanner makes many revolutions in the area of the same tracks and virtually all of the blocks in a field can be recovered in successive revolutions. Inner correction can be used, but complete outer codes cannot be assembled during track crossing, so outer correction is powerless.

In a D-1 machine developed by Sony a D-1 transport is fitted with track-following head assemblies in place of the usual playback heads. Each head shoe carries four heads, tracing four adjacent tape tracks, instead of the usual two heads. The extra heads mean that a jump from one segment to another can be obtained by head switching. Jumping takes place in the quarter revolution when the head is out of contact with the tape. The heads are subject to approximately 5000g due to the high rotational speed. Nevertheless thay can be deflected with a conventional piezoelectric element.

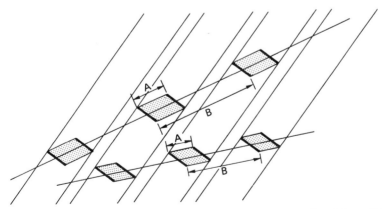

Figure 9.11 In shuttle, the heads cross tracks randomly, but the proportion of data which are readable is independent of the speed. If the sync blocks are shorter than the minimum track length played at the highest speed, then data can be recovered at all speeds. The angles here are exaggerated for the purpose of illustration. Even at 30× normal speed about 5 sync blocks can be recovered per track crossed. In practice the head can read for slightly longer than is indicated here because a slight tracking error will only reduce the signal-to-noise ratio.

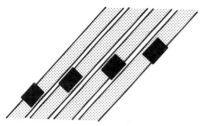

Figure 9.12 Four heads are fitted to one arm, but the spacing is not even. Two heads are offset to one side of the track, two to the other. A tracking error causes the level of the signals from one pair of heads to fall and the signal from the other pair to rise.

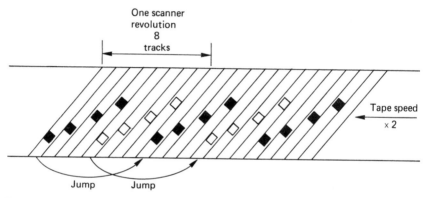

Figure 9.13 Since there are four heads per arm instead of two, all tape tracks can be read at ×2 speed. Each head arm must jump by two tracks while it is out of contact with the tape.

Figure 9.12 shows that the heads are not evenly spaced, but are slightly offset from the track centres. This causes a differential variation in RF signal strength if the tracking is not central, and a tracking error signal can be derived.

At normal speed, only the inner two heads are operational, but in variable speed, all heads function. Figure 9.13 shows that at 2 × normal speed all tape tracks can be followed. The heads will need to be deflected by a sawtooth waveform as the track angle is incorrect at 2 × speed, and a two-track jump will be required on every revolution as the sawtooth resets. The playback logic selects the required data to produce alternate entire fields. At other speeds the heads will need to jump on an irregular basis as the deflection builds up.

9.9 The D-2 format

The D-2 format was the first production composite digital recorder. It used the same ¾ inch cassette shell as D-1, but the tape was replaced with a 1600 Oe metal particle formulation. A further increase in density was achieved by incorporating azimuth recording. This became standard on all later formats. The Ampex DCT format records data-reduced 4:2:2 component video on a development of the NTSC D-2 transport as will be seen in Section 9.19.

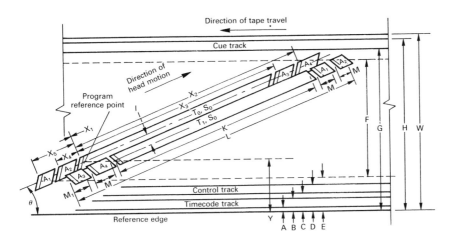

525/60		Millimetres	
Dimensions		Nominal	Tolerance
A	Timecode track lower edge	0.2	±0.1
B	Timecode track upper edge	0.7	±0.1
C	Control track lower edge	1.0	±0.1
D	Control track upper edge	1.5	±0.05
E	Program area lower edge	1.807	Derived
F	Program area width	16.1	Derived
G	Cue track lower edge	18.2	±0.1
H	Cue track upper edge	18.9	±0.1
I	Helical track pitch	0.0391	Ref.
K	Video sector length	132.49	Derived
L	Helical track total length	150.78	Derived
M_1	Audio sector length	4.13	Derived
M	Audio sector length	4.01	Derived
P_1	Control track	107.66	±0.3
P_2	Cue/timecode track	108.41	±0.3
W	Tape width	19.01	±0.015
X_1	Location of start of video sector	0	±0.1
X_2	Location of start of audio sector A_4	137.57	±0.1
X_3	Location of start of audio sector A_3	133.03	±0.1
X_4	Location of start of audio sector A_2	4.54	±0.1
X_5	Location of start of audio sector A_1	9.08	±0.1
Y	Program area reference	2.80	Basic
		Degrees	
Dimensions		Nominal	Tolerance
θ	Track angle	6.1296	Basic
$\alpha 0$	Azimuth angle (track 0)	+14.97	±0.17
$\alpha 1$	Azimuth angle (track 1)	−15.03	±0.17

Figure 9.14 The dimensions of the D-2 format for 525/60 and 625/50 use.

625/50		Millimetres	
Dimensions		Nominal	Tolerance
A	Timecode track lower edge	0.2	$\pm$0.1
B	Timecode track upper edge	0.7	$\pm$0.1
C	Control track lower edge	1.0	$\pm$0.1
D	Control track upper edge	1.5	$\pm$0.05
E	Program area lower edge	1.797	Derived
F	Program area width	16.1	Derived
G	Cue track lower edge	18.2	$\pm$0.1
H	Cue track upper edge	18.9	$\pm$0.1
I	Helical track pitch	0.0352	Ref.
K	Video sector length	135.39	Derived
L	Helical track total length	150.71	Derived
M_1	Audio sector length	3.47	Derived
M	Audio sector length	3.37	Derived
P_1	Control track	106.02	$\pm$0.3
P_2	Cue/timecode track	106.70	$\pm$0.3
W	Tape width	19.01	$\pm$0.015
X_1	Location of start of video sector	0	$\pm$0.1
X_2	Location of start of audio sector A_4	139.63	$\pm$0.1
X_3	Location of start of audio sector A_3	135.82	$\pm$0.1
X_4	Location of start of audio sector A_2	3.80	$\pm$0.1
X_5	Location of start of audio sector A_1	7.61	$\pm$0.1
Y	Program area reference	2.63	Basic
		Degrees	
Dimensions		Nominal	Tolerance
θ	Track angle	6.1326	Basic
$\alpha0$	Azimuth angle (track 0)	+14.97	$\pm$0.17
$\alpha1$	Azimuth angle (track 1)	$-$15.03	$\pm$0.17

Figure 9.14 Continued.

The dimensions of the D-2 format are shown in Figure 9.14. The audio blocks are placed at the ends of the tracks, and the fields begin and end with whole tracks. In a typical transport, two pairs of heads are positioned at 180° apart on a scanner which uses a wrap of just over half a turn. The head pairs trace the tape alternately, so that in stunt mode each has almost half a revolution in which to jump. As the tape speed increases, the audio will no longer be necessary, and the heads can begin to jump in the audio blocks at the end of the track, and continue to settle during the audio blocks at the beginning of the track.

The wide disparity between the subcarrier frequencies of NTSC and PAL leads to different segmentation being used in each case. The fundamental unit in the D-2 format is the segment, which consists of a pair of tracks, 0 and 1, one of each azimuth type. The first recorded track in a field is always a type 0 track, in which the azimuth is rotated clockwise by 14.97° from perpendicular when looking at the magnetic coating side of the tape. In a type 1 track, the azimuth is rotated 15.03° anticlockwise.

Figure 9.15(a) shows that in PAL, four segments of 76 lines each record a total of 304 lines per field[4], whereas in NTSC, shown in Figure 9.15(b), three segments of 85 lines each record a total of 255 lines per field.[5] The segment and track numbering is also shown. The control track necessary for segmented

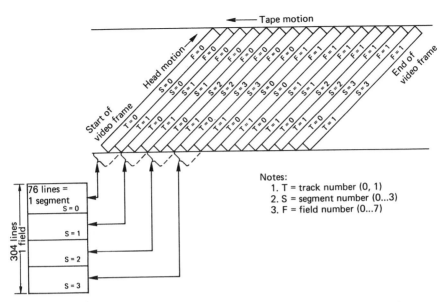

Figure 9.15(a) PAL segmentation in D-2. Four segments of 76 lines are necessary to record one field. The numbering scheme needed to recreate correctly framed pictures is shown here. The field number reflects the eight-field sequence of PAL. Audio blocks are omitted for clarity.

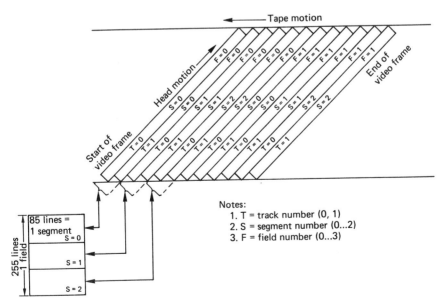

Figure 9.15(b) NTSC segmentation in D-2. Three segments of 76 lines are necessary to record one field. The numbering scheme needed to recreate correctly framed pictures is shown here. The field number reflects the four-field sequence of NTSC. Audio blocks are omitted for clarity.

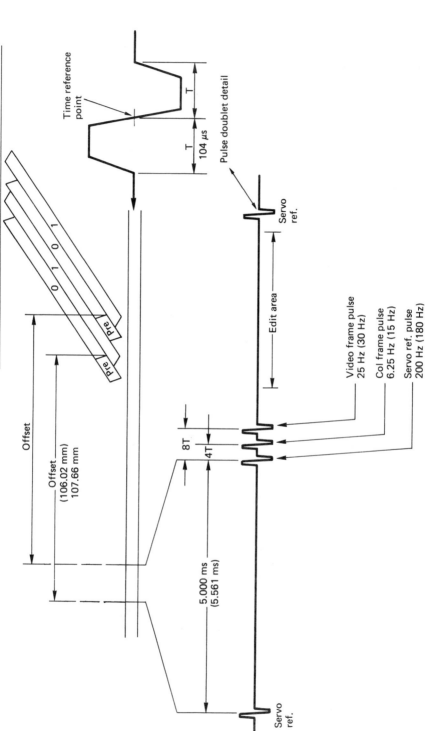

Figure 9.15(c) The control track of D-2 contains a servo reference pulse at segment rate, but the pulses are offset from the beginning of the segment, which is at the end of the preamble in the video sector. Servo pulse may be followed by colour frame pulse or video frame pulse as appropriate. Figures are for PAL, NTSC in brackets.

operation must convey segment, colour frame and frame information. Figure 9.15(c) shows that there is an event in the control track once per segment, and there are three positions in which a control track pulse can occur. A pulse is always present in the first position, and is used to control the capstan servo so that the segments will be properly traced on replay. The second pulse will occur once per colour frame, and the third pulse will occur once per frame. When tape travel initially starts, the capstan speed will slip until a control track colour frame pulse coincides with a pulse from the reference colour framer. At this point the capstan phase-locked loop will be closed, and the chroma phase of the replay signal will match that of the reference. The frame pulses allow the picture to be reassembled from segments correctly when playback is not colour framed, for example in TSO (Tape Speed Override) mode.

In a scanner of the type normally used, having opposing pairs of heads, two rotations per field will be needed in PAL, and one and a half rotations per field will be necessary in NTSC, giving scanner speeds of 100 Hz and 90/1.001 Hz respectively.

The tape speed does not differ between the formats, so that the playing time remains the same for both. The different scanner speeds result in the two formats having different track angles. The track widths are in inverse proportion to the scanner speeds, so the PAL track at 35 μm is 90% of the width of the NTSC track at 39 μm. A common transport can be used, having one helix angle, but the heads fitted will need to be specific to the format.

9.10 Distribution and concealment

Data to be recorded are divided equally between the two heads which are active at any one time. This process is called distribution, and is necessary because one head could not sustain the necessary data rate alone.

Figure 7.8 showed the concept of distribution, which ensures that in both rows and columns, alternate samples are recorded by a different head. If samples from a given head are lost for any reason, each lost sample is surrounded on four sides by samples from the other head. In the case of complete loss of signal from one head, due perhaps to clogging, it is still possible to produce a picture of reasonable quality from the remaining head.

9.11 Interleave and shuffle

The conflicting requirements mean that compromise is inevitable in the design of the shuffling process, to give a balanced performance in different operating modes.

Figure 9.16(a) shows the sector array of D-2 PAL, and Figure 9.16(b) shows the equivalent in NTSC. Outer codes are vertical columns, and six inner codes are formed along each row. In normal play, an error which is too large to be correctable will have to be concealed. Since the outer codes contain four redundancy symbols, each can correct four symbols by erasure. This corresponds to 4 bytes per column of the sector array. The largest data loss which can be handled will be when this damage is experienced in every column of the array, so the correctable burst error-size is given by multiplying the number of columns in the sector array by four. The resulting figures are 1824 bytes for PAL and 2040 bytes for NTSC. These figures are for video data only; the actual size of the burst

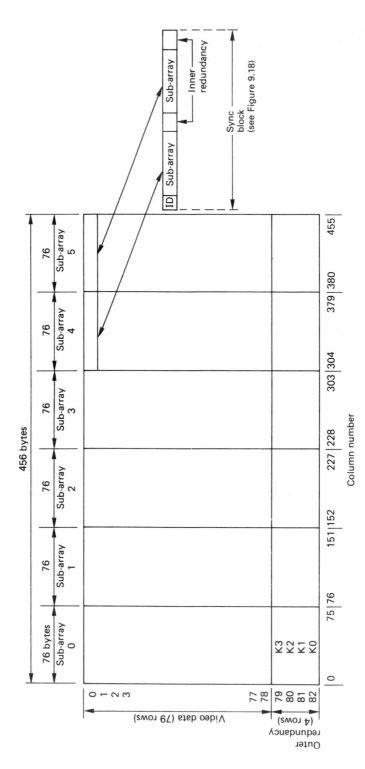

Figure 9.16(a) The sector array of D-2 PAL contains columns which are outer codewords. Rows are read, and two horizontal subarrays are used to construct a sync block by adding inner redundancy and ID codes. The video section of the track will thus contain $83 \times 3 + 249$ sync blocks. Array reading begins at the bottom so the outer redundancy appears at the beginning of the track. Data distributed over two such tracks (0 and 1) make a segment. Four segments make a field.

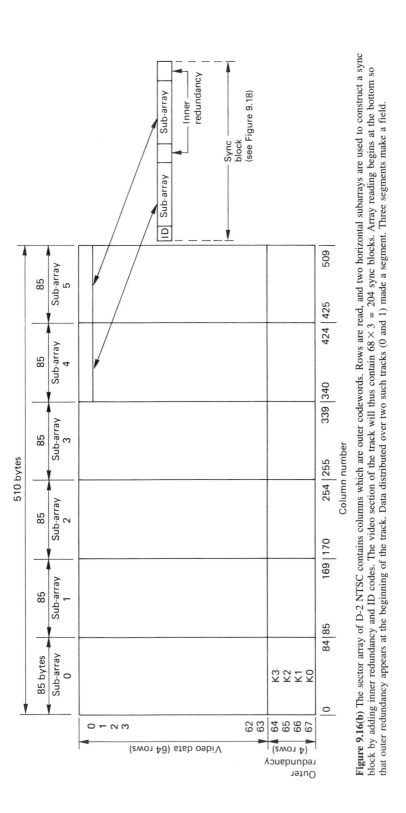

Figure 9.16(b) The sector array of D-2 NTSC contains columns which are outer codewords. Rows are read, and two horizontal subarrays are used to construct a sync block by adding inner redundancy and ID codes. The video section of the track will thus contain $68 \times 3 = 204$ sync blocks. Array reading begins at the bottom so that outer redundancy appears at the beginning of the track. Data distributed over two such tracks (0 and 1) made a segment. Three segments make a field.

will be larger because the length of the track involved also contains sync and ID patterns and inner redundancy for 12 sync blocks. The maximum correctable burst corresponds to about 13 mm of track length, or a longitudinal tape scratch of about 1.4 mm width.

If this condition is exceeded, total correction is no longer possible, and rows of flagged erroneous data will appear in the sector array. Concealment will become necessary, but the eye is adept at detecting patterns, and would perceive the shape of the concealment area if no steps were taken to reduce its visibility.

In fact the concealment patterns are made irregular by using shuffling.

9.12 Implementing the shuffle in PAL

The shuffle uses the same principles in both standards, but with different parameters. To avoid confusion, this section contains the PAL parameters, whereas Section 9.13 contains the same text but with the parameters for NTSC. The shuffle process falls into two main stages, permuting the order of samples within sector array columns, and then permuting the order of the columns. These will be dealt with in turn.

One possible implementation of the first shuffle stage is shown for PAL in Figure 9.17(a).

The source of information is a memory which sequentially stores samples from the distributor. In each line it will thus have 474 samples. Samples from each line are to be distributed over six outer code blocks, but the distribution is permuted, and the permutation changes from line to line throughout the 76 lines of the segment.

An incoming byte-rate clock controls the system. This clock operates a counter/divider which divides by 79 before resetting. As this is the number of samples in an outer block, it provides the block address, and the reset will increment a block count. The block counter/divider divides by six, the number of blocks in a line, and in turn the reset drives the line counter which counts the 76 lines in a segment.

Operation begins with all of the accumulators cleared. The byte accumulator adds 60 every time it is clocked, and so produces 60 × the byte number. In the first block the other accumulators will remain zero, so only this value passes to the modulo-474 circuit which subtracts integer multiples of 474 until the output no longer exceeds 474. Part of the calculation sequence is shown in the diagram, where it will be seen that successive source addresses are six samples apart. The intervening five samples will go into other blocks. The source address is used to obtain a sample from the pixel memory, and the byte count is used to place the sample in the correct place in the block. In this way a permuted block is assembled.

At the end of the first block, the byte counter resets, clearing the byte accumulator and incrementing the block counter. This causes the block accumulator to add 79 to the previously cleared state. The source address now becomes 60 × the byte address plus 79 × the block address. The process continues until all six blocks of the first line are complete, when the block count will reset, clearing the block accumulator and incrementing the line count. This causes the line accumulator to add 83 to the previously cleared value, so the full source address is given by 60 × the byte count plus 79 × the block count plus

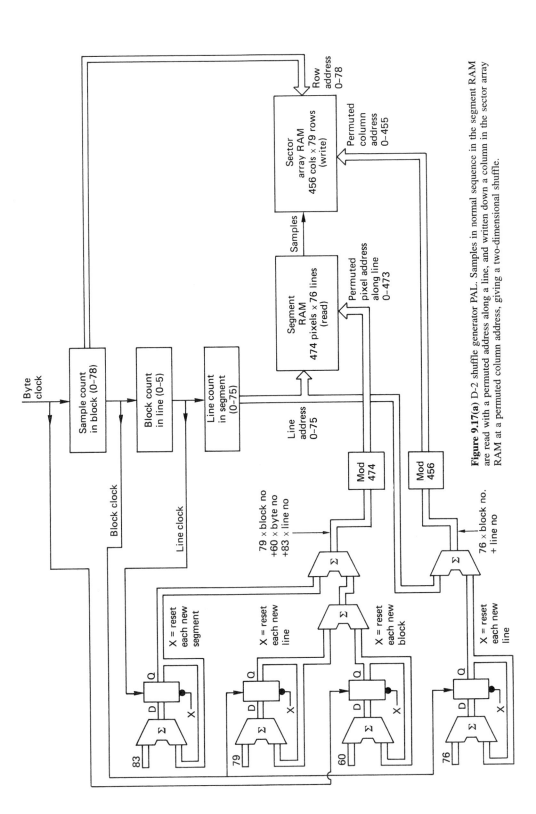

Figure 9.17(a) D-2 shuffle generator PAL. Samples in normal sequence in the segment RAM are read with a permuted address along a line, and written down a column in the sector array RAM at a permuted column address, giving a two-dimensional shuffle.

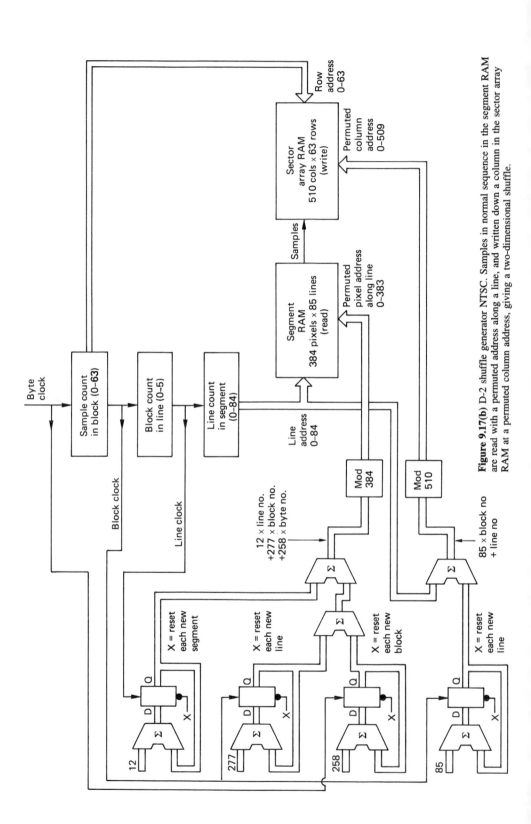

Figure 9.17(b) D-2 shuffle generator NTSC. Samples in normal sequence in the segment RAM are read with a permuted address along a line, and written down a column in the sector array RAM at a permuted column address, giving a two-dimensional shuffle.

$83 \times$ the line count. This process continues throughout the whole segment, until 456 blocks have been assembled.

The second stage of the shuffle is to permute the column number in the sector array. Figure 9.17(a) also shows that the block-rate clock also operates a second accumulator which multiplies the block number by 76. To the output of this is added the line number, and the result is taken modulo-456, since 456 is the number of columns in the sector array. This produces the column address into which the blocks produced by the mapping process are written. The row address is equal to the byte address within the block. The shuffle process is then complete, and the outer redundancy can be added on the columns, and the inner redundancy and ID codes can be added to the rows. The array contents are then ready to be recorded.

9.13 Implementing the shuffle in NTSC

The shuffle process falls into two main stages, permuting the order of samples within sector array columns, and then permuting the order of the columns. These will be dealt with in turn. One possible implementation of the first shuffle stage is shown for NTSC in Figure 9.17(b).

The source of information is a memory which sequentially stores samples from the distributor. In each line it will thus have 384 samples. Samples from each line are to be distributed over six outer code blocks, but the distribution is permuted, and the permutation changes from line to line throughout the 85 lines of the segment.

An incoming byte-rate clock controls the system. This clock operates a counter/divider which divides by 64 before resetting. As this is the number of samples in an outer block, it provides the block address, and the reset will increment a block count. The block counter/divider divides by six, the number of blocks in a line, and in turn the reset drives the line counter which counts the 85 lines in a segment.

Operation begins with all of the accumulators cleared. The byte accumulator adds 258 every time it is clocked, and so produces $258 \times$ the byte number. In the first block the other accumulators will remain zero, so only this value passes to the modulo-384 circuit which subtracts integer multiples of 384 until the output no longer exceeds 384. Part of the calculation sequence is shown in the diagram, where it will be seen that successive source addresses are six samples apart. The intervening five samples will go into other blocks. The source address is used to obtain a sample from the input memory, and the byte count is used to place the sample in the correct place in the block. In this way a permuted block is assembled.

At the end of the first block, the byte counter resets, clearing the byte accumulator and incrementing the block counter. This causes the block accumulator to add 277 to the previously cleared state. The source address now becomes $258 \times$ the byte address plus $277 \times$ the block address. The process continues until all six blocks of the first line are complete, when the block count will reset, clearing the block accumulator and incrementing the line count. This causes the line accumulator to add 12 to the previously cleared value, so the full source address is given by $258 \times$ the byte count plus $277 \times$ the block count plus $12 \times$ the line count. This process continues throughout the whole segment, until 510 blocks have been assembled.

The second stage of the shuffle is to permute the column number in the sector array. Figure 9.17(b) also shows that the block-rate clock also operates a second accumulator which multiplies the block number by 85. To the output of this is added the line number, and the result is taken modulo-510, since 510 is the number of columns in the sector array. This produces the column address into which the blocks produced by the mapping process are written. The row address is equal to the byte address within the block. The shuffle process is then complete, and the outer redundancy can be added on the columns, and the inner redundancy and ID codes can be added to the rows. The array contents are then ready to be recorded.

9.14 The D-2 sync block

The inner codes are designed to correct random errors and to detect the presence of burst errors by declaring the whole inner block bad. There is an optimum size for an inner code: too small and the redundancy factor rises; too large and burst errors are magnified, as are errors due to losing sync.

One row of the product block is too large to be one inner code, and so it is split into six inner code blocks. The dimensions of these are chosen to give adequate correction performance. However, individually identifying each inner code would raise the recording overheads. In shuttle, a geometric calculation reveals the shortest length of track which will be recovered at maximum tape speed, and this determines that it is not necessary to identify every inner codeword. Accordingly one sync block contains two inner codewords, but only one ID code. Three sync blocks then form one complete row of the sector array.

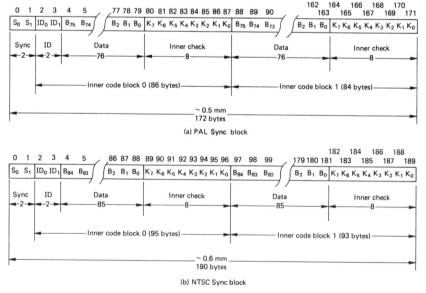

Figure 9.18 The sync blocks of D-2 contain two codewords but only one ID code which forms part of the first codeword. As a result, the first code block is 2 bytes longer than the second.

Figure 9.18(a) shows a PAL sync block. A 2 byte synchronizing pattern serves to phase the data separator and the deserializer. Following this is a 2 byte ID code which uniquely identifies this sync block in an eight-field sequence. The first data block of 76 bytes then follows, and the 8 bytes of inner redundancy are calculated over the ID code as well as the data, so a random error in the ID can be corrected. The first codeword is thus 86 bytes long. The second inner code block is 2 bytes shorter because it contains no ID. The entire sync block occupies just over half a millimetre of track.

Figure 9.18(b) shows an NTSC sync block. A 2 byte synchronizing pattern serves to phase the data separator and the deserializer. Following this is a 2 byte ID code which uniquely identifies this sync block in a four-field sequence. The first data block of 85 bytes then follows, and the 8 bytes of inner redundancy are calculated over the ID code as well as the data, so a random error in the ID can be corrected. The first codeword is thus 95 bytes long. The second inner code block is 2 bytes shorter because it contains no ID. The entire sync block occupies nearly two-thirds of a millimetre of track.

9.15 Miller^2 code in D-2

The details of channel coding have been treated in Chapter 4 and so this section confines itself to the implementation in D-2.

Miller^2 code has the same density ratio but half the jitter window of RNRZ, all other things being equal, and so might be thought inferior. In practice this turns out not to be the case because the narrow spectrum of Miller^2 is less stringent about equalization, the smaller ratio of run lengths causes less peak shift, and the higher clock content eases the task of the data separator. Thus in practice the performance of Miller^2 may be inferior under accurate tracking conditions, but the performance will not fall so rapidly with the onset of tracking error, and may actually be better than RNRZ during mistracking.

The main advantage of Miller^2 is, however, that it makes guard-band-less recording possible, minimizing tape consumption. It is also capable of erasure by overwrite, and early D-2 machines had no flying erase heads.

The encoding rules of Miller^2 require that a transition will be recorded in the centre of all data ones and between successive zeros, but in the case of an even number of ones between zeros, the transition of the last one is omitted.

These coding rules are used to generate a variety of patterns used for synchronizing the data separator and identifying the location of the head.

Figure 9.19 shows that the run-up pattern or preamble is obtained by feeding alternating ones and zeros to the channel coder. This results in a frequency of half the maximum, since only the ones result in a transition. This frequency will suffer fewer losses, and so will be readily detectable on replay. The transitions all indicate the centre of the bit cell and the PLO can easily synchronize to them. This run-in pattern precedes nearly every sector.

Figure 9.19 also shows that if a bit pattern of 011 is repeatedly presented to the channel coder, the last coding rule is invoked, and the transition due to the second one is omitted, resulting in a frequency of one-third the maximum. This is the lowest frequency which Miller^2 code can generate, and is very easily detectable with a simple filter. This pattern is used only at the beginning of the first segment of a field. It is incorporated in order to simplify the construction

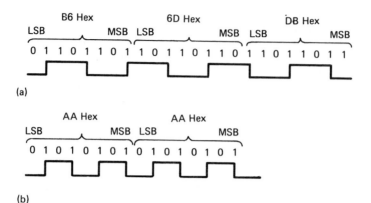

Figure 9.19 (a) Under the coding rules of Miller^2, the transition due to the last one in an even number of ones is omitted, so that a repeated sequence of data bits 011 will generate only one transition. This represents the lowest frequency possible in Miller^2, and is used to identify uniquely the first segment in a field. (b) The alternation of data ones and zeros produces a frequency of half the maximum which is ideal for bringing the phase-locked loop in the data separator into lock.

of automated systems where several transports share a single signal system. Each transport need only have a simple preamplifier and tuned circuit to detect the field run-in, and so it can, in conjunction with the control track and timecode, synchronize the scanner and colour-frame the capstan without the presence of a signal system. A cut between two tapes in two transports can thus be made by switching the input to a single signal system at the transport preamplifiers.

9.16 Synchronization and identification

Each sync block contains two inner codewords, and is the smallest quantum of data on the track to which the playback channel can synchronize independently. The sync pattern of D-2 is $30F5_{16}$, and is in fact the same pattern as is used for D-1.

Once symbol synchronizing is achieved, it is then possible to read the inner code blocks, and the first of these contains the ID code and reveals which sync block has been recovered. In normal play this will be the one after the previous one, but in shuttle, the sequence will be unpredictable. In shuttle, samples from any sync block properly recovered can be put in the correct place in a frame store by reference to the ID code.

Figure 9.20(a) shows that the information recorded in the ID code is split into two parts. The first byte is the sync block number in the track, and the second identifies the sector. The V/A bit specifies whether the block is audio or video, and the T bit specifies which track of the parallel pair. The segment bits determine which segment out of four for PAL and three for NTSC is present, and the field bits specify the position in the eight- or four-field sequences to help colour framing.

Figure 9.20(b) shows the sync block numbering within the segment for PAL, and Figure 9.20(c) shows the equivalent for NTSC.

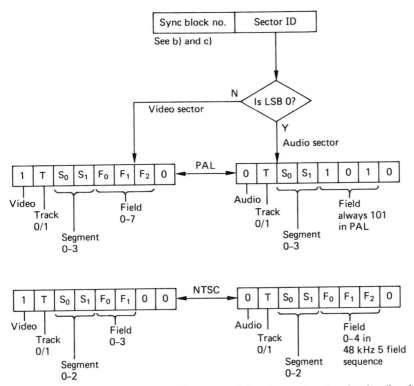

Figure 9.20(a) The ID code splits into 2 bytes: one of these is a number, the other describes the type of sync block and its position in the sequence. For video blocks the position in colour framing and segmentation sequences is shown. In PAL, the audio blocks only reflect the segmentation, whereas in NTSC the position in the five-field audio sequence (see Chapter 8) is shown. ID code is protected because it is part of the first codeword in the sync block.

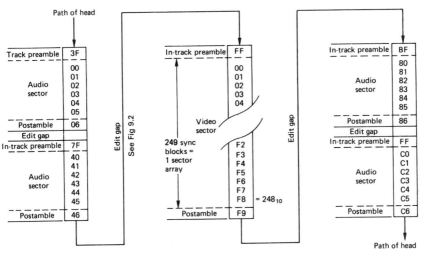

Figure 9.20(b) PAL ID numbering in the first byte of the ID code uniquely identifies every sync block in a sector. Second byte then determines which sector.

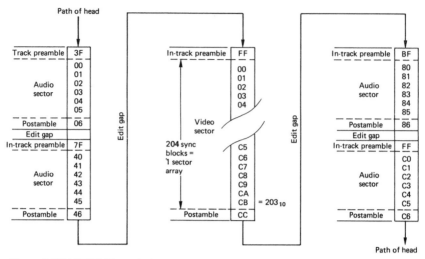

Figure 9.20(c) NTSC ID numbering in the first byte of the ID code uniquely identifies every sync block in a sector. Second byte then determines which sector.

9.17 Gaps, preambles and postambles

Each slant track in D-2 is subdivided into five sectors, two of audio at each end, and one of video in the centre. It is necessary to be able to edit any or all of the audio channels independently of the video. For this reason short spaces are left between the sectors to allow write current to turn on and off away from wanted data. Since the write current can only turn off at the end of a sector, it follows that the smallest quantum of data which can be written in the track at one time is a whole sector, although the smallest quantum which can be read is a sync block.

A preamble is necessary before the first sync block in a sector to allow the phase-locked loop in the data separator to lock. The preamble also contains a sync pattern and ID code so that the machine can confirm the position of the head before entering the sector proper. At the end of the sector a postamble containing an ID code is written before the write current is turned off. The pre- and postamble details can be seen in Figure 9.21.

The space between two adjacent sectors is known as an edit gap, and it will be seen in Figure 9.21 to begin with the postamble of the previous sector and end with the preamble of the next sector. Editing may result in a discontinuity nominally in the middle of the gap. There is some latitude, but the new recording must not begin so early that the postamble at the end of the previous sector is damaged, and at least 20 bytes of preamble must be written before the sync pattern at the beginning of the next sector, because it will not be possible to maintain continuity of bit phase at an edit, and the PLL must resynchronize.

In fact the length of the postamble, gap and preamble combined is exactly equal to the length of one sync block, which simplifies the design of the sequencer which controls the track recording. This is half the length of a gap in D-1, and is possible because the erase-head timing is independently controlled in D-2.

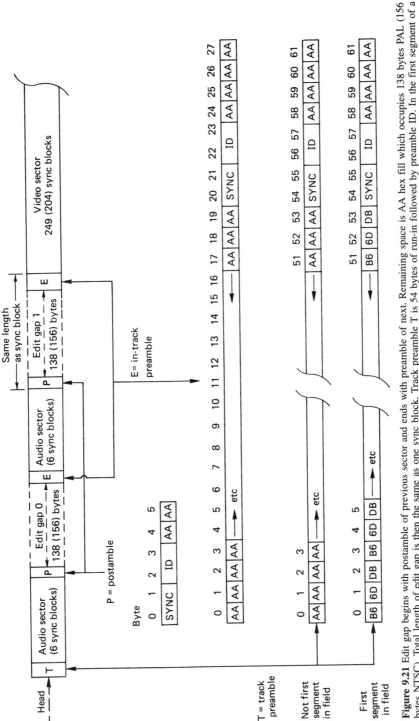

Figure 9.21 Edit gap begins with postamble of previous sector and ends with preamble of next. Remaining space is AA hex fill which occupies 138 bytes PAL (156 bytes NTSC). Total length of edit gap is then the same as one sync block. Track preamble T is 54 bytes of run-in followed by preamble ID. In the first segment of a field, run-in pattern is changed to B6, 6D, DB sequence (see Figure 9.19).

9.18 D-2 block diagram

Figure 9.22 shows a typical block diagram of the record section of a D-2 machine, where the inputs will consist of a composite video signal and four audio channels. Audio and video can be analog or digital, and most machines incorporate converters which can be bypassed if a digital input is available. Whichever input is used, the input video will always control the timing of the recording circuitry. In the case of a digital input, the $4 \times F_{sc}$ clock accompanying the data will be used to derive the symbol clock for much of the recorder. In the case of an analog input, the video burst will be fed to a phase-locked loop which generates the sampling clock locally.

The video data are distributed over two logical channels as was shown in Figure 7.8.

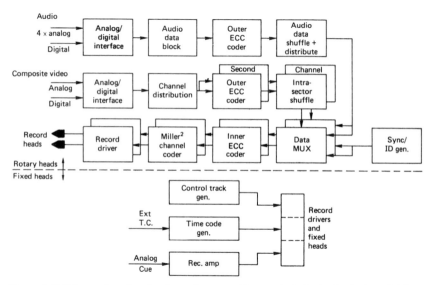

Figure 9.22 D-2 record section showing major stages. Note particularly the distribution of video over two channels, and the merging of the audio and video data into common inner coding circuits.

The distribution process results in each logical channel having half of the original number of samples in each line: 474 in PAL and 384 in NTSC. Each of these lines will be interleaved into six outer codewords, such that samples in the same codeword are six samples apart in the channel, and 12 samples apart on the television line. This is done by calculating the sample address along the line as a function of the block number and the byte number within the block. The first stage of the shuffle is obtained by changing the address calculation from line to line so that samples in the same place in an outer block on an adjacent line will have come from a different position along the line. This interleave/shuffle process results in blocks of 79 samples in PAL and 64 samples in NTSC. Then 4 bytes of Reed–Solomon redundancy are calculated on each block to make it into a codeword. The size of the outer codewords is equal to the height of the sector array memory, and outer codewords form columns in the sector array. Adjacent outer blocks do not form adjacent columns due to the second stage of the shuffle. In this, the column number is a function of the line number as well as the block number.

Eventually the sector array will be filled with columns of outer codewords, and it is then read in rows which are used to form inner codewords.

Each row results in six inner codewords, and two inner codewords are used in each sync block. The first codeword in the sync block is extended to protect the ID code and so it is 2 bytes longer than the second codeword.

There will be 249 video sync blocks in a PAL track and 204 video sync blocks in an NTSC track. In both channels, the reading of the sector array begins at the bottom, so that the four rows of outer code redundancy are placed at the beginning of the track. In the case of channel 0, readout continues in descending row order, but the memory readout sequence is modified for channel 1 so that a linear tape scratch crossing both tracks in the same place does not result in an identical corruption pattern in the two channels and so that a more random shuffle is effected in shuttle.

The audio processing is shown in parallel with the video processing, and uses a distribution scheme to spread samples in all channels over both heads and double recording to compensate for the fact that the audio blocks are small. This is explained more fully in Chapter 8.

The inner code generation, ID generation, serializing and Miller^2 channel coding are common to both audio and video, which effectively share the same circuitry, heads and tracks in a time multiplex.

At the beginning of a segment, the audio and video to be recorded have been interleaved and shuffled and are held in RAM so that they can be made available at the appropriate time.

Input to the serializer will initially be from the sync generator which produces the preamble at the beginning of the track. The serializer input then receives audio sync blocks until the end of the first audio sector, when the edit gap will be written. Following the preamble at the end of the edit gap, the second audio sector will be written, followed by another edit gap. After this edit gap, video sync blocks will be written, followed by a second edit gap and the second pair of audio sectors.

Figure 9.23 shows the replay system. Following the channel decoder, the sync detector phases the shift register in the deserializer so that the serial bit stream is correctly assembled into a parallel byte stream.

Inner blocks are checked by the inner decoder, which therefore also checks the ID code in the first inner block of a sync block. With 8 bytes of redundancy, the inner decoder could correct up to four random errors, but this would be at the expense of too many miscorrections. Accordingly, the inner code corrects up to three random errors, and a larger number are handled by declaring the entire inner code to be corrupt. An error flag is attached to every symbol in the block. Inner blocks are written into the sector array and de-shuffled, and any burst errors are converted to single-byte errors dotted around the array. These are accompanied by the error flags from the inner decoder, and so the 4 bytes of redundancy in the outer codes can correct four errors by erasure. If there are more than four error flags in an outer code, the symbols will be flagged as uncorrectable, and concealment must be used. When the two channels are combined the concealment process takes place.

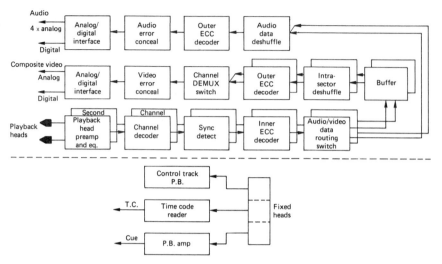

Figure 9.23 D-2 replay section. Two replay channels handle both audio and video as far as inner code error correction, and the data router then splits the audio and video to separate outer code processing.

The samples are now in their original sequence and can be output digitally or fed to a converter.

The audio samples are corrected by the inner and outer codes as for video, but as there are two copies of all audio data, any error-free data will be used to reassemble output samples.

9.19 The Ampex DCT format

The Ampex DCT (Digital Component Technology) format records data-reduced 8 bit 4:2:2 component video on a development of the D-2 transport. The intrafield data reduction system is based on the discrete cosine transform having eight pixel by four pixel blocks and uses approximately 2:1 reduction. The DCT transport is designed to be dual standard, which means that it can be configured from the control system menu to record either 525/60 or 625/50 signals. The same segmentation as D-2 is used, i.e. three segments per field for 60 Hz resulting in a drum speed of 90 Hz, and four segments per field for 50 Hz resulting in a drum speed of 100 Hz. It will be recalled that in D-2 the linear tape speed is independent of input standard and this required different track widths and heads. As DCT has a dual-standard transport, a common head width must be used and this is the same as in NTSC D-2. With 60 Hz input the same tape speed as D-2 is obtained, but with 50 Hz input the higher drum speed means that the linear speed will be higher and the playing time is slightly reduced.

Figure 9.24 shows that the track layout differs from D-2 in that the audio blocks are moved to the centre of the track between divided video blocks. As the data to be recorded have been data reduced, the error-correction system is correspondingly more powerful.

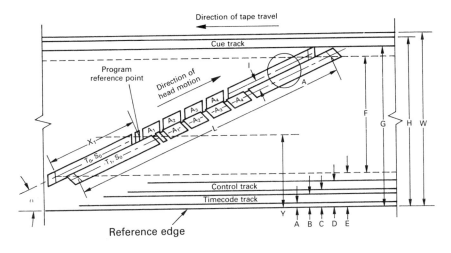

	DCT dimensions (mm)	Nominal	Tol (±)	Min	Max
A	Timecode track lower edge	0.2	0.1	0.1	0.3
B	Timecode track upper edge	0.7	0.1	0.6	0.8
C	Control track lower edge	1.0	0.1	0.9	1.1
D	Control track upper edge	1.5	0.05	1.45	1.55
G	Cue track lower edge	18.2	0.1	18.1	18.3
H	Cue track upper edge	18.9	0.1	18.8	19.0
	Head 1 track width	39.1	4	35.1	43.1
	Head 2 track width	39.1	4	35.1	43.1
	Head 3 track width	39.1	4	35.1	43.1
P1	Control track	160.720	0.3	160.420	161.020
P2	Cue/timecode track	160.720	0.3	160.420	161.020
	Flying erase head width 1/2 (μm)	79	5	84	74
	Flying erase head width 3/4 (μm)	79	5	84	74
	Erase head centring 1/2 (μm)	Centre	6	−6	6
	Erase head centring 3/4 (μm)	Centre	6	−6	6
X	Program ref. point	0	0.1	−0.1	0.1
	Tape speed – 525/60 (mm/s)	131.700	0.263	131.437	131.963
	Tape speed – 625/50 (mm/s)	146.459	0.293	146.166	146.752
Y	Ref. edge to program reference (mm)	8.500			

Figure 9.24 The dimensions of the DCT format.

Whilst further details of the format have not been released at the time of writing, from a conceptual standpoint the block diagram of the machine is broadly similar to that of Digital Betacam.

9.20 The D-3 format

The D-3 format is a composite digital format which records the same data as D-2. In fact dubs should be possible between two machines adhering to the composite digital interface standard described in Chapter 3. Whilst the data to be recorded are the same, there is otherwise little in common as D-3 uses ½ inch tape. The

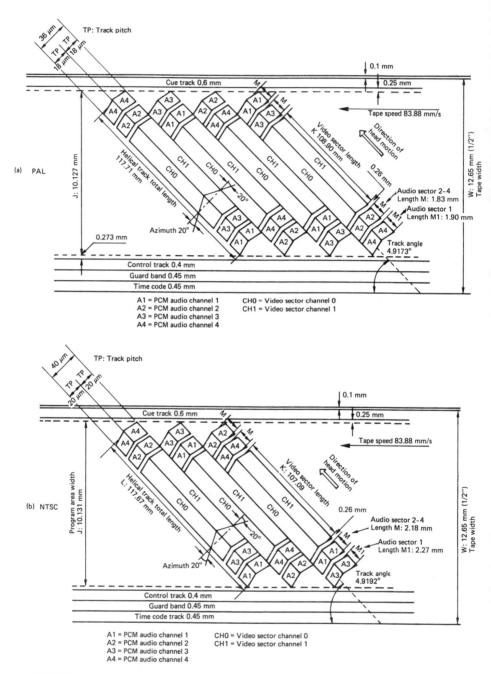

9.25 D-3 uses segmented recording where one video field is recorded on several tracks. At (a) the PAL format requires four segments or eight tracks for one field, whereas at (b) NTSC requires only three segments because the lower subcarrier frequency results in less data per line and there are fewer lines per field.

fundamental unit in the D-3 format is the segment, which consists of a pair of tracks, 0 and 1, one of each azimuth type. These can be seen in Figure 9.25. Note that the tracks are slanted the opposite way to D-2 because the tape descends the drum and is brought back to the cassette plane on the exit side. In D-2 the tape is taken below the cassette plane on the entry side and climbs the drum.

The first recorded track in a field is always a type 1 track, in which the azimuth is rotated anticlockwise by 19.983° from perpendicular when looking at the magnetic coating side of the tape. In a type 0 track, the azimuth is rotated 20.017° clockwise.

Figure 9.26(a) shows that in PAL, four segments holding the equivalent of 76 lines each record a total of 304 lines per field, whereas in NTSC, shown in Figure 9.26(b), three segments holding the equivalent of 85 lines each record a total of 255 lines per field. The segment and track numbering is also shown. It should be stressed that, unlike D-2, the data contained in a field are shuffled prior to segmentation, so the contents of a given segment could have come from anywhere in the field.

The control track necessary for segmented operation must convey segment, colour frame and frame information. Figure 9.26 also shows that the control track in PAL uses a 100 Hz waveform where the rising edge should occur coincident with a given scanner angle to allow capstan phase control. There are, however, three duty cycles which can be used in the control track waveform. A 50% duty

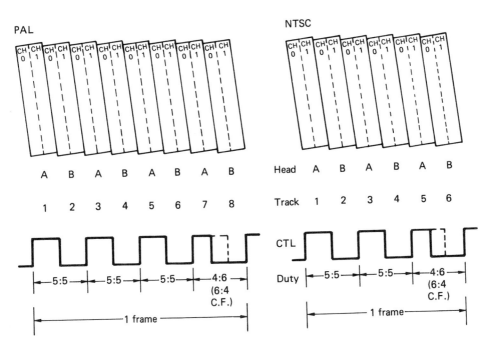

Figure 9.26 The D-3 control track uses one flux change per segment (or one cycle per scanner revolution). Normally the CTL duty cycle is 5:5 but at the end of every frame the duty cycle become 4:6 so that the segments can be put back in the correct frames. At the end of a colour frame, every two frames in NTSC or every four frames in PAL, CTL duty cycle changes to 6:4 to denote the colour frame flag.

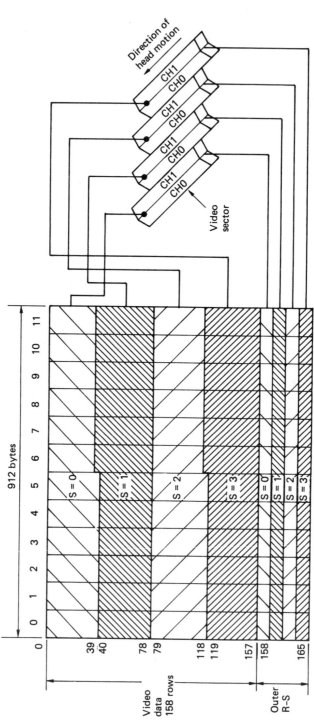

Figure 9.27(a) The field array of PAL D-3. Following distribution (Figure 9.36) the 948 samples per line become 474 samples per channel. Three columns of the array shown here hold 474 samples. Eight redundancy bytes are added to each column to form outer codes. The rows of the array are split into 12 parts and each has an ID pattern and redundancy added to make an inner code which occupies one sync block. The array is recorded on one of the tracks of four segments. The second array is recorded on the other tracks. Outer redundancy is recorded first in each track.

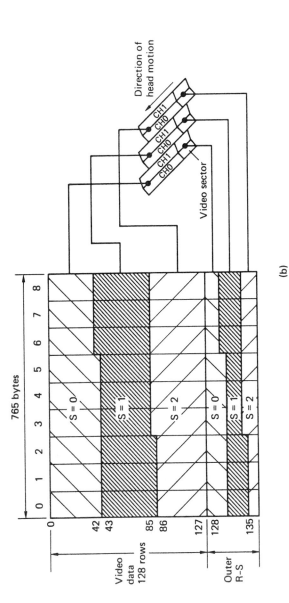

Figure 9.27(b) The field array of NTSC D-3. Following distribution (Figure 9.36) the 768 samples per line become 384 samples per channel. Three columns of the array shown here hold 384 samples. Eight redundancy bytes are added to each column to form outer codes. The rows of the array are split into nine parts and each has an ID pattern and redundancy added to make an inner code which occupies one sync block. The array is recorded in one of the tracks of three segments. Outer redundancy is recorded first in each track.

cycle indicates a segment pulse, whereas a 40% cycle indicates a frame pulse every eight segments, so that the segmentation can be properly reversed on replay. A 60% duty cycle indicates a colour frame pulse every four frames. In NTSC the frequency will be 90/1.001 Hz, frame pulses will be every six segments and the colour frame pulse will be every two frames.

9.21 The product code

Figure 9.27(a) shows the field array of D-3 PAL, and Figure 9.27(b) shows the equivalent in NTSC. Outer codes are vertical columns and three of these are necessary to contain the samples from one TV line after distribution. Data are recorded on tape by passing horizontally across the array to form inner codewords which are placed sequentially along the track. One row of the segment array is made into 12 inner code blocks in PAL and nine in NTSC, and this reduces error magnification due to small bursts. Each array will be recorded on four different tracks for PAL, three for NTSC. Two arrays are needed to record one field. Each array is recorded in tracks of the same azimuth type. The outer redundancy is distributed evenly over the tracks. Since the outer codes contain eight redundancy symbols, each can correct eight symbols by erasure. This corresponds to 8 bytes per column of the field array. The largest data loss which can be handled will be when this damage is experienced in every column of the array, so the maximum correctable burst-error size is given by multiplying the number of columns in the sector array by eight. The resulting figures are $912 \times 8 = 7296$ data bytes for PAL and $765 \times 8 = 6120$ data bytes for NTSC. These figures are for video data only; the actual size of the burst will be larger because the length of the track involved also contains sync and ID patterns and inner redundancy.

As the field array is spread over several tracks, the length of a correctable tape defect along the track depends upon the number tracks over which the defect spreads. Figure 9.28 shows that if the error is due to a helical scratch or a particle of debris passing under the head, it will be restricted to one track only and the correctable track length will be a maximum. If the defect is a linear tape scratch affecting all tracks, the correctable length of the defect is given by dividing the field array correction power by the number of tracks in which the array is recorded (three or four).

The maximum correctable single-track burst corresponds to about 19 mm of track length, or a longitudinal tape scratch of about 1.6 mm width.

If these conditions are exceeded, total correction is no longer possible, and rows of flagged erroneous data will appear in the field array. Concealment will become necessary and the concealment patterns are made irregular by the de-shuffle.

In shuttle, sync blocks will be recovered at random, and the shuffle means that when a sync block is successfully read, the pixels it contains are spread over the field, so the frame store will be updated all over instead of just in certain areas. The twinkling effect on picture-in-shuttle is caused by the shuffle.

9.22 Implementing the product code and shuffle – PAL

Whilst the same principles are used in both line standards, the parameters are different. To avoid confusion, this section contains the PAL parameters, whereas Section 9.23 contains the same text but with the parameters for NTSC.

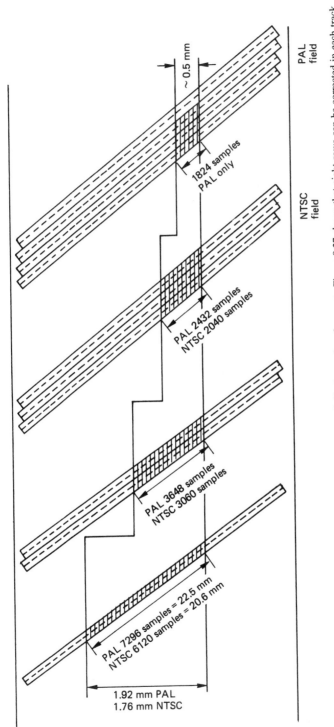

Figure 9.28 Error-correcting performance of D-3. For a single-segment helical scratch, reference to Figure 9.27 shows that eight rows can be corrected in each track by outer codes. This corresponds to 8 × 912 = 7296 samples (PAL) or 8 × 765 = 6120 samples (NTSC). In the case of a scratch along the tape, the maximum correction per field array must be divided by the number of tracks affected. In NTSC there are six tracks per field so a sustained scratch of 2040 samples can be corrected. In PAL there are eight tracks per field so a sustained scratch of 1824 samples can be corrected. This could be up to about 0.5mm wide.

The two-dimensional shuffle is obtained using two one-dimensional shuffles, one each side of the outer redundancy coder. The outer check bytes are not, however, shuffled, but are kept together so that they can be recorded at the beginning of the sectors.

There are two virtually identical channels running in parallel, one for each head, so the input to each process consists of half the samples from each of 304 lines. Each distributed line contains 474 samples, and these will be clocked into the process at $2 \times F_{sc}$.

Figure 9.29 shows one possible implementation of the shuffle process. Each TV line is split into a set of three outer blocks (Oblk). One outer block forms a column in the product code array, so there are three times as many columns as there are TV lines recorded ($304 \times 3 = 912$).

The incoming clock drives a divide-by-three counter which produces the parameter Oblk. As the outer block count changes between samples, successive samples in the input sequence will be distributed around the set of three outer blocks. As there is a two-channel distribution in addition to this process, samples in a given block will be six samples apart on the TV line.

The carry output of the divide-by-three stage drives an accumulator which adds 59 on each clock. The clock is also divided by 158 to provide a pulse once per line to reset the accumulator and clock the line counter.

The parameter Oblk is multiplied by 72, the line count is multiplied by 82 and these values are added to the accumulator output and the sum is expressed modulo-158. The result is a pseudo-random permuted row address where the incoming sample at that instant will be stored. This produces the vertical component of the shuffle. In order to produce a two-dimensional maximum distance shuffle, the column address is also permuted, but the horizontal shift stays the same for each TV line.

As an incoming line is distributed over three blocks, the parameter Oblk also needs to control the column address to put sequential input samples into three different columns. It will be seen from the figure that the line address and Oblk generate the column address. For a given TV line, the line address is constant, and the sequencing of Oblk will place samples in three complete columns.

Once the columns of the memory have been filled, the outer error correction coder can generate outer redundancy terms. Each column contains 158 samples, and 8 bytes of redundancy are added to make the column 166 symbols high.

The contents of the field array are written to four tape tracks by reading the array in rows and adding redundancy to produce inner codewords which occupy tape sync blocks. The 912 column array is split into 12 subarrays of 76 columns each. Reading across one subarray at a time produces 76 byte blocks to which 8 bytes of redundancy are added to make inner codewords. The addition of a sync pattern and ID code makes the codeword into a sync block. As there are 166 rows in the array and 12 sync blocks per row, there are a total of 1992 sync blocks to be recorded; 1896 of these are data and 96 are outer check symbols. As the outer redundancy is shared equally among the tracks, each records 498 sync blocks, 474 being data and 24 being outer code.

It will be seen from Figure 9.27(a) that the sync blocks are numbered beginning with 0 at top left in the field array and proceeding along rows.

The redundancy is recorded at the beginning of each track by selecting an appropriate sync block address in the memory which is a function of the segment address. In segment 0, the address will be 1896, the beginning of the outer check

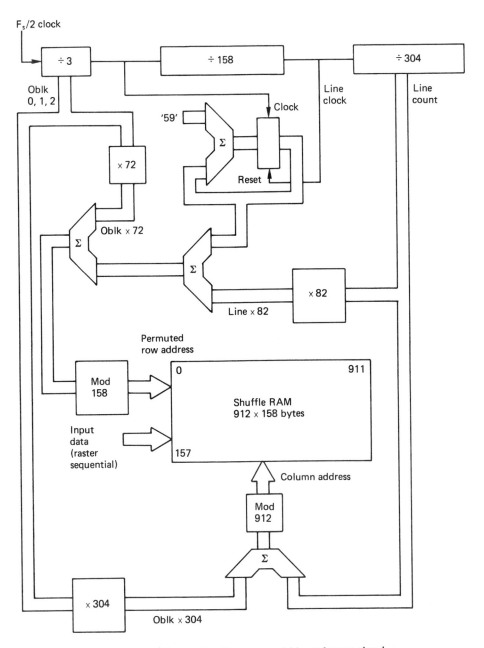

Figure 9.29 PAL D-3 shuffle implementation. Raster sequential input data are placed non-sequentially in the shuffle RAM by permuting row and column addresses to give a two-dimensional shuffle. See text for details.

symbols. As there are 24 outer check sync patterns in each track, the next segment will begin with address 1896 + 24 = 1920 and the one after that with 1896 + 48 and so on.

Following the recording of the outer check sync blocks at the beginning of the track, one-quarter of the data sync blocks (474) are recorded in the rest of the track. The starting sync block address is obtained by adding 474 times the segment address. The address is further modified by adding 711 for an odd track so that adjacent data in a track pair are non-adjacent on the screen. The starting address is further modified by the field number in the colour framing sequence in order to reduce the probability of stale data in shuttle.

As the 76 byte data contents of each sync block are read from the array memory, they are sent via the inner coder circuit which adds 8 bytes of inner check symbols. The inner coder is shared with the audio data.

9.23 Implementing the product code and shuffle – NTSC

The two-dimensional shuffle is obtained using two one-dimensional shuffles, one each side of the outer redundancy coder. The outer check bytes are not, however, shuffled, but are kept together so that they can be recorded at the beginning of the sectors.

There are two virtually identical channels running in parallel, one for each head, so the input to each process consists of half the samples from each of 255 lines. Each distributed line contains 384 samples, and these will be clocked into the process at $2 \times F_{sc}$.

Figure 9.30 shows one possible implementation of the shuffle process. Each TV line is split into a set of three outer blocks (Oblk). One outer block forms a column in the product code array, so there are three times as many columns as there are TV lines recorded ($255 \times 3 = 765$).

The incoming clock drives a divide-by-three counter which produces the parameter Oblk. As the outer block count changes between samples, successive samples in the input sequence will be distributed around the set of three outer blocks. As there is a two-channel distribution in addition to this process, samples in a given block will be six samples apart on the TV line.

The carry output of the divide-by-three stage drives an accumulator which adds 107 on each clock. The clock is also divided by 128 to provide a pulse once per line to reset the accumulator and clock the line counter.

The parameter Oblk is multiplied by 78, the line count is multiplied by 46 and these values are added to the accumulator output and the sum is expressed modulo-128. The result is a pseudo-random permuted row address where the incoming sample at that instant will be stored. This produces the vertical component of the shuffle. In order to produce a two-dimensional maximum distance shuffle, the column address is also permuted, but the horizontal shift stays the same for each TV line.

As an incoming line is distributed over three blocks, the parameter Oblk also needs to control the column address to put sequential input samples into three different columns. It will be seen from the figure that the line address and Oblk generate the column address. For a given TV line, the line address is constant, and the sequencing of Oblk will place samples in three complete columns.

Once the columns of the memory have been filled, the outer error-correction coder can generate outer redundancy terms. Each column contains

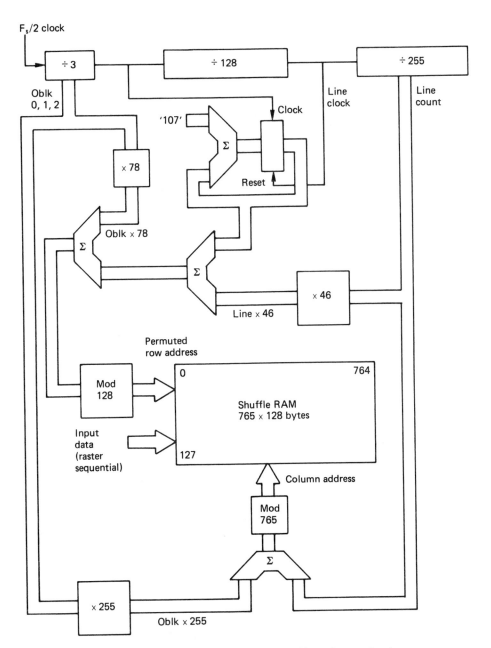

Figure 9.30 NTSC D-3 shuffle implementation. Raster sequential input data are placed non-sequentially in the shuffle RAM by permuting row and column addresses to give a two-dimensional shuffle. See text for details.

128 samples, and 8 bytes of redundancy are added to make the column 136 symbols high.

The contents of the field array are written to three tape tracks by reading the array in rows and adding redundancy to produce inner codewords which occupy tape sync blocks. The 765 column array is split into nine subarrays of 85 columns each. Reading across one subarray at a time produces 85-byte blocks to which 8 bytes of redundancy are added to make inner codewords. The addition of a sync pattern and ID code makes the code word into a sync block. As there are 136 rows in the array and nine sync blocks per row, there are a total of 1224 sync blocks to be recorded; 1152 of these are data and 72 are outer check symbols. As the outer redundancy is shared equally among the tracks, each records 384 sync blocks, 360 being data and 24 being outer code.

It will be seen from Figure 9.27 that the sync blocks are numbered beginning with 0 at top left in the field array and proceeding along rows.

The redundancy is recorded at the beginning of each track by selecting an appropriate sync block address in the memory which is a function of the segment address. In segment 0, the address will be 1152, the beginning of the outer check symbols. As there are 24 outer check sync patterns in each track, the next segment will begin with address 1152 + 24 = 1176 and the one after that with 1152 + 48 and so on.

Following the recording of the outer check sync blocks at the beginning of the track, one-third of the data sync blocks (384) are recorded in the rest of the track. The starting sync block address is obtained by adding 384 times the segment address. The address is further modified by adding 576 for an odd track so that adjacent data in a track pair are non-adjacent on the screen. The starting address is further modified by the field number in the colour framing sequence in order to reduce the probability of stale data in shuttle.

As the 85 byte data contents of each sync block are read from the array memory, they are sent via the inner coder circuit which adds 8 bytes of inner check symbols. The inner coder is shared with the audio data.

9.24 The D-3 sync block

The inner codes are designed to correct random errors and to detect the presence of burst errors by declaring the whole inner block bad. There is an optimum size for an inner code: too small and the redundancy factor rises; too large and burst errors are magnified, as are errors due to losing sync.

One row of the product block is too large to be one inner code, and so it is split into 12 or nine inner code blocks. The dimensions of these are chosen to give adequate correction performance. One sync block contains one inner codeword and an ID code; 12 or nine sync blocks then form one complete row of the sector array.

Figure 9.31(a) shows a PAL sync block. A 2 byte synchronizing pattern serves to phase the data separator and the deserializer. Following this is a 2 byte ID code which uniquely identifies this sync block in an eight-field sequence. The data block of 76 bytes then follows, and the 8 bytes of inner redundancy are calculated over the ID code as well as the data, so a random error in the ID can be corrected. The codeword is thus 86 bytes long. The entire sync block occupies about a quarter millimetre of track.

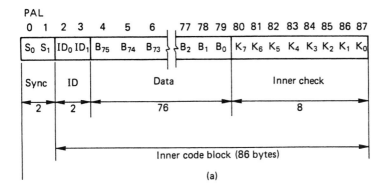

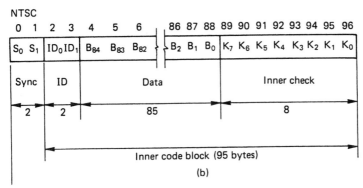

Figure 9.31 D-3 sync blocks (a) PAL and (b) NTSC. Each begins with the sync pattern 97F1 which is not randomized. The 2 byte ID, the data and the 8 bytes of inner check symbols are all randomized prior to EFM coding. The same block structure is used in both audio and video sectors.

Figure 9.31(b) shows an NTSC sync block. A 2 byte synchronizing pattern serves to phase the data separator and the deserializer. Following this is a 2 byte ID code which uniquely identifies this sync block in a four-field sequence. The data block of 85 bytes then follows, and the 8 bytes of inner redundancy are calculated over the ID code as well as the data, so a random error in the ID can be corrected. The codeword is thus 95 bytes long.

9.25 Synchronization and identification

Each sync block contains an inner codeword and is the smallest quantum of data on the track with which the playback channel can synchronize independently. Synchronization takes place on three levels: to the bit, to the symbol and to the sync block.

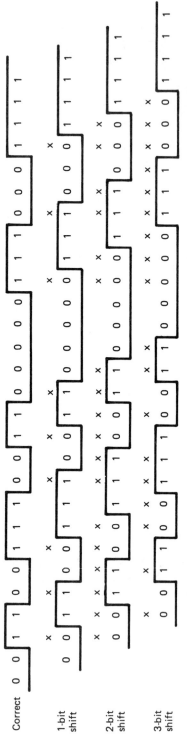

Figure 9.32 The sync pattern of D-3 is given by passing the 16 bit data pattern 97F1$_{16}$ through the EFM coder. This gives the waveform shown at top. This waveform has a variety of run lengths and it is unlikely that the pattern would be detected at the wrong time. It can be seen above that the difference between the correct timing and a variety of channel-bit shifts results in a large number of bit changes, shown by a cross.

Once bit synchronism has been achieved at the preamble, the serial data have to be correctly divided up into 14 bit symbols in order to decode the original samples. This is word synchronization, and is achieved by the unique pattern which occurs at the beginning of every sync block. Detection of this pattern resets the divide-by-eight counter which deserializes the data. It will also be used to preset the derandomizer to the correct starting value. The sync pattern of D-3 is $97F1_{16}$. Figure 9.32 shows that this pattern differs from itself shifted by as many bits as possible to reduce the possibility of false sync generation. Within a sector, sync patterns occur at regular spacing, so it is possible for the replay circuitry to predict the arrival of the sync pattern in a time window.

Once symbol synchronizing is achieved, it is then possible to read the inner code blocks, and the first 2 bytes contain the ID code and reveals which sync block has been recovered.

Figure 9.33(a) shows that the information recorded in the ID code is split into two parts. The first byte and bit 0 of the second is the 9 bit sync block number in the track; the remaining 7 bits of the second byte identify the sector. The V/A bit specifies whether the block is audio or video. The segment bits determine which segment out of four for PAL and three for NTSC is present, and the field bits specify the position in the eight- or four-field sequences to help colour framing.

Figure 9.33(b) shows the sync block numbering within the segment for PAL, and Figure 9.33(c) shows the equivalent for NTSC.

The ID bytes are randomized along with the data and redundancy in the sync block.

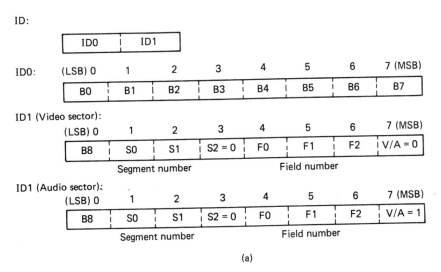

(a)

Figure 9.33(a) D-3 ID pattern consists of 2 bytes, ID0 and bit 0 of ID1 form a 9-bit block address. Bit 7 of ID1 is the video/audio flag and determines the type of sector. Remainder of the data carries field number (0–3 NTSC, 0–7 PAL) and segment number (0–2 NTSC, 0–3 PAL). Audio segment number requires only 2-bit code: thus S2 = 0.

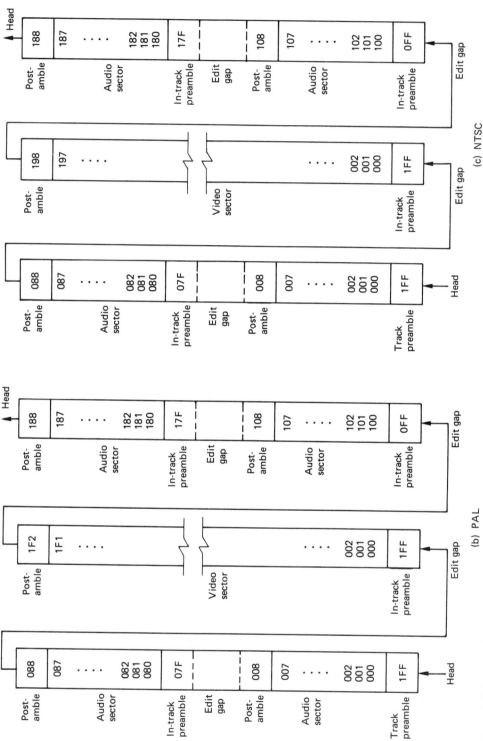

Figure 9.33(b) Showing ID code numbering to identify individually every sync block in the track. PAL video sector has more...

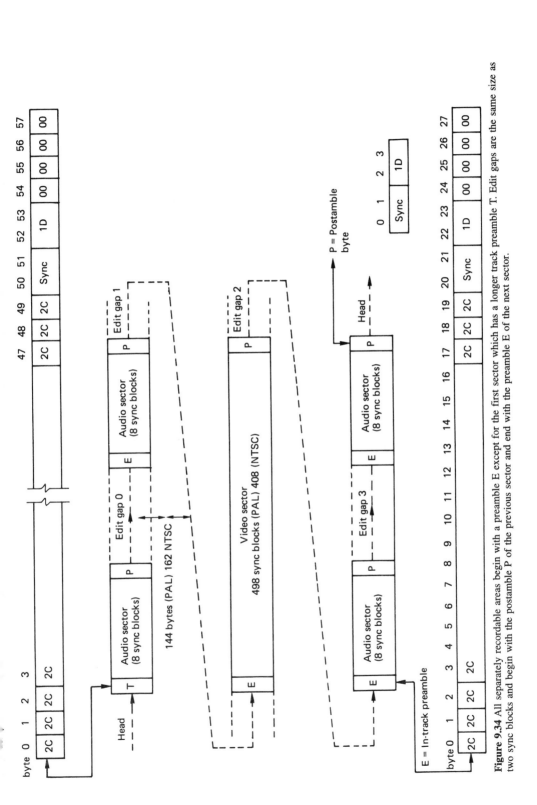

Figure 9.34 All separately recordable areas begin with a preamble E except for the first sector which has a longer track preamble T. Edit gaps are the same size as two sync blocks and begin with the postamble P of the previous sector and end with the preamble E of the next sector.

9.26 Gaps, preambles and postambles

Each slant track in D-3 is subdivided into five sectors, two of audio at each end, and one of video in the centre. It is necessary to be able to edit any or all of the audio channels independently of the video. As in other formats, edit gaps are left between the sectors to allow write current to turn on and off away from wanted data.

A preamble is necessary before the first sync block in a sector to allow the phase-locked loop in the data separator to lock. The preamble also contains a sync pattern and ID code so that the machine can confirm the position of the head before entering the sector proper. At the end of the sector a postamble containing an ID code is written before the write current is turned off. The pre- and postamble details can be seen in Figure 9.34.

The space between two adjacent sectors is known as an edit gap, and it will be seen in Figure 9.34 to begin with the postamble of the previous sector and end with the preamble of the next sector. Editing may result in a discontinuity nominally in the middle of the gap. There is some latitude, but the new recording must not begin so early that the postamble at the end of the previous sector is damaged, and at least 20 bytes of preamble must be written before the sync pattern at the beginning of the next sector, because it will not be possible to maintain continuity of bit phase at an edit, and the PLL must resynchronize.

In fact the length of the postamble, gap and preamble combined is exactly equal to the length of two sync blocks, which simplifies the design of the sequencer which controls the track recording.

9.27 Block diagram of a D-3 machine

Figure 9.35 shows a typical block diagram of the record section of a D-3 machine[6], where the inputs will be composite video and four audio channels. Audio and video can be analog or digital, and most machines incorporate converters which can be bypassed if a digital input is available. Whichever input is used, the input video will always control the timing of the recording circuitry. In the case of a digital input, the $4 \times F_{sc}$ clock accompanying the data will be used to derive the symbol clock for much of the recorder. In the case of an analog input, the video burst will be fed to a phase locked loop which generates the sampling clock locally.

The video data are distributed over two logical channels as shown in Figure 9.36.

The distribution process results in each logical channel having half of the original number of samples in each line: 474 in PAL and 384 in NTSC. Each of these lines will be interleaved into three outer codewords, such that samples in the same codeword are six samples apart on the television line. The first stage of the shuffle is obtained by changing the address calculation from line to line so that samples in the same place in an outer block on an adjacent line will have come from a different position along the line. This interleave/shuffle process results in blocks of 158 samples in PAL and 128 samples in NTSC. Then 8 bytes of Reed–Solomon redundancy are calculated on each block to make it into a codeword. The size of the outer codewords is equal to the height of the field array memory, and outer codewords form columns in the field array. Adjacent outer

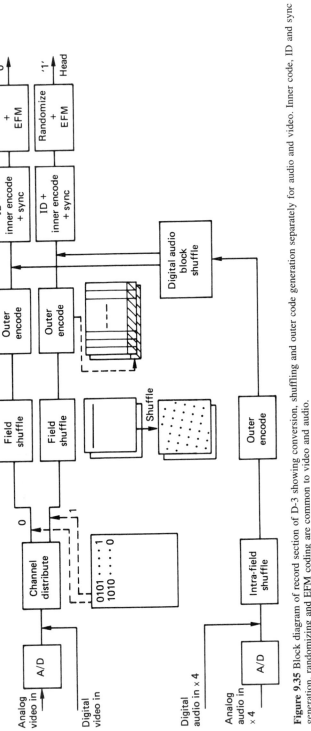

Figure 9.35 Block diagram of record section of D-3 showing conversion, shuffling and outer code generation separately for audio and video. Inner code, ID and sync generation, randomizing and EFM coding are common to video and audio.

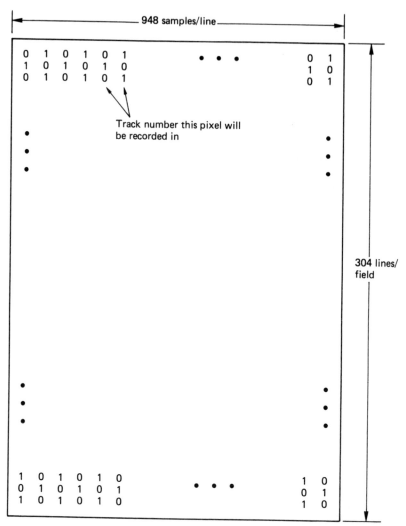

Figure 9.36 Distribution scheme for PAL D-3 (NTSC similar) shows that alternate pixels in two dimensions are recorded by alternate heads. Loss of one head signal allows interpolation from the remaining data.

blocks do not form adjacent columns due to the second stage of the shuffle. In this, the column number is a function of the line number as well as the block number.

Eventually the sector array will be filled with columns of outer codewords, and it is then read in rows which are used to form inner codewords.

Each row results in 12 or nine inner codewords, and one inner codeword is used in each sync block. The codeword is extended to protect the ID code.

There will be 498 video sync blocks in a PAL track and 408 video sync blocks in an NTSC track. In both channels, the reading of the field array begins at the bottom, so that the outer code redundancy is placed at the beginning of the track.

The memory readout sequence is modified for channel 1 so that a linear tape scratch crossing both tracks in the same place does not result in an identical corruption pattern in the two channels and so that a more random shuffle is effected in shuttle.

The audio processing is shown in parallel with the video processing, and uses a distribution scheme to spread samples in all channels over both heads and over 100% redundancy to compensate for the fact that the audio blocks are small. This is explained more fully in Chapter 8. There is no video-like shuffle, and a regular array is used to form a product block. Audio samples have longer wordlength than video samples, so the outer coding of the audio is somewhat different to the video, but the dimensions of the product block are such that the audio inner codewords are identical in size to the video inner codewords, so that common processing can be used.

As in most DVTRs, the inner code generation, ID generation, serializing, randomizing and channel coding are common to both audio and video, which effectively share the same circuitry, heads and tracks in a time multiplex.

At the beginning of a segment, the audio and video to be recorded have been interleaved and shuffled and are held in RAM so that they can be made available at the appropriate time.

Input to the serializer will initially be from the sync generator which produces the preamble at the beginning of the track. The serializer input then receives audio sync blocks until the end of the first audio sector, when the edit gap will be written. Following the preamble at the end of the edit gap, the second audio sector will be written, followed by another edit gap. After this edit gap, video sync blocks will be written, followed by a second edit gap and the second pair of audio sectors.

Figure 9.37 shows the replay system. The sync detector phases the shift register in the deserializer so that the serial bit stream is correctly assembled into 14 bit channel symbols for 14, 8 decoding and phases the derandomizer.

Inner blocks are checked by the inner decoder, which therefore also checks the ID code. The 14, 8 decoder can also generate error flags if a 14 bit channel pattern is detected which is not in the codebook. With 8 bytes of redundancy, the inner decoder could correct up to four random errors, but this would be at the expense of too many miscorrections. Using flags from the channel decoder helps to make the inner code more reliable. If the inner code correcting power is exceeded, this will be handled by declaring the entire inner code to be corrupt. An error flag is attached to every symbol in the block. Inner blocks are written into the field array and de-shuffled, and any burst errors are converted to single-byte errors dotted around the array. These are accompanied by the error flags from the inner decoder, and so the eight bytes of redundancy in the outer codes can correct 8 errors by erasure. If there are more than eight error flags in an outer code, the symbols will be flagged as uncorrectable, and concealment must be used. When the two channels are combined the concealment process takes place.

The samples are now in their original sequence and can be output digitally or fed to a converter.

The audio samples are corrected by the inner and outer codes as for video.

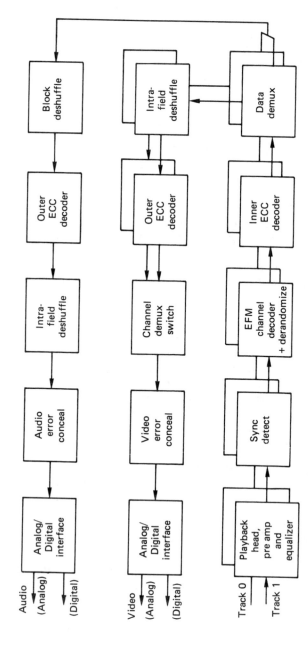

Figure 9.37 Replay block of D-3. Common circuitry is used for audio and video EFM demodulation and inner error correction. Data are then demultiplexed to separate audio and video signal paths.

9.28 The D-5 format

The D-5 format is actually two formats, one for each standard frame rate. The D-5 transport and much of the associated circuitry is designed in a generic manner so that various forms of input signal can be recorded after suitable formatting. The bit rate of about 300 megabits per second allows D-5 to record 525 or 625 line colour difference signals sampled to CCIR-601 without the use of data reduction. With 4:3 aspect ratio pictures having a luminance sampling rate of 13.5 MHz, 10 bit resolution is available; 16:9 aspect ratio pictures using a luminance sampling rate of 18 MHz can also be handled but with 8 bit resolution. With a suitable external data reduction unit, extended or high definition signals can be recorded.

A D-5 recorder is basically a double-speed D-3 machine which can also play D-3 format tapes if fitted with appropriate composite circuitry. For component recording, the scanner speed stays the same as in a D-3 machine of the same line standard, but the linear tape speed is doubled and extra heads on the scanner come into use, recording four tracks per segment as shown in Figure 9.38. The same length of tape is used in the cassettes and so the playing time will be halved in comparison with D-3.

The shortest recorded wavelength in D-5 is 0.64 µm which is shorter than that in D-3 which is 0.77 µm. In order to maintain signal quality, D-5 uses 1800 Oersted tape instead of the 1600 Oersted tape of D-3. It is intended that in the future only 1800 Oersted tape will be supplied for use with either format. The identification hole combinations in the cassette have been extended to cover the use of higher-coercivity tape.

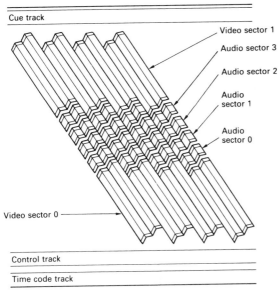

Figure 9.38 The D-5 format has four tracks per segment. Note edit gap alignment as per D-3 which allows quadruple-width erase head.

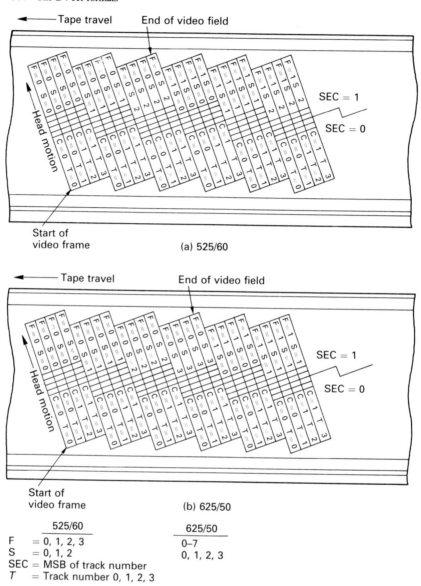

Figure 9.39 The segmentation of D-5. Each segment has four tracks, and three or four segments are necessary to record a field.

The segmentation of 525 line D-5 is shown in Figure 9.39(a) where it will be seen that three segments containing 12 tracks are required to record a field in one and a half drum revolutions. In 625 line D-5, shown in (b), four segments containing 16 tracks are required to record a field in two drum revolutions. The segment numbering scheme is also shown. The control track details are shown in Figure 9.40. Like D-3, the duty cycle of the control track pulses is changed for framing and colour framing purposes.

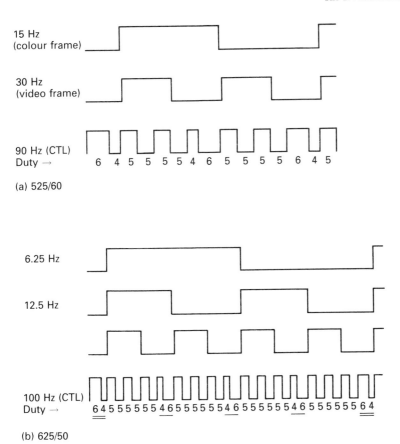

15 Hz
(colour frame)

30 Hz
(video frame)

90 Hz (CTL)
Duty →   6   4 5   5   5 5 4   6   5   5   5   5   6   4 5

(a) 525/60

6.25 Hz

12.5 Hz

100 Hz (CTL)
Duty →   6 4 5 5 5 5 5 5 4 6 5 5 5 5 5 5 4 6 5 5 5 5 5 5 4 6 5 5 5 5 5 5 6 4

(b) 625/50

Figure 9.40 The control track of D-5 uses duty cycle modulation for framing and colour framing; (a) shows the timing for 525/60 and (b) for 625/50.

The same audio data rate is required in D-3 and D-5, whereas the latter has twice as many tracks per unit time. As a result the audio blocks of D-5 are shorter. In addition the audio blocks have been moved to the centre of the tape where there is greater resistance to tracking error.

For simplicity the D-5 format has as much commonality with D-3 as possible. The same EFM channel coding is used with randomizing, and the same sync block structure is used containing an identical inner error-correcting code structure (see Section 9.24).

9.29 Input formatting

The processing of D-5 relies heavily on techniques developed for D-3 which is an 8 bit format. For simplicity, the processing of D-5 retains the 8 bit internal wordlength, but is based upon 18 MHz luminance sampling. In D-5, 16:9 input data can only be accepted with 8 bit wordlength, and these are handled directly; 4:3 inputs with a luminance sampling rate of 13.5 MHz can be accepted with 10 bit resolution, but require reformatting.

Input samples of 10 bits are split into two parts by removing the least significant 2 bits. The upper 8 bits are treated as a sample. The pairs of bits removed from four samples are assembled into an 8 bit pseudo-sample. The pairs of bits removed from the three samples (Y, C_R, C_B) in a co-sited pixel are arranged to be in the same pseudo-sample to minimize the effect of uncorrectable errors.

The 10 bit to 8 bit formatting is reversed on replay prior to the output, but within the machine data have an 8 bit structure.

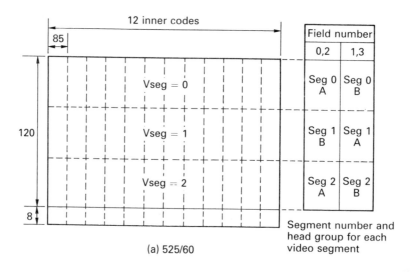

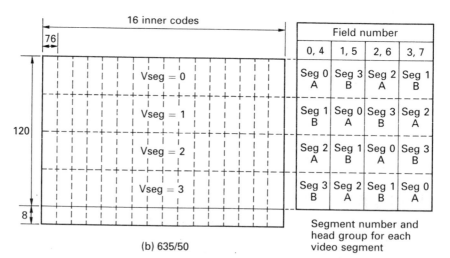

Figure 9.41 In 525/60 shown at (a) the data arrays are recorded in three segments, whereas at (b) data arrays in 625/50 are recorded in four segments. The segment numbering is rotated from one field to the next.

9.30 Distribution strategy

Distribution is designed to reduce the bit rate in a given channel and to permit effective concealment in the case of a head clog. Any distribution will reduce the bit rate, and so the distribution strategy is determined by the requirements of concealment. As the input to D-5 is component digital video, the constraints on distribution discussed in connection with the D-1 format are equally valid here.

In component video, alternate pixels are co-sited. An error in any one of the three samples in a co-sited pixel is potentially visible, but if all three samples are in error there is still only one pixel in error. It follows that samples from co-sited pixels should be recorded in the same channel and with the same head so that a head clog causes the minimum number of pixels to be lost. Loss of distributed samples would result in three times as many pixels in error. This approach is consistent with the requirement for picture-in-shuttle, in which sync blocks are recovered from tape randomly. If all three components are not present in the same sync block, pixels in the frame store cannot be updated properly.

From the distributed input samples in one field period the error correction strategy constructs four large, parallel Reed–Solomon product codes, one for each of the four channels. The D-5 drum carries two record-head bases, A and B, mounted 180° apart, and these each carry four heads, 0 through 3. Each half revolution of the drum sweeps four heads across the tape to create one segment. Although the tracks are interrupted physically by the central audio blocks, logically they are not, and one half revolution writes one video segment. In 525/60 one and a half revolutions are required to write one field using three video segments. In 625/50 two revolutions are required to write one field using four video segments. Figure 9.41 shows that one product block is carried in a track having the same position in three or four successive segments. The distribution process follows an algorithm which allocates incoming pixels on an individual basis to one of the four channels. Pixels are also distributed between the video segments so that the loss of a given tape track causes errors which are spread spatially over the whole field. The distribution process also ensures that if one head of the eight clogs, the pixels which are lost are surrounded by pixels which are recovered from the other seven heads.

Figure 9.42(a) shows how the input distribution works in 18 MHz mode. The incoming 4:2:2 data are demultiplexed into four sample types, Y_{odd}, Y_{even}, C_R and C_B and there will be 480 bytes of each type in one input line. These data are distributed over the four recording channels so that there will be 120 bytes in each. In 525/60, shown at (b), each line will be split into three parts, called subsegments, by the segmentation, whereas in 625/50, shown at (c), each will be split into four subsegments. The distribution process allocates incoming samples between the subsegments in such a way that adjacent input pixels will be recorded in a different segment. The four sample types form four adjacent columns in the product code.

Figure 9.43 shows how 10 bit samples are handled. The two LSBs from four input samples are assembled into 8 bit pseudo-samples.

Figure 9.44 shows the result of the distribution strategy of D-5 for both 525 and 625 line versions. The relationship between head and screen position is shown at (a). The effect of the loss of a single head is shown at (b). The luminance value of the missing pixel XX can be obtained by interpolation from

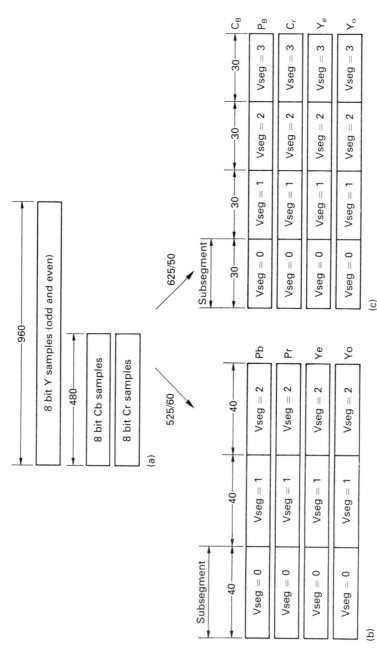

Figure 9.42 The input distribution scheme of D-5. Input pixels at (a) are demultiplexed into sample types. Samples are distributed over four channels and this diagram shows the distribution for one channel only. In 525/60, shown at (b), one quarter of the input line data of each sample type is divided into three subsegments. In 625/50, shown at (c) the division is into four subsegments. Each row here becomes a column in the main product code and so each subsegment will ultimately be recorded in a different tape segment.

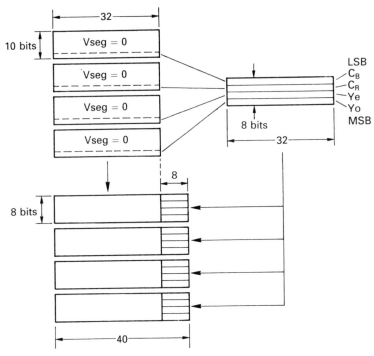

Figure 9.43 When ten-bit input data are supplied, the sampling rate is restricted to 13.5 MHz. This allows the data to be reformatted into 8 bit symbols by forming pseudo-samples from sets of 2 bits. Appending the pseudo-samples to the real samples results in the same subsegment structure as for 8 bit 18 MHz data. Example shown here is for 525/60; 625/50 is similar.

seven surrounding adjacent pixels shown in rectangles. The colour difference values accompany alternate luminance pixels, so concealment horizontally will be from pixels twice as far away, as shown in ellipses.

The effect of a three-head clog is shown at (c). Although three-eighths of the data are lost, concealment is still possible.

9.31 Error-correction strategy of D-5

Figure 9.45 shows the block diagram of a D-5 record channel and introduces the error correction system. Input samples are formatted into 8 bit data as shown in Section 9.29 and distributed over four channels as described in Section 9.30. A product code with two-dimensional shuffling is used as described in Chapter 7. The vertical dimension of the shuffle is known as intra-subsegment shuffling, which takes place after the input distribution.

Component digital video has no subcarrier, and large objects or flat fields give rise to areas of similar sample values. D-5 uses video randomizing prior to the error-correction system to increase the range of sample values to be recorded in comparison with the range of the input. Note that this video randomizing process is in addition to the randomizer in the channel coding process. The same randomizing polynomial is used (see Section 4.20) but the preset value of the

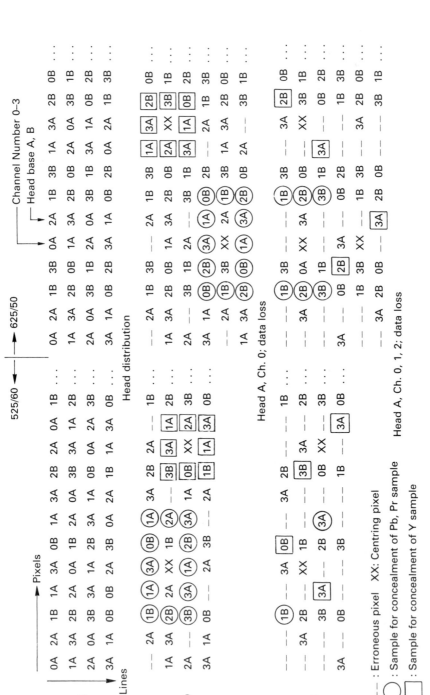

Figure 9.44 (a) Shows how input pixels are distributed over the eight heads in two sets of four. The result of a single head clog is shown at (b), where it will be seen that concealment is readily obtained. A three head clog is shown at (c) and concealment is still possible.

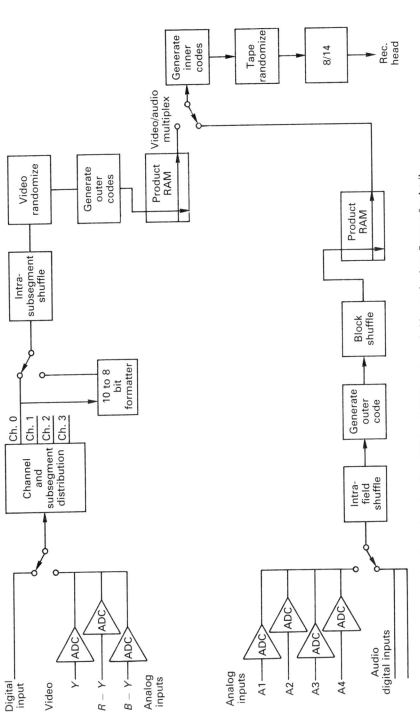

Figure 9.45 Block diagram of D-5 record section. Note 10 bit to 8 bit formatter and video randomizer. See text for details.

generator is changed as a function of the line number in order to prevent the two randomizers cancelling one another out. The effect of both randomizers together is effectively to eliminate the pattern sensitivity of the channel code so that the error rate is independent of picture content.

Following the vertical shuffle and randomizing, outer codewords are formed by adding redundancy to form columns in the product code. The horizontal component of the shuffle is obtained by writing the columns non-sequentially in the product code RAM.

The distribution of samples over the segments of four channels is carefully designed to give the best spatial relationship for concealment by keeping the samples corresponding to one pixel adjacent. In order to prevent the shuffle separating the samples from co-sited pixels, Y_{even}, C_R and C_B samples from the same line are subject to the same shuffle. Figure 9.46 shows how the data in each subsegment are shuffled by offsetting the memory address. The different shuffle of Y_{odd} samples can be seen.

The outer coder adds 8 bytes of redundancy to 120 byte input blocks and each is written into a column in the product code RAM. In both line standards, one line of input video is distributed over four adjacent columns in each product code. Data from the next line will not be written in the next four columns owing to the horizontal shuffling process. The column address is an algorithmic function of the line number so that adjacent lines of input video are recorded in widely separated sync blocks. The result of the vertical and horizontal shuffles in tandem is that all three samples of co-sited pixels remain on the same rows and in adjacent columns. When the RAM is read in rows they will be brought together in the same sync block.

Figure 9.41 showed the product code arrays for D-5. Four of these are required per field, one in each channel. Each row of the array is divided into 12 blocks of 85 bytes (525/60) or 16 blocks of 76 bytes (625/50). Each block is turned into an inner codeword by the addition of 8 bytes of redundancy. Inner codewords are

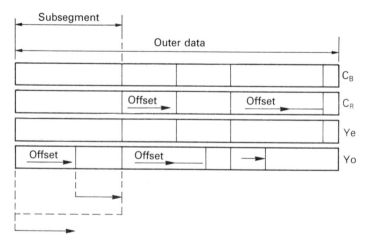

Figure 9.46 Intra-subsegment shuffling is achieved by offsetting the read address so that an end-around shift is obtained. Shown here is 525/60 case. Following this shuffle the subsegments are assembled into outer codewords.

recorded along the track as successive sync blocks. The sync blocks are identical to those used in D-3 and the channel coding scheme is also the same.

In 525/60 one and a half drum revolutions are required for a field and so the first segment of a field is naturally recorded alternately with A and B heads. This assists the use of interfield concealment. Two revolutions per field are required in 625/50 and so the head changeover does not occur naturally. It will be seen in Figure 9.41 that the same effect is obtained by reading video segments from the RAM in a different order in each field.

The audio data to be recorded are identical with those of D-3, and the product block formed on one field's worth of audio samples is the same. However, there are twice as many tracks in a field in D-5 and so the product block is distributed differently. In the 525 line version, the audio product block of each channel is recorded as 48 sync blocks distributed over 12 tracks which each contain an audio sector of four sync blocks. In the 625 line version the audio block is

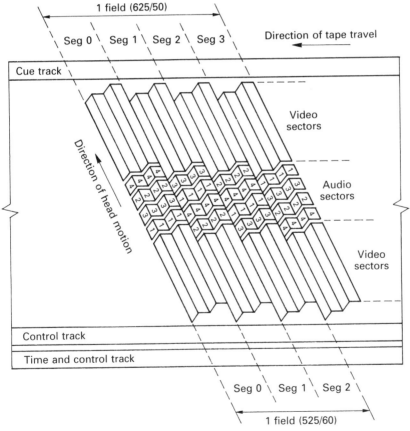

Figure 9.47 The audio channels are recorded in different sectors from segment to segment over a four-segment sequence in order to reduce the effect of tape scratches. Within the segment, the audio for a given channel is in the same sector to ease insert editing.

recorded as 64 sync blocks distributed over 16 tracks, again in audio sectors of four sync blocks. Figure 9.47 shows how the audio channel numbers are permuted throughout the field to resist tape scratches.

9.32 Synchronization and identification

The recording density of D-5 is higher than in D-3 and there are more sync blocks in each track. In addition there are now four tracks in a segment. The ID scheme of D-3 cannot accommodate the greater number of sync blocks, and so a new numbering scheme, shown in Figure 9.48, has been devised.

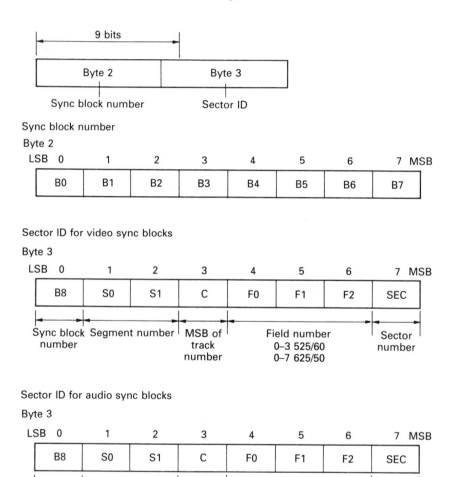

Figure 9.48 The ID code details of D-5. The sync block number requires 9 bits. Note the field number in video sectors is for colour framing. In audio the five field sequence of audio samples with respect to 59.94 field rate is recorded.

The ID code consists of 2 bytes which are broken into a 9 bit sync block number and a 7 bit sector ID as before. In D-3 the sector ID format had a bit which distinguished audio and video sectors. The bit in this position is now called the sector bit and is used to distinguish between the first and second halves of the

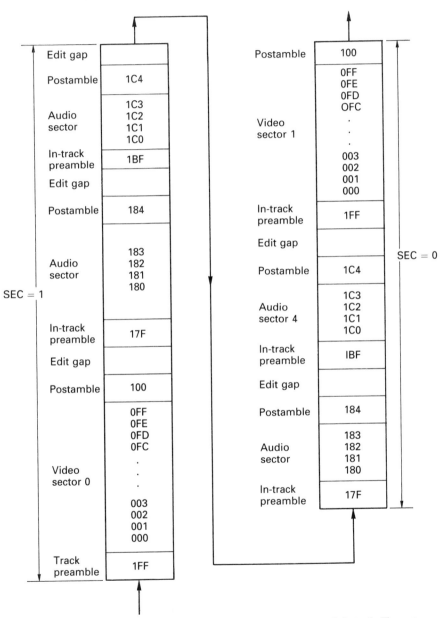

Figure 9.49 The sync block numbering scheme of D-5 depicted over one whole track. The sector number resolves ambiguity as block numbers are used twice. The number of sync blocks is the same in 525 and 625 line versions.

segment. The sector bit can be thought of as an extra sync address bit which doubles the address range. Each half contains one video block and two audio blocks. Audio and video are distinguished solely by having different sync block number ranges.

In D-3 there were two tracks per segment, and the use of azimuth recording meant that it was impossible to confuse the two tracks and no track number appeared in the ID. In D-5 there are four tracks per segment and so it is possible for the heads of two azimuth types to register with the tracks in two ways. Thus sector ID contains a bit which distinguishes the two azimuth pairs in the segment. This is the MSB of the track number within the segment.

The field and segment numbering scheme remains the same as in D-3.

Figure 9.49 shows the sync block numbering scheme throughout the track. There are the same number of sync blocks in both line standards. Note that each address appears twice; the sector bit resolves the ambiguity.

9.33 Digital Betacam

Digital Betacam (DB) is a component format which accepts 8 or 10 bit 4:2:2 data with 720 luminance samples per active line and four channels of 48 kHz digital audio having up to 20 bit wordlength. Video data reduction based on the discrete cosine transform is employed, with a compression factor of almost two to one (assuming 8 bit input). The audio data are uncompressed. The cassette shell of the $\frac{1}{2}$ inch analog Betacam format is retained, but contains 14 micrometre metal particle tape. The digital cassette contains an identification hole which allows the transport to identify the tape type. Unlike the other digital formats, only two cassette sizes are available. The large cassette offers 124 minutes of playing time; the small cassette plays for 40 minutes.

Owing to the trade off between SNR and bandwidth, which is a characteristic of digital recording, the tracks must be longer than in the analog Betacam format, but narrower. The drum diameter of the DB transport is 81.4 mm which is designed to produce tracks of the required length for digital recording. The helix angle of the digital drum is designed such that when an analog Betacam tape is driven past at the correct speed, the track angle is correct. Certain DB machines are fitted with analog heads which can trace the tracks of an analog tape. As the drum size is different, the analog playback signal is time compressed by about 9%, but this is easily dealt with in the timebase-correction process.[7] The fixed heads are compatible with the analog Betacam positioning. The reverse compatibility is for playback only; the digital machine cannot record on analog cassettes.

Figure 9.50 shows the track patterns for 525/60 and 625/50 Digital Betacam. The four digital audio channels are recorded in separate sectors of the slant tracks, and so one of the linear audio channels of the analog format is dispensed with, leaving one linear audio track for cueing.

Azimuth recording is employed, with two tracks being recorded simultaneously by adjacent heads. Electronic delays are used to align the position of the edit gaps in the two tracks of a segment, allowing double-width flying erase heads to be used. Three segments are needed to record one field, requiring one and a half drum revolutions. Thus the drum speed is three times that of the analog format. However, the track pitch is less than one-third that of the analog format, so the linear speed of the digital tape is actually slower. In 625/50, the track width

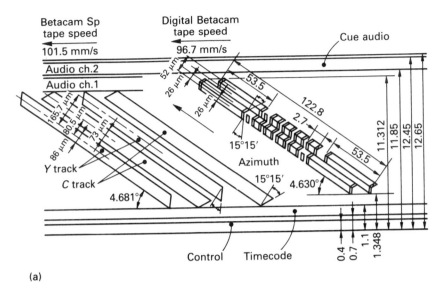

(a)

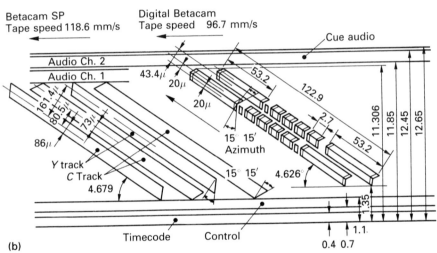

(b)

Figure 9.50 The track pattern of Digital Betacam, (a) for 625/50 and (b) for 525/60. Control and timecode tracks are identical in location to the analog format, as is the single analog audio cue track. Note the use of a small guard band between segments.

is 24 micrometres, with a 4 micrometre guard band between segments making the effective track pitch 26 micrometres, whereas in 525/60 the track width is 20 micrometres with a 3.4 micrometre guard band between segments making an effective track pitch of 21.7 micrometres. These figures should be compared with 18 micrometres for D-3/D-5 and 39 micrometres for D-2/DCT.

There is a linear timecode track whose structure is identical to the analog Betacam timecode and a control track shown in Figure 9.51 having a fundamental frequency of 50 Hz. Ordinarily the duty cycle is 50%, but this

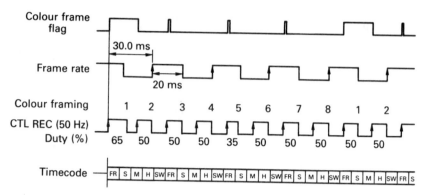

Figure 9.51 The control track of Digital Betacam uses duty cycle modulation for colour framing purposes.

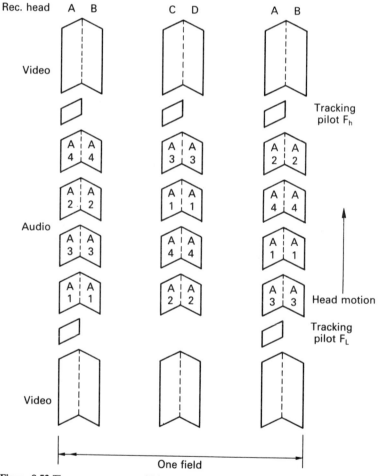

Figure 9.52 The sector structure of Digital Betacam. Note the tracking tones between the audio and video sectors which are played back for alignment purposes during insert edits.

changes to 65/35 in field 1 and 35/65 in field 5. The rising edge of the CTL signal coincides with the first segment of a field, and the duty cycle variations allow four- or eight-field colour framing if decoded composite sources are used. As the drum speed is 75 Hz, CTL and drum phase coincides every three revolutions.

Figure 9.52 shows the track layout in more detail. Unlike other digital formats, DB incorporates tracking pilot tones recorded between the audio and video sectors. The first tone has a frequency of approximately 4 MHz and appears once per drum revolution. The second is recorded at approximately 400 KHz and appears twice per drum revolution. The pilot tones are recorded when a recording is first made on a blank tape, and will be re-recorded following an assemble edit, but during an insert edit the tracking pilots are not re-recorded, but used as a guide to the insertion of the new tracks.

The amplitude of the pilot signal is a function of the head tracking. The replay heads are somewhat wider than the tracks, and so a considerable tracking error will have to be present before a loss of amplitude is noted. This is partly offset by the use of a very long-wavelength pilot tone in which fringing fields increase the effective track width. The low-frequency tones are used for automatic playback tracking.

With the tape moving at normal speed, the capstan phase is changed by steps in one direction and then the other as the pilot tone amplitude is monitored. The phase which results in the largest amplitude will be retained. During the edit preroll the record heads play back the high-frequency pilot tone and capstan phase is set for largest amplitude. The record heads are the same width as the tracks and a short-wavelength pilot tone is used such that any mistracking will cause immediate amplitude loss. This is an edit optimize process and results in new tracks being inserted in the same location as the originals. As the pilot tones are played back in insert editing, there will be no tolerance build-up in the case of multiple inserts.

The data reduction of DB[8] works on an intrafield basis to allow complete editing freedom and uses processes described in Chapter 4.

9.34 Block diagram of Digital Betacam

Figure 9.53 shows a block diagram of the record section of DB. Analog component inputs are sampled at 13.5 and 6.75 MHz. Alternatively the input may be SDI at 270 Mbits/s which is deserialized and demultiplexed to separate components. The raster scan input is first converted to blocks which are eight pixels wide by four pixels high in the luminance channel and four pixels by four in the two colour difference channels. When two fields are combined on the screen, the result is effectively an interlaced 8×8 luminance block with colour difference pixels having twice the horizontal luminance pixel spacing. The pixel blocks are then subject to a field shuffle. A shuffle based on individual pixels is impossible because it would raise the high frequency content of the image and destroy the power of the data reduction process. Instead the block shuffle helps the data reduction by making the average entropy of the image more constant. This happens because the shuffle exchanges blocks from flat areas of the image with blocks from highly detailed areas. The shuffle algorithm also has to consider the requirements of picture-in-shuttle. The blocking and shuffle take place when the read addresses of the input memory are permuted with respect to the write addresses.

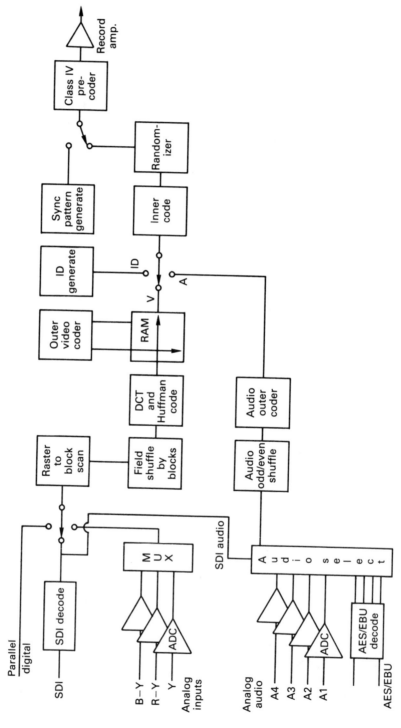

Figure 9.53 Block diagram of Digital Betacam record channel. Note that the use of data reduction makes this rather different to the block layout of full-bit formats.

Following the input shuffle the blocks are associated into sets of ten in each component and are then subject to the discrete cosine transform. The resulting coefficients are then subject to an iterative requantizing process followed by variable-length coding. The iteration adjusts the size of the quantizing step until the overall length of the ten coefficient sets is equal to the constant capacity of an entropy block, which is 364 bytes. Within that entropy block the amount of data representing each individual DCT block may vary considerably, but the overall block size stays the same.

The DCT process results in coefficients whose wordlength exceeds the input wordlength. As a result it does not matter if the input wordlength is 8 bits or 10 bits; the requantizer simply adapts to make the output data rate constant. Thus the compression is greater with 10 bit input, corresponding to about 2.4 to 1.

The next step is the generation of product codes as shown in Figure 9.54(a). Each entropy block is divided into two halves of 162 bytes each and loaded into

(a) Video ... 12 ECC blocks/field (2 ECC blocks/track)

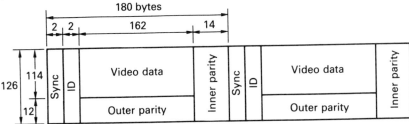

(b) Audio ... 2 ECC blocks/ (CH. × field)

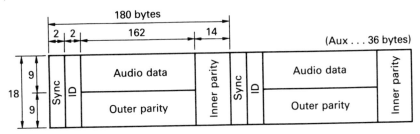

(c) Sync block

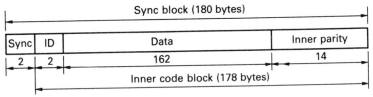

Figure 9.54 Video product codes of Digital Betacam are shown at (a); 12 of these are needed to record one field. Audio product codes are shown at (b); two of these record samples corresponding to one field period. Sync blocks are common to audio and video as shown at (c). The ID code discriminates between video and audio channels.

the rows of the outer code RAM which holds 114 such rows, corresponding to one-twelfth of a field. When the RAM is full, it is read in columns by address mapping and 12 bytes of outer Reed–Solomon redundancy are added to every column, increasing the number of rows to 126.

The outer code RAM is read out in rows once more, but this time all 126 rows are read in turn. To the contents of each row is added a 2 byte ID code and then the data plus ID bytes are turned into an inner code by the addition of 14 bytes of Reed–Solomon redundancy.

Inner codewords pass through the randomizer and are then converted to serial form for Class-IV partial response precoding. With the addition of a sync pattern of 2 bytes, each inner codeword becomes a sync block as shown in Figure 9.54(c). Each video block contains 126 sync blocks, preceded by a preamble and followed by a postamble. One field of video data requires 12 such blocks. Pairs of blocks are recorded simultaneously by the parallel heads of a segment. Two video blocks are recorded at the beginning of the track, and two more are recorded after the audio and tracking tones.

The audio data for each channel are separated into odd and even samples for concealment purposes and assembled in RAM into two blocks corresponding to one field period. Two 20 bit samples are stored in 5 bytes. Figure 9.54(b) shows that each block consists of 1458 bytes including auxiliary data from the AES/EBU interface, arranged as a block of 162×9 bytes. Outer code redundancy of 100% is obtained by adding 9 Reed–Solomon check bytes to each column of the blocks.

The inner codes for the audio blocks are produced by the same circuitry as the video inner codes on a timeshared basis. The resulting sync blocks are identical in size and differ only in the provision of different ID codes. The randomizer and precoder are also shared. It will be seen from Figure 9.52 that there are three segments in a field and that the position of an audio sector corresponding to a particular audio channel is different in each segment. This means that damage due to a linear tape scratch is distributed over three audio channels instead of being concentrated in one.

Each audio product block results in 18 sync blocks. These are accommodated in audio sectors of six sync blocks each in three segments. The audio sectors are preceded by preambles and followed by postambles. Between these are edit gaps which allow each audio channel to be independently edited.

By spreading the outer codes over three different audio sectors the correction power is much improved because data from two sectors can be used to correct errors in the third.

Figure 9.55 shows the replay channel of DB. The RF signal picked up by the replay head passes first to the Class IV partial response playback circuit in which it becomes a three level signal as was shown in Chapter 4. The three-level signal is passed to an ADC which converts it into a digitally represented form so that the Viterbi detection can be carried out in logic circuitry. The sync detector identifies the synchronizing pattern at the beginning of each sync block and resets the block bit count. This allows the entire inner codeword of the sync block to be deserialized into bytes and passed to the inner error checker. Random errors will be corrected here, whereas burst errors will result in the block being flagged as in error.

Sync blocks are written into the de-interleave RAM with error flags where appropriate. At the end of each video sector the product code RAM will be filled,

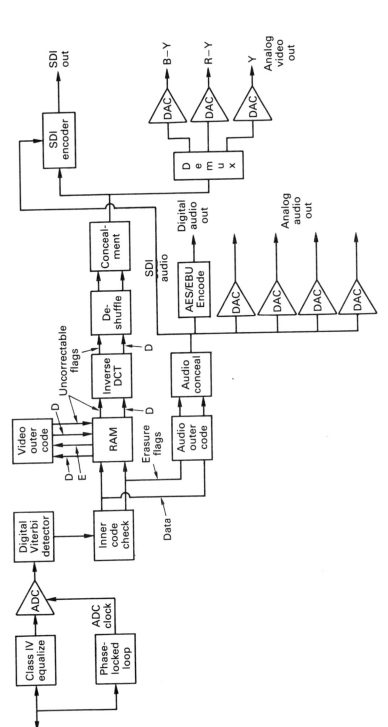

Figure 9.55 The replay channel of Digital Betacam. This differs from a full-bit system primarily in the requirement to deserialize variable-length coefficient blocks.

and outer code correction can be performed by reading the RAM at right angles and using the error flags to initiate correction by erasure. Following outer code correction the RAM will contain corrected data or uncorrectable error flags which will later be used to initiate concealment.

The sync blocks can now be read from memory and assembled in pairs into entropy blocks. The entropy block is of fixed size, but contains coefficient blocks of variable length. The next step is to identify the individual coefficients and separate the luminance and colour difference coefficients by decoding the Huffman-coded sequence. Following the assembly of coefficient sets the inverse DCT will result in pixel blocks in three components once more.

The pixel blocks are de-shuffled by mapping the write address of a field memory. When all of the tracks of a field have been decoded, the memory will

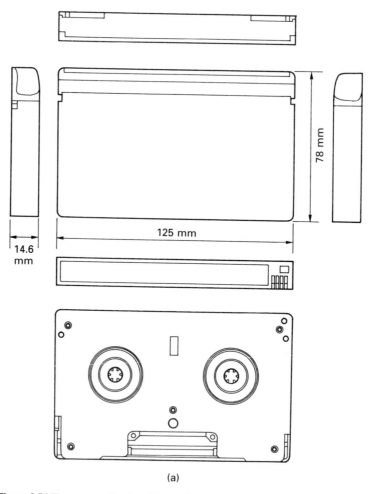

(a)

Figure 9.56 The cassettes developed for the ¼ inch DVC format. At (a) the standard cassette which holds 4.5 hours of program material. The small cassette, shown at (b) is intended for miniature equipment and plays for 1 hour.

contain a de-shuffled field containing either correct sample data or correction flags. By reading the memory without address mapping the de-shuffled data are then passed through the concealment circuit where flagged data are concealed by data from nearby in the same field or from a previous field. The memory readout process is buffered from the offtape timing by the RAM and as a result the timebase-correction stage is inherent in the replay process. Following conceal-ment the data can be output as conventional raster scan video either formatted to parallel or serial digital standards or converted to analog components.

9.35 The DVC Format

This component format uses quarter-inch wide metal evaporated (ME) tape which is only 7 micrometres thick in conjunction with data reduction to allow realistic playing times in miniaturized equipment. The format has jointly been developed by all the leading VCR manufacturers. Whilst intended as a consumer

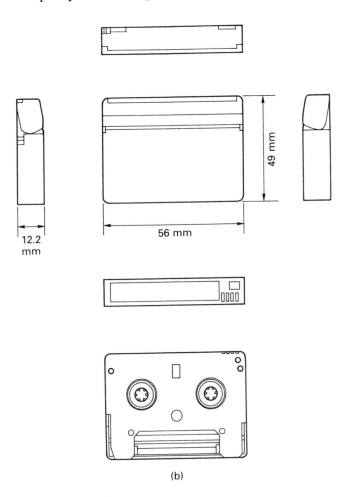

(b)

Figure 9.56 Continued.

format there is no doubt that it will also be used professionally for applications such as news gathering and simple production because of the low cost and small size. In addition to component video there are also two channels of 16-bit uniformly-quantized digital audio at 32, 44.1 or 48 kHz, with an option of four audio channels using 12-bit non-uniform quantizing at 32 kHz.

Figure 9.56 shows that two cassette sizes are supported. The standard size cassette offers 4½ hours of recording time and yet is only a little larger than an audio Compact Cassette. The small cassette is even smaller than an RDAT cassette yet plays for one hour. Machines designed to play both tape sizes will be equipped with moving reel motors. Both cassettes are equipped with fixed identification tabs and a moveable write-protect tab. These tabs are sensed by switches in the transport.

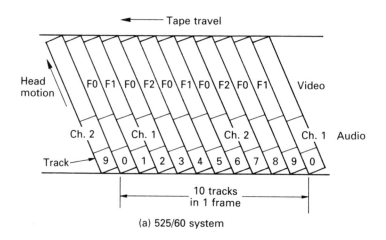

(a) 525/60 system

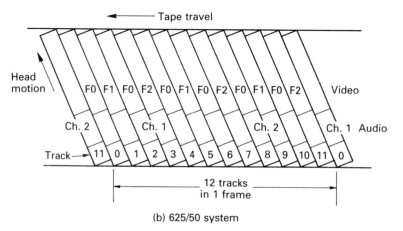

(b) 625/50 system

Figure 9.57 In order to use a common transport for 50 and 60 Hz standards the segmentation shown here is used. The segment rate is constant but 10 or 12 segments can be used in a frame.

DVC (Digital Video Cassette) has adopted many of the features first seen in small formats such as the RDAT digital audio recorder and the 8 mm analog video tape format. Of these the most significant is the elimination of the control track permitted by recording tracking signals in the slant tracks themselves. The adoption of metal evaporated tape and embedded tracking allows extremely high recording density. Tracks recorded with slant azimuth are only 10 μm wide and the minimum wavelength is only 0.49 μm resulting in a superficial density of over 0.4 Megabits per square millimetre.

Segmentation is used in DVC in such a way that as much commonality as possible exists between 50 and 60 Hz versions. The transport runs at 300 tape tracks per second; Figure 9.57 shows that 50 Hz frames contain 12 tracks and 60 Hz frames contain 10 tracks.

9.36 Tracking in DVC

The tracking mechanism relies upon buried tones in the slant tracks. From a tracking standpoint there are three types of track shown in Figure 9.58; F_0, F_1 and F_2. F_1 contains a low-frequency pilot and F_2 contains a high frequency pilot. F_0 contains no pilot tone, but the recorded data spectrum contains notches at the frequencies of the two tones. Figure 9.57 also shows that every other track will contain F_0 following a four-track sequence.

The embedded tracking tones are recorded throughout the track using the technique described in Section 4.19. Every 24 data bits an extra bit is added whose value has no data meaning but whose polarity affects the average voltage of the waveform. By controlling the average voltage with this bit, low frequencies can be introduced into the channel coded spectrum to act as tracking tones. The tracking tones have sufficiently long wavelength that they are not affected by head azimuth and can be picked up by the 'wrong' head. When a head is following an F_0 type track, one edge of the head will detect F_1 and the other edge will detect F_2. If the head is centralized on the track, the amplitudes of the two tones will be identical. Any tracking error will result in the relative amplitudes of the F_1 F_2 tones changing. This can be used to modify the capstan phase in order to correct the tracking error. As azimuth recording is used requiring a minimum of two heads, one head of the pair will always be able to play a type F_0 track.

In simple machines only one set of heads will be fitted and these will record or play as required. In more advanced machines, separate record and replay heads will be fitted. In this case the replay head will read the tracking tones during normal replay, but in editing modes, the record head would read the tracking tones during the pre-roll in order to align itself with the existing track structure.

9.37 DVC track layout

Figure 9.59 shows the track dimensions. The tracks are approximately 33 mm long and lie at approximately 9 degrees to the tape edge. A transport with a 180 degree wrap would need a drum of only 21 mm diameter. For camcorder applications with the small cassette this would allow a transport no larger than an audio 'Walkman'. With the larger cassette it would be advantageous to use time

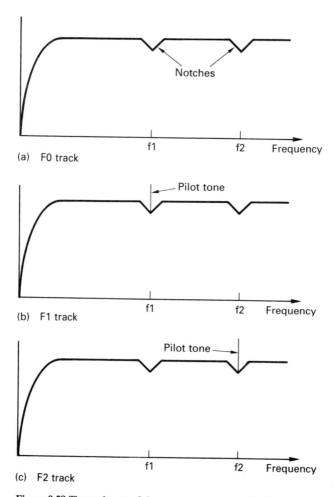

(a)   F0 track

(b)   F1 track

(c)   F2 track

Figure 9.58 The tracks are of three types shown here. The F_0 track (a) contains spectral notches at two selected frequencies. The other two track types (b), (c) place a pilot tone in one or other of the notches.

compression as shown in Section 6.5 to allow a larger drum with partial wrap to be used. This would simplify threading and make room for additional heads in the drum for editing functions.

The audio, video and subcode data are recorded in three separate sectors with edit gaps between so that they can be independently edited in insert mode. In the case where all three data areas are being recorded in insert mode, there must be some mechanism to keep the new tracks synchronous with those which are being overwritten. In a conventional VTR this would be the job of the control track.

In DVC there is no control track and the job of tracking during insert is undertaken by part of each slant track. Figure 9.59 shows that the track begins with the insert and track information (ITI) block. During an insert edit the ITI block in each track is always read by the record head. This identifies the position

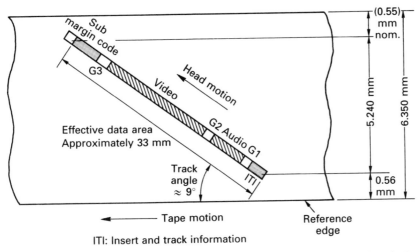

Figure 9.59 The dimensions of the DVC track. Audio. video and subcode can be independently edited. Insert and Track Information block aligns heads during insert.

of the track in the segmentation sequence and in the tracking tone sequence and allows the head to identify its physical position both along and across the track prior to an insert edit. The remainder of the track can then be recorded as required.

As there are no linear tracks, the subcode is designed to be read in shuttle for access control purposes. It will contain timecodes and flags.

9.38 DVC signal system

Figure 9.60 shows a block diagram of the DVC signal system. The input video is an eight-bit component digital according to CCIR-601, but compression of about 5:1 is used. Component video is required because compression is not practicable on composite signals. The colour difference signals are subsampled prior to compression. In 60 Hz machines, 4:1:1 sampling is used, allowing a colour difference bandwidth in excess of that possible with NTSC. In 50 Hz machines, 4:2:0 sampling is used. The colour difference sampling rate is still 6.75 MHz, but the two colour difference signals are sent on sequential lines instead of simultaneously. The result is that the vertical colour difference resolution matches the horizontal resolution. A similar approach is used in SECAM and MAC video. Studio standard 4:2:2 parallel or serial inputs and outputs can be handled using simple interpolators in the colour difference signal paths.

16:9 aspect ratio can be supported in standard definition by increasing the horizontal pixel spacing as is done in Digital Betacam. High definition signals can be supported using a higher compression factor.

As in other DVTRs, the error correction strategy relies upon a combination of shuffle and product codes. Frames are assembled in RAM, and partitioned into

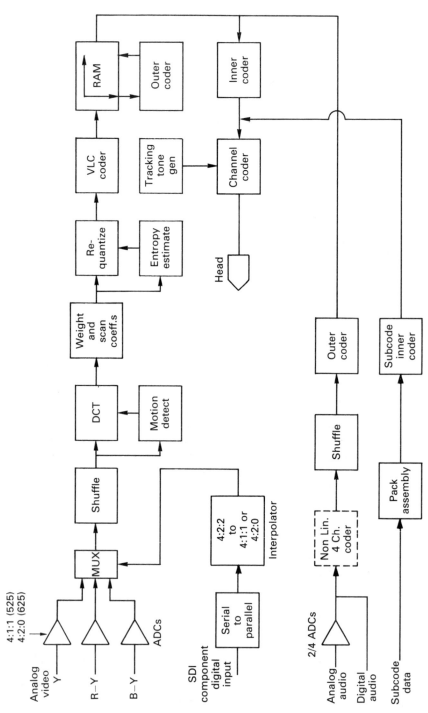

Figure 9.60 Block diagram of DVC signal system. This is similar to larger formats except that a high compression factor allows use of a single channel with no distribution.

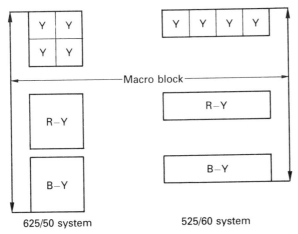

Figure 9.61 In DVC a macro block contains information from a fixed screen area. As the colour resolution is reduced, there are twice as many luminance pixels.

blocks of 8 × 8 pixels. In the luminance channel, four of these blocks cover the same screen area as one block in each colour difference signal as Figure 9.61 shows. The four luminance blocks and the two colour difference blocks are together known as a macro block. The shuffle is based upon re-ordering of macro blocks. Following the shuffle compression takes place. The compression system is DCT based and uses techniques described in Chapter 2. Compression acts within frame boundaries so as to permit frame accurate editing. This contrasts with the intra-field compression used in DB and DCT. Intra-frame compression uses 8 × 8 pixel DCT blocks and allows a higher compression factor because advantage can be taken of redundancy between the two fields when there is no motion. If motion is detected, then moving areas of the two fields will be independently coded in 8 × 4 pixel blocks to prevent motion blur. Following the motion compensation the DCT coefficients are weighted, zig-zag scanned and re-quantized prior to variable length coding. As in other compressed VTR formats the requantizing is adaptive so that the same amount of data is output irrespective of the input picture content. The entropy block occupies one sync. block and contains data compressed from five macro blocks.

The DVC product codes are shown in Figure 9.62. The video product block is shown at (a). This block is common to both 525 and 625 line formats. Ten such blocks record one 525 line frame whereas 12 blocks are required for a 625 line frame.

The audio channels are shuffled over a frame period and assembled into the product codes shown in Figure 9.6(b). Video and audio sync blocks are identical except for the ID numbering. The subcode structure is different. Figure 9.62(c) shows the structure of the subcode block. The subcode is not a product block because these can only be used for error correction when the entire block is recovered. The subcode is intended to be read in shuttle where only parts of the track are recovered. Accordingly only inner codes are used and these are much shorter than the video/audio codes, containing only 5 data bytes, known as a

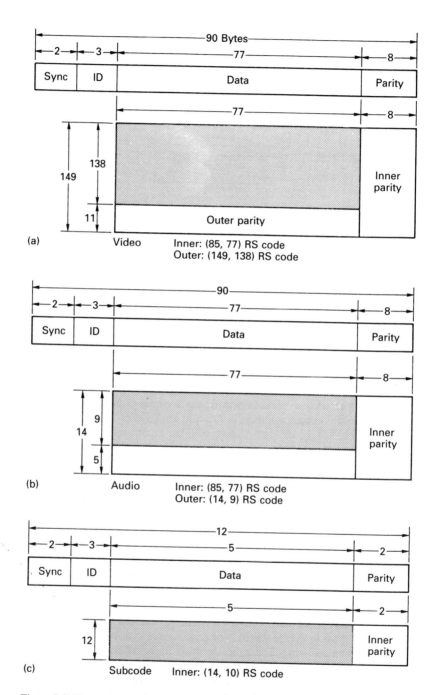

Figure 9.62 The product codes used in DVC. Video and audio codes at (a) and (b) differ only in size and use the same inner code structure. Subcode at (c) is designed to be read in shuttle and uses short sync blocks to improve chances of recovery.

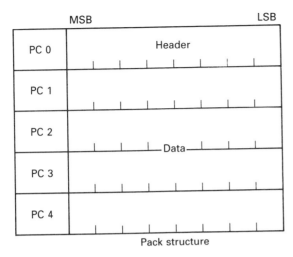

MSB   LSB

PC 0	Header
PC 1	
PC 2	Data
PC 3	
PC 4	

Pack structure

Figure 9.63 Structure of a Pack.

pack. The structure of a pack is shown in Figure 9.63. The subcode block in each track can accommodate 12 packs. Packs are repeated throughout the frame so that they have a high probability of recovery in shuttle. The pack header identifies the type of pack, leaving four bytes for pack data, e.g. timecode.

Following the assembly of product codes, the data are then channel coded for recording on tape. A scrambled NRZI channel code is used which is similar to the system used in D-1 except that the tracking tones are also inserted by the modulation process.

9.39 The future of DVTRs

Perhaps the main strength of digital video is the opportunities it offers which were denied to analog technology. These opportunities are in areas where no comparison with analog is possible.

The greatest opportunity is that once converted to the digital domain, video becomes data. Video data is indistinguishable from any other kind of data, and can take advantage of hardware and techniques developed elsewhere. Data can be recorded on many types of media having different characteristics.

There are many types of analog video signals – component, composite, 525 line, 625 line – and each type gave rise to an analog video recording format. This was inevitable because each signal required different bandwidth and/or had differing field rates. One tape track represented one field, and so there was a direct mechanical relationship between head speed and the video format.

On the other hand, there has never been such a connection in computer recording. Hard disks have constant-sized data blocks, but we have never been forced to write letters of constant length or store programs of constant length. Fitting variable-length data files into fixed-length storage blocks has been done for many years by a device called a formatter. As stated above, digitized video is only data, so it is not clear why different video standards require different recorders. It should be possible to have a generic data recorder which is capable of recording any line standard in conjunction with a suitable formatter.

There are some signs that this is beginning to happen. The first was the design of the D-1 format DVTR. The component digital sampling system has the same sampling frequencies in use for 525 and 625 line systems and therefore the data rate in the two systems is the same. The segmentation of D-1 was based on 300 segments a second, and this was divided down two ways. In 50 Hz systems, six segments make a field, whereas in 60 Hz systems, five segments make a field. As a result the head speed does not change going from 50 to 60 Hz. However, the D-1 format is unable to record composite digital data.

The compatibility between D-3 and D-5 is another interesting step. D-3 records composite sampled at four times subcarrier, which results in a data rate (NTSC) of almost half that of D-5 which records component digital. Certain D-5 machines can play D-3 tapes because the formats are basically similar. D-5 and D-3 use the same head speed, but D-5 has four tracks per segment and double the tape speed of D-3 which uses two tracks per segment. If a D-5 machine plays tape at D-3 speed, two of the heads in the segment align with the D-3 tracks. The D-5 machine, then, is a dual bit rate player. However, a 60 Hz D-5 can only play NTSC D-3 and a 50 Hz D-5 can only play PAL D-3. There is no 60/50 machine as was possible in D-1.

Current DVTRs edit by replacing recorded tape data on a field (or frame) accurate basis. Analog recorders had to work in that way, but digital recorders do not. They work that way because of conservatism. Quite a few DVTRs now offer the option of read–modify–write (RMW), also called pre-read, so that a tape can be played, altered and re-recorded in one pass. RMW allows editing to take place within the field. There is nothing magic about RMW; word processors have been doing it for years when retrieving a file to correct the spelling. The spelling corrections are not made by changing individual bytes on the disk block, but are made in memory prior to writing the file back to disk. In fact the word processor makes a better job of it because the size of the file has nothing to do with the size of the blocks on the hard disk.

Today's DVTRs only offer RMW as an option and the formats are designed to work without it. A DVTR with RMW does *not* need to be able to edit tape tracks to field accuracy. Tape editing to field accuracy is difficult with the narrow tracks of modern formats and all kinds of tricks with flying erase heads and guard bands are played to make it possible. In fact editability impairs recording density. An RMW DVTR could easily use tracks half as wide as those in current formats if it only edited physically every second or so at an interblock gap provided for the purpose. Editing to field accuracy or less would then only be possible using RMW. Current formats cannot offer this performance because they are not designed for RMW-only transports.

Halving the track width results in twice as much recording time on the same amount of tape, which has an economic advantage. However, half-width tracks also result in the tape speed being halved, and so a given duration of recording can be accessed in half the time.

The first video recorders used the quadruplex transverse scan-principle. These machines could not offer slow-motion modes with the analog technology of the day and helical-scan transports were developed instead. The longer tracks of helical scan allowed field-per-track recording and the larger drum allowed track-following heads for slow motion. DVTRs continue the helical scan tradition unnecessarily. In the digital domain slow motion is easier to perform, and using RAM buffers, there are innumerable data recorders in which the transport can only run at normal speed, but any data rate can be obtained by reading the memory as required and running the transport incrementally. There is then no need for a variable-speed transport and helical scan is no longer necessary. Transverse scan is much more compact than helical because the drum is much smaller and threading up is trivial. Incremental operation without head wear is possible by retracting the tape guide away from the drum when not actually transferring data. For a camcorder, transverse scan results in the smallest, lightest mechanism and the lowest power consumption. Tracking errors due to tape tension or temperature changes are inevitable in helical scan, but do not occur in transverse.

The point is that digital video is data like any other, but we cling to the notion that video is somehow different and make hardware which is based on analog constraints after such constraints have gone away. The main advantage of digital technology is freedom from technological restrictions. If we carry on in the same way when the restrictions are gone, the advantage is lost.

References:

1. BRUSH, R., Video data shuffling for the 4:2:2 DVTR. Presented at 20th SMPTE Television Conf. (Chicago, 1986), *SMPTE J.*, **95**, 1009–1016 (1986)
2. EGUCHI, T. and WILKINSON, J.H., The 4:2:2 component DVTR. An introduction to the world's first product. Presented at the 11th International Broadcasting Convention (Brighton, 1986), *IEE Conf. Publ. No. 268*, 57–62 (1986)
3. WILKINSON, J.H., The SMPTE type D-1 digital television tape recorder – error control. Presented at 20th SMPTE Television Conf. (Chicago, 1986) *SMPTE J.*, **95**, 1144–1149 (1986)
4. BRUSH, R., Design considerations for the D-2 PAL composite DVTR. *IERE Conf. Publ.*, **79**, 141–148
5. BRUSH, R., Design considerations for the D-2 NTSC composite DVTR. Presented at SMPTE Technical Conf. (Los Angeles, 1987)
6. AJ-D350 ½" Digital Studio VTR Technical Guide. Panasonic (1991)
7. HUCKFIELD, D., SATO, N. and SATO, I. Digital Betacam – The application of state of the art technology to the development of an affordable component DVTR. *Record of 18th ITS*, 180–199 (Montreux, 1993)
8. CREED, D. and KAMINAGA, K. Digital compression strategies for video tape recorders in studio applications. *Record of 18th ITS*, 291–301 (Montreux, 1993)

Index